MW00785392

PARTNERSHIPS AND LLCs

Tax Practice and Analysis

Second Edition

Thomas G. Manolakas
Robert Ricketts
Larry Tunnell

CCH INCORPORATED
Chicago

A WoltersKluwer Company

Editorial Staff

Production . . . . Diana Roozeboom

Index . . . . Lynn Brown

ISBN 0-8080-1252-5

4025 W. Peterson Ave.
Chicago, IL 60646-6085
1 800 248 3248
http://tax.cchgroup.com

To Thomas G. Manolakas,
tax practitioner, educator, author and colleague

Preface

Partnerships and LLCs: Tax Practice and Analysis will help readers understand the many facets of partnership and LLC taxation in a practical way. This book includes detailed reference material for the federal income taxation of partnerships and LLCs taxed as partnerships. It also discusses the taxation of state law partnerships with a separate commentary on the taxation of LLCs when there are actual or perceived issues that arise in applying Subchapter K of the Internal Revenue Code of 1986 to LLCs. In six parts, *Partnerships and LLCs: Tax Practice and Analysis* covers the critical concepts and issues of partnership and LLC practice. Individual parts focus on partnership characteristics, funding, taxation of operations, partner's share of partnership debt, disposition of partnership interest, and distributions. From choice of entity considerations to sales and liquidations, the breadth of partnership and LLC taxation is covered. Special attention is given throughout to the complex inner-workings of rules that bind, tax, and control these entity operations.

Partnerships and LLCs: Tax Practice and Analysis explains in detail the most important points of this challenging practice. The book is a mix of detailed explanations, illustrative examples and computations, and practical insights. Thoroughly footnoted to authority and organized to lead the reader from the basics to the complex, the book will assist those of all levels of experience.

January 2005

About the Authors

Author of the first edition, Thomas G. Manolakas, passed away in June 2004. The author held an LL.M. in Taxation and a J.D. from the New York University School of Law; an M.B.A. from the University of Southern California; and an M.S. in Taxation from Golden Gate University. Mr. Manolakas had been a member of the tax departments of the public accounting firms of Arthur Andersen and PricewaterhouseCoopers. He was tax counsel to the law firm Boutin, Dentino, Gibson, Di Giusto, Hodell & West in Sacramento, California. He was a visiting and adjunct tax professor at a number of universities, including the University of California, Hastings College of the Law; the University of Southern California, Graduate School of Business; and the University of San Diego School of Law. He was the author of several books on taxation and was widely regarded for his expertise in the broad spectrum of federal income taxation.

Robert Ricketts and Larry Tunnell, who will assume full authorship of the text in future editions, have revised the second edition of the book. Robert Ricketts is the Frank M. Burke Chair of Taxation and the Director of Accounting Programs at the Rawls College of Business at Texas Tech University. Larry Tunnell is an Associate Professor of Accounting at New Mexico State University in the College of Business Administration and Economics.

Contents

Contents in Detail

Paragraph

Part II — Funding the Partnership

Chapter 3 — Partnership Interest Received for Contribution of Property

Chapter 4 — Receipt of a Partnership Interest in Exchange for Services

Chapter 5 — Transactions Between a Partner and the Partnership

Paragraph

Chapter 5 —continued

Chapter 6 — Pre-Trade or Business Expenses

PART III — TAXATION OF OPERATIONS

Chapter 7 — Amount of Partnership Taxable Income

Chapter 8 — Character and Presentation of Partnership Taxable Income—The Pass-Through Concept

Paragraph

Chapter 8 —continued

Chapter 9 — Partners Take into Account the Partnership's Income or Loss

Paragraph

Chapter 9 —continued

PART IV — PARTNER'S SHARE OF PARTNERSHIP DEBT

Chapter 10 — Partner's Share of Partnership Debt

PART I

CONSIDERATIONS PRELIMINARY TO SELECTING THE PARTNERSHIP FORM OF OWNERSHIP

Chapter 1

Tax Definition of a Partnership

¶ 101 Introduction

Business activity may be conducted in various forms ranging from a sole proprietorship to a corporation. Along that continuum, a jointly held activity can be conducted as a tenancy in common, a general partnership, a limited partnership, a limited liability company, a limited liability partnership, an S corporation, a professional corporation, a C corporation, or a publicly traded partnership. Individuals must first choose their preferred form of doing business and then satisfy the requirements necessary to qualify for treatment as that form. The individual must take into account both tax and nontax considerations when selecting the form of doing business.

Often the taxpayer is treated as having made the same choice for both federal income tax purposes and all other purposes, including compliance with state and local tax and nontax rules. This is because the federal income tax definitions often coincide with the local jurisdiction's designation. For example, an incorporated operation cannot choose to be treated as unincorporated for tax purposes, although it can choose between being a C corporation or an S corporation. However, the status of a joint business arrangement as a partnership for federal income tax purposes is not always consistent with its characterization under state law. For example, partnerships and limited liability companies can elect to treat themselves as corporations. In addition, joint owners of property may be classified as tenants-in-common for non-income tax purposes, but as a partnership for federal income tax purposes. For federal income tax purposes, partnership status depends on the application of standards developed under the Internal Revenue Code.

Finally, while the income tax system often defines certain categories of entities that exist only for income tax purposes, such as S corporations, many types of state law classifications do not exist for income tax purposes. Examples are limited liability companies and limited liability partnerships. They may be treated as partnerships for partnership taxation purposes even though they share many characteristics with corporations (*e.g.*, limited liability, unlimited life, etc.). Therefore, it is important that the organization look to and satisfy the federal income tax definition of a partnership if such treatment is desired for federal tax purposes.

Under federal income tax law ". . . an unincorporated organization with two or more members is generally classified as a partnership for federal tax purposes if its members carry on a trade, business, financial operation, or venture and divide its profits."[1]

While the foregoing Internal Revenue Service definition can easily be used to distinguish a partnership from a sole proprietorship or joint ownership of personal-use recreational property, a more detailed description is often needed. One example is rental properties that are often held by tenants-in-common; under this circumstance, more detail is needed to determine if these are partnerships for federal income tax purposes. Penalties are risked or benefits may be missed by being unaware of the proper classification. Also, organizations classified as partnerships under the laws of local jurisdictions often resemble a co-ownership more than a partnership for federal income tax purposes. Thus, more detail is again needed to determine if these are partnerships for federal income tax purposes. This chapter discusses some of the more commonly encountered classification rules.

There are three general sets of regulatory rules that classify entities as a partnership versus something other than a partnership (*e.g.*, a corporation, trust or sole proprietorship):

- The rules which are commonly referred to as the "check-the-box" classification rules;[2]
- The "anti-abuse" rules;[3] and
- Rules which allow investment joint venturers to choose whether to be partnerships or tenancies-in-common.[4]

The names of the first two imply their general operation. The check-the-box regulations allow taxpayers to choose whether to treat partnerships and other unincorporated entities which are not partnerships (*e.g.*, LLCs) as corporations or partnerships for federal income tax purposes. The anti-

[1] IRS Pub. 541, Information on Partnerships.

[2] Reg. § § 301.7701-1, -2, and -3.

[3] Reg. § 1.701-2.

[4] Reg. § 1.761-2.

abuse rules allow the IRS to recharacterize something the taxpayer is treating as a partnership as something other than a partnership. The third rule allows simple partnerships that resemble jointly owned investments to elect to treat themselves not as partnerships, but as tenants-in-common for tax purposes.

In addition, there is substantive case law distinguishing a partnership from other business arrangements such as debtor-creditor or employee-employer relationships.

¶ 102 Classification of Partnerships

A business activity *incorporated* under the law of any state, federal, or foreign jurisdiction is treated as a corporation for federal income tax purposes. If the shareholders of that corporation prefer a tax treatment similar to a partnership, then they should make an S election. However, regulations provide that a jointly-owned, *unincorporated*, profit-motivated domestic business entity (such as limited liability companies and partnerships) may elect to be a corporation for tax purposes. They make this election by filing a Form 8832, Entity Classification Election. Filing the form is "checking the tax classification box."[5]

> ***Example 1-1.*** Clara and Ernie Majors are married and own a hardware store. Ernie operates the hardware store. He reports the tax results on Schedule C, Form 1040. The Majors would like to form an S corporation for federal income tax purposes, but they don't want the trouble and expense of incorporating and following the corporate formalities. Clara and Ernie enter into a partnership, contributing the hardware business and all related assets to the partnership. The partnership files Form 8832 electing to be a corporation for federal income tax purposes and then files Form 2553, Election by a Small Business Corporation Under Section 1362, and elects to be an S corporation. By electing to be classified as an S corproation, pass-through income (in excess of reasonable compensation) will not be subject to the self-employment or Medicare taxes.

If an eligible unincorporated organization does not elect to be a corporation, then it is by default a partnership for tax purposes. A single member unincorporated entity is treated as a disregarded entity unless it elects to be a corporation. It cannot be treated as a partnership. For example, a single member LLC owned by an individual will be treated as a sole proprietorship unless the individual elects to be treated as a corporation. Its business income and expenses will be reported on the individual's Schedule C Form 1040 and its rental income or loss will be reported on the individual's Schedule E, Form 1040. A corporation which owns a single

[5] The timing, effective dates and contents of the election are described in Reg. § 301.7701-3(c) and in the Instructions to Form 8832, Entity Classification Election.

member LLC would report its results as if it were a branch if it didn't elect to treat the LLC as a separate corporate subsidiary.

See sample Form 8832 in the Appendix.

301.7701-3 Regulations

(Effective for Entities Formed on or After January 1, 1997) [6]

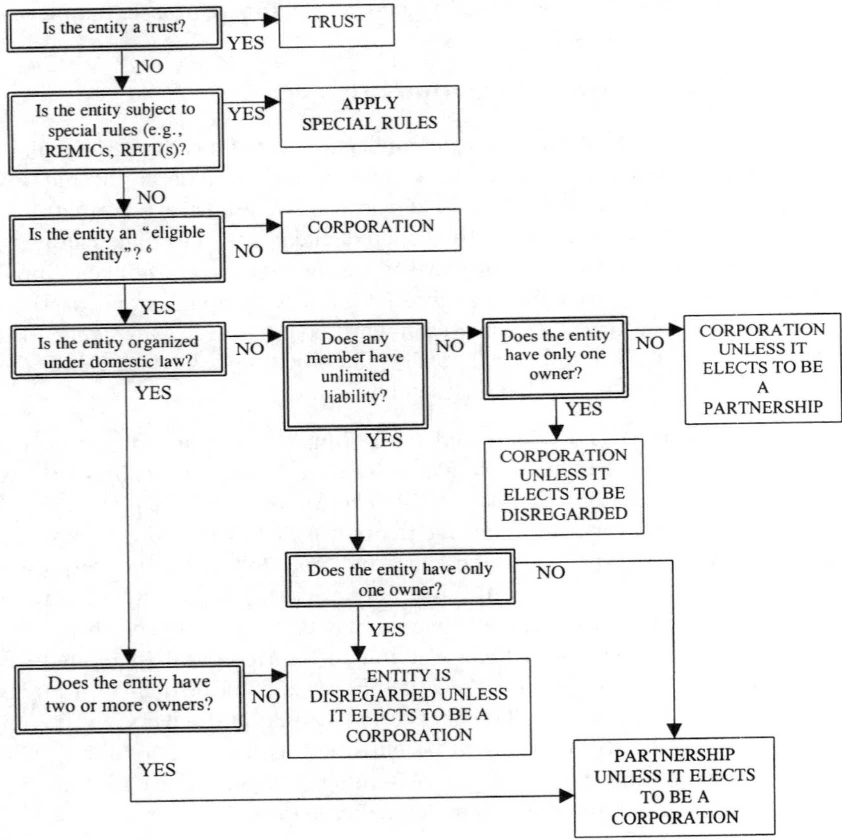

For entities in existence prior to January 1, 1997, their previously claimed classification will generally be respected for periods prior to that date if it was reasonable under the prior rules.[7]

[6] An "eligible entity" is any organization not deemed a corporation per Reg. § 301.7701-2(b)(1), (3), (4), (5), (6), (7), or (8).

[7] Reg. § 301.7701-3(h)(2).

¶ 103 Tax Issues Involving Classification of LLCs as Partnerships

The regulations require most jointly-owned unincorporated domestic business entities, such as limited liability companies (LLCs), to be treated as partnerships unless they elect corporate status.[8] Applying the partnership tax rules to an entity which is not a partnership does not normally present an additional layer of complexity for tax planning and compliance. The tax practitioner simply ignores the entity's nontax status, as an LLC for example, and applies the partnership tax rule to the issue at hand. However, complications can arise in applying statutory and regulatory rules mostly written in the mid-1950s and almost all written before 1990. These rules were intended to apply to common law partnerships and not to other forms of business. For example, general or limited partners may be treated differently for some partnership tax purposes. In the case of state law partnerships, it has been normally routine to identify who are the general partners and who are the limited partners and apply the appropriate tax rule accordingly. However, in the case of an LLC, for example, no member is legally a limited or general partner. All the members resemble limited partners from a limited liability standpoint, while all members who are managers resemble general partners from an operational standpoint.

Another example involves classifying partnership debt as recourse versus nonrecourse for purposes of allocating the debt among the partners for partnership interest and at-risk purposes. Generally, recourse debt is allocated to the partners who bear the risk of paying the creditors if the partnership fails to pay them. In contrast, nonrecourse debts (in the case of the at-risk rules' "qualified nonrecourse debt") are allocated among all partners, general and limited.[9] In either case, these rules, while relatively straightforward when applied to partnerships, become less clear when applied to non-partnership entities, such as LLCs, that elect to be classified as partnerships for federal income tax purposes.

Some of the quirks of applying partnership tax rules to nonpartnerships have been clearly addressed by statute or regulations while others have not. Of the addressed issues, some of the older provisions have laid out clear rules which probably would be different if the drafters were considering LLC implications. Some of the newer rules have consciously considered the LLC implications. This is a developing area. This section outlines some of the more commonly encountered problems in applying the partnership tax rules to LLCs. Additional issues which may arise in other contexts are discussed throughout the book at points where the application of partnership tax rules to LLCs is unclear. If there is no separate discussion, there is no recognized issue related to application of a partnership tax rule to an LLC.

---

[8] Reg. §§ 1.301.7701-2 and -3.

[9] Reg. § 1.752-3(a).

.01 *Liability Treatment Under Code Sec. 752*

A partner's basis in his or her partnership interest is important for many purposes. Examples include:

- Basis determines the extent of losses that may be deducted by a partner in a given year;[10] and
- Distributions of money in excess of a partner's basis are taxable to the partner. For example, a decrease in a partner's share of partnership liabilities is treated as a distribution of money, and therefore, if the "deemed" distribution exceeds a partner's tax basis, that partner must recognize gain.

Determining an LLC member's share of LLC debt is essentially a two-step process. First, the debt must be classified at the entity level as either recourse or nonrecourse. Second, the partnership liability sharing rules contained in the regulations must be applied.[11] In the case of recourse debt, debt is allocated to the persons who bear the economic risk of loss of that liability. In the case of nonrecourse debt, the regulations employ a three-tier allocation scheme which assumes the nonrecourse debt is secured by property.

A partnership liability is recourse if any partner or related person bears the "economic risk of loss" for that liability.[12] A partner bears the economic risk of loss with respect to a partnership liability if the partner (or a person related to the partner) would be obligated to make a payment to a partnership creditor or a contribution to the partnership with respect to a partnership liability and would not be entitled to reimbursement under circumstances in which all the partnership's liabilities were due and payable in full and all the partnership's assets were worthless. Recourse liabilities, as mentioned, are allocated among the persons who bear the economic risk of loss for those liabilities. Absent special circumstances, an LLCs debt is classified as nonrecourse debt under these rules.

A partnership liability is a nonrecourse liability if no partner bears the economic risk of loss with respect to that liability.[13] Partnership nonrecourse liabilities are allocated in accordance with a three-tier approach under which each partner's share of nonrecourse debt is the sum of: (1) each partner's share of Code Sec. 704(b) "minimum gain;" (2) each partner's share of Code Sec. 704(c) "minimum gain;" and (3) each partner's share of "excess" nonrecourse liabilities, which are allocated among the partners in accordance with their profits interests. Code Sec. 704(b) minimum gain is roughly defined as the amount by which a partnership's nonrecourse debt's total principal exceeds the total tax basis or if different the book value of the securing property. Code Sec. 704(c) minimum gain is equal to the lesser of the excess of the book value of the property serving as collateral for the

---

[10] Code Sec. 704(d).

[11] Reg. § § 1.752-1 through -5.

[12] Reg. § 1.752-1(a)(1).

[13] Reg. § 1.752-1(a)(2).

loan over its tax basis, or the excess of the debt over the tax basis of the securing property. The debt allocation rules normally result in allocating an amount of debt equal to total Code Sec. 704(b) minimum gain based upon a partnership's loss sharing ratio (normally the partner's share of depreciation) with the remainder allocated by reference to profit sharing ratios.[14]

LLCs. Quantifying a member's share of LLC liabilities is a function of applying the existing partnership liability allocation regulations. The problem is that debts that are normally recourse to a state law partnership's general partners are effectively nonrecourse to all LLC members (unless guaranteed by one or more LLC members). These debts are treated as nonrecourse for partnership tax purposes. The regulatory method for allocating nonrecourse debt among the partners assumes that nonrecourse debt is secured by property. The relationship between the total amount of nonrecourse debt and the total basis of partnership property securing the nonrecourse debt determines how the debt is allocated among the partners. The operation of these rules when the debt is unsecured is not explained by the regulations.

.02 Passive Loss Limitation Rules

Code Sec. 469(a)(1)(A) disallows a deduction for net passive activity losses incurred by individuals, trusts, estates, and personal service corporations. A passive activity net loss generally is the amount by which passive activity deductions for the taxable year exceed passive activity gross income for the year.[15] A passive activity means any non-real estate operator's rental activity and any activity that involves the conduct of any trade or business and in which the taxpayer does not *materially participate*.[16] A natural person may deduct up to $25,000 of passive activity losses attributable to all real estate activities with respect to which that individual *actively participated* during the year and satisfies other requirements.[17] Generally, an individual is treated as materially participating in an activity for a taxable year if he or she meets one of seven tests:

1. The individual participates for more than 500 hours;
2. The individual's participation constitutes substantially all of the participation of all individuals;
3. The individual participates for more than 100 hours, and that participation is not less than that of any other individual;
4. The activity is a significant participation activity and the individual's aggregate participation in all significant participation activities exceeds 500 hours;

[14] See Chapter 10.

[15] Code Sec. 469(d)(1); Temp. Reg. § 1.469-2T(b)(1).

[16] Code Sec. 469(c)(1).

[17] Code Sec. 469(i)(1), (2).

5. The individual materially participated for any five taxable years during the 10 immediately preceding taxable years;

6. The activity is a personal service activity and the individual materially participated for any three preceding taxable years; or

7. Based on all facts and circumstances, the individual participates on a regular, continuous, and substantial basis.[18]

A limited partner is deemed to materially participate only by qualifying under tests (1), (5) or (6).[19] For this purpose, a "limited partner" includes an individual whose liability for obligations of the partnership is limited, under the law of the state in which the partnership is organized, to a determinable fixed amount, such as capital contributions and contractual obligations to make additional capital contributions.[20]

Except as provided in regulations, no interest as a limited partner in a limited partnership shall be treated as an interest in which the taxpayer actively participates.[21] A partnership interest is not treated as a limited partnership interest if the individual is also a general partner at all times during the year.[22]

LLCs. An interest in an LLC certainly falls within the literal definition of a limited partnership interest.[23] Commentators have argued that manager-members should not be treated as limited partners for purposes of the material participation test since they are allowed to participate in management, unlike limited partners.[24]

S Corporation Observation. By contrast, an S corporation shareholder may satisfy any of the seven tests.

.03 Methods of Accounting

A taxpayer may compute taxable income under any number of specified "permissible methods" of accounting, including cash or accrual.[25] See ¶ 202. However, Code Sec. 448 prohibits the use of the cash method of accounting by the following entities:

- C corporations other than qualified personal service corporations and those with less than $5,000,000 of gross receipts;
- Partnerships with C corporation partners, unless the partnership has gross receipts of less than $5,000,000; and
- Tax shelters.[26]

---

[18] Temp. Reg. § 1.469-5T(a).
[19] Temp. Reg. § 1.469-5T(e)(2).
[20] Temp. Reg. § 1.469-5T(e)(3)(i)(B).
[21] Code Sec. 469(i)(6)(C).
[22] Temp. Reg. § 1.469-5T(e)(3)(ii).
[23] Temp. Reg. § 1.469-5T(e)(3)(i)(B).
[24] Jordan and Kloepfer, *The Limited Liability Company: Beyond Classification*, 69 TAXES 203, 210 (1991).
[25] Code Sec. 446(c).
[26] Code Sec. 448(b).

LLCs. An LLC that is classified as a tax shelter must use the accrual method. Code Sec. 448(d)(3) refers to Code Sec. 461(i)(3) for the definition of "tax shelter," which provides that a tax shelter is any of the following:

- An enterprise (other than a C corporation) if at any time interests have been offered for sale in an "offer required to be registered" with any federal or state agency.
- Any "syndicate."[27]
- Any "tax shelter."[28]

Required to be registered. An enterprise interest sale offer required to be registered means any enterprise (other than a C corporation) if at any time interests in such enterprise have been offered for sale in any offering required to be registered with any federal or state agency having the authority to regulate the offering of securities for sale.[29] An offering is "required to be registered" if, under applicable federal or state law, failure to file a notice of exemption from registration would result in violation of applicable federal or state law (regardless of whether notice is in fact filed).[30]

> ***Example 1-2.*** California Corporations Code, Section 25102(f), exempts from registration private placements if sales of the security are made to no more than 35 persons, all of whom have a preexisting personal or business relationship with the issuer or any of its partners, officers, directors, or controlling persons, or are "sophisticated" in financial matters, and the securities are not advertised. Although as a matter of practice most practitioners file a "Section 25102(f) Notice" with the California Department of Corporations, Corporations Code Section 25102(f) does not require a filing of a notice to qualify for exemption. Failure to file the notice does not cause the loss of the exemption. Thus, qualified private placements in California are not required to be registered and thus are not tax shelters under the rules above.

In most jurisdictions, an LLC membership interest must be a "security" for the registration rules to be applicable. Not all LLC interests are securities. This depends on whether the membership interest is an "investment contract." In California, for example, Section 25019 of the Corporate Securities Law, provides that every interest in an LLC will be a security, unless the person claiming the exemption can prove that all of the members are actively engaged in the management of the LLC.

In a private letter ruling, a law firm LLC represented that it has not ever and will not ever offer any interest in itself for sale to the general

[27] Within the meaning of Code Sec. 1256(e)(3)(B).

[28] As defined in Code Sec. 6662(d)(2)(C)(ii).

[29] Temp. Reg. § 1.448-1T(b)(1)(i).

[30] Temp. Reg. § 1.448-1T(b)(2).

public. Based on that representation, the LLC was held not to be an enterprise.[31]

Syndicate. "Syndicate" means any partnership or other entity other than a C corporation if more than 35 percent of the losses of the entity during the taxable year are *allocable* to limited partners or limited entrepreneurs (as defined in Code Sec. 446(e)(2)).[32] "Losses" means the excess of the deductions allocable to the enterprise over the amount of income recognized by the enterprise under its tax method of accounting, excluding gains or losses from the sale of capital assets or Code Sec. 1221(2) assets.[33] The regulations use the word *allocated* rather than *allocable.*[34]

An interest in any entity is not treated as held by a limited partner or a limited entrepreneur in five situations, including any period during which the interest is held by an individual who actively participates at all times during the period in the management of the entity, or if the interest is held by an individual who actively participated in the management of the entity for a period of not less than five years. However, note that the interests must be held by an individual. That could create a problem for a professional LLC converted from a partnership with professional corporations.[35]

An LLC will not be a "syndicate" if either it has no losses, so that there are none to be allocated, or at least 65 percent of any losses are allocated to persons who actively participate in management and are consequently not limited partners or limited entrepreneurs.

---

[31] IRS Letter Ruling 9321047 (2-25-93). See also IRS Letter Ruling 9328005 (12-21-92), and IRS Letter Ruling 9432018 (5-16-94) (firm provided management and operation of property).

[32] Code Sec. 1256(e)(3)(B).

[33] Temp. Reg. § 1.448-1T(a)(4). See IRS Letter Ruling 8911011 (12-14-88), which held that with respect to profit years, a limited partnership will not be a "syndicate" within Code Sec. 1256(e)(3)(B) because "there will be no losses allocable to partners" whether limited or otherwise. IRS Letter Ruling 9321047 (2-25-93) used "allocated" rather than "allocable" in paraphrase of the statute, but made no ruling on that point. See also IRS Letter Ruling 9328005 (12-21-92). IRS Letter Ruling 9415005 (1-10-94) adopted that interpretation and held in the case of a law firm that had consistently reported taxable income rather than loss, that the firm would not be a syndicate for any year in which it does not incur losses. This is a significant ruling for an LLC that cannot meet the active participation requirement.

[34] Temp. Reg. § 1.448-1T(a)(4).

[35] Code Sec. 1256(e)(3)(B), (C). See IRS Letter Ruling 9432018 (5-16-94). All of the members were represented to be actively engaged in the business of managers held that the LLC meets the active participation requirements. IRS Letter Ruling 9321047 (2-25-93). Although the agreement provided for members to elect five managers as the management committee with authority to conduct business for the firm and provided that all members would be required to vote in order for the firm to take certain actions, including the following: election of members to the management committee and compensation committee; removal of a member from either committee; admission of a member or provisional member; dismissal of a member; amendment of the Agreement; dissolution of the firm; major decisions; and approval of compensation committee recommendations subject to prescribed procedures. Based on the representation that the members would continue to engage in the practice of law and participate in the various described management activities, it was held that the LLC will meet the active participation requirements. IRS Letter Ruling 9328005 (12-21-92). An executive committee managed the LLC, but vote of all members was required for the LLC to take certain actions: admit or expel a member; determine compensation of members; make expenditures in excess of a specified amount; borrow funds in excess of a specified amount; open or close a branch office; change the name of the LLC or the location of its principal office; sell or otherwise dispose of all or substantially all of the assets of the LLC; dissolve the LLC; and amend the agreement under which the LLC is operated. In addition, "each member will, in varying degrees, participate in the following management activities attributable to the Business": handling client relations; supervising services provided to clients; billing, collecting and negotiating fees; participating in business and practice development activities; staffing projects, including the selection and use of specialists; and supervising, training, and evaluating LLC employees. Participation in the "various management activities set forth above" was held to constitute active participation.

Tax shelter. "Tax shelter" within the meaning of Code Sec. 6662(d)(2)(C)(iii) is any arrangement whose principal purpose is the avoidance or evasion of federal income tax.

The cash method is also not available for a partnership that has a C corporation as a partner.[36] However, for purposes of this rule, a qualified personal service corporation is treated as an individual, not a C corporation. That exception is important to a professional partnership, including a C corporation, that converts to an LLC. Further, the cash method is available if the partnership's gross receipts do not exceed $5,000,000.[37]

Accounting for inventories and accrual basis. When, in the opinion of the Secretary, it is necessary to use inventories to clearly determine the income of the taxpayer, the taxpayer must account for inventories.[38] Generally a taxpayer is required to account for inventories when the production, purchase, or sale of merchandise is an income-producing factor in the taxpayer's business.[39] In addition, in any instance in which it is necessary to account for inventories, the accrual method of accounting must be used with regard to purchases and sales unless the taxpayer uses a method of accounting which, in the opinion of the service, clearly reflects income.[40]

The IRS has provided administrative relief from the above provisions for qualifying "small business taxpayers." Under the "small business taxpayer" exception, certain small businesses are allowed to use the cash method of accounting even if the production, purchase, or sale of merchandise is an income-producing factor in the taxpayer's business. A qualifying small business taxpayer is any taxpayer with "average annual gross receipts" of $10,000,000 or less that is not prohibited from using the cash method under Code Sec. 448 (C corporations, partnerships with corporate partners, and tax shelters).[41]

Rev. Proc. 2001-10 provides that the Commissioner will exercise his or her discretion to except a qualifying taxpayer with average annual gross receipts of $1,000,000 or less from the requirements to use an accrual method of accounting under Code Sec. 446 and to account for inventories under Code Sec. 471.[42] Tax shelters are not eligible for this exception. Rev. Proc. 2001-10 provides procedures for taxpayers to follow to get automatic consent for this exception.

.04 Audit Issues—Tax Matters Partner

Tax partnerships, including LLCs treated as partnerships, are subject to the unified audit and litigation procedures contained in Sections 6221–6234, unless they are:

---

[36] Code Sec. 448(a)(1).
[37] Code Sec. 448(b)(3).
[38] Code Sec. 471.
[39] Reg. § 1.471-1.
[40] Reg. § 1.446-1(c)(2).
[41] Rev. Proc. 2002-28, 2002-1 CB 815.
[42] Rev. Proc. 2001-10, 2001-1 CB 272.

- Electing large partnerships,[43] or
- Small partnerships.[44]

The unified audit and litigation procedures require the partnership to appoint a general partner as its tax matters partner.[45] The tax matters partner is the person the IRS will deal with in connection with the unified procedures.

LLCs. The Internal Revenue Code does not define a general partner. If the term were deemed to mean a partner with personal liability for the organization's liabilities, then in an LLC there would be no one whom the partners may designate.[46] Under Code Sec. 6231(a)(7), the partners may designate only a general partner as the "tax matters partner" for purposes of partnership audits. If there is no general partner, the IRS is authorized to designate the tax matters partner.[47] Final regulations under Code Sec. 6231 governing the designation of tax matters partners were finalized on December 23, 1996, and are effective for all designations of tax matters partners on or after that date. Under the regulations, only member-managers of LLCs can be designated as the tax matters partner.[48]

.05 Self-Employment Taxes

A limited partner's share of income from a partnership, other than guaranteed payments for services under Code Sec. 707(c), is not subject to self-employment tax (*i.e.*, the income is excluded from "net earnings from self-employment").[49]

LLC members who are treated as limited partners for purposes of Code Sec. 1402(a)(13) cannot take into account their distributive shares that are not subject to Social Security tax for purposes of calculating their retirement plan contributions. For purposes of qualified retirement plans under Code Sec. 401, the term "employee" includes a "self-employed individual."[50] "Self-employed individual" means an individual who has "earned income."[51] "Earned income" means net earnings from self-employment (as defined in Code Sec. 1402(a)).[52] The deduction for retirement plan contributions by self-employed individuals is based upon earned income.[53]

---

[43] Code Secs. 771-777.

[44] Code Sec. 6231(a)(1)(B) (ten or fewer partners, each being a natural person or an estate, no partner being a nonresident alien and the partnership makes no special allocations).

[45] Code Sec. 6231(a)(7) and (8).

[46] See *Transpac Drilling Venture v. United States*, CA-FC, 94-1 USTC ¶ 50,067, 16 F3d 383, in which court held that limited partners who were designated as general partners for the "limited purpose only" of being tax matters partners did not qualify. But see Rev. Proc. 89-12, 1989-1 CB 798, which defines "general partner" to include a person with significant management authority relative to the other members.

[47] Code Sec. 6231(a)(7).

[48] Reg. § 301.6231(a)(7)-2(a).

[49] Code Sec. 1402(a)(13). IRS Letter Ruling 9110003 (12-4-90) held that strict compliance with the state limited partnership act was required for an inactive member of a partnership with limited management rights to qualify as a "limited partner" for purposes of the Code Sec. 1402(a)(13) exclusion.

[50] IRS Letter Ruling 9432018 (5-16-94).

[51] See Samuel P. Starr, *LLC Members May Be Liable for Tax on Self-Employment and Fringe Benefits*, 1 J. LIMITED LIABILITY COMPANIES 2, 51 (1994).

[52] Code Sec. 401(c)(1)(A).

[53] Code Sec. 401(c)(1)(B).

LLCs. Initially, the IRS ruled that if an LLC is classified as a partnership under Code Sec. 7701, its active members will be treated as general partners for self-employment tax purposes.[54] The ruling stated that a member "actively engaged" in the LLC's professional service business would not be treated as a limited partner under Code Sec. 1402(a)(13) and the member's distributive share of income from the LLC would therefore be treated as net earnings from self-employment.[55]

Proposed Regulations. Two sets of proposed regulations have provided guidance on this issue.[56] The first set of proposed regulations issued on December 29, 1994 have since been withdrawn. Under these proposed regulations, where an LLC is member-managed, it is possible for certain LLC members to be treated as limited partners who are not subject to self-employment tax.[57] A member is treated as a limited partner under these proposed rules if:

1. The member is not a manager; and
2. The LLC could have been formed as a limited partnership in the same jurisdiction, and the member could have qualified as a limited partner under the local limited partnership act.[58]

Thus, this proposed rule put a premium on the LLC members' "participation in control" under the local limited partnership rules.

Under these rules, any LLC members that "participate in the control" of the partnership might be treated as general partners under state law as to certain creditors (if the LLC were treated as a partnership for state law purposes). Therefore, assuming partnership tax treatment for federal tax purposes, a self-employment tax would be imposed on that participating LLC member.

Proposed regulations were again issued under Code Sec. 1402 early in 1997;[59] they provide that an individual will generally be treated as a limited partner unless he or she:

1. Has personal liability [60] for the debts of or claims against the partnership by reason of being a partner;
2. Has authority to contract on behalf of the partnership under the statute or law pursuant to which the partnership is organized; or
3. Participates in the partnership's trade or business for more than 500 hours during the taxable year.[61]

---

[54] Code Sec. 401(c)(2)(A).
[55] Code Sec. 404(a)(8).
[56] Prop. Reg. § 1.1402(a)-18.
[57] Prop. Reg. § 1.1402(a)-18(a). See also IRS Letter Rulings 9525058 (3-28-95) and 9423018 (3-11-94).
[58] Prop. Reg. § 1.1402(a)-18(b).
[59] Prop. Reg. § 1.1401-2(d).
[60] As defined in Reg. § 301.7701-3(b)(2)(ii).
[61] Prop. Reg. § 1.1402(a)-2(h)(2).

If, however, substantially all of the activities of a partnership involve the performance of services in the fields of health, law, engineering, architecture, accounting, actuarial science, or consulting, any individual who provides services as part of that trade or business will not be considered a limited partner.

These proposed regulations allow an individual who is not a limited partner for Code Sec. 1402(a)(13) purposes to nonetheless exclude from net earnings from self-employment a portion of his or her distributive share if the individual holds more than one class of interest in the partnership. The proposed regulations permit an individual that participates in the trade or business of the partnership to bifurcate his or her distributive share by disregarding guaranteed payments for services. In each case, however, such bifurcation of interests is permitted only to the extent the individual's distributive share is identical to the distributive share of partners who qualify as limited partners under the proposed regulation (without regard to the bifurcation rules) and who own a substantial interest in the partnership. Together, these rules exclude from self-employment income amounts that are demonstrably returns on capital invested in the partnership.

Section 935 of the Taxpayer Relief Act of 1997 [62] prohibits issuance of temporary and final regulations under Code Sec. 1402(a)(13) before July 1, 1998. This period has elapsed, but there is still no official controlling guidance as to which members of an LLC will be treated as limited partners for purposes of the self-employment tax and other earned income issues. Tax practitioner's approaches to this problem have varied widely. One position is that, based upon the definition of a limited partner as per the passive loss rules, all the members are limited partners.[63] Another is the possibility of following the approach provided in one of the two sets of proposed regulations. Finally, there is the possibility that no members are limited partners until the IRS issues regulations which expand the definition of limited partner beyond its literal meaning.

.06 Liquidation Payments Under Code Sec. 736

Before the Revenue Reconciliation Act of 1993,[64] payments made in liquidation of the interest of any retiring partner or deceased partner attributable to goodwill and unrealized receivables could be treated as a distributive share or guaranteed payment giving rise to a deduction or its equivalent for the benefit of the remaining partners.[65] That special treatment has been limited to payments made to a general partner in a partnership in which capital is not a material income-producing factor.[66] The House Committee report accompanying the Act makes clear that the special rule was intended to preserve the prior law treatment for personal service businesses (*e.g.*, accountants, lawyers, doctors, architects).

---

[62] P.L. 105-34.

[63] Temp. Reg. § 1.469-5T(e)(3)(B).

[64] P.L. 103-66.

[65] Code Sec. 736(a).

[66] See Code Sec. 736(b)(3).

LLCs. In order for these rules to apply to personal service LLCs, the retiring or deceased member would have to be treated as a "general partner."[67] "General partner" is not defined, and it is unclear whether an LLC member will be considered a general partner for purposes of Code Sec. 736(b)(3).

.07 At-Risk Rules

Generally, under Code Sec. 465 losses incurred by individuals and certain closely held corporations from an activity are deductible only to the extent of the aggregate amount with respect to which the taxpayer is at risk with respect to that activity.[68] Except in the case of "qualified nonrecourse financing," a taxpayer is at risk with respect to amounts borrowed for use in an activity only to the extent that he or she is personally liable for repayment of such amounts, or has pledged property as security for the debt.[69] If a taxpayer guarantees repayment of an amount borrowed by another person for use in an activity, the guarantee does not increase the taxpayer's amount at risk. Even if the guarantor pays the debt, the amount at risk is not increased until the taxpayer has no remaining legal rights against the primary obligor.[70]

A taxpayer is considered at risk with respect to his or her share of any qualified nonrecourse financing that is secured by real property used in the activity.[71] Qualified nonrecourse financing is generally nonseller financing with respect to which no person is personally liable for repayment.[72] A partner's share of the partnership's qualified nonrecourse financing is determined under Code Sec. 752.[73]

LLCs. At-risk basis for recourse liability exists only to the extent that any partner or related person bears the economic risk of loss. Nonrecourse debt which is secured by LLC real property that is restricted to the security may be qualified nonrecourse financing. However, the at-risk rules describe nonrecourse debt as financing with respect to which "no person" (instead of 'no member' or 'related person') is personally liable for repayment.[74] In the case of an LLC, the issue was whether recourse debt for which the LLC itself was personally liable could be treated as nonrecourse debt and, therefore, qualified nonrecourse debt if all the requirements were met.

In 1998, the Treasury Department clarified this issue.[75] The regulations under Code Sec. 465 provide a "tailored" definition of nonrecourse debt for purposes of classification as qualified nonrecourse debt.[76] In the case of a partnership, the debt will be considered nonrecourse if:

- The only person personally liable to repay the financing is the partnership;

[67] Code Sec. 736(b)(3)(B).
[68] Code Sec. 465(a)(1).
[69] Code Sec. 465(b)(2).
[70] Prop. Reg. § 1.465-6(d).
[71] Code Sec. 465(b)(6).
[72] Code Sec. 465(b)(6)(B)(iii).
[73] Code Sec. 465(b)(6)(C).
[74] Code Sec. 465(b)(6)(B)(iii).
[75] T.D. 8777, 1998-2 CB 219.
[76] Reg. § 1.465-27(b)(1)(iii).

- The partnership holds only real estate and incidental property; and
- The lender may proceed against only such property to collect on the financing in a default or default-like situation.[77]

Limited partners will, of course, not be considered at-risk with respect to other recourse debt. This could create an unwelcome surprise for partnerships converting to LLCs when the owner's at-risk amount becomes a negative member since recapture for the negative amount is required.[78]

¶ 104 IRS Reclassification

On December 29, 1994, the Internal Revenue Service issued regulations under Code Sec. 701 providing anti-abuse rules under Subchapter K. The regulations provide that the intent of Subchapter K is to permit taxpayers to conduct business for joint economic profit through a flexible arrangement that accurately reflects the partners' economic arrangement without incurring an entity level tax. The regulations add that implicit in the intent of Subchapter K are the following requirements:

- The partnership must be bona fide and each transaction or series of related transactions must be entered into for a substantial business purpose;
- The form of each transaction must be respected under substance over form principles; and
- Except as otherwise provided in the regulations, the consequences to each partner from operations and transactions between the partner and the partnership must accurately reflect the partners' economic agreement and clearly reflect the partner's income.[79]

The IRS can recast a transaction involving a purported partnership as if it were not a partnership if (1) the partnership is formed or availed of with a principal purpose of substantially reducing the present value of the partners' aggregate federal tax liability, and (2) the reduction occurs in a manner inconsistent with the intent of Subchapter K. If both requirements are met, the IRS can:

- Disregard the partnership in whole or in part and treat the partnership activity as owned by one or more partners;
- Treat one or more purported partners as not being partners;

[77] Reg. § 1.465-27(b)(4). There is a similar rule provided for single-member LLCs which are treated as disregarded entities. Reg. § 1.465-27(b)(5).

[78] Code Sec. 465(e).

[79] Reg. § 1.701-2(a). Prior to amendment, the regulations also applied to taxes other than income taxes. However, the IRS has announced that the rule will be amended to apply solely to income taxes. Announcement 95-8, 1995-7 IRB 56.

- Adjust the method of accounting of the partnership or a partner to clearly reflect income;
- Reallocate the partnership's income; or
- Otherwise adjust the tax treatment of the partners or the partnership.[80]

In determining whether a partnership was formed or availed of with a principal purpose of tax avoidance, the purported business purpose should be compared with the tax benefits resulting from the transaction. The regulations provide that the following illustrative factors should be considered in determining whether a transaction can be recast:

- The present value of the partners' aggregate tax liability is substantially less than if the partners conducted the business directly;
- The present value of the partners' aggregate tax liability is substantially less than if the purportedly separate transactions are aggregated and treated as a single transaction;
- One or more partners who are necessary to the claimed results have a nominal interest, are substantially protected from any risk of loss, or have little or no participation in the profits other than a preferred return for the use of capital;
- Substantially all the partners are related;
- Allocations comply with the literal requirements of Code Sec. 704(b) but are inconsistent with the purpose of Code Sec. 704(b);
- The benefits and burdens of ownership of property contributed are in substantial part retained by the contributing partner or a related partner; or
- The benefits and burdens of ownership of partnership property are in substantial part shifted to the distributee before or after the property is actually distributed.[81]

Eleven examples are used to illustrate the application of the above concepts. The examples cover a wide range of issues—Subchapter C, Subchapter S, foreign tax credits, special allocation of stock dividends, using Subchapter K provisions to duplicate losses, etc. In one example, a partnership is used to avoid the recognition of gain under the investment company provision of Code Sec. 351(e) and the liabilities-in-excess-of-basis rules of Code Sec. 357(c). The IRS concludes that the transaction cannot be recast under paragraph (b) of the regulations.[82]

---

[80] Reg. § 1.701-2(b).
[81] Reg. § 1.701-2(c).
[82] Reg. § 1.701-2(d), Ex. 4.

Regardless of whether a taxpayer has a tax avoidance intent or purpose, the IRS can treat a partnership as an aggregate of its partners to carry out the purpose of any Internal Revenue Code provision or Treasury regulation unless a Code provision or regulation prescribes the treatment of a partnership as an entity and clearly contemplates that treatment and the associated tax results.[83] For example, the interest deduction limitations of Code Sec. 163(e)(5) applicable to a corporation issuing debt and the extraordinary dividend rules of Code Sec. 1059 applicable to a corporate shareholder apply to corporations that are partners in a partnership that issues debt or holds stock.[84]

When an issue that may be affected by the regulation is considered in an examination, application of the regulation must be coordinated with both the Issue Specialist on the Partnership Industry Specialization Program Team and the IRS National Office.[85] The anti-abuse rules generally apply to transactions entered into on or after May 12, 1994.[86]

¶ 105 Tenancy in Common Distinguished

Even though a jointly held unincorporated activity is not treated as a corporation under the criteria discussed at ¶ 102, partnership status does not necessarily follow. Co-ownership of property, by itself, need not create a partnership for tax purposes. Co-ownership coupled with an expense-sharing arrangement is also not a partnership. If, however, the co-owners "actively and jointly" pursue a business activity, then a tax partnership is deemed to exist.[87] The taxpayers have some control over whether a jointly owned financial venture is treated as a partnership. If the financial venture amounts to an *actively* conducted business, then it *must* be accounted for as a partnership. If a lower level of activity is presented it can be treated as *either* a partnership or co-tenancy.

Intent. In the absence of an actively conducted business, classification as a partnership for tax purposes is determined by the intent of the owners. If the relevant facts and circumstances indicate an intent to operate as a partnership, then there is a partnership for tax purposes. Relevant factors include: (1) the existence of a partnership agreement; (2) filing partnership tax returns; (3) how title to property is taken; and (4) the owners ability to separately sell their shares of the property.

For example, joint investments in raw land, stock, and collectibles can be reported as a partnership or each owner can separately report his or her share of income and expenses, depending upon whether the owners have

[83] Reg. § 1.701-2(e).

[84] Reg. § 1.701-2(f), Exs. 1 and 2.

[85] Announcement 94-87, 1994-27 IRB; Preamble to Final Regulations, T.D. 8588, 1995-1 CB 109.

[86] The special rules of paragraph (e) apply to transactions on or after December 29, 1994. Reg. § 1.701-2(g).

[87] Reg. §§ 1.761-1(a) and 301.7701-1(a)(2). In the case of a husband and wife jointly owning a business, partnership treatment would seem to be required if both operated the business. If only one operates the business, his or her name would appear as the proprietor on Schedule C, Profit or Loss From Business, for Form 1040, U.S. Individual Income Tax Return.

determined that they intend to create a partnership or they merely intend joint ownership. If the parties wish to make their intentions clear, they should consider a Code Sec. 761 election. This election ensures the arrangement is treated as a tenancy in common in spite of a partnership agreement, filing partnership tax returns, and other factors which otherwise might result in partnership treatment. This election is discussed in the next paragraph. However, two CPAs conducting a joint practice and sharing in income and expenses must be reported as a partnership. The regulations under Code Sec. 761 allow only ventures not involving an active business to elect not to be treated as a partnership. This is available either in the first year of operations or after any number of years of reporting the venture as a partnership.

There are at least three important reasons for correctly determining whether a jointly owned activity is a partnership or a mere co-tenancy:

1. A partnership is required to file an informational tax return.[88] There is a penalty for failure to file this return unless it is due to reasonable cause.[89]

2. Where a partnership is deemed to exist, it must generally make all tax elections (*e.g.*, the election to expense property under Code Sec. 179, the election to defer recognition of gain in an involuntary conversion, etc.).[90] Elections made by the individual partners will generally be ineffective.[91]

3. A co-owner of realty is entitled to tax-free like-kind exchange treatment when the co-owner swaps his or her ownership interest for other realty if the statutory requirements under Code Sec. 1031 are met. However, a partner is not eligible for tax-free like-kind exchange treatment when the partner exchanges his or her partnership interest either for another partnership interest or for a direct interest in realty.[92]

Rental—Investment of active business? Jointly owned rental operations pose a frequently encountered special problem. Some rentals resemble passive investments and others are operated as active businesses. For example, a joint venture operating an assisted living facility is actively involved in a business and must file tax returns as a partnership. On the other hand, either co-ownership or partnership treatment is appropriate

[88] Form 1065, U.S. Partnership Return of Income. See Code Sec. 6031.

[89] Code Sec. 6698. "Reasonable cause" has been interpreted as including the failure to file by any small partnership that historically has failed to file returns. See H.R. Rep. No. 1445, 95th Cong., 2d Sess., 75 (1978); Rev. Proc. 81-11, 1981-1 CB 651. Domestic general partnerships with no more than 10 partners who are all individuals and where no special allocations are made are not subject to the penalty. However, the exception may not apply for purposes of state income tax.

[90] Code Sec. 703(b).

[91] See, for example, *M.H.S. Company, Inc. v. Commr.*, 35 TCM 733, Dec. 33,843(M), TC Memo. 1976-165 (elections made by the partners to roll over gain realized in an involuntary conversion were not recognized).

[92] Code Sec. 1031(a)(2)(D).

when there is a long-term investment in raw land held for future appreciation which is net leased for farming or grazing to offset carrying expenses.

Absent a demonstrated intent to conduct activity as partners, a co-ownership arrangement, not a partnership, is deemed to exist when two persons who join together as co-owners of an apartment project negotiate and execute leases, collect rents and other payments from tenants, and only perform those services customary to the maintenance of apartments.[93]

One factor used in determining whether co-owners of property must be treated as partners is whether a co-owner provides significant services, either directly or through an agent. If such services are provided, then a partnership may be deemed to exist. The definition of significant service, for a purpose other than those pertaining to Subchapter K, may be useful here. These normally include all services rendered to a customer that are primarily for that particular customer's convenience, rather than services usually or customarily rendered in connection with the rental property's use.[94] Supplying maid service, for example, would not likely constitute usual or customary service, whereas furnishing heat and light or cleaning public areas are not considered "additional services" rendered to an occupant. Thus, for example, when valet parking, maid and food service are provided at a retirement facility, co-ownership is likely to constitute a partnership, regardless of the owners' subjective intent. The co-ownership of an apartment complex when such "additional services" are not provided allows the co-owners to avoid Subchapter K status if they wish to do so.

When co-ownership of real or personal property exists and such property is leased out to third parties, the use of a "net lease" helps ensure the avoidance of partnership status. If the owners wish to avoid partnership status, the lessee and not the lessor should be responsible for providing any required "additional services" and the rent reduced accordingly. In all cases, however, the net lease's terms must be considered before the issue of partnership status can be decided. Use of a "net lease" by itself does not necessarily preclude partnership treatment. If the owners wish to report as a partnership, the absence of an actively conducted business does not preclude them from partnership status. It is a one-way street—too much activity precludes partnership status, but too little does not.

¶ 106 Election to Be Excluded from Subchapter K

In general, joint ventures and other unincorporated organizations may be excluded from Subchapter K at the election of the partnership by all the members.[95] However, the organization must be formed:

1. For investment purposes only and not for the active conduct of a business;

[93] Rev. Rul. 75-374, 1975-2 CB 261.

[94] Temp. Reg. § 1.469-1T(e)(3)(ii). This provision governs the distinction between rental deemed passive and rental operations sufficiently active to be deemed nonpassive.

[95] Code Sec. 761(a).

2. For the joint production, extraction, or use of property, but not for the purpose of selling services or property produced or extracted; or,

3. By dealers in securities for a short period for the purpose of underwriting, selling, or distributing a particular issue of securities.[96]

Additionally, each member of such organization must be able to adequately determine his or her individual income without the necessity of computing partnership taxable income.

.01 *Investment Partnerships*

A partnership qualifies as an "investing partnership" if:

- The owners can compute their income without the necessity of computing partnership taxable income;[97]
- The owners own the property as co-owners;
- The venture consists of co-owners who reserve the right to separately acquire or dispose of their interests in any property acquired; and
- The co-owners must not use the jointly held property to actively conduct business or irrevocably authorize a representative to purchase, sell, or exchange the investment property. Each participant can, however, separately delegate such authority for a period of one year or less.[98]

A common example of such an arrangement is an equal partnership making an investment in unimproved land when title is held in the partner's names rather than the partnership's name. A strong argument can be made that, according to the regulatory definition of a partnership (even absent such an election), an "investing partnership" need not be treated as a partnership for income tax purposes because of the lack of an actively conducted business. This would make the election especially redundant when no partnership agreement exists and partnership tax returns are not filed. However, given the uncertain effect accorded by judicial decisions of the parties' intentions and representations to third parties, an election in certain circumstances may be wise even when there is no formal partnership agreement and partnership returns are not filed. Where such returns have been voluntarily filed, an election to discontinue partnership status would be prudent from an administrative standpoint. The IRS should be notified that the group does not intend to treat itself as a partnership for tax purposes.

---

[96] *Id.*

[97] *I.e.*, profits and losses are allocated per capital accounts and no special allocations are present.

[98] Reg. § 1.761-2(a)(2).

These requirements must be met to be eligible for this safe harbor election not to be treated as a partnership. This will sometimes require modifying the business arrangement among the owners and changing title to the property. Modifications to the agreement among the partners can, for tax purposes, be treated as retroactive to the first day of the partnership's taxable year if made by the unextended due date for the partnership tax return.[99]

.02 Joint Production

Participants in a joint production, extraction, or property-use arrangement must also be co-owners (either in fee, under lease, or through another form of contract granting exclusive operating rights), must reserve the right to separately dispose of their interests, and must not jointly sell services or properties either produced or extracted. Each separate participant, however, may delegate authority to sell his or her share of the produced or extracted properties for a period not greater than the minimum needs of the industry or one year (whichever is less).[100]

.03 How Election Is Made

The election is made by filing a timely partnership return for the first taxable year for which an exclusion from Subchapter K is desired with an attached statement in lieu of the numerical information required by Form 1065, U.S. Partnership Return of Income.[101] If all members desire at the time of the organization's formation that it not be taxed as a partnership, they can instead all sign such an agreement and the participants owning substantially all interests must report tax-related items from the venture on their individual returns.[102] The latter method is commonly used by joint venturers of a passive investment, especially in real estate.

¶ 107 Shared Expenses Distinguished

Generally, a partnership does not exist if a joint undertaking is made for the sole purpose of sharing expenses.[103] When, for example, two or more persons construct a ditch to drain surface water from their properties, partnership status will not result.[104] This is true even though the properties are used in separately conducted businesses. It is joint control over the combined business and profit sharing that results in partnership status for tax purposes.

It is not uncommon for two or more professionals to share office expenses, such as rent, supplies, a secretary's salary (even though the secretary is actually an employee of only one of the professionals), utilities and phone service, and still avoid partnership classification. It is most important that each participant personally continue to serve his or her own

[99] Code Sec. 761(c).
[100] Reg. § 1.761-2(a)(3).
[101] This includes an extended tax return. See Reg. § 1.761-2(b)(2)(i).
[102] See Reg. § 1.761-2(b)(2)(ii).
[103] Reg. § § 1.761-1(a) and 301.7701-1(a)(2).
[104] Reg. § 301.7701-1(a).

clients, maintain separate records and bank accounts, and process separate billings, if applicable, in his or her own name. Partnership status for income tax purposes would ultimately result if the professionals hold themselves out as partners to third parties, conduct their business under their combined names, or pool their money and share profits. In order to assess the parties' true intent, courts have examined objective evidence such as whether the professionals kept joint books or employed joint employees, and whether they previously filed partnership returns. Whenever such an arrangement is recharacterized as a partnership, a new tax entity arises that results in a computation of taxable income subject to the provisions of Subchapter K.[105]

Even if the co-owners who share expenses have a noncash profit motive, the carrying on of a business activity indicates partnership status. This issue was raised in *Madison Gas & Electric v. Commissioner*,[106] when three electric companies agreed to jointly build, operate, and own as tenants-in-common a nuclear power plant. Madison Gas & Electric believed that it had merely entered an expense-sharing arrangement because none of the co-venturers shared a joint cash profit motive: both the electricity produced and the expenses incurred by the plant were divided among the three utilities in accordance with their respective ownership interest, and each utility had the option to either use or sell its share of the electricity produced. The relevant regulations provide that "tenants-in-common . . . may be partners if they actively carry on a trade or business, financial operation, or venture, and divide the profits thereof."[107] Contrary to Madison Gas & Electric's belief, however, the Seventh Circuit affirmed the Tax Court's controversial decision that a partnership existed. It held that "the fact that the profits are not realized in cash until after the electricity has been channeled through the individual facilities of each participant does not negate their joint profit motive nor make the venture a mere expense-sharing arrangement."

Thus, all previously deducted expenditures associated with the plant before it became operational would be required to be capitalized under Code Sec. 195 at the partnership level, and all revenues and other expenses became subject to partnership provisions. Similar expense-sharing arrangements found in areas such as oil and gas, mining, research and development, and cattle breeding are not exempt from this often criticized joint noncash profit rule.

---

[105] Reg. § 301-7701-1(a)(2).

[106] *Madison Gas & Electric v. Commr.*, 72 TC 521, Dec. 36,142 (1979), aff'd, CA-7, 80-2 USTC ¶ 9754, 633 F2d 512.

[107] Reg. § § 1.761-1(a) and 301.7701-1(a)(2).

¶ 108 Employment Relationships Distinguished

When two or more persons actively conduct a trade or business with an intention to share profits, but one party lacks a proprietary interest, an employment relationship and not a partnership is likely to exist. Although some elements of a partnership can also be found in many employment relationships (such as profit sharing, shared management control, or jointly provided services and/or capital), an employment arrangement is not a partnership for federal income tax purposes. Some courts have focused on the degree of managerial control vested with a person in determining whether he or she is a partner or an employee.[108] These decisions give weight to the parties' prior activities indicating whether a partnership was or was not intended. However, even if substantial managerial discretion is vested in a person, he or she may nevertheless be an employee, agent, or independent contractor for tax purposes if the person has no substantial interest in the venture's capital and if the person has no real liability for a proportionate share of the venture's losses.[109]

Generally, the courts have concluded that when one party (usually the provider of capital) has the power to terminate the arrangement and keep the business, an employment relationship exists.[110] Moreover, whenever a provider of services is compensated by a profit-sharing arrangement, at least one of the other partnership elements (such as sharing of losses, capital interest, or mutual control) must not be present in order for that individual to avoid partner status.[111] Though two parties may share profits, for example, and execute a "partnership agreement" while holding themselves out as "partners," no partnership relationship exists if the provider of services has no vested interest in the venture capital.[112] Additional evidence judicially considered in determining partner or employee status include:[113]

1. The agreement between the parties and execution thereof;
2. The manner in which the principal parties represent themselves to third parties;
3. Capital contributed or other capital interest held by each participant;

---

[108] *E.C. James v. Commr.*, 16 TC 930, Dec. 18,253 (1951), aff'd per curiam, 52-2 USTC ¶ 9378, 197 F2d 813; *Est. of R.D. McDaniel v. Commr.*, 20 TCM 1551, Dec. 25,111(M), TC Memo. 1961-302; *J.J. Finch v. Commr.*, 14 TCM 692, Dec. 21,109(M), TC Memo. 1955-179.

[109] *P.E. Dorman v. U.S.*, CA-9, 61-2 USTC ¶ 9773, 296 F2d 27; *Est. of C.M. Smith v. Commr.*, CA-8, 63-1 USTC ¶ 9268, 313 F2d 724; *C.L. Pounds v. U.S.*, CA-5, 67-1 USTC ¶ 9191, 372 F2d 342.

[110] See *I.L. Rosenburg v. Commr.*, 15 TC 1, Dec. 17,759 (1950); *R.O. Wheeler v. Commr.*, 37 TCM 883, Dec. 35,198(M), TC Memo. 1978-208; Rev. Rul. 75-43, 1975-1 CB 383.

[111] See *Est. of C.M. Smith v. Commr.*, CA-8, 63-1 USTC ¶ 9268, 313 F2d 724; *R.W. Ewing v. Commr.*, 17 TCM 626, Dec. 23,042(M), TC Memo. 1958-115; *P.E. Dorman v. Commr.*, CA-9, 61-2 USTC ¶ 9773, 296 F2d 27; *R.O. Wheeler v. Commr.*, 37 TCM 883, Dec. 35,198(M), TC Memo. 1978-208; *Est. of H. Kahn v. Commr.*, CA-2, 74-2 USTC ¶ 9524, 499 F2d 1186.

[112] *P.E. Dorman v. U.S.*, CA-9, 61-2 USTC ¶ 9773, 296 F2d 27.

[113] *Commr. v. W.O. Culbertson, Sr.*, SCt, 49-1 USTC ¶ 9323, 337 US 733, 69 SCt 1210; *Commr. v. F.E. Tower*, SCt, 46-1 USTC ¶ 9189, 327 US 280, 66 SCt 532.

4. The manner in which the participants kept the books of account;

5. The sharing of losses (rather than profits);

6. Mutual control over the business activities;

7. Restrictions placed on each participant; and

8. Whether or not partnership returns were filed.

In *Wheeler v. Commissioner,*[114] the Tax Court found that a partnership existed for tax purposes when two taxpayers joined together to acquire and develop real estate because a proprietary interest was held by both coventurers, and an intent to form and operate a partnership was shown. One party was to provide the capital and the other the necessary skill and management for the project. The IRS contended that the taxpayer's relationship was that of an employer-employee, whereby the provider of capital, apparently in a manner similar to an independent contractor, merely hired the provider of services to develop and manage the properties. However, the Tax Court based its decision on the fact that the provider of services, in a manner appropriate for a partner, not an employee, reported long-term capital gains from the sale of certain properties.

The major areas that left some doubt as to the status of the relationship in *Wheeler* were situations when the provider of capital was to bear all losses, title to the properties was held solely in his name, and the provider of services was, among other constraints, restricted in his authority to borrow or lend money on behalf of the venture. The court decided, however, that such restrictions merely served as protection for the other partner's capital advances and that holding title to all properties and bearing all losses were, by themselves, insufficient to cancel partnership status.[115] In addition, the provider of capital was also restricted in his authority, though not as severely as the provider of services, and this indicated a reciprocal protective device. The court concluded that contributions of skill and expertise were essential elements of the business.

It is important to note that when a provider of services has substantial management authority and contributes skill, expertise, or credibility necessary for the success of an otherwise valid partnership, then that individual may be a partner and retain partnership status for tax purposes even without a contribution of capital.[116]

---

[114] *R.O. Wheeler v. Commr.,* 37 TCM 883, Dec. 35,198(M), TC Memo. 1978-208.

[115] See Rev. Rul. 54-84, 1954-1 CB 284.

[116] See *R.T. Jensen v. Commr.,* 40 TCM 1058, Dec. 37,181(M), TC Memo. 1980-335; *R.O. Wheeler v. Commr.,* 37 TCM 883, Dec. 35,198(M), TC Memo. 1978-208.

¶ 109 Creditor-Debtor Relationships Distinguished

Factors likely to influence recognition of a valid debtor-creditor relationship include:

1. Legally required repayments made with interest, which are relatively certain, suggest debt is present; in contrast, equity contributions are subject to the risks of business activity;[117]
2. The existence of a written agreement or evidence of indebtedness;[118]
3. Whether a prudent third-party lender would make the same loan to a "debtor" under similar circumstances;[119]
   a. The way in which the loan terms reflect upon the transaction—are they arm's length?
   b. The manner in which the "creditor" ensures payment, including the amount of security for the loan;
   c. The manner in which the "creditor" enforces payments that are actually delinquent;
4. The extent of the role of the "creditor" in management;
5. The possibility of an underlying intent to profit from the activity other than by merely receiving interest;
   a. Whether equity "kicker" adds to the stated interest;
   b. The way in which the equity kicker compares with the fixed interest in terms of amount;
   c. The convertibility of loan into an equity interest; and
6. The testimony from outside parties with regard to any intention to act as creditor and debtor.

Although the practice of issuing equity participation loans has traditionally been used as one method of financing real estate acquisitions, it has also been used in other lending arrangements. In equity participation loans, lenders seek compensation by sharing in the profits of an undertaking they finance. This "equity kicker" is typically used for the purpose of making the loan a feasible undertaking for both the lender (possible additional interest) and the borrower (below-market fixed financing).[120] The borrower should consider how much control to give the lender. If the lender can exercise excessive control, then the lending arrangement may be

[117] See *E.C. Hartman v. Commr.*, 17 TCM 1020, Dec. 23,271(M), TC Memo. 1958-206.

[118] See *E. Mayer v. Commr.*, 13 TCM 391, Dec. 20,281(M), TC Memo. 1954-14.

[119] See *Astoria Marine Construction Co. v. Commr.*, 4 TCM 278 Dec. 14,438(M), TC Memo. 1945.

[120] The profit share is treated as interest if a true debtor-creditor relationship exists.

recharacterized as a partnership. In the case of financed acquisitions, the purchaser is generally entitled to basis in property purchased with borrowed funds. In addition, in the case of partnership borrowing, each partner's basis in the partnership would also normally include his or her share of the debt, which would, in turn, limit each partner's ability to deduct partnership losses.[121] If the "loan" were treated as a contribution to a partnership, the "borrower" would not be credited with basis attributable to the "borrowed" proceeds. The "lender would be treated as having contributed the "loaned" funds to the partnership. He or she would have basis for a contribution of money to a partnership. Because the partnership would have no debt, the "borrower" would have no share of partnership debt from the arrangement and would have basis for only his or her actual contributions; for example, he or she would have basis in the partnership interest for any down payment he or she made on the purchased property. In addition, no interest deduction would be allowed to the partnership because for tax purposes there would be no debt. The payments by the partnership to the "lender" could be deducted as guaranteed payments for use of capital,[122] or as distributions and/or an allocation of profits, if any. An example of excessive control would be the creditor's right to authorize all expenditures and to inspect, consult, and review the operation at all times.[123]

In *Stanchfield v. Commissioner*,[124] the Tax Court decided that the taxpayer's actions constituted those of a partner rather than a creditor. Stanchfield "loaned" money to a construction firm and was paid money as a surety for various jobs. In return, he was to receive one half of the profits, but no agreement was made regarding losses. The IRS asserted that the losses resulting from such loans and surety payments amounted to a nonbusiness bad debt and should be treated as short-term capital losses because Stanchfield was not a partner in the construction company of which his son-in-law was president. The Court, however, found it unlikely that "a canny businessman with a substantial amount of commercial experience would have advanced or caused to be advanced $111,000 and extended himself as surety and guarantor merely for the purpose of charging interest on the advance of loans." Rather, the Court determined that these acts were performed with the intention and expectation of making a joint profit. In reference to the lack of managerial services that Stanchfield contributed, the Court stated that although he did not personally sign any construction contracts, hold himself out as a partner to third parties, nor, for that matter, actually file partnership returns with the firm, he was not prevented from being treated as a partner for income tax purposes. He had contributed necessary money and financing skills to the partnership and this resulted in partner status even though he did not consider himself to be

[121] Code Sec. *752*.

[122] Code Sec. *707*(c).

[123] See *D.G. Haley v. Commr.*, CA-5, 53-1 USTC ¶ 9350, 203 F2d 815, rev'g and rem'g 16 TC 1509, Dec. 18,408 (1951), Acq. 1952-1 CB 2; see also Notice 94-47, 1994-1 CB 357, and Notice 94-48, 1994-1 CB 357.

[124] *A.L. Stanchfield v. Commr.*, 24 TCM 1681, Dec. 27,635(M), TC Memo. 1965-305.

a partner. In addition, since the funds he had advanced to the partnership were subordinated to other creditors, this was another factor indicating they constituted contributions rather than loans to the partnership.

In contrast, the Tax Court held that the taxpayer in *Astoria Marine Construction Co. v. Commissioner* [125] was merely a debtor and not involved in a partnership arrangement. In this case, Watzek, a supplier to Astoria, loaned the firm money so that it could fulfill a shipbuilding contract. The terms stated that upon completion of the project, Watzek was to receive the principal and 6-percent interest, subject to a special scale that allowed him to participate in the profits. He did not take part in any management decisions, knew nothing of boat building, and stated that it would have been foolish for him to enter into a partnership relationship with Astoria because of its dubious financial condition. His primary intention was to make Astoria a better customer for his lumber business. The IRS allowed Watzek, rather than Astoria, the loss sustained from the project because the venture had partnership characteristics. The Tax Court disagreed, stating that a creditor-debtor relationship existed regardless of the fact that a profit-sharing arrangement had been made. Therefore, any loss from the contract was rightfully Astoria's.

¶ 110 Lessor-Lessee Relationships Distinguished

Lessor-lessee relationships pose problems similar to that of creditor-debtor arrangements; if the lessor retains too much control over the operation of an active trade or business, a partnership is likely to arise. This is especially true when a lessor has management authority, such as the right to approve business decisions.[126] However, merely sharing in gross receipts or profits derived from leased property in accordance with a leasing agreement will not ordinarily create a partnership for tax purposes.[127] A lessor will run the risk of being deemed a partner, however, in a situation when profits which are to be shared are retained by a lessee and not distributed until requested by the lessor. This relationship may become particularly susceptible to scrutiny when the lessor uses the cash method of accounting and the lessee uses the accrual method. In addition, if the landlord shares a risk of loss from the operation of the tenant's business other than nonpayment of rent, the arrangement suggests a partnership agreement.[128]

---

[125] *Astoria Marine Construction Co. v. Commr.*, 4 TCM 278, Dec. 14,438(M), TC Memo. 1945.

[126] See *D.G. Haley v. Commr.*, CA-5, 53-1 USTC ¶ 9350, 203 F2d 815, rev'g and rem'g 16 TC 1509, Dec. 18,408 (1951), Acq., 1952-1 CB 2.

[127] See Reg. §§ 301.7701-3(a) and 1.761-1(a).

[128] But see *Myra Foundation*, CA-8, 67-2 USTC ¶ 9617, 382 F2d 107.

Chapter 2

Selection of Taxable Years and Accounting Methods

¶ 201 Introduction

A partnership is an entity for purposes of choosing an accounting method and a taxable year. However, the pass-through characteristics of partnership taxation have resulted in Congress enacting rules which limit a partnership's choice of taxable year and accounting method.

¶ 202 Taxable Year

.01 General Rules

Each partner must compute his or her annual individual taxable income by including his or her distributive share of the partnership's income and guaranteed payments for the taxable year of the partnership that ends with or within his or her own tax year.[1] This rule, standing alone, provides the partner with an opportunity to defer up to 11 months of income earned by the partnership from taxation until the next year.

> ***Example 2-1.*** Fred Dreer, a calendar year partner of a January 31 year-end partnership, will include his share of the partnership's income earned from February 1 of the prior calendar year in his computation of the current year's tax liability. This is an 11-month deferral of the prior year's February income until the next year's taxable income calculations.

Code Sec. 706(b)(1) imposes limitations on the use of this deferral opportunity. A partnership is required to show a business purpose for adopting a taxable year other than one specifically defined by statute.

In the absence of a business purpose for another taxable year, the partnership must adopt as its "required year:"

1. The taxable year of its partners who have an aggregate interest in partnership profits and capital of greater than 50 percent;[2]

---

[1] Code Sec. 706(a).

[2] Code Sec. 706(b)(1)(B)(i). A majority interest tax year is the tax year of one or more partners having (on that day) a total interest in partnership profits and capital of more than 50%. Generally, the testing day is the first day of the partnership's tax year. A partnership that changes to a majority interest tax year will not be required to change to

2. The taxable year of all its principal partners, if a year described in 1, above, does not exist;[3] or

3. The calendar year or such other period as the Secretary may prescribe in regulations, if a year described in (1) or (2), above, does not exist.[4]

These rules, which minimize the partnership's potential as an income deferral vehicle for the partners, are mandatory unless the partnership can show a valid business purpose for another taxable year, makes a Code Sec. 444 election, or elects to use a 52-53-week taxable year that ends with reference to its required taxable year or a taxable year elected under Code Sec. 444.[5]

If the partnership can show a business purpose for a year other than those listed above, it may be adopted as its year. This is a partnership level test as opposed to the partner level test required without a business purpose. The legislative history indicates that when 25 percent or more of the taxpayer's gross receipts for a 12-month period are recognized in the last two months of a period and this has occurred for three consecutive 12-month periods, then this period will be considered to be a natural business year, and the partnership will be deemed to have a business purpose for adopting such natural business year as its taxable year.[6] This three-year test focuses on the partnership's business rather than the partnership's operation of the business. For example, if the business was operated as a sole proprietorship and converted to a partnership by the addition of a new owner, the operating results of the proprietorship are used.

Finally, if the partnership wishes to adopt a year other than a required year as determined by the partners' year-ends or its business purpose year-end as determined by the timing of the partnership's gross receipts, it can elicit a year allowed by Code Sec. 444 if it makes the required payments and satisfies Code Sec. 444's additional rules.

> ***S Corporation Observation.*** An S corporation must use a calendar year unless it has a business purpose for a fiscal year, makes a Code Sec. 444 election, or elects to use a 52-53-week taxable year that ends with reference to its required taxable year or a taxable year

(Footnote Continued)

another tax year for either of the two tax years following the year of change. Code Sec. 706(b)(4).

[3] Code Sec. 706(b)(1)(B)(ii). A principal partner is one who has an interest of 5 percent or more in the partnership's profits or capital.

[4] Code Sec. 706(b)(1)(B)(iii). The Secretary has provided for the year which produces the least deferral of income.

[5] Reg. § 1.706-1(b)(2)(ii).

[6] This qualification is based upon Rev. Proc. 83-25, 1983-1 CB 689. While satisfaction of this rule will entitle the partnership to the relevant fiscal year, the legislative history indicates that failure should not preclude such a year. H.R. Rep. No. 841, 99th Cong., 2d Sess. II-319 (1986); see Rev. Rul. 87-57, 1987-2 CB 117.

elected under Code Sec. 444.[7] The presence of a business purpose is determined under the same rules as partnerships.[8]

.02 *Majority Interest Required Taxable Year*

Generally, a partnership must have the same tax year as that of its majority partners. The majority partners are those partners having the same tax year and whose combined interest in partnership capital and profits is greater than 50 percent. The ownership of certain foreign partners and a partner who is tax exempt is disregarded in determining the majority interest.[9] The majority interest is established on the first day of the partnership's taxable year; but the Secretary of Treasury may allow the partnership to test for majority interest on some other date.[10] However, before an alternate date will be allowed, the partnership must show that the date is representative of the current ownership interest of the partnership. If a partnership is required to change its tax year to that of its majority partners, it is not required to change again for either of the two years following the year of the change.[11]

> ***Example 2-2.*** The ABC Partnership was formed by Mary Alar and Graham Bowman who report their income on a calendar year and who each own 25% of partnership capital and profits. The other 50% is owned by a Cann Corporation which reports its income on a fiscal year ending on June 30. There is no combination of partners with the same taxable year-end with a majority interest in the partnership, and there are therefore no majority partners.

> ***Example 2-3.*** Assume the same facts as in Example 2-2, except that Cann Corporation owns only 49% of partnership capital and profits. Mary and Graham own 51%. The two individual partners are now majority partners and the partnership must use a calendar year.

.03 *Principal Partner Required Taxable Year*

If there is no one year-end that a majority of the partners share, the partnership must adopt the same tax year as that of all its principal partners. A principal partner is one who owns at least 5 percent of partnership capital or profits. If the principal partners have different tax years, the partnership must adopt a year that results in the least amount of deferred income to the partners.[12]

If a partnership has both majority partners and one or more principal partners, the partnership must adopt the tax year of the majority partners.

> ***Example 2-4.*** The ABC Partnership is a limited partnership with 30 individual limited partners and a corporate general partner. Each limited partner owns a 3% interest in partnership capital and profits.

---

[7] Reg. § 1.1378-1(a).

[8] Code Sec. 1378; Rev. Proc. 2002-39, 2002-22 IRB 1046.

[9] Reg. § 1.706-1(b)(5), (6).

[10] Code Sec. 706(b)(4)(A).

[11] Code Sec. 706(b)(4)(B).

[12] Reg. § 1.706-1(b)(2)(i)(C).

The corporate general partner owns the remaining 10% interest in capital and profits. Twenty-five of the 30 individual limited partners (representing 75% of the capital and profits interest in the partnership) have calendar year-ends. The other five have fiscal year-ends ending September 30. The corporate general partner, who is the only principal partner, has a fiscal year ending on June 30. The partnership must adopt the calendar year used by the majority of its partners rather than the June 30 year-end used by its principal partner.

.04 Calendar Year or Required Year Prescribed by Regulations

If there is no year-end that can satisfy the majority interest test and the principal partner test, the partnership must select a year-end (from among the partners' year-ends) resulting in the least aggregate deferral of income to the partners. The partnership does not have the option of choosing between a calendar year or the year of least aggregate deferral of income.[13] In determining the appropriate year-end under this rule, both the year-end and the profits interest of each partner must be taken into account.[14]

The determination of the least aggregate deferral of income is made by multiplying each partner's profits interest for the year by the number of months of deferral that would arise through the selection of the proposed tax year.[15] Months of deferral for this purpose are counted by going forward from the proposed partnership year-end to the partners' year-ends, using the information available at the beginning of the current tax year (unless the partners have made voluntary changes in their year-ends [16]). After testing each proposed tax year, the tax year that produces the least aggregate deferral of income is the "required year." If more than one partner's year-end produces the same aggregate deferral, the partnership can use either partner's year-end as its required year-end. If one of the qualifying taxable years is also the partnership's existing taxable year, the partnership must use its existing taxable year.[17] However, once the year-end is chosen, the partnership cannot change to another year-end of equal deferral.[18] The majority interest rule and the principal partners rule look at partners' interests in capital and/or profits. The least aggregate deferral rule looks only at the partners' interests in profits.

A special *de minimis* rule provides that if the tax year with the least aggregate deferral produces an aggregate deferral that is less than .5 when compared to the aggregate deferral of the partnership's existing tax year,

---

[13] Reg. § 1.706-1(b)(2)(i)(C).

[14] However, any tax-exempt partner who had no taxable income from the partnership in the preceding year is disregarded. Likewise, a tax-exempt entity that was not a partner in the preceding year is also disregarded if the partner will have no taxable income from the partnership in the current year. Reg. § 1.706-1(b)(5).

[15] Reg. § 1.706-1(b)(3)(i).

[16] IRS Letter Ruling 8907042 (11-23-88).

[17] Reg. § 1.706-1(b)(3)(i).

[18] *Id.*

the existing tax year will be treated as the tax year with the least aggregate deferral. Thus, no change in tax year is necessary or permitted.[19]

Partnerships subject to the least aggregate deferral rule must determine the tax year-end with the least aggregate deferral every year if the partners' profits interests or year-ends change. The only exception is the *de minimis* rule.

Example 2-5. The SD Partnership has two equal partners, Sam Burns and Danny Ferrer, and reports its income on a fiscal year ending June 30. Sam reports his income on a fiscal year ending June 30 and Danny reports his income on a fiscal year ending July 31. For the taxable year beginning July 1, the partnership will be required to retain its fiscal year since a year ending June 30 results in the least aggregate deferral of income to the partners. This determination is made as follows:

Year End	*Int.*	*Mos. Def.*	*Int. Def.*
June 30 Fiscal Year			
Sam 6/30	50%	0	0
Danny 7/31	50%	1	.5
Aggregate Deferral			.5
July 31 Fiscal Year			
Sam 6/30	50%	11	5.5
Danny 7/31	50%	0	0
Aggregate Deferral			5.5

The partnership must choose June 30th as its fiscal year. It cannot choose a calendar year.

Example 2-6. Corporations *A*, *B*, *C*, and *D* operate a partnership. *A* has an April 30 year-end, *B* has a July 31 year-end, *C* has a November 30 year-end, and *D* has a December 31 year-end. *A*, *B*, and *C* each own 30% of the partnership; *D* owns 10%. The determination of which year-end the partnership must use is made as follows:

Partner	*Partner's Year-end*	*Profits Interest*	*Months Deferred*	*Deferral*
A's April 30 Year-end				
A	4/30	.3	0	.0
B	7/31	.3	3	.9
C	11/20	.3	7	2.1
D	12/31	.1	8	.8
Aggregate Deferral				3.8
B's July 31 Year-end				
A	4/30	.3	9	2.7
B	7/31	.3	0	.0
C	11/30	.3	4	1.2
D	12/31	.1	5	.5
Aggregate Deferral				4.4

[19] Reg. § 1.706-1(b)(3)(iii).

C's Nov. 30 Year-end				
A	4/30	.3	5	1.5
B.	7/31	.3	8	2.4
C	11/30	.3	0	.0
D	12/31	.1	1	.1
Aggregate Deferral				*4.0*
D's Dec. 31 Year-end				
A	4/30	.3	4	1.2
B.	7/31	.3	7	2.1
C	11/30	.3	11	3.3
D	12/31	.1	0	.0
Aggregate Deferral				*6.6*

Since the April 30 year-end yields the least aggregate deferral of income, the partnership must select an April 30 year-end for its "required year.

.05 Changes in Required Taxable Years

The partnership's "required year" can change for three reasons:

1. The partners holding majority interests change (or their year-ends change);[20]
2. The principal partners change; or
3. The year-end with the least aggregate deferral changes.[21]

A change in the partnership's "required year" is treated as automatically approved by the IRS.[22] For "required year" changes, there is no four-year spread relief from "income bunching" that occurs because of short period returns. Annualization of the short period income is not required.[23] Unless the partnership has obtained approval for its natural business year, a change in a partner's year-end will often force the partnership to change its year-end.

A partnership that wants to adopt, change, or retain its annual accounting period must complete and file a current Form 1128 with the Director, IRS Center, Attention: ENTITY CONTROL, where the taxpayer files its federal income tax return. No copies of Form 1128 are required to be sent to the national office. In addition, the partnership must attach a copy of the Form 1128 to the partnership's Form 1065 for the first year the change is effective.[24]

If a partnership using the majority interest rule must change its year under that rule, it will not be required to change again for two years following the year of change.[25] However, if the partnership's year-end is required by the principal partner rule, and the year-end of its principal

[20] A consistency rule may avoid the need to change in some cases.

[21] There is a consistency rule and a *de minimis* rule that may avoid the need to change in some cases.

[22] Rev. Proc. 2002-38, 2002-1 C.B. 1037.

[23] Reg. § 1.706-1(b)(8)(i)(B).

[24] Rev. Proc. 2002-38, Sec. 7.02(1), 2002-22 IRB 1037.

[25] Code Sec. 706(b)(4)(B).

partners change requiring a change in the partnership's year-end, the two year retention of the old year is not allowed. Partnerships who have a taxable year dictated by the least aggregate deferral of income rule must change years under these rules on an ongoing basis unless the change would produce an aggregate deferral that is less than 0.5 when it is compared to the aggregate deferral for the prior year.[26] It must be remembered that if a year-end is based upon a partnership business purpose, the year-end of its partners is irrelevant.

.06 Business Purpose Taxable Year—The Natural Business Year

A partnership's natural business year is determined by applying a mechanical 25-percent gross receipts test over a three-year period. The gross receipts test is based on the three most recent 12-month periods ending with the last month of the requested fiscal year. To pass the test, gross receipts from sales and services for the last two months of each of the three 12-month periods must exceed 25 percent of the total gross receipts for that 12-month period. If the partnership qualifies for more than one natural business year, the year-end producing the highest three-year average percentage of gross receipts for the final two months is the partnership's natural business year.[27]

For purposes of this test, the period covered by the "three most recent years" is the three-year period ending with the last month for the requested new tax year-end and before the filing of the request for a year-end change. For example, if a partnership wants to adopt or change to an August 31 year-end in 2005, the three "most recent years" are the three years ending on August 31, 2005.[28]

Example 2-7. The ABC Partnership, which is newly formed but operates a business which has been in existence many years, wants to adopt an August 31 year-end. The gross receipts for the three most recent years for the 12-month period ending August 31 and a two-month period ending August 31 are:

		12-Month	*2-Month*
Year 1—	9/1/2002 to 8/31/2003	$270,000	
	7/1/2003 to 8/31/2003		$73,000
Year 2—	9/1/2003 to 8/31/2004	310,000	
	7/1/2004 to 8/31/2004		80,000
Year 3—	9/1/2004 to 8/31/2005	340,000	
	7/1/2005 to 8/31/2005		86,000

Since more than 25% of the gross receipts (27%, 25.81%, and 25.29% respectively) occurred in the last two months for all three prior years, the partnership's natural business year ends in August. Thus,

[26] Reg. § 1.706-1(b)(3)(iii).

[27] Rev. Proc. 2002-38, 2002-22 IRB 1037. See this also for additional guidance on the natural business year exception. The revenue procedure provides that, even though the 25% test is met, the IRS is not required to accept a request to change to a natural business year.

[28] *Id.*, 5.05.

the August 31 year-end can be adopted by filing Form 1128, Application to Adopt, Change or Retain a Tax Year, with the IRS by the due date, including extensions, of the partnership's tax return for the first year the new year end is effective.[29] If the change is approved, a short period return is required for the short year ending August 31.

Once a natural business year has been selected, the partnership may be required to periodically demonstrate that it continues to satisfy the 25-percent gross receipts test.[30]

In addition to the approval granted to a partnership requesting a taxable year conforming to a year meeting the 25-percent test, the partnership may request approval of a natural business year characterized by a general facts and circumstances analysis. However, the IRS anticipates that approval of a natural business year under this facts and circumstances test will be granted only in rare and unusual circumstances. The following factors will not ordinarily be sufficient to establish that the business purpose requirement for a particular taxable year has been met:

1. The use of a particular year for regulatory or financial accounting purposes;

2. Hiring patterns—for example, a firm that typically hires staff during certain times of the year;

3. The use of a particular year for administrative purposes, such as the admission or retirement of partners, promotion of staff, and compensation or retirement arrangements with staff or partners; and

4. The fact that a particular business involves the use of price lists, model years, or other items that change on an annual basis.[31]

A partnership seeking to retain, change, or adopt a tax year on the basis of the business purpose test must file Form 1128 by the due date (not including extensions) of the federal income tax return for the first effective year.[32]

Newly formed partnerships attempting to obtain approval of other than a required tax year on the basis of a business purpose can make a backup Code Sec. 444 election.[33] The backup election, which will become effective if the requested business purpose year-end is denied, is made by filing Form 8716, Election to Have a Tax Year Other Than a Required Tax Year, and typing or printing "BACKUP ELECTION" on the top of the form. However, if the Form 8716 is filed on or after the date the Form 1128

[29] *Id.*, 7.01.
[30] *Id.*, 6.05.
[31] Rev. Proc. 2002-39, 2002-1 C.B. 1046, 5.02(1)(b).
[32] *Id.*, 6.02.
[33] Temp. Reg. § 1.444-3T(b)(4).

is filed, Form 8716 must have printed or typed across the top "FORM 1128 BACKUP ELECTION."[34]

If the partnership has changed, or will change, its taxable year solely because its current taxable year no longer qualifies as a natural business year under either Rev. Proc. 2002-38 or Rev. Proc. 2002-39, its partners might qualify to spread their short-period taxable income over four years. In order for its partners to qualify, the following requirements must be met: (1) the partnership's short taxable year must have ended on or after May 10, 2002, but before June 1, 2004, (2) the partner's taxable income for one year would, except for this four-year spreading, have included partnership income from two partnership years, and (3) the income of the partnership for the short taxable year must have exceeded its expenses.[35]

.07 Adopting a Taxable Year Other Than a "Required Year" or "Natural Business" Year-End

The combination of the allowable required years and the narrow definition of a business purpose year has resulted in the overwhelming majority of partnerships controlled by individual partners being forced to use a calendar year.

In order to provide some relief to many forced conversions to calendar years, Congress enacted a procedure whereby S corporations, personal service corporations, and partnerships could adopt or retain otherwise unpermitted fiscal years.[36] Under Code Sec. 444, such entities are entitled to a one-time election to select a taxable year other than one the Internal Revenue Code requires.[37] Newly formed partnerships that would otherwise be obligated to use a required year may elect a fiscal year having a deferral period of three months or less.[38] If no election is made, the partnership must use the taxable year the Code requires.

However, an election under Code Sec. 444 is not without cost. Each year that an election under Code Sec. 444 is in effect, partnerships must make a "required payment," which is an amount that crudely approximates the tax deferral arising from the fiscal year.[39] Since each year's

[34] If the requested year is denied, a backup election is activated by filing Form 8752, Required Payment or Refund Under Section 7519, and making the required payment. The form must be filed and the required payment made by the later of (1) the normal due date of the required payment, or (2) 60 days from the date the IRS denies the business purpose year-end request. In filing the Form 8752 to activate the backup election, the partnership must type or print "ACTIVATING BACKUP ELECTION" on the top of the form. Temp. Reg. § 1.444-3T has additional guidance on backup elections.

[35] Rev. Proc. 2003-79, 2003-45 IRB 1036.

[36] The Omnibus Budget Reconciliation Act of 1987, P.L. 100-203, Act § 10206.

[37] Code Sec. 444(a). The election is made by the entity. Code Sec. 444(d)(1).

[38] Code Sec. 444(b)(1). An entity that came into existence before 1986 could elect to retain the taxable year it used for its last taxable year beginning in 1986. Code Sec. 444(b)(3). The election must have been made for the first tax year beginning after 1986, and must have been made by July 26, 1988. The Omnibus Budget Reconciliation Act of 1987, P.L. 100-203, Act § § 10206(d) and 444(b)(2). Alternatively, existing partnerships could change to a new taxable year that provides for a deferral period that does not exceed the lesser of three months or the deferral period of the year that was being changed. A deferral period consists of the number of months between the close of a taxable year elected and the close of the taxable year that would otherwise be required. Code Sec. 444(b)(4).

[39] Code Secs. 444(c)(1) and 7519. No payment is required unless the required payment exceeds $500. Code Sec. 7519(a)(2). A partnership that establishes a business purpose for its adoption of a fiscal year is not subject to the required payment rules.

required payment is adjusted to account for the required payment of the prior year,[40] the taxpayer is, in effect, required to maintain a noninterest-bearing account with the IRS.

> ***S Corporation Observation.*** The Code Sec. 444 rules applying to partnerships are virtually identical to those that apply to S corporations.

A partnership that has made the Code Sec. 444 election must file Form 8752, Required Payment or Refund Under Section 7519, with which any required payment is forwarded or refund requested.[41] A payment must be made if the amount remaining on deposit is less than the required amount. A refund is available if it exceeds this amount. If, for example, a calendar year is the partnership's required year, the required deposit amount is calculated by first determining that portion of the partnership's desired taxable year which elapses before the beginning of the calendar year and then dividing this number of months by twelve. This is the deferral ratio.

> ***Example 2-8.*** A fiscal year ending September 30 results in three months of the income earned during a calendar year being taxable to the partners in the next calendar year. This is a 25% deferral ratio.

The total amount that is required to be on deposit is based upon the taxable income of the previous fiscal year, the "net base-year income." The amount of the deposit is calculated by applying the highest individual tax rate plus one percent to the amount of taxable income deemed deferred during the last year. This deemed deferred income is determined by multiplying the deferral ratio by the "net base-year income."[42] This amount of income is in effect the average income deferred in the previous taxable year.

> ***Example 2-9.*** New partnership FGH elects a September 30 year-end under Code Sec. 444; there is no required payment because there is no net base-year income.[43] If, however, in the partnership's second taxable year ending on September 30 it has taxable income equaling $100,000, the deferred income is $25,000 [44] and the required payment is $10,150.[45] If, in the third year, the taxable income is $200,000, the required payment is an *additional* $10,150.[46]

Due to the fact that the base period's taxable income can be reduced through deductible payments to partners made after the deferral period, a special provision prevents these amounts from reducing base-year income unless they have been paid in the deferral period.[47]

---

[40] See Code Sec. 7519(b).

[41] The due date is May 15 of the calendar year which follows the calendar year in which the applicable year begins. Temp. Reg. § 1.7519-2T(a)(4)(ii).

[42] Both the tax rate and the percent of deferred taxable income taken into account are subject to a phase-in through 1989 for some entities in existence in 1986. Code Sec. 7519(d)(4).

[43] Temp. Reg. § 1.7519-1T(b)(4).

[44] 25% × $100,000.

[45] (39.6% + 1%) × $25,000.

[46] [29% × (25% × $200,000)] − $10,150 = $10,150; or $20,300, less the prior year's required payment of $10,150.

[47] Taxable income is first grossed up by the deferral period's allocable share of such payments and then reduced by the payments actually made during the deferral period. Code Sec. 7519(d)(1)(B).

.08 Code Sec. 444 Election

Code Sec. 444 election options for newly formed partnerships. A new partnership can make a Code Sec. 444 election for its first tax year. The only limitation is the deferral period, with respect to the "required year," can be no more than three months. For example, if the "required year" is the calendar year, a new partnership can elect September 30, October 31, or November 30 as its year-end.[48]

If the partnership fails to make the election for the first year and uses the "required year," it cannot make a later Code Sec. 444 election to change to a new year-end.[49]

Code Sec. 444 election options after the first year. An existing partnership using a "required year" cannot make a Code Sec. 444 election to change its tax year. However, an existing partnership using a Code Sec. 444 year-end can elect to retain its existing year-end if its "required year" changes. However, the deferral period of the retained year with respect to the new "required year" cannot exceed three months.[50]

Partnerships using years based on a natural business year/business purpose can elect to change their year-ends under Code Sec. 444. The only limitation is that the deferral period of the new year cannot exceed the shorter of (1) three months, or (2) the deferral period of the existing tax year being changed.[51]

The Code Sec. 444 filing requirements. A Code Sec. 444 election is made by filing Form 8716 (Form 1128 is not required). Form 8716 must be filed by the earlier of (1) the 15th day of the fifth month following the month that includes the first day of the tax year for which the election will first be effective, or (2) the due date, without extensions, of the income tax return for the first year resulting from the Code Sec. 444 election. Additionally, a copy of Form 8716 must be attached to the partnership return for the first tax year for which the election is made. Form 8716 needs to be filed only for the first year that the election applies.[52]

A partnership failing to file a timely election may still be able to elect under Code Sec. 444. Revenue Procedure 92-85 provides an automatic 12-month extension of time to file a Code Sec. 444 election.[53] To take advantage of this extension, the partnership must file Form 8716 within 12 months of the original deadline for filing the Form 8716. In addition, the following statement must be at the top of the form: "FILED PURSUANT TO REV. PROC. 92-85." The Form 8716 should be sent to the same address where the original election would have been sent if the filing had been timely made. No user fees are required.

---

[48] Code Sec. 444(b)(1).

[49] Code Sec. 444(b)(2)(B); Temp. Reg. § 1.444-1T(b)(4)(ii).

[50] Code Sec. 444(b)(1); Temp. Reg. § 1.444-1T(b)(4).

[51] Code Sec. 444(b)(2).

[52] Temp. Reg. § 1.444-3T.

[53] Rev. Proc. 92-85, 1992-2 CB 490; Reg. § 301.9100-2(a)(2)(i).

If the automatic extension provisions of Revenue Procedure 92-85 are used, all partners must report their income in a manner consistent with the election for the year it is made and for all subsequent years.

Once a Code Sec. 444 election has been made, it remains effective until terminated. The Code Sec. 444 election terminates upon the occurrence of any of the following events:

1. The partnership voluntarily or involuntarily changes to its required tax year-end. (A voluntary change can be made without the consent of the IRS.)

2. The partnership liquidates or is deemed to be liquidated under Code Sec. 708.

3. The partnership willfully fails to make the necessary required payments (under Code Sec. 7519).

4. The partnership becomes a member of a tiered structure.[54]

When the election is terminated, the partnership must file a short period return for the required year by its due date. An extension of time to file the return can also be obtained. The return should have "SECTION 444 ELECTION TERMINATED" across the top.

Once a Code Sec. 444 election has been terminated, the partnership cannot make another Code Sec. 444 election for any future period.[55] When a partnership with a Code Sec. 444 election terminates due to the sale or exchange of 50 percent or more of the total interest in partnership capital and profits within a 12-month period, its Code Sec. 444 election is terminated. It is unclear if the "old" partnership's terminated Code Sec. 444 election prevents the "new" partnership from making a Code Sec. 444 election. If a Code Sec. 444 election is terminated, the partnership is again subject to the "required year" rules.

> ***LLC Observation.*** When a state law partnership converts to an LLC there is no termination for partnership taxation purposes. Therefore all elections including the Code Sec. 444 election remain effective.

See sample Form 1128 and Instructions in the Appendix.

.09 52-53-Week Taxable Year

In order to reduce the compliance burden of partnerships that keep their books on a 52-53-week fiscal year, a 52-53-week taxable year is allowed. A partnership is eligible to elect a 52-53-week taxable year if the partnership uses a 52-53-week fiscal year, and the year would otherwise satisfy the requirements of Code Sec. 441 and the related regulations. For

[54] Reg. § 1.444-1T(a)(5)(i).

[55] Code Sec. 444(d)(2)(B).

example, a taxpayer that is required to use a calendar year under Reg. § 1.441-1(b)(2)(i)(D) is not eligible.[56]

The 52-53-week year must always end on the same day of the week, and must always end on either (1) the date on which that day of the week last occurs in the calendar month, or (2) the date on which that day of the week falls which is nearest to the last day of the calendar month.

> ***Example 2-10.*** If a partnership elects a taxable year ending always on the last Friday in November, then for the year 2004, the taxable year would end on November 26, 2004. On the other hand, if the partnership had elected a taxable year ending always on the Friday nearest to the end of November, then for the year 2004, the taxable year would end on December 3, 2004.[57]

If both a partnership and a partner use a taxable year ending with reference to the same month, the partner could potentially get a deferral of their share of the partnership's income. For example, if the partnership's taxable year always ends on November 30, but the partner's taxable year always ends on the last Friday in November, then the partner would often get a deferral of the partnership income. To keep partners from getting this deferral, the regulations provide a special rule to follow when a partnership or a partner, or both, use a 52-53-week taxable year and the taxable year of the partnership and the partner end with reference to the same calendar month. Under these circumstances, for purposes of determining the taxable year in which items from the partnership are taken into account by the partner, the partner's taxable year is deemed to end on the last day of the partnership's taxable year.[58]

A newly formed partnership may adopt a 52-53-week taxable year without the approval of the Commissioner if the year ends with reference to either the taxpayer's required taxable year (as defined in Reg. § 1.441-1(b)(2)) or the taxable year elected under Code Sec. 444.[59] In order to adopt a 52-53-week taxable year, a partnership must file with its Form 1065 for its first taxable year a statement indicating (1) the calendar month with reference to which the 52-53-week taxable year ends, (2) the day of the week on which the taxable year will end, and (3) whether the taxable year will always end on the last occurrence of that day of the week in the calendar month, or the occurrence of the day of the week that is nearest to the last day of the calendar month.[60]

¶ 203 Accounting Method

Code Sec. 448, which was first added to the Internal Revenue Code in 1986, denies some partnerships and C corporations the right to use the cash receipts and disbursements accounting method even when it otherwise

[56] Reg. § 1.441-2(a)(3).
[57] Reg. § 1.441-2(a)(4).
[58] Reg. § 1.441-2(e).
[59] Reg. § 1.441-2(b)(1)(i).
[60] Reg. § 1.441-2(b)(1)(ii).

properly reflects income.[61] In the case of partnerships, it applies to tax shelters and partnerships with a C corporation as a partner.

The rule does not apply to partnerships (which are not tax shelters) with a corporate partner if, in years beginning after December 31, 1985, the partnership itself does not have average gross receipts of more than $5,000,000 for the preceding years.[62] It also does not apply if the C corporation partner is a "qualified personal service corporation."[63]

A C corporation is any corporation that is not an S corporation. Thus, a C corporation for this purpose includes a regulated investment company, a real estate investment trust, a trust having unrelated business income, and a corporation exempt from tax under Code Sec. 501(a) to the extent it has unrelated business income. A tiered arrangement with a C corporation partner in an upper-tier partnership results in the reclassification of all the lower-tier partnerships as partnerships with a C corporation partner.[64]

> ***Example 2-11.*** The ABC Partnership has four partners. Three are individuals, and the fourth is the XYZ Partnership. Their average gross receipts exceed $5,000,000. XYZ has three partners—two individuals and a C corporation. Since XYZ has a C corporation partner, and it also owns an interest in ABC, the ABC Partnership is treated as having a C corporation partner and is precluded from using the cash method.

A partnership with a C corporation partner can use the cash method if the partnership meets a gross receipts *de minimis* test (unless the partnership is a tax shelter). If the partnership's average gross receipts for the preceding three tax years do not exceed $5,000,000, it can use the cash method.[65] If a partnership has not been in existence three years, the test period includes the number of years the partnership has been in existence. Partnerships must annualize gross receipts from short tax years before making the computation. Gross receipts are computed using the partnership's tax accounting methods for the year the receipts were recognized, and include total sales of goods or services, investment income (including tax-exempt income), and gains from the sale of assets (the asset's gross sales price is reduced by its basis).[66]

Tax shelters are prohibited from using the cash method without exception.[67] For this purpose, a tax shelter is defined as:

---

[61] Code Sec. 448(a). Effective for taxable years beginning after December 31, 1986.

[62] Code Sec. 448(c).

[63] Code Sec. 448(b)(2). A "qualified personal service corporation" is defined in Code Sec. 448(d)(2) as a corporation in which substantially all the activities consist of performing services in certain specified fields, and which is owned by employees performing those services for the corporation or by certain related persons. The permitted fields of activity are health, law, engineering, architecture, accounting, actuarial science, the performing arts, and consulting. Excluded are services where compensation is contingent on the consummation of a transaction, such as sales or brokerage services.

[64] Temp. Reg. § 1.448-1T(a)(3).

[65] Temp. Reg. § 1.448-1T(f)(1).

[66] Temp. Reg. § 1.448-1T(f)(2)(iv).

[67] Code Sec. 448(a)(3).

1. An enterprise in which interests have been offered for sale in any offering required to be registered under state or federal law;[68]

2. All partnerships in which limited entrepreneurs are allocated more than 35 percent of the losses for the taxable year;[69] or

3. Any arrangement that has as its principal purpose the avoidance or evasion of the federal income tax.[70]

Under the second provision above, a tax shelter includes any entity, other than a C corporation, that allocates more than 35 percent of its *losses* to limited entrepreneurs (limited partners or similar persons).[71] In determining whether a partnership or other entity has losses, the gains or losses from the sale of capital assets and depreciable or real property used in a trade or business are not taken into account. This 35-percent test is an annual test, and has no impact unless the partnership actually experiences a tax loss for the year in question.[72]

LLC Observation. The recent popularity of Limited Liability Companies (LLCs) has raised the question of whether LLCs can use the cash method of accounting. An LLC classified as a partnership for tax purposes can use the cash method when it meets the other tests (*i.e.*, the LLC has no C corporation as a member and is not a tax shelter). However, a blanket assumption that all LLCs can use the cash method is not appropriate, particularly where the LLC will experience tax losses. In Private Letter Rulings, the IRS has permitted certain LLCs to use the cash method.[73] The question is whether the LLC members are limited entrepreneurs for purposes of the 35-percent rule. In each of the letter rulings issued, the LLC was a service entity, and all but one of the LLCs practiced law or accounting. Furthermore, each LLC represented in its ruling request that all members would be active participants in the business. It appears this representation was critical to the IRS's determination that the members were not "limited entrepreneurs," thereby avoiding classification as a syndicate. How the IRS would rule if a nonservice LLC were involved or if all members did not actively participate in the business remains unclear. This is still a developing area of the tax law. For a discussion of the tax accounting options of an LLC, see ¶ 103.03.

---

[68] Code Sec. 461(i)(3)(A). This definition also encompasses any "offering" subject to a notice or filing requirement with any state or federal agency. This definition includes all entities—not only those formed with tax avoidance as a motive. Nevertheless, these entities cannot use the cash method of accounting. Temp. Reg. § 1.448-1T(b)(2).

[69] Code Secs. 461(i)(3)(B) and 1256(e)(3)(B). See Reg. § 1.448-1T. A partnership may be required to change its method of accounting in a loss year.

[70] Code Secs. 461(i)(3)(C) and 6661(b)(2)(C)(ii).

[71] Code Sec. 1256(e)(3)(B).

[72] Temp. Reg. § 1.448-1T(b)(3); IRS Letter Ruling 8911011 (12-14-88). Code Sec. 1256(e)(3)(C) lists exceptions which can remove certain limited partnerships from the tax shelter definition even though more than 35% of the losses are allocable to limited partners. IRS Letter Ruling 8911011 contains an excellent summary of these exceptions.

[73] IRS Letter Rulings 9321047 (2-25-93), 9328005 (12-21-92), 9350013 (9-15-93), and 9412030 (12-22-93).

PART II

FUNDING THE PARTNERSHIP

Chapter 3

Partnership Interest Received for Contribution of Property

¶ 301 Introduction

When there is an exchange of a taxpayer's property for replacement property, Code Sec. 1001 provides that the difference between the basis of the relinquished property and the value of the replacement property is gain realized. This realized gain is recognized unless a nonrecognition provision defers the taxable event. When property is transferred to a partnership in exchange for a partnership interest, Code Sec. 721 and related provisions provide the basic nonrecognition rules. The application of these rules is discussed in this chapter.

¶ 302 General Rule: Contribution of Property Is Treated as a Tax-Free Exchange of Property for a Partnership Interest

Code Sec. 721 provides that if property is contributed to a partnership in exchange for an interest in that partnership, gain or loss is not recognized. This is the result regardless of whether the contribution is made to the partnership upon formation or at a later date. Also, unlike contributions to corporations, control by the contributors is not an issue.

> ***S Corporation Observation.*** Contributions to an S corporation in exchange for stock are taxable unless shareholders owning 80 percent or more of the outstanding stock make contributions to the S corporation in the same transaction.[1]

.01 Basis of Partner's Partnership Interest and Partnership's Property

In keeping with the general pattern of nonrecognition provisions, Code Sec. 722 requires that the partner take an "exchanged basis" in the

---

[1] Code Sec. 351.

partnership interest equal to the basis of the contributed property.[2] In the majority of contributions, the value of the partnership interest will approximate the contributed property's value. If the interest is sold, the partner will then recognize gain or loss in the amount not taxed on the exchange of the original property for the partnership interest. Under Code Sec. 723, the partnership takes a "transferred basis" in the contributed property equal to the contributing partner's basis.[3] If the partnership later sells the property, it will recognize the deferred gain or loss. This gain or loss will be allocated to the partner who originally contributed the property under Code Sec. 704(c), thus increasing his or her basis in the partnership interest by a like amount.[4] Therefore, if the contributing partner sells his partnership interest after the partnership sells the contributed property, the gain or loss recognized will not reflect the gain or loss built into the contributed property.

This system is designed to insure that gain or loss deferred under Code Sec. 721 upon the contribution of property to the partnership is ultimately recognized by the contributor-partner, either when the partnership disposes of the contributed property or when the partner disposes of the partnership interest, but not both. The partnership must take care, however, to insure that this gain is not recognized twice. For example, if the partner sells his or her interest in the partnership before the partnership disposes of the contributed property, he or she will recognize the built-in gain or loss at that time. If the partnership does not take preventative action, by making a Code Sec. 754 election, it will recognize the same gain or loss again when it subsequently disposes of the contributed property.[5] The Code Sec. 754 election allows the partnership to adjust its basis in its assets (under Code Sec. 743(b)) to reflect the gain or loss recognized by the contributor-partner on the sale of his or her partnership interest.

> ***Observation.*** The seemingly simple rules of Code Secs. 721, 722, and 723 providing tax-free treatment for partnership organizations and creating a separate entity for tax purposes create tremendous tax complexity in the partnership rules. This is because before the partnership's formation, the members own their assets directly and personally report income or loss related to that asset. After the contribution, the partnership is the first tax accounting level for the income or loss produced by the assets, even though the income or loss flows to the partners. However, the partner's interest in the partnership is a newly created intangible asset which merely represents the partners' indirect ownership interest in the underlying assets' value. This creates a second potential tax accounting level for taxing the same income twice

[2] Code Sec. 7701(a)(44).

[3] Code Sec. 7701(a)(43).

[4] In the case of a C corporation there is always a double taxation of any appreciation. This result will occur in the context of partnership taxation only where the partner sells his or her partnership interest before the partnership sells the property and there is no Code Sec. 754 election in effect.

[5] This gain or loss will be allocated to the contributing partner's successor-in-interest (the partner who purchased his or her interest) under Code Sec. 704(c).

when the partnership distributes cash to the partners or when a partner sells the partnership interest.

The objective of the partnership taxation rules is that income or loss generated at the entity level is to be taxed only once and at the partner level. Most of the complexity of the partnership tax rules is caused by rules neutralizing the tax effects of creating two levels of ownership for the same activity.

These rules range from being relatively simple in operation and purpose to complex in operation and obscure in purpose. The simplest rules are the Code Sec. 705 basis adjustments. A partner's basis in his or her interest is increased by the partner's share of taxed income so that when the partner sells his or her interest or the partnership distributes the previously taxed income the partner is not taxed again. The partner's partnership interest basis is also increased by his or her share of tax exempt interest so that the accumulated tax exempt interest is not taxed when the interest is sold or the partnership distributes tax exempt interest to him or her. Likewise, nondeductible noncapitalized expenditures reduce the basis of the partnership interest. The spent funds have reduced the value of the interest. If the interest's basis were not also reduced, the expenditure would become indirectly deductible. Lastly, deductible losses reduce basis in a partnership interest because otherwise a second loss would arise on the sale of the interest. These basic partner-level adjustments ensure that income and loss are taken into account only once, tax exempt interest remains untaxed, and nondeductible expenditures remain undeducted. These rules are the primary method for entity-level and owner-level tax accounting and are coordinated to provide for a single pass-through level taxation for partnerships.

> ***S Corporation Observation.*** It is commonly said that S corporations are corporations taxed like partnerships. This statement is true only as an approximate general comparison with a C corporation, but this statement is literally the situation with respect to basis adjustments to the shareholder's stock for the S corporation's income or loss. The S corporation rules are simply a cross reference to the partnership rules.[6]

In the case of partnership taxation, additional layers of tax complexity are added by way of rules which further attempt to neutralize the tax effects of creating the partnership as a tax reporting entity separate from its owners. For example, a partnership can make a Code Sec. 754 election to allow the purchaser of a partnership interest to receive the tax attributes that would be received if he or she had purchased an interest in the partnership's assets directly (*e.g.*, depreciation deductions based on the fair market value of partnership properties, etc.).

---

[6] Code Sec. 1367(a).

At a partnership's formation, the total of the partnership's basis in its properties (generally referred to as "the inside basis") will equal the total of the partners' bases in their partnership interests (generally referred to as "the outside basis"). This is because each partner's basis in his or her partnership interest is equal to the partnership's basis in the assets a partner contributed. Also, the partnership's basis in the assets is equal to the partners' former basis in the assets. Therefore, both the aggregate basis of the partnership interests to the partners and the aggregate basis of the assets to the partnership are derived from the same source and are equal. This equality between aggregate inside and outside basis is not often disturbed as a result of operations or nonliquidating distributions.[7] For example, as previously described, the partnership's taxable income increases its inside basis because it represents a net inflow of assets. The inside/outside basis equality is continued because Code Sec. 705 requires each partner to increase his or her outside basis for the partner's allocated share of the income. Similar but opposite adjustments result in retaining the inside/outside basis equality in the event of partnership losses.[8] Many events can cause the inside/outside basis equality to terminate. An example is the sale of a partnership interest when, absent a Code Sec. 754 election by the partnership, the partnership's total basis in all its assets (the inside basis) remains unchanged but the aggregate outside basis is changed by the difference between the new and old partner's bases in the partnership interest. This change will usually equal the seller's gain or loss on the sale. However, if there is a Code Sec. 754 election in effect, the equality between inside and outside basis normally continues even though there is a sale (or liquidation) of one of the interests in the partnership. For example, in the case of a sale, the partnership adjusts its basis in its assets to reflect the buying partner's basis in his or her partnership interest.[9]

It can be observed that when aggregate inside and outside basis become unequal, aggregate outside basis is the true total tax investment the partners have in the partnership. It can also be observed that an event creating an inside and outside basis disparity will, with one exception, be an event which allows a Code Sec. 754 election. This one exception is when a partner's distributive share of partnership loss exceeds the basis of the partnership interest. If the election is not made, the taxable income generated by the partnership will not take into account the partners' true investment in the partnership. The pass-through income will be either larger or smaller than the partners' true tax investment should reflect. If a Code Sec. 754 election is made, then aggregate inside will be made equal to

[7] Nonliquidating cash distributions in excess of the partner's basis in his or her partnership interest and distributions of partnership property with a basis to the partnership in excess of the partner's basis in his or her interest will cause inside and outside basis to part company.

[8] The inside/ outside basis equality helps the partnership to achieve conduit status. The partnership's income or loss is taken into account only once and this is at the partner level.

[9] Code Sec. 743(b).

outside basis and the partnership's taxable income will truly reflect the partners' tax investment in the partnership.

Example 3-1. *Inside/outside basis continuing equality.* Upon formation of a partnership, the partners make the following contributions:

Partner	*Asset*	*FMV*	*Tax Basis*	*Built-In Gain (Loss)*
Kathleen	Cash	$100	$100	$ 0
Heather	Blackacre	200	300	(100)
Anne	Whiteacre	300	150	150
		$600	*$550*	*$50*

The partnership has a total initial basis in these assets of $550. After the contribution, the partnership's books of account used in computing taxable income are initially as follows:

Assets	*Tax Basis*
Cash..............................	$100
Blackacre	300
Whiteacre	150
	$550
Liabilities	$ 0

Tax Capital Accounts	*Tax Basis*	*Partnership Interest Basis*
Kathleen	$100	$100
Heather	300	300
Anne	150	150
	$550	*$550*

Note that the above partnership's tax basis capital account balance can be incorrectly confused with capital accounts kept according to financial accounting standards. The latter accounts are frequently referred to as "book capital accounts." The partnership's financial accounting books, including book capital accounts, are used in calculating its economic performance. These accounts have initial entries reflecting the *value* of contributions. This allows the partnership to credit each partner with the value of his or her contribution on its financial accounting books. It also requires the partnership to account to the partners for the *value* of the contributions received.

The partnership's initial "book accounting" balance sheet appears as follows:

Assets	*Book Value*
Cash..............................	$100
Blackacre	200
Whiteacre	300
	$600

Liabilities	$ 0
Capital Accounts	
Kathleen	$100
Heather	200
Anne	300
	$600

Comparison of Tax Basis of Interests and Book Capital Accounts

Partner	***Book Value***	***Tax Basis***
Kathleen	$100	$100
Heather	200	300
Anne	300	150
	$600	*$550*

During the first year, the partnership has the following items of cash receipts and expenses which arise from the only partnership activities and there are no other items of income or expense:

Gross Receipts	$900
Expenses	(600)
Net Income	*$300*

Assuming that the partnership agreement calls for an equal division of partnership profits, the book accounting balance sheet at the end of the first year appears as follows:

Assets	***Book Value***
Cash	$400
Blackacre	200
Whiteacre	300
	$900
Liabilities	$ 0
Capital Accounts	
Kathleen	$200
Heather	300
Anne	400
	$900

If the partnership is liquidated on the first day of year two and its assets have market values equaling their book values, each partner can expect to receive cash or property with a value equaling his or her ending book capital account.

The year-end partnership *tax* balance sheet appears as follows:

Assets	***Tax Basis***
Cash	$400
Blackacre	300
Whiteacre	150
	$850

Liabilities	$ 0	

Capital Accounts	*Tax Basis*	*Partnership Interest Basis*
Kathleen	$200	$200
Heather	400	400
Anne	250	250
	$850	*$850*

In the examples above the aggregate tax basis of the asset's $550 started out equal to the aggregate basis of the partnership interests. This equality is continued after the first year of income. Three hundred dollars of net income increases both aggregate inside and outside basis to $850. The potential for taxing this previously taxed $300 is eliminated by basis adjustments to the partners' partnership interests.

Example 3-2. *Inside/outside basis inequality after sale of a partnership interest.* If in the above example Anne sells her partnership interest at the end of Year 1 to Dale for its value of $400, Anne has $150 in gain and Dale has a basis in the interest of $400.

Assets	*Tax Basis*
Cash	$400
Blackacre	300
Whiteacre	150
	$550

Liabilities	$ 0

Tax Capital Accounts	*Tax Basis*	*Partnership Interest Basis*
Kathleen	$200	$200
Heather	400	400
Dale	250	400
	$850	*$1,000*

Anne's $150 gain from the sale of her partnership interest represents only her share of the partnership's untaxed net appreciation in Whiteacre and Blackacre. Anne's $100 share of the partnership's $300 first year income is not taxed again because Anne's $100 partnership interest basis increase offsets $100 of sales price.

After Anne's sale of her interest to Dale, the ABD partnership's aggregate inside basis of $850 is $150 less than the aggregate outside basis of $900. The true tax investment the partners have in the partnership operation is $1,000. This is their aggregate basis in their partnership interests. However, for purposes of reporting the partnership's results of operations, the partnership's tax basis in the operation is only $850. This disparity can cause the net tax results of its operations to exceed what would be the result if the partnership were credited with a full $1,000 basis in its assets. This would cause the partnership to over-report the amount of net income by under-reporting its expenses. The partnership's depreciation expense or cost of goods sold offset would not adequately reflect the new partner's tax investment in the partnership. For example, here Dale has $100 tax investment in her indirect one-third share of Whiteacre. However, her one-third share of the partnership's basis is $0. In the absence of any partnership tax rule neutralizing this situation, if the partnership sold Whiteacre for $300, Dale would report the entire partnership gain of $150. This is because Dale steps into the shoes of Anne for purposes of Code Sec. 704(c). Dale would have tax gain even though the property was sold for the same price she indirectly paid for it when purchasing her partnership interest.

When inside and outside basis are unequal, a Code Sec. 754 election is available unless the disparity is caused by partnership losses that exceed a partner's basis in his or her interest basis and are being carried over at the partner level by that partner.

If the partnership makes a Code Sec. 754 election, aggregate inside and outside basis will become equal and the partnership's taxable income will reflect the true taxable income of the partners. If a Code Sec. 754 election is not made, the partnership's net income for tax purposes will not reflect the partners' true tax investment in the assets. However, in the absence of a Code Sec. 754 election, Code Sec. 704(c)'s rules will, under some circumstances, produce a result similar to a Code Sec. 754 election for an incoming partner but offsetting adjustments for the continuing partners.

Example 3-3. *Effect on income allocation of built-in gain upon entry of a new partner by way of a cash contribution.* The PLS Partnership, which has been in operation for a few years, was capitalized with cash contributions by Pam, Larry and Simon. Its current balance sheet is as follows:

Assets	*Tax Basis*	*FMV*
Cash	$350	$350
Blackacre	70	250
Whiteacre	150	300
	$570	*$900*
Liabilities	$0	

Tax Capital Accounts	*Tax Basis*	*Partnership Interest Basis*
Pam	$190	$190
Larry	190	190
Simon	190	190
	$570	*$570*

Aggregate inside and outside basis are both $570.

Allan is admitted as an equal partner for a contribution of $300. Whether or not there is a Code Sec. 754 election in effect, the resulting partnership balance sheet is as follows:

Assets	*Tax Basis*	*FMV*
Cash	$650	$650
Blackacre	70	250
Whiteacre	150	300
	$870	$1,200
Liabilities	$ 0	

Tax Capital Accounts	*Tax Basis*	*Partnership Interest Basis*
Pam	$190	$190
Larry	190	190
Simon	190	190
Allan	300	300
	$870	$870

The entry of Allan as a new partner through a cash contribution has not affected the equality between inside and outside basis. However, if Whiteacre is sold for $300, the partnership has taxable gain of $150. A Code Sec. 754 adjustment is available only on the entry of a new partner by purchase or inheritance. Under Code Sec. 704(b), the partnership must allocate $150 to the continuing partners and zero to Allan.[10]

S Corporation Observation. When there is a purchase of stock in an S corporation or entry of a new shareholder through a contribution to the corporation, there is no mechanism to adjust the S corporation's basis in its assets or allocate its income to reflect the purchase price. There is also no Code Sec. 704(c) type income allocation method which taxes the built-in gain of the assets to the continuing shareholders and not the new shareholder.

.02 Holding Period of a Partner's Partnership Interest and a Partnership's Property

A partner must add ("tack") the holding period of contributed capital and Code Sec. 1231 assets to the holding period of his or her partnership interest received in exchange for contributing such assets.[11] A partnership interest received for contributions of other property starts the day after it is received. The partnership interest will, therefore, have a fragmented holding period when a combination of assets is contributed. The partnership includes in its holding period the contributor's holding period for all types of contributed assets.[12]

[10] Reg. § 1.704-1(b)(4)(i) and (b)(5), Ex. 14 and 18.

[11] Code Sec. 1223(1).

[12] Code Sec. 1223(2).

¶ 303 Depreciation Methods

The depreciable property's basis and the depreciation method and recovery period carries over to the partnership, and the partnership is subject to potential depreciation recapture.[13] When the partnership eventually sells the contributed property, it may be required to recapture depreciation deductions.[14] To the extent the gain on a subsequent sale represents the difference between the fair market value of the Code Sec. 1245 property and the adjusted tax basis at the time of contribution, that gain (including the recapture) will be allocated to the contributing partner under Code Sec. 704(c).

¶ 304 Contributions of Encumbered Property

The results to the partners and the partnership itself described above are affected if the contributed property is encumbered by liabilities. In order to determine the effect on the partners, both the contributing partner and the other partners should treat the contribution of encumbered property as consisting of two separate successive steps:

1. First, the existence of the debt is ignored and the results of the contribution are analyzed as described above—the effect to the contributing partner is an increased basis for his or her partnership interest in the amount of the contributed property's basis. This will have no effect on the outside bases of the other partners.

2. Second, the debt is then taken into account. Each partner has a deemed cash contribution or distribution depending upon whether the total of the liabilities transferred to the partnership results in a net increase or a decrease in his or her liabilities.[15] This calculation is made for all partners regardless of whether or not an individual partner is contributing property to the partnership. Partners with deemed cash contributions will increase their basis by this amount,[16] and partners with deemed cash distributions will reduce their basis by the amount of this distribution.[17] If any partner has a deemed distribution in excess of his or her basis, as determined in step (1) above, such excess is reported as gain.[18] It is treated as gain from the sale of a partnership interest. This is capital gain in most instances, however, Code Sec. 715(b) may apply and result in ordinary income. The crux of the analysis is determining how much the encumbered property's contribution increases or decreases each partner's share of the partnership's liabilities.

---

[13] Code Sec. 1223(2).

[14] Prop. Reg. § 1.168-5.

[15] Reg. §§ 1.1245-2(c)(2) and 1.1250-3(c)(3).

[16] See Code Sec. 752.

[17] See Code Sec. 722.

[18] Code Secs. 705(a) and 733.

Before a partnership takes over a partner's liabilities, that partner's total liabilities can be categorized as consisting of his or her share of the partnership's liabilities, for which the partner is indirectly responsible, plus his or her own separate nonpartnership liabilities, for which the partner is directly responsible. When encumbered property is contributed to a partnership and the partnership agrees to become primarily liable for paying the debt, the contributing partner's nonpartnership-related liabilities for which he or she is directly responsible decrease by the amount of such debt. This debt relief is treated as a cash distribution from the partnership. In taking over this liability, however, the partnership has a simultaneous increase in its total indebtedness by the same amount. When a partnership's total debt increases, then each partner is treated as if each made a cash contribution to the partnership to the extent of his or her share of that new debt. This is because each partner, including the contributing partner contributing the encumbered property, is treated as if he or she is responsible for the portion of partnership debt allocated to the partner under Code Sec. 752.

A contribution of encumbered property by one of the partners, therefore, causes each of the other partners to be treated as if each had made a cash contribution to the partnership equal to his or her share of the increased partnership debt. This increases his or her basis by that amount. The contributor of the encumbered property is also treated as having made a cash contribution for his or her share of the increased partnership indebtedness, but each partner is also considered to have received an offsetting cash distribution for the amount of the debt for which each partner is no longer primarily responsible. When the partnership has no other indebtedness, the partner contributing encumbered property will typically have a net deemed distribution of money equal to the debt shifted from him or herself to the other partners. The net distribution is first applied to reduce his or her basis in the partnership interest, and any excess over this amount is treated as gain. In short, the contributor of the encumbered property is treated as having received a cash distribution in the amount of his or her net debt relief and the other partners are each treated as having made a cash contribution for their share of the same amount.

Example 3-4. *C* is invited to join the AB equal general partnership. Before *C* is admitted, the partnership's balance sheets are as follows:

AB Partnership

Assets	*Tax Basis*	*FMV*
Cash	$500	$500
Stock	50	50
Greenacre	550	550
	$1,100	*$1,100*

Liabilities	$ 0	$ 0
Capital		
A	$550	$550
B	550	550
	$1,100	*$1,100*

A and *B* each have a tax basis in their partnership interests of $550. *C* contributes Purpleacre to the partnership, which has a tax basis and value of $850, and is made an equal one-third partner in capital, profits, and losses. The property is encumbered by a recourse indebtedness of $300, which the partnership assumes. When analyzing the tax consequences of this contribution of encumbered property, the first step is to account for the property contribution as if there were no debt relief. The results are as follows:

ABC Partnership

Assets	*Tax Basis*	*FMV*
Cash	$500	$500
Stock	50	50
Greenacre	550	550
Purpleacre	850	850
	$1,950	*$1,950*
Liabilities	$ 0	$ 0
Capital		
A	$550	$550
B	550	550
C	550	550
	$1,950	*$1,950*

A and *B* continue to have a $550 basis in their partnership interests and *C*'s partnership interest basis is $850. The debt is then taken into account in the second step as follows:

ABC Partnership

Assets	*Tax Basis*	*FMV*
Cash	$500	$500
Stock	50	50
Greenacre	550	550
Purpleacre	850	850
	$1,950	*$1,950*
Liabilities	$300	$300
Capital		
A	$550	$550
B	550	550
C	550	550
	$1,950	*$1,950*

A and *B* are each treated as if they made a $100 cash contribution and their bases are each increased from $550 to $650 (note that this is equal to their tax capital accounts plus one-third of the debt). *C* is treated as if he received a $300 cash distribution and made a $100 cash contribution, for a net cash distribution of $200 and his basis in his partnership interest is reduced from $850 to $650. Also, his capital account now reflects the $550 net book value of his contribution.

Computing the amount of the contributing partner's deemed cash distribution is relatively straightforward. It is the gross amount of debt shifted from the partner to the partnership. It is immaterial whether the contributing partner remains personally liable for repayment on the partnership's default or whether the partnership itself becomes personally liable. Secured debt is treated as the obligation of the securing property's owner.[19]

Computing the offsetting deemed cash contribution is more involved. An increase in a partner's share of partnership liabilities is treated as a cash contribution. This requires a comparison of the partner's share of partnership liabilities before the partnership acquired the new indebtedness to his or her share afterward. Naturally, if the contributing partner was not a member of the partnership before the contribution of the encumbered property, his or her share of the partnership's debt is zero immediately before the contribution. Partnership recourse and nonrecourse liabilities are allocated among the partners according to separate sets of rules. Due to Code Sec. 752's method of allocating nonrecourse debt among partners, it appears that it is impossible for a contribution of property subject to nonrecourse debt to result in gain to the contributor. These rules are discussed in Chapter 10.

Observation. The preparer of the partnership's tax return does not have the responsibility to compute partner level gain caused by contribution of encumbered property. The contributing partner is responsible. The preparer of the partnership's tax return has the responsibility to determine each partner's share of partnership debt. The contributing partner may use the partnership's K-1s to find his or her net debt relief treated as a deemed money distribution. The partner contributing the encumbered asset may simply compare his or her share of partnership debt as reported on the K-1 for the year-end immediately prior to the contribution to the share of debt for the year-end of the property contribution. If the partner was not a partner in the previous year, his or her share of debt was zero. If there is an increase, it is a deemed money contribution. This deemed money contribution is offset against the partner's debt taken over by the partnership and any net debt relief is a deemed money distribution. If

[19] Code Sec. 731(a).

this deemed money distribution exceeds his basis in the partnership interest, the excess is gain.

When a partner contributes property to a partnership with liabilities sufficiently in excess of basis to trigger gain for the contributor, accounting aberrations arise:

Example 3-5. The ABC equal partnership was originally funded with cash contributions from *A*, *B* and *C*. It holds debt-financed long-term investments in real estate. The partners each have a $400 basis in their partnership interests. Its balance sheets are as follows:

ABC Partnership

Assets	***Tax Basis***	***FMV***
Cash	$400	$400
Blackacre	600	700
Whiteacre	200	400
	$1,200	*$1,500*
Liabilities		
(recourse)	$600	$600
Capital		
A	$200	$300
B	200	300
C	200	300
	$1,200	*$1,500*

D is admitted to the partnership as a one-fourth equal partner in exchange for a contribution of investment property, Greenacre, with a value of $1,500, a basis of $300, and encumbered by a recourse debt of $1,200, which the partnership assumes. *D*'s results are as follows:

Step 1:		
D's basis in his partnership interest under Code Sec. 722		$300
Step 2:		
D's deemed cash distribution	($1,200)	
D's deemed cash contribution	450	
Net deemed cash distribution		*(750)*
D's basis for his partnership interest		$ *0*
D's gain		$450

A, *B*, and *C* shares of partnership debt have increased from $200 each to $450 each, increasing their bases in the partnership interests by $250.

The ABCD partnership's balance sheets are as follows:

ABCD Partnership

Assets	*Tax Basis*	*FMV*
Cash	$400	$400
Blackacre	600	700
Whiteacre	200	400
Greenacre	300	1,550
	$1,500	*$3,000*
Liabilities	$1,800	$1,800
Capital		
A	$200	$300
B	200	300
C	200	300
D	(900)	300
	$1,500	*$3,000*

The aggregate basis of the ABCD partnership for its assets (inside basis) is $1,500. The aggregate basis of the partners in their partnership interests is $1,950 (3 × $650 + $0). This is a disparity of $450. When there is such a disparity, the aggregate outside basis is the partner's true tax investment in the partnership's assets. Generally, a Code Sec. 754 adjustment is available when such a disparity occurs. The Code Sec. 754 adjustment will eliminate the disparity. Here, if a Code Sec. 754 election was in effect, the partnership would be allowed to increase its basis in Blackacre, Whiteacre, and Greenacre by a total of $450 under Code Sec. 734(b)(1)(A).

Partner *D* has a $900 negative balance in his tax capital account. This reflects the excess of the debt encumbering the property he contributed over the tax basis of such property. When added to his share of the partnership's debt, $450, his tax basis in the partnership interest appears to be $(450). Note that this is the amount of gain recognized by *D* on contribution of the property to the partnership.[20] Partner *D*'s basis in his partnership interest is, however, zero.

S Corporation Observation. Code Sec. 357 governs the contribution of encumbered property to an S corporation. The rules of Code Sec. 357(c) treat debt relief in excess of the basis of contributed property as gain. Unlike the partnership rules discussed above, the shareholder is not allowed to offset debt relief with any share of corporate debt. As a result, if four shareholders each contributed an asset with a zero basis subject to $100 of recourse debt, each has $100 of gain under Code Sec. 357(c). If they had contributed the same assets to an equal, general partnership and their shares of the $400 partnership debt were $100 each, there would be no *net* relief and no deemed money contribution or distribution and therefore no gain.

[20] Code Sec. 752(c).

¶ 305 Contributions Requiring Special Consideration

Code Sec. 721 provides an exception to the general rule that, when there is an exchange of property, the realized gain or loss resulting from the difference between the value of property received and the basis of the property transferred must be reported in the year of the exchange. If Code Sec. 721 applies, the taxation of this realized gain or loss is deferred. Code Sec. 721 also has its exceptions. When they apply, gain or loss is recognized in the year of contribution. This section discusses some common exceptions. It also covers contributions that may initially appear to be excluded from the nonrecognition provisions of Code Sec. 721, but in fact are qualified for its provisions.

.01 Property Subject to Depreciation Recapture

The depreciation recapture provisions generally require that when recapture property is transferred the potential recapture amount is taxed.[21] These sections specifically state that they generally override any other conflicting Internal Revenue Code provision.[22] Therefore, to avoid recapture on a disposition of recapture property, either Code Sec. 1245 or 1250 must specifically make exception for the transfer from the recapture requirement. The applicable provisions do provide that a contribution of recapture property to a partnership will not itself trigger recapture.[23] The partnership succeeds to the potential for recapture. However, if gain is incurred at the time of the transfer (*e.g.*, under Code Sec. 731(a) or 707), some of or all the gain is characterized as depreciation recapture.[24]

Code Sec. 1245 gain on contribution. Generally, capital gain is triggered by Code Sec. 731(a) upon receipt of a deemed cash distribution in excess of the partner's basis in contributed property (including deemed cash contributions under Code Sec. 752(a)).[25] However, if recapture property is involved, at least part of the gain is recharacterized as ordinary income. The gain is divided between capital and ordinary based on the fair market value of recapture property versus other property contributed. If half the value of the contributed property is recapture property, half the gain is ordinary income from Code Sec. 1245 recapture and half the gain is capital.[26] This provision gives no consideration to whether the liabilities giving rise to the gain recognition are associated with either the recapture or nonrecapture property.[27]

Partnership recognizes Code Sec. 1245 gain. The depreciable property's basis and the depreciation method and recovery period carries over to the new partnership, and the partnership is subject to potential

[21] Note that if the partnership had a Code Sec. 754 election in effect, it would increase both *D*'s tax capital account and its tax basis in its assets by $450. This would result in a deficit of only $(450) in *D*'s tax capital account; when added to his share of debt, it would yield his correct tax basis in the partnership interest of zero.

[22] Code Secs. 1245(a) and 1250(a).

[23] Code Secs. 1245(d) and 1250(i).

[24] Code Secs. 1245(b)(3) and 1250(d)(3).

[25] Code Sec. 731(a) triggers gain on the contribution of property to the partnership when encumbered property is contributed and the partner's net debt relief exceeds the contributed property's basis.

[26] Reg. § 1.731-1(a)(3).

[27] Reg. §§ 1.1245-4(c)(1) and 1.1250-3(c)(1).

depreciation recapture.[28] When the partnership eventually sells the contributed property, it may be required to recapture depreciation deductions previously claimed either before or after the contribution of such property to the partnership.[29] To the extent the gain on a subsequent sale represents the difference between the fair market value of the Code Sec. 1245 property and the adjusted tax basis at the time of contribution, that gain including the recapture will be allocated to the contributing partner under Code Sec. 704(c).[30]

.02 *Property Subject to Investment Tax Credit Recapture*

As a general rule, when an investment credit has been claimed in the year property is placed in service and there is an "early disposition" of such property, some portion of the credit must be recaptured as additional tax in the year of such "early disposition."[31] The statute provides an exception for what is considered to be "a mere change in the form of conducting the trade or business, so long as the property is retained in such trade or business as investment credit property and the taxpayer retains a substantial interest in such trade or business."[32] When the early disposition is a partnership contribution, the contributing partner will not be required to recapture an investment tax credit if the partnership continues to use the property in the same business as operated by the contributing partner, and the contributing partner retains a substantial interest in the partnership. The regulations, under the predecessor provision, indicate that a 50-percent interest is substantial.[33] Case law has ruled that a seven-percent interest is not substantial.[34] There is no other authority defining the limits of a substantial interest between these extremes; the author's experience indicates that a greater than 20-percent interest in capital and profits will likely avoid recapture. An interest in the partnership below this amount justifies concern that conflict with the IRS may be encountered. If recapture is avoided, it is the contributing partner who must recapture the credit if the partnership disposes of the property within the original prescribed period of recapture.[35]

.03 *Accounts Receivable*

Accounts receivable of either a cash- or accrual-basis taxpayer are property and may be transferred free of taxation pursuant to Code Sec. 721.[36] The contributor's basis in the accounts receivable will become the partnership's transferred basis in the receivables, and the contributor's adjusted basis in the partnership interest will be derived from this same amount. The partnership will report income if its collections of these

---

[28] Reg. § 1.1245-4(c).

[29] Prop. Reg. § 1.168-5.

[30] Reg. § § 1.1245-2(c)(2) and 1.1250-3(c)(3).

[31] Reg. § 1.1245-1(e).

[32] Code Sec. 50(a)(1). An "early disposition" is a retention of the tax credit property less than a statutory time period, which varies with the property's type.

[33] Code Sec. 50(a)(4) flush language.

[34] Reg. § 1.47-3(f)(6), Ex. 5 (withdrawn).

[35] *J. Soares v. Commr.*, 50 TC 909 Dec. 29,138 (1968).

[36] Reg. § 1.47-3(f)(5)(i) (withdrawn).

receivables exceed their transferred basis. The partnership must allocate this income to the contributor to the extent the value of the accounts receivable exceed their basis at the time of contribution.[37] Any excess of collections over the value of the accounts receivable at the date of contribution may be allocated according to the partnership agreement. However, any income from the accounts receivable allocated to other partners must be reflected in their capital accounts and ultimately distributed to them.

> ***Observation.*** The contributor need not report all the income from the receivables. Their value at contribution will often be less than their face amount. The partnership agreement can allocate any amount collected above the initial value of the receivables to any partner. This, however, will increase his or her capital account and share of the partnership's assets.

.04 Third-Party Notes Being Reported on the Installment Method

Dispositions of notes being reported on the installment method normally trigger recognition of gain to the holder.[38] Installment obligations, however, are property within the meaning of Code Sec. 721. Therefore, the partner is not required to treat the contribution of such notes to the partnership as a disposition. The partnership will continue to report the gross profit on the installment method.[39] However, to the extent the value of the note exceeds its tax basis at the time of contribution, gross profit subsequently recognized by the partnership on receipt of payments on the note must be allocated to the contributor.[40] The remainder of the gross profit can be allocated according to the partnership agreement.

.05 Third-Party Notes Not Being Reported on the Installment Method

When a cash-basis taxpayer receives a note that is not being reported on the installment method, the note must be taken into income at its fair market value on the date received. An accrual-basis taxpayer takes the same note into account at its face amount. In either case, the amount reported as income becomes the note's basis and is recovered as payments are received. The later contribution of such note to a partnership, in exchange for a partnership interest, is not a taxable event. The note's remaining basis will become both part of the contributor's basis in his or her partnership interest and the partnership's basis in the note. If the subsequent collections on the note exceed its transferred basis, then the partnership will incur taxable income. This income must be allocated to the

[37] See Rev. Rul. 80-198, 1980-2 CB 133. This revenue ruling, like most authority in this area, involves a contribution to a corporation but, due to the similarities the partnership provisions share with the corporate provisions, most practitioners assume that a partnership contribution will receive the same treatment. See also IRS Letter Ruling 8251114 (9-23-82).

[38] Code Sec. 704(c).

[39] Code Sec. 453B.

[40] Reg. § § 1.721-1(a) and 1.453-9(c)(2).

contributor to the extent that the note's value exceeded its basis at the time of its contribution to the partnership.

> ***S Corporation Observation.*** Because there is no Code Sec. 704(c) counterpart in the S corporation rules, a contribution of accounts receivable, notes receivable, or other appreciated assets will result in all the shareholders reporting a portion of the pre-contribution built-in gain inherent in the contributed property. On the other hand, a contribution of depreciated assets allows all the shareholders to share in the pre-contribution built-in loss.

.06 Partner's Personal Obligations

The prevailing view has been that a partner's contribution of his or her own personal obligation produces neither additional basis in his or her partnership interest nor an increased capital account. The regulations specifically provide that for book capital accounting purposes this is true whether or not it is secured by property or a letter of credit. The obligation is treated as a promise to provide funds in the future. It does not constitute a current contribution of property or money within the meaning of Code Sec. 721.[41]

A controversial Ninth Circuit Court of Appeals case has cast some doubts about the view that no basis arises from a contribution of a partner's own note to a partnership.[42] The case specifically involved a contribution of property with liabilities in excess of basis to a corporation. The Commissioner issued a deficiency notice based on Code Sec. 357(c), which in the corporate context requires the contributing shareholder to report gain to the extent of the excess of the liabilities assumed by the corporation over the basis of the assets contributed by the shareholder. However, the shareholder had also contributed his own note to the corporation for which he claimed he had a fair market value basis. This would have avoided the application of Code Sec. 357(c). The court held for the taxpayer but *in dicta* indicated that its holding would not apply to S corporations and partnerships. The cause of the court's reservations about the opinion's application to S corporations is inexplicable because Code Sec. 357(c) applies identically to C and S corporations. Its reservation about the application of this holding to partnerships also seems unfounded. The rationale given for the court's decision under the facts of the corporate situation also applies to partnerships. The court was concerned that if the contributing shareholder had no basis in the note, then under Code Sec. 362, the corporation would have no basis in the note either. If the note was either paid by the

[41] Code Sec. 704(c).

[42] The regulations specifically provide that the partner will receive an increase in his or her capital account only when the partner pays the note or the note is sold. Reg. § 1.704-1(b)(2)(iv)(*d*)(*2*). If a personal note did constitute property for purposes of Code Sec. 721, the prevailing view is that the result would be similar because the note would have a zero basis in the hands of the maker. If the regulation's approach to a partner's contribution of his or her own note to a partnership is followed for basis and gain or loss purposes, a partner has a zero basis in the note and this will carry over to the partnership upon contribution. The Partner's basis in his or her partnership interest will be increased by the same amount—zero.

shareholder when the corporation held it or if the corporation sold the note, the corporation would have income for what was essentially a contribution of money. In the case of a partnership, the same problem arises. If the partnership has no basis in the note, when it is paid or sold, the partnership will have income. This income must be allocated to the partner under Code Sec. 704(c). The partner is taxed on what is essentially a contribution of money to the partnership. It could be argued that he or she should receive basis in the partnership interest for both the income allocated to him or her and the payment on the note. The partner would ultimately receive a gain offset or a loss reflecting both the income reported and the money paid to the holder of the note. He or she would have no net income from contribution of the note and payment.

There are two problems with this approach. First, there are timing disparities. The partner would have income when the note is sold and the offsetting adjustment only when the partnership interest is sold or there is a distribution which takes into account the increased partnership interest adjusted basis. Second, any income recognized by the partnership on receipt of payments on the note (allocated to the contributing partner under Code Sec. 704(c)) will likely be ordinary. In contrast, the additional basis in the partner's interest in the partnership associated with recognition of this gain will likely produce an offset to capital gains or produce a capital loss.

Another approach to the situation which might prove successful is treating the payment of the note and the encumbered property contribution as part of the Code Sec. 351/721 contribution. The regulations under Code Sec. 351 treat all transfers which are interdependent as part of the same contribution.

.07 Personal-Use Property

A partner's contribution of property which, before the contribution, was not considered investment or business property also receives nonrecognition treatment.

Partnership's basis. When property formerly used by the partner for personal purposes is converted to business or investment use by the partnership, the partnership takes the lower of the property's fair market value at the time of contribution, or the contributing partner's adjusted basis, as its basis for computing depreciation.[43] Although there is no authority directly on point, the partnership's basis for loss computations related to the property should be the lower of fair market value or the partner's basis at the time of contribution. For gain computations, the partnership would use the partner's basis plus or minus the basis adjustments attributable to the partnership ownership. There may be situations where using the gain basis

[43] *D.J. Peracchi v. Commr.*, CA-9, 98-1 USTC ¶ 50,374, 143 F3d 487.

produces a loss and the loss basis produces a gain. In such cases, the partnership will report neither gain nor loss.

Partner's basis. Although there is no authority directly on point concerning the partner's computation of loss on the sale of his or her partnership interest, the partner's basis in his or her partnership interest should likewise not include the amount by which the contributed property's basis exceeded its value at the time of contribution. For purposes of limiting a partner's deductible share of partnership loss to the adjusted basis of his or her partnership interest,[44] the exchanged basis should be limited to fair market value. With respect to the computation of gain, both the partner's basis in his or her interest and the partnership's basis in its assets include the contributor's entire basis. For purposes of computing gain on receipt of money distributions in excess of a partner's basis in his or her partnership interest,[45] the exchanged basis should be a carryover basis without reference to the contributed property's fair market value.

.08 Investment Partnerships

While Code Sec. 721(a) provides the general rule that no gain or loss is recognized on the contribution of property to a partnership, an exception found in Code Sec. 721(b) provides that contributions to investment partnerships are ineligible for nonrecognition treatment. The intent of Code Sec. 721(b) is to tax partnership contributions that are intended to achieve (or have the effect of achieving) investment diversification for the contributing partners.[46] The partnership rule runs parallel to a similar rule for corporations.[47]

Asset ownership test. A partnership (general, limited, or an LLC) is not classified as an "investment company partnership" unless nonidentical assets are contributed, and after the contributions, more than 80 percent of the value of the assets is held for investment and consists of:

- Money (if to be used for investing purposes);
- Stocks and other equity interests in a corporation;
- Evidences of indebtedness;
- Options, forward or future contracts;
- Notional principal contracts and derivatives;
- Foreign currencies;
- Interests in precious metals;

[44] *L.Y.S. Au v. Commr.*, 40 TC 264, Dec. 26,110 (1964), aff'd per curiam, CA-9, 64-1 USTC ¶ 9447, 330 F2d 1008.

[45] Code Sec. 704(d).

[46] Code Sec. 731(a).

[47] S. Rep. No. 938, 94th Cong., 2d Sess., pt 2, at 43, 44 (1976).

- Investments in regulated investment companies (mutual funds);
- Real estate investment trusts (REITs);
- Publicly traded partnerships; or
- Other assets considered investments under Code Sec. 351(e)(1).[48]

Diversification test. There also must be meaningful diversification for the investment company rule to come into play. In IRS Letter Ruling 9608026,[49] a limited partnership among related parties was formed. One partner contributed publicly traded securities with significant value, while the others contributed cash worth less than one percent of the total value of the contributions. The partner contributing the securities did not diversify his portfolio, because he was the only significant contributor. Since diversification cannot be achieved without at least two significant contributors, Code Sec. 721(b) did not apply.[50]

In addition, diversification must result from partner contributions rather than from later partnership transactions. In IRS Letter Ruling 9607005,[51] several related parties contributed publicly traded securities and a small amount of cash to form a limited partnership. The partnership immediately borrowed funds and acquired additional securities which had the effect of diversification. However, since the diversification was achieved with borrowed funds rather than by virtue of partner contributions, Code Sec. 721(b) did not apply. This was the case even though the partnership's borrowing and subsequent security purchases were planned when the partnership was formed.

Finally, note that if all contributing partners contribute diversified portfolios of stock and securities, Code Sec. 721(b) should *not* apply. This is because diversification is already present *before* the contributions. Accordingly, the act of contributing a diversified portfolio of investment assets to a partnership does not result in diversification for the contributing partners.[52]

Gain but not loss. If appreciated property is contributed to an investment company partnership, the gain is recognized by the partner upon contribution. However, the general nonrecognition rule still applies to property which has declined in value. The character of any gain recognized under this rule is determined by reference to the character and holding period of such property in the partner's hands just prior to the contribution.

> ***Example 3-6.*** Sam Talangbayan owns TGM Company common stock (traded on the NYSE). He paid $10,000 for the stock, which is

[48] Code Sec. 351(e).
[49] Code Sec. 721(b); Reg. § 1.351-1(c)(1).
[50] IRS Letter Ruling 9608026 (11-21-95).
[51] See also Reg. § 1.351-1(c)(5).
[52] IRS Letter Ruling 9607005 (11-7-95).

currently valued at $50,000. Tom Mitchell owns MGT Company preferred stock and convertible debentures (traded on the NASDAQ). He paid $25,000 for the convertible debentures and $10,000 for the preferred stock. The stock and debentures have a $50,000 combined value. Sam and Tom decide to diversify their investment risks associated with these investments, so they each contribute their securities to TGMGT Partners (an equal general partnership).

Because TGMGT is an investment company, upon contribution Sam must recognize gain of $40,000 and Tom must recognize gain of $15,000. Sam's initial basis in his partnership interest is $50,000, as is Tom's.[53] The partnership's basis in the securities is equal to their fair market value on the contribution date, and the partnership's holding period begins on that date.[54]

.09 *Depreciation Methods*

The general rule under Code Sec. 721 is that no gain or loss is recognized on property transferred to a partnership in exchange for a partnership interest. When depreciable property is contributed in a tax-free exchange, the partnership is treated as if it stepped into the transferor partner's shoes. The partnership must use the transferor's depreciation method and remaining depreciable life.

If a partner recognizes gain on a contribution of encumbered property to a partnership because of net debt relief in excess of the basis of the contributed property, absent a Code Sec. 754 election in effect for the year of contribution, the partnership's basis in the property is the partner's basis. There is no basis increase allowed to the partnership for the gain recognized by the partner. This is true even though, in effect, the partnership is purchasing a portion of the asset through assumption of the partner's debt.

Observation. If the partners agree that the basis to the partnership should reflect the debt, they should consider a sale to the partnership.

If there is a Code Sec. 754 election in effect to the extent that a partner's net debt relief causes gain to be recognized on the contribution, and the property's basis in the partnership's hands exceeds its basis in the transferor's hands, the increase in basis is treated by the partnership as a separate asset placed in service on the date of contribution.

Example 3-7. Carla Smith contributed depreciable residential real property purchased in 1990 to the QRS partnership in exchange for a 10% interest therein. Due to excessive debt, she recognized a $50,000 gain on the transfer. The original cost of the property, acquired in January 1990, was $300,000. Carla assigned $25,000 of this

[53] Reg. § 1.351-1(c)(6).

[54] Code Sec. 722.

cost to the land, and $275,000 to the building. She transferred the property to the partnership on May 1, 2000. Since the property is 27.5-year property, Carla's depreciation deductions have been $10,000 per year (with the exception of 1990 in which she was allowed only 11.5/12 of this amount). The partnership will take a carryover basis in the property and will continue to depreciate it over the remaining 17.5 years of its depreciable life. For 2000, Carla will claim 4/12 of the deduction ($3,333), and the partnership will claim 8/12 ($6,667). If the partnership has a Code Sec. 754 election in effect, and this is the partnership's only capital or Code Sec. 1231 asset, it will increase its basis in this property by $50,000 (the amount of gain recognized by Carla on the transfer). This increase will be treated as newly acquired property (acquired May 1, 2000) and will be depreciated, straight-line, over 27.5 years beginning on that date. See ¶ 1703.

.10 Suspended Losses

Property contributed to a partnership may have related losses that were not deductible by the contributing partner because of statutory limitations. For example, the losses could have been suspended because of the Code Sec. 465 at-risk rules or the Code Sec. 469 passive activity rules. Any losses suspended by Code Secs. 465 or 469 prior to the contribution of the related activity remain with the contributing partner and are not transferred to the partnership.[55] If the activity produces income in the partnership's hands, it will be either passive income or "income from a former passive activity" which can be offset by any of the activity's unused passive activity deductions from a prior year.[56] All income generated by the activity on the partnership's hands results in an additional at-risk amount.

---

55 Code Sec. 723.

56 Prop. Reg. § 1.456-67(b); Code Sec. 469(g).

Chapter 4

Receipt of a Partnership Interest in Exchange for Services

¶ 401 Introduction

The nonrecognition provisions that apply to the receipt of a partnership interest in exchange for a property contribution do not apply to one who receives a partnership interest in exchange for services. The rules governing both the service partner's and the partnership's results are relatively well defined to the extent that the service partner gets an interest in the partnership's capital. The law governing the receipt of a future profits interest is less clear cut.

A partner is treated as receiving a partnership interest in capital if upon its receipt he or she would have "an interest that would give the holder a share of the proceeds if the partnership's assets were sold at fair market value and the proceeds were distributed in a complete liquidation of the partnership."[1] A profits interest is a share in the results of future operating results and future appreciation in the partnership's assets.

Upon receipt of an interest in partnership capital in exchange for services, the service partner must recognize income equal to the fair market value of the partnership interest received. Note that fair market value is usually not the same as the amount credited to the partner's tax basis capital account in the partnership's books. Also note that the fair market value of the interest is not necessarily equal to the partner's share of capital plus or minus the product of his or her profit or loss sharing ratio, multiplied by the built-in gain or loss of the partnership assets. Valuation discounts for lack of control and marketability should be considered.

> ***Observation.*** Practitioners have often observed that the IRS position may overstate the value of the partnership interest. This is because for a partner there are restrictions on control over his or her share of the assets and the partner's partnership interest is less marketable than simply having separate ownership of property having a value equal to his or her share of the cash value of the assets.

---

[1] Rev. Proc. 93-27, 1993-2 CB 43.

¶ 402 Capital Interest Received

.01 *Results to Service Partner*

An interest in capital that vests in the service partner immediately is valued and treated as personal service income on the date of receipt.[2] For this purpose, an interest is vested if it either is transferable or it is not subject to a substantial risk of forfeiture. If the partnership interest received by the service partner does not vest immediately, but rather is contingent, for example, upon the occurrence of future events (*e.g.*, fully leasing a vacant office building, the partnership reaching a specified level of profitability, etc.) and is not transferable until that date, then the service partner recognizes no income with regard to receipt of the partnership interest until it is vested. At that time, the service partner will recognize compensation income equal to the value of the partnership interest received, as measured at the vesting date.

The service partner may elect, under Code Sec. 83(b), to ignore the contingency associated with receipt of the partnership interest and include the partnership interest in income when initially received and measured at its initial value. Partners making this election cannot take into account the risk of forfeiture or lack of transferability in valuing the interest. Moreover, if the interest is subsequently forfeited, no deduction for the loss will be allowed to such partners even though they have basis in the now forfeited interest [3] (in an amount equal to the amount previously included in income).

> ***Example 4-1.*** On January 1 of Year 1, Kali is granted an equal one-fourth interest in the ABCD partnership for her agreement to find tenants for the partnership's newly constructed office building. This interest is subject to the condition that it is forfeited back to the partnership in the event that the building is not at least 50% leased as of January 1 of Year 2 and 75% leased as of August 17 of Year 2.

Such a partnership interest would be considered subject to a substantial risk of forfeiture. Unless the service partner elects, within 30 days of receiving the interest, to value and report the interest as income in the year received rather than when it is vested, the interest is not taxable until the risk of forfeiture lapses.[4]

There are two benefits of electing to be taxed in the year of receipt:

- The recipient avoids recognizing subsequent appreciation in the partnership interest as compensation income when the interest becomes vested, and

[2] Code Sec. 83(a).

[3] Code Sec. 83(b)(1).

[4] Reg. § 1.83-2(b).

- Any amounts received as partnership distributions are not recharacterized as compensation (because the service partner is recognized as a partner).[5]

The Code Sec. 83(b) election is especially beneficial when the initial value of the partnership interest received by the service partner is relatively low or when the difference between that value and the amount paid, if any, for that interest (in addition to services provided) is relatively small. In either case, little income will be recognized at the time the Code Sec. 83(b) election is made, and if the partnership interest subsequently appreciates, the appreciation will not be taxed to the partner as compensation.

Example 4-2. Eddie Horton received a 5% interest in MidCity Associates, a partnership formed to construct and manage an office tower. The interest is contingent upon Eddie's ability to find tenants for the newly constructed office tower. Construction of the building was recently completed at a total cost of $1.2 million. The partnership's debts total $1,000,000. Thus, if Eddie makes the election under Code Sec. 83(b) to recognize income from the transaction now, he will report at most $10,000 as compensation. This amount may be further reduced by lack of marketability or lack of control discounts. Any gains subsequently recognized upon disposition of the interest would then be taxed as capital gain.

A Code Sec. 83(b) election must, as stated, be made no later than 30 days after the date on which the property is transferred and may be made prior to the transfer.[6] The written election must be separately filed with the Internal Revenue Service Center office where the service provider regularly files income tax returns. The service provider must also attach a copy of the election to his or her income tax return for the year of the transfer [7] and must furnish a copy to the person for whom services are performed.[8]

Until the interest vests, the regulations provide for a curious result when the Code Sec. 83(b) election is not made: the service partner is not considered a partner for tax purposes.[9] It is unclear how to give effect to this regulatory pronouncement and no specific official guidance has been offered. One choice would be to interpret the regulations literally and simply ignore the service partner's membership in the partnership, and, to the extent cash and property are paid to him, he or she would be treated as an employee or independent contractor. The payment would not be subject to the special rules applying to partnership payments to partners under Code Sec. 707(a) and Code Sec. 707(c). Payments would be deducted by the partnership and would be personal services income to the partner. They would not be considered distributions of distributive shares of income.

[5] The service partner is also treated as a partner for purposes of allocating partnership income and loss.

[6] Reg. § 1.83-2(b).

[7] Reg. § 1.83-2(c).

[8] Reg. § 1.83-2(d).

[9] Reg. § 1.83-1(a)(1).

Another approach, apparently more popular but with less regulatory support, is to simply ignore this provision and treat a forfeitable partnership interest the same as any other vested partnership interest.

It is clear to all tax practitioners who follow the subject closely that this situation has not been adequately analyzed by the taxing authorities. It is presently unclear how to give effect to the regulations, and the IRS has offered no guidance. Traditionally, however, the IRS Commissioner has not been shy to retroactively penalize actions inconsistent with later defined rules. Most practitioners who wish to avoid this risk elect Code Sec. 83(b) and include the value of the interest in income in the year received. The regulations clearly provide that the service partner is then treated as a partner for tax purposes.

.02 Results to Partnership

When the interest is vested, the partnership is treated as if it transferred a partitioned tenancy-in-common interest in its property to the service partner as compensation for his or her past or future services. It is entitled to a deduction for the value of the capital interest paid to the service partner unless a cash payment to an independent party for such services would be nondeductible. This deduction is allocable to the continuing partners other than the service partner in proportion to their respective indirect interests in the partnership property transferred. The total deduction allowed to the partnership is equal to the value of the property deemed transferred to the service partner.[10] Therefore, each continuing partner's deduction will equal the reduction in his or her interest in the liquidated value of the partnership. The service partner's income will equal his or her increased interest in the liquidated value of the partnership.[11]

Since the partnership is treated as if it transferred an undivided tenancy-in-common interest in its own property to the partner in exchange for services, it must realize gain or loss on the portion of its property used to pay for the services. This gain or loss is allocated to the same partners who are allocated the deduction because they are the partners who used their share of appreciated or depreciated property to pay for services.

The situation can be viewed as if the partnership paid an undivided interest in the partnership's property to the service partner who, therefore, takes it with a basis equal to its fair market value. He or she, in turn, is treated as having contributed such property back to the partnership in exchange for a partnership interest. The partnership therefore takes as its

[10] Often admission of a new partner is accounted for by reallocating the existing capital account values among the new and existing partners. However, when this accounting procedure is used, each partner's tax deduction will equal his or her capital account reduction only if the partnership balance sheet, including the partners' capital accounts, is stated in terms of the asset's current values excepting goodwill. A service partner's receipt of an interest in goodwill represents only a share of the current estimate of future profitability and is treated as a receipt of an interest in future partnership profits and is described at ¶ 403.

[11] The partnership must comply with Form 1099 or W-2 reporting requirements to qualify for the deduction to avoid withholding. See Reg. § 1.83-6(a)(2).

transferred basis for this portion of the property its fair market value. The net effect to the basis of the partnership's property is that it is changed by the gain or loss realized by the partnership. The portion of the partnership's property treated as paid to the service partner is stepped up or down in basis for the amount of gain or loss recognized by the partnership. This portion of the partnership's property will have a basis equal to its value. The benefit or burden of this step up or down in basis should be, and probably is, required to be allocated to the service partner in accordance with Code Sec. 704(c) considerations.

Example 4-3. The ABC partnership was formed by cash contributions and has been holding undeveloped investment realty for long-term appreciation. Its balance sheet is as follows:

ABC Partnership

Assets	***Tax Basis***	***FMV***
Real Estate	$90,000	$120,000
Liabilities	$ 0	$ 0
Capital		
A	$30,000	$40,000
B	30,000	40,000
C	30,000	40,000
	$90,000	*$120,000*

Kali, a real estate developer, is admitted as an equal unrestricted one-fourth partner for his promise to produce a feasibility study related to subdividing and marketing the partnership's property. Assuming no discounts for lack of control and marketability, Kali has personal service income of $30,000 and a basis in her partnership interest of $30,000.[12] Assuming Code Sec. 263A does not require capitalizing such a payment, the partnership has a $30,000 deduction.[13] This deduction should be allocated to *A, B,* and *C* only because it arose before Kali became a partner.[14] The partnership has capital gain of $7,500.[15] This gain is also allocated only to *A, B,* and *C* for the same reason that the $30,000 deduction is allocated to them alone. It is the continuing partners who have used their share of the value of the assets to pay *A.* They should be allowed the deduction and be required to report gain from using the share of their appreciated assets to pay Kali. The resulting partnership balance sheet is as follows:

---

[12] One-fourth total value of the partnership (1/4 × $120,000 = $30,000).

[13] The partnership is treated as paying Kali with property. The property paid to Kali for her services has a value of $30,000 (1/4 × $120,000).

[14] Code Sec. 706(d). There is a possibility that the deduction arose as Kali became a partner and not before. However, it must be emphasized that *A, B* and *C* are bearing the economic burden of the shift of a portion of the property's value to Kali. They may want the deduction.

[15] The partnership is treated as selling one-fourth of the real estate with a value of $30,000 and a basis of $22,500.

ABCD Partnership

Assets	***Tax Basis***	***FMV***
Real Estate	$97,500 [16]	$120,000
Liabilities	$ 0	$ 0
Capital		
A [17]	$22,500	$30,000
B	22,500	30,000
C	22,500	30,000
Kali [18]	30,000	30,000
	$97,500	*$120,000*

¶ 403 Profit Interest Received

As discussed in the previous section, a partner's receipt of a capital interest for services is governed by a complex set of rules that are relatively well established. In contrast, the rules governing a profit interest allowed to a partner in exchange for services are less clear cut. The general framework has been established, but the details of application remain unsettled.

Before 1971, tax practitioners were understandably confident that a profits interest allocated to a partner, in exchange for a promise of future services or in payment for past services, would be taken into account in the year the partnership realized that partner's share of income or loss. The reasons underlying this mistaken confidence were simple. First, valuing an expected interest in future results is usually impossible. Second, even if a profits interest could be valued and this amount reported when the right to share in future profits was established, what could be done in the year that share of income materialized? If the service partner was required to again include his or her share of the income, the partner would have reported the same income twice, first as an estimated amount and second when the actual amounts became known.[19] Also, what if the estimated value did not materialize? The partner will have reported ordinary income in an early year followed by a capital loss in later years. Unfortunately, bad facts and administrative shortsightedness have resulted in bad law. Consequently, the government's right to tax a profits interest to the recipient in the year the right becomes part of the partnership agreement has been established.[20]

Case law provides the most important potential limitation to the IRS's authority to require reporting the receipt of the profits interest itself as

[16] The real estate's basis is three-fourths of the ABC partnership's basis of $90,000, or $67,500 plus Kali's $30,000 cost basis in the real estate.

[17] *A, B,* and *C*'s capital accounts, values, and basis in their interests are reduced by one-fourth. This is the portion of their interest in the partnership transferred to Kali. This is their original capital account of $30,000 less their $10,000 share of the deduction plus their $2,500 share of income.

[18] Kali's capital account of $30,000 represents her share of the basis of the real estate. Kali is treated as having received one-fourth share worth $30,000 as payment for services and then contributing it to the partnership. This results in a capital account and basis of $30,000.

[19] Because the service partner will increase his or her basis in the partnership interest by the income reported on both occasions, his or her future taxable income will potentially be reduced by the amount of the over-reporting. Eventually, therefore, when the partner receives the benefit of this increased basis, the temporary over-reporting will have reversed itself.

[20] *S. Diamond v. Commr.*, 56 TC 530, Dec. 30,838 (1971), aff'd, CA-7, 74-1 USTC ¶ 9306, 492 F2d 286, 290.

personal services income. The profits interest must be taken into account in the year in which it is created when it has a "determinable market value." The leading decision in this area observes that "[s]urely in many if not the typical situation it will have only speculative value, if any."[21] Due to the obvious problems with reasonably valuing the profits interest through forecasts of future operations, the IRS has taken another approach. The IRS has ruled that the receipt of the right is not taxable if:

1. The partnership does not have a substantially certain stream of income;

2. The interest is held two years; and

3. The partnership interest is not publicly traded.[22]

The occurrence of the event that causes the interest to become substantially vested also will not be taxable if the above three requirements are met and the following three are also met:

1. The partnership and the service provider treat the service provider as a partner from the date the interest is granted, and the service provider recognizes his or her distributive share of partnership income, gain, loss, deduction, and credit in computing income tax liability for the entire period during which the service provider has the interest;

2. Neither the partnership nor any of the partners take any deductions for the value of the interest, either upon the grant of the interest or at the time that the interest becomes substantially vested; and

3. The other conditions stated in Rev. Proc. 93-27 are satisfied.[23]

Although the IRS's position certainly reduces the frequency with which taxpayers will need to resolve the issue before taking a reporting position, it doesn't eliminate it. For example, service partners who receive a profits interest in a partnership which owns property subject to a net lease or service partners who sell their interests within two years will still have to show that the interest had no ascertainable value when received to avoid reporting ordinary income in the year the partnership interest was received rather than capital gains when it was sold.

In addition to the problem, discussed in the previous section, of whether one who has a nonvested profits interest is a partner for tax

[21] *Id.* See *D.B. St. John v. U.S.*, DC Ill., 84-1 USTC ¶ 9158. By using a liquidation value approach, the court held the ascertainable value to be zero. See also *Campbell v. Commr.*, CA-8, 91-2 USTC ¶ 50,420, 943 F2d 815, rev'g 59 TCM 236, Dec. 46,493(M), TC Memo. 1990-162.

[22] Rev. Proc. 93-27, 1993-2 CB 343. See also GCM 36346 (1975).

[23] Rev. Proc. 2001-43, 2001-2 CB 191.

purposes, other practical results remain uncertain which are not cured by a Code Sec. 83(b) election.[24] If the expected profits interest is taxed before it has materialized, is it taxed again when it is earned? Additionally, can the partnership take a deduction for the value of the profits interest transferred to the partner?[25]

[24] See discussion at ¶ 402.01 regarding Reg. § 1.83-2(b) and partners' receipt of capital interest.

[25] See generally, Cuff, *New Partner in Professional Service Partnership Faces Unforeseen Tax Problems*, 64 *J. Taxn.* 302 (1986).

Chapter 5

Transactions Between a Partner and the Partnership

¶ 501 Introduction

In keeping with the entity/aggregate tension of the partnership taxation rules, transfers between the partnership and the partner are subject to rules which recognize the partnership as an entity separate from the partner, but take into account the fact that the partner is to some extent dealing with him- or herself. This chapter discusses the tax treatment of actual and deemed sales between the partnership and partner.

¶ 502 Tax Treatment of Sale of Property to the Partnership by a Partner

.01 Sale at a Gain

If any person considered to be related to the partnership, whether a partner or not, sells property to the partnership that does not qualify as a capital asset in the *partnership's* hands, the gain will be treated as ordinary income.[1] The same result occurs when the sale is by the partnership to the related party. Examples of property commonly affected by this provision are depreciable realty and subdivided real estate which will be developed and sold to the public.

Persons are considered to be related to the partnership if they own, directly or indirectly, more than 50 percent of the partnership's profit *or* capital interests. A person is considered to indirectly own partnership interests if those interests are owned by the following other persons:

1. Brothers,
2. Sisters,
3. Spouse,

[1] Code Sec. 707(b)(2).

4. Ancestors, or

5. Lineal descendants.[2]

A partnership interest held by a corporation, partnership, estate, or trust is considered to be owned proportionately by, or for, its shareholders, partners, or beneficiaries.[3]

.02 *Sale at a Loss*

No loss may be recognized on the sale of property between a partnership and a person owning, directly or indirectly, more than 50 percent of the interest in capital or profits of the partnership.[4] Indirect ownership is defined under Code Sec. 267(c) as described above.[5] Following the structure of Code Sec. 267, the buyer of property in this situation takes a cost basis equal to the price he, she or it paid to acquire the property even though the loss realized by the seller is not recognized. However, when the buyer subsequently disposes of the property, any gain realized in that transaction may be offset by the disallowed loss previously realized by the seller. The gain offset should be treated as tax exempt income for partnership interest adjusted basis purposes. If the disallowed loss exceeds the subsequently realized gain (or if there is no gain subsequently realized on disposition), the excess loss is permanently erased.

> ***Example 5-1.*** Hilary Martin owns 60% of the capital and profits interests in Marlow Partners. This year, her son, Steve, sold property to the partnership for its appraised value of $275,000. Steve's tax basis in the property was $315,000. Because he is deemed to own the 60% interest in the partnership owned by Hilary, his $(40,000) loss is disallowed under Code Sec. 707(b)(1). However, the partnership's tax basis in the property will be equal to the $275,000 price it paid. If it subsequently sells the property for, say, $325,000, it will report gain of only $10,000 (its $50,000 realized gain offset by Steve's $40,000 disallowed loss). Note that if it later sells the property for only $300,000, it will report no gain or loss. Its $25,000 realized gain will be offset by the previously disallowed loss, but no deduction will be allowed for the remaining, "unused" loss.

> ***Observation.*** A question remaining unanswered is whether the partner who had the burden of the disallowed loss can be specially allocated the benefit of the offset to the partnership's taxable income. Although the situation is very much like a built-in Code Sec. 754(c) loss, neither the Code Sec. 704(b) or (c) regulations address the issue.

---

[2] Code Secs. 707(b)(3) and 267(c).

[3] Code Secs. 707(b)(3) and 267(c)(1).

[4] Code Sec. 707(b)(1). Losses are also disallowed on the sale of property between two partnerships if the same persons own (directly or indirectly) more than 50 percent of the profits or capital interests in the two partnerships.

[5] For this purpose, Code Sec. 707(b)(3) provides for the application of Code Sec. 267(c), "other than paragraph (3) of such section."

¶ 503 Property Contributions Treated as Disguised Sales

.01 In General

The traditional method of tax accounting for property contributions and distributions allowed sellers of property to structure sales as property contributions coupled with (subsequent) distributions. The sellers and buyers could take the position that a bona fide contribution and an unrelated distribution had occurred and report the transaction under those more favorable rules rather than as sales. The IRS was left the difficult task of detecting the "plan" and proving that the transactions taken as a whole amounted to a sale. These disguised sales could take the form of money sales when funds were "distributed" soon after a property "contribution." The sale could also be made in exchange for other property. For example, a taxpayer could contribute property *A* to a partnership and receive property *B* as a distribution in liquidation of his interest. Or, property *A* could be distributed to another partner in liquidation of his interest, leaving the partnership with only property *B* as its principal asset and the taxpayer as its principal partner. Under the traditional contribution and distribution rules of partnership taxation, the swap would be tax-free. Three provisions have been enacted to treat these types of transactions as disguised sales: Code Secs.707(a)(2)(B), 704(c)(1)(B) and 737.

> ***S Corporation Observation.*** There is no counterpart to the partnership disguised sale rules in the S corporation arena. However, the potential for abuse is not as available. If a shareholder receives any property other than stock in exchange for a contribution of property to a regular or S corporation, such property is treated as "boot" and generates immediate tax consequences. Distributions to a shareholder subsequent to the contribution of property to the S corporation must generally be pro rata unless they are structured as a stock redemption. Stock redemptions are treated by the shareholder as a sale of his or her stock, which trigger immediate tax consequences. In addition, distributions of appreciated property are a taxable event to an S or C corporation.[6]

.02 Contributions Related to Distributions—The Facts and Circumstances Test of Code Sec. 707(a)(2)(B)

An abuse that was addressed in The Tax Reform Act of 1984 [7] was that of property contributions that are disguised sales between partners or between the partnership and the "contributing" partner. Code Sec. 707(a)(2)(B) deals with disguised sales carried out by means of a contribution to the partnership entity followed by a subsequent distribution to the partner by recharacterizing the transaction as a sale. The "disguised sale

[6] Code Sec. 311(b).

[7] The Tax Reform Act of 1984, P.L. 98-369, 98th Cong., 2d. Sess. (July 18, 1984).

between partners" technique demonstrated in the example below was used by taxpayers in a number of reported cases.[8]

> ***Example 5-2.*** *A* owns land with a $100,000 fair market value and basis of $60,000. *B* is interested in developing the land but *A* does not want to recognize the gain on sale of the land. They form an equal partnership in which *A* contributes the land and *B* contributes $50,000 and a financing commitment. After the money is obtained to finance the development, the partnership distributes $50,000 of cash to *A*. Since *A*'s basis is $60,000, *A* recognizes no gain on the transaction. This is true even though in the IRS's view *A* had, in essence, sold a half interest in this property to *B*, which should have resulted in a gain of $20,000. *A* is using his entire basis in the land to offset a gain on sale of one-half the land.

> ***Example 5-3.*** *A* owns land with a $100,000 fair market value and a basis of $60,000. The BC partnership is interested in developing the land and *A* is willing to sell it for BC's installment note. Under the installment method of reporting this sale, *A*'s reporting ratio would be 60% and *A* would report 60% of each payment as capital gain. ABC instead arranged the sale as a contribution to the ABC partnership and an installment liquidation of *A*'s interest. Under the partnership distribution rules, cash distributions are first treated as recoveries of *A*'s $60,000 basis in his interest before he reports any capital gain.[9] *A* is in effect receiving cost recovery reporting for the installment sale.

Prior to implementation of Code Sec. 707(a)(2)(B), the IRS was explicitly authorized in the regulations under Code Sec. 731 to recharacterize as sales contributions which were followed by related distributions.[10] The IRS argued that the substance of such transactions was a sale and that the tax treatment should correspond to the substance. The courts, however, often held that taxpayers had simply structured a transaction to achieve favorable tax results. The cases hinged on the importance of the particular property to the business of the partnership and the necessity of financial success before the partner contributing property could recover his or her entire investment. As an example, there is the case of *Otey v. Commissioner*,[11] in which the Tax Court pointed out that, without the contributed property, there was no partnership property, and Otey had no guarantee of recovering his property's value from a buyer. Code Sec. 707(a)(2)(B) now states, as did the prior regulations, that when such a transaction, viewed as a whole, is properly characterized as a sale, then the transaction is treated as a sale and governed by Code Sec. 707(a)(1). The legislative history of the

[8] *J.H. Otey, Jr. v. Commr.*, 70 TC 312, Dec. 35,167 (1978), aff'd per curiam, CA-6, 80-2 USTC ¶ 9817, 634 F2d 1046; *Barenholtz v. Commr.*, 77 TC 85, Dec. 38,070 (1981) (holding that there was a taxable sale).

[9] Code Sec. 731(a).

[10] Reg. § 1.731-1(c)(3).

[11] *J.H. Otey, Jr. v. Commr.*, 70 TC 312, Dec. 35,167 (1978), aff'd per curiam, CA-6, 80-2 USTC ¶ 9817, 634 F2d 1046.

section provides the following factors to be considered in determining whether the net effect of the transaction is a disguised sale:

1. A partner wishing to avoid sale treatment must bear risk of failure of the business venture;

2. A transitory partner status in the partnership is a factor suggesting that a "contribution" is really a sale; and

3. A short time period between the contribution and distribution is a factor suggesting that a "contribution" is really a sale.[12]

The legislative history of Code Sec. 707(a)(2) authorizes the Treasury Department to prescribe new regulations to more specifically carry out these purposes. On April 24, 1991, the IRS issued proposed regulations listing a number of factors that may tend to prove the existence of a disguised sale;[13] on September 25, 1992, the IRS finalized these regulations. The final regulations include most of the concepts of the proposed regulations. The final regulations are effective for property transfers considered part of a sale occurring after April 24, 1991.[14]

General rules. The general rules provide that a transfer of property to a partnership, coupled with a concurrent or subsequent transfer of money or other consideration to the contributing partner (including the assumption of the partner's liability or taking the property subject to the liability), will be treated, not as two separate transactions, but as a *sale*, in whole or in part, of the property to the partnership if:

1. The transfer of money or other consideration would *not* have been made but for the transfer of property; and

2. In cases in which the transfers are not made simultaneously, the subsequent transfer is not dependent on the entrepreneurial risks of partnership operations.[15]

The regulation adopts a test of ten facts and circumstances to determine whether either of the foregoing two rules apply.[16]

The facts and circumstances taken into account in determining whether a disguised sale has occurred are:

1. The reciprocal transfer's timing and amount are determinable with reasonable certainty;

2. The partner has a legally enforceable right to the reciprocal transfer;

3. The right to the reciprocal transfer is secured;

---

[12] S. Rep. No. 169, 98th Cong., 2d Sess., 226-30 (1984).

[13] Prop. Reg. §§ 1.707-3, -4, -5, and -6.

[14] See Notice 92-46, 1992-2 CB 375, for circumstances when the proposed regulations apply to transactions occurring after April 24, 1991, but before the final regulations were issued.

[15] Reg. § 1.707-3(b)(1).

[16] Reg. § 1.707-3(b)(2).

4. Another party is legally obligated to make contributions to the partnership to permit the partnership to make the reciprocal transfer;

5. Another party is legally obligated to loan money to the partnership to permit the partnership to make the reciprocal transfer;

6. The partnership is obligated to borrow amounts necessary to permit the reciprocal transfer;

7. The partnership holds money or other liquid assets, beyond the reasonable needs of the business, that are expected to be available to make the reciprocal transfer;

8. The partnership distributions, allocations, or control of partnership operations is designed to effect an exchange of the burdens and benefits of ownership of property;

9. Transfers of money or other consideration by the partnership to the partner which are disproportionately large in relationship to the partner's general and continuing interest in partnership profits indicates a reciprocal transfer; and

10. A distribution that is in no event returnable indicates a reciprocal transfer.[17]

Presumptions. If within two years of a property contribution to a partnership the partnership transfers money or other property to the partner, the transfers are presumed to be a sale of the property to the partnership unless the facts and circumstances clearly establish that the transfers do not constitute a sale.[18] With certain exceptions, the regulations require tax return disclosure of any distributions to a property contributor made within two years of the property contribution.[19]

See sample Form 8275, Disclosure Statement, in the Appendix.

If the transfers of property and money are *more* than two years apart, then there is a presumption that a "sale" did *not* take place. However, if two or *less* years separate the transactions, then there is a presumption that a disguised sale did occur. Both these presumptions are rebuttable.

> ***Example 5-4.***[20] A transfers property to a partnership with a value of $4,000, and receives an interest in the partnership and $3,000 in cash. His basis in the property is $1,200. Under Code Sec. 707(a)(2)(B):
>
> - Three-fourths of the transaction is treated as a "sale" ($3,000/$4,000), and one-fourth as a "contribution."

---

[17] *Id.*

[18] Reg. § 1.707-3(c).

[19] Either the distributee partner files Form 8275, Disclosure Statement, or an attachment to his or her Form 1040, U.S. Individual Income Tax Return, described in the regulations in lieu of Form 8275. Reg. § § 1.707-3(c)(2) and 1.707-8.

[20] Reg. § 1.707-3(f), Ex. 1.

- A must recognize gain as follows:

Sale proceeds	$3,000
Basis (3/4 × $1,200)	(900)
Gain	$2,100

- *A* has made a contribution of property with a value of $1,000 and a basis of $300 (one-fourth each of $4,000 and $1,200, respectively). Note that *A*'s percentage interest in the partnership is ignored, and indeed not even mentioned, in the above results.

- The partnership has purchased a three-fourths interest in the property and has a basis of $3,300 ($3,000 cost basis plus a $300 transferred basis).

If multiple properties are transferred to the partnership, the computation of the "sale" and "contribution" amounts are allocated to the various properties in proportion to their respective fair market values.

Special rules for guaranteed payments, preferred returns, cash flow distributions, and preformation expenditures. The legislative history of Code Sec. 707(a)(2)(B) indicates that the disguised sale rules are not intended to prevent partners from receiving guaranteed priority or preferential distributions in return for their capital contributions.[21] In the context of disguised sale determinations, the critical issue relating to preferred returns and guaranteed payments is whether they represent merely a return *on* the recipient's contributed capital or, instead, are designed to serve as a return *of* all or a portion of the recipient's contributed capital. In the case of a return *on* capital, such an interest does not provide a means of withdrawing the transferor's equity in the contributed property and can be disregarded in the disguised sale analysis. In the case of a return *of* capital, the payment does reduce the transferor-partner's equity interest in the partnership and must be taken into account in the disguised sale analysis.

Guaranteed payments and preferred returns—definition. The term "guaranteed payment for capital," as used in the regulations, means any payment to a partner by the partnership that is determined without regard to partnership income and is for the use of that partner's capital.[22] The term "preferred return," as used in the regulations, refers to a partner's right to preferential distributions of partnership cash flow matched, to the extent available, by an allocation of partnership income.[23]

Guaranteed payments presumed not to be sales proceeds. A guaranteed payment for capital made to a partner will not be treated as part of a sale of property under the regulations.[24] This exclusion applies whether or

[21] See H.R. Rep. No. 432, Pt. 2, 98th Cong., 2d Sess., 1216, 1218, 1221 (1984); S. Rep. at 231.

[22] Reg. § 1.707-4(a)(1).

[23] Reg. § 1.707-4(a)(2).

[24] Reg. § 1.707-4(a)(1)(i).

not the guaranteed payment is made within two years of the transferor's contribution of property to the partnership.[25]

For purposes of Code Sec. 707(a)(2) and the regulations thereunder, a payment is presumed to be a guaranteed payment for capital [26] if it is:

- Characterized by the parties as a guaranteed payment for capital;
- Determined without regard to income of the partnership; and
- Reasonable.

This presumption can be rebutted only by facts and circumstances clearly establishing that the payment is not a guaranteed payment for capital and is part of a sale.[27]

A payment to a partner that is characterized by the parties as a guaranteed payment for capital but that is not reasonable will be presumed not to be a guaranteed payment for capital.[28] This presumption will apply whether or not the guaranteed payments are made within two years of the transferor's contribution of property to the partnership.[29] This presumption can be rebutted only by facts and circumstances clearly establishing that the payment is a guaranteed payment for capital.[30]

Reasonable preferred payments presumed not sales proceeds. A transfer of money to a partner that is characterized by the parties as a preferred return and that is reasonable is presumed not to be part of a sale of property to the partnership.[31] This presumption can be rebutted only by facts and circumstances (including the likelihood and expected timing of the matching allocation of income or gain to support the preferred return) clearly establishing that the transfer is part of a sale.[32]

Reasonable in amount. A transfer of money that is made to a partner that is characterized as a guaranteed payment for capital or a preferred return is reasonable only to the extent that:

- The transfer is made to the partner pursuant to a written provision of a partnership agreement that provides for payment for the use of capital in a reasonable amount; and
- The payment is made for the use of capital only after the date on which that provision is added to the partnership agreement.[33]

A transfer of money that is made to the partner during any partnership taxable year and is characterized as a preferred return or guaranteed

[25] Reg. § 1.707-4(a)(1)(ii).
[26] *Id.*
[27] *Id.*
[28] Reg. § 1.707-4(a)(1)(iii).
[29] *Id.*
[30] *Id.*
[31] Reg. § 1.707-4(a)(2).
[32] *Id.*
[33] Reg. § 1.707-4(a)(3)(i).

payment for capital is reasonable in amount if the sum of any preferred return and any guaranteed payment for capital that is payable for that year does not exceed the amount determined by multiplying either (1) the partner's unreturned capital at the *beginning* of the year or, at the partner's option, (2) the partner's weighted average capital balance for the year (with either amount appropriately adjusted, taking into account the relevant compounding periods, to reflect any unpaid preferred return or guaranteed payment for capital that is payable to the partner) by the safe harbor interest rate for that year.[34] Regardless of the partnership's risk profile, the safe harbor interest rate for a partnership's taxable year equals 150 percent of the highest applicable federal rate in effect at any time from the time that the right to the preferred return or guaranteed payment for capital is first established pursuant to a binding, written agreement among the partners through the end of the taxable year.[35] A partner's unreturned capital equals the excess of the aggregate amount of money and the fair market value of other consideration (net of liabilities) contributed by the partner to the partnership over the aggregate amount of money and the fair market value of other consideration (net of liabilities) distributed by the partnership to the partner other than transfers of money that are presumed to be guaranteed payments for capital, reasonable preferred returns, or operating cash flow distributions (described below).[36]

A partner is likely to elect to use the weighted average capital balance where a partner contributes additional capital to the partnership after the beginning of the year, exceeding any distributions received during the year, inasmuch as this method will increase the amount of reasonable guaranteed payments and/or preferred returns. Conversely, a partner who makes no additional contributions and receives distributions reducing capital during the year would prefer to use the unreturned capital at the beginning of the year.

Presumption rebutted. As stated, the presumption that a reasonable preferred return is not part of a disguised sale and the presumption that a reasonable guaranteed payment is a guaranteed payment for capital are both subject to rebuttal based upon a showing of facts and circumstances that clearly establish to the contrary. In rebutting these presumptions, the regulations appear to be most focused on whether the preferred return or guaranteed payment is merely an income preference or has the potential to return to the recipient some portion of his or her investment. The regulations, in the case of preferred returns and guaranteed payments, do not seem concerned with the degree of entrepreneurial risk associated with any such income preference. Since, absent special circumstances, neither a preferred return nor a guaranteed payment has the capacity to reduce the recipient's capital investment, they are distinguishable from other cash

[34] Reg. § 1.707-4(a)(3)(ii).

[35] *Id.*

[36] *Id.*

flow distributions that do have such capacity. There is nothing inherently offensive about a preferred return or a guaranteed payment, assuming reasonableness, whether received with respect to cash or property. As with preferred stock, they merely represent an income preference generally found in a situation where one partner has traded off a participation in the upside in return for a more secure cash flow.[37]

If, however, the deduction for a reasonable guaranteed payment is disproportionately allocated to the recipient thereof, the payment effectively reduces the partner's equity interest and is therefore converted from a return *on* capital to a return *of* capital. The same is true when the parties agree to a reasonable preferred return that is not expected to be matched with income, or such matching is not expected to occur until the distant future. Once the character of these income preferences has been changed in this manner, as in the case of any other distribution of capital, entrepreneurial risk considerations must be applied. In such cases, if the IRS can also establish that the funding of such income preferences has been secured or supported by arrangements with a partner or third parties that insulate such payments from the risks of the partnership's business, the favorable presumptions would likely be overridden and the provisions of Reg. § 1.707-3 applied.

For example, a partnership agreement may provide for a guaranteed payment paid with respect to a transferor partners' capital which is (1) limited in duration, (2) charged entirely against the cash flow otherwise distributable to the transferee partner, and (3) expressly subject to credit support provided by the transferee partner. Moreover, if the partnership or the partner had purchased the property from the contributing partner in an installment sale, applying a market interest rate would have resulted in payments approximating the guaranteed payments. Such arrangement insures a reduction in the transferor partner's capital and a concomitant build-up in the transferee partner's capital of a predetermined amount (much like the shift of equity accompanying a sale). Therefore, the combination of these circumstances are sufficient to override the favorable presumption otherwise extended to a guaranteed payment that is reasonable in amount. The payments actually result in a return of, rather than a return on, capital due to the economic effect of disproportionately burdening the transferee partner's cash flow.[38]

In addition, though the regulations do not address this circumstance, when a nonsimultaneous distribution is found to be a related transfer and a portion of the partner's contributed property is deemed sold, it would appear that any preferred returns or guaranteed payments previously made with respect to that portion of the recipient partner's capital that is

---

[37] Thus, a preferred return that is matched with gross income (a low risk source) should be as acceptable as a preferred return matched with net income (a potentially high risk source, depending upon its components). A preferred return matched with gross income is similar to many guaranteed payments (though still less secure than others).

[38] Reg. § 1.707-4(a)(4), Ex. 2.

deemed sold would also be characterized, in whole or in part, as payments with respect to such sale. The partner would be treated as receiving installment sale payments and the partnership would get basis for its obligation to make the payments.[39]

Operating cash flow distributions. An operating cash flow distribution received in connection with a contribution of property to a partnership is presumed not to be part of a sale of such property to the partnership.[40] This presumption will apply whether or not the operating cash flow distributions are made within two years of the transferor's contribution of property to the partnership.[41] Such presumption can be rebutted only by facts and circumstances clearly establishing that the distribution is part of a sale transaction.[42]

Operating cash flow distribution defined. Transfers of money by a partnership to a partner during the taxable year will be presumed to be operating cash flow distributions for purposes of the regulations to the extent that:

- Such distributions are not presumed to be guaranteed payments for capital;
- Such distributions are not reasonable preferred returns;
- Such distributions are not characterized by the parties as distributions to the recipient partner acting in a capacity other than as a partner; and
- Such distributions do not exceed the product of (1) the net cash flow of the partnership from operations from the year, multiplied by (2) the lesser of the partner's percentage interest in overall partnership profits for that year or the partner's percentage interest in overall partnership profits for the life of the partnership.[43]

The net cash flow of the partnership from operations for a taxable year is an amount equal to the taxable income or loss of the partnership arising in the ordinary course of the partnership's business and investment activities, *increased* by:

- Tax exempt interest;
- Depreciation;
- Amortization;
- Cost recovery allowances; and

---

[39] *Id.* The only undesirable aspect of the example is that it did not provide insight into the relative weight given to each of the above circumstances.

[40] Reg. § 1.707-4(b)(1).

[41] *Id.*

[42] *Id.*

[43] Reg. § 1.707-4(b)(2)(i).

- Other non-cash charges deducted in determining such taxable income;

and *decreased* by:

- Principal payments made on any partnership indebtedness;
- Property replacement or contingency reserves actually established by the partnership;
- Capital expenditures when made from other than these reserves or from borrowings, the proceeds of which are not included in operating cash flow; and
- Any other cash expenditures (including preferred returns) not deducted in determining such taxable income or loss.[44]

In determining a partner's operating cash flow distributions for any taxable year, the partner may use the partner's smallest percentage interest under the terms of the partnership agreement in any material item of partnership income or gain that the partnership may realize in the three-year period beginning with such taxable year.[45] This provision is intended to serve merely as a safe harbor for taxpayers and is not intended to preclude a taxpayer from using a different percentage in determining its operating cash flow distributions.[46]

The preamble to the final regulations states that, if a transfer of operating cash flow exceeds the amount allowed under the operating cash flow distribution presumption described above,[47] the transfer will qualify for the presumption up to the amount allowed under the presumption.[48] The excess or portion of the transfer that does not qualify as an operating cash flow distribution is tested under the facts and circumstances test, subject to any presumptions that may apply.[49]

> ***Example 5-5.*** Joe Baxter contributed property with a tax basis of \$100,000 and a fair market value of \$200,000 to newly formed Baxter Brothers Partnership. In exchange, Joe received a 20% general partnership interest. For the partnership's first year of operations, it reported \$200,000 of taxable income, of which \$40,000 (20%) was allocated to Joe. At year-end, he received a distribution of \$60,000 from partnership cash flows. Because this distribution exceeded Joe's share of cash flows, the excess will likely be treated by the IRS as a disguised payment under Code Sec. 707. Joe will likely be treated as having sold 10% (20,000/200,000) of the contributed asset, and will be required to recognize a \$10,000 gain (10% of the built-in gain interest in the property at the date of contribution).

[44] *Id.*
[45] Reg. § 1.707-4(b)(2)(ii).
[46] *Id.*
[47] Reg. § 1.707-4(b)(2)(i).
[48] See the Preamble to Final Regulations, T.D. 8439, 1992-2 CB 126.
[49] *Id.*

Post-year-end distribution requirement. The proposed regulations provided that excludible guaranteed payments for capital, preferred returns, and operating cash flow distributions would lose their character unless distributed no later than 75 days after the end of a taxable year.[50] The final regulations eliminate this distribution deadline. Therefore, a payment that initially qualifies for an exclusion will not lose the benefit of qualification even if it is retained for distribution in a later year.

Special rule for reimbursements of preformation expenditures. A transfer of money or other consideration by a partnership to a partner will not be treated as part of a sale of property by the partner to the partnership under the regulations to the extent that the transfer to the partner is made to reimburse the partner for certain capital expenditures incurred before property is contributed to the partnership.[51]

Preformation capital expenditures defined. To qualify for this special rule, the capital expenditures must meet the following conditions:

- The capital expenditures are incurred during the two-year period preceding the transfer by the partner to the partnership; and

- The capital expenditures are incurred by the partner with respect to:

  - Partnership organization and syndication costs described in Section 709 of the Internal Revenue Code; or

  - Property contributed to the partnership by the partner, but only to the extent the reimbursed capital expenditures do not exceed 20 percent of the fair market value of such property at the time of the contribution. However, the 20 percent of value limitation does not apply if the fair market value of the contributed property does not exceed 120 percent of the partner's adjusted basis in the contributed property at the time of contribution. If these rules are satisfied, 100 percent of the reimbursement of capital expenditures that otherwise satisfy the requirements of the regulations are excepted from disguised sale treatment.[52]

The proposed regulations left some question as to whether the exception would apply at all if the reimbursement exceeded 20 percent of the fair market value. The language was modified in the final regulations to provide that in the case of a reimbursement that exceeds 20 percent of the fair market value of the contributed property, the reimbursement qualifies for the exception to the extent of 20 percent of value.

---

[50] Prop. Reg. § 1.707-4(c).

[51] Reg. § 1.707-4(d).

[52] See the Preamble to Final Regulations, T.D. 8439, 1992-2 CB 126.

Planning. The preformation expenditure rule provides substantial flexibility to taxpayers holding appreciated property in need of capital improvements. In tandem with the disguised sale rules governing the sale/contribution of encumbered property with qualified liabilities incurred in the acquisition or improvement of a contributed property,[53] these rules allow a taxpayer to withdraw potentially all of his or her equity in a property acquired and/or improved within the preceding 24 months (assuming the taxpayer could finance up to 80 percent of its acquisition costs and improvement with a qualified liability). However, this rule is in need of clarification on several points.

The preformation expenditure rule is clearly related to the disguised sale qualified liability rule,[54] and yet there is no expressed interface between the two rules. As a result, a literal application of the two rules can result in a doubling-up of the benefits realized by a taxpayer. For example, it would appear that the 20-percent limitation in the preformation expenditure rule can be literally read to relate to the full fair market value of the contributed property, not reduced by qualified liabilities incurred in funding the same capital expenditures being reduced under such rule. If the transferor financed more than 80 percent of the acquisition and improvement of the contributed property within 24 months of its transfer to a partnership, it would appear that the transferor can actually use this rule as a means of withdrawing equity from the improved property itself or other property contributed along with the improved property.

> ***Example 5-6.*** *A* owns a property that has appreciated from $2 million to $5 million in value. *A* spends $5 million on improvements to such property financed 100% with a qualified (recourse) liability. The property has a value of $10 million, as improved. *B* contributes $7 million of cash to partnership AB for a 70% interest therein. *A* contributes the improved property to AB for a 30% interest therein. AB assumes the $5 million liability and distributes $2 million cash to *A*. AB immediately repays the $5 million assumed liability. Technically, the preformation expenditure rule should safe harbor the $2 million distribution from disguised sale treatment even though all of the capital expenditures were funded with a qualified liability.[55] The $2 million distribution is actually a withdrawal of a portion of *A*'s "historic" equity in the property and should be taxable as disguised sales proceeds.

> ***Example 5-7.*** *A* owns unencumbered property *X* with a fair market value of $5 million and a tax basis of $2 million. *A* acquires property *Y* with a fair market value of $5 million—financing 100% of such purchase on a recourse basis. *A* contributes *X* and *Y* (subject to the debt) to partnership AB and receives from AB a distribution of $2

[53] Reg. § 1.707-5(a)(6)(i)(C).

[54] *Id.*

[55] Otherwise exempted from disguised sale treatment under Reg. § 1.707-5.

million and a Code Sec. 704(b) book capital account of $3 million. *B* contributes $5 million to AB and AB immediately repays the qualified liability transferred by *A*. Though it would appear that *A* has effectively sold 40% of property *X* to AB for a $1.2 million gain, this transaction does not appear to be subject to recharacterization under the final regulations.

Though it seems that the 20-percent fair market value limitations should apply to the value of only the property upon which the capital expenditures were incurred, it is not clear whether improvements to real property should be treated as separate property for this purpose.

The reference to capital expenditures should be clarified as to whether a capital expenditure (*i.e.*, a cost giving rise to a benefit extending over a 12-month or greater period) that is currently deductible for federal income tax purposes due to a special allowance still qualifies as a capital expenditure under this rule (*e.g.*, intangible drilling cost deductions). Since the character of these expenditures is not affected by the allowance of the deduction such items should qualify.

Clarification should also be provided in the case where the property to be contributed to a partnership is an interest in another existing partnership. More specifically, in this context, do capital contributions made within the prior 12 months constitute capital expenditures with respect to the contributed partnership interest? Does it matter when the expenditure at the level of the existing partnership being funded through such capital contributions is itself a capital expenditure? In this context, are capital expenditures limited to organizational costs, syndication costs, and other "outside" costs associated with the acquisition of such interest?

It is difficult to understand the limitations imposed on the preformation expenditure rule (*i.e.*, the 24-month and 20-percent value limitations) in light of the fact that no such limitations are applied to the related qualified liability rule under the disguised sale rules.[56] Assuming that it is clarified under the preformation expenditure rule that historical equity cannot be withdrawn from an encumbered property using the double-dipping method outlined above, there does not appear to be justification for such bias. It merely encourages taxpayers to fund their capital expenditures with as much debt financing as possible.

Other exceptions. The regulations provide that other types of transfers or payments to a partner may be excepted from treatment as part of a sale, by revenue ruling or other guidance published in the Internal Revenue Bulletin. The Preamble to the final regulations suggests that disguised sale payments do not include loans, repayments, and guaranteed payments for services.[57]

---

[56] Code Sec. 1.707-5(a)(6)(i)(C).

[57] Reg. § 1.707-4(e); T.D. 8439, 1992-2 CB 126.

Debt relief deemed sales proceeds. Regulation § 1.707-5 delineates the rules for determining how much, if any, "sale" consideration is received by the partner when the partnership assumes his or her liabilities or takes the transferred properties subject to them.

Deemed sale price. Unless the liability is a "qualified liability" (see below), the "deemed distribution" arising from allocation of a portion of such liability among the other partners will be treated as a payment subject to the disguised sale rules.

If, after a transfer of property, the partnership incurs debt and within 90 days distributes all or part of the proceeds to the contributing partner, then the "sale" amount [58] is not the total cash distributed, but only the portion thereof which is attributable to the liability shares of the other partners.[59]

The portion of the distribution attributable to the contributing partner is thus treated as a "regular" distribution.

> ***Example 5-8.*** Kali transfers property to a partnership with a value of $4,000. She receives no actual money distribution, but the partnership assumes a $3,000 recourse liability (which is not a qualified liability) in connection with the transfer of the property. Assume further that Kali has a 33-1/3% interest in the partnership. Her basis in the property is $1,200.
>
> - Kali is deemed to have sold an interest in the property for $2,000 (66-2/3% of the $3,000 liability attributable to the other partners). This sales price is 50% of the total property value of $4,000. Hence, Kali's gain is:
>
> | | |
> |---|---:|
> | Sales price . . . . | $2,000 |
> | Cost (50% × $1,200) . . . . | (600) |
> | Gain . . . . | *$1,400* |
>
> - Kali is also deemed to have contributed property to the partnership in exchange for a partnership interest with a value of $2,000 and a basis of $600 subject to a $1,000 recourse liability. For purposes of determining the partner's share of partnership debt, the partnership debt is $4,000.

Qualified liability relief not deemed sales proceeds. A "qualified liability" is one which is not greater than the fair market value of the property and was incurred by a partner:

- More than two years prior to the transfer of the property and who has encumbered the property during this period; or

[58] For purposes of Reg. § 1.707-3.

[59] Reg. § 1.707-5(b). Note that the rules of Temp. Reg. § 1.163-8T apply to "trace" the financing proceeds into the hands of the partner.

- Within two years of the property transfer, who has encumbered the property during the period, and was *not* incurred in anticipation of the transfer and based on the facts and circumstances was incurred:[60]

    1. For the purpose of providing funds, the expenditure of which was capitalized to the property; or

    2. In the ordinary course of the business in which the property was used, and substantially all of the assets used in such business are transferred to the partnership.[61]

Summary. The foregoing has only been a brief explanation of the more straightforward circumstances giving rise to disguised sales. The regulations contemplate more exotic situations.

Another area of contention is "disguised payments for services." Here, the concern is that ordinary-income compensation for services is converted to capital gain, or that the partnership is avoiding capitalizing service compensation. However, proposed regulations on the subject have not yet been issued.[62]

> ***Example 5-9.*** The ABC partnership engages *C*, an architect, to design and supervise construction of improvements to its properties. If the partnership paid *C* with cash, the payments would be capitalized into the basis of the improvements. Instead, they admit him as a partner for rendering the future services of designing and construction supervision. His income allocation would have the effect of allowing the other partners a deduction for his services and if he sells his interest, he will have capital gain.

The "disguised sale" rationale is also manifested in Code Sec. 704(c)(1)(B) (Distribution of Contributed Property to Partners other than the Contributing Partner) and in Code Sec. 737 (Distribution of Property to a Partner with Built-In Gain).

.03 Partner Contributes Property and Partnership Distributes It to Another Partner—Code Sec. 704(c)(1)(B)

Prior to the implementation of Code Sec. 704(c)(1)(B),[63] it was relatively simple for a seller of property to avoid gain by contributing it to a partnership that distributed it to another partner (the buyer) leaving the partnership with the property the buyer had contributed (the purchase price).

---

[60] There are requirements of notification to the IRS under Reg. § 1.707-5 that are similar to those under Reg. § 1.707-3.

[61] Reg. § 1.707-5(a)(6).

[62] Reg. § 1.707-2 has been reserved therefore.

[63] The Omnibus Budget Reconciliation Act of 1989, P.L. 101-239, 101st Cong., 1st Sess. Code Sec. 704(c)(1)(B) applies to any property contributed to a partnership after October 3, 1989. The regulations apply to distributions on or after January 9, 1995.

Example 5-10. *A* owns Blackacre, which has a fair market value of $100 and basis of $10. The BCDE Partnership wishes to buy and develop Blackacre, but *A* neither wants to recognize gain on the property's sale nor to participate in a Code Sec. 1031 like-kind exchange. A new ABCDE Limited Partnership is formed with *A* contributing Blackacre, *B* contributing $100, and *C, D* and *E* contributing $1 each. Blackacre is then distributed to *B* in liquidation of his interest. *B* recognizes no gain and takes a basis of $100 in Blackacre. The ACDE partnership continues as an investment partnership with *A* as the general partner holding a 99% interest. Its sole asset is $103.

Background. The stated purpose of Code Sec. 704(c)(1)(B) is to prevent partners from escaping the anti-gain shifting rule of Code Sec. 704(c)(1)(A) by simply distributing the contributed property to another partner who may receive a full basis step-up in the property in a liquidating distribution.[64]

Recognition of gain or loss. If property contributed by one partner is distributed to another partner within seven years of its contribution, the contributing partner (or his or her successor) [65] recognizes gain or loss in an amount (and character) equal to the gain or loss that would have been allocated to the contributing partner under Code Sec. 704(c)(1)(A) if the partnership had sold the property to the distributee at its fair market value at the time of the distribution.[66]

The amount of gain or loss recognized by the contributing partner may vary depending on the particular method the partnership uses in making allocations of built-in gain or loss [67] because the amount of remaining built-in gain or loss may vary depending on the particular method of allocation adopted.[68]

The regulations provide that property a partnership receives in exchange for contributed property in a nonrecognition transaction is treated as the contributed property. This result is consistent with the built-in gain or loss rules in general.[69] The regulations also provide that the successor in interest of a contributing partner is treated as the contributing partner.[70] For example, if the contributing partner subsequently sells his or her interest to another partner, the new partner will be treated as the contributor of any property previously contributed by the selling partner. Any gain or loss allocated to the transferee partner under Code Sec. 704(c)(1)(B) may be offset, however, if the partnership has a Code Sec. 754 election in effect.[71] This result is consistent with built-in gain or loss rules in general.

[64] H.R. Rep. No. 101-247, 101st Cong., 1st Sess., 406 (1989). In this case, the continuing partners could avoid a Code Sec. 734(b) step-down in the basis of the retained noncontributed property by not making a Code Sec. 754 election in such year.

[65] Code Sec. 704(c)(1).

[66] Code Sec. 704(c)(1)(B)(i) and (ii). For property contributed to the partnership prior to June 9, 1997, the time period is five years rather than seven years. The Taxpayer Relief Act of 1997, P.L. 105-34, Act § 1063(a).

[67] Code Sec. 704(c)(1)(B); Reg. § 1.704-3.

[68] See Reg. § 1.704-4(a)(5), Exs. 1-3.

[69] Reg. §§ 1.704-4(d)(1) and 1.704-3(a)(8).

[70] Reg. § 1.704-4(d)(2).

[71] Reg. §§ 1.704-4(e)(3) and 1.704-3(a)(7).

Character of gain or loss. The regulations provide that the character of the contributing partner's gain or loss is determined as if the property had been sold by the partnership to the distributee partner. Thus, if the distributee partner holds more than a 50-percent capital or profits interest in the partnership, any gain recognized by the contributing partner is ordinary income if the property is not a capital asset when held by the distributee partner.[72]

In addition, because the property is treated as having been sold by the partnership to the distributee partner, the regulations provide that any loss that would have been disallowed under the related party rules [73] had the distributed property actually been sold to the distributee partner will be disallowed under Code Sec. 704(c)(1)(B) as well.[74]

Basis rules. *Contributing partner's basis in his or her partnership interest.* The contributing partner recognizing gain or loss under Code Sec. 704(c)(1)(B) is entitled to increase the basis, or required to decrease the basis, of his or her partnership interest by the amount of gain or loss recognized under Code Sec. 704(c)(1)(B).

Partnership's basis in Code Sec. 704(c) built-in gain or loss property. The partnership is entitled to increase the basis, or required to decrease the basis, of the contributed property by the gain or loss required to be recognized by the contributing partner under Code Sec. 704(c)(1)(B). The basis adjustment to the property is deemed made prior to the distribution, after which the usual distribution rules are applied to the distributee.[75]

> ***Example 5-11.*** Christine Williams contributed nondepreciable realty with a tax basis of $45,000 and a fair market value of $75,000 to the Williams Sisters Partnership in exchange for a 25% interest therein. Three years later, when the property's value had increased to $90,000, it was distributed to another partner in partial liquidation of her interest in the partnership. Upon distribution of this property to another partner, Christine will be required to recognize the still remaining built-in gain of $30,000 inherent in the property at the date she initially contributed it to the partnership. This gain will increase both Christine's basis in her partnership interest and the partnership's basis in the property she contributed. Thus, subject to the limitations of Code Sec. 732(a)(2),[76] the distributee partner will take a $75,000 basis in the property received.

These adjustments are taken into account in determining (1) the noncontributing partner's basis in the property distributed to that partner,

---

[72] Reg. § 1.704-4(b)(2); Code Sec. 707(b)(2).

[73] Code Sec. 707(b)(1).

[74] Reg. § 1.704-4(b)(2), Ex.

[75] Reg. § 1.704-4(e)(2); S. Rep. No. 101, 101st Cong., 1st Sess., 197 (1989). This portion of the legislative history and Code Sec. 737 regulations will have less importance because the current Code Sec. 708 regulations do not create a deemed property distribution as part of a technical termination occurring after May 9, 1997.

[76] Under Code Sec. 732(a)(2), the distributee partner's basis in the distributed property cannot exceed her basis in her partnership interest immediately prior to receipt of the distribution.

(2) the contributing partner's basis in any property distributed to that partner in the same transaction (except to the extent that the distributed property is like-kind property subject to a special rule discussed below), (3) the basis adjustments, if any, to partnership property by a partnership with a Code Sec. 754 election in effect, and (4) the amount of the contributing partner's gain under Code Sec. 731 or Code Sec. 737 on a related distribution of money or property, respectively, to the contributing partner.

Special rules for constructive termination of partnerships. The 1989 Senate Finance Committee Report (the "Senate Report") states that "parties will recognize gain in connection with the distribution of partnership property within 5 years following the constructive termination, *to the extent of their respective shares of the pre-termination appreciation or depreciation in the value of the partnership property that is not already required to be allocated to the original contributor (if any) of the property.*"[77] Thus, the Senate Report appears to indicate that a Code Sec. 708(b)(1)(B) termination would start a new seven-year period running with respect to built-in gain (*i.e.*, appreciation), even gain accruing in property between the date it was acquired by the terminated partnership and the date it was deemed contributed to the reconstituted partnership pursuant to the Code Sec. 708(b)(1)(B) termination. The December 22, 1995, regulations begin a new seven-year period for post-contribution changes in the value of partnership property whenever there is a termination of the partnership under Code Sec. 708(b)(1)(B).[78] Thus the 1995 regulations required that there be maintained with respect to a contributed property two or more seven-year periods whenever a Code Sec. 708(b)(1)(B) termination occurs prior to the lapse of the original seven-year period.

> ***Example 5-12.*** Assume that Partner *A* contributes Blackacre, with a fair market value of $100 and a basis of $0, to partnership AB on January 1 of Year 1. If AB is terminated on January 1 of Year 4, when Blackacre has a fair market value of $150, AB must maintain under Code Sec. 704(c)(1)(B) two separate seven-year periods with respect to Blackacre (with a fair market value of $150 and a basis of $0):
>
> 1. A seven-year period that expires on January 1 of Year 7, with respect to the precontribution appreciation of $100, and
> 2. A seven-year period that expires on January 1 of Year 11, with respect to the post-contribution appreciation of $50.

[77] Emphasis added. Reg. § 1.704-4(a)(4)(ii). For property contributed to the partnership after June 9, 1997, the time period is seven years. The Taxpayer Relief Act of 1997, P.L. 105-34, Act § 1063(a).

[78] Reg. § 1.704-4(a)(4)(ii) and (c)(3); Preamble to T.D. 8642, 1996-1 CB 126. For property contributed to the partnership prior to June 9, 1997, the time period is five years rather than seven years. The Taxpayer Relief Act of 1997, P.L. 105-34, Act § 1063(a).

In fact, AB could technically have as many as seven separate seven-year periods maintained with respect to Blackacre under Code Sec. 704(c)(1)(B) (assuming a termination occurs every 12 months).

The Senate Report also appears to confirm and the regulations state that once a Code Sec. 704(c)(1)(B) seven-year period has expired, a constructive termination will not make Code Sec. 704(c)(1)(B) applicable again to the original built-in appreciation. Thus, in Example 5-12, if the termination of AB had occurred after January 1 of Year 10, the new Code Sec. 704(c)(1)(B) seven-year period would commence only with respect to the post-contribution appreciation of $50 upon the deemed contribution of Blackacre (with a fair market value of $150 and basis of $0) to reconstituted AB (*i.e.*, the period with respect to Blackacre's precontribution appreciation of $100 would not be revived).[79]

On May 8, 1997, the regulations were modified and now provide that in the case of a technical termination, after May 9, 1997, under Code Sec. 708(b)(1)(B), "A subsequent distribution of Section 704(c) property by the new partnership to a partner of the new partnership is subject to Section 704(c)(1)(B) to the same extent that the distribution by the terminated partnership would have been subject to Section 704(c)(1)(B)."[80]

Contributor receives like-kind property in same distribution. The regulations provide a special rule under Code Sec. 704(c)(2) for cases in which the contributing partner receives like-kind property no later than the earlier of (1) 180 days following the date of the distribution of contributed property to another partner, or (2) the due date (determined with regard to extensions) of the contributing partner's income tax return for the taxable year of the distribution to the other partner. Under this rule, the gain that otherwise would be recognized by the contributing partner under Code Sec. 704(c)(1)(B) is reduced by the amount of built-in gain or loss in the distributed like-kind property in the hands of the contributing partner. The amount of the built-in gain or loss is determined by reference to the contributing partner's basis in the property immediately after the distribution.[81] The regulations provide that the basis in the distributed like-kind property in this situation is determined without taking into account any increase in the basis of the contributing partner's partnership interest for any gain recognized under Code Sec. 704(c)(1)(B).[82] This special rule implements the statutory objective of not requiring gain or loss on distributions where gain or loss would not have been recognized on an exchange outside of a partnership. When gain or loss is not recognized in exchanges of like-kind property outside of partnerships, the built-in gain or loss on the exchanged property is generally preserved in the property received in the exchange. To the extent that this built-in gain or loss is not preserved in the

[79] Reg. § 1.704-4(a)(4)(ii).

[80] Reg. § 1.704-4(b)(3); see also Reg. § 1.704-4(a)(4)(i).

[81] Code Sec. 732(a) or (b).

[82] Reg. § 1.704-4(d)(3).

case of a distribution of property by the partnership, the exception does not apply.

Overlap of Code Sec. 704(c)(1)(B) and Code Sec. 737. Code Sec. 737 applies when a partner receives a distribution from the partnership of property other than property he or she originally contributed. Under Code Sec. 737, upon receipt of the distributed property, any built-in Code Sec. 704(c) gain inherent in the property originally contributed by such partner is triggered to the extent that the *value* of the property received in the distribution exceeds the partner's tax basis in his or her partnership interest. Like Code Sec. 704(c)(1)(B), Code Sec. 737 applies only to distributions received in the seven-year period following the initial contribution of appreciated property to the partnership.

> ***Example 5-13.*** Alfred Johnson contributed nondepreciable real estate with a fair market value of \$150,000 (tax basis \$80,000) to the Sun Country Partnership in exchange for a 20% partnership interest. Three years later, he received a distribution of other real estate from Sun Country with a tax basis of \$70,000 and a fair market value of \$115,000. This distribution reduced his interest in the partnership from 20% to 10%. At the date of the distribution, Sun Country still owned the property contributed by Alfred. Under Code Sec. 737, Alfred must recognize \$25,000 gain on receipt of the property distribution from Sun Country. This gain, which reflects the excess of the value of the property received by Alfred (\$115,000) over his basis in his partnership interest (\$90,000) will increase the partnership's tax basis in the property Alfred originally contributed. The tax basis of this property is now \$105,000 (\$80,000 + \$25,000), leaving a remaining Code Sec. 704(c) built-in gain for Alfred of only \$45,000 (\$150,000 date of contribution value minus \$105,000 adjusted tax basis).

Code Sec. 704(c)(1)(B) and Code Sec. 737 will often overlap. Certainly, if the property distributed to the contributing partner itself contains built-in (precontribution) appreciation and such property was originally contributed to the partnership by another partner, the distribution of any portion of such property to the contributing partner during the seven years following the contribution of such distributed property will result in the partner who contributed such distributed property also recognizing Code Sec. 704(c) gain under Code Sec. 704(c)(1)(B).

Overlap of Code Sec. 704(c)(1)(B) and Code Sec. 707(a)(2)(B). Under the disguised sale rules of Code Sec. 707(a)(2)(B), the determination of whether a sale, rather than a contribution, of an asset has occurred depends largely upon the entrepreneurial risk to which such asset is subject in the hands of the partnership and the degree of certainty as to timing and amount with which the contributing partner can forecast the ultimate distribution of cash or some other asset to such partner in the future (taking into account the entrepreneurial risks that exist during the period preceding such distribution).[83]

If, based on relevant facts and circumstances a sale is found to have occurred under Code Sec. 707(a)(2)(B), the regulations are clear that such sale is deemed for all tax purposes to have occurred at the outset on the initial conveyance of the property to the partnership.[84] The regulations deem the contributing partner to have received a payment right, rather than a partnership interest, at the time and any subsequent related distribution of cash or property to the contributing partner will be characterized as a payment in satisfaction of the partnership's obligation arising out of the sale and not as a distribution.[85] Thus, the related distribution of cash or property that constitutes part of a disguised sale transaction is not a distribution to a partner acting in his or her capacity as a partner. Any such distribution is not subject to Code Sec. 731.

There appears to be no overlap between the disguised sale regulations and Code Sec. 704(c)(1)(B). Once the IRS is successful in recharacterizing a transaction as a disguised sale of the appreciated property, all Code Sec. 704(c)(1)(B) built-in gain with respect to that property is eliminated. The contributing partner would already be characterized as having sold the property to the partnership (or the other partner) at the outset and having triggered a recognition of the built-in gain. Because the timing and magnitude of the gain recognition under the two rules usually will differ, and because the IRS's opportunity to successfully apply the disguised sale recharacterization will vary greatly depending upon the facts of each case, the IRS can be expected to assert both theories of recharacterization as alternatives on audit or in litigation. They should not, however, overlap.

General observations. Code Sec. 704(c)(1)(B) will not apply in the following cases:

- A distribution of the contributed property back to the contributing partner (or his or her successor in interest);[86]
- A distribution of contributed property to a noncontributing partner, if coupled with the distribution of a noncontributed property of a like kind (under Code Sec. 1031) to the contributing partner not later than the earlier of 180 days after the date of distribution of the contributed property or the due date for the contributing partner's tax return for the year in which the distribution was made;[87]
- An election under Code Sec. 761(a) to be excluded from Subchapter K;

[83] Reg. § 1.707-3(b)(2).
[84] Reg. § 1.707-3(a)(2).
[85] *Id.*
[86] Code Sec. 704(c)(1)(B).
[87] Code Sec. 704(c)(2).

- The distribution of a contributed property more than seven years after its contribution;
- The distribution of a noncontributed property to a contributing partner;[88]
- Distributions to a partner other than in his or her capacity as a partner (*e.g.*, transactions or distributions subject to Code Sec. 707(a) or Code Sec. 751(b));[89]
- Transfers by the transferee partnership of all of its assets to a second partnership coupled with the transferee partnership's distribution of the second partnership's interests to its partners. However, the second partnership is subject to Code Sec. 704(c)(2);[90] and
- Incorporation of the partnership.[91]

The regulations also provide that Code Sec. 704(c)(1)(B) does not apply to the distribution of a portion of contributed property to a noncontributing partner in a complete liquidation of the partnership if a portion of the contributed property is distributed to the contributing partner and that portion has unrecognized gain or loss in the hands of the contributing partner, determined immediately after the distribution, at least equal to the built-in gain or loss that would have been allocated to the contributing partner under Code Sec. 704(c)(1)(A) on a sale of the contributed property by the partnership at the time of the distribution. This exception is consistent with the purpose of Code Sec. 704(c)(1)(B) to prevent the shifting of built-in gain or loss among partners because no shift has occurred in this limited situation.[92]

.04 *Partner Contributes Property and Partnership Distributes Other Property to the Partner—Code Sec. 737*

Code Sec. 737 [93] addresses partnership distributions of property to a partner within seven years of a contribution of other property to the partnership by the same partner.[94] The 1992 legislative history (the "legislative history") accompanying the enactment of Code Sec. 737 noted that "the committee is concerned that a partner who contributes appreciated property to a partnership may be able to avoid or defer the recognition of gain with respect to that property through the mechanism of having the partnership distribute other partnership property to him in partial or complete redemption of his interest while the partnership continues to own the contributed property."[95] Code Sec. 737 thus appears to have been

---

[88] But see Code Sec. 737.

[89] Reg. § 1.704-4(a)(2).

[90] Reg. § 1.704-4(c)(4).

[91] Reg. § 1.704-4(c)(5).

[92] Reg. § 1.704-4(c)(2).

[93] Enacted by the Energy Policy Act of 1992, P.L. 102-486. Code Sec. 737 applies to partnership distributions of appreciated property on or after June 25, 1992. The regulations apply to distributions on or after January 9, 1995.

[94] For property contributed to the partnership prior to June 9, 1997, the time period is five years rather than seven years. The Taxpayer Relief Act of 1997, P.L. 105-34, Act § 1063(a).

[95] See H.R. Rep. No. 11, 102d Cong., 2nd Sess. Code Sec. 3004.

intended to serve as a backstop to the gain recognition provisions under Code Sec. 704(c)(1)(B) which are primarily concerned with taxpayers avoiding the recognition of Code Sec. 704(c) built-in gain by distributing a contributed (appreciated) property to a noncontributing partner. Both Code Sec. 737 and Code Sec. 704(c)(1)(B), in turn, serve as back-ups to the disguised sale rules in Code Sec. 707(a)(2)(B). The effective date of Code Sec. 737 was retroactive in that it piggybacks off of the effective date rule of Code Sec. 704(c)(1)(B). Code Sec. 737 therefore applies to any property contributed to the partnership after October 3, 1989.

> ***Example 5-14.*** *A* owns Blackacre, which has a fair market value of $100 and a basis of $10. The BCDE Partnership wishes to buy and develop Blackacre. *A* neither wants to recognize gain on a sale of Blackacre, nor is willing to participate in a Code Sec. 1031 like-kind exchange. The new ABCDE partnership is formed with *A* contributing Blackacre and *B, C, D* and *E* contributing $25 each. The partnership invests its cash in $100 of investment grade artwork, which is distributed to A in liquidation of his interest. *A* has no gain and his basis in the investment artwork is $10. If the partnership has a Code Sec. 754 election in effect for the year of *A*'s liquidating distribution, Blackacre has a positive adjustment to its basis of $90.[96]

The Tax Reform Act of 1984 [97] made mandatory the application of Code Sec. 704(c) allocations as a means of prohibiting the shifting of a contributed property's built-in gain or loss from a contributing partner to a noncontributing partner. In 1989, Code Sec. 704(c)(1)(B) was enacted to prohibit the avoidance of Code Sec. 704(c) by requiring that built-in gain or loss be recognized upon the distribution of a contributed property having Code Sec. 704(c) built-in gain or loss to a noncontributing partner. (This recognition avoidance potential was generally present only if the partnership had failed to make a Code Sec. 754 election such that no Code Sec. 734(b) adjustment was available to adjust the inside basis of the noncontributed property). The policy of Code Sec. 737, enacted in 1992, if related at all to the Code Sec. 704(c) rules, seems to be to prohibit the shifting of Code Sec. 704(c) built-in gain or loss from a contributed property kept by the partnership to a noncontributed property distributed to the former owner of the contributed property. It is akin to the Code Sec. 707(a)(2)(B) disguised sale rules.

Mechanics. If a partner contributes appreciated property to a partnership and receives a distribution of other property from the partnership within seven years of such contribution, the contributing partner shall recognize gain equal to the lesser of:[98]

1. An amount equal to the excess, if any, of the fair market value of the distributed property (other than money) over the part-

[96] Code Sec. 734(b)(1)(B).
[97] P.L. 98-369.
[98] Code Sec. 737(b).

ner's adjusted tax basis in his or her partnership interest, immediately prior to the distribution, reduced (but not below zero) by any money received in the distribution; and

2. The net remaining precontribution gain of the contributing partner.[99]

Net precontribution gain. The net precontribution gain of the contributing partner is equal to the net gain (if any) that the contributing partner would have recognized, pursuant to Code Sec. 704(c)(1)(B), if all property that the contributing partner had contributed to the partnership within seven years of the distribution, and which the partnership still held immediately prior to the distribution, was distributed by the partnership to another partner.[100] For this purpose, built-in losses inherent in any property contributed within the preceding seven-year period will be netted against built-in gains in any other such property in determining net precontribution gain.[101]

Basis rules following application of Code Sec. 737. *Contributing partner's basis in partnership interest.* The adjusted basis of a partner's interest in a partnership is increased by any gain which that partner is required to recognize under Code Sec. 737. For purposes of determining the basis of distributed property, the increase in the contributing partner's basis in his or her partnership interest is deemed to occur immediately prior to the distribution of property.[102]

Partnership's basis in contributed property following application of Code Sec. 737. The partnership is entitled to increase the basis of the contributed built-in gain property by any gain the contributing partner is required to recognize pursuant to Code Sec. 737.[103]

Character of gain. Any gain recognized under Code Sec. 737 is in addition to gain recognized under Code Sec. 731 and the character of gain is determined by the "proportionate character of the net precontribution gain."[104] The character is determined at the partnership level as if the distributed property had been sold to an unrelated party.[105]

Code Sec. 737 not triggered if contributed property distributed back to the contributor. The purpose of Code Sec. 737 is to tax disguised sales; its provisions should not apply to distributions of the same property contributed to the partnership. Code Sec. 737(a), however, has application to all distributions. Code Sec. 737(d) provides an exception to any gain recognition if the property distributed was previously contributed by the same partner.

---

[99] Reg. § 1.737-1(a)(1); Code Sec. 737(a)(1) and (2).

[100] Code Sec. 737(b)(1).

[101] See legislative history, H.R. Rep. No. 11, 102nd Cong., 2nd Sess., § 3004 (1992).

[102] Code Sec. 737(c)(1); Reg. § 1.737-3(b).

[103] Code Sec. 737(c)(2); Reg. § 1.737-3(c).

[104] Code Sec. 737(a); Reg. § 1.737-1(d).

[105] Compare Code Sec. 704(c)(1)(B).

If a contributed asset is distributed back to the contributing partner, that asset will neither be:

- Taken into account in determining the fair market value of the distributed property for purposes of calculating Code Sec. 737 gain, nor
- Taken into account in determining net precontribution gain.[106]

If the contributed asset that is distributed back to a contributing partner consists of an interest in an entity (*e.g.*, a corporation) the exception noted above shall not apply to the extent the value of the entity is attributable to property contributed to it after such property was contributed to the partnership.[107]

Constructive terminations of partnerships. The legislative history of Code Sec. 737 and the regulations make clear that a constructive distribution of partnership property to a contributing partner pursuant to a Code Sec. 708(b)(1)(B) termination under the pre-May 8, 1997, Code Sec. 708 regulations will not result in a recognition of Code Sec. 704(c) gain to the contributing partner under Code Sec. 737.[108] In fact, the Conference Report states that a constructive termination under Code Sec. 708(b)(1)(B) does not change the application of the sharing requirements of Code Sec. 704(c) to precontribution gain with respect to property contributed to the partnership before the termination.

The legislative history further states that "parties will recognize gain in connection with the distribution of partnership property within 5 years following the constructive termination, *to the extent of their respective shares of the pretermination appreciation in the value of the partnership property that is not already required to be allocated to the original contributor (if any) of the property.*"[109] Thus, the legislative history appears to indicate that a Code Sec. 708(b)(1)(B) termination will start a new seven-year period running with respect to built-in gain (*i.e.*, appreciation), even gain accruing in property between the date it was acquired by the terminated partnership and the date it was deemed contributed to the reconstituted partnership pursuant to the Code Sec. 708(b)(1)(B) termination.[110] This concept of a new seven-year period with respect to this post-acquisition appreciation leads to several problems.

[106] Code Sec. 737(d)(1); Reg. § 1.737-2(d)(1).

[107] Code Sec. 737(d)(1); Reg. § 1.737-2(d)(1) and (2). Presumably, this exception to the exception applies only if the property contributed by the partnership to the entity is not itself property that was originally contributed by the contributing partner to which the interest in the entity is distributed.

[108] Reg. § 1.737-2(a).

[109] Emphasis added. See legislative history, H.R. Rep. No. 11, 102nd Cong., 2nd Sess., § 3004 (1992). For property contributed to the partnership after June 9, 1997, the time period is seven years. The Taxpayer Relief Act of 1997, P.L. 105-34, Act § 1063(a). This portion of the legislative history and Code Sec. 737 regulations will have less importance because the current Code Sec. 708 regulations do not create a deemed property distribution as part of a technical termination occurring after May 9, 1997.

[110] The regulations seem to adopt this approach indirectly through a cross reference to the Code Sec. 704(c)(1)(B) rules. See Reg. § 1.737-2(a) cross reference to "similar" rules of Reg. § 1.704-4(c)(3).

The legislative history appears to require that there be maintained with respect to a contributed property two or more seven-year periods whenever a Code Sec. 708(b)(1)(B) termination occurs prior to the lapse of the original seven-year period maintained under Code Sec. 737.

Example 5-15. Assume that Partner *A* contributes Blackacre, with a fair market value of $100 and a basis of $0, to partnership AB on January 1 of Year 1. If AB is terminated on January 1 of Year 2, when Blackacre has a fair market value of $150, it would appear that AB must maintain under Code Sec. 737 two separate seven-year periods with respect to Blackacre (with a fair market value of $150 and a basis of $0):

1. A seven-year period that expires on January 1 of Year 7, with respect to the precontribution appreciation of $100; and

2. A seven-year period that expires on January 1 of Year 8, with respect to the postcontribution appreciation of $50.

In fact, AB could technically have as many as seven separate seven-year periods maintained with respect to Blackacre under Code Sec. 737 (assuming a termination occurs every 12 months).

The legislative history also appears to confirm that once a Code Sec. 737 seven-year period has expired, a constructive termination will not make Code Sec. 737 applicable again to the original built-in appreciation. Thus, in the example above, if the termination of AB had occurred after January 1 of Year 7, the new Code Sec. 737 seven-year period would commence only with respect to the postcontribution appreciation of $50 upon the deemed contribution of Blackacre (with a fair market value of $150 and a basis of $0) to reconstituted AB (*i.e.*, the period with respect to Blackacre's precontribution appreciation of $100 would not be revived).

On May 8, 1997, the Code Sec. 737 regulations were modified and now provide that in the case of a technical termination, after the date under Code Sec. 737, "[a] subsequent distribution of Section 704(c) property by the new partnership to a partner of the new partnership is subject to Section 737 to the same extent that the distribution by the terminated partnership would have been subject to Section 737."[111]

Effective date. Code Sec. 737 applies to partnership distributions of appreciated property on or after June 25, 1992. The regulations apply to distributions on or after January 9, 1995. A seven-year period applies to contributions after June 8, 1997, and five years for distributions prior to that date.

[111] Reg. § 1.737-2(a).

Without more, this effective date provision could have been construed to result in Code Sec. 737 retroactively applying to properties contributed to a partnership as far back as June 25, 1987 (five years prior to a distribution date of June 25, 1992). That would precede the October 3, 1989, effective date of Code Sec. 704(c)(1)(B).

But since gain recognition is limited to net precontribution gain that would otherwise be recognized under Code Sec. 704(c)(1)(B), Code Sec. 737 can apply only to properties contributed to a partnership after October 3, 1989, the effective date of Code Sec. 704(c)(1)(B) (including properties constructively contributed to a reconstituted partnership upon the termination of a partnership formed prior to October 3, 1989, but terminated after such date).

The only justification for any retroactive effective date for Code Sec. 737 appears to be based upon the policy that Code Sec. 737 is a necessary compliment to Code Sec. 704(c)(1)(B) in shoring up the Code Sec. 704(c) mandate that built-in gains inherent in contributed properties not be allowed to shift from a contributing partner to a noncontributing partner. Code Sec. 737 actually only implements a policy against shifting built-in gains from one property to another and is more akin to a backstop to Code Sec. 707(a)(2)(B) than Code Sec. 704(c)(1)(B).

Overlap of Code Sec. 737 and Code Sec. 707(a)(2)(B). The determination for Code Sec. 707(a)(2)(B) purposes of whether a sale, rather than a contribution, of an asset to a partnership has occurred depends largely upon the entrepreneurial risk to which the contributing partner is subject while a participant in the partnership. The more entrepreneurial risk such partner is subject to, and the lesser the degree of certainty with which the contributing partner can predict the amount and timing of any ultimate distribution of cash or some other asset in the future, the higher the probability that such partner's initial conveyance to the partnership will be characterized as a contribution and not a sale.[112]

If, based on relevant facts and circumstances, a sale is found to have occurred, the Code Sec. 707 regulations are clear that such sale is deemed for all tax purposes to have occurred at the time of the initial conveyance of the property to the partnership.[113] Those same regulations deem the contributing partner to have received a payment right, rather than a partnership interest, at that time and any subsequent related transfer of cash or property to the contributing partner will be characterized as a payment in satisfaction of the partnership's purchase obligation arising out of the disguised sale.[114]

Thus, the related distribution of cash or property that constitutes part of a disguised sale transaction is not a distribution to a partner acting in a

---

[112] Reg. § 1.707-3(b)(2).

[113] Reg. § 1.707-3(a)(2).

[114] *Id.*

partner capacity. No such distribution is subject to characterization as a partnership distribution under Code Sec. 731.

An interface between the disguised sale regulations and Code Sec. 737 is not required. Once the IRS is successful in recharacterizing a suspect contribution to a partnership as a disguised sale or exchange of the contributed property to the partnership, Code Sec. 737 should have no application to the partnership's related transfer to the partner taxable under Code Sec. 707(a)(2)(B). The contributing partner would already be characterized as having engaged in a taxable exchange of the appreciated property with the partnership (or the other partner) at the outset and having triggered a recognition of the built-in gain. In other words, there would be no net precontribution gain to recognize under Code Sec. 737; nor would there be a distribution to the contributing partner (in a partner capacity) to trigger application of Code Sec. 737.

Because the timing and magnitude of the gain recognition under the two rules likely will differ, and because the IRS's opportunity to successfully apply the disguised sale recharacterization will vary greatly depending upon the particular facts of each case, the IRS can be expected frequently to assert both theories of recognition independently (assuming the suspect distribution is within the prescribed seven-year period). The two provisions should not, however, overlap.

Overlap of Code Sec. 737 and Code Sec. 704(c)(1)(B). A contributing partner is required to recognize Code Sec. 704(c) built-in gain inherent in a contributed property when such property is distributed to a noncontributing partner within seven years of the date of its contribution.[115]

Code Sec. 704(c)(1)(B) and Code Sec. 737 will often overlap. Certainly, if the property distributed to the contributing partner itself contains built-in (precontribution) appreciation and such property was originally contributed to the partnership by another partner, the distribution of any portion of such property to the contributing partner during the seven years following the contribution of such distributed property will result in the partner who contributed such distributed property also recognizing Code Sec. 704(c) gain under Code Sec. 704(c)(1)(B). Such provisions generally require a full recognition of all the precontribution appreciation inherent in all of the partnership's properties.[116]

Code Secs.704(c)(1)(B) and 737 appear to interact appropriately and do not appear to be in need of any further clarification in this regard.

Planning. Code Sec. 737 requires only that the contributing partner recognize gain if the fair market value of the property distributed exceeds the adjusted basis of the distributee partner's interest in the partnership. Thus, for example, a contribution of property to increase that partner's

[115] Code Sec. 704(c)(1)(B).

[116] Reg. § 1.737-1(c)(2)(iv).

basis in its partnership interest in order to avoid recognition of gain under Code Sec. 737 will be respected. A partner may be able to contribute built-in loss property, immediately prior to a partnership distribution, in order to reduce the net precontribution gain inherent in that partner's contributed properties. Such self-help strategies, however, would still need to avoid the disguised sale rules in Code Sec. 707(a)(2)(B). The partnership could consider also obtaining loans which increase the partners' bases in their interests.

A distributee partner is not taxed under Code Sec. 737 to the extent that the partner receives a distribution of property he or she previously contributed.[117] Further guidance may be warranted in this area. To the extent that the partnership makes modifications to the contributed property (*i.e.*, land developed and held for resale), it is not clear whether such property retains its character as previously contributed property or is somehow fragmented into contributed and noncontributed components. In addition, though not clear, Code Sec. 737 should not apply to the extent a partner receives a distribution of property fungible with the property that he or she contributed.

Code Sec. 737 does not except certain distributions of partnership property other than distributions of previously contributed property.[118] Assuming the partnership were incorporated within seven years after the contribution of appreciated property, the substituted basis property is the functional equivalent (at least to the extent of the value associated with the exchanged property) of the property contributed by the partner. The exception for distributed property under Code Sec. 737(d)(1) takes into account substituted basis property where the partnership received this substituted basis property in exchange for property contributed by the partner and the partnership later distributes the substituted basis property to the contributing partner.[119] Therefore, Code Sec. 737 does not apply to a distribution of the stock of a corporation which owns as its only asset, property previously contributed by the distributee.

Code Sec. 737 applies to an incorporation of the partnership involving an actual distribution of property by the partnership to the partners followed by a contribution to a corporation.[120] Code Sec. 737 does not apply, however, to the extent that the property actually distributed to a partner was previously contributed to the partnership by that partner.[121] Code Sec. 737 does not apply to an incorporation of a partnership by methods not involving an actual distribution of partnership property to the partners, provided that the incorporation is followed by a complete liquidation of the partnership as part of the same plan or arrangement as the incorporation.[122] The explanation of provisions to the proposed regulations states

---

[117] Code Sec. 737(d)(1).
[118] *Id.*
[119] Reg. §§ 1.737-2(d)(3) and 1.757-2(e), Ex. 2.
[120] Reg. § 1.737-2(c).
[121] Reg. § 1.737-2(d).
[122] Reg. § 1.737-2(c).

that Code Sec. 737 does not apply to these situations because the partners are converting their partnership interests into a stock interest in the corporation in a nonrecognition transaction and, under the rules of either Code Sec. 732 or Code Sec. 358, the built-in gain in a partner's partnership interest is preserved in the stock received by the contributing partner. While incorporation by means of a distribution of partnership property to the partners results in the same conversion of a partnership interest into stock of a corporation, that method of incorporation involves an actual distribution of property to the partners.[123] In this case, the form of incorporation the partners choose governs the tax consequences of incorporation, including the application of Code Sec. 737.

The regulations provide that a related distribution of property the distributee partner previously contributed to the partnership is not taken into account in determining the amount of the excess distribution or the partner's net precontribution gain.[124]

Example 5-16.[125] On January 1 of Year 1, *A*, *B*, and *C* form partnership ABC as equal partners. *A* contributes the following nondepreciable real property to the partnership:

	FMV	*Adjusted Tax Basis*
Property A1	$20,000	$10,000
Property A2	10,000	6,000

A's total net precontribution gain on the contributed property is $14,000 ($10,000 on Property A1 plus $4,000 on Property A2). *B* contributes $10,000 cash and Property B, nondepreciable real property with a fair market value and adjusted tax basis of $20,000. *C* contributes $30,000 cash. On December 31 of Year 3, Property A2 and Property B are distributed to *A* in complete liquidation of *A*'s interest in the partnership. Property A2 was previously contributed by *A* and is therefore not taken into account in determining the amount of the excess distribution or *A*'s net precontribution gain. The adjusted tax basis of Property A2 in the hands of *A* is also determined under Code Sec. 732 as if that property were the only property distributed to *A*. As a result of excluding Property A2 from these determinations, the amount of the excess distribution is $10,000 ($20,000 fair market value of distributed Property B less $10,000 adjusted tax basis in *A*'s partnership interest). *A*'s net precontribution gain is also $10,000 ($14,000 total net precontribution gain less $4,000 gain with respect to previously contributed Property A2). *A* therefore recognizes $10,000 of

[123] See Explanation of Provisions, NPRM PS-76-92 and PS-51-93, 60 FR 2352, 2355 (1/ 9/ 95).

[124] Reg. § 1.737-2(d)(1).

[125] Reg. § 1.737-2(e), Ex. 1. Assume, for purposes of the example, unless otherwise indicated, that partnership income equals partnership expenses (other than depreciation deductions for contributed property) for each year of the partnership, the fair market value of the partnership property does not change, all distributions by the partnership are subject to Code Sec. 737, and all partners are unrelated.

gain on the distribution, the lesser of the excess distribution or the net precontribution gain.

Consistent with Code Sec. 737(d)(1), the regulations also provide for a limitation in the case of a distribution of a previously contributed interest in an entity. It is intended to prevent a partner from avoiding Code Sec. 737 by contributing an interest in an entity to the partnership and having the partnership contribute property to that entity, followed by a distribution of an interest in the entity to the contributing partner under the previously contributed property exception.[126] This rule does not apply to the extent that the property contributed by the partnership to the entity was contributed by the same partner that contributed the interest in the entity because, in that case, the distributee partner is receiving only a distribution of property that it previously contributed to the partnership.

Code Sec. 737 does not apply to the extent that Code Sec. 751(b) applies to a distribution.[127] Thus, Code Sec. 751 will supersede Code Sec. 737 to the extent a portion of the distribution is recharacterized as a sale or exchange under Code Sec. 751(b). Code Sec. 737 would still appear to apply to the portion of any distribution actually treated as a Code Sec. 731 distribution under Code Sec. 751(b).

Where the partner receives a distribution of other property encumbered by a liability, the partner's assumption of responsibility for that liability is treated under Code Sec. 752(a) as a contribution of cash to the partnership. This deemed contribution increases the partner's basis in his or her partnership interest. This basis increase technically occurs upon the distribution (and not immediately before such distribution). Since Code Sec. 737 refers to the contributing partner's basis in the partnership interest "immediately prior" to the distribution, it may be unclear whether the deemed contribution alleviates the partner's recognition of gain under Code Sec. 737. However, in two previous (unrelated) revenue rulings, the IRS has indicated that the basis adjustment associated with a deemed contribution under Code Sec. 752(a) occurs immediately prior to the distribution of encumbered property which triggers that adjustment.[128] Thus, the assumption of debt by a partner in connection with a Code Sec. 737 distribution should alleviate the gain recognized under that section as well.

There are certain instances where Code Sec. 737 will require recognition of built-in gain which is still embedded in the contributed property (*i.e.*, no shift of such gain to the distributed property has occurred). This generally occurs when the noncontributed property being distributed to the contributing partner has appreciated since its acquisition by the partnership. In this case, gain recognition by Code Sec. 737 cannot be justified on any tax policy ground but, by its terms, it applies nonetheless.

---

[126] Reg. § 1.737-2(d)(2). See Explanation of Provisions, NPRM PS-76-92 and PS-51-93, 60 FR 2352, 2355 (1/ 9/ 95).

[127] Code Sec. 737(d)(2).

[128] See Rev. Rul. 79-205, 1979-2 CB 255, and Rev. Rul. 87-120, 1987-2 CB 161.

Chapter 6

Pre-Trade or Business Expenses

¶ 601 Introduction

A partnership's deduction for expenses incurred prior to commencing operations confronts two obstacles:

1. There is no partnership trade or business and therefore a Code Sec. 162 expense is not allowed; and

2. A majority of the expenditure will benefit a future taxable year and therefore is potentially a capital expenditure under Code Sec. 263.

Organization, syndication, business investigation and start-up expenditures are four examples of these expenses which are commonly encountered in a partnership context. The rules governing the tax treatment of these expenditures are discussed in this chapter.

¶ 602 Organization and Syndication Expenses—Code Sec. 709

Prior to the Tax Reform Act of 1976,[1] Tax Court decisions dealt with the deductibility of expenses of forming a partnership and of selling interests in the partnership. A number of cases held that legal fees incurred in the organization of the partnership were capital expenditures and could not be deducted.[2]

.01 Organization Expenses

Code Sec. 709(a), added by the Tax Reform Act of 1976, clearly disallows all deductions for amounts paid or incurred to organize a partnership. However, with respect to organizational expenses incurred before October 22, 2004 (the date of enactment of the American Jobs Creation Act of 2004),[3] Code Sec. 709(b) permits the partnership to elect to amortize these expenses over a period not less than 60 months beginning in the

---

[1] The Tax Reform Act of 1976, P.L. 94-455.

[2] *A. Wolkowitz v. Commr.*, 8 TCM 754, Dec. 17,168(M) (1949); *Meldrum & Fewsmith, Inc. v. Commr.*, 20 TC 790, Dec. 19,801 (1953); *M.E. Wildman v. Commr.*, 78 TC 943, Dec. 39,093 (1982).

[3] P.L. 108-357.

month in which the partnership commences business. Up to $5,000 of organizational expenses incurred after October 22, 2004 may be deducted in the taxable year in which the trade or business begins. However, the $5,000 amount is reduced (but not below zero) by the amount that all organizational expenses, including those amortizable over not less than 60 months, exceed $50,000. Any additional organizational expenses are amortizable over the 180-month period that begins with the inception of the trade or business.[4] Making the election is essential to obtaining the deduction.[5] The election is irrevocable and the period chosen cannot be changed.

Definition of organization expenses. Code Sec. 709(b)(2) defines organizational expenses as expenditures which are:

1. Incident to the creation of the partnership;
2. Chargeable to a capital account; and
3. Are of a character which, if expended incident to the creation of a partnership having an ascertainable life, would be amortized over such life.

These expenditures must be for the creation of the partnership and not syndication costs incurred in selling the partnership interests or business start-up costs or investigatory costs. Partnership organizational expenses are capitalized expenses incurred on the partnership's formation.[6] Examples of these costs include:

1. Legal fees incurred in drafting the partnership agreement;
2. Filing fees for registering the partnership with the state and local authorities; and
3. Accounting fees for services incident to the organization of the partnership. For example, setting up the partnership's accounting system.

The distinction between organizational expenses and syndication costs is important because organizational expenses can be amortized but syndication costs cannot. Investigatory expenses and start-up costs are not amortized under Code Sec. 709(b), but are amortized under Code Sec. 195 (as discussed at ¶ 603).

Eligible organization expenses. Organizational expenditures eligible for the deduction and amortization election are limited to expenditures incurred during the period that begins within a reasonable time before the partnership began business and ends with the original due date, not including extensions, of the tax return for the year in which the partnership

[4] Code Sec. 709(b)(1), as amended by the American Jobs Creation Act of 2004; Committee Report on the American Jobs Creation Act of 2004, Sec. 902.

[5] See *G.H. Driggs v. Commr.*, 87 TC 759, Dec. 43,419 (1986).

[6] Code Sec. 709(b).

begins business operations.[7] Organizational expenses incurred outside this time period (such as costs incurred after the due date of the tax return for the year in which the business began) are required to be capitalized as nondeductible and nonamortizable partnership expenditures. This is true regardless of whether the partnership makes an otherwise valid amortization election. However, if the partnership makes a proper election, it is permitted to file an amended return to add organizational expenses incurred prior to the original due date of the tax return but inadvertently omitted from the election statement.[8]

If the partnership uses the cash method of accounting, no amortization or deduction is allowed for organizational expenses incurred until it is paid. However, in the year when the expense is paid, the partnership is allowed to add the prior year amortization deduction that would have been allowed had the expense been paid in the year incurred to the amortization deduction claimed in the year of payment.[9] The wording of Reg. § 1.709-1(b)(1) indicates that the $5,000 deduction would also be allowed in the year of payment, if later than the year it is incurred. The result is that the total deduction and amortized expense for the partnership is unaffected by whether or not it uses cash or accrual basis accounting. The accounting method only affects the timing of the amortization deduction.

As previously stated, organizational expenses not covered by an election—either because they are incurred too early, too late, or because the election is not made—are treated as nondeductible capital expenditures of the partnership. They are not deductible and do not reduce the partner's outside bases in their partnership interests. Thus, the tax benefit associated with these costs will not be realized until the partners are liquidated or the partners sell their partnership interests. At that date, the partners' bases will be higher than they would have been had the expenditures been deductible; consequently, they will recognize less gain (or more loss) on the sale or liquidation of their interests.

The time period in which the expenditures must be incurred in order to qualify as "incident to the creation" of the partnership includes a "reasonable time" before the partnership begins business. The end of the period is the date (without extension) for the filing of the partnership return for the taxable year in which the partnership begins business. The beginning of this time period is somewhat ambiguous. There is no authority or guidance as to what is a reasonable time before the partnership begins business. The end of the period is precisely defined, but it can be unreasonable. It is easy to imagine organizational expenses which can be incurred much later than the due date for filing the first partnership tax return. For example, a partnership which converts to a limited partnership or a partnership that converts to an LLC will incur organizational expenses incident to such a "reorgani-

[7] Reg. § 1.709-2(a).
[8] Reg. § 1.709-1(c).
[9] Reg. § 1.709-1(b).

zation;" clearly, these will be incurred well after the filing date for the original partnership's initial return.

The Code Sec. 709(b) election. The election to deduct and amortize organizational expenses is made by attaching a statement to the partnership return for the year in which the partnership commences business operations. The election must be made with a timely filed (including extensions) return.[10] The statement must describe each organizational expense incurred (whether or not paid), its amount and date, the date the partnership business begins, and the selected amortization period not less than 60 months, if applicable. Presumably future regulations will require a similar indication of the amounts to be deducted and the amount to be amortized over 180 months, if applicable. A cash basis partnership must indicate the amount paid during the taxable year. As long as the partnership has made a valid election in the year the business commences, the partnership can later amend the return for that year to add amortized expenses inadvertently omitted.

The amortization deduction. A partnership can elect to amortize its organizational expenses over a period of 60 months or more. The partnership can select any amortization period as long as it is at least 60 months. The amortization period starts in the month the partnership begins business. If the election is not properly made, the partnership's organizational costs are required to be capitalized and treated as nondeductible expenditures.

The date on which the partnership begins business is therefore important for three reasons:

1. First, the reasonable time before the partnership begins business starts the period during which eligible organizational expenses must be incurred.

2. Second, the due date for the tax return which includes this date is the last date on which organizational expenditures can be incurred.

3. Third, it is the month in which the partnership is first allowed to amortize the organizational expenditures.

For purposes of amortizing organizational expenses, the partnership is considered to begin business in the month in which it was in the state of readiness to do the business for which it was organized. The acquisition of operating assets necessary to conduct the contemplated business is a primary factor in determining when the partnership's business begins. Mere administrative actions, such as signing the partnership agreement or registering to do business in the state, do not constitute the beginning of business for this purpose.

[10] Reg. § 1.709-1(c).

The regulations deal with the beginning of business as follows:

> The determination of the date a partnership begins business for purposes of section 709 presents a question of fact that must be determined in each case in light of all the circumstances of the particular case. Ordinarily, a partnership begins business when it starts the business operation for which it was organized. The mere signing of a partnership agreement is not alone sufficient to show the beginning of business. If the activities of the partnership have advanced to the extent necessary to establish the nature of its business operations, it will be deemed to have begun business. Accordingly, the acquisition of operating assets which are necessary to the type of business contemplated may constitute beginning business for these purposes. The term "operating assets," as used herein, means assets that are in a state of readiness to be placed in service within a reasonable period following their acquisition.[11]

Part VI of Form 4562, Depreciation and Amortization, is used to report the amortizable tax basis of the partnership's qualifying organizational expenses, the amortization period, and the allowable amortization expense for a particular year. The Code Section cited as authority for the deduction on Form 4562 is Code Sec. 709(b). Form 4562 is required to be attached to Form 1065, U.S. Partnership Return of Income. The deduction for amortization expense, however, is carried from Form 4562 into the main body of the Form 1065. If, for example, the partnership is involved in trade or business, the deduction is claimed on the other deductions line on page one of Form 1065. If the partnership is involved in multiple activities, the deduction should be allocated between the activities using a reasonable method of allocation. For example, it may be allocated based upon the fair market values of the respective assets in the different activities.

LLC Observation. A partnership which converts to a limited liability company is not terminated. Therefore, for tax purposes a new partnership is not created. It is likely that the IRS will contend that these expenses may not be amortized under Code Sec. 709(b)(2)(A) if they are incurred after the due date of the continuing partnership's initial tax return. Case law prior to the enactment of Code Sec. 709 by the Tax Reform Act of 1976 [12] treated these expenses as nondeductible capital expenditures.[13] The IRS can be expected to take the position that the tax consequences of conversion are governed by these decisions.

.02 Syndication Costs

Code Sec. 709(a) denies any deduction for amounts paid and incurred "to promote the sale of (or to sell) an interest in such partnership." The selling expenses are commonly referred to as syndication expenses. Unlike organizational expenses, the regulations specifically provide that the deduction and amortization election under Code Sec. 709(b) is not available for syndication expenses.[14] Syndication expenses include all those connected

[11] Reg. § 1.709-2(c).

[12] P.L. 94-455

[13] *A. Wolkowitz v. Commr.*, 8 TCM 754, Dec. 17,168(M) (1949); *Meldrum & Fewsmith, Inc. v. Commr.*, 20 TC 790, Dec. 19,801 (1953); *M.E. Wildman v. Commr.*, 78 TC 943, Dec. 39,093 (1982).

[14] Rev. Rul. 89-11, 1989-1 CB 179. Even if the syndication effort is abandoned, the IRS's position

with the issuing and marketing of interests in the partnership. Examples of syndication expenses are:[15]

1. Brokerage fees;
2. Registration fees;
3. Legal fees of an underwriter, place management, an issuer for securities advice and for advice pertaining to the adequacy of tax disclosure in the prospectus;
4. Accounting fees for preparation of representations to be included in the offering materials; and
5. Printing costs of the prospectus, placement memorandum, and other selling and promotional material.

Legal or accounting expenses involving tax matters may be incurred by a partnership in the process of being formed. Depending upon the facts and circumstances, such expenses may be:

- Currently deductible ordinary and necessary business expenses;
- Costs of organizing the partnership that are not deductible under Code Sec. 709, but amortizable under Code Sec. 709(b)(1); or
- Nondeductible syndication expenses.

An example of currently deductible legal expense is the cost of the tax opinion incurred at the formation of a partnership relating to the Code Sec. 704(c) implications arising because the partners have already contributed appreciated property. Also, the partnership's payment for a tax opinion related to the application to the partnership of the at-risk rules under Code Sec. 465 would be currently deductible. Legal costs arising from planning for the contribution to the partnership of property, the agreed value of which differs from its adjusted basis in the hands of the contributor, may be required to be capitalized as either organization or syndication expenses. Costs of preparing the partnership agreement related to such contributions would be organization expenses. Costs related to selling the partnership interests would be syndication expenses.[16]

¶ 603 Investigation, Acquisition, and Start-Up Expenses—Code Secs. 195 and 263

Prior to the 1980 enactment of Code Sec. 195,[17] expenses incurred prior to a taxpayer's carrying on a trade or business were held to be nondeductible under Code Secs. 162 and 212.[18]

(Footnote Continued)

is that the accrued syndication costs are not deductible.

[15] Reg. § 1.709-2(b).

[16] *R.C. Honodel v. Commr.*, CA-9, 84-1 USTC ¶ 9133, 722 F2d 1462.

[17] P.L. 98-605.

[18] *F.B. Polachek v. Commr.*, 22 TC 858, Dec. 20,453 (1954), and Code Sec. 162; *Richmond Television Corp. v. U.S.*, CA-4, SCt, 65-2 USTC ¶ 9724, 382 US 68, 86 SCt 233; and Code Sec. 162; *A.A. Aboussie v. U.S.*, CA-8, 85-2 USTC ¶ 9860, 779 F2d 424, and Code Sec. 162; *J.K. Johnson v. Commr.*,

Code Sec. 195 was directed at two distinct failures arising in the application of Code Secs. 162, 212, and 167 to start-ups. First, these provisions permitted a deduction only in the context of a "trade or business" type activity and this was interpreted to preclude a deduction until such activity commenced. Second, to the extent that amounts could not be identified with the acquisition of specific assets having determinable useful lives, recovery was postponed until the trade or business terminated, or was sold or exchanged in a taxable transaction. As the House Ways and Means Committee noted:

> Under present law, costs incurred prior to the commencement of a business normally are not deductible because they are not incurred in carrying on a trade or business. The start-up or pre-operating costs must be capitalized and often can not be depreciated or amortized because no ascertainable life can be established for these costs. However, the capitalized costs may be covered for purposes of measuring gain or loss on the disposition of the business.[19]

There are two categories of Code Sec. 195 expenses:

1. Investigation expenses; and
2. Pre-opening/start-up expenses.

Prior to October 22, 2004, the date of enactment of the American Jobs Creation Act of 2004, partnerships could elect to amortize Code Sec. 195 expenses over a period of not less than 60 months, beginning with the month in which the partnership commenced its trade or business. With respect to Code Sec. 195 expenses incurred after October 22, 2004, up to $5,000 of these expenses may be deducted in the taxable year in which the trade or business begins. However, the $5,000 amount is reduced (but not below zero) by the amount that all Code Sec. 195 expenses (including those incurred prior to October 22, 2004) exceed $50,000. Any additional organizational expenses are amortizable over the 180-month period that begins with the commencement of the trade or business.[20]

.01 Investigation Expenses

The first question in determining the treatment of an investigation expenditure is whether the expenses in question are incurred to expand the present business or are costs incurred in entering into a new business. Expenses incurred in expanding a taxpayer's current business are deductible currently as trade or business expenses.

Costs of investigating "new business." Assuming that the partnership is entering into a new business and not expanding an old business, the question is what expenses are allowed to be capitalized under Code Sec. 195 and deducted or amortized, and what expenses must be capitalized as

(Footnote Continued)

CA-6, 86-2 USTC ¶ 9534, 794 F2d 1157; *M.H. Fishman v. Commr.*, CA-7, 88-1 USTC ¶ 9137, 837 F2d 309, and Code Sec. 212; *G.S. Sorrell, Jr. v. Commr.*, CA-11, 89-2 USTC ¶ 9521, 882 F2d 484, and Code Sec. 212. The capitalization and amortization rules for start-up expenses also apply to Code Sec. 212 activities, but only if the activity is engaged in anticipation of such activity becoming an active trade or business. Code Sec. 195(c)(1)(A)(iii).

[19] H. Rep. No. 96-1278 at 3, 1980-2 CB 709.

[20] Code Sec. 195(b), as amended by the American Jobs Creation Act of 2004; Committee Report on the American Jobs Creation Act of 2004, Sec. 902.

acquisition expenses of the business assets and must be depreciated over the assets' useful lives. The House Ways and Means Committee described Code Sec. 195 start-up costs as, "[u]nder the provision, eligible expenses consist of investigatory costs incurred in reviewing a prospective business prior to a final decision to enter that business."[21]

The IRS describes investigatory expenditures as follows:

> Expenditures incurred in the course of a general search for, or investigation of, an active trade or business in order to determine *whether* to enter a new business and *which* new business to enter (other than costs incurred to acquire capital assets that are used in the search or investigation) qualify as investigatory costs that are eligible for amortization as start-up expenditures under § 195. However, expenditures incurred in an attempt to acquire specific businesses do not qualify as start-up expenditures because they are acquisition costs under § 263. The nature of the cost must be analyzed based on all the facts and circumstances of the transaction to determine whether it is an investigatory cost incurred to facilitate the *whether* and *which* decisions, or an acquisition cost incurred to facilitate consummation of an acquisition.[22]

The IRS also stated that:

> we believe the reference to a final decision describes the point at which a taxpayer makes its own decision whether to acquire a specific business, and subsequently incurs costs in an effort to consummate the acquisition. At that point the general and preliminary investigation ceases and the taxpayer initiates its acquisition process. Costs incurred in connection with this process must be capitalized.[23]

It is settled that during the acquisition process there will be a point in time when expenses cease being capitalized and deducted or amortized under Code Sec. 195 and start being capitalized under Code Sec. 263 as cost of acquiring the business itself. According to a pre-Code Sec. 195 ruling:

> a taxpayer will be considered to have entered into a transaction for profit if, based upon all the facts and circumstances, the taxpayer has gone beyond the general investigatory search . . . to focus on the acquisition of a specific business or investment . . . Expenses incurred in the course of a general search for a preliminary investigation of a business or investment involve expenses related to the decision of whether to enter a transaction and which transaction to enter . . . Once the taxpayer has focused on the acquisition of a specific business or investment, expenses that are related to acquire such business or investment are capital in nature [.] [24]

In the case of an investigatory expense incurred in acquisition of a partnership interest by a partner, the amortization deduction is taken by the partner.

Business expansion expenses. As noted above, start-up expenses do not include the costs involved in expanding an existing business. These amounts are currently deductible under Code Sec. 162. However, even in the case of an expansion of an existing business, if the expenses are incurred in connection with the acquisition of assets, Code Sec. 263 requires capitalization in the cost basis of those assets. In the case of a partnership, the test

---

[21] H. Rep. No. 96-1278 at 10, 1980-2 CB 712. Of course, if the business never begins, Code Sec. 195 never comes into play. See, *e.g., R.I. Koenig v. Commr.*, 75 TCM 2484, Dec. 52,743(M), TC Memo. 1998-215.

[22] Rev. Rul. 99-23, 1999-20 IRB 3.

[23] IRS Technical Advice Memorandum 199901004 (9-28-98).

[24] Rev. Rul. 77-254, 1977-2 CB 63.

of whether there is an existing business which is being expanded is applied at the partnership level.[25] For example, if two individuals who are already engaged in a hardware business join together in a partnership to jointly open up a new store and incur expansion expenses in seeking a new location for the hardware business, the partnership would be considered to be in a new trade or business even though from the partners' standpoint this could be considered a mere expansion of the existing hardware business. The partnership itself was not in the business before and now it is. There is also a question of fact whether a partnership with an established ongoing business is expanding the existing business or is entering a new business. Factors which could imply expansion of the business would be geographically extending the business or vertical integration. Factors indicating a new trade or business might include involvement in marketing products that differ significantly from the products currently being marketed or marketing the same products to new and different customers. For example, a distributor of flowers who is currently working in the wholesale market who opens up a retail shop might be considered to be entering into a new business.

.02 Pre-opening Start-Up Expenses

As mentioned, there are two classes of Code Sec. 195 expenses. In addition to investigatory costs discussed above, there are also start-up costs. Start-up costs are incurred after the decision has been made to establish a particular business and before the time a new business begins. Examples include:

- Advertising;
- Wages paid to employees who are being trained and to instructors;
- Travel and other expenses incurred in lining up prospective distributors, suppliers or customers; and
- Salaries or fees paid or incurred for executives, consultants, and/or similar professional services.

These expenses are sometimes referred to as "pre-opening expenses." Code Sec. 195 applies only to expenses which have a trade or business requirement as a prerequisite to deductibility and are not capitalized under another provision of the Internal Revenue Code. For example, marketing expenses and the cost of training employees are deductible under Code Sec. 162 if the partnership is already engaged in the trade or business to which they relate. *Richmond Television Corporation v. United States* involved a corporation formed to construct and operate a television station and is a

[25] *Madison Gas and Electric Co. v. Commr.*, CA-7, 80-2 USTC ¶ 9754, 633 F2d 512, aff'g 72 TC 521, Dec. 36,142 (1979); *R.C. Goodwin v. Commr.*, 75 TC 424, Dec. 37,502 (1980), aff'd without published opinion, CA-9, 691 F2d 490.

good example of start-up expenditures.[26] During the three years the application to the Federal Communications Commission for a permit to engage in that activity was pending, the taxpayer conducted a training program to train staff available once the permit was granted. The training expenses incurred between the decision to establish a business and the actual beginning of the business operations were disallowed as a deduction because the taxpayer was not "carrying on" a trade or business when the expenses were incurred.[27] But, if such expenses are now incurred before business begins, they are subject to the provisions of Code Sec. 195.

Expenses which are deductible in the absence of an existing business are deductible without reference to Code Sec. 195's requirements. Code Sec. 195 does not apply to interest and taxes deductible under Code Secs. 163 and 164 because they are deductible whether or not there is a related trade or business. They are not Code Sec. 195 expenses even though a deduction for these expenses may be disallowed under another provision of the Internal Revenue Code. For example, they may be required to be capitalized under Code Sec. 263, even though the partnership is engaged in active trade or business.[28] Interest capitalized under Code Sec. 263A is not amortized under Code Sec. 195.

Start-up period. For purposes of Code Sec. 195, the start-up period begins with the end of the investigatory phase of whether to enter the business or which business to enter and it ends when the associated trade or business is actively conducted. The start-up period ends and amortization begins at the point when the partnership is engaged in an *active* trade or business. The question of when a taxpayer is actively engaged in a trade or business is a facts and circumstances determination. Generally, taxpayers are considered to be actively engaged in a trade or business when they actually begin earning revenue from that trade or business. In contrast, a taxpayer may begin depreciating an asset when it is in a state of readiness to be used in that business, as he or she is considered to have placed the asset in service in a trade or business. Similar rules apply under Code Sec. 709, which allows the taxpayer to begin amortizing organizational expenses when the partnership is ready to begin conducting business; under that section, the trade or business is deemed to begin when the partnership is in a position to begin doing business. However, Code Sec. 195 requires an active trade or business.

.03 Unamortized Investigation and Start-Up Expenses

Like organizational costs not fully amortized when the partnership liquidates, unamortized start-up expenses can be deducted as an ordinary loss under Code Sec. 165 if the trade or business is completely disposed of

[26] *Richmond Television Corp. v. U.S.*, SCt, 65-2 USTC ¶ 9724, 382 US 68, 86 SCt 233.

[27] Expenditures had to be capitalized and could have been amortized if the asset acquired had a limited life. The year involved was before the enactment of Code Sec. 195.

[28] However, interest and taxes may be required to be capitalized under some other Code sections, such as Code Sec. 263A.

before such costs have been fully amortized.[29] It is possible that an in-kind distribution of trade or business operating assets to one or more of the partners in liquidation of their partnership interests should be considered a complete disposition of the trade or business for these purposes. The rules provide for a deduction of the unamortized expenses only if the taxpayer *completely* disposes of the trade or business generating the expenditures before the end of the amortization period.

.04 Code Sec. 195 Procedure

The election. The statute provides that "[a]n election under subsection (b) shall be made not later than the time prescribed by law for filing the return for the taxable year in which the trade or business begins (including extensions thereof)."[30] The regulations, however, provide that the election may be filed with the return for the taxable year in which the taxpayer's active trade or business begins, or any prior taxable year.[31] The regulations were intended to simplify the filing of a Code Sec. 195 election. First, if a taxpayer is uncertain as to the year in which the active trade or business begins, he or she need not file an election for each possible year. Rather, a Code Sec. 195 election for a particular trade or business will be effective if the trade or business becomes active in the year for which the election is filed or in any subsequent year. Second, the regulations also allow taxpayers who have made timely elections under Code Sec. 195 to file a revised statement with a subsequent return to include any start-up expenditures not included in the original statement. Although the amortization election may be made for a partnership year prior to the year in which its active trade or business begins, the amortization itself cannot begin until the taxpayer actively conducts a trade or business.[32]

Tax return presentation. Start-up expenses are included within the definition of "amortizable property" in the instructions to Form 4562, Depreciation and Amortization. The required information is entered in Part VI, Capital Amortization, of Form 4562, and from there the current year's deduction for rental trade or business activity flows through the "Other Deductions" line on page 1 of Form 1065 (not the "Depreciation" line). Therefore, the current year's deduction for start-up expenses is included in the computation of the partnership's ordinary income or loss for operations.

---

[29] Code Sec. 195(b)(2).

[30] Code Sec. 195(d)(1).

[31] Reg. § 1.195-1(b).

[32] This odd rule results from the amendment to Code Sec. 195 by the Deficit Reduction Act of 1984, P.L. 98-369 (Act § 94(a)). This change requires a trade or business to be actively conducted for the start-up period to end (and for the amortization period to begin); but Code Sec. 195(d)(1), which deals with the time for the amortization election, was not changed. As a result, the statute still provides that, as under pre-1984 law, the election must be filed for the year in which the partnership's business begins, without regard to when the active conduct begins.

SUMMARY TABLE FOR TAX TREATMENT OF PRE-OPENING EXPENSES

	Organizational Expenses	*Syndication Costs*	*Investigation and Start-up Expenses*
Proper year to make election.	In tax year business begins.	Not applicable.	In any tax year up to the year the active trade or business begins.
Proper time to begin deduction and/or amortization.	In month partnership begins business.	Not applicable.	In month *active* conduct of business operation begins.
Treatment if partnership liquidates.	If election applies, partnership takes ordinary loss deduction under Code Sec. 165. If election does not apply, partnership has no loss but the partners have increased loss or reduced gain on liquidation.	Capitalized amount will reduce partner's capital gain or increase capital loss on liquidation of his or her interest.	If election applies, partnership takes ordinary loss deduction under Code Sec. 165. If election does not apply, partnership has no loss but the partners have increased loss or reduced gain on liquidation.
Treatment of capitalized amounts for which election is not available or no election applies.	Permanently capitalized. No tax benefit until partner sells interest or partnership liquidates. At that time, capitalized amount will reduce partner's capital gain or increase capital loss.	Permanently capitalized. No tax benefit until partner sells interest or partnership liquidates. At that time, capitalized amount will reduce partner's capital gain or increase capital loss.	Permanently capitalized. No tax benefit until partner sells interest or partnership liquidates. At that time, capitalized amount will reduce partner's capital gain or increase capital loss.

PART III

TAXATION OF OPERATIONS

Chapter 7

Amount of Partnership Taxable Income

¶ 701 Introduction

Generally, in computing its taxable income, the partnership takes into account the same items of income and deduction during the year as does an individual. The partnership, however, is required to present its taxable income in a specified format very different from that of an individual. The partnership must separately state the net amounts of the items of income and deductions enumerated in Code Sec. 702. These separately stated amounts are items subject to special limitations or treatment that could affect the calculation of a partner's nonpartnership deductions or income from other sources. The statute's effect is that each partner is to take into account his or her share of the partnership's net amount of each of these items. Any special limitation is applied at the partner level and is computed with reference to the partner's share of the partnership's items together with the partner's items of the same type from other sources. Code Sec. 702(a) requires that the partnership separately state its net amounts from the following sources:

1. Long-term capital gains and losses.
2. Short-term capital gains and losses.
3. Code Sec. 1231 gains and losses.
4. Charitable contributions.
5. Dividends that are taxed as net capital gains or are eligible for the dividends received deduction.[1]
6. Income taxes paid to foreign countries.
7. Other items required by the regulations.

Examples of items the regulations add are the following:

1. Recoveries of bad debts and taxes.

---

[1] Code Sec. 243.

2. Gains from wagering.

3. Nonbusiness expenses.

4. Medical and dental expenses.

5. Items specially allocated.

6. Any amount that, if separately taken into account by any partner, would result in an income tax liability for that partner different from that which would result if that partner did not take the item separately into account.[2]

Administrative pronouncements and case law add other types of income and deductions that must be separately stated. In preparing the partnership's tax return, these separately stated items are listed on Schedule K of the partnership tax return (Form 1065, U.S. Partnership Return of Income). The remaining amounts of income and deduction that are not separately stated are taken into account by simply netting them on line one of Form 1065, Schedule K.

Example 7-1. The equal AB partnership has the following items of income and deductions for its taxable year:

Gross rents		$250,000
Depreciation	$100,000	
Maintenance expenses	40,000	
Property taxes	10,000	
Insurance	5,000	
Property management fees	30,000	
		(185,000)
Net rental income		*$65,000*
Gains from selling investment land		40,000
Partnership's taxable income		*$105,000*
Charitable deductions		$10,000

The partnership's taxable income is $105,000, but this net amount never appears on its tax return. The partnership must separately state its net rental income of $65,000 because this is per se passive income from nonreal estate operations.[3] and each partner's passive losses from other sources are deductible only to the extent of his total passive income from all sources. The capital gains of $40,000 must also be separately stated because a partner's capital losses are deductible only to the extent of his capital gains from all sources (plus $3,000 for individuals). The partnership's charitable contributions are not deductible by the partnership but must be stated separately because each individual partner can deduct these amounts only if his total charitable contributions do not exceed the percentages of adjusted gross income specified in Code Sec. 170.

[2] Reg. § 1.702-1(a)(8)(i), (ii).

[3] Code Sec. 469(c)(7).

S Corporation Observation. An S corporation calculates and presents its taxable income in the same manner as does a partnership.[4]

¶ 702 Both Entity and Aggregate Rules Apply

The computation and treatment of partnership taxable income has many similarities to both treating it as an entity separate from its owners and a joint ownership through a tenancy-in-common of individuals. For example, there is no income tax imposed on the partnership form of conducting business. But the combined net income for the jointly owned activity is computed and reported by the partnership on Form 1065.

Partnerships are treated as entities for purposes of making most elections (such as choice of accounting methods) that affect the computation of pass-through items, and for certain procedural purposes.[5] Partnerships are treated similar to tenants-in-common or as an aggregation of individual owners for other purposes; for example, the Code Sec. 469 passive loss limits and the Code Sec. 465 at-risk limits apply at the partner level. This is commonly referred to as the entity and aggregate aspects of partnership taxation. The statute, regulations and other guidance sometimes treat a partnership as an entity distinct from its owners. This mimics C corporation taxation where the shareholders and the corporation generally are two separate and distinct taxpayers. As mentioned, other partnership rules treat the partners as if they were tenants-in-common in the jointly owned venture. This is an aggregate approach to partnership taxation. In some situations, there is a choice whether to use an entity rule or an aggregate rule. For example, a purchaser of a partnership interest has a new cost basis in his or her interest, but not a cost basis in his or her share of the assets. This is an entity rule. However, the partner receives a cost basis in his or her share of the assets if a Code Sec. 754 election is in effect. This is in essence an election to use an aggregate rule.

Another example of treating a partnership as an aggregate is that each partner's gross income includes his or her share of the partnership's gross income.[6] The regulations and instructions for Form 1065 do not specifically provide for this item to be separately stated. However, examples of its importance to partners include:

- Requirement to file a tax return.[7]
- Application of six-year statute of limitations for omitting more than 25 percent of gross income.[8]
- Tax imposed on S corporations with excess investment income and termination of such a corporation's S election.[9]

Other examples of an "aggregate" approach to partnership taxation include:

---

[4] Code Sec. 1366(a).
[5] See Code Secs. 703(b), 6221 and following.
[6] Code Sec. 702(c).
[7] Code Sec. 6012(a).
[8] Code Sec. 6501(e).
[9] Code Secs. 1375 and 1362(d)(3).

- Partners are required to report their shares of partnership profit or loss regardless of whether the partnership makes a distribution to them or they pay money to the partnership.[10]

- The character of the income, gain, loss, deduction or credit at the partnership level is passed through to the partners.[11]

- Some elections are made at the partner level:[12]

  1. The Code Sec. 901 election;
  2. Election to deduct certain mining exploration expenditures;[13]
  3. Election related to cancellation of indebtedness income;[14] and
  4. Elections related to nonresident and foreign corporation investments on United States rental realty.[15]

Other examples of an "entity" approach to partnership taxation include:

- An S corporation shareholder may deduct his or her share of losses only to the extent of his or her basis in the stock and the basis he or she has in loans made to the corporation.[16] Loans made by a partnership to an S corporation owned by the partners are not considered as loans by its partners to the S corporation.[17]

- Partnership income is computed at the entity level;[18]

- The partnership files a tax return reporting its taxable income;[19]

- The partnership has its own accounting method;[20]

- The partnership has its own taxable year;[21] and

- The partnership makes most of the elections affecting the computation of its taxable income. A partial list of the elections made at the partnership level follows:

  1. Depreciation elections;[22]
  2. Inventory method;[23]
  3. Election to rollover involuntary conversion gains;[24]

---

[10] Code Secs. 702(a) and 704.
[11] Code Sec. 702(a) and (b).
[12] Code Sec. 703(b).
[13] Code Sec. 617.
[14] Code Sec. 108(b)(5) and (c)(3).
[15] Code Secs. 871(d)(1) and 882(d)(1).
[16] Code Sec. 1366(d) and (d)(1)(B).
[17] *E.J. Frankel v. Commr.*, 61 TC 343, Dec. 32,250 (1973).
[18] Code Sec. 703(a).
[19] Code Sec. 6031.
[20] Code Sec. 703(b).
[21] Code Sec. 706.
[22] Prop. Reg. § 1.168-5(e)(7).
[23] Code Sec. 472.
[24] Code Sec. 1033.

4. Election to expense a limited amount of depreciable basis in year of acquisition;[25]
5. Election not to use the installment method for reporting installment sales;[26]
6. Election to amortize organizational expenses;[27]
7. Election to adjust the basis of partnership assets following certain distributions (Code Sec. 734(b)) or transfers of interests in the partnership (Code Sec. 743(b));[28] and
8. Election to apply self-charged interest deduction rule.[29]

.01 *Involuntary Conversions*

The entity-level application of Code Sec. 1033 to involuntary conversions is an example of the surprising and sometimes unfair results which can occur when the partnership is treated as a separate entity and the actions of the partners are disregarded. If gain is realized when partnership property is involuntarily converted, the partnership itself must reinvest in similar or related property to enjoy the nonrecognition provision of Code Sec. 1033.[30]

> ***Example 7-2.*** The ABCD partnership has an insured building with a value of $100,000 and zero adjusted basis. It is completely destroyed by fire. The insurer pays the partnership $100,000 resulting in a $100,000 realized involuntary conversion gain. If the partnership liquidates and each partner reinvests in property which would qualify under Code Sec. 1033 for nonrecognition, the entire gain is taxed. If the ABCD partnership is not liquidated and it reinvests $100,000 in qualified property, no gain is recognized.

If an individual suffering an involuntary conversion purchases an interest in a partnership which owns qualifying property, the purchase fails to qualify for Code Sec. 1033 treatment.[31] If the individual already owned a partnership interest in a different partnership and that partnership invested in qualifying property, there would be no deferral under Code Sec. 1033.

If the condemned property is encumbered, the IRS has ruled that a partner must recognize gain under Code Sec. 731 if there is a reduction in partnership debt which causes a reduction of a partner's share of that debt to exceed his or her partnership interest basis, even though the partnership satisfies Code Sec. 1033's requirements.[32]

> ***Example 7-3.*** The equal AB partnership's insured building with a value of $100,000 and basis of zero is subject to a debt of $100,000

---

[25] Code Sec. 179.
[26] Code Sec. 453.
[27] Code Sec. 709.
[28] Code Sec. 754.
[29] Prop. Reg. § 1.469(7)(f).
[30] *T.K. McManus v. Commr.*, 65 TC 197, Dec. 33,483 (1975), aff'd, CA-9, 78-2 USTC ¶ 9748, 583 F2d 443; *M. Demirjian v. Commr.*, CA-3, 72-1 USTC ¶ 9281, 457 F2d 1.
[31] *M.H.S. Co., Inc. v. Commr.*, 35 TCM 733, Dec. 33,843(M), TC Memo. 1976-165, aff'd, CA-6, 78-1 USTC ¶ 9442, 575 F2d 1177.
[32] Rev. Rul. 81-242, 1981-2 CB 147; Rev. Rul. 94-4, 1994-1 CB 196.

and is completely destroyed by fire in Year 1. Prior to the fire, each partner's basis in his interest is zero. The insurer pays $100,000 in insurance proceeds to the lender in Year 1 and in the next taxable year the partnership purchases qualifying replacement property with a value of $100,000 subject to a debt of $100,000. The IRS has ruled that *A* and *B* each have a deemed money distribution of $50,000 on the last day of the partnership taxable year in which the debt was paid in Year 1. Under these facts, because each partner's basis is zero, each has a gain of $50,000. If the partnership had borrowed $100,000 for any purpose by the close of the tax year in which the insurance company paid the lender, there would have been no gain.

.02 Code Sec. 1244 Stock

The application of Code Sec. 1244 is another example of an entity approach. Code Sec. 1244 allows the owner of qualifying stock a limited amount of ordinary loss when the stock is worthless or is sold at a loss. A partnership qualifies for the ordinary loss treatment if it satisfies the requirements of Code Sec. 1244.[33] However, if the partnership distributes the stock to its partners, they do not qualify for an ordinary loss because Code Sec. 1244 treatment applies only to original holders of the stock. Therefore, even though they are the original owners from an aggregate view of partnership taxation, Code Sec. 1244 adopts an entity view and the partnership itself, not the partners, are the original owners.[34]

.03 Prepaid Expenses

Prepaid expenses are deductible only if after taking the deduction into account income is clearly reflected.[35] If a partnership prepays expenses, the distortion of income test is applied at the partnership level [36] and probably also at the partner level.[37]

¶ 703 Calculation of the Amount of the Partnership's Taxable Income

With a few exceptions, a partnership's taxable income is computed by taking into account the same items of income, gain, loss, deduction, and credit as required of an individual.[38] The characterization and timing rules are also, with a few exceptions, based upon the rules applied to individuals rather than corporations.[39] For example, because a partnership's taxable income is to be computed as if it were an individual, a partnership is entitled to treat losses realized on the disposition of small business corporation stock as defined in Code Sec. 1244 as ordinary losses.[40]

---

[33] Code Sec. 1244 treatment is not available to S corporations. *V.D. Rath v. Commr.*, 101 TC 196, Dec. 49,266 (1993).

[34] Reg. § 1.1244(a)-1(b)(2); *J. Prizant v. Commr.*, 30 TCM 817, Dec. 30,923, TC Memo. 1971-196.

[35] Code Sec. 446(b).

[36] *B. Resnick v. Commr.*, 66 TC 74, Dec. 33,761 (1976), aff'd, CA-7, 77-1 USTC ¶ 9451, 555 F2d 634.

[37] *R.E. Clement v. U.S.*, CtCls, 78-2 USTC ¶ 9566, 580 F2d 422, 217 CtCls 495; *J.R. Parks v. U.S.*, DC Tex., 77-1 USTC ¶ 9404, 434 FSupp 206.

[38] Code Sec. 703(a); Reg. § 1.703-1(a)(1).

[39] Trusts, estates, and S corporations also adopt as a starting point the rules provided for individuals. Code Secs. 641(b) and 1363(b).

[40] *V.D. Rath v. Commr.*, 101 TC 196, Dec. 49,266 (1993). However, if the stock is distributed to the partners, they are not entitled to an ordinary loss. Reg. § 1.1244(a)-1(b)(2); *J. Prizant v. Commr.*, 30 TCM 817, Dec. 30,923(M), TC Memo. 1971-196.

S Corporation Observation. The Tax Court has held [41] that an S corporation is not entitled to an ordinary deduction under Code Sec. 1244 for losses incurred on the worthlessness or sale of otherwise qualified small business corporation stock under Code Sec. 1244.

Many situations fall under a category of exceptions found in Code Sec. 703(a) when a partnership does not treat itself as an individual. The Code section provides, for example, that the partnership is not allowed the deduction for:

1. Personal exemptions;
2. Taxes paid or accrued to foreign countries;
3. Charitable contributions;
4. Net operating loss carryovers;
5. Additional itemized deductions provided in Code Secs. 211 and following; and
6. Depletion with respect to oil and gas wells.

The disallowance of personal exemptions and net operating loss carryovers or carrybacks prevents a double deduction for these amounts. The partners and the partnership do not both get personal exemptions or their equivalents. The partnership's negative taxable income passes through to its partners and is part of any net operating loss that it may cause to a partner. There is no second carryover at the partnership level.

The other disallowed expenses are simply part of the process of separating them from the partnership's other items of income and loss and testing their treatment at the partner level.

In addition to these statutory disallowances, the regulations prevent the partnership from taking a deduction for a capital loss carryover.[42] The reason for the disallowance is the same as the reason for denying net operating loss deductions—to prevent two deductions for the same loss—one at the partnership level and the other at the partner level.

Other exceptions to treating a partnership as an individual are found within specific provisions throughout the Internal Revenue Code governing the timing and character of various items of income or deduction. However, if the partnership-level treatment of an item has not been specifically addressed in the Internal Revenue Code, it follows rules accorded to an individual taxpayer.

It is sometimes difficult to classify items of income or expense as partnership or partner items. When there is doubt about whether a partner or a partnership is the earner of the income, the general rule is that income is reported by the partnership if it is reasonably associated with the

[41] *V.D. Rath v. Commr.*, 101 TC 196 , Dec. 49,266 (1993).

[42] Reg. § 1.703-1(a)(2)(vii).

partnership's business activity.[43] Income from property is taxed to the beneficial owner and not necessarily the record owner.[44]

It is common for a partnership agreement to require partners to assign certain types of outside service income to the partnership. The IRS has ruled [45] and the Tax Court has held [46] that the partner must report the income himself even if the income is from services similar to services rendered by the partnership. If service income is properly reportable by a partner but turned over to the partnership, and the service partner's share of the income is less than the amount taxed to him, a partner level deduction may be in order.[47]

The general rule is that the partnership must deduct its expenses even though they are paid by a partner.[48] If, however, the partner is personally responsible for the expense and not entitled to reimbursement, the partner appears to be entitled to the deduction. The relevant authority for this position treats the partner as if he or she were engaged in the partnership's activities directly.[49] The partnership and partners may in effect shift a partnership deduction to a partner. If the partnership makes a deductible guaranteed payment subject to Code Sec. 707(c) to the partner and specially allocates such deduction to the payee partner, there is no net income to the partner. The partner then is entitled to a deduction for his or her "unreimbursable" partnership expense.[50] As long as the expenses are the type that the partner is expected to pay without reimbursement, the partner can deduct the expenses on Schedule E.[51] Unreimbursed expenses would include unreimbursed home office deductions under Code Sec. 280A.[52]

¶ 704 Payments to a Partner

With proper planning, payments to a partner for services (salary, wages, commissions), the use of property (rent, royalties), or the use of capital (interest) may be deductible by the partnership or simply treated as a method of income allocation. If payments are made to a partner acting in a nonpartner capacity, the treatment of the payment is governed by Code Sec. 707(a). If payments are made to a partner acting as a partner, but without regard to partnership profits, they are guaranteed payments governed by Code Sec. 707(c). Code Sec. 707(a) and (c) payments are part of

[43] *S.B. Schneer v. Commr.*, 97 TC 643, Dec. 47,803 (1991).

[44] Rev. Rul. 55-39, 1955-1 CB 403; Rev. Rul. 54-84, 1954-1 CB 284.

[45] Rev. Rul. 64-90, 1964-1 CB 226; Rev. Rul. 80-338, 1980-2 CB 30; IRS Letter Ruling 9514008 (1-4-95).

[46] *W.B. Mayes v. Commr.*, 21 TC 286, Dec. 19,994 (1953).

[47] See Rev. Rul. 64-90, 1964-1 CB 226.

[48] *H.K. Stevens v. Commr.*, 46 TC 492, Dec. 28,026 (1966), aff'd per curiam, CA-6, 68-1 USTC ¶ 9174, 388 F2d 298; IRS Technical Advice Memorandum 8442001 (5-14-84).

[49] IRS Technical Advice Memorandum 9316003 (12-23-92). If the partnership agreement or partnership practice requires a partner to bear the burden of partnership business expenses, he is entitled to a Section 162 deduction. The partner cannot deduct expenses for which he was entitled to, but failed to seek reimbursement. *F.S. Klein v. Commr.*, 25 TC 1045, Dec. 21,573 (1956).

[50] See IRS Technical Advice Memorandum 9330001 (4-1-93).

[51] Per the Schedule E instructions, these expenses are reported on a separate line in the same manner as partner-level interest expense incurred in debt traced to the purchase of a partnership interest.

[52] Rev. Rul. 94-24, 1994-1 CB 87.

the partnership's aggregated nonseparately stated taxable income calculation unless they are specially allocated. If payments made to a partner acting as a partner are dependent on the level of partnership profits, the payments are first treated as a special allocation of income to that partner under Code Sec. 704 and then as a distribution of that income under Code Sec. 731.

A partnership generally classifies its payments to a partner into one of three categories:

- Code Sec. 707(a) payments;
- Code Sec. 707(c) payments; or
- A distributive share of the partnership's income.

As a general rule, Code Sec. 707(a) tends to treat the payment as if it were made to a nonpartner. At the other extreme, payments which are not classified as Code Sec. 707(a) or (c) payments are ignored as "payments" and are considered distributive shares of the partnership's income coupled with a distribution. Code Sec. 707(c) payments are treated as distributive shares for some purposes and are treated as payments to nonpartners for other purposes. The following chart summarizes the continuum of comparative attributes and treatment of these payments.

Nonpartner-type activity; Payment to partner reflects fair market value compensation; not partnership income.	Partner-type activity; Payment reflects fair market value compensation, not partnership income.	Partner-type activity; Payment is share of partnership income not necessarily fair market value compensation.
Code Sec. 707(a) Payment	***Code Sec. 707(c) Payment***	***Code Sec. 704(a) Allocation with a Code Sec. 731 Distribution***
Partnership deduction if not capitalized under Code Sec. 263—but not before the day the partner must include payment in income.	Partnership deduction based solely on its accounting method if not capitalized under Code Sec. 263.	No partnership deduction but reduction in other partners' income simultaneous with payee's partner's income.
Partnership deduction and partner income are simultaneous; partner's income is ordinary—he receives a Form 1099 if applicable.	Partnership deduction and partner's income simultaneous; partner's income is ordinary and the partner income is reported on his or her K-1.	Income's character flows from partnership level.

Classification of a payment as a deduction or profit-sharing arrangement is based upon its purpose and the method used in calculating its amount. If the payment is deductible in computing the partnership's taxable income, the timing of the deduction will also vary depending upon whether or not the partner is paid for fulfilling his or her duty as a partner in contrast to acting in a nonpartner capacity. A nondeductible payment to a partner which is treated as a distributive share of income (*e.g.*, under Code Secs. 704(a)/731) will, in many respects, result in the functional equivalent of a deduction from the viewpoint of the other partners. If the payment is not deductible, it is instead considered a method of allocating the partnership's taxable income, but the ultimate effect of allocating income to a partner is the functional equivalent of allowing the other partners a deduction. Often correctly classifying these various payments to ensure their proper tax treatment is inordinately complex in comparison to the differences in tax effect ultimately accorded to such classification.

LLC Observation. Although a limited liability company (LLC) resembles a corporation in many non-income tax respects, an LLC member is not treated as an employee for tax purposes unless there is a special treatment specified by the Internal Revenue Code. Even though the LLC member would generally be a common law employee, the LLC does not treat Code Sec. 707(a) or (c) payments for services as payroll. For example, the LLC does not issue an annual Form W-2, nor does it withhold any taxes or make Social Security tax payments.

S Corporation Observation. S corporation payments to shareholders for services fall into three categories. They are treated as payments to employees if the shareholder is an employee under the general common law rules. They are treated as paid to an independent contractor if the shareholder's work does not create an employer/employee relationship. The payments are distributions if they are paid on account of stock ownership, including payments received by the shareholder in excess of what would be deemed "reasonable compensation" for services rendered are treated as distributions. As such they are nontaxable to the shareholder to the extent of his or her stock basis; once basis is fully recovered, any remainder is generally treated as capital gain.

.01 Payments to Partners as Compensation for Services or Property Not Required as a Condition of Partner Status

Definition. If a partner engages in transactions with the partnership in a capacity other than as a partner, the partner is treated as if he or she were not a member of the partnership with respect to that transaction. Such transactions include loans of money or property, property rentals, sales of property, and providing certain services.[53] Payments made to partners for the use of the partner's money or property, or for "support"

[53] Reg. § 1.707-1(a).

services, are normally deductible by the partnership. They are known generally as Code Sec. 707(a) payments. For example, the tax results of a partnership payment for leasing a partner's property are typically clear. The partnership deducts rent and the partnership reports rent. If a partnership borrows money from a partner, it deducts and the partner reports interest. The definition of support services is not precise, but generally it includes services not required of the partner by the partnership agreement or because of his or her partner status. They are usually services that are not central to the partnership's main function.[54] If the partnership agreement requires certain services to be rendered by a partner as a condition of his or her partner status, amounts paid to the partner which are not dependent on partnership income would normally be classified as guaranteed payments under Code Sec. 707(c) rather than Code Sec. 707(a) payments. However, if an analysis of the surrounding facts and circumstances shows that there was no business purpose or effect for that portion of the partnership agreement and there was a tax avoidance motive and effect, the provision would be ignored. If the partnership agreement is silent as to who should perform certain services, but there is a contract between the partnership and a partner that allows the partner to perform certain services for a limited time period, this would be strong evidence that the partner is performing nonpartner activities and the payment is a Code Sec. 707(a) payment. It is the contract of employment, not his or her partner status, that both allows and requires that the partner perform the services. If the partner fails to adequately perform his or her duties, the partner will lose his or her employment but not his or her partnership interest. For example, payments received by a general partner for managing the partnership's office buildings, which are its major assets, would not normally be considered Code Sec. 707(a) payments if these services are required by the partnership agreement. The general partner's profit-sharing arrangement, or guaranteed payment, compensates him or her for these expected services. However, payments to a limited partner for providing bookkeeping services for the partnership would qualify as Code Sec. 707(a) payments, if the partnership agreement did not require the services of the limited partner. An important characteristic of Code Sec. 707(a) payments is that they are normally determined by reference to the value of the services or property provided rather than the partnership's profits or losses.

Tax accounting. The partnership is allowed a deduction for a Code Sec. 707(a) payment only if it is a deductible expenditure. As to the proper year for the partnership to claim the deduction, two requirements must be satisfied:

- First, the amount must be currently deductible under the partnership's method of accounting. For example, a cash

[54] Technically, the statutory issue is whether the facts and circumstances indicate that the partner is "acting in his capacity as a partner."

method partnership must have paid the amount to the partner. An accrual method partnership must have satisfied the "all events" and "economic performance" tests.[55]

- Second, under Code Sec. 267, the partnership generally cannot claim a deduction for a payment to a partner until the day the partner must report the payment as income. For example, an accrual method partnership cannot claim a deduction in the current year for a payment which is to be made to a cash method partner in the following year.

Code Sec. 707(a) payments are deductible by a partnership that has an accounting method different from that of the partner on the later of these two days: (1) the day on which such an amount is deductible according to the partnership's normal accounting method, or (2) the day the partner must include such payment in gross income.[56]

Normally, the partner's taxable income and the partnership's deduction will occur on the same day, which is dictated by the day the partner is required to include the amount as income under his or her normal accounting method whether the partnership is using a cash or accrual basis tax accounting method.

Example 7-4. Partner *A*, who is a calendar-year, cash-method taxpayer, performs noncapitalized Code Sec. 707(a)-type services for the ABC partnership calendar-year, accrual-basis partnership in Year 1. *A* receives payment in Year 2. Partner *A* must include personal services income in his Year 2 individual tax return whether or not the partnership is required to capitalize the expenditure. The partnership may deduct the amount in Year 2.

Example 7-5. Partner *A*, who is a calendar-year, accrual-method taxpayer, performs noncapitalized Code Sec. 707(a)-type services for the ABC partnership calendar-year, *cash*-basis partnership in Year 1. The partnership pays *A* in Year 2. Partner *A* has income in Year 1 whether or not the partnership is required to capitalize the expenditure. ABC deducts the expenditure in Year 2 if capitalization is not required. This is the only situation when *A*'s income and the partnership's deduction will not occur simultaneously.

Example 7-6. The same facts as Examples 7-4 and 7-5, except both the partnership and partner are cash-method taxpayers. *A* has income and ABC has a deduction in Year 2.

Example 7-7. The same facts as Examples 7-4 and 7-5, except both are using the accrual-method of accounting. *A* has income and ABC has a deduction in Year 1.

55 Code Sec. 461(h).

56 Code Sec. 267(a) and (e). The partnership always uses a Form 1099 to report these payments to the service partner. Form W-2 is not used even though the partner might be a common law employee, and therefore no withholding of income or payroll tax is required.

.02 Guaranteed Payments

Definition. "Guaranteed payments" are those payments made to a partner for acting in his or her capacity as a partner when the amount is determined independent of the partnership's operating results. These amounts are also known as "Section 707(c) payments" and can represent either payment for services rendered or for use of the partner's capital. The primary reason for making a Code Sec. 707(c) payment is the same as the reason for granting a partner a profits interest. He or she is providing essential services or capital to the partnership. However, in contrast to the normal consideration for these "partner activities," the amount of the payment is determined by reference to the value of the services or property provided rather than by reference to partnership profits. The use of "guaranteed payments" allows more flexibility to the partnership in recognizing the varying contributions of services and capital provided by different partners toward producing the partnership's overall profitability.

> ***Example 7-8.*** The ABC partnership is owned by a group of CPAs who do both tax and audit services. *A*, *B*, and *C* are the founding senior partners who are well known and active in the business community. They are chiefly responsible for acquiring and retaining new clients. The junior partners perform and supervise most of the work. The partnership wishes to have an income sharing arrangement which both compensates the partners for time spent doing client work and recognizes other considerations. They agree upon a guaranteed Code Sec. 707(c) hourly payment for client-chargeable time spent and an equal division of profits for the partnership's income in excess of this amount.

> ***Example 7-9.*** The ABC limited partnership holds unimproved unused land for long-term investment and future development. The success of this venture depends heavily on both capital and development activity. The partners agree that the limited partners should receive a compounded cumulative Code Sec. 707(c) guaranteed payment for capital equal to the percentage increase in the Consumer Price Index plus 3% times their yearly ending capital accounts as a return on their invested capital. Partnership profits in excess of this amount will be allocated 50% to the service partners and the remainder to the limited partners in proportion to their ending capital accounts.

Guaranteed payments for use of a partner's capital are similar to interest payments, but the partnership has no duty to repay the principal at a specified date as required in the case of an actual debt. These amounts are paid to partners in consideration for their continued *investment* in the partnership. In the case of payments for services, the partnership agreement must require these activities or they must otherwise be considered central to the partnership's main activity. If the partner has both the right and duty to perform the services under the partnership agreement as opposed to a separate contract between the partner and partnership, it is a "guaranteed payment" under Code Sec. 707(c) unless there is strong evidence to the contrary. For example, a fixed payment received by a general partner for supervising the partnership as required by the partnership agreement would normally qualify as a guaranteed payment. In contrast, payments received by a limited partner for performing an isolated consulting task would not qualify unless there were additional factors strongly evidencing that it was his or her duty as a partner to consult with the partnership. The latter payment should be considered a Code Sec. 707(a) payment as described earlier.

As mentioned, a guaranteed payment is a payment made in exchange for "partner-type activity," including the use of a partner's invested capital. However, the amount of the payment is calculated without reference to the partnership's profit or loss. The literal language of Code Sec. 707(c) refers to a payment "determined without regard to the income of the partnership." Payments measured by reference to *gross receipts* have been held ineligible for Code Sec. 707(c) treatment.[57] The IRS has ruled that despite these decisions the taxpayer may treat payments dependent upon gross rentals as guaranteed payments if they otherwise qualify for such treatment.[58] A guaranteed payment is a hybrid. It is similar to a Code Sec. 707(a) payment because its amount is calculated independent of partnership results. However, unlike a Code Sec. 707(a) payment, it represents payment for something a partner is expected to make available to the partnership: necessary services and capital. Therefore, in this respect, it resembles an income allocation.

Tax accounting. The hybrid nature of a guaranteed payment is reflected in its tax treatment. Like a Code Sec. 707(a) payment, the partnership is entitled to a deduction if a cash payment to an independent party would have been deductible. Timing of the deduction is governed by the partnership's accounting method alone. The partnership is allowed to deduct this amount only from its ordinary income, and the partner, in turn, characterizes the income as ordinary.[59] The partner must include the agreed upon payment as income on the last day of the partnership's year in which the partnership takes the payment into account. This date is determined by the partnership's method of accounting and is independent of the partner's tax accounting method.[60] Guaranteed payments are considered Code Sec. 162 trade or business expenses but are subject to capitalization under the general rule of Code Sec. 263.[61] Therefore, in the case of a deductible Code Sec. 707(c) payment, the partner's treatment is similar to a partner's treatment of a distributive share of income even though, in the case of a Code Sec. 707(c) payment, the partnership may be allowed a

[57] *E.T. Pratt v. Commr.*, 64 TC 203, Dec. 33,189 (1975), aff'd, CA-5, 77-1 USTC ¶ 9347, 550 F2d 1023.

[58] Rev. Rul. 81-300, 1981-2 CB 143; see also S. Rept. No. 169, 98th Cong., 2d Sess. 230 (1984).

[59] The partnership does not use a Form 1099 or W-2 to report Section 707(c) payments to the partner. Because Section 707(c) payments are an income share, they are reported on the partner's K-1.

[60] Reg. § 1.707-1(c).

[61] Code Sec. 707(c). Both Section 707(a) payments and distributive shares of income can also be subject to capitalization under Section 263.

deduction. The net result is often very similar to treating the guaranteed payment as a distributive share of the partnership's ordinary income. In short, the partnership treats a Code Sec. 707(c) payment very much like it treats a 707(a) payment, but the partner treats it very much like a share of the partnership's ordinary income. There is no direct authority governing the results if a partnership pays the guaranteed amount with appreciated or depreciated property. Code Sec. 707(c) provides that the amount is treated as paid to a nonpartner for purposes of Code Secs. 61 and 162 only—for other purposes it is an income share and a distribution.[62]

As mentioned, a Code Sec. 707(c) payment is similar to a Code Sec. 707(a) payment in that the deduction and income resulting from Code Sec. 707(c) payments are ordinary in character and the partner's income occurs simultaneously with the partnership's deduction. However, in the case of the Code Sec. 707(c) payment, the timing of the partner's income is governed by the year the partnership takes the deduction. In the case of the 707(a) payment, the reverse is true. The timing of the partnership's 707(a) deduction is deferred until the partner must include the payment as income.[63]

Example 7-10. Partner *A*, who is a calendar-year, cash-method partner, performs noncapitalized Code Sec. 707(c)-type services for the ABC partnership calendar year accrual-basis partnership in Year 1. The partnership makes the payment in Year 2. ABC will deduct the amount in Year 1. Partner *A* must include the amount in Year 1 taxable income whether or not the partnership is required to capitalize the expenditure.

Example 7-11. Partner *A*, who is a calendar-year, accrual-method partner, performs noncapitalized Code Sec. 707(c)-type services for the calendar-year, cash-basis ABC partnership in Year 1. The partnership makes the payment in Year 2. ABC will deduct the payment in Year 2. Therefore, *A* will include the payment in Year 2 taxable income whether or not the partnership is required to capitalize the expenditure.

Example 7-12. The same facts as Examples 7-10 and 7-11 above, except that both the partnership and the partner use the cash-accounting method. The partnership deducts the payment in Year 2 and, therefore, the partner must include this amount as income for Year 2.

Example 7-13. The same facts as Examples 7-10 and 7-11 above, except that both the partnership and the partner use the accrual-accounting method. The partnership deducts the payment in Year 1 and, therefore, the partner has income in Year 1.

A Code Sec. 707(c) guaranteed payment generally will not affect the computation of a partner's distributive share of partnership income. How-

[62] *U.S. v. T.C. Davis*, SCt, 62-2 USTC ¶ 9509, 370 US 65, 82 SCt 1190.

[63] Code Sec. 267(e)(1).

ever, complications arise when the partner is entitled to the greater of a specified guaranteed salary payment or a fixed percentage of partnership income computed before the guaranteed payment is taken into account.

Example 7-14. The ABC cash method partnership (a law firm) agreement provides that *A* is to receive one-third of the ordinary income of the partnership, as determined before any guaranteed payment is taken into account, but not less that $21,000. In addition, he is to receive one-third of the losses after taking into account the guaranteed payment. Capital gains and losses are to be shared equally. The ordinary income of the partnership is $90,000—long term capital gains (LTCG) are $30,000 and short-term capital gains (STCG) are $9,000. *A* is entitled to $30,000 (1/3 of $90,000) as his distributive share of partnership income. No part of this sum constitutes a guaranteed payment since the distributive share is more than the $21,000 guaranteed payment.[64] *A* would also include his share of LTCG ($10,000) and STCG ($3,000) in his distributive share.

Example 7-15. Assume the same facts as in Example 7-14, except the partnership's ordinary income is only $30,000. *A*'s distributive share of partnership income is $10,000 (1/3 of $30,000). Since the partnership agreement entitles *A* to not less than $21,000, the remaining $11,000 is payable to *A* as a guaranteed payment.[65]

	A	*B*	*C*
Guaranteed Payment	$11,000	$ 0	$ 0
Distributive's Share of Income	10,000	4,500	4,500
Total Income Reported by Partner	*$21,000*	*$4,500*	*$4,500*

This example effectively allocates the $22,000 deduction for the guaranteed payment equally between *A*, *B*, and *C*. There is no express prohibition which would deny the ABC partnership from specially allocating the deduction. However, allocating the $11,000 deduction to *A* would economically eliminate his guaranteed minimum and allocating the deduction to *B* and *C* would increase *A*'s net share to more than $21,000.

Under these circumstances, the importance to *A* of whether the amount is a special allocation of a $21,000 distributive share or a guaranteed payment of $21,000 is slight provided that partnership capital gains are separately allocated.

Code Sec. 267(a)(2) does not apply because the $10,000 is a distributive share which is taxable to *A*, whether or not paid, despite his method of accounting (and is not a deduction to the partnership), and the $11,000, although deductible if paid, is subject to Code Sec. 707(c). *A* would continue to report his allocable share of LTCG and STCG.

[64] Reg. § 1.707-1(c), Ex. 2.

[65] *Id.*

Example 7-16. Assume the same facts as in Example 7-14, except the partnership's ordinary income is only $12,000. Relying on the regulations, *A* would have a distributive share of $4,000 (1/3 of $12,000) and a guaranteed payment of $17,000 ($21,000 – $4,000).[66] However, after taking the guaranteed payment into account, the partnership suffers a loss of $5,000 ($12,000 – $17,000) and thus there are not partnership profits from which to allocate a share to *A.*

Profits	$12,000
Code Sec. 707(c)	(17,000)
Code Sec. 702(a)(8)	*$(5,000)*

It has been suggested that the regulation does not go far enough and that the solution may be to treat the entire payment to the partner as a guaranteed payment whenever the partnership's income before deducting the guaranteed payment is less than the guaranteed payment. Losses then can be ratably shared among the partners.[67] Using this approach, *A* would have a guaranteed payment of $21,000 and a distributive share of partnership loss in the amount of $3,000 (1/3 of the $9,000 loss after subtracting the $21,000 guaranteed payment from the $12,000 of partnership income).

Profits before guaranteed payment	$12,000
Code Sec. 707(c)	(21,000)
Partnership taxable income— $(3,000) to each of *A, B,* and *C* [68]	*$(9,000)*

A guaranteed payment is:

- Not a share of profits for purposes of identifying the partnership's required taxable year.[69]
- Not a share of profits for the special rules on the taxation of sales between a partnership and its partners.[70]
- Not a share of profits for purposes of the partnership's technical termination upon the sale of interests in that partnership.[71]
- Not subject to income or payroll tax (FICA and FUTA) withholding.[72]
- Subject to the tax on self-employment income unless the partnership is not engaged in a trade or business [73] or the payment

[66] *Id.*

[67] McKee, Nelson, & Whitmire, *Federal Taxation of Partnerships and Partners,* ¶ 13.03[3] (1997).

[68] Another approach that could be provided for in the partnership agreement is that *A* shares only in additional loss items—those not attributable to his guaranteed payment. Thus, the $9,000 loss should be shared only by *B* and *C* ($4,500 each). The partnership agreement should be made clear on this point. A method of arriving at this result is to take the Section 702(a)(8) loss of $5,000, after determining that a $17,000 guaranteed payment is required, and giving *A* a priority positive distributive share of $4,000 of gross receipts which increases the total loss to $9,000, which is shared by *B* and *C* equally.

[69] Code Sec. 706(b)(1)(B); Reg. § 1.707-1(c).

[70] Code Sec. 708(b); Reg. § 1.707-1(c).

[71] Code Sec. 708(b); Reg. § 1.707-1(c).

[72] Reg. § 1.707-1(c); see Rev. Rul. 69-184, 1969-1 CB 256.

[73] A guaranteed payment is net income from self-employment *only* if the partnership is engaged in a trade or business. Reg. § 1.1402(a)-1(b). For this purpose, a partnership engaged in the business of renting real estate appears to be considered engaged in a trade or business (see Reg. § 1.1402(c)-1) even though real estate rental income is generally excluded from the definition of net income from self-employment. Code Sec. 1402(a)(1); Reg. § 1.1402(a)-4. Therefore, a partner receiving a guar-

is a guaranteed payment for the use of capital paid to a limited partner.

- Earned income for purposes of contributions to a qualified deferred compensation plan.
- Nonpassive interest income for purposes of the Code Sec. 469 passive loss rules if paid for the use of capital.[74]
- Nonpassive compensation income for purposes of the Code Sec. 469 passive loss rules if paid for services.[75]

Observation. If the payee partner does not materially participate in the partnership's activity or if the partnership's activity is per se passive then this essentially self-charged amount may increase a pass-through passive loss which cannot be offset with the guaranteed payment. Although the self-charged character of these payments arguably qualifies for the "self-charged interest" rules of Proposed Reg. § 1.469-7 if the guaranteed payment is for capital, the self-charged aspect will probably be ignored if the payment is for services.

According to the IRS,[76] premiums a partnership pays for accident and health insurance coverage on behalf of its partners are deemed guaranteed payments for services to the partners—provided the premium payments are paid for services rendered as partner, and the payments are determined without regard to partnership income. As guaranteed payments, the premiums are deductible by the partnership and included in the recipient partners' gross income. While the partner cannot exclude the premiums from income, the partner can deduct a percentage of the cost of the premiums on his or her individual income tax return in arriving at adjusted gross income (Line 26, Form 1040) under Code Sec. 162(1)—assuming the Code Sec. 162(1) requirements are met.

As noted above, guaranteed payments constitute ordinary income to the recipient, but are not salary or wages for employment tax purposes.[77] Since the payments are not wages, they are not subject to income tax withholding or Social Security withholding requirements.[78]

Because guaranteed payments, from the partnership's point of view, are treated as payments to nonpartners, they have no net direct impact on the recipient partner's tax basis and Code Sec. 704(b) book capital ac-

(Footnote Continued)

anteed payment from a partnership engaged in the business of renting real estate may have net income from self-employment, even though he would not have net income from self-employment if he engaged in the same activity as an individual. However, the IRS has ruled that a one-fourth partner in a partnership owning an office building, who performs services for the partnership and receives as remuneration "a specified amount each week from the gross rents collected," is not subject to the self-employment tax on either his distributive share or the weekly amount. Rev. Rul. 64-220, 1964-2 CB 335. The Worksheet for Figuring Net Earnings (Loss) From Self-Employment treats a dealer in real estate's rental income as self-employment income if it is received in the course of a trade or business as a real estate dealer, but the worksheet treats all Section 707(c) guaranteed payments other than guaranteed payments made to limited partners for use of capital as self-employment income.

[74] Reg. § 1.469-2(e)(2)(ii).

[75] *Id.*

[76] Rev. Rul. 91-26, 1991-1 CB 184.

[77] FICA and FUTA; Rev. Rul. 69-184, 1969-1 CB 256.

[78] Code Sec. 3402.

count.[79] Partnership income is reduced by the guaranteed payments and each partner's share of the deduction reduces his or her basis in the partnership interest is reflected in his or her capital account. Neither the income nor the payment flows through the partnership's or recipient partner's Schedule K-1 capital account reconciliation.[80] Obviously, if a payment is *not* a guaranteed payment, the distribution and related allocation of income will decrease and increase, respectively, the partner's tax basis in his or her partnership interest—and the amounts will flow through the partner's Schedule K-1 capital account reconciliation. The guaranteed payments do appear in Schedule M-1 in reconciling the partnership's taxable Net Income (Loss) with its Code Sec. 704(b) or other book accounting income (loss). The guaranteed payment is part of the partnership's tax net income, but not part of the partnership's book income. The Code Sec. 707(c) payment is not considered a distribution for purposes of "Analysis of Partners' Capital Account" on Schedule K-1, Item J.

Guaranteed payments for capital—Are they just ordinary income or are they interest? The passive activity regulations characterize guaranteed payments for services and capital as nonpassive income.[81] These regulations treat a guaranteed payment for services as wages and a guaranteed payment for capital "as the payment of interest."[82] This provision implies that *both* the partnership and partner treat a guaranteed payment for use of capital as interest.[83] These regulations were promulgated to separate passive activity income and loss from nonpassive activity income and loss. Interest income is considered to be portfolio income and therefore not passive income. The ultimate result of following a confusing set of cross-referenced provisions is that a Code Sec. 707(c) guaranteed payment for capital is investment income for purposes of the limitations relating to deducting the investment interest.[84] Guaranteed payments for capital are also treated as interest for purposes of capitalizing construction period interest.[85] The Instructions for Form 1065, U.S. Partnership Return of Income, refer to a guaranteed payment for capital as "interest."[86] This is true even though the guaranteed payment is not paid for the use of money the partnership owes to a creditor. However, the instructions say such amounts should not be shown as interest on the Form 1065 but as a guaranteed payment on line 10 of page one. The IRS appears in most situations to want the partnership not to treat a guaranteed payment for capital as interest, but for the partner to treat the income as interest.[87]

---

[79] The portion, if any, of the partnership's deduction allocable to the recipient partner will affect his capital account. Reg. § 1.704-1(b)(2)(iv)(*o*).

[80] Item J, Schedule K-1, and Schedule M-2, Form 1065.

[81] Whether the payment is for services or capital, the partner's income is not passive, but the deduction may increase the passive loss (or decrease the passive income) of the partners who do not materially participate.

[82] Reg. § 1.469-2(e)(2).

[83] It is unclear whether the self-charged interest rules will apply because there is no lending transaction.

[84] Section 163(d)(5) defines an investment as "property which produces income of a type described in Section 469(e)(1)." Section 469(e)(1) includes interest, and Reg. § 1.469-2(e)(2) specifically says a guaranteed payment for capital is interest.

[85] Reg. § 1.263-9(c)(2)(iii).

[86] See also GCM 36702 (April 12, 1976).

[87] *Id.*

The guaranteed payment regulations treat guaranteed payments as shares of the partnership's ordinary income without any reference as to whether the payment is for services or capital.[88] With regard to the partnership's Form 1065, mechanically the payment can't be a share of partnership interest income because its interest income is separately stated as part of portfolio income or loss and the guaranteed payment is an expense in arriving at the partnership's nonseparately stated net income. While the regulations provide only that a guaranteed payment is treated as a share of the partnership's ordinary income, the tax return preparation process goes one step further and results in its being a share of only *nonseparately* stated ordinary income.

The Form 1065 is further misleading. Guaranteed payments for services and capital are lumped together as a single deduction in arriving at the partnership's net nonseparately stated income.[89] For compliance purposes, the partnership's total income to be allocated to the partners as guaranteed payments,[90] and as each partner's share of the partnership's total guaranteed payments, are stated as single lump sums without distinguishing between payments for capital and services.[91] Forms 1065 and K-1 would be cleaner if they treated guaranteed payments for capital and services separately.

The Instructions for Form 1065 create additional uncertainty as to the proper treatment of guaranteed payments. The Worksheet For Figuring Net Earnings (Loss) From Self-Employment treats all guaranteed payments other than those paid to a limited partner for use of capital as self-employment income.[92] Reg. § 1.1402(a)-1(b), issued before the enactment of Code Sec. 1402(a)(13), indicate that guaranteed payments are self-employment income whether they are paid for services or the use of capital. Code Sec. 1402(a)(13) now provides that only Code Sec. 707(c) payments for services "actually rendered" are subject to self-employment tax. This maze of conflicting rules can lead to surprising results. For example, guaranteed payments to general partners for the use of capital may be capitalized as construction period *interest* by the partnership, but be considered *earned income* subject to self-employment tax at the partner level.

[88] Reg. § 1.707-1(c).
[89] Form 1065, page one, line 10.
[90] Form 1065, Schedule K.
[91] Form 1065, Schedule K-1.
[92] Code Sec. 1402(a)(13).

Line 14a. Net Earnings (Loss) From Self-Employment

Schedule K. Enter on line 14a the amount from line 5 of the worksheet.

Schedule K-1. Do not complete this line for any partner that is an estate, trust, corporation, exempt organization, or individual retirement arrangement (IRA).

Enter in box 14 of Schedule K-1 each individual general partner's share of the amount shown on line 5 of the worksheet and each individual limited partner's share of the amount shown on line 4c of the worksheet, using code A.

Line 14b. Gross Farming or Fishing Income

Enter on line 14b the partnership's gross farming or fishing income from self-employment. Individual partners need this amount to figure net earnings from self-employment under the farm optional method in Section B, Part II of Schedule SE (Form 1040). Enter each individual partner's distributive share in box 14 of Schedule K-1 using code B.

Line 14c. Gross Nonfarm Income

Enter on line 14c the partnership's gross nonfarm income from self-employment. Individual partners need this amount to figure net earnings from self-employment under the nonfarm optional method in Section B, Part II of Schedule SE (Form 1040). Enter each individual partner's share in box 14 of Schedule K-1 using code C.

Worksheet Instructions

Line 1b. Include on line 1b any part of the net income (loss) from rental real estate activities from Schedule K, line 2, that is from:

1. Rentals of real estate held for sale to customers in the course of a trade or business as a real estate dealer or
2. Rentals for which services were rendered to the occupants (other than services usually or customarily rendered for the rental of space for occupancy only). The supplying of maid service is such a service; but the furnishing of heat and light, the cleaning of public entrances, exits, stairways and lobbies, trash collection, etc., are not considered services rendered to the occupants.

Lines 3b and 4b. Allocate the amounts on these lines in the same way Form 1065, page 1, line 22, is allocated to these particular partners.

Line 4a. Include in the amount on line 4a any guaranteed payments to partners reported on Schedule K, line 4, and Schedule K-1, box 4, and derived from a trade or business as defined in section 1402(c). Also include other ordinary business income and expense items (other than expense items subject to separate limitations at the partner level, such as the section 179 expense deduction) reported on Schedules K and K-1 that are used to figure self-employment earnings under section 1402.

Credits and Credit Recapture

Note. Do not attach Form 3800, General Business Credit, to Form 1065.

Low-Income Housing Credit

Section 42 provides a credit that can be claimed by owners of low-income residential rental buildings. If the partners are eligible to take the low-income housing credit, complete and attach Form 8586, Low-Income Housing Credit; Form 8609, Low-Income Housing Credit Allocation Certification; and Schedule A (Form 8609), Annual Statement, to Form 1065.

Note. If part or all of the credit reported on lines 15a or 15b is attributable to additions to qualified basis of property placed in service before 1990, report on an attachment to Schedules K and K-1 the amount of the credit on each line that is attributable to property placed in service (a) before 1990 and (b) after 1989.

Line 15a. Low-Income Housing Credit (Section 42(j)(5))

Enter on line 15a the total low-income housing credit for property with respect to which a partnership is to be treated under section 42(j)(5) as the taxpayer to which the low-income housing credit was allowed.

If the partnership invested in another partnership to which the provisions of section 42(j)(5) apply, report on line 15a the credit reported to the partnership on Schedule K-1 (Form 1065), box 15, code A.

Schedule K-1. Report in box 15 of Schedule K-1 each partner's distributive share of the low income housing credit reported on line 15a of Schedule K using code A. If the partnership has credits from more than one rental activity, identify on an attachment to Schedule K-1 the amount for each separate activity. See *Passive Activity Reporting Requirements* on page 13.

Line 15b. Low-Income Housing Credit (Other)

Enter on line 15b any low-income housing credit not reported on line 15a. This includes any credit reported to the partnership on Schedule K-1 (Form 1065), box 15, using code B.

Schedule K-1. Report in box 15 of Schedule K-1 each partner's distributive share of the low income housing credit reported on line 15b of Schedule K using code B. If the partnership has credits from more than one rental activity, identify on an attachment to Schedule K-1 the amount for each separate activity. See *Passive Activity Reporting Requirements* on page 13.

Line 15c. Qualified Rehabilitation Expenditures (Rental Real Estate)

Enter on line 15c the total qualified rehabilitation expenditures related to rental real estate activities of the partnership. Also complete the applicable lines of Form 3468, Investment Credit, that apply to qualified rehabilitation expenditures for property related to rental real estate activities of the

Worksheet for Figuring Net Earnings (Loss) From Self-Employment

1a	Ordinary business income (loss) (Schedule K, line 1)	1a			
b	Net income (loss) from certain rental real estate activities (see instructions)	1b			
c	Other net rental income (loss) (Schedule K, line 3c)	1c			
d	Net loss from Form 4797, Part II, line 17, included on line 1a above. Enter as a positive amount	1d			
e	Combine lines 1a through 1d	1e			
2	Net gain from Form 4797, Part II, line 17, included on line 1a above	2			
3a	Subtract line 2 from line 1e. If line 1e is a loss, increase the loss on line 1e by the amount on line 2	3a			
b	Part of line 3a allocated to limited partners, estates, trusts, corporations, exempt organizations, and IRAs	3b			
c	Subtract line 3b from line 3a. If line 3a is a loss, reduce the loss on line 3a by the amount on line 3b. Include each individual general partner's share in box 14 of Schedule K-1, using code A			3c	
4a	Guaranteed payments to partners (Schedule K, line 4) derived from a trade or business as defined in section 1402(c) (see instructions)	4a			
b	Part of line 4a allocated to individual limited partners for other than services and to estates, trusts, corporations, exempt organizations, and IRAs	4b			
c	Subtract line 4b from line 4a. Include each individual general partner's share and each individual limited partner's share in box 14 of Schedule K-1, using code A			4c	
5	Net earnings (loss) from self-employment. Combine lines 3c and 4c. Enter here and on Schedule K, line 14a			5	

-28- Instructions for Form 1065

The correct treatment to be accorded a guaranteed payment for the use of capital as interest, self-employment income, or other income is dependent upon the issue at hand. If the partnership prefers that such payments be treated as interest for all tax purposes, the partners should consider loaning capital to the partnership and receiving interest.[93] The interest payment will be a Code Sec. 707(a) payment and subject to the timing provisions of Code Sec. 267, but the partnership is not entitled to a deduction until the day the partner must report the interest income.

.03 *Payments Not Governed by Code Sec. 707(a) or (c)*

If a payment cannot be classified as falling within the definition of either Code Sec. 707(a) or (c), then it will be treated as part of the partnership's agreement regarding the distribution of profits. For example,

[93] Naturally, this will change the economic arrangement. The partnership owes a partner debt whether or not the money is lost. A capital account is reduced by a partner's share of loss.

a payment made for services required by the partnership agreement that are normally performed by a partner, the amount of which is based on a percentage of partnership net income, will be deemed a distributive share of partnership income. The partnership is not allowed a deduction, but the ultimate effect is very similar to that of a Code Sec. 707(c) payment. The service partner's income is included in the year in which the partnership year ends, and the other partners' shares of the partnership's taxable income are reduced by this amount in the same year. The allocation reduces the other partners' shares of income even though a salary payment for the same type of service would have been capitalized.[94] Code Sec. 707(c) payments, however, are always reported as ordinary income by the partner and are always treated as a deduction from ordinary income by the partnership. In contrast, if the payment is treated as a distributive share of partnership income, then the partner will be treated as having received a pro rata share of each type of partnership income.

Finally, the partner's basis is increased by his or her share of the partnership's income and then decreased by the actual payment. The payment is treated as a distribution of income previously credited to his or her capital account.

> ***Example 7-17.*** Cynthia Bond is a partner in the equal ABC Partnership who uses the cash method of accounting and reports her taxable income on the calendar year. She performs services in Year 1 for ABC, which employs the cash method of accounting and calendar year as well. The partnership agreement provides that Cynthia is to receive 25% of the partnership's net nonseparately stated income in Year 1 as payment for special services of managing the partnership's activities as required by the agreement. The remaining net income is divided equally between Cynthia, Brad Olson and Andy Napolitano, the other partners. The partnership has $400 of ordinary income in Year 1 and makes no payments. ABC makes a $100 payment to Cynthia in Year 2 for her services in Year 1. An analysis of its calculation indicates that it is governed by neither Code Sec. 707(a) nor (c). The result is as follows:

Partnership Results—Year 1

Partnership gross income	$400
Deductions	0
Partnership taxable income	$400
Special allocation to Cynthia [95]	(100)
Amount divided equally	$300

[94] Code Sec. 707(a)(2)(A) provides that if an allocation of income for services and a distribution, when viewed together, are property characterized as a transaction occurring between the partnership and a partner acting other than in his capacity as a member of the partnership, then the allocation and distribution are treated as a Section 707(a) payment. However, there are no regulations, rulings, cases, or other guidance concerning when and how this provision applies.

[95] Required by Code Sec. 702 to be separately stated. Reg. § 1.702-1(a)(9).

Partners' Taxable Income—Year 1

	Andy	*Brad*	*Cynthia*
Special allocation to Cynthia	$ 0	$ 0	$100
Share of partnership income not specially allocated	100	100	100
Total	*$100*	*$100*	*$200*

Assuming that the results of operations in Year 2 are the same as in Year 1, but because Cynthia renders no special services in Year 2, the partnership makes no special allocation to her, the results are as follows:

Partnership Results—Year 2

Partnership gross income	$400
Deductions	0
Partnership taxable income	*$400*
Special allocation to Cynthia	0
Partnership income divided equally	*$400*

Partners' Taxable Income—Year 2

	Andy	*Brad*	*Cynthia*
Special allocation	$ 0	$ 0	$ 0
Share of partnership income not specially allocated	133	133	133
Total	*$133*	*$133*	*$133*

The $100 payment to Cynthia in Year 2 is a distribution and results in gain only if it exceeds her basis.

Example 7-18. Assume the same facts as Example 7-17, but the payment qualifies as a Code Sec. 707(c) payment. Since the partnership is a cash method taxpayer, it deducts the payment in Year 2. Year 1 results are as follows:

Partnership Results—Year 1

Partnership gross income	$400
Deductions	0
Partnership taxable income	*$400*
Special allocation to Cynthia	0
Amount divided equally	*$400*

Partners' Taxable Income—Year 1

	Andy	*Brad*	*Cynthia*
Special allocation to Cynthia	$ 0	$ 0	$ 0
Share of partnership income not specially allocated	133	133	133
Total	*$133*	*$133*	*$133*

Assuming that the results of operations in Year 2 are the same as Year 1, the results are as follows:

Partnership Results—Year 2

Partnership gross income	$400
Deductions	(100)
Partnership taxable income	*$300*
Special allocation to Cynthia	0
Partnership income divided equally	*$300*
Cynthia's ordinary income from the guaranteed payment	$100

The $100 payment to Cynthia in Year 2 is treated as a distribution and results in gain only if it exceeds her basis in her partnership interest.

Partners' Taxable Income—Year 2

	Andy	*Brad*	*Cynthia*
Special allocation	$ 0	$ 0	$ 0
Share of partnership income	100	100	100
Guaranteed payment	100	0	0
Total	*$200*	*$100*	*$100*

Two-Year Summary—Special Allocation vs. Guaranteed Payment

	Special Allocation			*Guaranteed Payment*		
	Andy	*Brad*	*Cynthia*	*Andy*	*Brad*	*Cynthia*
Year 1						
Guaranteed payment	$ 0	$ 0	$ 0	$ 0	$ 0	$ 0
Special Allocation	0	0	100	0	0	0
Share of income not specially allocated	100	100	100	133	133	133
Year 2						
Guaranteed payment	0	0	0	0	0	100
Special allocation	0	0	0	0	0	0
Share of income not specially allocated	133	133	133	100	100	100
Total	*$233*	*$233*	*$333*	*$233*	*$233*	*$333*

The ultimate effect is to reduce Brad and Andy's taxable income, regardless of whether it is classified as a Code Sec. 704/ 731 income allocation and payment, as in Example 7-17, or a Code Sec. 707(c) payment, as in this example. The classification may, however, alter the timing of when the effects take place. Naturally, the character of income reported by Cynthia and the other partners can also be affected by the classification.

If the payment was classified as a Code Sec. 707(a) payment, the results under the example's assumptions would be the same as those for the Code Sec. 707(c) example, except the payment would be labeled a payment for services rather than a guaranteed payment.

.04 Summary: Is This "Much Ado About Very Little"?

In short—the answer is *usually yes.* In the case of all three classifications, the payee's income and the other partners' reductions in shares of partnership income occur simultaneously. This eliminates the group's ability to generate a partnership deduction without a partner having offsetting income. In the case of a Code Sec. 707(a) payment, the partnership generally deducts the payment when the partner reports the income under his or her accounting method. Otherwise, when the payment is a guaranteed payment or a distributive share of income, the payee partner has income at the time his or her payment is subtracted from the other partners' shares of the partnership's taxable income under the partnership's accounting method.

The timing of the partnership's deduction and the partner's income will be the same regardless of which of the three categories the payment falls into if:

1. Both the partnership and the partner are using the cash method of accounting;
2. They both use the calendar year as their taxable year; and
3. The payment is made to the partner during the same year the services or capital is provided by the partner to the partnership.

Similarly, if both the partnership and partner are accrual-method taxpayers using the same taxable year, classification of the payment will not alter the timing regardless of when payment is made. In other cases, the partnership's deduction may be deferred beyond the year in which it normally would be allowed or the partner may have reportable income before he or she is paid. Finally, the income and deduction are always ordinary in the case of Code Sec. 707(a) and (c) payments. However, if the payment does not fit either of these categories and is treated as a share of partnership income, some portion could be, for example, capital gains or Code Sec. 1231 gains. In years in which capital gains are taxed at the same effective rate as ordinary income, this distinction should make little difference in the partners' tax liabilities.

Although in a majority of the situations the correct classification of a payment to a partner will have little if any effect on the partner's tax liability, there are circumstances when there can be an important difference to both the payee partner and the partnership.

Example 7-19. The ABC limited partnership is an accrual method, calendar-year owner and operator of commercial real property. Partner *A* receives 5% of net rental income as payment for his services. It is payable on March 30 of the partnership's following year. If the partnership agreement requires that he perform these duties and receive compensation as an obligation of being a general partner, any payment is a Code Sec. 707(c) payment. *A* must report the guaranteed payment in the year the partnership accrues the expense. Any part of the expense the partnership accrues during the year is taxable to *A* even though he is not paid until March 30 of the following year.

Example 7-20. Assume the same facts as Example 7-19 except that the partnership agreement makes no reference to *A*'s duties as a property manager or payment for such duties. Instead there is a separate five-year contract with *A* to manage the partnership properties with compensation equal to 5% of the net rental income. The payment is a Code Sec. 707(a) payment. If *A* is a cash basis taxpayer, he includes the payment in income on March 30 and the partnership may not deduct the payment until its taxable year which includes March 30.

Observation. Any cash method partner who receives a K-1 from a partnership showing a Code Sec. 707(c) guaranteed payment for a year in which the partner has not received an actual cash payment should review the partnership agreement. If the partnership agreement has not provided for an employment relationship, the payment might be misclassified. If there is a contract outside of the partnership agreement, the payment is probably a Code Sec. 707(a) payment. This means the partner need not report the payment until he or she is paid and the partnership can't deduct the payment until the partner is paid.[96]

See sample page 2 of Form 1065 and page 1 of Schedule K-1 in the Appendix.

[96] Form 8088, Missing Information Necessary to Complete Adjustment Request, should be filed notifying the IRS that the partner's tax position is inconsistent with the partnership's tax position.

Chapter 8

Character and Presentation of Partnership Taxable Income—The Pass-Through Concept

¶ 801 Introduction

A partnership is not a separate tax-paying entity. Rather, the partnership's income (or loss) is passed through to its partners, who then compute their tax liabilities based on the rates in Code Sec. 1.[1]

Generally, as discussed in Chapter 7, a partnership computes its taxable income in the same manner as do individuals.[2] Once computed, the partnership's items of income, loss, deduction, or credit are passed through to partners for inclusion in their taxable income for their tax year in which the taxable year of the partnership ends.[3] Items that may have potentially varying tax consequences to particular partners must be separately stated;[4] all other items are aggregated and passed through as a net lump sum.[5] These items are allocated among the partners in accordance with the partnership agreement.[6] The partnership's pass-through items retain the character they possessed at the partnership level; for example, tax-exempt interest earned by the partnership is treated as tax-exempt interest in the hands of the partners.[7]

S Corporation Observation. In contrast to the flexibility extended to partners, who can make disproportionate or special allocations of tax items if such allocations have "substantial economic

[1] Code Sec. 703(a).
[2] *Id.*
[3] Code Sec. 706(a).
[4] Code Sec. 703(a)(2).
[5] Code Sec. 702(a)(1) and (8).
[6] Code Sec. 704(a). In contrast, the pro rata share of a shareholder of an S corporation is determined by allocating an equal portion of each item to each day of the corporation's taxable year, and then dividing that amount by the shares outstanding on the day. Code Sec. 1377(a)(1). As in the case of partnerships, the IRS has the authority to make adjustments to the amounts passed through where such is necessary to reflect the value of services or capital provided by a family member of one or more shareholders. Code Secs. 704(e) and 1366(e).

[7] Code Sec. 702(b).

effect," special allocations of tax items among the S corporation shareholders are not allowed.[8]

Generally, a partner increases his or her basis by the amount of taxable and tax-exempt income passed through, and decreases his or her basis (but not below zero) by items of loss and deduction and any expenses of the partnership that were not deductible in computing its taxable income and which were not properly chargeable to capital account (for example, life insurance premiums paid to insure the lives of the partners).[9]

¶ 802 General Rule—Entity-Level Characterization

The character of a tax item realized by a partnership "shall be determined as if such item were realized directly from the source from which realized by the partnership, or incurred in the same manner as incurred by the partnership."[10] Although this language has been the subject of academic discussion, the generally accepted view is that the character of the item is determined by reference to partnership-level factors.[11]

> ***Example 8-1.*** A real estate dealer who trades in apartment buildings is a limited partner in a partnership that owns an apartment building it has managed for 20 years. The partnership sells the building under circumstances such that its gain is considered Code Sec. 1231 gain. Each partner's share, including the real estate dealer's, is taxed as Code Sec. 1231 gain.

¶ 803 Characterization of Gain (Loss) on Disposition of Contributed Property

Except as provided by Code Sec. 724, the character of the partnership's income is determined at the partnership level.[12] The partner's status is not controlling. Code Sec. 724 modifies partnership level characterization for three categories of contributed property: (1) unrealized receivables, (2) inventory items, and (3) capital loss property. Different rules are provided for each category. Substituted basis property received in exchange for such contributed property is treated as if it were the contributed property.[13]

---

[8] S corporations can in effect "specially allocate" amounts of income among their owner-employees only through salary adjustments. Amounts of income allocated among shareholders can also be altered through changes in stock ownership. The shareholders must, however, transfer their stock during the year for the allocation to be effective because the S corporation's income is allocated among the shareholders based upon the number of days they have owned the shares. In contrast, partnership income is allocated according to the partnership agreement, including amendments made by the due date of the tax return. It is possible, therefore, for the partners to wait until the tax year is complete before deciding how to allocate the partnership's income among themselves. In the case of an S corporation, unlike a partnership, it is impossible to allocate a particular item of income or deduction. Depreciation, for example, is required to be shared by all the shareholders based upon their stock ownership.

[9] Code Sec. 705.

[10] Code Sec. 702(b).

[11] *U.S. v. J.A. Basye*, SCt, 73-1 USTC ¶ 9250, 410 US 441, 93 SCt 1080. The opposite interpretation is that a partner treat partnership items as if he or she generated them directly. For example, a partner who was a dealer in land would treat the partnership's land sale as if it were his or her sale, ordinary income being the likely result. The entity-level partnership characterization rule is described in Rev. Rul. 67-188, 1967-1 CB 216. See also *E.G. Barham v. U.S.*, DC Ga., 69-1 USTC ¶ 9356, 301 FSupp 43.

[12] Code Sec. 702(b).

[13] Code Sec. 724(d)(3). There is an exception for property which is contributed by the partnership to a corporation in an exchange qualifying for Code Sec. 351. Code Sec. 724(d)(3)(B).

Any gain or loss recognized by the partnership on the disposition of what is considered an "unrealized receivable" in the hands of the contributing partner will be ordinary income.[14] If Code Sec. 724 did not exist, this would normally be the same result.

Inventory items retain their ordinary income taint under Code Sec. 724(b) for five years after their contribution to the partnership. After that period, the character of the contributed property to the partnership is determined at the partnership level. As a result, sale by the partnership of property that was inventory in the hands of the partner who previously contributed such property to the partnership within five years of its contribution will result in ordinary income for the entire amount of the gain. Appreciation existing at the time of the contribution is taxed to the contributor under Code Sec. 704(c), and the remainder is ordinary income allocated according to the partnership agreement. The term "inventory" includes all property held primarily for sale by the contributing partner and any other asset which, upon sale by the contributing partner, would not be considered a capital or Code Sec. 1231 asset.[15]

"Capital loss property" includes any capital asset held by the contributing partner which had an adjusted basis in excess of its fair market value immediately before it was contributed to the partnership.[16] If the partnership sells such property at a loss, Code Sec. 724(c) requires the built-in loss at the time of the contribution to retain its character as a capital loss for a period of five years from the date of the contribution. Any additional loss accruing while the property is held by the partnership is characterized at the partnership level.

¶ 804 Presentation of a Partnership's Taxable Income

Although a partnership accounts for roughly the same items of income and deduction as an individual, the format in which it reports this information is quite different. An individual first subtracts from his or her gross income the sum of his or her "above the line" deductions. This subtotal is the individual's "adjusted gross income."[17] An individual next reduces adjusted gross income by the sum of any "itemized deductions."[18] The resulting *single* number is taxable income.[19] A partnership reports the results of the taxable year's operations differently. It separately lists the net amount of any item of income, loss, or deduction that could affect the various partners differently.[20] For example, tax-exempt interest income and other tax exempt income are each separately stated. The net amount of each type of nondeductible expenditure is separately listed.[21] Any item of a

[14] Code Sec. 724(a) and (d). "Unrealized receivables" are defined generally in Code Sec. 751(c) as rights to payment for goods or services that have not been previously included in income, provided that the payment would have been treated as ordinary income. It also includes depreciation recapture under Code Secs. 1245(a) and 1250(a).

[15] Code Secs. 724(d)(2) and 751(d).

[16] Code Sec. 724(c).

[17] Code Sec. 62. An individual income tax return (Form 1040) will take these deductions into account on page one or its supporting schedules.

[18] Itemized deductions are all deductions not enumerated in Code Sec. 62.

[19] Code Sec. 63.

[20] The net amount of each item is shown on a separate line of Schedule K (Form 1065, U.S. Partnership Return of Income).

[21] These items are reported separately on Schedule K. Each partner will decrease his or her partnership interest adjusted basis for his or her share of nondeductible expenditures and increase his or her partnership interest adjusted basis for tax-exempt income.

partnership's income or deduction which is specially allocated to a particular partner is separately stated even though absent the special allocation it need not have been separately stated. The remainder of the partnership's items of income, loss, and deduction are simply aggregated as one net number.[22] Unlike an individual, a partnership's taxable income is not reduced to one number.[23] This section discusses which items of partnership income and deduction must be separately stated.

¶ 805 Separately Stated Items

The law provides only that a partnership must separate its items of income, loss, and deduction that could, by their nature, affect the various partners differently.[24] But it is also necessary to inform the partners of their shares of nontaxable income and expenditures that are not deductible by the partnership. Normally, the partnership tax return preparer will probably not separately report to the partners each item that might conceivably constitute a separately stated item of income, loss, and deduction. It is therefore not unlikely that partners may need to request additional information in order to prepare their returns.

A partnership is denied certain deductions.[25] In most cases the result is clear. The partnership acts in a manner similar to that of a nominee. It reports the amount and nature of the nondeductible expenditure to the partners, and its intermediary status is ignored. The partners are simply treated as if they had paid the amounts directly.[26] Because the partners' bases are reduced by nondeductible expenditures, these payments are often dealt with as if the partnership first distributed these amounts and then the partners made the payments themselves.[27]

---

[22] This net number is calculated on page one of the Form 1065 and is the first entry on Schedule K.

[23] When it is necessary for a partner to know his or her gross income from all sources such gross income includes the partner's pro rata share of the partnership's gross income. Code Sec. 702(c). This amount is not normally part of the information provided with the partner's K-1.

[24] Code Sec. 702(a)(1)-(8).

[25] Code Sec. 703(a)(2).

[26] The partners are required to reduce partnership interest adjusted basis by their share of the expenditure. Code Sec. 705(a)(2)(B). This is because the partnership no longer has the money and its ownership interests are therefore less valuable. If a partnership interest adjusted basis reduction were not required the partner would have a loss or reduced gain on the sale of his or her ownership interests and this would result in a second tax benefit for the same expenditure. The result is very similar to treating the partnership as having distributed the nondeductible amount to the partner who paid it to the ultimate payee. The partnership interest's basis should, however, be reduced only once, not for both the nondeductible expenditure and the deemed distribution.

[27] The partners will be required to reduce their bases in their partnership interests by their allocable shares of nondeductible expenditures. Code Sec. 705(a)(2)(B). Absent this basis adjustment the partners would receive a tax benefit for expenditures that should be denied at both the partner and partnership level. For example, neither the partnership nor partner should be entitled to deduct expenses incurred to produce tax-exempt income. If a partnership's funds have been spent providing life insurance the interests in the partnership have been reduced in value by the amount of the expenditures. If the partner's basis in their interests is not reduced by the expenditure, subsequent sale of the partnership interest will generate additional loss or a reduced amount of gain in the amount of the expenditure. For amounts that are deductible by the partner but not by the partnership, absent a basis reduction to the partnership interests, a double tax benefit will be generated by items passed through to the partner and deducted by him or her. Investment expenses other than interest are an example of a possible double deduction if no basis adjustment is made. Code Sec. 212 allows an individual to deduct such expenditures, but a partnership is disallowed Code Sec. 212 expenses. A deduction that is allowed to an individual by Code Sec. 212 is specifically disallowed to a partnership. The tax return for a partnership requires these expenses be separately stated. (Schedule K, Form 1065.) The individual partner deducts these amounts along with his or her other itemized deductions. If he or she is not required to reduce his or her ownership interest's basis by the expenditure, the ownership interest's sale at its reduced value caused by the expenditure will generate a loss or a reduced amount of gain reflecting such expenditures as an additional tax benefit.

There is a slim technical distinction between a partnership's nondeductible separately stated item of expenditure and a separately stated deductible partnership expenditure. The ultimate result is normally the same whether the item is a separately stated partnership deduction or a separately stated nondeductible amount. There is only one narrow practical distinction between nondeductible expenditures that are separately stated and deductible expenditures that are separately stated. The possible difference exists in the application of the basis limitation on the deductibility of losses. A partner's "distributive share of partnership loss (including capital loss) shall be allowed only to the extent of the adjusted basis of such partner's interest in the partnership."[28] A literal interpretation of the basis limitation rules would conclude that the partner of a partnership is not subject to those rules for his share of the partnership's nondeductible expenditures.[29]

.01 Deduction for Personal Exemptions

Although a partnership typically computes its deductions in the same manner as an individual, it is not entitled to a deduction for a personal exemption. There is no partnership expenditure and no reduction in the basis of the partnership interests, and the item is simply disregarded.

.02 Deduction for Foreign Taxes and Taxes of U.S. Possessions Allowed Under Code Secs. 164(a) and 901

Technically, this expenditure is not deductible by a partnership.[30] These taxes paid by a partnership pass through to its partners who then elect to either deduct the taxes or take a foreign tax credit.[31] It is treated as if the partnership distributed the funds to pay the taxes and the partners paid the tax. The partner's share of foreign income, deduction, foreign taxes and other information is entered on the partnership's Form 1065, Schedule K, lines 16i-m, "Foreign Transactions," and reported to the partner on Schedule K-1, box 16, "Foreign Transactions."

.03 Charitable Contribution Deduction

A partnership is not officially entitled to deduct a contribution to a charitable organization.[32] The partnership, however, must separately state its total net contributions to each separate category of charity as defined by Code Sec. 170. It must also identify the type of property contributed because the information could affect a shareholder's individual income tax calculation.[33] Each partner then combines the contributions passed through from the partnership and other pass-through entities with any of the year's

---

[28] Code Sec. 704(d).

[29] Conversely, if expenditures disallowed at the partnership level are deductible by the partner only to the extent of his or her basis, the carryover rules of Code Sec. 704(d) should provide an unlimited carryover even though they are not components of a net operating loss within the meaning of Code Sec. 172.

[30] Code Sec. 703(a).

[31] These are nondeductible expenditures and therefore the basis of the partnership interests are reduced. The partners' capital accounts are also reduced for their shares of the taxes.

[32] Code Sec. 703(a)(2)(C). Even though charitable contributions are not deductible by a partnership, Schedule K specifically lists it among its separately stated amounts. The partnership informational tax return treats a charitable contribution as if it were a separately stated partnership deduction.

[33] An individual's deduction for gifts to charities is limited to various percentages of his or her adjusted gross income. The specific percentage is governed by the type of charity and also whether cash or property is gifted. Code Sec. 170(b) and (e).

other charitable contribution pass-throughs and his or her direct contributions to compute the year's allowed charitable contribution deduction. The partner is treated as having received a money distribution for whatever share of the contribution was paid on his or her behalf. The partner's capital account and basis in his or her interest are reduced by this amount. The partnership enters the total amount of these payments on Form 1065, Schedule K, line 13a, "Contributions." Each partner's share of this amount is shown on Schedule K-1, box 13, "Other deductions." The partnership must provide a copy of its Form 8283, Noncash Charitable Contribution, to every partner if the value of an item or a group of similar items exceeds $5,000, even if the amount allocated to each partner is $5,000 or less.

.04 Code Sec. 172—Net Operating Deduction, and Code Sec. 1212—Capital Loss Carrybacks and Carryovers

These amounts are not carried over or back by the partnership.[34] A partnership's inability to carry net operating losses forward generally does not affect its partners. If the loss clears the basis, at risk, and passive loss rules, and the partner does not have sufficient current income to absorb the loss, he or she is allowed to individually carry the unused losses forward or back.[35]

.05 Code Sec. 611—Oil and Gas Well Depletion

A partnership cannot take a deduction for oil and gas depletion. Instead, oil and gas depletion is passed through and computed at the partner level.[36]

.06 Dividends

For purposes of determining the tax on long-term capital gains, "qualified dividend income" is added to net capital gain and adjusted net capital gain.[37] However, in computing the tax on dividends, the qualified dividend income cannot be offset by any capital losses.[38] The net effect of these rules is to tax qualified dividend income at either a 5 percent or 15 percent rate, depending on what the taxpayer's marginal tax rate is. If the taxpayer's marginal tax rate on taxable income is 15 percent or below, the tax rate on qualified dividend income is 5 percent. If the taxpayer's marginal tax rate on taxable income is above 15 percent, qualified dividend income will be taxed at 15 percent.[39] "Qualified dividend income" consists of dividends received from domestic and qualified foreign corporations, but only if the taxpayer held the stock for at least 61 days of the 121-day period beginning 60 days before the ex-dividend date.[40] The partnership separately states its qualified dividend income on Form 1065, Schedule K, line 6b, "Qualified

[34] Code Sec. 703(a); Reg. § 1.703-1(a)(2)(vii). The partnership loss reduces the partners' basis in their interest whether or not it is disallowed by the at-risk rules (Code Sec. 465) or the passive loss rules (Code Sec. 469).

[35] Code Sec. 172. If the losses are disallowed at the partner level because they are suspended under the basis, at-risk, or passive limitations, the losses are not available to a partner for net operating loss carryback but are carried over for an unlimited time until the partner has sufficient basis, at-risk amount, or passive income.

[36] Code Sec. 613A(c)(7)(D).

[37] Code Secs. 1(h)(3)(B) and 1(h)(11)(A).

[38] Code Sec. 1(h)(3).

[39] Code Sec. 1(h).

[40] Code Sec. 1(h)(11)(B).

dividends." Each partner's share of qualified dividend income is shown on Schedule K-1, box 6b, "Qualified dividends."

The deduction allowed under Code Sec. 243 to corporations for a percentage of the dividends received from other corporations is not allowed to a partnership because its taxable income is computed as if it were an individual. Corporate partners will separately determine their eligibility for this deduction. The corporate partner will not be required to reduce basis for this amount. The partnership separately states its ordinary dividend income [41] on Form 1065, Schedule K, line 6a, "Ordinary dividends." Each partner's share of ordinary dividends is shown on Schedule K-1, box 6a, "Ordinary dividends."

.07 Code Sec. 212—Expenses for the Production of Income

These amounts are not classified as a partnership deduction but they are separately stated and passed through to the partners as is discussed in ¶ 805.16 and ¶ 805.28.

.08 Code Sec. 213—Medical Expenses

A partnership is not allowed a deduction for expenditures for medical expenses as a *medical expense.* If a partnership pays medical costs for the benefit of its nonpartner employees it is able to deduct the payments as additional compensation. If it pays these amounts for the benefit of a service partner under a Code Sec. 104 self-insured health plan or Code Sec. 105 insured health plan, the IRS's position is that they are deemed Code Sec. 707(c) guaranteed payments.[42] If the medical payments are for the benefit of a nonservice partner or if the IRS's position is not followed, such payments are treated as money distributions to the affected partner. The partner's basis and capital account are reduced accordingly and the partner is entitled to any applicable deduction as if he or she paid the expense directly. See the detailed discussion of fringe benefits at ¶ 805.27.

.09 Code Sec. 215—Alimony

A partnership is not allowed an alimony deduction. If a partnership pays alimony for the benefit of its employees or its service partners, it may be able to deduct the payments as additional compensation or treat them as a money distribution.[43] If these amounts are paid on behalf of a partner who does not perform services, the payment is treated as a distribution to such partner. The partners' basis in his or her partnership interest and capital account are reduced by the alimony payment.

.10 Code Sec. 216—Deduction for Taxes, Interest, and Business Depreciation by a Cooperative Housing Corporation Tenant-Partner

If an individual service partner owns stock in the cooperative housing corporation and the partnership pays amounts to the cooperative on behalf

[41] Code Sec. 702(5).

[42] The compensation to a service partner would be treated as a Code Sec. 707(c) payment. Rev. Rul. 91-26, 1991-1 CB 184.

[43] Rev. Rul. 91-26, 1991-1 CB 184.

of its service partner, it may be able to deduct the payments as Code Sec. 707(a) or (c) guaranteed payments.[44] If these amounts are paid on behalf of a partner who does not perform services, they should be treated as a distribution to such partner. When it is the partnership that owns the stock and pays these amounts but a partner uses the space there is no official guidance as to the results. The most likely treatment is that these amounts should be separately stated and passed through to the partners. The treatment generally accorded to items paid by a partnership which are not deductible by it but may be deductible by its partners is simply to pass the item through to the partner. The partnership enters the total amount of these payments on Form 1065, Schedule K, line 13e, "Other deductions." Each partner's share is shown on Schedule K-1, box 13, "Other deductions."

.11 *Code Sec. 217—Moving Expenses*

A partnership is not allowed a moving expense deduction. If a partnership pays these amounts for the benefit of its nonpartner employers it is additional compensation. If it pays these amounts to its service partners, it may be able to deduct the payments as Code Sec. 707(a) or (c) guaranteed payments.[45] If these amounts are paid on behalf of a partner who does not perform services, the payments are treated simply as distributions. The partner for whom the partnership paid the expenses is treated as receiving a distribution equal to the expenses paid. His or her capital account and basis in his or her partnership interest are reduced by this amount.

.12 *Code Sec. 219—Retirement Savings*

A partnership is not allowed a deduction for contributions to a plan for its benefit. If a partnership contributes amounts for the benefit of its service partners, it may be able to deduct the payments as Code Sec. 707(a) or (c) guaranteed payments.[46] If these amounts are paid on behalf of a partner who does not perform services, the payment is treated as a distribution.

.13 *Trust or Estate Partner*

All depreciation deductions must be separately stated if a trust or estate is a partner.[47]

.14 *Rental Real Estate Activities*

Income and expenses attributable to these activities flow through to the partners as real estate rental activity. Passive losses incurred in rental real estate activities are subject to a special $25,000 deduction allowance in excess of passive income at the general partner level depending upon the level of the partner's adjusted gross income and whether he or she "actively participates" in the rental activity.[48] Also, taxpayers in a real property business who materially participate in any real estate rental activity treat income or loss from that activity as nonpassive.[49] The partnership has the obligation to define the boundaries of its various activities. The partner

[44] *Id.*
[45] *Id.*
[46] *Id.*
[47] Rev. Rul. 74-71, 1974-1 CB 158.
[48] Code Sec. 469(i).
[49] Code Sec. 469(c)(7).

then may group activities conducted directly and through other Code Sec. 469 entities with the activities of the partnership. Once the partnership has set the boundaries of its activities, the partner may not treat portions of the partnership's activities as separate activities. He or she may only combine his or her share of the partnership defined activity with other activities to form an activity with wider borders than the partnership's.[50]

.15 *Rental Activities Other Than Real Estate*

Income and expenses attributable to non-real estate rental activities flow through to the partners as passive without the special $25,000 allowance or the active income treatment available to real estate operators described in the previous paragraph. The partnership also has the obligation to define the boundaries of these various activities. The partner then may group activities conducted directly and through other Code Sec. 469 entities with the activities of the partnership. Once the partnership has set the boundaries of its activities, the partner may not treat portions of the partnership's activities as separate activities. He or she may only combine his or her share of the partnership defined activity with other activities to form an activity with wider borders than the partnership's.[51]

.16 *Portfolio (Investment) Income and Related Deductions Other Than the Interest Deduction*

These amounts are not taken into account in computing passive income and loss.[52] The partner takes his or her share of these partnership items into account with such items from other sources for purposes of the investment interest limitations.[53] Types of income in this category include: interest, dividends, royalty and annuity income not derived in the ordinary course of business, and gain from disposition of property producing such income. Expenses other than interest directly related to producing portfolio (investment) income and losses incurred on the disposition of portfolio (investment) assets are the only deductions in this category.[54] Portfolio (investment) expense other than interest expense is a common example of an expenditure that is not deductible by the partnership but is separately stated.[55] Form 1065, Schedule K, requires the partnership to separately state dividend and royalty income on Form 1065, Schedule K, lines 6 and 7. "Qualified" dividends are entered on line 6b of Schedule K and box 6b of Schedule K-1, and all taxable ordinary dividends are entered on line 6a and box 6a, respectively, of Schedules K and K-1. "Qualified" dividends are dividends that meet certain holding period and other requirements, and are taxed at capital gains tax rates. Net short-term capital gains and losses are entered on line 8 of Schedule K and box 8 of Schedule K-1, "Net short-term capital gain (loss)." Net long-term capital gains and losses are entered on line 9a and box 9a, respectively, of Schedules K and K-1. Unrecaptured section 1250 gains and collectibles gains are entered on lines 9c and 9b,

[50] Reg. § 1.469-4(d)(5)(i).
[51] *Id.*
[52] Code Sec. 469(e)(1)(A). Working capital is considered a portfolio (investment) asset. Code Sec. 469(e)(1)(B).
[53] Code Sec. 163(d).
[54] Code Sec. 163(d)(4)(C) and (5)(B).
[55] Code Sec. 67(c).

respectively, of Schedule K. The partnership's total remaining gross portfolio income is entered on line 11 of Schedule K, "Other income." The partnership must attach a schedule showing the composition of the income entered on line 11. The partnership enters portfolio income which is also investment income on line 20a of Schedule K. With the exception of oil and gas ventures, portfolio income and investment income are the same.[56] All Code Sec. 212 expenses directly related to producing portfolio income are entered on Schedule K, line 13b. The partnership must attach a schedule showing the composition of the Code Sec. 212 portfolio expenses entered on Schedule K, line 13b. The partnership enters the portion of portfolio expense which is also investment expense on Form 1065, Schedule K, line 20b. Investment expenses are also included on Schedule K, line 13b. With the exception of oil and gas ventures, the amount entered in line 20a is the same as line 13b.[57]

.17 Code Sec. 1231 Gains and Losses

The partnership's net Code Sec. 1231 gain or loss is separately stated on Form 1065, Schedule K, line 10, "Net Section 1231 gain (loss)." The partnership's net Code Sec. 1231 gain or loss from rental activity should be specified. Each partner is allowed to treat his or her net share of the partnership's Code Sec. 1231 gains and losses as if they were a direct result of his or her sales activity. The Code Sec. 1231 character is determined at the partnership level but each partner combines his or her net share of the partnership's Code Sec. 1231 gains and losses with such gains and losses from all other sources.[58] Gain characterized as ordinary income under recapture provisions [59] which is not required to be specially allocated is not separately stated and is therefore netted with the other nonseparately stated items on page one of Form 1065. The partnership's total ordinary nonrental income from this source is entered on Form 1065, line 6, "Net gain (loss) from Form 4797, part II, line 18."[60] Recapture income from rental activities is part of the net income or loss from rental activity. Code Sec. 1231 requires a preliminary netting of gains and losses from thefts and casualties of trade and business assets.[61] If this preliminary netting results in a loss, each loss is treated as an ordinary loss and it is not part of the general Code Sec. 1231 netting process. A partnership which has casualty and theft gains and losses should report two net Code Sec. 1231 amounts—the net gain or loss from casualties and thefts and the net of the remaining Code Sec. 1231 transactions. The partnership net income or loss from involuntary conversions due to casualties or thefts are shown on Form 1065, Schedule K, line 11, "Other income (loss) attach Schedule."

---

[56] Code Sec. 163(d)(5).

[57] *Id.*

[58] This is reported on the *partner's* Form 4797, Sales of Business Property.

[59] The most commonly encountered examples are the depreciation recapture provisions of Code Secs. 1245 and 1250. Reg. § 1.1245-1(e)(2), for example, requires the recapture to be allocated to the partnership interest which received the depreciation deduction.

[60] The partnership's recapture of Code Sec. 179 expense is entered on Form K-1, box 20, but not on Form 1065, line 6.

[61] Code Sec. 1231(a)(4)(C).

.18 *Capital Gains and Losses*

Short and long-term capital gains and losses are each separately netted and stated as two net amounts.[62] The reporting procedure for partnership capital gains and losses and other portfolio income and expenses is discussed at ¶ 805.16

.19 *Interest Deductions*

Business, rental, and investment interest. The partnership's deductible interest expense must be traced to its various activities.[63] Interest paid for borrowed funds is traced to the partnership's purchase of, or investment in, its various activities. The potential activities to which the debt is traced under these regulations include:

1. Real estate rental activities;
2. Nonreal estate rental activities;
3. Trade or business activities in which it does not materially participate;
4. Trade or business activities in which it does materially participate;
5. Trade or business activities in which it does materially participate but formally did not materially participate [64]; and
6. Its investments in portfolio assets.

With the exception of interest expense on debt traced to investments (portfolio assets), the interest expense related to each of the above activities must be aggregated with the other related expenses and netted against income from the activity.[65] The net result for each activity after taking into account the interest and other expenses related to that activity is separately stated.[66]

Interest on partnership debt which is traced to purchasing portfolio assets is separately stated on the partnership's Form 1065, Schedule K, line 13c, "Investment interest expense" and not on line 13b, "Deductions related to portfolio income." The interest on partnership debt traced to purchasing investment assets which are not portfolio assets is separately reported on Form 1065, Schedule K, line 13e, "Other Deductions." Line 13e may be used when the partnership has interest traced to working interests in oil and gas property.[67] Each partner's share of partnership interest expense traced to purchasing portfolio assets is shown on Schedule K-1, box 13.

[62] These net amounts are calculated on the partnership's Schedule D (Form 1065) and flow through to the *partner's* Schedule D.

[63] The interest allocation rules contained in Temp. Reg. § 1.163-8T apply to individuals, partnerships, and S corporations.

[64] A former passive activity. Code Sec. 468(f).

[65] Interest traced to investments (portfolio assets), other expenses directly connected with producing investment income (portfolio income), and investment income (portfolio income) are separately stated as three distinct totals.

[66] The boundaries of the partnership's various activities are defined by the partnership. Reg. § 1.469-4(d)(5). The partner then may group activities conducted directly and through entities. Reg. § 1.469-4(d)(5)(i).

[67] Code Secs. 163(d)(5)(A)(ii) and 469(c)(3).

Construction interest. Interest on debt incurred or continued for construction is capitalized as part of the constructed asset's cost during the construction period. This includes both interest on debt directly traced to construction and debt assigned to construction under the "avoided-cost" allocation system enacted by The Tax Reform Act of 1986.[68] The avoided-cost system is used to temporarily assign nonconstruction related debt to construction during the construction period. This is debt which, prior to commencement of construction, had been traced to other activities under the tracing rules.[69] Theoretically, if the partnership could have repaid a debt (and therefore not incurred the interest expense) instead of making construction payments, the interest must be capitalized under the avoided-cost method. With respect to partnerships, interest capitalization requirements are applied first at the partnership level and then at the partner level.[70] The partnership subtracts from its accumulated construction expenditures its debt directly traced to construction. Construction expenditures in excess of debt directly traced to construction (excess construction costs) are considered to have been provided by the partnership's remaining debt under the avoided-cost method. If such construction expenditures exceed the partnership's remaining debt any excess is treated as received from any partner borrowing. When construction costs exceed all partnership debt, the partners are subject to the interest capitalization rules as if they had paid any construction expenditures in excess of the partnership's debt with partner-level borrowing.[71] The partnership reports each partner's share of the excess of construction costs over the partnership's debt allocated to construction costs on the Partner's K-1, other information, box 20, with a description. Each partner is required to capitalize interest on debt previously traced to other activities during the construction period in an amount equal to his or her share of the partnership's construction costs in excess of his or her share of the partnership's debt. The partner is to maintain a "deferred asset" consisting solely of the capitalized interest attributable to his or her portion of the partnership's construction expenditures in excess of its debt.[72] The deferred asset is accounted for in the same manner as the partnership accounts for the constructed asset. The partner is allowed to treat any remaining capitalized cost as partnership interest adjusted basis if he or she disposes of his or her partnership interest.[73] The complexities of the partner-level deferred asset treatment may often be avoided by an

[68] P.L. 99-514; Code Sec. 262A(f).

[69] Debt traced to personal use, qualified residence debt, and debt incurred or continued to produce tax-exempt income is not reassigned to construction. Reg. § 1.263A-9(a)(4).

[70] Code Sec. 263A(f)(2)(C).

[71] Notice 88-99, 1988-2 CB 422.

[72] De minimis rules provide that the partner may ignore the partnership's activities if: (1) he or she owns 20% or less of the partnership interests; and (2) the partner's share of the construction expenditures in excess of its debt are $250,000 or less. Notice 88-99, 1988-2 CB 422.

[73] Under the avoided-cost method of debt allocation, a partner who incurs construction expenditures is also required to capitalize interest on debt directly traced to construction as well as interest on debt not traced to construction to the extent that construction expenditures exceed debt directly traced to construction. For this purpose the partner's share of the partnership's debt is considered to be his or her debt. The result is that he or she may be required to capitalize some or all of his or her share of the partnership's interest expense. In practice this may require the partner to request that the partnership separately state interest normally included in determining the net results of its various activities.

When a partner owning 20% or less of the partnership interests is engaged in construction and receives pass-through interest expense of less than $25,000, the interest capitalization rules will not apply to the interest expense passed through from the partnership. Notice 88-99, 1988-2 CB 422.

election to capitalize otherwise deductible expenditures at the partnership level.[74]

Tax exempt income and related expenses including interest on debt borrowed to produce tax-exempt income. Interest on debt incurred or continued for the purchase or carrying of obligations producing tax-exempt income is disallowed.[75] Expenses other than interest allocable to producing tax exempt income are disallowed.[76] The interest expense disallowed, the related tax-exempt income, and any other expense allocable to producing tax-exempt income are separately stated. The partnership's total tax exempt interest is entered on Form 1065, Schedule K, line 18a, "Tax-exempt interest income." Each partner's share of the partnership's tax exempt interest income is shown on Schedule K-1, line 19. The partnership total tax exempt income other than interest is entered on Form 1065 Schedule K, line 18b, "Other tax exempt income." Each partner's share of the partnership tax exempt income other than interest is shown in Schedule K-1, box 18. The partnership's total expenses allocable to tax exempt income other than the interest expense are entered on Form 1065, Schedule K, line 18c, "Nondeductible expenses." Each partner's share of the partnership total expense allocable to producing tax exempt income other than the interest expense is shown on Schedule K-1, box 18. Absent a "direct relationship," very little authority addresses the issue of whether interest paid or incurred by a partnership and passed through to a partner could be attributed to tax-exempt obligations held by the partner, or whether tax-exempt obligations held by the partnership could be treated as purchased or carried by a partner incurring interest expense on individual debt.[77]

Interest on distributed debt. It is not uncommon for a partnership to borrow funds to make distributions to partners. When a partnership applies the tracing rules to outstanding debt it may be traceable to a distribution to the partners. Under the interest tracing rules, if debt incurred by a partnership is traced to a distribution, the partnership itself cannot determine the character of the interest expense. Instead, the partners must characterize a portion of interest expense flowed through to them based on their use of the distributed funds unless the partnership chooses the alternative treatment.[78] The partnership enters the total interest paid or incurred on funds borrowed traced to a distribution to the partners on Form 1065, Schedule K, line 13e, "Other deductions."[79] The partnership's

[74] See Notice 88-99, 1988-2 CB 422.

[75] Code Sec. 265(a)(2).

[76] Code Sec. 265(a)(1).

[77] *B.P. McDonough*, 36 TCM 213, Dec. 34,277(M), TC Memo. 1977-50, aff'd, CA-4, 78-2 USTC ¶ 9490, 577 F2d 234. Tax-exempt interest income and interest expense of partners and partnership is aggregated for Code Sec. 265(2) purposes. See also *O. Phipps v. U.S.*, CtCls, 75-1 USTC ¶ 9399, 206 CtCls 583, 515 F2d 1099. Tracing debt from its source to its use is done in accordance with case law rather than the tracing regulations. See generally Rev. Proc. 72-18, 1972-1 CB 740.

[78] Notice 88-20, 1988-1 CB 487. The total interest expense should be entered on the partnership's Form 1065, Schedule K, line 11 [now line 13e], "Other Deductions." Each partner's share of the interest expense should be included on line 11 [now line 13e] on Schedule K for "Other Deductions." A schedule should also be attached to the K-1 listing all distributions to the shareholder to which debt proceeds are traced indicating the amount of the debt proceeds and interest expense allocated to each distribution. See also Notice 89-35, 1989-1 CB 675.

[79] If the partner who received the distribution transfers his or her partnership interest, an interesting but unanswered question arises. Should the buyer be required to ascertain the seller's treatment and continue it, or can this be looked at as if it were a leveraged or boot-strapped acquisition? If the latter alternative is correct the new owner's share of the debt is treated as if it were incurred on debt

alternative is to allocate the debt proceeds among the entity's other expenditures during the taxable year to the extent that debt proceeds have not otherwise been allocated to such expenditures. There is no special election to use this alternate allocation method. The interest expense allocated to the partnership's activities is reported on Form 1065 and flows through to the individual partner's K-1 in box 13.

Interest on debt used to retire a partner. There is no formal guidance concerning the allocation of debt used to finance the retirement of a partner. The ultimate result of a debt-financed retirement is that the continuing partners have indirectly borrowed to purchase an increased ownership interest in the partnership. If the interest expense treatment is forced into the Code Sec. 736 pattern, the interest on borrowed money that is distributed to the partner and classified as Code Sec. 736(b) payments should be treated as interest on distributed borrowed money. However, the retiring partner would not get an allocation of any share of the interest deduction and the continuing partners should not have their treatment of the interest dependent upon the retiring partner's use of the funds. The partnership is allowed an election to treat the funds as if they had been spent on partnership activities.[80] Interest paid for the use of borrowed money that is paid to the retired partner and classified as a Code Sec. 736(a)(1) "distributive share" of income cannot be classified under the normal rules. This payment is neither a partnership distribution nor an expense. It is an income share under Code Sec. 736(a). The tracing rules do not classify debt traced to a share of income as a use of borrowed money. Interest on indebtedness traced to a Code Sec. 736(a)(2) "guaranteed payment" possibly could be considered as debt incurred to pay a Code Sec. 162 expense.[81] If so, it would be a nonseparately stated interest expense traced to the partnership's business.

However, whether the payments are Code Sec. 736(a) or (b) payments, they are being made to acquire the retiring partners' share of the partnership assets. It would be reasonable to treat the debt as traced to purchasing the retired partner's interest in the partnership assets. The continuing partners would treat this indirect purchase of the underlying assets the same as a direct purchase of his or her partnership interest.[82] The remaining partners should be entitled to treat the interest as paid on indebtedness incurred to purchase the retiring partner's share of unrealized receivables, goodwill, and other property. What is clear is that interest on borrowed funds traced to payments to retire a partner are not covered by official guidance.[83]

Partnership interest paid on debt owed to a partner—Self-charged interest. When a partner lends money to the partnership, the

(Footnote Continued)

traced to the purchase of the partnership's assets. Notice 89-35, 1989-1 CB 675.

[80] Notice 88-20, 1988-1 CB 487, and Notice 89-35, 1989-1 CB 675.

[81] Reg. § 1.707-1(c).

[82] Notice 89-35, 1989-1 CB 675.

[83] If funding for the ex-partner's liquidating distributions were provided by the retiring partner accepting an interest-bearing note from the partnership, the "interest" payments are not considered interest. They are considered part of the money distributed under Code Sec. 736.

partner both receives interest income and is allocated a share of the partnership's interest deduction. Absent a special rule, and assuming the loan proceeds are used in the partnership's activities classified as passive for the lending partner, the interest income would be portfolio interest income and the interest expense would be a passive deduction. Accordingly, the interest expense would not be available to offset the interest income. If the partner borrows from a third party to make the loan to the partnership, however, the interest expense on the third-party loan would be a portfolio deduction, which would offset the portfolio income paid by the partnership.[84]

Congress did not intend for these types of lending transactions to cause these unfavorable results.[85] The Conference Committee Report to The Tax Reform Act of 1986 refers specifically to loans between a pass-through entity and its owners.[86]

> Under certain circumstances, the interest may essentially be "self-charged," and thus lack economic significance . . . Under these circumstances, it is not appropriate to treat the transaction as giving rise both to portfolio interest income and to passive interest expense. Rather, to the extent that a taxpayer receives interest income with respect to a loan to a pass-through entity in which he or she has an ownership interest, such income should be allowed to offset the interest expense passed through to the taxpayer from the activity for the same taxable year.

With respect to loans from the partner to the partnership, in general, certain owner/lender self-charged interest income is recharacterized as passive income, thus allowing the use of self-charged interest expense to offset self-charged interest income.[87] The recharacterization rules apply to both interest received from direct partner loans to the partnership and indirect loans when an S corporation shareholder lends money to a partnership in which the S corporation is a partner and the lending shareholder has a direct or indirect "qualifying interest" (a 10 percent ownership interest). When the recharacterization rules apply, the "applicable percentage" of the partner's interest income from interest paid by the borrowing partnership is recharacterized as passive income from the pass-through entity's activity. In addition, the "applicable percentage" of the partner's related interest expenses is treated as a passive activity deduction.[88] The partner's applicable percentage is determined by dividing the partner's share of the

[84] A similar problem is created when a loan in the opposite direction is made. When a partnership lends money to its partner, the partner both incurs an interest deduction and is allocated a share of the partnership's interest income. Absent a special rule, and assuming the partner invests the loan proceeds in a passive activity, his or her share of the partnership interest income would be portfolio income and the interest expense would be a passive deduction even if the partnership's other income items were passive to the partner. Accordingly, the interest expense would not be available to offset the interest income. If instead the partner invests the loan proceeds in a portfolio investment, or if the partnership borrows from a third party to make the loan to the partner, the interest expense on the third-party loan would be a portfolio deduction, which would offset the portfolio income.

[85] Inequitable results of a similar nature are apparently acceptable. For example, if a partnership conducts a passive activity and pays one of its partners a fee for services, the partner would have compensation income and could have a passive activity loss attributable to the partnership's passive activities. The self-charged interest rules do not permit the salary to be offset by the passive activity loss.

[86] H.R. Rep. No. 841, 99th Cong., 2d Sess. II-146-II-147 (1986) (Conference Report to P.L. 99-514); See also Staff of the Joint Committee on Taxation, *General Explanation of the Tax Reform Act of 1986* (Blue Book), at p. 233, n. 26 (similar rule for loans from the entity to its owners) and S. Rep. No. 841, 99th Cong., 2d Sess. II-146 to 147 (1986).

[87] Reg. § 1.469-7.

[88] Reg. § 1.469-7(c)(2).

self-charged interest deductions that constitute passive activity deductions by the greater of (1) the partner's share of total self-charged interest deductions (regardless of whether these deductions are treated as passive activity deductions), or (2) the partner's income from interest charged to the partnership.[89] The partnership should include each partner's share of the partnership's self-charged interest expense on Schedule K-1, line 25, "Supplemental information."

The recharacterization rules in the regulations do not apply if the partnership (rather than the partner) elects not to have self-charged treatment apply.[90] The election is made for a taxable year by attaching a written statement to the partnership's return or amended return for the taxable year. It applies to all loan transactions between the pass-through entity and its direct or indirect owners for all subsequent taxable years that end before the date on which the election is revoked.[91] The election can not be revoked without the consent of the IRS.[92]

With respect to loans from the partnership to a partner, if certain requirements are satisfied, a partner's "applicable percentage" of self-charged interest income of the partnership attributable to loans made by the partnership to its partners is recharacterized as passive activity gross income. The applicable percentage of the partner's share of related interest expenses is treated as a passive activity deduction.[93] The self-charged interest rules relating to loans from a partnership are applicable only if:

1. The partnership has interest income arising from loans made to its partners ("self-charged interest income");
2. A partner owns a direct or qualifying indirect interest [94] in the partnership sometime during the partnership's taxable year and has deductions for interest paid to the partnership; and
3. The partner's deduction for interest charged by the partnership is included in his or her passive activity deductions.[95]

A partner's applicable percentage is equal to his or her passive activity deductions for interest charged by the partnership, divided by the greater of (1) the partner's deduction for all interest that the partnership charges the partner (regardless of whether the deductions are treated as passive activity deductions), or (2) the partner's share of the partnership's self-charged interest income.[96] The partnership should include each partner's share of self-charged interest income on Schedule K-1, box 20, "Other Information."

---

[89] Reg. § 1.469-7(c)(3).

[90] Reg. § 1.469-7(g)(1). The self-charged interest rules may be undesirable because (1) of the administrative burden associated with the application of the rules; (2) in certain circumstances the application of the rules produces no benefit; or (3) the recharacterization of the interest income may have adverse consequences for certain partners. The partnership-level nature of the election out could cause serious conflicts among the partners of a partnership—*e.g.*, if one partner has investment interest carryovers under Code Sec. 163(d) and the other partners do not.

[91] Reg. § 1.469-7(g)(2) and (3).

[92] Reg. § 1.469-7(g)(4).

[93] Reg. § 1.469-7(d)(2).

[94] Reg. § 1.469-7(c)(1).

[95] Reg. § 1.469-7(c)(1)(iii).

[96] Reg. § 1.469-7(c)(3).

.20 *Interest and Royalty Income*

The partnership separately states its total interest and royalty income on Form 1065, Schedule K, on lines 5 and 7, respectively. Each partner's share of the partnership interest and royalty income is shown on Schedule K-1, boxes 5 and 7.

.21 *Cancelled Debt Income*

In general, a partnership's cancellation of indebtedness income (COD) is reported as separately stated ordinary gross income. The partnership enters its total COD on Form 1065, Schedule K, line 11, "Other Income." Each partner's share of the partnership COD is reported on Schedule K-1, box 11, "Other income." It is ordinary income derived from the activity to which the debt is traced under the tracing rules.[97]

Sources of cancelled debt income. The following are examples of situations when, absent special circumstances making an exclusion from gross income available, a partnership may incur cancellation of indebtedness income:

1. A reduction in the principal amount of its liability.

2. A material modification of the debt. For example, a reduction in the interest rate on outstanding debt. A change in the interest rate may be a material modification in the existing debt requiring the partnership to treat the original debt as if it had been refinanced with the new debt. When new debt is issued in satisfaction of existing debt the partnership is treated as if it paid the existing debt with an amount of money equal to the "issue price" of the new debt instrument.[98] Therefore, the issuance of the new debt will generate discharge of indebtedness income if the issue price is less than the balance of the old debt.[99] However, new debt with an interest rate at least equal to the applicable federal rate will not result in debt discharge income.

3. When a person related to the debtor directly or indirectly acquires debt from a person who is not related to the debtor, debt discharge income may result.[100] The amount of the income equals the excess of the face amount of the debt over its value.[101]

---

[97] Temp. Reg. § 1.163-8T. Thus, if the debt proceeds had been traced to the partnership's trade or business activity it would be reported as "Other income" one page one of Form 1065.

[98] Issue price is defined in Code Sec. 1274 as the present value of all payments to be made with respect to the obligation (stated interest and principal) at a discount factor equal to the "applicable federal rate." The applicable federal rate is published through monthly revenue rulings.

[99] Code Sec. 108(e)(11); Reg. § 1.1001-3(a). Added to Code Sec. 108(e) by Act § 11325(a)(1) of P.L. 101-508 (The Omnibus Budget Reconciliation Act of 1990), generally applies to debt instruments issued after October 9, 1990.

[100] Code Secs. 267(b) and 707(b)(1) define a related party for this purpose.

[101] Code Sec. 108(e)(4). An indirect related party acquisition includes when an unrelated person acquires the debt in anticipation of becoming related. Reg. § 1.108-2(c).

In a number of circumstances, however, the Internal Revenue Code provides specific exceptions to the general rule that cancellation of indebtedness triggers income to the debtor.[102] Income realized from the forgiveness of indebtedness is excluded:

1. If the discharge occurs in a Title 11 case;[103]
2. To the extent the debtor remains insolvent;[104]
3. If the debt was incurred incident to the purchase of property and the seller/creditor reduces the amount of the debt when the debtor is solvent;[105]
4. If it is a discharge of qualified farm debt of a solvent farmer;[106]
5. Payment of the debt would have been deductible;[107] or
6. The debt is "qualified real property business indebtedness."

Foreclosures, etc., and cancelled debt income. When debt is secured by the partnership property and the partnership transfers that property to the lender as part of the cancellation, the exclusion provisions for *cancelled debt* may be partially or completely inapplicable. This is the result whether the property is transferred in a foreclosure, a voluntary transfer to the secured creditor (a deed in lieu), or an indirect transfer to the secured creditor by way of an abandonment.[108] The entire amount of a nonrecourse debt cancelled in connection with the property's transfer is treated as amount realized for its sale. Therefore, no cancellation of debt income is generated when property subject to a nonrecourse debt is transferred in whole or partial satisfaction of the debt. The transfer of property by a debtor in partial or whole satisfaction of a recourse debt is treated as payment of the debt to the extent of the property's value. Gain or loss, but not cancellation of debt income, is realized on the difference between the property's value and its adjusted basis.[109] Any excess of the debt over the fair market value of the transferred property generates cancellation of debt

---

[102] Code Sec. 108. In addition to the statutory exclusions from gross income provided for cancelled debt there are a number of judicial decisions which may expand the possibilities for not reporting cancelled debt income. These decisions generally predate the Bankruptcy Tax Act of 1980 (P.L. 96-589) and their viability is not certain. See Code Sec. 108(e)(1).

[103] Code Sec. 108(a)(1)(A) and (d)(2). Title 11 of the United States Code federal bankruptcy proceedings. A debtor who is in a bankruptcy proceeding is entitled to the statutory bankruptcy exclusions even if he or she is solvent immediately after the debt discharge within Code Sec. 108's definition.

[104] Code Sec. 108(a)(1)(B) and (3). Insolvency is defined as the excess of liabilities over the fair market value of assets. A debtor who is not in bankruptcy is entitled to this statutory exclusion only to the extent the discharge does not cause the fair market value of his or her assets to exceed his or her remaining debt. There is some question as to how goodwill and an individual's "exempt assets" are accounted for. Exempt assets are those which the bankrupt individual is allowed to keep after a bankruptcy. See Code Sec. 522 of the Bankruptcy Code. The cases of *R.S. Cole v. Commr.*, 42 BTA 1110, Dec. 11,364 (1940); *Fifth Avenue-14th Street Corp. v. Commr.*, CA-2, 45-1 USTC ¶ 9115, 147 F2d 453; *Est. of B.M. Marcus v. Commr.*, 34 TCM 38, Dec. 33,012(M), TC Memo. 1975-9; and *C.L. Hunt v. Commr.*, 57 TCM 919, Dec. 45,833(M), TC Memo. 1989-335, have all held that exempt assets are not taken into account in determining the fair market value of the debtor's assets after the debt discharge for purposes of the insolvency exception. The judicial reasoning is that the debt discharge does not free up these assets because they are assets the debtor can keep even if the debts are not discharged. The IRS's position is that exempt assets are included in the solvency determination. IRS Technical Advice Memorandum 199935002 (5-3-99); IRS Letter Ruling 199932013 (5-4-99).

[105] Code Sec. 108(e)(5). The property is treated as if it were purchased for the reduced price.

[106] Code Sec. 108(g).

[107] Code Sec. 108(e)(2).

[108] Reg. § 1.1001-2(c), Ex. 8; Rev. Rul. 90-16, 1990-1 CB 12; *M.L. Middleton v. Commr.*, 77 TC 310, Dec. 38,124 (1981), aff'd per curiam, CA-11, 82-2 USTC ¶ 9713, 693 F2d 124 (abandonment); *J.W. Yarbro v. Commr.*, CA-5, 84-2 USTC ¶ 9691, 737 F2d 479, cert. denied, 489 US 1189, 105 SCt 959 (abandonment); and Rev. Rul. 76-111, 1976-1 CB 215.

[109] Rev. Rul. 90-16, 1990-1 CB 12.

income if and when the debt becomes uncollectible. Gain generated by a partnership's transfer of its encumbered assets to its creditors will be taxable to the partners whether or not the partnership or the partner is insolvent or bankrupt. Seldom can this gain be offset with an ordinary loss from the abandonment of a worthless partnership interest. The gain generates basis in the partnership interest which could, possibly, generate more worthless partnership interest loss. However, the deemed money distribution resulting from the liquidated partnership's debt under Code Sec. 752(b) would probably result in the liquidation being treated as capital gain or loss on a liquidating distribution rather than an abandonment of a worthless partnership interest. Any basis not recovered through the deemed money distribution would be a capital loss.[110]

Assuming the gain and debt are allocated in the same manner, the basis increase resulting from the gain will be offset by the deemed cash distribution associated with the reduction in the partner's share of partnership debt. Even though the income from the foreclosure may be offset by a loss on dissolution of the partnership interest, a net tax liability can be generated when the pass-through gain is ordinary and the loss is capital or if the income is passed through in a year prior to the loss on the worthless partnership interest.

Example 8-2. *Partnership debt is recourse.* The equal ABC partnership has the following balance sheet:

ABC Partnership

Assets	***Tax Basis***	***FMV***
Blackacre	$30,000	$60,000
Liabilities		
(recourse)	$90,000	$90,000
Capital		
A	$(20,000)	$(10,000)
B	(20,000)	(10,000)
C	(20,000)	(10,000)
	$(60,000)	*$(30,000)*

ABC partnership deeds Blackacre to the lender in lieu of a foreclosure and the remaining debt is cancelled. The results to the ABC partnership are as follows:

	Deemed Sale	***Cancelled Debt Income***
Deemed Sales Price	$60,000	$30,000
Adjusted Basis	(30,000)	
Gain	*$30,000*	

The ABC partnership separately reports the $10,000 gain and $10,000 cancelled debt income for each partner.

[110] Code Secs. 731(a) and 741.

Each partner's result is as follows:

Beginning partnership interest basis	$10,000
Increase for gain	10,000
Increase for cancelled debt income	10,000
Subtotal	*$30,000*
Reduction in debt share deemed distribution	(30,000)
Ending basis	$ 0
Gain/Loss	$ 0

Observation. Each partner's basis in his or her partnership interest is increased by the cancelled debt income whether or not it is excluded from the partner's income under Code Sec. 108.[111]

Example 8-3. Partnership debt is nonrecourse. If the debt had been nonrecourse, the results would have been as follows:

	Deemed Sale	*Cancelled Debt Income*
Deemed Sales Price	$90,000	$ 0
Adjusted Basis	(30,000)	
Gain	*$60,000*	

The ABC partnership separately states $20,000 gain for each partner and the result is as follows:

Beginning partnership interest basis	$10,000
Increase for gain	20,000
Increase for cancelled debt income	0
Subtotal	*$30,000*
Reduction in debt share deemed distribution	(30,000)
Ending basis	$ 0
Gain/Loss	$ 0

Example 8-4. Assume the same facts as in Example 8-2, except that the ABC partnership allocated the cancelled debt income (COD) differently than the partners shared in debt under Code Sec. 752 and that the allocation has substantial economic effect or its equivalent under Code Sec. 704(b). Assume the COD is allocated 50% to *A* and the remainder equally to *B* and *C*. The result would have been as follows:

	A	*B*	*C*
Beginning partnership interest basis	$10,000	$10,000	$10,000
Increase for gain	10,000	10,000	10,000
Increase for cancelled debt income	15,000	7,500	7,500
Subtotal	*$35,000*	*$27,500*	*$27,500*
Reduction in debt share deemed distribution	(30,000)	(30,000)	(30,000)
Ending basis	*$5,000*	*$ 0*	*$ 0*
Gain	$ 0	$2,500	$2,500

A's unrecovered basis will be a capital loss if the partnership is terminated as part of the transaction. Partners *B* and *C* each have a capital gain of $2,500.

[111] Code Sec. 705(a)(1)(A) and (B).

The insolvency/bankruptcy exclusion of cancelled debt income. Tax attributes must be reduced if cancelled debt is excluded from gross income by the statutory provisions for bankrupt or insolvent persons.[112] In the context of a partnership debt it is the partner's insolvency or bankruptcy that qualifies each partner for an exclusion, and tax attributes are reduced at the partner level.[113] The partnership's insolvency or bankruptcy is irrelevant. When a partner, but not the partnership, files bankruptcy and the partner's liability for his or her share of partnership debt is discharged, but the partnership remains liable for the entire debt, there is a deemed cash distribution to the bankrupt partner (and a deemed cash contribution by those partners whose responsibility for repayment of the debt has increased).[114] If this deemed distribution exceeds the partner's basis, there is gain for the excess.[115] The holder of the partnership interest at year end must report the gain.[116]

> ***S Corporation Observation.*** In the case of an S corporation, the exclusion is available if the S corporation is insolvent without regard to the solvency of the shareholders.[117]

> ***LLC Observation.*** For nontax purposes, an LLC provides protection from creditors that is comparable to a shareholder's protection from the creditors of the corporation. From an income tax standpoint, if the LLC is treated as a partnership, its solvent/nonbankrupt members will incur taxable income when the creditors are not paid. Although a tax liability for not paying the debts is certainly less expensive than paying the debts, the members should be aware of the tax consequences. They will not normally be walking away from the activity free of all financial obligations.

With one exception, tax attributes must be reduced in the following order:

1. *Net operating losses.* A partner's net operating losses (NOLs) for the taxable year of the discharge are reduced first and then carryovers to that year are reduced in the order in which they arose.[118]

2. *General business credit.* A partner's tax credit carryovers are reduced in the same order in which they were taken into account. For credits earned in years beginning after December 31, 1986, the credits are reduced by 33-1/3 percent of the dollar amount of cancelled debt.

3. *Minimum tax credit.* Credit available on the first day of the next taxable year.[119]

---

[112] The attribute reductions are made after a determination of the debtor's tax liability for the years of discharge. Code Sec. 108(b)(4)(A).

[113] Code Sec. 108(d)(6).

[114] Code Sec. 752(b).

[115] Code Sec. 731(a).

[116] IRS Letter Ruling 9619002 (1-31-96).

[117] Code Sec. 108(d)(7)(A).

[118] Code Sec. 108(b)(2)(A) and (4)(B).

[119] Code Sec. 108(b)(2)(C).

4. *Capital loss carryovers.* A partner's net capital losses for the taxable year of the discharge are reduced first and then carryovers to that year are reduced in the order they arose.[120]

5. *Basis reduction.* The debtor's property basis is reduced according to the provisions of Code Sec. 1017. The order of the basis reduction of assets is prescribed by the regulations.[121] No basis reduction is required for property exempted from the bankruptcy proceedings by Code Sec. 522 of Title 11 of the United States Code.[122] The basis adjustments are treated as depreciation for purposes of Code Sec. 1245 and as "additional depreciation" (accelerated) for purposes of Code Sec. 1250, whether or not the property is Code Sec. 1245 or Code Sec. 1250 property.[123]

6. *Passive activity loss and credit carryovers.*

7. *Foreign tax credit carryovers.* Any carryover to or from the taxable year of discharge allowed under Code Sec. 33. For credits earned in years beginning after December 31, 1986, the credits are reduced by 33-1/3 percent of the dollar amount of cancelled debt.

The reduction in each category of carryovers is made in the order of taxable years in which the items would be used, with the order determined as if the debt discharge amount were not excluded from income. The reductions are made after the computation of the current year's tax.[124]

Bankrupt and insolvent persons, including partners, can avoid the statutory order of attribute reduction only by making an election to first reduce the basis of depreciable assets to zero and then resume the statutory order of attribute reduction for any remaining cancelled debt excluded from income by the insolvency and bankruptcy provisions. The partner can elect to apply any portion of the required attribute reduction to reduce the basis of the depreciable property before resuming the statutory order.[125] A partner's partnership interest is considered depreciable property to the extent of his or her share of the partnership's depreciable property.[126]

Observation. Although reducing the basis of depreciable property for excluded cancelled debt income before following the statutory tax attribute reduction pattern is elective, it is an election which is generally made.

---

[120] Code Sec. 108(b)(2)(A) and (4)(B).

[121] Reg. § 1.1017-1. (1) Real property used in the trade or business or held for investment that secured the discharged debt immediately before the discharge; (2) property (other than inventory, notes and accounts receivable) used in the trade or business; (3) any other property (other than inventory, notes and accounts receivable) used in the trade or business; (4) inventory, notes and accounts receivable used in the trade or business; (5) property held for the production of income; (6) other property.

[122] Code Sec. 1017(c)(1).

[123] Code Sec. 1017(d).

[124] Code Sec. 108(b)(4)(A). The tax attributes are available for the calculation of the tax liability for the taxable year of discharge. In all cases, the reductions are made as of the first day of the succeeding year. Thus, gain or loss on property sold during the discharge year is not affected by any basis reduction. Property acquired any time during the discharge year and held on the first day of the next year is eligible for basis reduction.

[125] Code Sec. 108(b)(5). An election is available to treat real property held for sale to customers (dealer property) as depreciable property. Code Sec. 1017(b)(3)(E).

[126] But the partnership is required to reduce the basis of its depreciable property by the same amount. Code Sec. 1017(b)(3)(C).

The regulations provide guidance for treating partnership interests as depreciable property if an election is made not to use the general attribute reduction rules. As a general rule, a partner can independently determine whether to request that the partnership reduce his or her share of depreciable basis in partnership property enabling him or her to treat the partnership interest as depreciable property (or depreciable real property in the case of qualified real property business indebtedness). However, a partner must request consent if the partner owns (directly or indirectly) more than 50 percent of the partnership's capital and profits interest or if the partner receives a distributive share of cancellation of indebtedness income from the partnership. The partner's request must be made before the due date (including extensions) for filing his or her federal income tax return for the tax year in which he or she has the cancellation of indebtedness income.[127]

The partnership generally is free to grant or deny its consent. The partnership, however, is required to grant consent if requests are made by partners owning (directly or indirectly) an aggregate of more than 80 percent of the partnership capital and profits or five or fewer partners owning (directly or indirectly) an aggregate of more than 50 percent of the capital and profits interests.[128] A partnership that consents to a basis reduction must include a consent statement with its Form 1065 for the tax year following the year that ends with or within the tax year the taxpayer excludes the COD income. The partnership must also provide a copy of that statement to the affected partner(s) on or before the due date of the taxpayer's return (including extensions) for the tax year in which the taxpayer partnership and the amount of (1) the reduction to the partner's proportionate interest in the adjusted basis of the partner's depreciable property, or (2) depreciable real property, whichever is applicable.[129] For taxable years beginning before January 1, 2003, this statement should also be attached to the partner's timely filed (including extensions) tax return for the year in which the income is excluded under Code Sec. 108(a). For later years, the statement should be retained and be available for inspection.[130]

Form 982, Reduction of Tax Attributes Due to Discharge of Indebtedness (and Section 1082 Basis Adjustment), must be filed and signed by the partner whenever debt discharge income is excluded from gross income. The special basis reduction elections are also made on Form 982.

In applying the partner-level tax attribute reduction rules, a partnership interest is treated as depreciable property to the extent of the partner's interest in the partnership's depreciable property.[131] The basis reduction in the depreciable partnership property is an adjustment to the basis of partnership property only with respect to the electing partner. No adjustment is made to the common basis of partnership property. For purposes of income, deduction, gain, loss and distribution, the partner will have a special basis for those partnership properties for which the basis was

[127] Reg. § 1.1017-1(g)(2)(ii)(A).
[128] Reg. § 1.1017-1(g)(2)(ii)(c).
[129] Reg. § 1.1017-1(g)(2)(iii).
[130] Temp. Reg. § 1.1017-1T(g)(2)(iii)(B).
[131] Code Sec. 1017(b)(3)(C).

adjusted under Code Sec. 1017. The recovery of adjustments to the basis of the partnership property for the partner making this election is recovered in the manner described in Reg. § 1.743-1.[132] In effect, the partnership records a negative basis which is amortized as an offset to depreciation specially allocated to the electing partner or as additional gain on the property's disposition which may be reported partially as ordinary income.[133] Adjustments to the basis of partnership property are treated in the same manner and have the same effect as an adjustment to the basis of partnership property under Code Sec. 743.[134]

As mentioned, eligibility for Title 11 and insolvency exclusions provided for debt discharge income is tested at the partner level.[135] The solvency or bankruptcy of the partnership is irrelevant to the exclusion of the forgiveness of indebtedness income at the partner level.[136] Tax attribute reduction is likewise applied at the partner level.[137] If a partner is bankrupt or insolvent and does not recognize cancellation of indebtedness income, the partner may make the election to reduce his or her basis in depreciable property before reducing other tax attributes.[138] No new taxable entity is created when a partnership files a bankruptcy petition.[139] This tax provision should not be confused with the bankruptcy provisions, other than income tax, providing that a new entity, the bankruptcy estate, is created for the administration of the bankruptcy rules. The partnership continues to file a Form 1065 according to its normal taxable year.[140] If a partner who is an individual is bankrupt, a new taxable estate is created.[141] His or her partnership interest is treated as owned by the estate but there is deemed not to be a transfer of his or her interest.[142] Therefore, there is no possibility that the partnership will terminate under Code Sec. 708(b)(1)(B), and all income is taxed to the estate.

Qualified real property business indebtedness exclusion of cancelled debt income. Taxpayers other than C corporations may elect to exclude from gross income certain discharge of qualified real property business indebtedness if they are not bankrupt and not insolvent.[143] The amount so excluded cannot exceed the basis of certain depreciable real property of the taxpayer and is treated as a reduction in the basis of that property.

Qualified real property business indebtedness is indebtedness that:

1. Is incurred or assumed in connection with real property used in a trade or business;

2. Is secured by that real property; and

---

[132] Reg. § 1.1017-1(g)(2)(v)(B).

[133] Code Sec. 1017(d). S. Rep. No. 1035, 96th Cong., 2d Sess. (1980), at 14.

[134] Reg. § 1.1017-1(g)(2)(v)(C).

[135] Code Sec. 108(d)(6).

[136] If cancelled debt is not eligible for exclusion at the partner level its partners are responsible for the tax liability generated by the debt discharge.

[137] Code Sec. 108(d)(6).

[138] Code Sec. 108(d)(7). See Form 982, Reduction of Tax Attributes Due to Discharge of Indebtedness.

[139] Code Sec. 1399. A separate taxable estate is created for an individual bankruptcy proceeding but not for corporations or partnerships.

[140] The trustee of the partnership's Chapter 7 bankruptcy estate is responsible for filing returns due after the petition is filed.

[141] Code Sec. 1398(a).

[142] Code Sec. 1398(f).

[143] Code Sec. 108(a)(2).

3. With respect to which the taxpayer has made an election under this provision.[144]

Indebtedness incurred or assumed on or after January 1, 1993, is not qualified real property business indebtedness unless it is either:

1. Debt incurred to refinance qualified real property business debt incurred or assumed before that date (but only to the extent the amount of such debt does not exceed the amount of debt being refinanced), or

2. Qualified acquisition indebtedness.[145]

Qualified real property business indebtedness does not include qualified farm indebtedness.

Qualified acquisition indebtedness is debt incurred to acquire, construct, or substantially improve real property that is secured by such debt, and debt resulting from the refinancing of qualified acquisition debt, to the extent the amount of such debt does not exceed the amount of debt being refinanced.[146]

The amount excluded under the provision with respect to the discharge of any qualified real property business indebtedness may not exceed the excess of (1) the outstanding principal amount of such debt (immediately before the discharge), over (2) the fair market value (immediately before the discharge) of the business real property serving as security for the debt. For this purpose, the fair market value of the property is reduced by the outstanding principal amount of any other qualified real property indebtedness secured by the property immediately before the discharge.

> ***Example 8-5.*** Assume that Individual *J* owns a building worth $150,000, used in his trade or business, that is subject to a first mortgage securing a debt of *J*'s of $110,000 and a second mortgage securing a second debt of *J*'s of $90,000. *J* is neither bankrupt nor insolvent and neither debt is qualified farm indebtedness. *J* negotiates with his second mortgagee to reduce the second mortgage debt to $30,000, resulting in discharge of indebtedness income in the amount of $60,000. Assuming that *J* has sufficient basis in business real property to absorb the reduction (see below), *J* can elect to exclude $50,000 of that discharge from gross income. This is because the principal amount of the discharged debt immediately before the discharge (*i.e.*, $90,000) exceeds the fair market value of the property securing it by $50,000 (*i.e.*, $150,000 of free and clear value less $110,000 of other qualified business real property debt or $40,000). The remaining $10,000 of discharge is included in gross income.

The amount excluded under this provision may not exceed the aggregate adjusted bases (determined as of the first day of the next taxable year or, if earlier, the date of disposition) of depreciable real property held by

[144] Code Sec. 108(c)(3).
[145] Code Sec. 108(c)(3).
[146] Code Sec. 108(c)(3).

the taxpayer immediately before the discharge, determined after any reductions under subsections (b) and (g) of Code Sec. 108. Depreciable real property acquired in contemplation of the discharge is treated as not held by the taxpayer immediately before the discharge.[147]

The amount of debt discharge excluded under the provision reduces the depreciable realty's basis, following the rules of Code Sec. 1017. See the discussion earlier in this section.

The deemed distribution [148] arising from the reduction in a partner's share of partnership liabilities attributable to the discharge of partnership debt is treated as follows. The allocation of an amount of excluded debt discharge income to a partner results in that partner's basis in the partnership being increased by such amount.[149] The reduction in a partner's share of partnership liabilities caused by the debt discharge also results in a deemed distribution,[150] which in turn results in a reduction [151] of the partner's basis in his or her partnership interest. This basis reduction is separate from any reduction in basis of the partner's interest under the provision—*i.e.*, the basis reduction that occurs as a result of treating the partnership interest as depreciable real property to the extent of the partner's proportionate interest in the depreciable real property held by the partnership (provided the partnership makes a corresponding reduction in the basis of depreciable partnership real property with respect to that partner).

> ***S Corporation Observation.*** In applying these rules to income from the discharge of indebtedness of an S corporation, the election is made by the S corporation,[152] and the exclusion and basis reduction are both made at the S corporation level.[153] The shareholders' stock basis is not adjusted by the amount of debt discharge income that is excluded at the corporate level. As a result of these rules, if an amount is excluded from the income of an S corporation under this provision, the income flowing through to the shareholders will be reduced (compared to what the shareholders' income would have been without the exclusion). Where the reduced basis in the corporation's depreciable property later results in additional income (or a smaller loss) to the corporation because of reduced depreciation or additional gain (or smaller loss) on disposition of the property, the additional income (or smaller loss) will flow through to the shareholders at that time, and will then result in a larger increase (or smaller reduction) in the shareholder's basis than if this provision were not available. Thus, these rules simply defer recognition of income by the shareholders.

If depreciable real property, the basis of which was reduced under these rules, is disposed of, then for purposes of determining the amount of recapture under Code Sec. 1250: (1) any such basis reduction is treated as a deduction allowed for depreciation, and (2) the determination of what

---

[147] Code Sec. 108(c)(2)(B).
[148] Code Sec. 752.
[149] Code Sec. 705.
[150] Code Sec. 752.
[151] Code Sec. 733.
[152] Code Sec. 1363(c).
[153] Code Sec. 108(d)(7).

would have been the depreciation adjustment under the straight line method is made as if there had been no such reduction. Thus, the amount of the basis reduction that is recaptured as ordinary income is reduced over the time the taxpayer continues to hold the property, as the taxpayer forgoes depreciation deductions due to the basis reduction.[154]

.22 *Code Sec. 179 and Additional First-Year Depreciation*

A taxpayer is entitled to deduct up to $100,000 ($25,000 in tax years beginning after 2007) of amounts paid during any taxable year beginning before 2008 for tangible personal property used in a trade or business.[155] The $100,000 maximum is reduced by the excess of (1) qualifying property placed in service over (2) $400,000.[156] The $100,000 and $400,000 amounts are indexed for inflation. For tax years beginning in 2005, for example, those amounts are $105,000 and $420,000, respectively.[157] The $100,000 ($25,000) limit applies at both the partnership and partner levels.[158] This limitation means that a partnership's total Code Sec. 179 deduction cannot exceed $100,000 and that a partner's individual Code Sec. 179 deduction (taking into account his or her share of the Code Sec. 179 deduction from the partnership and Code Sec. 179 deductions from his or her other activities) may not exceed $100,000. In addition to the $100,000 limit there is an active trade or business income limitation. The Code Sec. 179 deduction cannot create an overall trade or business loss at either the partnership level or the partner level.[159] Neither the partner's nor the partnership's Code Sec. 179 deduction can exceed its net active trade or business taxable income from all sources.[160] The limits are applied first at the partnership level and amounts in excess of only the active trade or business income limit are carried over at the partnership level.[161] There is no carryover provision for amounts exceeding the $100,000 limit.[162]

> ***Observation.*** An allocation of a Code Sec. 179 expense from a partnership to a partner who exceeds the $100,000 limit is in effect an income allocation. This is because even though the deduction is disallowed, partnership interest adjusted basis is reduced which causes more gain or less loss on sale of the interest.

The partnership must, however, reduce its basis in its qualifying assets (for which the election was made) by the entire expense elected.[163] The partnership selects the properties and the apportionment of cost that is subject to any carryover.[164] If the partnership disposes of Code Sec. 179 property while there is a related carryover it is added to the property's basis.[165] Code Sec. 179 deductions that have survived the gamut of the

---

[154] The provision is effective with respect to discharges after December 31, 1992, in taxable years ending after that date.

[155] This amount is reduced if more than $400,000 ($200,000 after 2005) of such property is placed in service during the year.

[156] Code Sec. 179(b)(2).

[157] Rev. Proc. 2004-71, Sec. 3.18, 2004-50 IRB.

[158] Code Sec. 179(d)(8).

[159] Code Sec. 179(b)(3).

[160] For this purpose, net taxable income excludes any suspended deduction or net operating loss carryover but includes Code Sec. 1231 gains (or losses) from sales and interest from working capital. Reg. § 1.179-2(c)(1). Active income requires meaningful participation in management or operations in a Code Sec. 162 activity. Reg. § 1.179-2(c)(6)(i). A passive investor's income does not qualify. Reg. § 1.179-2(c)(6)(ii). Rental activity other than a net-lease arrangement seems to satisfy this test. Reg. § 1.179-1(h)(2), Ex.

[161] Code Sec. 179(b)(3); Reg. § 1.179-2(c)(2).

[162] Reg. § 1.179-3(b)(1).

[163] Reg. §§ 1.179-1(f)(2) and -3(g)(2).

[164] Reg. § 1.179-3(e).

[165] Reg. § 1.179-3(g)(3).

partnership-level limits are tested with the same limits and carryover rules at the partner level. The partner's basis in the partnership interest is reduced by the full amount allocated from the partnership whether or not the partner can deduct or carryover the amount allocated.[166] If the partner disposes of his or her interest while there is a related carryover it is added to his or her basis in the partnership interest.[167] The partnership enters its total Code Sec. 179 deduction on Form 1065, Schedule K, line 9, "Section 179 expense deduction." Each partner's share of the Code Sec. 179 expense is shown on Schedule K-1, line 9, "Section 179 expense deduction."

New property with a MACRS recovery period no longer than 20 years, acquired after May 5, 2003 and before January 1, 2005, is eligible for additional first year depreciation of 50 percent of the property's basis.[168] The basis that the 50 percent is applied to is the basis remaining after reducing it by the Code Sec. 179 expense taken, if any. Regular MACRS depreciation can be taken on the basis remaining after reducing the basis by the Code Sec. 179 expense and the additional first year depreciation. The partnership can elect to take no additional first year depreciation[169] or to take a reduced depreciation percentage of 30 percent of the remaining basis.[170] To make this election, the partnership must attach a statement to its return indicating the class of property for which it is making the election and that the partnership is either (1) electing to deduct the 30 percent special allowance or (2) electing not to claim any special allowance at all for all of that property in that class placed in service during the tax year.[171]

.23 Recovery of Previously Deducted Amounts

Partnership recoveries of amounts deducted in prior years must be separately stated.[172] The separately stated amount is tested for exclusion at the partner level under Code Sec. 111.[173] The partnership enters its total recoveries of previously deducted amounts on Form 1065, Schedule K, line 7, "Other income." Each partner's share of this amount is shown on Schedule K-1, line 7, "Other income." This amount is reported by a partner who is an individual on Form 1040, line 21, only to the extent it reduced taxable income in a prior year.

.24 Alternative Minimum Tax Information

Both individuals and some corporations are subject to the alternative minimum tax (AMT).[174] The base for the AMT is alternative minimum taxable income (AMTI), which is generally equal to taxable income modified by adjustments [175] and preferences.[176] When the AMT exceeds the taxpayer's regular tax liability, the excess is an additional tax. When the reverse is true, a credit is available if the difference is due to a timing adjustment which either accelerated income or deferred deductions and caused an AMT liability in an earlier year.

---

[166] Reg. § 1.179-3(h)(1).

[167] Reg. § 1.179-3(h)(2). There is no partner-level carryover for Code Sec. 179 expenses exceeding the $20,000 limit.

[168] Code Sec. 168(k)(4).

[169] Code Sec. 168(k)(2)(C)(iii).

[170] Code Sec. 168(k)(4)(E).

[171] Instructions to Form 4562 (2003), p. 3.

[172] Reg. § 1.702-1(a)(8)(i).

[173] See *T.A. Frederick v. Commr.*, 101 TC 35, Dec. 49,165 (1993) (S corporation case).

[174] Code Sec. 55.

[175] Code Sec. 56.

[176] Code Sec. 57.

Timing adjustments are amounts of income or deductions which are reported in different years for AMT and regular tax purposes. For example, depreciable basis is generally recovered faster for regular tax than AMT. In earlier years, AMTI will exceed regular taxable income; in later years the reverse is true. Timing adjustments include:

- Depreciation deductions.[177]
- Mining and development costs.[178]
- Long-term contract income.[179]
- AMT net operating loss deduction.[180]
- Amortization of pollution control facilities.[181]

The partnership should report separately to each partner his or her share of AMT income, gain and deduction for each separately stated regular tax amount affected. The partnership may make an election to use the 150 percent declining balance method of depreciation to avoid a depreciation adjustment for personal property placed in service after 1998. Any difference in AMTI and regular taxable income generated by the partnership should result in a different basis in the partnership interest for regular tax and AMT purposes. Therefore, if the partner sells his or her partnership interest which has an AMT/regular tax basis difference, the partner will have this difference reflected in the gain or loss computed for AMT and regular tax purposes.[182]

The partnership enters the total difference between the amount of depreciation for AMT purposes and regular tax purposes as a positive or negative number on Form 1065, Schedule K, line 17a, "Post-1986 depreciation adjustment." Each partner's share of this adjustment is shown on Schedule K-1, box 17. Positive adjustments are added to the partner's share of partnership income for AMT purposes. The reverse is done with negative adjustments. The net difference in any gains or losses from the disposition of property because of different bases for AMT and regular tax are reported on the partnership's Form 1065, Schedule K, line 17b, "Adjusted gain or loss." Each partner's share of the net difference from gains and losses from the disposition of property for AMT and regular tax are shown on Schedule K-1, box 17, "Alternative minimum tax (AMT) items." The partnership's total tax preferences and adjustments, other than depreciation and gain and loss adjustments, are entered on Form 1065, Schedule K, line 17f, "Other AMT items (attach statement)." The partnership must attach a schedule showing each partner's share of these items. Each partner's Schedule K-1 shows his or her share of each of these items on Schedule K-1, box 17, "Alternative minimum tax (AMT) items." The partnership should attach a schedule showing the composition of these items.

---

[177] Code Sec. 56(a)(1).
[178] Code Sec. 56(a)(2).
[179] Code Sec. 56(a)(3).
[180] Code Sec. 56(a)(4).
[181] Code Sec. 56(a)(5).

[182] It is possible that the IRS will object to this analysis. It may take the approach that Code Sec. 56(a)(6) allows AMT basis only for property directly subject to AMT depreciation.

.25 Self-Employment Income

Each general partner has self-employment income for his or her share of the partnership's trade or business income. However, a limited partner's distributive share is not treated as net earnings from self-employment.[183] But guaranteed payments to limited partners for services rendered do constitute earned income for purposes of the self-employment tax. A partner includes his or her share of self-employment income in his or her year with or within which the partnership's year ends.[184] If a partner dies, his or her self-employment income includes only the portion of the year ending on the first day of the month following his or her death.[185] There is net income from self-employment *only* if the partnership is engaged in a trade or business.[186] For this purpose, a partnership engaged in the business of renting real estate appears to be considered engaged in a trade or business.[187] The Worksheet for Figuring Net Earnings (Loss) From Self-Employment treats the taxpayer's rental income as self-employment income only if it is received in the course of the taxpayer's trade or business as a real estate dealer. The partnership enters its total self-employment income on Form 1065, Schedule K, line 14a. It represents the amount of partnership income reported elsewhere in the tax return which should be classified as earned income; thus, the amount reported on this line is *not* treated as additional income by the partners. Each partner's share of the self-employment income is shown on Schedule K-1, box 14.

LLPs and LLCs. Code Sec. 1402(a)(13) excludes a limited partner's share of partnership income from Social Security taxation. Limited partners are subject to Social Security taxation for payments by the partnership to them for services. There is currently no definitive guidance as to who among members of an LLC or LLP is a limited partner for Code Sec. 1402(a)(13) purposes. However, proposed regulations treat a partner in a tax partnership as a limited partner unless he or she (1) has personal liability for the debts of the entity, (2) has the authority to contract on behalf of the entity, or (3) participates more than 500 hours in the partnership during the year.[188] With respect to LLPs, IRS Letter Ruling 200403056 addresses the issue of whether certain retirement payments to the partner of a professional LLP are self-employment income, and rules that they are not if they meet the requirements of Code Sec. 1402(a)(10). The letter ruling does not, however, identify the characteristics that would indicate that a partner in an LLP is a limited partner.

.26 Compensation Paid to Service Partners

Partnership payments to a partner for independent contractor type services which are subject to Code Sec. 707(a) are not subject to withholding. The deduction is not separately stated unless it is specially allocated.

[183] Code Sec. 1402(a)(13).
[184] Reg. § 1.1402(a)-2(e).
[185] Code Sec. 1402(f).
[186] Reg. § 1.1402(a)-1(b).
[187] Code Sec. 1402(a)(1); Reg. § 1.1402(a)-4; see Reg. § 1.1402(c)-(1), even though real estate rental income is generally excluded from the definition of net income from self-employment.
[188] Prop. Reg. § 1.1402(a)-2(h)(2)(iii).

The payment to the partner is reported on a Form 1099 and not the partner's K-1 or Form W-2. A partner who receives payments from the partnership for required partner/employee type services rendered which are determined without regard to partnership profits (guaranteed payments under Code Sec. 707(c)) is not regarded as an employee of the partnership for purposes of withholding. The partnership's deduction for guaranteed payments is not separately stated unless it is specially allocated. The partnership's total guaranteed payments are deducted on Form 1065, line 10. Unlike Code Sec. 707(a) payments, Code Sec. 707(c) payments made to a partner are not reported on Form 1099, but rather appear as a separately stated amount on Schedule K-1, box 4. For more detail related to the deductibility timing, character, and other treatment of payments to partners, see ¶ 704. Compensation paid to any employee other than a partner is subject to withholding for income tax purposes and is also subject to withholding for FICA [189] and FUTA [190] purposes. Liability is imposed under such provisions with respect to "wages." The term "wages" is defined by Code Secs. 3121(a) and 3306(b) as "all remuneration for employment." The definition of wages for purposes of withholding is similar.

> ***LLC Observation.*** Although for nontax purposes LLCs resemble corporations, for federal income tax purposes they are treated as partnerships. The rules described immediately above apply in the same manner to LLCs and LLPs.

.27 Fringe Benefits

Employee fringe benefits generally consist of property or services provided directly or indirectly to or for an employee as a salary or wage supplement. One of the advantages of a C corporation is that it permits an owner/employee of the business to participate in certain fringe benefits provided for employees and receive the same favorable tax benefits. The value of many of these benefits is excluded from the employee's income by specific statutory provisions but the corporation is entitled to deduct the cost. Two major questions related to this subject are:

1. What are fringe benefits?
2. How do partnerships treat fringe benefits?

There is no inclusive definition of "employee fringe benefit." Subchapter K of the Internal Revenue Code, dealing with the tax treatment of partners and partnerships, contains no direct reference to "employee fringe benefits." The general rule is that partners do not qualify for the exclusions afforded certain employee fringe benefits due to the absence of an employer-employee relationship.[191] Absent an official definition of a fringe benefit in the partnership provisions, other sections of the Code must be examined to arrive at a definition of "employee fringe benefits." Such an examination reveals that although there is no statutory definition, the

[189] Code Sec. 3101, et seq.
[190] Code Sec. 3301, et seq.
[191] See the legislative history of Code Sec. 707(c).

legislative history of Code Sec. 1372 does list five employee benefits that Congress considers to be fringe benefits.[192]

1. The former $5,000 death benefit exclusion set forth in former Code Sec. 101(b).
2. The exclusion from income of amounts received by the taxpayer from an accident and health plan as set forth in Code Sec. 105(b), (c) and (d).[193]
3. The exclusion from income of amounts paid by an employer to an accident and health plan as provided in Code Sec. 106.
4. The exclusion of the cost of up to $50,000 in group term life insurance on an employee's life provided by Code Sec. 79.[194]
5. The exclusion from income of meals or lodging furnished for the convenience of the employer set forth in Code Sec. 119.

There are a number of benefits that partnerships and a C corporations can make available to their partners or shareholders, which might be considered fringe benefits for this purpose, that are deductible by the partnership or C corporation but not taxable to the partners or shareholders. These employee benefits are available to partner/partnership arrangements because the applicable code provision treats the partner as an employee.[195] These employee benefits include:

1. Group legal services plans.[196]
2. Employer-provided educational assistance.[197]
3. Child and dependent care assistance.[198]
4. No-additional-cost services.[199]
5. Qualified employee discounts.[200]
6. Working conditions fringe benefits.[201]
7. De minimis fringe benefits.[202]

---

[192] H.R. Rep. No. 826, 97th Cong., 2d Sess. (1982), note 2 at 21 S. Rep. No. 640. 97th Cong., 2d Sess. (1982), note 2 at 22. It should be noted that the list includes only items that are statutorily excluded from the employee's income.

[193] Code Sec. 105(g).

[194] Reg. § 1.79-0.

[195] For purposes of qualified retirement plans, Code Sec. 401(c)(1) treats self-employed individuals with earned income, including partners, as employees. Code Sec. 401(c)(2) defines earned income by reference to Social Security taxes imposed by Code Sec. 1401. This definition of an employee is incorporated by reference in several employee fringe benefit provisions.

[196] Code Sec. 120(d)(1) defines an employee by reference to Code Sec. 401(c)(1). The partnership is considered an employer of any partner/ employee. Code Sec. 120(d)(2).

[197] Code Sec. 127(c)(2) defines an employee by reference to Code Sec. 401(c)(1). The partnership is considered an employer of any partner/ employee. Code Sec. 127(c)(3). However, not more than 5% of the cost of these benefits may be provided for the group of greater-than-5% partners. Code Sec. 127(b)(3).

[198] Code Sec. 129(e)(3) defines an employee by reference to Code Sec. 401(c)(1). The partnership is considered an employer of any partner/ employee. Code Sec. 129(e)(4). However, not more than 25% of amounts spent for dependent care assistance can be provided for greater-than-5% partners. Code Sec. 129(d)(4).

[199] Code Sec. 132(b). Reg. § 1.132-1(b)(1) provides that "any partner who performs services for the partnership is considered employed by the partnership."

[200] Code Sec. 132(c). Reg. § 1.132-1(b)(1) provides that "any partner who performs services for the partnership is considered employed by the partnership."

[201] Code Sec. 132(d). Reg. § 1.132-1(b)(2)(ii) provides that "any partner who performs services for the partnership is considered employed by the partnership."

[202] Code Sec. 132(e). Reg. § 1.132-1(b)(4) defines an employee as any recipient of a fringe benefit.

8. On-premises athletic facilities.[203]

9. Qualified retirement plans.[204]

There is no definition of an employee under Code Sec. 125 for cafeteria plans. Proposed Regulations [205] include present and former employees as employees but specifically reject the deferred compensation [206] definition. This seems to exclude partners working for the partnership.

In addition, partners are not employees for purposes of the qualified transportation fringe benefit.[207] It is unclear whether or not partners are employees with respect to the qualified moving expense or the qualified retirement service fringe benefits.[208] With respect to qualified retirement service fringe benefits, the related definition of a qualified plan indirectly indicates that a partner would be considered an employee.[209]

The 1982 legislative history also explains Congress' impression of how a partnership treats a fringe benefit for tax purposes.

> Under the bill, the treatment of fringe benefits of any person owning more than 2% of the stock of the corporation will be treated in the same manner as a partner in a partnership. Thus, for example, amounts paid for medical care of a shareholder-employee *will not be deductible by the corporation (by reason of Sections 1363(b)(2) and 703(a)(2)(E)),* will be deductible by that individual only to the extent personal medical expenses will be allowed as an itemized deduction under Section 213. However, similar amounts paid by the corporation on behalf of shareholders owning 2% or less of the corporation may be deducted as a business expense.[210]

The 1982 legislative history created confusion as to how a partnership is to treat fringe benefits. Traditionally, however, payment of fringe benefits for partners have been treated as a nondeductible deemed distribution which reduces the partner's basis in his or her interest and which the partner treats as if the partner paid directly. If there is a deemed money distribution, partnership interest basis has no net change. Assuming that the insured partner's share of income is the same as his share of the insurance expense, it is first increased by the income not offset by the disallowed expense and then reduced by the deemed distribution.

Revenue Ruling 91-26 clarified the IRS's view of the correct treatment of fringe benefits provided to service partners.[211] The fringe benefits are treated as additional compensation to the service partner. Thus, such payments are treated as guaranteed payments under Code Sec. 707(c) which are treated by the service partner as ordinary earned income. Since the service partner is treated as if he or she then paid for the fringe benefits directly, the partner may be entitled to deduct them on his or her personal return (*e.g.*, as self employed medical insurance, medical expenses, etc.).

---

[203] Code Sec. 132(h)(5). Reg. § 1.132-1(b)(3) provides that "any partner who performs services for the partnership is considered employed by the partnership."

[204] Code Secs. 401-420.

[205] Prop. Reg. § 1.125-1, Q&A 4.

[206] Code Sec. 401(c).

[207] Reg. § 1.132-9, Q. 24.

[208] Code Sec. 132(g), (m).

[209] Code Secs. 132(m)(3), 219(g)(5), 401(a)(1), and 401(c)(1).

[210] Emphasis added. H.R. Rep. No. 826, 97th Cong., 2d Sess., 21 (1982); S. Rep. No. 640, 97th Cong., 2d Sess., 22 (1982). It is likely that the emphasized portion of the text should have been deleted. The conjunction "and" is needed and the explanation of the Subchapter S Revision Act of 1982 (P.L. 97-354) prepared by the Staff of the Joint Committee on Taxation (Sept. 8, 1982) omits this language.

[211] Rev. Rul. 91-26, 1991-1 CB 184.

.28 Code Sec. 212(3)—Tax Return Preparation Expenditures

A partnership must file a return for each taxable year beginning with the year in which it receives income or incurs expenditures allowable as deductions, unless the partnership is excluded from filing because it has no income, deductions, or credits for federal income tax purposes for the year.[212] In addition, a partnership that elects out of the partnership rules of Subchapter K does not have to file a partnership return, except that the partnership must file a return containing the information required by Reg. § 1.761-2(b)(2)(i).[213] Finally, a partnership that derives all of its income from the holding or disposition of tax-exempt obligations or shares in a regulated investment company that pays exempt-interest dividends and that the IRS has excepted from the partnership reporting requirements does not have to file a partnership return.[214]

The partnership return must be filed on or before the fifteenth day of the fourth month following the end of the partnership's taxable year.[215] An automatic three month extension is allowed upon filing an application.[216] The return must be filed in the district in which the partnership has its principal office or place of business within the United States.[217]

The return must be signed by a partner, and any partner's signature is prima facie evidence of his or her authority to sign the return on behalf of the partnership.[218] The return must state (1) the partnership's gross income and allowable deductions; (2) the names and addresses of all partners; and (3) the amount of each partner's distributive share of partnership income, loss, and so forth.[219]

The failure of a partnership to file a timely return subjects it to a penalty unless the partnership can show that the failure was due to reasonable cause. The penalty equals $50, multiplied by the number of persons who were partners in the partnership during any part of its taxable year, multiplied by the number of months (or fraction thereof) during which the failure to file continues (but not in excess of five months). The penalty is assessed against the partnership, and the deficiency procedures in Code Secs. 6211 and 6216 are inapplicable.[220]

The legislative history of the penalty provisions of Code Sec. 6698 states that the reasonable cause test is intended to protect "small partnerships" (those with ten or fewer partners) from the penalty as long as each partner reports his or her share of partnership income and deductions.[221] The IRS has announced that any domestic partnership with ten or fewer partners that comes within the exceptions provided in Code Sec.

---

[212] Reg. § 1.6031(a)-1(a)(3).
[213] Reg. § 1.6031(a)-1(c)(1)(i).
[214] Reg. § 1.6031(a)-1T(a)(3)(ii).
[215] Reg. § 1.6031-1(e)(2).
[216] Temp. Reg. § 1.6081-2T.
[217] Reg. § 1.6031-1(e)(1).
[218] Code Sec. 6063.
[219] Reg. § 1.6031-1(a)(1).
[220] Code Sec. 6698; see *F.E. Bader v. United States*, ClsCt, 86-1 USTC ¶ 9432, 10 ClsCt 78. In *Christian Laymen in Partnership, Ltd. v. United States*, DC Okla., 90-1 USTC ¶ 50,042, a district court held that the entire Code Sec. 6698 penalty must be paid before a refund suit can be brought. A partial payment (one month of the penalty) does not satisfy the "divisible tax" rule. The significance of this holding is magnified because the ordinary deficiency procedures are inapplicable to this penalty. Effectively, the partners must pay the entire penalty asserted before they are entitled to their day in court.

[221] See HR Rep. No. 1445, 95th Cong., 2d Sess., 75 (1978).

6231(a)(1)(B) (part of the partnership level audit adjustment procedures [222]) will be considered to have met the reasonable cause test and will not be subject to Code Sec. 6698 if it establishes that all partners timely reported their full shares of all partnership items. If a partnership consisting of ten or fewer partners does not satisfy these requirements, it may show other reasonable cause for failure to file a timely return.

A partnership must furnish to its partners a copy of the information shown on the partnership's return "as may be required by regulations." Temporary Regulations issued in 1988 require the partnership to furnish to each person who was a partner at any time during the taxable year a written statement including the partner's distributive share of partnership income, gain, loss, deduction or credit, and any other information required by the form or accompanying instructions.[223] The statement must be furnished on or before the due date for the partnership return (determined with regard to extensions).[224] The partnership must assume that a nominee (other than a clearing agency) is actually the beneficial owner of the interest if the nominee fails to furnish to the partnership the requisite statement containing information about the beneficial owner.[225]

In the case of an individual, the miscellaneous itemized deductions for any taxable year are allowed only to the extent that the aggregate of such deductions exceeds two percent of adjusted gross income.[226] Itemized deductions include an individual's deduction under Code Sec. 212(3) for amounts paid or incurred "in connection with the determination, collection, or refund of any tax."[227] An individual's share of a pass-through entity's expenditures are disallowed to the extent they would have been disallowed under the itemized deduction rule if he or she paid them directly.[228] The regulations list "tax counsel fees and appraisal fees" as examples of itemized deductions allowed by Code Sec. 212(3) [229] and therefore subject to the restrictions limiting itemized deductions. The regulations also provide an example of a partnership's generic Code Sec. 212 expense being passed through to its partners.[230] Finally, the regulations require that fees incurred for "income tax return preparation or income tax advice" by a nonpublicly offered regulated investment company (RIC), which is another type of pass-through entity, are to be passed through as itemized deductions. Most practitioners, however, take the position that the costs of preparing a partnership's Form 1065 are not incurred "in connection with the determination, collection, or refund of any tax." They are deducted as the partnership's accounting fees related to its business or its other activities.[231]

---

[222] Rev. Proc. 84-35, 1984-1 CB 509.

[223] Code Sec. 6031(b); Temp. Reg. § 1.6031(b)-1T(a)(1) and (3).

[224] Temp. Reg. § 1.6031(b)-1T(b).

[225] Temp. Reg. § 1.6031(b)-1T(a)(2).

[226] Code Sec. 67(a).

[227] Code Sec. 63(d) defines an itemized deduction. Code Sec. 67 limits them to the excess of 2% of adjusted gross income. Code Sec. 212(3) allows an individual's deduction for his or her income tax related expenditures.

[228] Code Sec. 67(c)(1).

[229] Temp. Reg. § 1.67-1T(a)(1)(iii).

[230] Temp. Reg. § 1.67-2T(b)(2). The example states only that they "are expenses to which section 212 applies."

[231] See Rev. Rul. 92-29, 1992-1 CB 20, in support of this position. It allows expenses in preparing business-related schedules as business deductions.

The partnership enters its nonseparately stated items of income on Form 1065, lines 1-7, and its nonseparately stated deductions on lines 9-20. The net nonseparately stated income is entered on line 22 and on Form 1065, Schedule K, line 1. Each partner's share of this nonseparately stated income is shown on Schedule K-1, box 1.

.29 Income Attributable to Domestic Production Activities

For tax years beginning after December 31, 2004, Code Sec. 199 allows a deduction of up to 9 percent of a taxpayer's income from domestic production activities. The actual percentage allowed is 3 percent for years beginning in 2005 and 2006, 6 percent for 2007 through 2009, and 9 percent for 2010 and later years. The deduction is calculated by multiplying the applicable percentage above by the lesser of (1) the qualified domestic production activities income of the taxpayer for the taxable year, or (2) taxable income for the taxable year (or adjusted gross income, if the taxpayer is an individual).[232] However, the amount of the deduction for any taxable year can not exceed 50 percent of the W-2 wages of the taxpayer for the taxable year.[233]

In general, domestic production activities under Code Sec. 199 include any lease, rental, license, sale, exchange, or other disposition of tangible personal property which was manufactured, produced, grown, or extracted by the taxpayer in whole or in significant part within the United States. Also allowed as domestic production activities are film, electricity, natural gas, or potable water produced by the taxpayer in the United States, construction performed in the United States, and engineering or architectural services performed in the United States for construction projects in the United States.[234]

In the case of partnerships and other pass-through entities, Code Sec. 199 will be applied at the partner (or other owner) level, under rules to be promulgated by the Secretary of the Treasury.[235] However, Code Sec. 199 specifically requires that partners will be allocated W-2 wages from the partnership (for purposes of the W-2 wage limitation) equal to the lesser of:

1. The partner's allocable share of partnership wages, or

2. 2 times 9 percent of the partnership's qualified domestic production activities income allocated to the partner for the taxable year.[236]

The deduction, with one adjustment, is allowed in computing alternative minimum taxable income.[237] However, the deduction is not allowed in computing income from self-employment.[238]

---

232 Code Sec. 199(a)(1), (d)(2).
233 Code Sec. 199(b)(1).
234 Code Sec. 199(c)(4).
235 Code Sec. 199(d)(1).
236 Code Sec. 199(d)(1)(B).
237 Code Sec. 199(d)(6).
238 Code Sec. 1402(a)(16).

¶ 806 Reporting Taxable Income for Large Partnerships/ LLCs

Special rules allow electing large partnerships to compute their taxable incomes using a simplified method. Under this method, the Schedule K-1 received by the partners/LLC members is structured much like Form 1099, which investors are accustomed to receiving. The partnership/LLC's income, loss, and credits are to be reported by the partner/member in the following categories:

1. Taxable income or loss from passive loss limitation activities,
2. Taxable income or loss from other activities,
3. Net capital gain (or net capital loss)—
   a. To the extent allocable to passive loss limitation activities, and
   b. To the extent allocable to other activities,
4. Tax-exempt interest,
5. Applicable net AMT adjustment separately computed for—
   a. Passive loss limitation activities, and
   b. Other activities,
6. General credits,
7. Low-income housing credit,
8. Rehabilitation credit,
9. Foreign income taxes,
10. The credit for producing fuel from a nonconventional source, and
11. Other items to the extent that the Secretary determines that the separate treatment of such items is appropriate.[239]

A large partnership/LLC will file Form 1065-B, rather than Form 1065. As implied from the above categories, all capital gains and losses are netted at the partnership/LLC level. Net long-term capital gain (loss) is divided between passive and other activities, and reported separately to the partners/members. In contrast, any excess of net short-term capital gain over net long-term capital loss is consolidated with the partnership's other taxable income and is not separately reported.

Similarly, electing large partnerships consolidate general credits and separately report them to partners/members as a single item. Partners and LLC members report their shares as a current year general business credit. Other credits are claimed by the partnership/LLC itself, rather than being passed through to partners or LLC members. For example, the refundable credit for federal tax paid on fuels and the refund or credit for tax paid on

[239] Code Sec. 772(a).

undistributed capital gains of a regulated investment company or a real estate investment trust are taken by the partnership and thus are not separately reported to partners. The partnership/LLC also recaptures the investment credit and low-income housing credit.

.01 *Eligibility*

To be eligible, a partnership or LLC must have had at least 100 partners during the *preceding* taxable year.[240] Thus, a partnership/LLC may not elect to use the simplified rules in its first tax year. In determining the number of partners or LLC members in the prior year, *service* partners are not counted.[241] For this purpose, a service partner is any partner/member who must perform substantial services in connection with the entity's activities, or who has performed such services in past years. Indeed, *service partnerships* or LLCs are not allowed to elect to be treated as large partnerships. A service partnership/LLC is one for which "substantially all" of the partners/members are:

1. Individuals performing substantial services in connection with the entity's activities,
2. Personal service corporations with the owner-employees performing the services,
3. Retired partners/members who had previously performed the services prior to retirement, or
4. Spouses of any of the above.

Commodities partnerships—those whose principle business consists of trading in commodities (other than inventory as defined in Code Sec. 1221(a)(1)) or in commodity options, futures or forwards—are also ineligible to elect large partnership status.

.02 *Making the Election*

The election to be treated as a large partnership is made by filing Form 1065-B, rather than Form 1065. The election is applicable beginning with the first year in which Form 1065-B is filed, and remains in effect for all future years as long as the partnership or LLC continues to have 100 or more partners or members.

240 Code Sec. 775(a)(1)(A).

241 Code Sec. 775(b)(1).

Chapter 9

Partners Take into Account the Partnership's Income or Loss

¶ 901 Introduction

After the partnership has assembled its income and deductions in the prescribed format, as described in Chapters 7 and 8, every partner is required to take into account his or her share of each item. The income/loss allocation rules consist of two major subdivisions:

1. Discretionary tax allocations of partnership generated income and loss; and

2. Mandatory tax allocations of gain or loss built into partnership property which must be allocated to the partners who owned the property when the built-in gain or loss arose.

Discretionary tax allocations are treated under Code Sec. 704(b). Mandatory tax allocations must comply with Code Sec. 704(c). Under Code Sec. 704(b), the partnership may allocate any item of taxable income or loss in any manner the partners desire so long as the tax allocation reflects the manner in which they are sharing the economics that generated the related tax item. Under Code Sec. 704(c), the partnership must allocate built-in gain or loss to the partners who suffer or benefit from the property's appreciation or depreciation according to one of the methods prescribed by the regulations.

With respect to Code Sec. 704(b) tax allocations, the partnership can market tax allocations which must be accepted as valid by the IRS if it satisfies a series of requirements specified by the regulations. These allocations are generally referred to as "safe harbor" allocations. If the partnership does not satisfy the requirements necessary for a safe harbor allocation, it must be able to prove that its tax allocation is consistent with the related economic allocation of income or loss from the same source. These tax allocations are generally referred to as "facts and circumstances" allocations or "partner's interest in the partnership" allocations. There is a safe harbor allocation if the partnership agreement has "substantial economic effect" or is "deemed to be in accordance with the partner's economic interest in the partnership" as defined by the regulations, otherwise there is a facts and circumstances allocation.

In addition to these two major types of taxable income and loss allocations, there are also rules governing allocations of income and loss:

- Upon transfer of a partnership interest;
- In family partnerships;
- Upon depreciation recapture; and
- Credits.

¶ 902 Allocating the Partnership Income in Accordance with the Partnership Agreement

If the partnership agreement's allocation has "substantial economic effect," a partner's share is determined simply by reference to the allocation of the various items of income and deduction made by the partnership agreement.[1] The agreement is considered to retroactively include all changes made by the due date of the partnership tax return (excluding extensions).[2] If, however, the agreement's allocation of any item lacks "substantial economic effect," such item is allocated according to the various partners' economic interests, if any, in the item of income or deduction.[3] Due to the imprecision of this facts-and-circumstances analysis, as well as the Commissioner's presumption of correctness in determining its

[1] Code Sec. 704(a).
[2] Code Sec. 761(c).
[3] Code Sec. 704(b)(2).

meaning, it is imperative that the agreement have substantial economic effect or its equivalent if the partners wish to be certain of the validity of their tax allocations if their economic arrangement is hazy.

.01 Substantial Economic Effect

The "substantial economic effect" test is intended to ensure that if a tax deduction allowed for a partnership expense involves a possible economic risk of loss to the partnership itself, then that tax deduction is allocated to the specific partner who is most likely to bear the economic burden of that loss. It is also intended to ensure that taxable income is allocated only to partners most likely to enjoy the potential of the economic benefit from the transaction generating the taxable income.

In many situations none of the partners risk the potential economic loss associated with a deduction. For example, when an expense is paid with nonrecourse borrowed funds, neither the partnership nor any partner bears personal responsibility for repayment; the lender has the economic risk in the event that the partnership's business will not generate the funds to repay the loan. In these "nonrecourse debt deduction" situations, the partnership's allocation is not tested under the "substantial economic effect" test. The allocation, however, may be deemed to be in accordance with the various partners' economic interests under one of the alternative tests described below in ¶ 902.02.

The "substantial economic effect" test has two parts:

1. Does the agreement have "economic effect"?

2. If the agreement has "economic effect," is that economic effect "substantial"?

Economic effect. The regulations provide that an agreement has economic effect if it (1) has economic effect under the general rule, (2) meets the alternate test for economic effect, or (3) has economic effect equivalence. These three rules govern the allocation of deductions that arise from contributions and those allowed because of borrowed funds for which one or more partners has personal liability for repayment. These are deductions for which members in the partnership will bear the economic loss associated with the tax deductions if the venture is a failure. These three rules also govern the allocation of taxable income other than reversals of nonrecourse debt deductions.

General rule. The general rule requires that three tests be met. The partnership agreement or local law must provide that:[4]

[4] Reg. § 1.704-1(b)(2)(ii)(*b*).

1. The partners' capital accounts must be "properly" maintained in accordance with the accounting rules contained in the regulations (Code Sec. 704(b) accounting);

2. Liquidating distributions must be made in accordance with the capital accounts that have been properly maintained; and

3. Partners with a deficit in their capital accounts must be required, either by local law or the partnership agreement, to restore such amount to the partnership upon liquidation of their interests.

LLC Observation. An LLC member is not, as a general rule, responsible under local law for additional capital contributions. Therefore, in the case of an LLC there must generally be an explicit unlimited capital account make-up provision to qualify for economic effect under the general rule.

The general rule is intended to require that the partners who are allocated tax deductions that involve a possible economic loss to the partnership itself suffer the potential economic burden of the loss. It also ensures that partners who are allocated income enjoy the potential economic benefit from such allocation. The capital accounts are the scoreboard that keeps track of the partners' interests in the book value of the partnership's assets. If there is no agreement to the contrary, limited partners are not responsible for restoring a negative capital account balance to zero upon liquidation of the partnership. As long as all limited partners have positive capital accounts, the first two requirements will ensure that the economic result approximately matches the tax allocation. This is because increased or decreased positive balances in the partners' capital accounts represent an increased or reduced interest in the book value of the partnership's assets. The third requirement primarily affects a limited partner's loss allocation, which would cause or increase a negative capital balance. The first two requirements alone theoretically result in a reduced claim on the book value of the partnership's assets by the partner claiming the deduction, including limited partners. Once a limited partner has a zero capital account, however, he or she theoretically has no further claim on the partnership's assets. Requiring that the limited partner reduce his or her capital account for additional tax deductions allocated to that partner would have no economic effect unless the partner is required to repay the deficit. The general rule, however, takes an all or nothing approach. All three requirements must be satisfied. Even though the absence of a deficit capital account make-up requirement is economically important only if there is a deficit capital account, the regulations conclude that the general rule is not satisfied unless there is an unlimited deficit capital account make-up requirement that will apply when there is a deficit capital account. The regulations require that without a deficit capital account make-up provision in the partnership agreement, the tax deduction is properly allocated to the partners actually bearing the economic risk of the book accounting loss.[5]

> ***LLC Observation.*** If the agreement requires Code Sec. 704(b) accounting and liquidating distributions in accordance with capital accounts, when members' capital accounts are positive, the facts and circumstances analyses under the "partners economic interest in the partnership" test is likely to conclude that although there is not a "safe harbor" allocation under Code Sec. 704(b), because of the absence of an unlimited deficit capital account make-up provision, the tax allocation is valid. This is because it is allocated to the partner who has the economic benefit or burden related to the tax allocation. However, when a loss allocation creates a negative capital, two possibilities are present. First, if the total LLC debt exceeds the aggregate basis of the recurring property, the deduction is a nonrecourse debt deduction unless one of the members is personally liable for the debt. Nonrecourse deductions cannot have substantial economic effect and safe harbor allocations are made in accordance with rules discussed in ¶ 902.02. Second, the validity of a deficit capital account make-up agreement is a matter of state law. The rules of each state must be separately consulted.

The "alternate economic effect" test, however, as discussed immediately below, provides that if the agreement satisfies the first two of the "economic effect" tests of the general rule, but the agreement lacks an unlimited deficit capital account make-up provision, then the allocation "will be considered to have economic effect . . . to the extent such allocation does not cause or increase a deficit balance in such partner's capital account" in excess of the partner's contribution requirement. The regulations contain additional requirements for the alternate test such as a "qualified income offset" requirement which are discussed in the next section.[6]

An essential requirement for satisfying both the general rule's economic effect test and the alternate economic effect test is that capital accounts must be "properly" maintained. The regulations contain almost 10 pages of small type defining how capital accounts are to be "properly" maintained.[7] In general, they require that the partners' contributions and distributions be recorded in their "book" capital accounts at fair market value, net of liabilities, at the time of the contribution or distribution.[8] In addition to *requiring* that contributed and distributed property be revalued

[5] Reg. § 1.704-1(b)(1)(ii).

[6] Reg. § 1.704-1(b)(2)(ii)(*d*).

[7] Reg. § 1.704-1(b)(2)(iv).

[8] Reg. § 1.704-1(b)(2)(iv)(*d*) and (*e*).

for proper capital account maintenance, the regulations *allow* the partnership to revalue the partnership's other property at any time money or other property is either contributed to, or distributed from, the partnership. This revaluation, which is reflected in the partners' *book* capital accounts only, may be by agreement among the partners or any other reasonably reliable method. The book accounting required for a safe harbor Code Sec. 704(b) tax allocation is discussed in ¶ 902.04.

"Alternate" economic effect test. Provided the partnership agreement meets the general rule's first and second requirements for economic effect, if:

1. A partner to whom an allocation is made *is not required to restore his or her deficit capital account balance* or is obligated to restore only a limited dollar amount of such deficit balance, and

2. The *partnership agreement* contains a special capital account adjustment provision and a "*qualified income offset*,"

then an allocation to the partner will be considered as having economic effect to the extent that the allocation *does not cause or increase a deficit balance in such partner's capital account* (in excess of any deficit balance that the partner is obligated to restore) as of the end of the partnership tax year to which such allocation relates.[9]

Capital account adjustments. In order to determine whether the partner's capital account will fall below the partner's limited deficit capital account make-up requirement, special adjustments must be made to the capital account. The partner's capital account must first be reduced by:

1. Certain expected allowable depletion deductions;[10]

2. Allocations of loss and deduction that, as of the end of such year, are expected to be made to such partner under Code Sec. 704(e)(2) (family partnership rules), 706(d) ("varying interest") rules, and certain gain or loss deemed to occur under Code Sec. 751;[11] and

3. Distributions that, as of the end of such year, are "*reasonably expected" to be made to such partner* (to the extent that such distributions are expected to exceed offsetting increases to the partner's capital account that are also reasonably expected to be made).[12]

---

[9] Reg. § 1.704-1(b)(2)(ii)(d)(1).
[10] Reg. § 1.704-1(b)(2)(iv)(*k*).
[11] Reg. § 1.704-1(b)(2)(ii)(d)(5).
[12] Reg. § 1.704-1(b)(2)(ii)(d)(6).

The purposes of adjustment 3 above to the partner's capital account in determining whether the allocation will cause or increase a deficit capital account in excess of the partner's limited deficit capital account make-up requirement is to prevent the partnership from delaying a distribution to the year following a loss year, so that the partner will have sufficient capital to absorb a current year loss allocation.

> ***Example 9-1.*** At year end, George Doug has a capital account of $25 (and basis in excess of $50) and the partnership is required under the partnership agreement to distribute to him $25 at the beginning of the following year (the partnership is expected to be able to meet its requirement). George's share of partnership losses is $25. Under the partnership agreement, George is not required to make up a negative capital account. The partnership may not allocate the loss to George (even though at the time of the allocation he has sufficient capital to cover) because the required distribution is reasonably expected to be made and *prior to the allocation of the loss* George's capital account must be reduced by the amount of the distribution, even though the distribution is to occur in the following year.

Qualified income offset provision. The partnership agreement must provide that a partner who "unexpectedly" receives an adjustment, allocation, or distribution that results in a deficit capital account in excess of the partner's limited deficit capital account make-up requirement will be allocated items of *gross* income and gain in an amount and manner sufficient to eliminate such deficit as quickly as possible. This is known as a "qualified income offset" provision in the agreement.[13]

Economic effect equivalence. Allocations made to a partner that do not otherwise have economic effect under the general rule or the alternate test, but somehow produce economic results which are identical to those that would have been produced if it had complied with the stated rules, are deemed to have economic effect. This is tested by a deemed liquidation at year end. If the economic results to a partner would be the same as those under the prescribed rules, that partner's allocation has economic effect.[14]

Substantiality. The drafters of the regulations realized that it would be possible for the partnership agreement to comply with the economic effect tests, but, through timing and/or character allocations, it would still be possible for an allocation to reduce the partners' individual overall tax burdens without affecting their economic arrangement with respect to their claims on the partnership's results of operations.

The regulations provide that:

> the economic effect of an allocation is not substantial if, at the time the allocation (or allocations) becomes part of the partnership agreement, (1) the

[13] Reg. § 1.704-1(b)(2)(ii)(d)(3).

[14] Reg. § 1.704-1(b)(2)(ii)(i).

> after-tax consequences of at least one partner may, in present value terms, be enhanced compared to such consequences if the allocation (or allocations) were not contained in the partnership agreement, and (2) there is a strong likelihood that the after-tax consequences of no partner will, in present value terms, be substantially diminished compared to such consequences if the allocation (or allocations) were not contained in the partnership agreement.[15]

Shifting allocations. Even though the partnership agreement may satisfy all elements of economic effect, it is clear that this careful mixing of income types results in no actual economic effect.[16]

> ***Example 9-2.*** Anne and Bob Hevrdjes make up an equal partnership which incurs $100 of long-term capital gains and $100 of ordinary income during the year. Anne has a large capital loss carryover from prior years and partner Bob has a large net operating loss carryover. Rather than allocating each item of income equally between them, the partnership agreement is modified for this year to allocate the capital gains to Anne and the ordinary income to Bob.
>
> With or without the provision allocating long-term capital gains and ordinary income to separate partners, each has a $100 increase to his or her capital account. If the allocation were valid, it would reduce each of the partners' current tax liability when compared with the results of allocating half of each type of income to each of them.

Transitory allocations. Allocations may lack substantiality because they merely shift tax consequences, as in the previous example, or because they are transitory in nature. Transitory allocations are allocations of income or deductions in an earlier year with an allocation of reasonably expected offsetting results in later years. Specifically, the regulations[17] provide that an allocation is not substantial if there is a strong likelihood that:

1. The organized allocation will be substantially offset by an offsetting allocation; and

2. The total tax liability of the partners for the years of the original and offsetting allocations is less than if the allocations were not made.

The regulations add that if an allocation has the effect of offsetting an earlier allocation, the combination will be presumed to lack substantiality unless the taxpayer can prove that there was not a strong likelihood that the offset would occur.

---

[15] Reg. § 1.704-1(b)(2)(iii)(*a*).
[16] Reg. § 1.704-1(b)(2)(iii)(b).
[17] Reg. § 1.704-1(b)(2)(iii)(c).

In addition, the regulations treat an original and offsetting allocation as substantial if at the point of the original allocation there is a strong likelihood that the offsetting allocation will not in "large part" be made within five years after the original allocation.[18]

> ***Example 9-3.*** Oak and Pyle are equal partners in the OP general partnership. Both partners expect to have the same marginal tax bracket for several years, but Oak has a NOL carryforward that will expire at the end of OP's second tax year (2001). To permit Oak to take advantage of the NOL carryforward, the partners agree to allocate all the partnership net taxable income to Oak for 2000 and 2001. Beginning in 2002, future partnership net taxable loss is to be allocated to Oak, and future partnership net income is allocated to Pyle, until the allocation of income to Oak in the first two years is offset. The partnership agreement requires properly maintained capital accounts, distributions to be made in accordance with capital accounts, and restoration of deficit capital accounts to satisfy the economic effect test. The partnership's income is primarily from highly rated corporate bonds that are expected to produce sufficient income in 2002 through 2006 to offset the allocation of partnership income to Oak in the first two years. Although the allocations have economic effect, the effect is transitory, making the allocations insubstantial. The predictable income from the bonds creates a strong likelihood that the net increases and decreases to the partners' capital accounts will be the same at the end of 2006 with or without the allocations and the partners' total taxes will be reduced by the allocations.[19]

Allocations of depreciation in early years with a chargeback of an offsetting amount of gain to the partner on disposition of the asset is an example of what would be a transitory allocation except that it is specifically exempted from this prohibition against transitory allocations. In this case, the regulations create a nonrebuttable presumption that the partnership's property is worth its book value.[20] The property's value is deemed to decrease by the amount of the depreciation allowable and an offsetting gain allocation is deemed not to be reasonably expected.

[18] Reg. § 1.704-1(b)(2)(iii)(c)(2).
[19] Reg. § 1.704-1(b)(5), Ex. (8)(ii).
[20] Reg. § 1.704-1(b)(2)(iii)(*c*)(2). Its value is presumed to decrease by any depreciation claimed.

EQUITY AND RECOURSE DEBT DEDUCTIONS

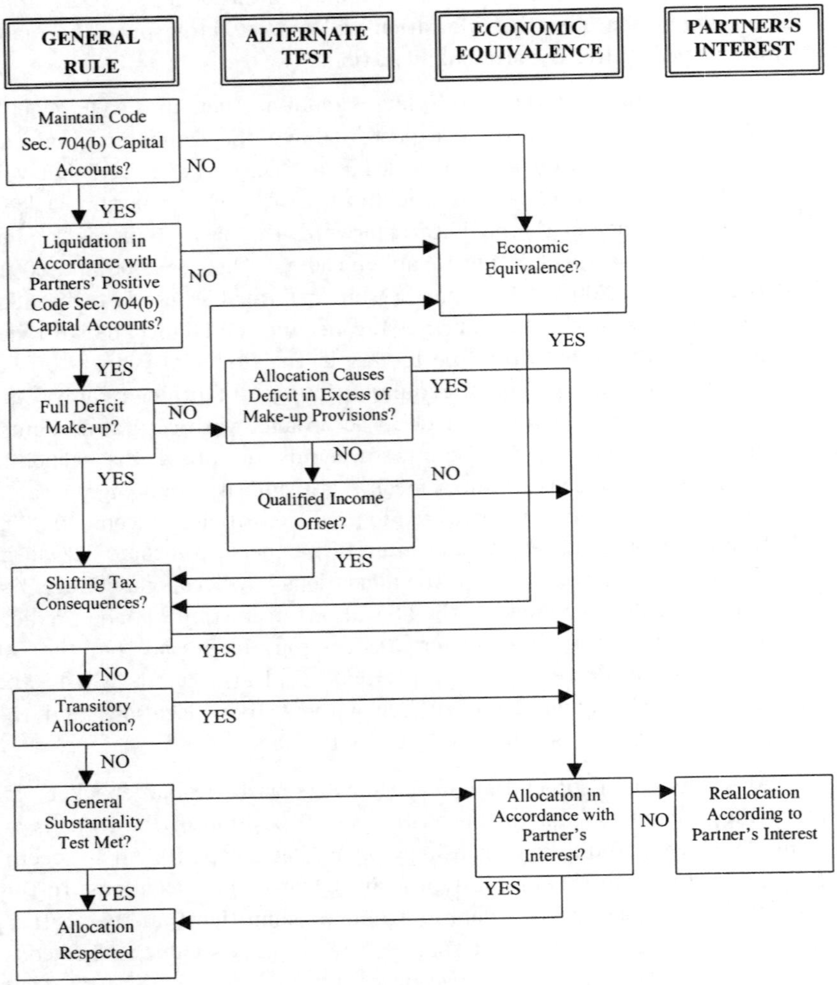

GENERAL RULE | ALTERNATE TEST | ECONOMIC EQUIVALENCE | PARTNER'S INTEREST

Maintain Code Sec. 704(b) Capital Accounts? NO → Economic Equivalence? YES ↓

Liquidation in Accordance with Partners' Positive Code Sec. 704(b) Capital Accounts? NO → Economic Equivalence? YES ↓

Full Deficit Make-up? NO → Economic Equivalence?; NO → Allocation Causes Deficit in Excess of Make-up Provisions? YES ↓

Allocation Causes Deficit in Excess of Make-up Provisions? YES → Allocation in Accordance with Partner's Interest?; NO ↓ Qualified Income Offset?

Qualified Income Offset? NO → Allocation in Accordance with Partner's Interest?; YES → Shifting Tax Consequences?

Economic Equivalence? YES → Shifting Tax Consequences?

Shifting Tax Consequences? YES → Allocation in Accordance with Partner's Interest?; NO ↓

Transitory Allocation? YES → Allocation in Accordance with Partner's Interest?; NO ↓

General Substantiality Test Met? → Allocation in Accordance with Partner's Interest?; YES ↓

Allocation in Accordance with Partner's Interest? NO → Reallocation According to Partner's Interest; YES → Allocation Respected

Allocation Respected

.02 *Allocations Deemed to Be in Accordance with the Partners' Interests in the Partnership—Nonrecourse Deductions and Minimum Gain*

The regulations are predicated upon the assumption that allocations of losses and deductions attributable to nonrecourse debts cannot have substantial economic effect. The regulations assume that there can be no economic effect upon the partners because it is the lender who bears the risk that the partnership will lose the borrowed funds.[21] The regulations provide a test for determining when the allocation will be *deemed* to be

[21] Reg. § 1.704-2(b)(1).

made in accordance with the partners' economic interests in the partnership. If this test is met, the agreement will have the functional equivalent of "substantial economic effect."[22] While there are other requirements that must be satisfied, the most fundamental is that the deductions derived from nonrecourse financing must be allocated in a manner reasonably consistent with the allocation of other significant items of income or deductions that have met the economic effect test. In short, the nonrecourse debt deductions must be allocated in a manner reasonably consistent with other material items of income or deductions generated by recourse debt or contributed equity.

> ***LLC Observation.*** Nonrecourse debt is defined as a debt for which "no partner or related person bears the economic risk" as defined by the regulations.[23] In the case of an LLC, the partners are protected from most creditors by operation of the state's LLC statute. Therefore, unless a partner assumes an economic risk under Reg. § 1.752-2 with respect to an LLC's liabilities all debt financed deductions must satisfy the nonrecourse debt deduction rules described in this section.

The allocation of deductions attributable to nonrecourse debt will be *deemed* to be in accordance with the partners' interests if the following conditions are met:[24]

1. Equity and recourse deductions have economic effect. This condition is met if either (a) the three mechanical tests of economic effect are satisfied (proper maintenance of capital accounts, liquidating distributions made in accordance with these properly maintained positive capital accounts, and, upon liquidation of a partner's interest, a deficit capital account make-up requirement), or (b) the alternate test is satisfied (the first two of the three mechanical tests are met and deduction allocations causing deficit capital accounts are not allowed);

2. The partnership agreement provides for the allocation of nonrecourse deductions and is reasonably consistent with allocations of deductions, from the same source, which do have substantial economic effect;

3. The partnership agreement states that if there is a reduction in the amount of minimum taxable gain, the partners who have taken deduction allocations attributable to nonrecourse debts must also be allocated items of income equal to their reduced share of the minimum gain; and

---

[22] *Id.*

[23] Reg. §§ 1.704-2(b)(3) and 1.752-1(a)(2).

[24] Reg. § 1.704-2(e).

4. All other (other than nonrecourse) material allocations and capital account adjustments under the partnership agreement are valid.

Minimum gain. Naturally, the first question to be answered is: when is a partnership allocating nonrecourse deductions? Unless the partnership is allocating nonrecourse deductions, the substantial economic effect rules governing the validity of the partnership's allocations govern. It is only when the partnership is allocating nonrecourse debt deductions that this special rule must be satisfied. This special rule, governing the validity of the partnership's allocations of nonrecourse debt deductions, is not a rule that is in addition to those governing the allocation of other partnership deductions. It is a substitute rule that, alone, governs the validity of nonrecourse debt deductions. A partnership is considered to be incurring deductions arising from borrowed funds (recourse and nonrecourse), in general, when the securing property's basis (or "book" value, if the two differ) is less than the secured debt. The regulations create a new concept, "minimum gain," based upon the regulations under Code Sec. 1001.[25] Under these regulations, upon the disposition of property secured by nonrecourse indebtedness, the debtor's amount realized includes the entire outstanding balance of the nonrecourse indebtedness, regardless of the fair market value of the underlying property. Thus, the Code Sec. 704(b) regulations recognize that once the book value of the property serving as collateral for a nonrecourse loan falls below the outstanding balance of that loan, the borrower will, at some point in the future, recognize gain at least equal to the excess of the debt over the book value of the securing property.[26] Thus, if nonrecourse deductions cause a partner's capital account to fall below zero by this amount, there will be a guaranteed amount of future income (minimum gain) at least sufficient to restore the capital account to zero. No partner's capital deficit can exceed his or her share of partnership minimum gain (in absolute value) unless the partner is obligated to restore deficit capital balances to zero.

The amount of nonrecourse deductions which are allocated under this rule for a partnership year equals the net increase in "partnership minimum gain," reduced by distributions of the proceeds of nonrecourse debt that is distributed.[27] Partnership minimum gain is the total gain which would be realized for all property subject to the nonrecourse debt.[28] Nonrecourse deductions consist first of depreciation, but if they exceed the partnership depreciation they consist of a pro rata share of other partnership losses, deductions and other nondeductible noncapitalized expenditures.

[25] Reg. § 1.1001-2. See in particular Examples 7 and 8.

[26] Abandonment or foreclosure of the property securing the nonrecourse loan is treated as a sale of such property to the nonrecourse lender for the outstanding balance of the debt.

[27] Reg. § 1.704-2(c).

[28] Reg. § 1.704-2(d) and (b)(2).

Example 9-4. *Nonrecourse deductions.* Sam Selan and Tom Thompson each contribute $100,000 to form ST Partnership. ST purchases a building for $800,000 with the $200,000 cash and a $600,000 *nonrecourse* note. The partnership agreement provides for all three tests of economic effect. The partnership has taken tax and book depreciation on the building equal to $450,000 so that it now has an adjusted basis and book value of $350,000. Other than depreciation deductions, the partnership's taxable income has equaled its deductible expenses. All annual allocations of the depreciation have been charged to Sam. The capital accounts at the end of the current year are as follows:

	Sam	*Tom*
Capital account, beginning	$100,000	$100,000
Depreciation	(450,000)	0
Capital account, ending	*$(350,000)*	*$100,000*

Assuming, as the regulations do, that the property's value decreases by the amount of the partnership's book depreciation, the first $200,000 of depreciation is the amount for which the partnership, and indirectly, the partners, bears the economic burden of loss. Sam bears the risk of the first $100,000 of assumed decrease in the property's value. If the property is sold for $700,000, the creditor is paid $600,000, Tom is entitled to receive his ending capital account which is the remaining $100,000, and Sam is entitled to his ending capital account of zero. Because of Sam's deficit capital account make-up requirement he also bears the economic risk of the second $100,000 of depreciation deductions. If the partnership sells the property for its presumed value of $600,000, all of the partnership's money is paid to the creditor. Upon liquidation, Sam is required to contribute his deficit capital account of $100,000 to the partnership which is distributed to Tom in satisfaction of his ending capital account. Sam has suffered the risk that the property will devalue by the depreciation deductions allocated to him.

Any risk of decrease in value due to depreciation beyond $200,000 is borne by the creditor. This is also the point at which the amount of nonrecourse debt equals the basis of the securing property. If the debt remains at $600,000, any further basis reductions will first create and then increase the amount by which nonrecourse debt exceeds the basis of the recurring property. The yearly increase of this excess is partnership minimum gain and results in the partnership being treated as generating nonrecourse deductions in the amount of such increase. In this example, $450,000 of depreciation has been allocated to Sam since the property was purchased. If the property is sold for its book value (the regulation's presumed fair market value), the partnership would pay the creditor $350,000 and have no cash left to distribute to the partners. Under the partnership agreement, Sam is obligated to restore

$100,000 of his capital account to the partnership. Upon liquidation the partnership will distribute these funds to Tom, who has a $100,000 ending capital account when the partnership is liquidated. Sam's deficit capital account in excess of $100,000 is meaningless. In this example, if ST were liquidated at the end of the current year and Sam were actually liable to restore $350,000 to ST, $250,000 of the restoration would lack real economic content. Of $350,000 contributed to the partnership by Sam, Tom would get $100,000 to satisfy his positive capital account balance. The other $250,000 presumably would be returned to Sam. The third requirement of economic effect, it follows, would not be satisfied. The requirement to restore a negative capital account balance which is to be paid to partners with positive capital account balances cannot be met. This is because $250,000 of Sam's recontribution is not distributed to recourse creditors or to partners with a positive capital balance. There are none. The $250,000 contribution would be returned to Sam who does not have a positive account balance. Thus, the third of the mechanical tests for economic effect cannot be met, even though the partnership agreement contains a deficit capital account make-up provision.

The allocation of $250,000 cannot have substantial economic effect. In addition, the allocations of nonrecourse deductions cannot be considered to have economic effect under the "alternate test."[29] The regulations, however, allow a safe harbor allocation for nonrecourse deductions if the requirements described herein are satisfied. They are deductions that are *deemed* to have been allocated in accordance with the partners' economic interests in the partnership.

Minimum gain chargeback provision requirement. The minimum gain chargeback rules apply whenever there is a decrease in aggregate partnership minimum gain during the year. Partnership minimum gain decreases as reductions occur in the amount by which the aggregate partnership nonrecourse liability exceeds the aggregate adjusted tax basis of the encumbered property. Minimum gain chargeback is the allocation of income required by a net decrease in partnership minimum gain. Such allocations cannot have economic effect because the gain merely offsets the nonrecourse deduction previously claimed by the partnership. Thus, to avoid impairing the economic effect of other allocations, allocations under a minimum gain chargeback must be made to the partners that either were allocated nonrecourse deductions or received distributions or proceeds attributable to a nonrecourse debt.[30]

Thus, if there is a net reduction in the amount of partnership minimum gain, the partners who have taken deduction allocations attributable

[29] Reg. § 1.704-1(b)(2)(ii)(*d*).

[30] Reg. § 1.704-2(b)(2).

to nonrecourse debts must also be allocated items of income equal to their share of the reduction in minimum gain.[31]

However, a partner is not subject to minimum gain chargeback requirements to the extent his or her share of the net decrease in partnership minimum gain is caused by a guarantee, refinancing, or other change in the debt instrument causing it to become partially or wholly recourse debt or partner nonrecourse debt and the partner bears the economic risk of loss for the newly guaranteed, refinanced, or otherwise changed liability.[32]

In addition, a partner is not subject to the minimum gain chargeback requirement to the extent he or she contributes capital that is used to repay the nonrecourse liability or is used to increase the basis of the property subject to the nonrecourse debt.[33]

Minimum gain can be reduced by the cost of capital improvements and payment of debt principal. Surprising results can occur where cash or recourse liabilities are used to repay nonrecourse debt or make capital improvements.

Example 9-5. *Debt payment.* Ross Rindell and Sean Stein are partners in the RS Partnership and each has an equal interest in all items of income, gain, loss and deduction other than a special allocation of all depreciation to Ross. During all relevant years Sean has a positive capital account. The partnership agreement satisfies the first two requirements of economic effect, includes a qualified income offset, and a minimum gain chargeback provision. Ross's negative capital account and the partnership minimum gain at the end of Year 1 are $35,000 (the debt principal of $75,000 over the adjusted basis/book value of $40,000 of the property securing the nonrecourse debt). The partnership makes its first payment of $25,000 on the debt principal in February of the following year, Year 2. During Year 2, income equals deductions (excluding $10,000 of depreciation). Therefore, as of the end of Year 2, if there had been no debt repayment, Ross's deficit capital account would have remained equal to the minimum gain of $45,000. Depreciation of $10,000 is allocated, per the partnership agreement, to Ross.

After the debt payment has been made the capital accounts of the partners will not be affected. However, the partnership minimum gain has decreased $15,000 from negative $35,000 to $20,000. The current minimum gain is the excess of the remaining partnership debt of $50,000 over the remaining $30,000 book value/basis of the partnership property securing the debt. The partnership must—pursuant to its minimum gain chargeback provision—allocate $15,000 of income to Ross. When there is insufficient partnership income to allocate Ross

[31] Reg. § 1.704-2(f)(1).
[32] Reg. § 1.704-2(f)(2).
[33] Reg. § 1.704-2(f)(3).

the entire $15,000 chargeback, it carries forward to succeeding years.[34] Here, assuming the partnership has gross income of at least $15,000, it is allocated to Ross.

Identifying nonrecourse deductions where the partnership has both recourse and nonrecourse indebtedness. Nonrecourse deductions equal the increase in partnership minimum taxable gain, which in turn is the excess of the total partnership nonrecourse indebtedness over the basis/book value of all property securing such debt. When the property is secured by both recourse and nonrecourse debt, the nonrecourse debt rules apply only when the partnership is deducting amounts due to nonrecourse financing. If there is more than one debt secured by a single property an allocation of the basis/book value is necessary. Where the debts are of equal priority, the basis/book value is allocated according to their relative amounts. If they are of unequal priority the basis/book value is allocated first to the superior debt, then any excess is allocated to the inferior debt. The regulations allocate the property's basis to the liability with the higher priority first.[35] Thus, where the nonrecourse debt is junior to the recourse debt, nonrecourse deductions will be considered taken after those generated by contributions but before recourse loan deductions. The liability with the least priority under local law is, in effect, considered to be the first source of the deductions generated by debt.

Example 9-6. *A* is the general partner of the ABC limited partnership. The partnership agreement allocates income or loss other than depreciation equally and all depreciation to *C*. The partnership purchases improved real estate for $600,000. The terms are:

Cash paid with contributed funds	$200,000
Funds borrowed from third party (Recourse debt secured by realty with a first-trust deed)	100,000
Seller financing (Nonrecourse debt secured by the realty with a subordinated trust deed).	300,000
Property's basis	*$600,000*

In the first year, operating cash expenses are equal to operating income, and there is a net taxable loss of $100,000 due to depreciation. No principal payments are made toward the debts. As the property's year-end basis ($500,000) exceeds the securing debt ($400,000), no minimum gain is created. The tax loss is not a nonrecourse debt deduction. The partnership is bearing the risk of loss and the partnership agreement's allocation of the depreciation deduction must have substantial economic effect or it is allocated according to the facts-and-circumstances test.

In the second year, the operating results are the same. Again, because no minimum gain is created, the partnership is assumed to be incurring losses of its invested equity. The partnership agreement's

[34] Reg. § 1.704-2(f)(6) and (j)(2)(iii).

[35] Reg. §§ 1.704-2(d)(2)(ii) and 1.752-2.

allocation of the depreciation must have substantial economic effect to avoid a facts-and-circumstances allocation.

In the third year, the operating results are again the same as in the first two years. There is a $100,000 taxable loss. The outstanding debt of $400,000 now exceeds the property's basis of $300,000 by $100,000.

Debt		$400,000
Cost	$600,000	
Depreciation	(300,000)	
Adjusted basis		(300,000)
Debt exceeding basis		*$100,000*

Is it the recourse or nonrecourse debt which is exceeding basis? The regulations allocate the property's basis first to the most superior debt (for example, a first-trust deed), then to other debts in their declining order of priority. The liability with the least priority is allocated the property's basis last.[36] In this example, the third-party recourse debt is superior to the nonrecourse seller financing.

Total basis	$300,000
Less basis allocated to superior debt	(100,000)
Basis allocated to inferior nonrecourse debt	200,000
Inferior nonrecourse debt	(300,000)
Nonrecourse debt deduction (minimum gain)	*$100,000*

Since it is the third year in which "minimum gain" of $100,000 appears, the allocation of the depreciation deduction cannot have substantial economic effect. The depreciation deduction will be deemed to have been allocated according to the partners' interests in the partnership if it is allocated in a "manner that is reasonably consistent with allocations, which have substantial economic effect, of some other significant partnership item attributable to the property securing the nonrecourse liabilities of the partnership" and the other requirements for safe harbor nonrecourse debt deduction allocations are satisfied.[37] In this example, if *C* is allocated the depreciation deduction in year three, this nonrecourse debt deduction is consistent with allocations of deductions from the same source that have economic effect, namely depreciation for years one and two.

In the fourth and fifth years, if the results of operations are the same, the partnership's taxable losses are nonrecourse debt deductions. This is because each year the excess of the nonrecourse debt over the basis allocated to it, the minimum gain, grows larger. The basis is decreasing by the amount of the depreciation deduction and, in our example, the nonrecourse debt is remaining constant.

In the sixth year, if the results of operations continue to remain constant, the loss will not be a nonrecourse debt deduction and its

[36] Reg. § 1.704-2(d)(2).

[37] Reg. § 1.704-2(e)(2).

allocation by the partnership agreement must have substantial economic effect. This is because all the nonrecourse debt has been allocated to previous deductions. There is a nonrecourse debt deduction only to the extent of an *increase* in minimum gain. Minimum gain equals nonrecourse debt's excess over the basis allocated to it.

Example 9-7. The Cynthia and Samuel General Partnership is formed with equal contributions of $100,000 each, and all items of income, deduction, loss, and gain are shared equally except depreciation, which is allocated to Samuel. Cynthia is required to restore a negative capital account, however, Samuel is required to restore a maximum of $100,000. The first two requirements of economic effect are satisfied and the partnership agreement contains a qualified income offset and a minimum taxable gain chargeback provision with respect to Samuel. The partnership purchases a building for $1,000,000, using the contributions and $800,000 of borrowed funds. A bank has made a recourse loan of $600,000 which has priority over nonrecourse seller financing of $200,000. Excluding $100,000 of depreciation per year, income equals deductions.

Year 1's allocation of a net depreciation loss of $100,000 to Samuel is considered as having economic effect under the alternate test.[38]

Year 2's allocation has the same result.[39]

In Year 3, a minimum taxable gain is created. Debt ($800,000) exceeds basis/book value ($1,000,000 cost basis less $300,000 depreciation = $700,000) by $100,000.[40] Nonrecourse deductions are $100,000 because the economic burden of the deduction is borne by the creditor alone. The basis/book value of the partnership property is first allocated to the bank's superior priority debt of $600,000. Therefore, the $100,000 in remaining basis/book value is exceeded by $200,000 of nonrecourse debt.[41] The third year's allocation does not have economic effect. However, because the four requirements of Reg. § 1.704-2 are satisfied, the allocations are deemed to be in accordance with the partners' interests in the partnership. The requirements are satisfied as follows:

1. Equity and recourse deductions have economic effect. This condition is satisfied if either the three mechanical tests of economic effect are satisfied (proper maintenance of capital accounts, liquidating distributions made in accordance with these properly maintained positive capital accounts, and, upon liquidation of a partner's interest, an unlimited deficit capital account make-up requirement), or the alternate test is satisfied

[38] Reg. § 1.704-1(b)(2)(ii)(*d*).
[39] Reg. § 1.704-1(b)(2)(ii)(*c*)(*2*) and (*d*).
[40] Reg. § 1.704-2(d)(1).
[41] Reg. § 1.704-2(d)(2).

(the first two of the three mechanical tests are met and deduction allocations causing deficit capital account in excess of the partner's limited deficit capital account make-up requirement are not allowed);

2. The allocation of nonrecourse deductions is reasonably consistent with allocations of deductions, from the same source, which do have substantial economic effect;

3. The partnership agreement states that if there is a reduction in the amount of minimum taxable gain, the partners who have taken deduction allocations attributable to nonrecourse debt must be allocated items of income equal to their share of the minimum gain; and

4. All other (other than nonrecourse) material allocations and capital account adjustments under the partnership agreement are valid.

Comprehensive examples of nonrecourse debt deduction allocation.

Example 9-8.[42] *Comprehensive example—Basic fact pattern.* Unless otherwise provided, the following facts are assumed. LP, the limited partner, and GP, the general partner, form a limited partnership to acquire and operate a commercial office building. LP contributes $180,000, and GP contributes $20,000. The partnership obtains an $800,000 nonrecourse loan and purchases the building (on leased land) for $1,000,000. The nonrecourse loan is secured only by the building, and no principal payments are due for five years. The partnership agreement provides that:

- GP will be required to restore any deficit balance in GP's capital account following the liquidation of GP's interest (as set forth in Reg. § 1.704-1(b)(2)(ii)(b)(3)); and
- LP will not be required to restore any deficit balance in LP's capital account following the liquidation of LP's interest.

The partnership agreement contains the following provisions required by Reg. § 1.704-2(e):

- A qualified income offset (as defined in Reg. § 1.704-1(b)(2)(ii)(d)); a minimum gain chargeback (in accordance with Reg. § 1.704-2(f));
- A provision that the partners' capital accounts will be determined and maintained in accordance with Reg. § 1.704-1(b)(2)(ii)(b)(1); and

[42] Reg. § 1.704-2(m), Ex. 1.

- A provision that distributions will be made in accordance with partners' positive capital account balances (as set forth in Reg. § 1.704-1(b)(2)(ii)(b)(2)).

In addition, as of the end of each partnership taxable year, the items described in Reg. § 1.704-1(b)(2)(ii)(d)(4), (5), and (6) are not reasonably expected to cause or increase a deficit balance in LP's capital account.

The partnership agreement provides that, except as otherwise required by its qualified income offset and minimum gain chargeback provisions, all partnership items will be allocated 90% to LP and 10% to GP until the first time when the partnership has recognized items of income and gain that exceed the items of loss and deduction it has recognized over its life, and all further partnership items will be allocated equally between LP and GP. Finally, the partnership agreement provides that all distributions, other than distributions in liquidation of the partnership or of a partner's interest in the partnership, will be made 90% to LP and 20% to GP until a total of $200,000 has been distributed, and thereafter all the distributions will be made equally to LP and GP. In each of the partnership's first two taxable years, it generates rental income of $95,000, operating expenses (including land lease payments) of $10,000, interest expense of $80,000, and a depreciation deduction of $90,000, resulting in a net taxable loss of $85,000 in each of those years. The allocations of these losses—90% to LP and 10% to GP—have substantial economic effect.

	LP	*GP*
Capital account on formation	$180,000	$20,000
Less: net loss in Years 1 and 2	(153,000)	(17,000)
Capital account at end of Year 2	*$27,000*	*$3,000*

In the partnership's third taxable year, it again generates rental income of $95,000, operating expenses of $10,000, interest expense of $80,000, and a depreciation deduction of $90,000, resulting in a net taxable loss of $85,000. The partnership makes no distributions.

Alternative 1. *Calculation of nonrecourse deductions and partnership minimum gain.* If the partnership were to dispose of the building in full satisfaction of the nonrecourse liability at the end of the third year, it would realize $70,000 of gain ($800,000 amount realized less $730,000 adjusted tax basis). Because the amount of the partnership minimum gain at the end of the third year (and the net increase in partnership minimum gain during the year) is $70,000, there are partnership nonrecourse deductions for that year of $70,000, consisting of depreciation deductions allowable with respect to the building of $70,000. Pursuant to the partnership agreement, all partnership items comprising the net taxable loss of $85,000, including the $70,000 nonrecourse deduction, are allocated 90% to LP and 10% to

GP. The allocation of these items, other than the nonrecourse deductions, has substantial economic effect.

	LP	*GP*
Capital account at end of Year 2	$27,000	$3,000
Less: net loss in Year 3		
(without nonrecourse deductions)	(13,500)	(1,500)
Less: nonrecourse deductions in Year 3	(63,000)	(7,000)
Capital account at end of Year 3	*$(49,500)*	*$(5,500)*

The allocation of the $70,000 nonrecourse deduction satisfies requirement (2) of Reg. § 1.704-2(e) because it is consistent with allocations having substantial economic effect of other significant partnership items attributable to the building. Because the remaining requirements of Reg. § 1.704-2(e) are satisfied, the allocation of nonrecourse deductions is deemed to be in accordance with the partners' interests in the partnership. At the end of the partnership's third taxable year, LP and GP's shares of partnership minimum gain are $63,000 and $7,000, respectively. Therefore, LP is treated as obligated to restore a deficit capital account balance of $63,000, so that in the succeeding year LP could be allocated up to an additional $13,500 of partnership deductions, losses, and Code Sec. 705(2)(B) items that are not nonrecourse deductions.[43] Even though this allocation would increase a deficit capital account balance, it would be considered to have economic effect under the alternate economic effect test.[44] If the partnership were to dispose of the building in full satisfaction of the nonrecourse liability at the beginning of the partnership's fourth taxable year (and had no other economic activity in that year), the partnership minimum gain would be decreased from $70,000 to zero, and the minimum gain chargeback would require that LP and GP be allocated $63,000 and $7,000, respectively, of the gain from that disposition.

Alternative 2. *Illustration of reasonable consistency requirement.* Assume that instead of the allocation above, all partnership items are allocated 90% to the limited partner and 10% to the general partner until the partnership generates minimum gain. The partnership agreement provides that all nonrecourse deductions of the partnership will be allocated equally between LP and GP. Furthermore, at the time the partnership agreement is entered into, there is a reasonable likelihood that over the partnership's life it will realize amounts of income and gain significantly in excess of amounts of loss and deduction (other than nonrecourse deductions). The equal allocation of excess income and gain has substantial economic effect.

[43] Reg. § 1.704-2(g)(1).

[44] Reg. § 1.704-1(b)(2)(ii)(*d*).

	LP	*GP*
Capital account on formation	$180,000	$20,000
Less: net loss Years 1 and 2	(153,000)	(17,000)
Less: net loss in Year 3 (without nonrecourse deductions)	(13,500)	(1,500)
Less: nonrecourse deductions in Year 3	(35,000)	(35,000)
Capital account at end of Year 3	$*(21,500)*	$*(33,500)*

The allocation of the $70,000 nonrecourse deduction equally between LP and GP satisfies the reasonable consistency requirement because the allocation is consistent with allocations which will have substantial economic effect of other significant partnership items attributable to the building. Because the remaining requirements of a safe harbor nonrecourse debt deduction allocation are satisfied, the allocation of nonrecourse deductions is deemed to be in accordance with the partners' interests in the partnership. The allocation of the nonrecourse deductions—75% to LP and 25% to GP (or in any other ratio between 90% to LP/10% to GP and 50% to LP/50% to GP)—also would satisfy the reasonably consistent requirement.[45]

Alternative 3. *Allocation of nonrecourse deductions that fails reasonable consistency requirement.* Assume instead that the partnership agreement provides that LP will be allocated 99%, and GP 1%, of all nonrecourse deductions of the partnership. Allocating nonrecourse deductions this way does not satisfy the reasonably consistent requirement because the allocations are not reasonably consistent with allocations having substantial economic effect of any other significant partnership item attributable to the building. Therefore, the allocation of nonrecourse deductions will be disregarded, and the nonrecourse deductions of the partnership will be reallocated according to the partners' overall economic interests in the partnership, determined under Reg. § 1.704-1(b)(3)(ii).[46]

Alternative 4. *Pro rata capital contributions to pay down nonrecourse debt.* At the beginning of the partnership's fourth taxable year, LP contributes $144,000 and GP contributes $16,000 of additional capital to the partnership, which the partnership immediately uses to reduce the amount of its nonrecourse liability from $800,000 to $640,000. In addition, in the partnerships's fourth taxable year, it generates rental income of $95,000, operating expenses of $10,000, interest expense of $64,000 (consistent with the debt reduction), and a depreciation deduction of $90,000, resulting in a net taxable loss of $69,000. If the partnership were to dispose of the building in full satisfaction of the nonrecourse liability at the end of that year, it would realize no gain ($640,000 amount realized less $640,000 adjusted tax basis). Therefore, the amount of partnership minimum gain at the end of the year is zero, which represents a net decrease in

45 Reg. § 1.704-2(m), Ex. 1(ii).

46 *Id.*

partnership minimum gain of $70,000 during the year. LP and GP's shares of this net decrease are $63,000 and $7,000 respectively, so that at the end of the partnership's fourth taxable year, LP and GP's shares of partnership minimum gain are zero. Although there has been a net decrease in partnership minimum gain, LP and GP are not subject to a minimum gain chargeback.[47]

	LP	*GP*
Capital account at end of Year 3	$(49,500)	$(5,500)
Plus: contribution	144,000	16,000
Less: net loss in Year 4	(62,100)	(6,900)
Capital account at end of Year 4	*$32,400*	*$3,600*
Minimum gain chargeback carryforward	$ 0	$ 0

Alternative 5. *Loans of unequal priority.* Assume the basic facts except that instead of an $800,000 nonrecourse debt, the building the partnership acquired is secured by a $700,000 nonrecourse loan and a $100,000 recourse loan, subordinate in priority to the nonrecourse loan. The $700,000 adjusted basis of the building at the end of the partnership's third taxable year is allocated to the nonrecourse liability (with the remaining $30,000 allocated to the recourse liability) so that if the partnership disposed of the building in full satisfaction of the nonrecourse liability at the end of that year, it would realize no gain ($700,000 amount realized less $700,000 adjusted tax basis).[48] Therefore, there is no minimum gain (or increase in minimum gain) at the end of the partnership's third taxable year. If, however, the $700,000 nonrecourse loan were subordinate in priority to the $100,000 recourse loan, the first $100,000 of adjusted tax basis in the building would be allocated to the recourse liability leaving only $630,000 of the adjusted basis of the building to be allocated to the $700,000 nonrecourse loan. In that case, the balance of the $700,000 nonrecourse liability would exceed the adjusted tax basis of the building by $700,000, so that there would be $70,000 of minimum gain (and a $70,000 increase in partnership minimum gain) in the partnership's third taxable year.[49]

Alternative 6. *Nonrecourse borrowing; distribution of proceeds in subsequent year.* The partnership obtains an additional nonrecourse loan of $200,000 at the end of its fourth taxable year, secured by a second mortgage on the building, and distributes $180,000 of this cash to its partners at the beginning of its fifth taxable year. In addition, in its fourth and fifth taxable years, the partnership again generates rental income of $95,000, operating expenses of $10,000, interest expense of $80,000 ($100,000 in the fifth taxable year reflecting the interest paid on both liabilities) and a depreciation deduction of $90,000, resulting in a net taxable loss of $85,000 ($105,000 in the

[47] Reg. § 1.704-2(f)(3).
[48] Reg. § 1.704-2(d)(2).
[49] *Id.*

fifth taxable year reflecting the interest paid on both liabilities). The partnership has distributed its $5,000 of operating cash flow in each year ($95,000 of rental income less $10,000 of operating expense and $80,000 of interest expense) to LP and GP at the end of each year. If the partnership were to dispose of the building in full satisfaction of both nonrecourse liabilities at the end of its fourth taxable year, the partnership would realize $360,000 of gain ($1,000,000 amount realized less $640,000 adjusted tax basis). Thus, the net increase in partnership minimum gain during the partnership's fourth taxable year is $290,000 ($360,000 of minimum gain at the end of the fourth year less $70,000 of minimum gain at the end of the third year). Because the partnership did not distribute any of the proceeds of the loan it obtained in its fourth year during that year, the potential amount of partnership nonrecourse deductions for that year is $290,000. If the partnership had distributed the proceeds of that loan to its partners at the end of its fourth year, the partnership's nonrecourse deductions for that year would have been reduced by the amount of that distribution because the proceeds of that loan are allocable to an increase in partnership minimum gain.[50] Because the nonrecourse deductions of $290,000 for the partnership's fourth taxable year exceed its total deductions for that year, all $180,000 of the partnership's deductions for that year are treated as nonrecourse deductions, and the $110,000 excess nonrecourse deductions are treated as an increase in partnership minimum gain in the partnership's fifth taxable year under Reg. § 1.704-2(c).

	LP	*GP*
Capital account at end of Year 3 (including cash flow distributions)	$(63,000)	$(7,000)
Plus: rental income in Year 4	85,500	9,500
Less: nonrecourse deductions in Year 4	(162,000)	(18,000)
Less: cash flow distributions in Year 4	(4,500)	(500)
Capital account at end of Year 4	*$(144,000)*	*$(16,000)*

At the end of the partnership's fourth taxable year, LP and GP's shares of partnership minimum gain are $225,000 and $25,000, respectively (because the $110,000 excess of nonrecourse deductions is carried forward to the next year). If the partnership were to dispose of the building in full satisfaction of the nonrecourse liabilities at the end of its fifth taxable year, the partnership would realize $450,000 of gain ($1,000,000 amount realized less $550,000 adjusted tax basis). Therefore, the net increase in partnership minimum gain during the partnership's fifth taxable year is $200,000 ($110,000 deemed increase plus the $90,000 by which minimum gain at the end of the fifth year exceeds minimum gain at the end of the fourth year ($450,000 less $360,000)). At the beginning of its fifth year, the partnership distrib-

[50] Reg. § 1.704-2(c) and (h)(1).

utes $180,000 of the loan proceeds (retaining $20,000 to pay the additional interest expense). The first $110,000 of this distribution (an amount equal to the deemed increase in partnership minimum gain for the year) is considered allocable to an increase in partnership minimum gain for the year.[51] As a result, the amount of nonrecourse deductions for the partnership's fifth taxable year is $90,000 ($200,000 net increase in minimum gain less $110,000 distribution of nonrecourse liability proceeds allocable to an increase in partnership minimum gain), and the nonrecourse deductions consist solely of the $90,000 depreciation deduction allowable with respect to the building. As a result of the distributions during the partnership's fifth taxable year, the total distributions to the partners over the partnership's life equal $205,000. Therefore, the last $5,000 distributed to the partners during the fifth year will be divided equally between them under the partnership agreement. Thus, out of the $185,000 total distribution during the partnership's fifth taxable year, the first $180,000 is distributed, 90% to LP and 10% to GP, and the last $5,000 is divided equally between them.

	LP	*GP*
Capital account at end of Year 4	$(144,000)	$(16,000)
Less: net loss in Year 5 (without nonrecourse deductions)	(13,500)	(1,500)
Less: nonrecourse deductions in Year 5	(81,000)	(9,000)
Less: distribution of loan proceeds	(162,000)	(18,000)
Less: cash flow distribution in Year 5	(2,500)	(2,500)
Capital account at end of Year 5	*$(403,000)*	*$(47,000)*

At the end of the partnership's fifth taxable year, LP's share of partnership minimum gain is $405,000 ($225,000 share of minimum gain at the end of the fourth year plus $81,000 of nonrecourse deductions for the fifth year and a $99,000 distribution of nonrecourse liability proceeds that are allocable to an increase in minimum gain) and GP's share of partnership minimum gain is $45,000 ($25,000 share of minimum gain at the end of the fourth year plus $9,000 of nonrecourse deductions for the fifth year and an $11,000 distribution of nonrecourse liability proceeds that are allocable to an increase in minimum gain).

Alternative 7. *Debt priority—Partner guarantee of nonrecourse debt.* In the third year, LP and GP personally guarantee the "first" $100,000 of the $800,000 nonrecourse loan (*i.e.*, only if the building is worth less than $100,000 will they be called upon to make up any deficiency). Only $630,000 of the adjusted tax basis of the building is allocated to the $700,000 nonrecourse portion of the loan because the collateral will be applied first to satisfy the $100,000 guaranteed portion, making it superior in priority to the remainder of the loan.[52]

[51] Reg. § 1.704-2(h).

[52] Reg. § 1.704-2(d)(2).

On the other hand, if LP and GP were to guarantee the "last" $100,000 (*i.e.*, if the building is worth less than $800,000 they will be called upon to make up the deficiency up to $100,000), $700,000 of the adjusted tax basis of the building would be allocated to the $700,000 nonrecourse portion of the loan because the guaranteed portion would be inferior in priority to it.

Alternative 8. *Partner nonrecourse debt.* Assume instead that the $800,000 loan is made by LP, the limited partner. The $800,000 obligation does not constitute a nonrecourse liability of the partnership for purposes of Reg. § 1.704-2, the allocation rules, because LP, a partner, bears the economic risk of loss for that loan.[53] Instead, the $800,000 loan constitutes a partner nonrecourse debt. In the partnership's third taxable year, partnership minimum gain would have increased by $70,000 if the debt were a nonrecourse liability of the partnership. Thus, there is a net increase of $70,000 in the minimum gain attributable to the $800,000 partner nonrecourse debt deduction for the partnership's third taxable year, and $70,000 of the $90,000 depreciation deduction from the building for the partnership's third taxable year constitutes a partner nonrecourse deduction with respect to the debt.[54] This partner nonrecourse deduction must be allocated to LP, the partner that bears the economic risk of loss for that liability.[55]

Alternative 9. *Nonrecourse debt and partner nonrecourse debt of differing priorities.* As in Alternative 8, above, the $800,000 loan is made to the partnership by LP, the limited partner, but the loan is a purchase money loan that "wraps around" a $700,000 underlying nonrecourse (also secured by the building) not issued by LP to an unrelated person in connection with LP's acquisition of the building. Under these circumstances, LP bears the economic risk of loss with respect to only $100,000 of the liability.[56] Therefore, the $800,000 liability is treated as a $700,000 nonrecourse liability of the partnership and a $100,000 partner nonrecourse debt (inferior in priority to the $700,000 liability) of the partnership for which LP bears the economic risk of loss.[57] $70,000 of the $90,000 depreciation deduction realized in the partnership's third taxable year constitutes a partner nonrecourse deduction that must be allocated to LP.[58]

Example 9-9. *Comprehensive example.* Tammy Yong and Pam Zahn form YZ partnership, each contributing $100,000 in cash. YZ purchases a commercial building with a market value of $800,000 using $200,000 cash and $600,000 proceeds from a nonrecourse note. The partnership agreement states that all allocations will be properly reflected in the capital accounts and that all liquidating proceeds are, throughout the term of YZ, to be distributed according to the partners'

---

53 Reg. § 1.704-2(b)(4).
54 See Reg. § 1.704-2(i)(3).
55 See Reg. § 1.704-2(i)(1).
56 See Reg. § 1.752-2(f), Ex. 6.
57 See Reg. § 1.704-2(d).
58 See Reg. § 1.704-2(i)(2).

capital accounts. The agreement does not provide for the restoration of partners' negative capital account balances to the partnership. Tammy is to receive all cost recovery deductions relating to the building.

In Year 1, YZ has no net income or loss exclusive of book depreciation and cost recovery deductions of $80,000, computed using the straight-line method over 10 years.

	Tammy	*Pam*
Capital account, formation	$100,000	$100,000
Cost recovery	(80,000)	0
Capital account, 12/31/Year 1	*$20,000*	*$100,000*

The regulations create a nonrebuttable presumption that the value of the property declines by the amount of book depreciation. Therefore, the partners bear the risk of loss on the cost recovery deduction to the extent they are not attributable to nonrecourse debt. The nonrecourse debt rules are not applied until there is minimum gain (nonrecourse debt principal in excess of the adjusted basis (or book value if it is different than adjusted basis) of the property securing the debt). The allocation cannot have economic effect because there is no obligation to restore a deficit capital account upon liquidation. If the agreement contains a "qualified income offset" and the allocation, together with other expected downward capital account adjustments, will not cause a negative capital account, the allocation will be "considered" to have economic effect under the "alternate test." A "qualified income offset" merely requires that if there is an unexpected event that causes a deficit capital account, it will be eliminated "as quickly as possible."[59] Let us assume the agreement contains a qualified income offset and satisfies the other requirements of the alternate economic effect test.

In Year 2, YZ has another cost recovery deduction of $80,000 and no income or loss.

	Tammy	*Pam*
Capital account, 1/1/Year 2	$20,000	$100,000
Cost recovery	(80,000)	0
Capital account, 12/31/Year 2	*$(60,000)*	*$100,000*

The last $60,000 of the depreciation does not have substantial economic effect because Pam bears the risk of loss for that amount. Therefore, the $60,000 must be reallocated to Pam. If the partnership agreement had a provision requiring Tammy to restore $60,000, the allocation would be "considered to have economic effect" to the extent of the make-up provision.[60] Assume the partnership agreement re-

[59] Reg. § 1.704-1(b)(2)(ii)(*d*)(*3*).

[60] Reg. § 1.704-1(b)(2)(ii)(*c*)(*2*) and the "alternate test" Reg. § 1.704-1(b)(2)(ii)(*d*).

quires Tammy to restore a deficit capital account up to a maximum of $60,000, and satisfies the other requirements of the alternate economic effect test.

In Year 3, YZ capital accounts again incur cost recovery deductions of $80,000 and no income or loss.

	Tammy	*Pam*
Capital account, 1/1/Year 3	$(60,000)	$100,000
Cost recovery	(80,000)	0
Capital account, 12/31/Year 3	*$(140,000)*	*$100,000*

Pam again bears the risk of loss of the depreciation to the extent of $40,000.[61] She must be reallocated that portion of the deduction, in spite of the partnership agreement's allocation of the entire amount to Tammy. The $40,000 allocation would have economic effect (see year two discussion) if Tammy were obligated to restore a total negative capital account of at least $100,000 ($60,000 from Year 2 and $40,000 for Year 3). Let us assume the partnership agreement has such an agreement and satisfies the other requirements of the alternate economic effect test.

There is now a minimum taxable gain of $40,000 ($600,000 – $560,000), which means the partnership is considered to have $40,000 of nonrecourse deductions. Allocations of nonrecourse deductions cannot have economic effect. It is the creditor who bears the burden of a loss where the partnership liquidated and the property is sold for its presumed value, book value.[62] Briefly, such an allocation can be considered to be in accordance with the partners' interests in the partnership if four conditions are satisfied:

1. The first two requirements of the economic effect test are satisfied;

2. The nonrecourse deductions are reasonably consistent with allocations from the same source that have substantial economic effect;

3. Beginning the first year of the partnership in which there are nonrecourse deductions there is a minimum gain chargeback provision; and

4. All other material allocations are recognized under the regulations.

If in Year 3 the partnership agreement does have a provision requiring YZ to allocate gains and income to the partners equal to each partner's share of the net decrease in partnership minimum gain

[61] If the building were sold for its preserved value of $560,000 ($800,000 less three year's book/ tax depreciation totaling $240,000), the lender would be entitled to the cash sales proceeds and Pam would receive in liquidation only the $60,000 deficit capital account make-up Tammy agreed to in Year 2.

[62] Reg. § 1.704-2(b)(1).

at a time no later than the time the minimum taxable gain is reduced (a "minimum gain chargeback provision") and satisfies the other three requirements, then YZ can allocate $40,000 of the cost recovery deduction to Tammy, and the allocation will be deemed to be in accordance with the partners' interests in the partnership.

If these conditions are not satisfied, the allocation attributable to the nonrecourse debt ($40,000) to Tammy would not have economic effect or be deemed to be in accordance with the partners' interests. The nonrecourse debt portion of the allocation of the cost recovery deduction is required to be reallocated in accordance with Tammy and Pam's interests in the partnership. Here, it is likely that because most items are shared equally the nonrecourse deductions would be so allocated.

.03 Amendments to the Partnership Agreement

The partnership agreement consists of all agreements made among the partners concerning the partnership. These agreements may be oral or written and may or may not be included in an official partnership agreement document.[63]

If a partnership agreement is modified, a determination will be made as to whether the modification was part of the original agreement, prior allocations may be reallocated to conform with the new agreement, and future allocations may be made in accordance with the old agreement.[64]

Example 9-10. Partners Paul Peters, Quinn Qwenton and Rich Ryndak form a partnership, PQR by contributing cash of $15,000, $10,000, and $25,000, respectively. PQR purchases a machine for $40,000 cash. The PQR partnership agreement states that cost recovery on the machine is to be allocated 60% to Richard and 40% to Paul. All ordinary income and losses exclusive of depreciation are to be allocated 30% to Paul, 20% to Quinn and 50% to Rich. Capital gains and losses will be divided in the same manner as the ordinary items. The agreement also provides for the three requirements of the economic effect test. PQR elects to depreciate the machinery using the straight-line method over five years. In years one and two PQR generates losses of $20,000 and $10,000 respectively exclusive of the depreciation. In year three, PQR generates $10,000 of income exclusive of the depreciation. The allocations during the first three years all have substantial economic effect. According to the partnership agreement, the capital account adjustments for the first three years are as follows:

---

[63] Reg. § 1.704-1(b)(2)(ii)(*h*).

[64] Reg. § 1.704-1(b)(4)(vi).

PQR Partnership Cumulative Capital Account Adjustments Years 1–3

	Paul	*Quinn*	*Rich*
Capital account, beginning	$15,000	$10,000	$25,000
Year 1			
Depreciation	(3,200)		(4,800)
Loss.....................	(6,000)	(4,000)	(10,000)
Capital account, year end	*$5,800*	*$6,000*	*$10,200*
Year 2			
Depreciation	(3,200)		(4,800)
Loss.....................	(3,000)	(2,000)	(5,000)
Capital account, year end	*$(400)*	*$4,000*	*$400*
Year 3			
Depreciation	(3,200)		(4,800)
Income	3,000	2,000	5,000
Capital account, year end	*$(600)*	*$6,000*	*$600*

In Year 3 Paul, Quinn and Rich modify the terms of the partnership agreement, deleting the requirements to restore negative capital accounts upon liquidation. As a result of this modification, the depreciation allocation in Year 2 becomes invalid to the extent of the deficit in Paul's capital account for which Rich and Quinn have borne the economic burden. Starting in Year 2, loss allocation must be reallocated according to the partners' interests in the partnership rather than the terms of the partnership agreement. The regulations do not provide definitive guidance as to interpreting the partner's economic arrangement and the terms of each partnership agreement must be interpreted separately.

Four hundred dollars of the loss allocated to Paul in Year 2 and $200 in Year 3 will be reallocated to Quinn and Rich based upon the economic risk of loss each bears. The disallowed loss will be characterized as depreciation and operating loss based upon their relative amounts during each year. For example, in Year 2 depreciation represented 52% of the deductions allocated to Paul. Therefore $206 of the disallowed $400 will be considered depreciation.[65] The remainder of the loss, $194, will be miscellaneous. It is a question of interpretation, but the arrangement among the parties suggests that Quinn is not to be economically affected by the machine's depreciation.[66] Therefore, under this analysis, Rich bears the risk of the depreciation originally allocated to Paul. The remainder of the loss is shared between Quinn and Rich based upon their relative loss sharing ratios. Quinn will be

[65] (Depreciation ÷ Total Loss) × Loss disallowed
= Percent of loss from depreciation
($3,200/$6,200) × 400 = $206 depreciation

[66] The allocation in the partnership agreement indicates depreciation does not affect *Q*'s capital account.

allocated 29% and Rich will be allocated 71%.[67] A similar analyses is applied to Year 3.

In the event Years 2 and 3 were barred by the statute of limitations, the IRS would likely take the position that the economic effect of the modification requires that Paul be treated as having been specially allocated sufficient income to bring his capital account to zero.

.04 Code Sec. 704(b) Capital Account Accounting

Property contributions. Contributed property is valued at its *fair market value,* and the capital accounts of the partners are adjusted accordingly.[68]

Example 9-11. The equal ABC partnership has the following balance sheet:

Assets	Book Value	Tax Basis	
Cash	$100	$100	
Accounts Receivable	100	100	
Property, Plant and Equipment	100	100	
	$400	$350	
Liabilities	$ 0	$ 0	
Capital Accounts	Book Value	Tax Basis	PIAB*
A	$100	$100	$100
B	100	100	100
C	100	100	100
	$300	$300	$300

*Partnership Interest Adjusted Basis

Z is admitted as an equal partner upon his contribution of appreciated land. Its value is $100, but its adjusted basis is $50. The ABCZ partnership's balance sheet is as follows:

Assets	Book Value	Tax Basis	
Cash	$100	$100	
Accounts Receivable	100	100	
Property, Plant and Equipment	100	100	
Land	100	50	
	$400	$350	
Liabilities	$ 0	$ 0	
Capital Accounts	Book Value	Tax Basis	PIAB*
A	$100	$100	$100
B	100	100	100
C	100	100	100
Z	100	50	50
	$400	$350	$350

*Partnership Interest Adjusted Basis

[67] 70% = 29% to *Q*
50%/70% = 71% to *R*

[68] Reg. § 1.704-1(b)(2)(iv)(*d*).

Economic recognitions on property distributions. For *distributed* property, Code Sec. 704(b) accounting requires that the partners' capital accounts must first be adjusted by the *unrealized economic* income, gain, loss, or deduction inherent in that property (*i.e.*, the property is treated as if it were sold and the *economic* results (*not tax*, for there is no recognition for tax purposes), booked to the capital accounts based upon the partners' profit and loss sharing arrangement with respect to the distributed property).[69]

Example 9-12. *Non-liquidating property distribution (featuring negative book capital account).* The equal ABCD partnership has the following balance sheet:

Assets	*FMV*	*Code Sec. 704(b) Book Value*	*Tax Basis*
Cash	$100	$100	$100
Accounts Receivable	100	100	100
Property, Plant and Equipment	400	100	100
Land	200	100	100
	$800	$400	$400
Liabilities	$ 0	$ 0	$ 0

Capital Accounts	*Partner Liquidation Values*	*Code Sec. 704(b)*	*Tax Basis*	*PIAB**
A	$200	$100	$100	$100
B	200	100	100	100
C	200	100	100	100
D	200	100	100	100
	$800	$400	$400	$400

**Partnership Interest Adjusted Basis*

The ABCD partnership distributes the land to *A*, who retains his equal interest in profits and losses. The resulting balance sheet is:

Assets	*FMV*	*Code Sec. 704(b) Book Value*	*Tax Basis*
Cash	$100	$100	$100
Accounts Receivable	100	100	100
Property, Plant and Equipment	400	100	100
	$600	$300	$300
Liabilities	$ 0	$ 0	$ 0

[69] Reg. § 1.704-1(b)(2)(iv)(*e*)(*1*).

Capital Accounts	*Partner Liquidation Values*	*Code Sec. 704(b)*	*Tax Basis*	*PIAB**
A	$ 0	$(75)	$ 0	$ 0
B	200	125	100	100
C	200	125	100	100
D	200	125	100	100
	$600	$300	$300	$300

**Partnership Interest Adjusted Basis*

If the partnership uses Code Sec. 704(b) accounting in maintaining its books, the land is treated as if it were sold for $200, which generates a book (and tax) gain of $100. This is divided equally according to the partnership agreement. Each capital account, including *A*'s, is $125. *A*'s capital account is then reduced by the land's value of $200 to $(75). If the remaining partnership property were sold for its current value and the $300 gain divided equally, the partners would share the liquidation proceeds according to their ending capital accounts.

If the partnership uses tax accounting in maintaining its books and *A*'s capital account is reduced by the partnership's basis for the land, the partnership agreement must be modified. Whether the partnership uses book or tax accounting, *A, B,* and *C* must receive a special allocation of the first $300 of gain from the sale of the assets if they intend to remain equal partners.

Example 9-13. *Non-liquidating distribution creating negative tax basis capital account.* The equal ABCD partnership has the following balance sheet:

Assets	*FMV*	*Code Sec. 704(b) Book Value*	*Tax Basis*	*PIAB**
Cash.	$100	$100	$100	
Accounts Receivable.	100	100	100	
Property, Plant and Equipment	400	60	60	
Land	200	140	140	
	$800	$400	$400	
Liabilities	$ 0	$ 0	$ 0	

Capital Accounts	*Partner Liquidation Values*	*Code Sec. 704(b)*	*Tax Basis*	*PIAB**
A	$200	$100	$100	$100
B	200	100	100	100
C	200	100	100	100
D	200	100	100	100
	$800	$400	$400	$400

**Partnership Interest Adjusted Basis*

The ABCD partnership distributes the land to A, who retains his equal interest in profits and losses. The resulting balance sheet is:

Assets	***FMV***	***Code Sec. 704(b) Book Value***	***Tax Basis***	
Cash	$100	$100	$100	
Accounts Receivable	100	100	100	
Property, Plant and Equipment	400	60	60	
	$600	*$260*	*$260*	
Liabilities	$ 0	$ 0	$ 0	
Capital Accounts	***Partner Liquidation Values***	***Code Sec. 704(b)***	***Tax Basis***	***PIAB****
A	$ 0	$(85)	$(40)	$(40)
B	200	115	100	100
C	200	115	100	100
D	200	115	100	100
	$600	*$260*	*$260*	*$260*

**Partnership Interest Adjusted Basis*

Normally the partner who receives a nonliquidating distribution succeeds to the partnership's basis in the property as his basis.[70] However, this amount cannot exceed the partner's basis in his interest. *A*'s basis for the land is therefore $100. This is $40 less than the ABCD Partnership's former basis. The result is that the aggregate basis of the partnership's basis in its assets is $40 less than the partners' aggregate basis in their partnership interests. If the partnership had a Code Sec. 754 election in effect, the $40 Code Sec. 734(b)(1)(B) adjustment to the partnership's property, plant and equipment's basis would bring both aggregate inside and outside basis to $300 (and *A*'s tax basis capital account would be increased to zero).

For Code Sec. 704(b) accounting purposes, the partnership is treated as if it sold the land for $200. This would generate a book gain (but not a taxable gain) of $60. This hypothetical gain is allocated among the partners according to their agreed allocation of gain from the land's sale. Here the gain is shared equally, $15 per partner. This brings each partner's capital account, including *A*'s, to a total of $115. *A* is then treated as if he received a $200 cash distribution from the partnership. *A*'s ending Code Sec. 704(b) capital account is $(85). If the remainder of the partnership's property is sold and the gain divided equally, the ending capital accounts would equal the liquidation values. The liquidating cash distribution could be made in accordance with these ending capital accounts.

[70] Code Sec. 732(a)(1).

It would be appropriate to include in *A*'s Schedule K-1 that his basis in his partnership interest is $40 in excess of his tax basis capital account.

Example 9-14. *Retired partner's lingering Code Sec. 704(b) capital account after a liquidating distribution.* The ABCD Partnership has the following balance sheet:

Assets	*FMV*	*Code Sec. 704(b) Book Value*	*Tax Basis*	
Cash	$100	$100	$100	
Accounts Receivable	100	100	100	
Property, Plant and Equipment	400	100	100	
Land	200	100	100	
	$800	*$400*	*$400*	
Liabilities	$ 0	$ 0	$ 0	
Capital Accounts	*Partner Liquidation Values*	*Code Sec. 704(b)*	*Tax Basis*	*PIAB**
A	$200	$100	$100	$100
B	200	100	100	100
C	200	100	100	100
D	200	100	100	100
	$800	*$400*	*$400*	*$400*

**Partnership Interest Adjusted Basis*

The ABCD Partnership distributes the land to A in liquidation of his partnership interest. The resulting balance sheet is:

Assets	*FMV*	*Code Sec. 704(b) Book Value*	*Tax Basis*	
Cash	$100	$100	$100	
Accounts Receivable	100	100	100	
Property, Plant and Equipment	400	100	100	
	$600	*$300*	*$300*	
Liabilities	$ 0	$ 0	$ 0	
Capital Accounts	*Partner Liquidation Values*	*Code Sec. 704(b)*	*Tax Basis*	*PIAB**
A	$ 0	$(75)	$ 0	$ 0
B	200	125	100	100
C	200	125	100	100
D	200	125	100	100
	$600	*$300*	*$300*	*$300*

**Partnership Interest Adjusted Basis*

The Code Sec. 704(b) accounting rules contemplate the partnership maintaining the retired partner's capital account.[71] This will

[71] See Reg. § 1.704-1(b)(5), Ex. 14(vii).

create a compliance problem if Schedules L, M-1, and M-2 are kept according to Code Sec. 704(b) book values. This is because the instructions for Form 1065 regarding Schedules L, M-1, and M-2 require "[t]he amounts on Schedule M-2 should equal the total of the amounts reported in Item J of all the partners' Schedule K-1." *A* is no longer a partner and doesn't receive a K-1. This means the total partnership capital shown on the K-1s will be $375 rather than $300.

To resolve this problem, the regulations allow the partnership to "revalue" all its assets under Code Sec. 704(b) (for book purposes only). The revaluation will trigger an additional $300 of book gain (but no tax gain) which, when allocated equally among the partners (including *A*), will increase each of their capital accounts by $75. This increase will eliminate *A*'s capital account and allow him to be removed from the partnership's balance sheet.

Example 9-15. *Retired partner's lingering tax basis capital account after a liquidating distribution.* The ABCD Partnership has the following balance sheet:

Assets	*FMV*	*Code Sec. 704(b) Book Value*	*Tax Basis*	
Cash	$100	$100	$100	
Accounts Receivable	100	100	100	
Property, Plant and Equipment	400	60	60	
Land	200	140	140	
	$800	*$400*	*$400*	
Liabilities	$ 0	$ 0	$ 0	
Capital Accounts	***Partner Liquidation Values***	***Code Sec. 704(b)***	***Tax Basis***	***PIAB****
A	$200	$100	$100	$100
B	200	100	100	100
C	200	100	100	100
D	200	100	100	100
	$800	*$400*	*$400*	*$400*

**Partnership Interest Adjusted Basis*

The ABCD Partnership distributes the land to *A* in liquidation of his partnership interest. The resulting partnership balance sheet is:

Assets	*FMV*	*Code Sec. 704(b) Book Value*	*Tax Basis*
Cash	$100	$100	$100
Accounts Receivable	100	100	100
Property, Plant and Equipment	400	60	60
	$600	*$260*	*$260*

	Partner Liquidation Values	Code Sec. 704(b)	Tax Basis	PIAB*
Liabilities	$0	$0	$0	
Capital Accounts				
A	$0	$(85)	$(40)	$(40)
B	200	115	100	100
C	200	115	100	100
D	200	115	100	100
	$600	*$260*	*$260*	*$260*

Partnership Interest Adjusted Basis

The Code Sec. 704(b) accounting rules contemplate the partnership maintaining the retired partner's tax basis capital account as well as his Code Sec. 704(b) capital account.[72]

This will create a compliance problem for this partnership whether Schedules L, M-1, and M-2 are kept according to Code Sec. 704(b) or tax basis values. This is because the Instructions for Form 1065's Specific Instructions for Schedules L, M-1, and M-2 require "[t]he amounts on Schedule M-2 should equal the total of the amounts reported in Item J of all the partners' Schedule K-1." *A* is no longer a partner and receives no Schedule K-1. Therefore, the Schedule K-1 issued to partners will have a total partnership capital of $375 rather than $260.

As in the previous example, a revaluation of the partnership's assets for book purposes will eliminate *A*'s book capital account. Because he is no longer a partner, his tax capital account must be eliminated as well. If the partnership has a Code Sec. 754 election in effect (or makes one for the year of distribution), the resulting adjustments to the basis of its remaining assets will allow its books to balance without *A*'s deficit capital balance.

If the partnership does not have a Code Sec. 754 election in effect when the partnership uses tax-basis accounting in completing Schedules L, M-1, and M-2, a reasonable approach would be to show *A*'s ending capital tax basis account as "Other assets" and attach a schedule explaining that it represents unbooked appreciation of the partnership's assets used in valuing a former partner's liquidating distribution.

Debt. Property contributions and distributions are accounted for in the partner equity section of the Code Sec. 704(b) "book" balance sheet at the value of the property net of liabilities secured by such contributed or distributed property at the date of contribution or distribution (assuming the recipient takes the property subject to the liability).[73]

---

[72] *Id.*

[73] Reg. § 1.704-1(b)(2)(iv)(*b*)(*2*) and (*5*).

Example 9-16. Contribution of encumbered property. The equal ABC general partnership has the following balance sheet:

Assets	FMV	Code Sec. 704(b) Book Value	Tax Basis	
Cash	$100	$100	$100	
Accounts Receivable	100	100	100	
Property, Plant and Equipment	400	100	100	
	$600	$300	$300	
Liabilities	$ 0	$ 0	$ 0	
Capital Accounts	**Partner Liquidation Values**	**Code Sec. 704(b)**	**Tax Basis**	**PIAB***
A	$200	$100	$100	$100
B	200	100	100	100
C	200	100	100	100
	$600	$300	$300	

*Partnership Interest Adjusted Basis

The partnership admits *Z* as a new equal partner in exchange for his contribution of land with a gross value of $600 and encumbered by a recourse debt of $400. *Z*'s basis in the land is $200.

Assets	FMV	Code Sec. 704(b) Book Value	Tax Basis	
Cash	$100	$100	$100	
Accounts Receivable	100	100	100	
Property, Plant and Equipment	400	100	100	
Land	600	600	200	
	$1,200	$900	$500	
Liabilities	$ 0	$ 0	$ 0	
Capital Accounts	**Partner Liquidation Values**	**Code Sec. 704(b)**	**Tax Basis**	**PIAB***
A	$200	$100	$100	$100
B	200	100	100	100
C	200	100	100	100
Z	200	200	(200)	(200)
	$800	$500	$100	

*Partnership Interest Adjusted Basis

Z's contribution results in a deemed net money distribution to him of $300 ($400 relief of direct indebtedness under Code Sec. 752(b) offset by $100 increased share of partnership debt under Code Sec. 752(a)). The deemed distribution triggers a $100 taxable gain to *Z*. The aggregate basis of the partners in their partnership interests exceeds by $100 the partnership's basis in its assets. If a Code Sec. 754

election was in effect, the $100 Code Sec. 734(b) adjustment to the partnership's property basis would eliminate this disparity.

If *Z* sold his partnership interest for its net value of $200, the results are as follows:

Amount Realized ($200 cash sales price + $100 debt relief) . .	$300
Basis of partnership interest	0
Gain	*$300*

Z will have recognized the total original potential gain of $400 inherent in the land contributed to the partnership ($100 upon the encumbered land's contribution and $300 upon the partnership interest's sale).

This is another situation when a partner's adjusted basis in his or her partnership interest is not always equal to his tax basis capital account plus his share of debt. His negative capital account of $200 plus his debt share of $100 equals a negative $100.

Observation. Note that if the partnership makes a Code Sec. 754 election, this problem will be solved. If it does not, *Z* must add both his share of the partnership debt *and* the gain he recognized at the time of the property's contribution to his negative tax basis capital account to arrive at the tax basis of his partnership interest. This adjustment continues to be necessary after the partnership sells the land and *Z* has reported his pre-contribution appreciation of $400 under Code Sec. 704(k).

If the partnership maintains its books in accordance with Code Sec. 704(b) accounting rules and the partnership sells the land for $200 cash with the buyer assuming the debt, there will be no Code Sec. 704(b) book income and no changes to the partners' capital accounts. There will be taxable gain of $400, which is required to be allocated to *Z*. This will increase *Z*'s partnership interest adjusted basis to $400. Because the partnership debt has been reduced by $400, each of the partners has a deemed money distribution of $100 with the corresponding basis decrease in their partnership interests.

If the partnership maintains its books in accordance with tax basis accounting, sale of the land will increase *Z*'s capital account by $400 to $200. Because the partnership's accounting method will not change, the tax effects to *Z* and the other partners are the same as described in the preceding paragraph.

Observation. Note that the regulations under Code Sec. 704(b) require that the provisions of Code Sec. 704(c) be applied to gain subsequently recognized by the partnership on sale of the property, plant and equipment. For book and tax purposes, the first $300 of gain recognized upon the sale of these assets must be allocated to *A*, *B* and *C*, since this was the amount of built-in gain inherent in these assets when *Z* joined the partnership.[74] Of course, as noted previously, the partnership can recognize the book (but not the tax) gain immediately by revaluing its assets upon *Z*'s entry into the partnership. Revaluation is generally a good idea since it formalizes the partners' agreement on the fair market value of its assets as of the date of entry of the new partner(s), and brings their book capital accounts into conformity with their economic interests in the partnership's net assets.

Example 9-17. *Non-liquidating distribution of encumbered property.* The ABCD equal general partnership has the following balance sheet:

Assets	*FMV*	*Code Sec. 704(b) Book Value*	*Tax Basis*	
Cash	$100	$100	$100	
Accounts Receivable	100	100	100	
Property, Plant and Equipment	400	300	300	
Land	400	100	100	
	$1,000	*$600*	*$600*	
Liabilities				
Recourse	$200	$200	$200	
Capital Accounts	*Partner Liquidation Values*	*Code Sec. 704(b)*	*Tax Basis*	*PIAB**
A	$200	$100	$100	$100
B	200	100	100	100
C	200	100	100	100
D	200	100	100	100
Total Liability and Equity	*$1,000*	*$600*	*$600*	*$600*

**Partnership Interest Adjusted Basis*

The partnership distributes the land to *A*, who assumes the $200 liability which encumbers the land. The balance sheet is as follows:

Assets	*FMV*	*Code Sec. 704(b) Book Value*	*Tax Basis*
Cash	$100	$100	$100
Accounts Receivable	100	100	100
Property, Plant and Equipment	400	300	300
	$600	*$500*	*$500*
Liabilities	$ 0	$ 0	$ 0

[74] Reg. § 1.704-1(b)(4)(i), (2)(iv)(*g*)(*1*), and (5), Ex. 14(iv).

Capital Accounts	*Partner Liquidation Values*	*Code Sec. 704(b)*	*Tax Basis*	*PIAB**
A	$ 0	$(25)	$200	$200
B	200	175	100	100
C	200	175	100	100
D	200	175	100	100
	$600	*$500*	*$500*	*$500*

*Partnership Interest Adjusted Basis

A's $200 basis in his partnership interest is calculated as follows:

Beginning basis		$150
Deemed contribution for taking over the partnership's debt Code Sec. 752(c)	$200	
Deemed money distribution for share of partnership's debt reduction	(50)	
Net money contribution		150
Partnership interest adjusted basis before property distribution		300
Partnership's basis for distributed property		(100)
A's partnership interest adjusted basis after land distribution		*$200*

This would result in a $200 loss if he received nothing (the value of his interest) on a liquidating distribution or sold his interest for its net book value of zero. But he has the land with basis of $100 and value of $400. This represents a net gain of $100 ($300 gain from land sale less $200 loss from partnership interest sale or liquidation for zero value). This was the net gain potential that he would have recognized if he sold his partnership interest immediately before the distribution for $100.

A's post-distribution tax basis capital account is calculated as follows:

A's beginning capital account		$100
Plus partnership debt assumed by *A*[75]	$200	
Less partnership's basis in distributed property	(100)	100
A's post-distribution tax basis capital account		*$200*

A's post-distribution *book* capital account is calculated as follows:

A's beginning capital balance	$100
Plus share of gain on deemed sale of land (25%)	75
Plus partnership debt assumed by *A*	200
Less fair market value of distributed property	(400)
A's post-distribution 704(b) capital account	*$(25)*

Note that the partnership can, and generally should, revalue all its property (rather than just the land) upon the distribution to *A*. In such a case, it would recognize an additional book (but not tax) gain of $100

[75] There is no official guidance for tax basis capital account bookkeeping. Here, assumption of a partnership debt is treated as a money contribution.

on the plant, property and equipment which, when allocated among the partners, would increase *A*'s book capital account to zero and the other partner's book capital accounts to $200.

Each partner's basis in his partnership interest is equal to his tax basis capital account plus his share of the debt (zero in this example). However, the partners must recognize that their tax basis capital accounts are *not* used to govern rights to liquidating distributions. *A*'s tax basis capital account is $200, but if the partnership sold its assets and distributed the cash proceeds, *A* should receive nothing; *B*, *C* and *D* would each receive a one-third share of the $600 proceeds.

Transfer of a partnership interest. The Code Sec. 704(b) accounting rules require that the transferee step into the shoes of the transferor on transfer of a partnership interest.[76] If the partnership has a Code Sec. 754 election in effect for the year of a sale or exchange of a partnership interest, no adjustment is made to the partnership assets or to the capital account of the transferred interest.[77]

Distributions causing Code Sec. 734(b) adjustments. Adjustments to partners' capital accounts are required when Code Sec. 734(b) adjustments to the tax basis of partnership property is required. In a nonliquidating distribution, the partners' capital accounts are adjusted by the total amount of the basis adjustment. The adjustment is allocated around the partners capital accounts since they would share an equal amount of income, gain or loss had the property been sold by the partnership for its recomputed basis. The adjustment is presumably allocated among the assets in the same manner the tax allocation is made under Code Sec. 755. In a liquidating distribution, the entire basis adjustment is allocated to the capital account of the liquidated partner. In both a liquidating and non-liquidating distribution, the adjustment is, however, limited to the partnership's ability to allocate it to partnership property.[78]

Nondeductible, noncapital expenditures. A partner's capital account is reduced by the partner's share of nondeductible expenditures which are not capitalized. These expenses reduce cash available for distribution. Code Sec. 709 organization and syndication expenses are treated in this manner except to the extent of the amortization expenses.[79]

Guaranteed payments. Guaranteed payments are treated as an ordinary partnership expense. They reduce capital accounts based upon the partners' profit and loss sharing arrangement.[80]

Adjustments where guidance is lacking. Partnership transactions where Code Sec. 704(b) accounting is not specified are to be made in a manner which:

---

76 Reg. § 1.704-1(b)(2)(iv)(*l*).

77 Reg. § 1.704-1(b)(2)(iv)(*m*).

78 Reg. § 1.704-1(b)(2)(iv)(*m*)(*4*) and (b)(5), Ex. 14(vii).

79 Reg. § 1.704-1(b)(2)(iv)(*i*).

80 Reg. § 1.704-1(b)(2)(iv)(*o*).

1. Maintains the equality between assets and capital accounts plus liabilities;
2. Is consistent with the partners economic arrangement; and
3. Is based on federal tax accounting principles.

Optional revaluation of all property and capital accounts. On the contribution or distribution of property, the contributed or distributed property itself must be "revalued" to its fair market value for capital account maintenance purposes. This revaluation is *not* optional. In three situations under the capital account maintenance rules there is an *optional* adjustment allowed of *all* the partnership property, and, correspondingly, the capital accounts of all the partners, provided that the revaluation is for substantial non-tax business purposes:

1. Contribution of property (including money) to a partnership in exchange for a partnership interest;
2. Distribution of property (including money) from a partnership in exchange for a partnership interest; and
3. Grant of an interest in the partnership (other than a de minimis interest) on or after May 6, 2004, as consideration for the provision of services to or for the benefit of the partnership by an existing or new partner acting in a partner capacity;
4. Under "generally accepted industry accounting practices" where substantially all of the partnership's property (excluding money) is stock, securities, commodities, options, warrants, futures, or similar instruments that are readily traded on an established securities market.[81]

Revaluation procedures. If the partnership elects to revalue the partnership assets, the procedures are as follows:

1. The adjustments are based on the fair market value of the property on the date of adjustment.
2. The property is treated as sold, and "gain" or "loss" is recognized *for book purposes only* by subtracting the book value of the property from the fair market value of the property. There is no current tax recognition.
3. The gain or loss so determined is allocated among the partners on the basis of their economic agreement as provided in the partnership, and reflected in their capital accounts.
4. *Book* depreciation, amortization, and depletion, and book gain or loss for the revalued property, must be calculated as provided in the safe harbor regulations.[82]

[81] Reg. § 1.704-1(b)(2)(iv)(*f*).

[82] *I.e.*, as provided in Reg. § 1.704-1(b)(2)(iv)(*g*).

5. Allocation of *tax* depreciation, amortization, and depletion, and tax gain or loss must reflect the variation between the tax and book values and amounts under the same principles as apply to treatment of such variations under Code Sec. 704(c).[83] Income and loss concerning receivables and payables must be similarly handled.[84]

Decision to revalue. Much of the decision is based upon accounting considerations. Revaluation generally enhances the usefulness of the partnership's balance sheet. For example, revaluing the partnership's assets when a partner's interest has been liquidated by a cash distribution can avoid the unbalanced books problem caused by his or her ending capital account not being equal to the cash distribution. Revaluation will also cause the assets and capital accounts to more closely track fair market values rather than the residual of cost basis net of depreciation and other book adjustments to carrying values. This is especially useful to users of the balance sheet who understand little of historical cost accounting or have very little idea of the value of their partnership interest.

While the decision to revalue is "optional," the regulations contemplate that in the usual context the election will be made. If the election is not made then the partnership agreement must otherwise provide for effectively the same results as if the election had been made.[85] Otherwise, the regulations caution, there may be other tax ramifications outside of the allocation arena (*e.g.*, gift or compensation).[86]

The decision to revalue or not revalue partnership property under the election, and the decision to use the safe harbor or some other approach under the partners' interests in the partnership rules for handling the book depreciation, amortization, and depletion, may have extremely significant economic impact on the partners, and may not be decisions that are made only "for tax purposes." Partners should be extremely careful in making these decisions.

> ***Observation.*** If the partnership agreement allocates the entire depreciation deduction to one partner an increased book value of the depreciable asset will result in a larger book expense. This may result in a reduced share of the partnership's net income.

Accounting for a differential between book value and tax basis. The disparity between the Code Sec. 704(b) book value of partnership property and its tax basis is commonly referred to as a "book-tax differential." These book-tax differences are caused by adjustments to the Code Sec. 704(b) book values unmatched by a tax basis adjustment. A book-tax differential may be caused as previously mentioned by two types of Code Sec. 704(b) adjustments:

---

[83] Reg. § 1.704-1(b)(2)(iv)(*f*).

[84] Reg. § 1.704-1(b)(2)(iv)(*g*)(*2*).

[85] Reg. § 1.704-1(b)(5), Ex. 14(iv).

[86] Reg. § 1.704-1(b)(2)(iv)(*f*).

1. *Mandatory Code Sec. 704(b) adjustments.* If the contributing partner's basis for the asset is different than its value, the asset is recorded on the partnership's books at its value and the partner's capital account is increased by this same amount after reduction for liabilities shifted to the partnership in the transfer. This book-tax difference is considered built-in gain or loss under Code Sec. 704(c). As such, it must be taken into account by the contributing partner to the extent possible rather than shifted to the other partners. This is accomplished by allocating tax gain or loss on disposition of the property to the contributor. If the property is depreciable, the built-in gain or loss is taken into account over the asset's life in the form of reduced or increased depreciation allocations to the contributor.[87] See ¶ 903.03.

2. *Optional Code Sec. 704(b) adjustments.* If the partnership receives a contribution or makes a distribution, it is allowed, but not required, to adjust the Code Sec. 704(b) book values of its other property. This is true whether the distribution or contribution was of money or other property. Booking to value is also allowed in other circumstances if it conforms to "generally accepted industry accounting practice."[88]

Whether the Code Sec. 704(b) book-tax differential results from a mandatory or optional Code Sec. 704(b) adjustment, it must be accounted for in the same manner.[89] Whether or not the partnership makes the optional Code Sec. 704(b) book adjustments, it must allocate its income or loss in conformance with the concepts of Code Sec. 704(c) to the extent of its actual book-tax differential or its potential book-tax differential if mandatory or optional rebookings are not made.

Where the partnership property is revalued under Code Sec. 704(b) accounting rules, allocation of gain, loss and deductions attributable to the property cannot have economic effect, since the capital account adjustments are not equal to the tax gain or loss. Accordingly, the tax allocations must be determined in accordance with the facts and circumstances test (the partner's interest in the partnership rule). Such allocations will be deemed to be in accordance with the partner's interest in the partnership if the tax items are shared among the partners so as to take into account the difference between tax basis and book value in the manner provided in Code Sec. 704(c).[90]

Code Sec. 704(c)(1)(A) provides that partnership tax income, gain, loss, and deduction must be allocated among the partners to take account of the difference between the fair market value of property contributed to a partnership and its tax basis at the time of contribution. The principles

[87] See Reg. § 1.704-3.
[88] Reg. § 1.704-1(b)(2)(iv)(*f*).
[89] Reg. § 1.704-1(b)(2)(iv)(*g*)(*1*).
[90] Reg. § 1.704-1(b)(4)(i) and (1)(i).

under this section are no different from the principles applicable in working with this so-called book-tax differential under the Code Sec. 704(b) rules. Historically, the problem was more clearly recognized in the context of contributions to partnerships, and thus the independent existence of Code Sec. 704(c), but the regulations treat any book-tax differential in the same manner, however it arises, whether as a result of contribution of property, distribution of property, or some other revaluation of property for capital account purposes under the partners' interests in the partnership rules.

Book-tax differences must be reconciled by following the principles applicable under Code Sec. 704(c).[91] Under the safe harbor capital account maintenance rules, the amount of book depreciation, amortization, or depletion for a period must have the same relationship to the book value as the tax depreciation, amortization, or depletion concerning the property has to the tax basis of that property.[92] Note that Code Sec. 704(c) applies to the book-tax differential existing with respect to property contributed to the partnership. The book-tax differential concerning contributed property (*i.e.*, covered by Code Sec. 704(c)) and revalued property already held by the partnership (*i.e.*, covered by Code Sec. 704(b)) is identical, and the treatment should be the same under both provisions. For example, under Code Sec. 704(c), gain built into property contributed to a partnership must be allocated to the contributing partner when it is reorganized by the partnership. Similarly, if a new partner contributes cash to join a partnership which has built-in gain property, the built-in gain must be allocated to partners other than the new partner when the partnership recognizes the built-in gain. The second situation is often referred to as a "reverse Code Sec. 704(c) allocation." Consider the following two examples:

Example 9-18. *Straight forward Code Sec. 704(c) allocation.* The ABC general partnership has the following balance sheet:

Assets	*FMV*	*Code Sec. 704(b) Book Value*	*Tax Basis*
Cash	$300	$300	$300
Accounts Receivable	600	600	600
Property, Plant and Equipment	900	900	900
	$1,800	*$1,800*	*$1,800*
Liabilities	$ 0	$ 0	$ 0

[91] Reg. § 1.704-1(b)(2)(iv)(*g*)(*1*) and (4)(i). This is sometimes referred to as the "same method, same life" rule.

[92] Reg. § 1.704-1(b)(2)(iv)(*g*)(*3*). It is concerning the depreciation, amortization, and depletion of property for book purposes that partners most frequently may want to use capital account procedures that are at odds with the safe harbor requirement, relying, instead on the rules for partners' interests in the partnership. Compare former Reg. § 1.704-1(b)(2)(iv)(*g*)(*3*), as existed prior to September 9, 1986, with the current version. The former version allowed greater latitude concerning book depreciation, amortization, and depletion. The change was only with respect to the safe harbor requirements; the approaches allowed by the former regulation, and other approaches, may, under the proper circumstances, be valid under the partners' interests in the partnership rules.

Capital Accounts	Partner Liquidation Values	Code Sec. 704(b)*	Tax Basis	PIAB*
A	$600	$600	$600	$600
B	600	600	600	600
C	600	600	600	600
	$1,800	$1,800	$1,800	$1,800

*Partnership Interest Adjusted Basis

Z is admitted as an equal general partner in exchange for his contribution of unencumbered land with a value of $600 and basis of $450. After the contribution, the balance sheet is as follows:

Assets	FMV	Code Sec. 704(b) Book Value	Tax Basis
Cash	$300	$300	$300
Accounts Receivable	600	600	600
Property, Plant and Equipment	900	900	900
Land	600	600	450
	$2,400	$2,400	$2,250
Liabilities	$ 0	$ 0	$ 0

Capital Accounts	Partner Liquidation Values	Code Sec. 704(b)	Tax Basis	PIAB*
A	$600	$600	$600	$600
B	600	600	600	600
C	600	600	600	600
Z	600	600	450	450
	$2,400	$2,400	$2,250	$2,250

*Partnership Interest Adjusted Basis

Without regard to whether the partnership is keeping its books in conformance with Code Sec. 704(c), Code Sec. 704(c) requires that the precontribution gain inherent in the land of $150 be allocated to *Z* upon the subsequent sale or disposition of the land by the partnership (unless the land is sold for less than $600). When the property is sold for $600 or more, the special allocation will bring *Z*'s capital account equal to the other partners and any additional gain will be shared equally. The tax basis capital accounts will then reflect the intentions of the partners. If the property is sold for less than $150 gain, the tax allocation may not bring the capital accounts to equal and thus will not reflect the partners' stated intents of being equal partners from the time of *Z*'s admittance to the partnership. In that case, *Z* alone will have suffered the economic consequences of the decline in value from the agreed upon value existing when the property was contributed. For example, if the property is sold for $550 resulting in $100 of tax gain and $50 of lost value since its contribution, the partnership would allocate the entire taxable gain to *Z*, but the tax basis capital accounts should reflect equal values of $575 for all four partners.

If the balance sheet is kept according to Code Sec. 704(b) accounting procedures, the land's sale will result in a book-tax differential equal to *Z*'s Code Sec. 704(c) gain. The Code Sec. 704(b) capital accounts, however, will need no adjustments to keep them equal.

For example, if the land is sold for $550, there is a Code Sec. 704(b) book loss of $50, bringing each partner's capital account to $587.50. There is however, a tax gain of $100 and it is all allocated to *Z*'s Schedule K-1 as "Other income."

Example 9-19. *Reverse Code Sec. 704(c) allocation.* The ABC general partnership has the following balance sheet:

Assets	***FMV***	***Code Sec. 704(b) Book Value***	***Tax Basis***	***PIAB****
Cash	$ 0	$ 0	$ 0	
Accounts Receivable	300	300	300	
Property, Plant and Equipment	900	900	900	
Land	600	450	450	
	$1,800	*$1,650*	*$1,650*	
Liabilities	$ 0	$ 0	$ 0	
Capital Accounts	***Partner Liquidation Values***	***Code Sec. 704(b)***	***Tax Basis***	***PIAB****
A	$600	$550	$550	$550
B	600	550	550	550
C	600	550	550	550
	$1,800	*$1,650*	*$1,650*	*$1,650*

**Partnership Interest Adjusted Basis*

Z is admitted as an equal general partner in exchange for a $600 cash contribution. After the contribution, the balance sheet is as follows:

Assets	***Partner Liquidation Values and Code Sec. 704(b) Capital Accounts with Optional Adjustments***	***Code Sec. 704(b) Without Optional Adjustments***	***Tax Basis***
Cash	$600	$600	$600
Accounts Receivable	300	300	300
Property, Plant and Equipment	900	900	900
Land	600	450	450
	$2,400	*$2,250*	*$2,250*
Liabilities	$ 0	$ 0	$ 0

Without Capital Accounts	*Partner Liquidation Values and Code Sec. 704(b) Capital Accounts with Optional Adjustments*	*Code Sec. 704(b) Optional Adjustments*	*Tax Basis*	*PIAB**
A	$600	$550	$550	$550
B	600	550	550	550
C	600	550	550	550
Z	600	600	600	600
	$2,400	*$2,250*	*$2,250*	*$2,250*

**Partnership Interest Adjusted Basis*

Code Sec. 704(c) is not applicable to contributions unless contributed property has a basis different than its value. *Z* contributed cash. *Z*, however, is in the same theoretical situation as the continuing partners in a partnership receiving appreciated property from a new partner. If the land is sold for a $150 gain (the pre-admission appreciation) and the gain is divided equally, *Z* will report $37.50 of realized gain that was generated during *A*, *B*, and *C*'s ownership period. Potential gain will have been shifted from *A*, *B*, and *C* to *Z*. However, if the capital accounts reflecting this tax allocation are used in determining *Z*'s rights to liquidation proceeds, *Z* will be entitled to $637.50 in a liquidating distribution made according to ending capital accounts. While Code Sec. 704(c) does not address this situation, the Code Sec. 704(b) regulations do.[93] These regulations require that the pre-admission tax appreciation of $150 be allocated to *A*, *B*, and *C* when it is recognized.

If the partnership's books are kept on a tax basis or a Code Sec. 704(b) book basis with no election to revalue, this will require that both the tax and book gain from sale of the land be allocated first to *A*, *B*, and *C* to the extent of the first $150. Additional Code Sec. 704(b) book and tax gain can be allocated in any manner. The regulations caution that if the first $150 of book and tax gain are divided equally, *Z*'s $37.50 windfall will be examined and treated as a gift, salary, or other classification which represents the true intent of the parties. The regulations will treat an equal tax allocation coupled with no increase in the liquidating value of *Z*'s partnership interest as lacking economic effect.

If the partnership elects under Reg. § 1.704-1(b)(2)(iv)(*f*) to revalue its assets and capital accounts, the book-tax differential is treated in the same way as a Code Sec. 704(c) book-tax differential. Here the tax gain in excess of the book gain is allocated among *A*, *B*, and *C*.

[93] Reg. § 1.704-1(b)(4)(i), (2)(iv)(*f*), and (5), Ex. 14(vi).

S Corporation Observation. Subchapter S contains no counterpart to Code Sec. 704(c) and reverse Code Sec. 704(c) allocations. Therefore, all shareholders report a portion of any gain built into assets contributed to the corporation when the corporation recognizes the built-in gain. In addition when a new shareholder joins the corporation through a contribution to the corporation in exchange for stock, a portion of any gain built into the corporate property will be allocated to the new shareholder when the property is sold.

Example 9-20. *New partner contributes cash—Revaluation.* ABC partnership has one nondepreciable asset, which has a value of $300 and tax basis of $150. The three equal partners, *A*, *B* and *C*, each have capital accounts and tax basis of $50. *D* contributes $100 cash to the partnership in exchange for a 25% interest in partnership capital, profits and losses. If the partnership makes the election to revalue its assets under Reg. § 1.704-1(b)(2)(iv)(*f*), the book value of the existing partnership asset is increased to $300, its fair market value at the time of the adjustment. For purposes of adjusting the capital accounts of *A*, *B*, and *C*, the asset is treated as if it is sold for $300, with the partnership recognizing economic (not tax) gain of $150, which is allocated $50 to each of the three original partners, and their capital accounts are thereby increased to $100 each. Note that the property's tax basis remains at $150 (thus there is a $150 book-tax differential—the difference between the $300 book value and the $150 tax basis), and the tax basis of *A*, *B*, and *C* remains at $50 each. *D*'s capital account and tax basis are $100. If the property thereafter appreciates and is sold for $400, there is $100 of book gain and $250 of tax gain. The book gain would be allocated $25 to each partner. The first $150 of the tax gain would be allocated $50 to each of *A*, *B*, and *C*, "reconciling" the book-tax differential, and the last $100 is allocated $25 to each partner (*i.e.*, in the manner most consistent with the underlying economic allocation).[94] The partners' ending capital accounts (and tax bases) would be $125 each, reflecting their relative rights to the $500 cash now held by the partnership.

Example 9-21. *New partner contributes cash—No revaluation.* Assume the same facts as in the above example, except the partnership does not elect to revalue the asset. The book value of the property remains $150 and the capital accounts of *A*, *B*, and *C* remain at $50 each. *D*'s capital account is $100. Assume again that the property is sold for $400, generating a book *and* tax gain of $250. In this case, the only way to reconcile the economic gain on the sale with the partners' underlying agreement (*i.e.*, that they are all equal) is to allocate the first $150 economic gain $50 each to *A*, *B*, and *C* and the second $100

[94] Reg. § 1.704-1(b)(4)(i).

of gain equally to the four partners. The tax gain would be allocated in the same manner, so that the ending capital accounts and tax basis of all of the partners will be $125 each, the same as if the election had been made.[95]

Observation. When a new partner enters a partnership through a cash contribution, the effect of the Code Sec. 704(b) rules is similar to a new partner purchasing a partnership interest from a partner when the partnership has a Code Sec. 754 election in effect. The new partner's share of the taxable income is determined as if the adjusted basis of the partnership assets is equal to their value. The same is true of a property contribution except that the new partner will also have a Code Sec. 704(c) allocation to reflect any built-in gain or loss in the contributed property.

Ceiling rule limitation on allocations. An important limitation on the ability of partners to allocate income, gain, loss, and deduction among the partners is the "ceiling rule." Simply stated, the ceiling rule provides that the amount of income, gain, loss, and deduction from a transaction that may be allocated to a partner for tax purposes cannot exceed the amount of such item that the partnership actually incurs for tax purposes.[96] This simple statement belies the amount of complexity that the ceiling rule involves.

Effect of rule. The ceiling rule provides that in some circumstances the partnership may not receive tax profit, loss or depreciation from an asset equal to the corresponding economic profit, loss or depreciation that the partnership realized. The problem is best understood by example.

Example 9-22. Assume that Rick and Michele are the original partners in an equal partnership which owns Genneyre Acres, a mobile home park. The park has an adjusted basis of $6,000,000 and a value of $1,000,000. Austin and Teddie become 25% partners in the partnership through a contribution of $500,000 each. The park consequently increases in value and is sold for $4,000,000. Austin and Teddy have each enjoyed an economic benefit of $500,000 and Rick and Michelle have each suffered a $1,000,000 economic loss. There is neither sufficient taxable gain nor loss generated by the transaction to allocate an amount of partnership taxable gain or loss equal to the partners' economic gain or loss.

The effects of the ceiling rule can be and sometimes are required to be reduced or eliminated by "curative" or "remedial" allocations. These are discussed more thoroughly in ¶ 903.

---

[95] Reg. § 1.704-1(b)(5), Ex. 14(iv).

[96] Reg. § 1.704-1(c)(2)(i).

Code Sec. 704(b) accounting and Schedules L, M-1, M-2 and K-1. *Pre-1991.* Great confusion has existed over whether Schedule L on Form 1065 represents the tax basis or "book" value of the partnership assets, whether Schedules M-1 and M-2 use book values on line one rather than tax-basis values, and whether the "Partner's capital account analysis" box of Schedule K-1 is the individual partner's tax-basis or book capital account compilation (both excluding debt). The IRS and the forms themselves have been confused and a source of confusion for everyone else on this issue.

In 1976, for the first and only time, the IRS decided to require information concerning the partners' bases to be disclosed, and the Schedule K-1 for 1976 required disclosure of the applicable partner's year-end basis "as determined under Code Sec. 705." Apparently realizing that the basis-disclosure requirement would place a heavy burden on partnerships and that the necessary information may not be available to the partnership (*i.e.*, if a partnership interest was transferred), the IRS [97] issued supplemental instructions to Schedule K-1 requiring disclosure of basis for returns filed in 1977 only if either the partnership had nonrecourse loans or a partner whose interest was decreased or terminated during the year had a negative capital account at the end of the year. The supplemental instructions also provided that the partnership, in calculating the partners' bases, could rely on the information available to it, except the partnership was required to obtain the purchase price from transferees who were *admitted* to the partnership. The rules did not provide how the partnership was to meet its reporting requirement if the admitted partner cannot be required, under the partnership agreement, to disclose that information.

In all years subsequent to 1976, the Schedule K-1 has required "capital account" information plus information concerning the partner's shares of the partnership recourse and nonrecourse debt. However, even with the debt information, a partner's basis in the partnership cannot be confidently calculated from his or her K-1.

Until 1988, the instructions to Schedule L provided that for Schedule L "the amounts shown should agree with the partnership's primary books and records." Schedule M instructions, the predecessor to Schedules M-1 and M-2, referred to the partners' "capital account." Given that the partnership's "primary" books and records are the partnership's *economic* records, there seemed to be little question that the returns were intended to reflect book rather than tax capital account information on Schedules L, M and K-1. The instructions were, however, not clear on this point and many, if not most, schedules were prepared on a tax basis.

In 1988, the instructions to Schedule L were changed to provide:

> The amounts shown should agree with the partnership's primary books and records and should, therefore, reflect tax basis. Attach a statement showing

[97] Announcement 77-38, 1977-13 IRB 21; Internal Revenue News Release IR-1769 (1977).

> any difference. Balance sheet amounts shown on Schedule L should not be adjusted to reflect any revaluation under Regulations section 1.704-1(b)(2)(iv)(f).

Schedule M and the K-1 instructions continued to refer to the "partners' capital account."

In 1989, the instructions were changed again to eliminate the "and should, therefore, reflect tax basis" language. However, the instructions continued to prohibit making on the return the optional adjustments made to the capital accounts under the regulations. Thus, the instructions seemed to recognize that tax basis was not required, but also specifically prohibited use of the regulations' version of a book capital account, at least where there was a revaluation under the specific regulations cited.

About the best that could be said about this sorry history is that it was a mess. There was little consistency in how returns were being prepared—the information that the IRS (and partners) were obtaining was largely useless.

1991 Changes. Beginning in 1991, the IRS made fundamental changes to Form 1065 and the instructions, perhaps in an attempt to clear up the confusion.

Schedules M-1 and M-2. The 1991 Form 1065 provided for a Schedule M-1 "Reconciliation of Income per Books With Income Per Return" and a Schedule M-2 "Analysis of Partners' Capital Accounts." The "Analysis of Partner's Capital Account" line on the Schedule K-1 to the Form 1065 was coordinated to the Schedule M-2. These schedules were fundamentally different from their counterparts pre-1991, and the return was now clear that Schedules L, M-2, and Item J on the Schedule K-1 were to reflect the partnership Code Sec. 704(b) *book* capital account, income and basis amounts, and *not* partnership tax income and tax basis. The 1991 general instructions to Schedule M-2 provided, in full, as follows:

> Show what caused the changes in the partners' capital accounts during the tax year. Do ***not*** *use the rules for figuring the basis of a partner's interest when figuring the partners' capital accounts. Instead, follow the rules explained below to determine the partners' capital accounts.*
>
> The beginning and ending capital accounts should agree with the partnership's books and records *and the balance sheet amounts.* Attach a statement explaining any differences.
>
> Also, the amounts on Schedule M-2 should equal the total of the amounts reported in Item J of all the partners' Schedules K-1.
>
> See Regulations section 1.704-1(b)(2)(iv) for additional information on the rules for determining the partners' capital accounts.[98]

The regulations cited in the instructions are the regulations for explaining how to account for economic capital accounts for the Code Sec. 704(b) safe harbor establishing the economic effect of an allocation.

---

[98] Instructions for Form 1065 (1991), U.S. Partnership Return of Income, page 23.

1992 Changes. In 1992, the IRS again changed its position as to the accounting method to be used on Form 1065 Schedules L, M-1, M-2, and Schedule K-1, Item J.

The 1992 and following Instructions for Form 1065 provide as follows:

> **Schedule M-2—Analysis of Partners' Capital Accounts**
>
> Show what caused the changes during the tax year in the partners' capital accounts as reflected on the partnership's books and records. The amounts on Schedule M-2 should equal the total of the amounts reported in Item J of all the partners' Schedules K-1.
>
> The partnership may, but is not required to, use the rules in Regulations section 1.704-1(b)(2)(iv) to determine the partners' capital accounts in Schedule M-2 and Item J of the partners' Schedules K-1. If the beginning and ending capital accounts reported under these rules differ from the amounts reported on Schedule L, attach a statement reconciling any differences.[99]

Publication 541, Tax Information on Partnerships, states as follows:

> **Schedule M-2**
>
> Schedule M-2 is an analysis of the partners' capital accounts. It shows the total equity of all partners in the partnership at the beginning and end of the tax year and shows the adjustments that caused any increase or decrease. The total of all the partners' capital accounts is the difference between the partnership's assets and liabilities shown on Schedule L. A partner's capital account will not necessarily present the tax basis for an interest in the partnership.[100]

Exemption from preparing schedules. Not all partnerships are required to complete Schedules L, M-1, and M-2 and box N on the Schedule K-1. If a partnership's total receipts are less than $250,000, its total assets are less than $250,000, and its Schedules K-1 are filed with the return and furnished to the partners on or before the due date of the partnership return (including extensions), then the partnership is excused from completing Schedules L, M-1, M-2, and box N on the K-1.[101]

Caution. The lesson here, however, is that because of this long history of confusion, practitioners need to be careful in relying on the K-1 information concerning the "capital accounts" to be either tax basis or capital account information. The author further recommends, especially for a small partnership, attaching to the K-1 copies given to the partners of a balance sheet prepared using tax basis, which should clearly reflect that the partners' actual outside bases may be different than their tax basis capital accounts increased by their share of debt. For example, this would be true if there has been a transfer of a partnership interest. Although it is the

---

[99] Id., page 29.
[100] *Id.*, page 18.
[101] See Instructions to Form 1065, Schedule B, Question 5.

individual partner's responsibility to account for his or her basis, help from the partnership is sometimes necessary.

¶ 903 Allocations of Income and Deductions from Contributed Property—Code Sec. 704(c)

Before the Deficit Reduction Act of 1984,[102] income, deduction, gain, or loss relating to contributed property were allocated in accordance with the partnership agreement unless an election was made under former Code Sec. 704(c)(2). That election resulted in allocations taking into account the variations between the basis of contributed property and its fair market value at the time of contribution. Absent such an election, the general rule provided income-shifting opportunities between taxpayers and also generated potentially unfair effects on unwitting taxpayers who had entered into arm's-length transactions.

> ***Example 9-23.*** *A* and *B* enter into a partnership agreement in which *A*, a taxpayer with a 50% marginal income tax bracket, contributes property with a $10,000 basis and a $50,000 fair market value. *B*, a taxpayer with a 25% marginal income tax bracket, contributes $40,000 of cash. Partner *B* could argue that his contribution should be lower than *A*'s because of the inherent tax liability with respect to *A*'s property that *B* must eventually bear. However, in the case of related parties, it is important to note that the AB combination still benefits if half of the gain is taxed at *B*'s tax rate. This reduces the total tax liability on the gain from $20,000 (50% × $40,000) to $15,000 [(50% × $20,000) + (25% × $20,000)]; and, *B* could benefit by gaining a 50% partnership interest at a cost lower than 50% of the fair market value of the assets.
>
> In this situation under old law, *B* was disadvantaged if he was not well informed or advised because he might contribute $50,000 to obtain a 50% interest in the AB partnership. Furthermore, taxpayers who desired to shift income would take advantage of the general rule. Therefore, the elective rule of former Code Sec. 704(c)(2) was adopted as the mandatory rule of Code Sec. 704(c). Variations between basis and value at the time of contribution must be taken into account in allocations with respect to such property.

The purpose of the statute is to allocate gain or loss inherent in contributed property to the contributor and to allocate among the noncontributing partners only the gain or loss that accrues after the date of contribution.

The legislative history of the Deficit Reduction Act of 1984 [103] states that the taxpayers could rely on regulations under former Code Sec. 704(c)(2) for purposes of handling Code Sec. 704(c) allocations until new

[102] The Tax Reform Act of 1984, P.L. 98-369, 98th Cong., 2d Sess.

[103] *Id.*

regulations were issued.[104] The report also notes that examples which are necessary additions to these regulations include contributions of:

1. More than one item of property with built-in gain or loss by a single partner;

2. Property with built-in gain or loss by more than one partner;

3. Property with built-in gain that would constitute ordinary income under the various recapture provisions;

4. Property that is disposed of by the partnership for property with substituted basis;[105]

5. Property when there are disproportionate profit-and-loss-sharing arrangements contained in the partnership agreement; and

6. Property that is not disposed of before the contributing partner's disposition of his or her partnership interest or until it is worthless.

The (long awaited) Code Sec. 704(c) final regulations apply to property contributed to a partnership and to optional revaluations on or after December 21, 1993.[106]

Under the regulations, the partnership can use any reasonable method of taking into account built-in gains and losses so that the contributing partner receives the tax burdens and benefits of any built-in gain or loss. Two reasonable methods of making allocations under Code Sec. 704(c) are the "traditional method" and the "traditional method with curative allocations." A third reasonable method that is permissible under the regulations is the "remedial allocation method." Other reasonable methods are also acceptable.[107]

These rules apply on a property-by-property basis, with limited exceptions. Therefore, in determining whether there is a disparity between adjusted tax basis and fair market value, the built-in gains and losses inherent in items of contributed property cannot be aggregated. The partnership may use different methods with respect to different items of contributed property, but a single reasonable method is applied for each item of contributed property. The overall method or combination of methods must be reasonable based on the facts and circumstances.[108] For example, it may be unreasonable to use one method for appreciated property and another method for depreciated property. Similarly, it may be unreasonable to use the traditional method for built-in gain property contributed by a partner with a high marginal tax rate while using curative

---

[104] H.R. Rep. No. 861, 98th Cong., 2d Sess., 854-858 (1984).

[105] See Code Sec. 7701(a)(42).

[106] Reg. § 1.704-3(f).

[107] Preamble, T.D. 8500, 1994-1 CB 183.

[108] Reg. § 1.704-3(a)(2).

allocations for property contributed by a partner with a low marginal tax rate.[109]

> ***Comment.*** Code Sec. 704(c) and the regulations apply to property contributed to the partnership when there is a built-in gain or loss. Code Sec. 704(c) allocates the built-in gain or loss to the partner who owned the property when the gain or loss arose. When there is an acquisition of a partnership interest through a contribution when the partnership holds property with built-in gain or loss, the partnership's built-in gain or loss must be allocated to the partners who owned their partnership interest when the built-in gain or loss arose. These are Code Sec. 704(b) allocations and are generally referred to as "reverse Code Sec. 704(c) allocations"; see ¶ 902.04.

.01 Anti-abuse Rule

An allocation method (or combination of methods) is not reasonable if the contribution of property (or optional revaluation under Code Sec. 704(b)) and the corresponding allocation of tax items with respect to the property are made with a view to shifting the tax consequences of built-in gain or loss among the partners in a manner that substantially reduces the present value of the partners' aggregate tax liability.[110]

.02 Traditional Method

In general, the traditional method requires that when the partnership has income, gain, loss, or deduction attributable to Code Sec. 704(c) property (*i.e.*, property whose book value differs from the contributing partner's adjusted tax basis at the time of contribution), it must make appropriate allocations to the partners to avoid shifting the tax consequences of the built-in gain or loss. Thus, if the partnership sells Code Sec. 704(c) property and recognizes gain or loss, built-in gain or loss is allocated to the contributing partner.[111]

For Code Sec. 704(c) property subject to amortization, depletion, depreciation, or other cost recovery, the allocations of these deductions takes into account built-in gain or loss in the property. Thus, tax allocations to the noncontributing partners of depreciation with respect to Code Sec. 704(c) property must, to the extent possible, equal book allocations to those partners.[112]

The "traditional method" is the term applied to the historical rules which have existed under former Reg. § 1.704-1(c). Built-in gain or loss inherent in contributed property (Code Sec. 704(c) gain or loss) is attributable to the contributing partner (or, on the admission of a new partner with "book-up" or "book-down," to the existing partners). If the contributed property is disposed of in a non-taxable exchange, the property received with a substituted basis becomes Code Sec. 704(c) property. Taxable gain or

[109] *Id.*
[110] Reg. § 1.704-3(a)(10).
[111] Reg. § 1.704-3(b)(1).
[112] *Id.*

loss on disposition of the property and tax depreciation and other cost-recoveries must be allocated to the *non*-contributing partners so as to reflect their "views" of the property, *i.e.*, the *book* gain, loss, depreciation, etc. The "ceiling rule" remains part of the traditional method.

.03 Ceiling Rule Limitation

Total income, gain, loss, or deduction allocated to the partners for a taxable year with respect to a Code Sec. 704(c) property cannot exceed the total partnership income, gain, loss, or deduction with respect to that property for the taxable year (ceiling rule). If the partnership has no property whose allocations are limited by the ceiling rule, the traditional method is reasonable when used for all contributed property.[113]

Example 9-24.[114] *A* and *B* form an equal partnership. *A* contributes property with an adjusted basis of $5,000 and a fair market value of $10,000. *B* contributes $10,000 cash. The property is depreciated, for both book and tax purposes, on the straight-line method over the property's remaining recovery period of 10 years.

- *A* has an initial built-in gain of $5,000 ($10,000 − $5,000).
- Book depreciation of $1,000 per year is allocated $500 to both *A* and *B*. If the property had a fair market value adjusted basis, *B* also would have received $500 of tax depreciation. Tax depreciation, however, amounts only to $500 and must all be allocated to *B*.
- At the end of year one, the property has a book value of $9,000 and an adjusted basis of $4,500. *A*'s built-in gain has been reduced to the remaining book/tax differential of $4,500 ($9,000 − $4,500).
- If the property is sold at the end of Year 1 for $10,000, the book gain is $1,000, allocated $500 each to *A* and *B*. The tax gain, however, is $5,500. This is allocated $5,000 to *A* (his remaining $4,500 of built-in gain plus his $500 of book gain) and $500 to *B*.
- If the property is sold at the end of year one for less than $9,000, the entire tax gain, being less than the remaining built-in gain, is allocated to *A* and none to *B*. The ceiling rule prevents *B* from having a tax loss, even though he has a book loss.

Assuming a sales price of $7,000, there is a book loss of $2,000, allocated $1,000 each to *A* and *B*, and a tax gain of $2,500, all allocated to *A*.

[113] *Id.*

[114] Reg. § 1.704-3(b)(2), Ex. 1.

Comment. The effect of the Code Sec. 704(c) regulations is to allocate to the noncontributing partner tax depreciation based on the property's value over its remaining life.[115] This will normally result in the noncontributing partner's share of depreciation exceeding his share had the partnership purchased the property. It will also reduce his Code Sec. 704(b) capital account by his share of the property's depreciable value more quickly than if the partnership had purchased the property.

Example 9-25. *A* and *B* form an equal partnership. *A* contributes property with an adjusted basis of $4,000 and a fair market value of $10,000. *B* contributes $10,000 cash. The property is depreciated, for both book and tax purposes, on the straight-line method over the property's remaining recovery period of 10 years.

A has an initial built-in gain of $6,000 ($10,000 − $4,000). Book depreciation of $1,000 per year is allocated $500 to both *A* and *B*. If the property had been purchased, *B* also would have received $500 of tax depreciation. Tax depreciation, however, amounts to only $400 and must be totally allocated to *B*. The ceiling rule prevents *B* from having $500 of depreciation.

At the end of Year 1, the property has a book value of $9,000 and an adjusted basis of $3,600. *A*'s built-in gain has reduced to the remaining book/tax differential of $5,400 ($9,000 − $3,600).

If the property is sold at the end of Year 1 for $10,000, the book gain is $1,000, allocated $500 each to *A* and *B*. The tax gain, however, is $6,400. This is allocated $5,900 to *A* (his remaining $5,400 of built-in gain plus his $500 of book gain) and $500 to *B*.

If the property is sold at the end of Year 1 for less than $9,000 (book value), the entire tax gain, being less than the remaining built-in gain, is allocated to *A* and none to *B*. The ceiling rule prevents *B* from having a tax loss, even though he has a book loss.

.04 Traditional Method with Curative Allocations

To correct distortions created by the ceiling rule, a partnership may make reasonable curative allocations to reduce or eliminate disparities between book and tax items of noncontributing partners. A curative allocation is an allocation of income, gain, loss, or deduction for tax purposes that differs from the partnership's allocation of the corresponding book item. For example, if a noncontributing partner is allocated less tax depreciation than book depreciation with respect to an item of Code Sec. 704(c) property because of the ceiling rule, the partnership may make a curative allocation to that partner of tax depreciation from another item of partnership

[115] Reg. § 1.704-1(b)(2)(iv)(*g*)(*3*).

property to make up the difference, notwithstanding that the corresponding book depreciation is allocated to the contributing partner.[116]

To correct distortions created by the ceiling rule, a partnership may make reasonable curative allocations of *other* tax items of income, gain, loss or deduction, provided they are of the same *character* as the item limited by the ceiling rule. Thus, the non-contributing partners will have equal allocations of book and tax income, *i.e.*, the tax allocations will reflect their "view" of the contributed property. To be reasonable, a curative allocation of income, gain, loss, or deduction must be expected to have substantially the same effect on each partner's tax liability as the tax item limited by the ceiling rule. The expectation must exist at the time the Code Sec. 704(c) property is obligated to be (or is) contributed to the partnership.[117]

If a partnership does not have items sufficient in amount and character to equalize the non-contributing partners' book and tax allocations, the partnership may make the curative allocation in the next succeeding year that it has such sufficient items. However, the curative allocations must be made within a reasonable period of time, and, further, must be provided for in the partnership agreement for the year of contribution or revaluation.

A curative allocation is reasonable only to the extent that it does not exceed the amount necessary to avoid the distortion created by the ceiling rule for the current year and only if the items used have the same effect on the partners as the item affected by the ceiling rule. For example, if depreciation on a contributed asset is affected by the ceiling rule, only items of depreciation from other assets or ordinary income, and not capital gain, may be used as a curative allocation. There is an exception to the similar-in-character rule and yearly effect of the ceiling rule limit. If depreciation on a contributed asset has been limited by the ceiling rule and the asset is sold at a gain (*i.e.*, Code Sec. 1231 gain), it is not unreasonable to make a curative allocation of this gain to the contributing partner that takes into account the accumulated depreciation deficit allocated to the noncontributing partner. This amount exceeding the yearly ceiling rule limit and mismatching of character is available only if properly provided in the partnership agreement in effect for the year of contribution or revaluation.[118]

> ***Example 9-26.***[119] In the AB partnership of the previous example the $100 disparity between the book and tax depreciation allocated to *B* may be eliminated by a curative allocation of $100 of ordinary income to *A*, thereby reducing the ordinary income allocable to *B*. *B*'s net tax effect is now equal to his book position.

---

[116] Reg. § 1.704-3(c)(1).

[117] Reg. § 1.704-3(c)(3)(iii)(A).

[118] Reg. § 1.704-3(c)(3)(iii)(B) and (i).

[119] Reg. § 1.704-3(c)(4), Ex. 1.

While *A* has additional taxable income of $100, and his built-in gain remains at $5,400, the difference between his book and tax capital accounts is now equal to the built-in gain.

Assume the property is sold at the end of one year for $7,000, generating a book loss of $2,000, which would be a Code Sec. 1231 loss. In the absence of any other partnership 1231 gains or losses, there must be a curative allocation of another type of gain, loss, income or deduction available to give *B* which has substantially the same effect on his tax liability as his allocation of Code Sec. 1231 book loss.

.05 Remedial Allocation Method

A partnership may adopt the remedial allocation method by making reasonable remedial allocations to eliminate ceiling rule disparities between tax items of noncontributing partners and corresponding book items. Remedial allocations are tax allocations of income or gain that are offset by tax allocations of loss or deduction. These tax allocations are created by the partnership and have no effect on the partnership's book capital accounts.[120]

A partnership may adopt the remedial allocation method to eliminate the disparities caused by the ceiling rule. Under this method, the partnership makes a remedial allocation of income, gain, loss, or deduction to the noncontributing partner equal to the amount of the limitation caused by the ceiling rule and a simultaneous offsetting remedial allocation of deduction, loss, gain, or income to the contributing partner. Remedial allocations are not notional tax items created by the partnership solely for Code Sec. 704(c) and reverse Code Sec. 704(c) purposes. They are not a share of the partnership's taxable income or loss. Remedial items have the same effect as actual tax items on a partner's tax liabilities and the basis of the partnership interest.[121] As in the case of the traditional method with curative allocations, remedial allocations must have the same effect on the partners as the item limited by the ceiling rule.

A special rule applies for calculating book depreciation. The portion of the book basis up to the tax basis is recovered in the same manner as the tax basis. The remainder of the book basis is recovered using any available tax method and period for newly purchased property of the type contributed or revalued.[122]

Example 9-27.[123] *A* and *B* form an equal partnership. *A* contributes property with an adjusted basis of $4,000 and a fair market value of $10,000. *B* contributes $10,000 cash. The property has four years remaining on its 10-year recovery period. Under the remedial method, the partnership's book depreciation for each of the first four years equals $1,600 [$1,000 ($4,000 tax basis divided by four years) + $600

[120] Reg. § 1.704-3(d)(1).
[121] Reg. § 1.704-3(d)(4).
[122] Reg. § 1.704-3(d)(2).
[123] Reg. § 1.704-3(d)(7), Ex. 1.

($6,000 excess of book value over basis divided by 10 years)]. *A* and *B* are each allocated 50% of the book depreciation under the partnership agreement. For the first four years, *B* is allocated $800 of tax depreciation and *A* is allocated the remaining $200 of tax depreciation. No remedial allocations are made because the ceiling rule does not result in a book allocation of depreciation to *B* different from the tax allocation. At the end of Year 4, the capital accounts are as follows:

	A		***B***	
	Book	***Tax***	***Book***	***Tax***
Contribution	$10,000	$4,000	$10,000	$10,000
Depreciation	(3,200)	(800)	(3,200)	(3,200)
	$6,800	*$3,200*	*$6,800*	*$6,800*

Beginning in Year 5, the ceiling rule would cause an annual disparity of $300 between *B*'s book and tax capital accounts (tax depreciation is $0, but book depreciation is $600, allocated $300 each to *A* and *B*). Consequently, under the remedial method, the partnership must make remedial allocation of $300 of ordinary deductions (with the same character as depreciation) to *B* and $300 of ordinary income to *A*. At the end of Year 10, the capital accounts are as follows:

	A		***B***	
	Book	***Tax***	***Book***	***Tax***
Balances, End of Year 4	$6,800	$3,200	$6,800	$6,800
Book Depreciation.....	(1,800)	0	(1,800)	0
Remedial Allocation ...		1,800		(1,800)
	$5,000	*$5,000*	*$5,000*	*$5,000*

Note that the "traditional method with curative allocations" and the "remedial allocation method" look deceptively similar. They are, however, different.

As to depreciation:

- In the "traditional method with curative allocations," disparities between book and tax depreciation are "cured" over the remaining tax life of the property.

- In the "remedial allocation method," however, the book-tax disparity is "remedied" over the longer tax recovery period for new property.

Example 9-28. Assume the same facts as in the previous example. *A* and *B* form an equal partnership. *A* contributes property with an adjusted basis of $4,000 and a fair market value of $10,000. The property has four years remaining on its original 10-year recovery period. *B* contributes $10,000 of cash. The partnership adopts the traditional method with curative allocation for a Code Sec. 704(c) purpose.

A has an initial built-in gain of $6,000 ($10,000 – $4,000). The partnership's yearly book depreciation is $2,500 ($10,000/4 years). *B*'s share of the book depreciation is $1,250 per year. The partnership's yearly tax depreciation is $1,000 ($4,000/4 years).

Under the traditional method with curative allocations *B* is entitled to all the tax depreciation of $1,000 per year plus a curative allocation of $250 of other deductions of the same character which would otherwise go to *A*. The entire book/tax differential is taken into account in four years under the traditional method with curative allocation rather that ten years, as would be required under the remedial allocation method. During four years, A has received no depreciation and has reported $1,000 of *B*'s economic income, and *B* has received $4,000 of depreciation deduction and avoided paying tax on $1,000.

As to gain/loss from the sale of contributed property:

- The "traditional method with curative allocations" requires that if the property is sold at a tax gain (loss), but a book loss (gain), the disparity between the book and tax results *cannot* be cured by allocating a tax loss (gain) to the non-contributing partner unless that tax loss (gain) has been generated by the disposition of another asset which will have substantially the same effect on the partner's tax liability as the property sold.[124]

- Such is not the case with the "remedial allocation method." Thus, if property is sold at a tax gain but at a book loss, the non-contributing partners may be allocated a *loss* and the contributing partner an offsetting *larger gain* than the reported tax gain from the sale.

Example 9-29.[125] *A* and *B* form an equal partnership. *A* contributes land with an adjusted basis of $4,000 and a fair market value of $10,000; *B* contributes $10,000 cash. The property is later sold for $9,000, resulting in a capital gain of $5,000 and a book loss of $1,000. If provided for in the partnership agreement, a remedial allocation of a $500 capital loss to *B* with an offsetting remedial allocation of a $500 capital gain to *A* may be made, resulting in the following capital accounts:

	A		*B*	
	Book	***Tax***	***Book***	***Tax***
Contributions	$10,000	$4,000	$10,000	$10,000
Sale of land	(500)	5,000	(500)	0
Remedial Allocations		500		(500)
	$9,500	*$9,500*	*$9,500*	*$9,500*

[124] Reg. § 1.704-3(c)(3)(iii)(A).

[125] Reg. § 1.704-3(d)(7), Ex. 2.

.06 Special Rules

A partnership may disregard the mandatory allocations under Code Sec. 704(c), or only allocate gain or loss on the disposition of the property, if there is a "small disparity."[126] The disparity between the book values (FMV) and adjusted bases of all properties contributed by a partner within a single taxable year of the partnership is a "small disparity" if:

- The difference between the book values and adjusted bases of all items of contributed property is not more than 15 percent of their adjusted bases; and
- The total disparity for all such properties does not exceed $20,000.

For all purposes of Code Sec. 704(c), properties may be *aggregated* and treated as one item of property, as follows:

- All properties, except real estate that are included in the same general asset account under Code Sec. 168.
- Zero basis property other than real property.
- For partnerships that do not use a specific identification method of accounting, each item of inventory, other than securities.
- Other classes of property as published in the Internal Revenue Bulletin or permitted in a letter ruling.
- Special aggregation rules apply to securities partnerships.[127]

.07 Capital Account Analysis

Example 9-30. Using the facts of the AB partnership of the previous examples, the relationship between the book and tax capital accounts of the partners and of *A*'s built-in or deferred gain appear below. Assume one year has expired and that the partnership has ordinary income of $2,000 before depreciation. Under the "traditional method" and with "curative allocations":

	Capital A		*Capital B*	
	Book	*Tax*	*Book*	*Tax*
Contribution	$10,000	$4,000	$10,000	$10,000
Ordinary income	1,000	1,000	1,000	1,000
Depreciation	(500)	(0)	(500)	(400)
Traditional method	*$10,500*	*$5,000*	*$10,500*	*$10,600*
Differences	$5,500	$(100)		
Effect of ceiling rule	(100)	100		
Built-in gain	*$5,400*	*$ 0*		

[126] Reg. § 1.704-3(e).

[127] Reg. § 1.704-3(e)(3).

Traditional method, above . . .	$10,500	$5,000	$10,500	$10,600
Curative allocation of ordinary income		100		(100)
Balances as cured	*$10,500*	*$5,100*	*$10,500*	*$10,500*
Difference (equals built-in gain)	*$5,400*		*$ 0*	

¶ 904 Allocation of Partnership Income and Loss on Transfer of or Change in a Partner's Interest

On the transfer of a partnership interest, it is necessary to allocate partnership profit or loss between the transferor partner and the transferee partner. In addition, if a new partner is admitted to the partnership or a partner's interest is increased, reduced or liquidated, it is necessary to allocate the partnership's income or basis by taking into account the partners varying interest during the year. Generally, the taxable year of the partnership as a whole does not close on the transfer of a partner's interest.[128] Also, the taxable year of the partnership as a whole does not close upon the admission of a new partner, liquidation of a partner or change in a partner's interest in the partnership.[129] However, a partnership's taxable year closes on the date of sale with respect to a partner who terminates his or her entire partnership interest by transfer, death or liquidating distribution.[130] The terminated partner's distributive share of partnership income or loss for the short period, ending on the disposition date, is therefore included in his or her tax return for the taxable year that includes the sale date. Thus, if the sale occurs in December, a selling calendar year partner in a January fiscal-year partnership may be required to include as many as 23 months of partnership income in his or her income in the year of sale. The other partners will report on January 30 their share of only 12 months of operations.

If a partner transfers less than his or her entire interest in a partnership or is partially liquidated, the partnership year does not close with respect to the selling partner; the selling partner's distributive share of partnership income is includible in his or her taxable year, within which ends the normal partnership year-end by taking into account his or her varying interest in the partnership during its taxable year. Even though the income attributable to the portion of the partnership interest transferred is includible in the partner's income at the same time as the income attributable to the retained portion, any gain or loss on the transfer is determined by adding it to the basis of the portion of the partnership interest that is transferred. The regulations indicate that the basis of the portion of the interest that is transferred is adjusted to reflect the partnership profit and loss up to the date of sale.[131]

[128] Code Sec. 706(c)(1). This is true even though the transfer results in the partnership's technical dissolution under the *nontax* rules of most jurisdictions.

[129] Code Sec. 706(c)(1).

[130] Code Sec. 706(c)(2)(A).

[131] Reg. § 1.705-1(a)(1).

A transferring partner's distributive share of partnership income, gain, loss, deduction, and credit is determined by taking into account his or her "varying interest" in the partnership during the year of the sale. The regulations afford the partners a measure of flexibility in making this determination by providing two methods of allocation.[132] The first method provides for an "interim closing" of the partnership books whenever the partners' interests change, whereas the second (which requires "agreement among the partners") provides for the proration of partnership income, gain, loss, deduction, and credit over the entire taxable year of the partnership.[133] In addition, if a partner is liquidated, or there is a change in the partner's share of the partnership profits and losses during the year by contribution or distribution or otherwise, the partner's share of such profits and losses is determined by using the same two methods.[134]

> ***Example 9-31.*** On December 1 of Year 1, *D* buys *A*'s interest in the equal interest, calendar-year, accrual-basis ABC partnership that has incurred expenses totaling $360 for the year, $240 of which were accrued prior to December 1 of Year 1 and $120 in the month of December, and has accrued $360 of income equally over the taxable year.
>
> Under the "interim closing" method of allocation, *D*'s distributive share of the partnership's expenses is $40 (incurred during December of Year 1 after *D* bought the partnership interest), and *D*'s share of partnership income is $10. He accordingly incurs a $30 loss from the partnership. Under the second method of allocation, however, *D*'s share of partnership expenses is $10 (1/3 partner × 1/12 of the year × $360), and his share of partnership income is $10 (1/3 partner × 1/12 of the year × $360). Accordingly, *D* would report no income or loss from the partnership for Year 1.

Even though the buyer and seller's initial impression is that each will prefer the method of income allocation that will result in the least income, a closer analysis will reveal that the buyer is normally much more concerned with avoiding income than is the seller. For example, if the seller agrees to the method of income allocation that increases his or her share of the year's partnership income, the seller also increases basis in the partnership interest for an equal amount. This increased basis results in a decreased gain for the identical amount. The offsetting amounts occur in the seller's same taxable year. Typically the seller has no change in the amount of income, but will have less gain and more ordinary income. The net result is increased tax for the ordinary income/capital gains rate differential applied to the income shifted to him.

---

[132] Reg. § 1.706-1(c).

[133] Reg. § 1.706-1(c)(2).

[134] S. Rep. No. 938, 94th Cong., 2d Sess. 98 (1976); *Richardson v. Commr.*, 76 TC 512, Dec. 37,801 (1981), aff'd CA-5, 83-1 USTC ¶ 9109, 693 F2d 1189.

The buyer's increased income share also results in an increased basis for his or her partnership interest. But the buyer reports the income currently while most likely making use of the additional basis in the distant future. The present value of the tax benefit obtained from the basis adjustment is much less than the seller's. The buyer and seller should consider an increased price that would compensate the seller for any increased tax liability coupled with adopting an income allocation method that minimizes the buyer's share.

> ***Observation.*** The method of allocating partnership taxable income between the buyer and seller need not be consistent with any method used to fix the price paid for the partnership interest.

.01 Special Rules Limiting Loss Allocations on Transfer or Change in a Partner's Interest

Code Sec. 706(c)(2) was amended in 1976 to make it clear that Code Sec. 706's prohibition against "retroactive" allocations applies to partners who acquire interests by transfer from other partners as well as those who acquire or increase their interests by contributions.[135] Notwithstanding the 1976 amendments, the Congressional objective to prevent retroactive allocations largely went unrealized due to a number of techniques that were developed—paramount among these was the use of the closing of the books method of income allocation in tiered partnership arrangements and cash-basis partnerships.

Multitiered partnership structures were created when a parent partnership owned an interest in a subsidiary partnership that carried on the business activity. When a new partner purchased an interest in the parent partnership, the "interim closing" method of allocation was used and it was claimed that, since the parent partnership only realized its share of the subsidiary's income, gain, losses, and deductions on the last day of the subsidiary's taxable year, the incoming partner was entitled to a full distributive share of any losses incurred by the subsidiary. The IRS rejected this approach and took the position that the parent sustained the losses at the same time as the subsidiary partnership and that the subsidiary's losses could, accordingly, not be retroactively allocated.[136] However, Congress felt this area remained open to abuse by taxpayers. Partnerships also sought to make retroactive allocations by adopting the cash-basis method of accounting, utilizing the interim closing-of-the-books method, and deferring the payment of deductible expenses until near the close of the partnership's taxable year.[137]

---

[135] See General Explanation of the Tax Reform Act of 1976 (P.L. 94-455), Staff of the Joint Committee on Taxation, 94th Cong. 2d Sess., 91-94 (1976).

[136] Rev. Rul. 77-311, 1977-2 CB 218.

[137] The legislative history of the 1976 amendments to Code Sec. 706 seems to sanction this technique. However, the committee reports on the 1984 amendments to Code Sec. 706 refer to it as an area of abuse.

The Tax Reform Act of 1984 [138] attempted to combat the above-mentioned abuses by providing, in Code Sec. 706(d), specific rules for the determination of each partner's distributive share of items of income, gain, loss, deduction, or credit of the partnership when there is a change in any partner's interest during the partnership's taxable year. Code Sec. 706(d)(1) provides as a general rule that each partner's distributive share of the above items is to be determined by using any method prescribed by regulations that takes into account the varying interests of the partners in the partnership during the taxable year.

This general rule is, however, subject to two exceptions specified in Code Sec. 706(d)(2) and (3). Certain "allocable cash-basis items" must be prorated over the period to which they are attributable.[139] In addition, partnerships which are partners in another partnership must consider the income of that partnership as earned pro rata over the taxable year.[140]

The first exception applies only to partnerships using the cash-basis method of accounting. The "allocable cash-basis items" that must be prorated are (1) interest, (2) taxes, (3) payment for services or for the use of property, and (4) "any other item of a kind specified in regulations prescribed by the Secretary as being an item with respect to which the application of Code Sec. 706(d)(2) is appropriate to avoid significant misstatements of the income of the partners." Both the House Committee and the Senate Committee interpret significant misstatements of income as retroactive allocations to the partners. Any item within this category is to be assigned to each day in the period to which it is attributable.[141] The amounts so assigned are then apportioned among the partners in proportion to their interests in the partnership at the close of each day.[142] Both the House and the Senate Committee Reports make it clear that the determination of the period to which an expense is attributable for this purpose is to be made in accordance with "economic accrual principles." Thus, in effect, cash-basis partnerships are placed on the accrual method of accounting, but only for purposes of allocating income and deductions to incoming partners with respect to "allocable cash-basis items" which have been paid by the partnership. The partnership's deduction, however, is allowed only when the item is paid, even though the accrual system is used in determining which partners are entitled to that deduction.

If a payment of an allocable cash basis item is attributable to a year following the year of payment, it is assigned to the last day of the year of payment. All allocable cash-basis items that are attributable to periods before the current taxable year must be allocated entirely to the first day of the year in the case of items allocable to prior years, and entirely to the last day of the year in the case of items allocable to future periods.[143] Any

[138] The Tax Reform Act of 1984, P.L. 98-369.
[139] Code Sec. 706(d)(2).
[140] Code Sec. 706(d)(3).
[141] Code Sec. 706(d)(2)(A)(i).
[142] Code Sec. 706(d)(2)(A)(ii).
[143] Code Sec. 706(d)(2)(C).

portion of a *deductible* cash-basis item that is assigned in this manner to the first day of any taxable year is allocated among persons who are partners during the prior period to which the portion is attributable, in accordance with their varying interests in the partnership during such prior period, rather than in accordance with their interest on the first day of the year.[144] If, however, all or part of a deductible cash-basis item is allocated to persons who are no longer partners on the first day of the taxable year in which the items are taken into account, then such part of the item must be capitalized by the partnership and allocated to the basis of partnership assets under Code Sec. 755.[145] Capitalized expenditures that are allocated to basis under Code Sec. 755 will presumably be treated as Code Sec. 743(b) adjustments. As such, they will reduce the new partner's shares of partnership income. The effect of the basis adjustment will depend upon whether the regulations allocate the basis adjustments solely to the buying partners or treat them as common basis adjustments.

The Code Sec. 706(d)(2) provisions deny the partnership the ability to allocate the specified deductions that were generated prior to the new partner's admittance. These rules do not prohibit the partnership from allocating a disproportionate share of deductions to the new partners if they were generated after their admittance.

The application of Code Sec. 706(d)(2) to cash-method *income* items is unclear. While the focus of both the statute and the accompanying legislative history clearly is on cash-method *deduction* items, the definition of "allocable cash-method items" in Code Sec. 706(d)(2)(B) arguably includes income items. Code Sec. 706(d)(2)(B)(iv) includes any "item" specified by regulations and does not, by its terms, limit the regulations to deductible items. In addition, the general rule provided in Code Sec. 706(d)(1) refers to "items" as including both income and deduction.

> ***Comment.*** The combined expense of closing the books of the partnership and working with the allocable cash basis item rule may encourage more partnerships to use the easier method of prorating items rather than the more precise cut-off method.

If Code Sec. 706(d)(2) is applicable to income items, several questions arise. First, what is the relationship between Code Sec. 706(d)(2) and Code Sec. 751, which provides rules for dealing with shifts in the partners' interests in unrealized receivables? Second, what is a cash-method income item? As an example, does it include installment receivables under Code Secs. 453 and 453A? Third, what are the mechanical rules for assigning an "appropriate portion" of a cash-method income item to each day in the period to which it is attributable? Suppose, for example, that an accounting partnership: (1) accepts an engagement on January 1, receiving a retainer on that day; (2) performs services at various times through the following

[144] Code Sec. 706(d)(2)(D)(i).

[145] Code Sec. 706(d)(2)(D)(ii).

December; and (3) renders a statement for its fee (net of the retainer) on January 1 of the following year. To what days is the fee allocable? Is it necessary to account for the services rendered on a daily basis? Are the rules different if the fee eventually charged is result-oriented or is wholly contingent? If an income item is allocated to one who is no longer a partner, what adjustment is made to the partnership assets?

The requirement that partnership items must be determined and allocated to the partners on a *daily* basis can cause significant administrative burdens for partnerships if there are frequent changes in the partners' interests. In connection with the 1976 amendments,[146] the Conference Report suggests that this problem should be addressed by regulations that would allow "interim closing" on the fifteenth and last days of each month, rather than requiring daily closing.[147] Since 1976, in the absence of any new regulations under Code Sec. 706, many partnerships have used considerably more aggressive allocation techniques based on monthly or even quarterly closing. Typically, partnerships using these techniques allocate monthly or quarterly losses to the persons who are partners on the last day of the month or quarter without regard to whether they held their partnership interests for all or only a portion of the month or quarter. The validity of these techniques under the 1976 amendment is, of course, subject to serious question.

The Senate version of Code Sec. 706(d)(2) and (3) would have allowed partnerships to make an annual election to determine the varying interests of the partners by using a monthly convention that treats all changes in the partners' interests in the partnership during any month as occurring on the first day of the month. The Conference Committee to the Deficit Reduction Act of 1984 [148] removed this provision from the statute based on its understanding that the Treasury would provide, by regulation, a monthly convention to treat partners entering after the fifteenth day of a month as entering on the first day of the following month, and partners entering during the first 15 days of a month as entering on the first day of the month. During the discussion on the floor of the Senate that preceded approval of the final version of the 1984 Act, Senator Dole, chairman of the Senate Finance Committee, stated that the mid-month convention described in the Conference Report was not intended to restrict the Treasury's discretion to provide a more flexible convention by regulations when no abuse potential is present. He then stated that regulations could provide that, in nonabusive cases, any partner admitted to a partnership during a calendar month could, for purposes of the retroactive rules, be treated as having been admitted on the first day of such month.

---

[146] Tax Reform Act of 1976, P.L. 94-455.

[147] H.R. Rep. No. 861, 98th Cong., 2d Sess. 858 (1984).

[148] P.L. 98-369.

Code Sec. 706(d)(3) contains Congressional response to tiered partnership arrangements aimed at effecting retroactive allocations. It provides that when a parent partnership holds an interest in a subsidiary partnership and during the taxable year there is a change in any partner's interest in the parent partnership, then, except to the extent provided by regulations, the parent partnership's share of any item of income, gain, loss, deduction, or credit of the subsidiary partnership is to be apportioned over that portion of the taxable year during which the parent partnership had an interest in the subsidiary.[149] The effect of this amendment is to place the parent partnership effectively on a consolidated basis of accounting vis-à-vis the subsidiary partnership.

.02 Retroactive Allocations Among Newly Admitted and Continuing Partners

The partnership may not allocate items of income or deduction to a partner if they arose before he or she became a member of the partnership. Code Sec. 706(c)(2) was amended in 1976 [150] to make it clear that the prohibition against "retroactive" allocations applies to partners who acquire or increase their interests by contributions as well as those who acquire interests by transfer from other partners.[151] The legislative history of the 1984 changes in Code Sec. 706 explicitly approves the position of the Tax Court in *Kenneth E. Lipke v. Commissioner*.[152] *Lipke* indicates that retroactive allocations (or reallocations) of partnership income or loss among contemporaneous partners are permissible,[153] provided they are not related to the infusion of new capital into the partnership.[154] This is good news for legal, accounting, and other service partnerships, many of which traditionally have allocated their income after the end of their tax year.

¶ 905 Family Partnerships—Code Sec. 704(e)

Originally, "family" partnerships were an important means of diverting income from parents to their children.[155] In the past they engendered the largest portion of the litigation relating to the taxation of partnerships.

---

[149] This apparently confirms the IRS's position that losses in this situation are sustained by the parent partnership at the same time they are sustained by the subsidiary partnership. See Rev. Rul. 77-311, 1977-2 CB 218.

[150] Tax Reform Act of 1976, P.L. 94-455.

[151] A detailed discussion of allocating income between the new and continuing partners may be found at ¶ 905.

[152] *K.E. Lipke v. Commr.*, 81 TC 689, Dec. 40,528 (1983). See General Explanation of the Tax Reform Act of 1976 (P.L. 94-455), Staff of the Joint Committee on Taxation, 94th Cong., 2d Sess., 91-94. Code Sec. 761(c) defines a "partnership agreement" to include any modifications made prior to the due date for filing the partnership return and, under Code Sec. 704(a), a partner's distributive share is determined by the partnership agreement. On the surface, it appears that retroactive allocations to partners who increase or decrease their interest in the partnership's results through contributions or distributions may be possible through an amendment to the agreement. This result was not intended (see also Code Sec. 761(f)), but the legislative history of the Deficit Reduction Act of 1984 (P.L. 98-369) makes it clear that Code Sec. 761(c) still permits retroactive modifications to the partnership agreement that result in shifts of interests among the partners who are members for the entire taxable year, provided those shifts are not attributable to additional capital contributions. See General Explanation of the Revenue Provisions of the Deficit Reduction Act of 1984 (P.L. 98-369), Joint Committee on Taxation, 98th Cong., 2d Sess., 219.

[153] Under Code Secs. 706 and 761.

[154] See Rev. Rul. 77-310, 1977-2 CB 217.

[155] Prior to 1948, in which year income-splitting was authorized for all spouses, family partnerships were utilized primarily to divert income from one spouse to another. Act § 301 of the Revenue Act of 1948 (P.L. 471), providing for income-splitting between spouses, obviated the necessity for this device.

The income tax incentive to using family limited partnerships as a method of reducing the family's total income tax by diverting some of it to family members with lower marginal tax rules has diminished since the enactment of Code Sec. 704(e). In addition to Code Sec. 704(e), there are two major reasons for this change. First, effective in 1987, the tax on unearned income of a child under age 14 is computed at the parent's marginal tax rate.[156] Indeed, the statute allows the parent an election to claim the child's unearned income on the parent's tax return.[157] For purposes of taxing the unearned income of a child under 14 at the parent's highest tax rates, earned income includes wages, salaries, and other compensation for personal services. Therefore, unless the child renders services to or on behalf of the partnership, all the child's distributive share of partnership income is unearned income. Second, in prior years, family members could have a wide variation in their highest marginal tax rates. Historically, the highest individual income tax rates have reached as high as 90 percent. Currently the highest bracket is less than half that amount and the tax rates for individuals reach 28 percent at a relatively low level of income. In addition, if a trust holds the partnership interest, the trust is taxed at the highest individual rate on taxable income in excess of $9,550.

Family limited partnerships are currently popular mostly because of the estate and gift tax benefits they can provide. Using the proper planning for transfers of partnership interests, a donor has the potential to transfer partial interests in his or her business which have a discounted value for estate and gift tax purposes because of the partnership interest's lack of control and marketability. At the same time the donor can control the business in his or her capacity as a general partner. These family limited partnerships are subject to the income tax rules of Code Sec. 704(e) even though income tax planning was not an objective of forming the partnership.

> ***LLC Observation.*** Although an LLC may be treated as a partnership for income tax purposes, for estate planning purposes there may be differences in any discounts in valuation on account of lack of marketability. One factor in valuing this discount is the partner or members' right to liquidate his or her interest. In some jurisdictions, LLC members have rights to liquidate their interest that are superior to a limited partner. This would result in less of a valuation discount for the interest transferred. For estate and gift tax purposes, the only restrictions which are taken into account in valuing the LLC or partnership interest are those created by local law. Additional restrictions provided in the LLC or partnership agreement are disregarded.[158]

---

[156] Code Sec. 1(g).

[157] Code Sec. 1(g)(7).

[158] Reg. § 26.2704-2(b).

Code Sec. 704(e) provides a statutory rule for partnerships which follows two well-established principles of tax law. These principles are that income derived from property is to be taxed on the owner of the property,[159] and that income derived from services is to be taxed to the person performing the services.[160]

The family-partnership provisions of Code Sec. 704(e) are virtually the same as the amendments to the 1939 Code enacted in 1951 in order to assure that a bona fide owner of a capital interest in a family partnership in which capital is an income-producing factor will be respected as such.[161] They state that a person shall be recognized as a partner for income tax purposes "if he owns a capital interest in a partnership for which capital is a material income-producing factor, whether or not such interest was derived by purchase or gift from any other person."[162] In addition, they state that in a partnership in which capital is a material income-producing factor, a donee partner's distributive share of income under the partnership agreement shall be taxed to him or her except to the extent that such share is determined without allowance of reasonable compensation to the donor for his or her services to the partnership, and, to the extent that such share is attributable to donated capital, it is proportionately greater than the donor's share attributable to his or her capital.[163] For the purpose of these allocation provisions, an interest purchased from a member of the family is treated as a donated interest.[164]

---

[159] *E.T. Blair v. Commr.*, SCt, 37-1 USTC ¶ 9083, 300 US 5, 57 SCt 330. Compare cases dealing with the assignment of merely the income derived from property, *C.H. Harrison v. S.H. Schaffner*, SCt, 41-1 USTC ¶ 9355, 312 US 579, 61 SCt 759, and *G.T. Helvering v. P.R.G. Horst*, SCt, 40-2 USTC ¶ 9787, 311 US 112, 61 SCt 144. Compare cases where the donor or property retained control over the income therefrom, *Commr. v. J. Sunnen*, SCt, 48-1 USTC ¶ 9230, 333 US 591, 68 SCt 715, or the property itself *G.T. Helvering v. G.B. Clifford, Jr.*, SCt, 40-1 USTC ¶ 9265, 309 US 331, 60 SCt 554.

[160] *G.T. Helvering v. G.A. Eubank*, SCt, 40-2 USTC ¶ 9788, 311 US 122, 61 SCt 149, rehearing denied, 312 US 713 (1941); *R.H. Lucas v. G.C. Earl*, SCt, 2 USTC ¶ 496, 281 US 111, 50 SCt 241 (1930).

[161] The Revenue Act of 1951 (P.L. 183); Code Sec. 340; S. Rep. No. 1622, 83d Cong., 2d Sess. 384 (1954). In *Commr. v. W.O. Culbertson, Sr.*, SCt, 49-1 USTC ¶ 9323, 337 US 733, 69 SCt 1210, the Supreme Court reaffirmed the principle that income derived from property is taxable to the real owner of the property, and held therefore that a donee of property who invests it in a family partnership and exercises real control over the property and the disposition of the income derived therefrom can qualify as a true partner. However, some later lower court decisions, see, *e.g.*, *H. Feldman v. Commr.*, 14 TC 17, Dec. 17,425 (1950), aff'd, CA-4, 50-1 USTC ¶ 9122, 186 F2d 87; *W.S. Barrett v. Commr.*, 13 TC 539, Dec.17,231 (1949), aff'd, CA-1, 50-2 USTC ¶ 9501, 185 F2d 150, continue to hold that a wife would be recognized as a valid partner in her husband's enterprise only if she invested "capital originating with her" (see, *e.g.*, *G. Graber v. Commr.*, CA-10, 48-2 USTC ¶ 9409, 171 F2d 32, 35; *C.L. Canfield v. Commr.*, CA-6, 48-2 USTC ¶ 9337, 168 F2d 907, 913; cf. *F. Smith v. L. Henslee*, CA-6, 49-1 USTC ¶ 9216, 173 F2d 284), or performed "vital additional services" (see, *e.g.*, *S. Friedman v. Commr.*, 10 TC 1145, Dec. 16,461 (1948); *W.E. Grace v. Commr.*, 10 TC 1, Dec. 16,203 (1948)), although the opinion in the *Culbertson* case said that the Court's earlier opinions in *Commr. v. F.E. Tower*, SCt, 46-1 USTC ¶ 9189, 327 US 280, and *A.L. Lusthaus v. Commr.*, SCt, 46-1 USTC ¶ 9190, 327 US 293, on which the lower courts were relying, were being misinterpreted.

[162] Code Sec. 704(e)(1). The donee partner may be a corporation, all of whose stock is owned by the donor. *C. Turner v. Commr.*, 24 TCM 544, Dec. 27,344(M), TC Memo. 1965-101 (1965), appeal dismissed (CA-9, 1965); compare *L.F. Noonan v. U.S.*, CA-9, 71-2 USTC ¶ 9756, 451 F2d 992, aff'g per curiam 52 TC 907, Dec.29,725 (1969) ("shell" corporation disregarded, and its share of partnership income attributed to sole shareholder). For tax purposes, such a corporation may be treated as a donee partner even if, in form, it is the assignee of the donor's entire interest in the partnership, but is not substituted in his or her place as a partner and is not considered to be a partner under local law. *D.L. Evans v. Commr.*, 50 TC 40, Dec. 29,915 (1970), aff'd, CA-7, 71-2 USTC ¶ 9597, 447 F2d 547.

[163] Code Sec. 704(e)(2).

[164] Code Sec. 704(e)(3). The Internal Revenue Code limits "family" for this purpose to only a spouse, ancestors, lineal descendants, and trusts for the primary benefit of such persons. *G.A. Paul v. Commr.*, 16 TCM 752, Dec. 22,560(M), TC Memo. 1957-170. Note, however, that this limitation applies only to bona fide purchases, and that the allocation rules will apply to the purported purchase of a partnership interest by an individual only *collaterally related* to the seller (or unrelated)

Where capital is a material income-producing factor, the partnership's income must, as mentioned, include a reasonable payment to the donor as compensation for any services rendered for or on behalf of the partnership. When the donor is a partner, the payment is characterized as a Code Sec. 707(a) or 707(c) payment, depending upon the criteria discussed at ¶ 704. If the donor is not a partner, it is not clear whether Code Sec. 704(e) applies. A literal interpretation of the statutes implies that the donor must be paid reasonable compensation whether or not the donor remains a partner. If Code Sec. 704(e) does apply to a donor partner who is no longer a partner, the payment is treated as made to an unrelated employee or independent contractor. After the donor's reasonable compensation is taken into account, the partnership is free to allocate its remaining income in any manner with one exception. Based upon relative capital accounts, the donee's share of the partnership's income cannot exceed the donor's share. For this purpose, payments to the donee for services are not considered a share of income.[165] As a result, disproportionate distributions will not necessarily be considered a prime factor in determining whether a donee is a partner, but only in determining the extent to which the reallocation of income through the partnership will be recognized for income tax purposes. However, when an incoming donee partner receives a distributive disproportionate share, that part of his or her distributive share which is disproportionate will remain taxable to the donor.[166] What constitutes reasonable compensation paid to the donee is a facts and circumstances question.[167]

Despite the existence of these provisions, therefore, the questions of whether or not, in a particular case, "capital is a material income-producing factor" and whether or not the services of the donor have been reasonably compensated [168] still can create considerable uncertainty.

(Footnote Continued)

if the transfer has "any of the substantial characteristics of a gift." Reg. § 1.704-1(e)(3)(ii)(*b*). If the purchase does not have "the usual characteristics of an arm's-length transaction," it will be bona fide only if it is "genuinely intended to promote the success of the business by security participation of the purchaser in the business or by adding his or her credit to that of the other participants." Reg. § 1.704-1(e)(4)(ii).

[165] Reg. § 1.704-1(e)(3)(i)(b).

[166] *Bayou Verret Land Co. v. Commr.*, CA-5, 71-2 USTC ¶ 9713, 450 F2d 850, aff'g, rem'g and rev'g 52 TC 791, Dec. 29,744 (1969), Acq. (result only, as to a different issue).

[167] See Code Sec. 704(e)(2); Reg. § 1.704-1(e)(3)(i)(*c*). Under prior law, the IRS had contended that it could reallocate income in proportion to capital invested and services rendered. I.T. 3845, 1947-1 CB 66 (declared obsolete, Rev. Rul. 69-43, 1969-1 CB 310); see also Mim. 6767, 1952-1 CB 111 (declared obsolete, Rev. Rul. 69-31, 1969-1 CB 307). The courts, however, generally disagreed. *W.B. Woosley v. Commr*, CA-6, 48-1 USTC ¶ 9292, 168 F2d 330; *C.L. Canfield v. Commr.*, CA-6, 48-2 USTC ¶ 9337, 168 F2d 907; *R. Adams v. M.H. Allen*, DC Ga., 51-1 USTC ¶ 9300; *M.E. Trapp v. H.C. Jones*, DC Okla., 50-1 USTC ¶ 9101, 87 FSupp 415, aff'd on this point, CA-10, 51-1 USTC ¶ 9116, 186 F2d 951; *N.B. Drew v. Commr.*, 12 TC 5, Dec. 16,757 (1949), Acq., but cf. *D.L. Jennings v. Commr.*, 10 TC 505, Dec. 16,309 (1948), Acq.; *M. German v. Commr* 2 TC 474, Dec. 13,378 (1943), Acq. The Committee Report to the Revenue Act of 1951 (P.L. 183) states that after making "a reasonable allowance. . . for the services rendered by the partners. . . the balance of the income will be allocated according to the amount of capital which the several partners have invested." H.R. Rep. No. 586, 82d Cong., 1st Sess., 34 (1951). If the standards for determining reasonable compensation for members of a family partnership resemble those applied to stockholder-employees of corporations, considerable partnership income that is actually attributable to personal services, but which is in excess of "reasonable compensation for services," may be deflected to the donee. The Internal Revenue Code also provides that a partner's distributive share of partnership earnings need not be diminished merely because of his or her absence due to military service. Code Sec. 704(e)(2).

[168] *W.L. Peterson v. W.M. Gray*, DC Ky., 59-2 USTC ¶ 9692.

S corporation Observation. Like the family partnership rules of Code Sec. 704(e), Code Sec. 1366(e) permits the IRS to reallocate S corporation income among members of a "family"[169] if one or more of the S corporation's shareholders renders services or furnishes capital without receiving reasonable compensation in exchange for the services or capital. The significant difference between the Subchapter S family reallocation rule and the Subchapter K family reallocation rule is that the Subchapter S reallocation rule can apply to an undercompensated family member who does not have an ownership interest in the S corporation and who did not transfer any ownership interest to a family member.[170] The reallocation rule of Code Sec. 1366(e) was intended to prevent family members from shifting income among themselves to minimize tax liability.

Example 9-32. Picture Palace, an S corporation, has two equal shareholders, Leopold and Catalina, who are brother and sister. Their father, Fred, renders services to the corporation. In an attempt to shift income to Leopold and Catalina, Fred renders services to the corporation and is paid less than the reasonable value of the services. Under Code Sec. 1366(e), the IRS can apparently increase Fred 's gross income to reflect the additional compensation Fred should have received from the corporation and can apparently increase the compensation deductions to Leopold and Catalina, decreasing their income.

If one family member is undercompensated for capital provided to the corporation, Code Sec. 1366(e)(3) permits the IRS to reallocate items of income. Apparently, Code Sec. 1366(e) permits the IRS to reallocate income in a situation in which a parent provides capital to the corporation but does not receive a sufficient amount of stock in exchange for the property. In those same circumstances, the regulations under the gift tax provisions provide that the parent is treated as making a gift and is potentially liable for gift tax.[171]

.01 Capital as a Material Income-Producing Factor

The regulations state that capital is a material income-producing factor if a substantial portion of the gross income of the business is attributable to capital. Ordinarily, this will be deemed to be the case if the

[169] The term "family" is defined by reference to Code Sec. 704(e)(3), which provides that the family of any individual includes "only his spouse, ancestors, and lineal descendants, and any trusts for the primary benefit of such persons."

[170] Code Secs. 704(e) and 1366(e).

[171] See Reg. §25.2511-1(h)(1). Read literally, Code Sec. 1366(e) and the gift-tax regulations may mean that a shareholder who contributes excess capital to an S corporation could have both gift-tax liability and an additional share of income allocated to him. This result seems anomalous. If the gift-tax rules apply, it simply means that a shareholder transferred a share of the contributed property or a share of stock to another family member. Viewed in this manner, the contributions of the shareholders would be proportionate and not trigger application of Code Sec. 1366(e). Alternatively, since the shareholder providing services is not being adequately compensated, expect the IRS to argue that he or she is subject to income tax as if adequate compensation were received *and* gift tax as if it were subsequently transferred to the other "donee" shareholder(s).

business requires substantial inventories or substantial investment in plant, machinery, or equipment.[172]

The Tax Court, in a case involving the analogous requirements of former Code Sec. 1361, stated that "[c]apital will be deemed to be a material income-producing factor when it 'gives character to a sizable portion of the operations . . .' but if capital is utilized merely in the form of salaries, wages, or office rent it is not a material income-producing factor."[173]

A majority of the Tax Court, with eleven Judges disagreeing, held that capital was not a material income producing factor for purposes of Code Sec. 704(e)(1) in a family limited partnership which borrowed substantial sums necessary for its business of constructing homes.[174] The borrowings were secured by personal guarantees of the family head who, although not directly a partner, was president and principal stockholder of the sole corporate general partner. The Court majority, in attempting to distinguish "borrowed" capital from capital contributed directly to the partnership by its partners, was obviously straining to disallow a purported allocation of 90 percent of the partnership's profits to five limited partner family trusts created with nominal cash contributions. This decision is questionable and a more reasonable alternative on the facts would have been either to disregard the partnership as a sham, as suggested by the concurring Judges, or to have allocated partnership profits in proportion to capital contributions after allocating all borrowed capital to the corporate general partners, as suggested by the dissenting Judges.

A capital investment by a donee partner is not in itself sufficient to validate a family partnership where the investment is unnecessary to the business of the partnership.[175]

.02 Donor's Reasonable Compensation

In determining reasonable compensation, the regulations indicate that among other factors to be considered are the degree of managerial responsibility of each partner, the cost ordinarily necessitated in securing comparable services from a person with no capital interest in the partnership, and,

[172] Reg. § 1.704-1(e)(1)(iv). Compare Reg. § 1.1361-2(e)(2); *S.H. Hartman*, 43 TC 105, Dec. 27,022 (1964).

[173] *Fred J. Sperapani*, 42 TC 308, 334 (1964), appeal dismissed (CA-4, 1965); cf. *Payton v. United States*, CA-5, 425 F2d 1324, cert. denied, 400 US 957 (1970).

[174] *Carriage Square, Inc. v. Commr.*, 69 TC 119, Dec. 34,710 (1977).

[175] *A. Pogetto v. United States*, CA-9, 62-2 USTC ¶ 9660, 306 F2d 76; *U.S. v. J.R. Ramos*, CA-9, 68-1 USTC ¶ 9337, 393 F2d 618, cert. denied, 393 US 983, 89 SCt 454 (1968); *M.W. Grober v. Commr.*, 31 TCM 1179, Dec. 31,623(M), TC Memo. 1972-240 (nominal capital contributions from donees; 99% of required capital borrowed from corporation controlled by donor). Cf. the present provisions relating to earned income from foreign sources (Code Sec. 911(b)), which were derived from Code Sec. 116(a)(3) of the 1939 Code. See *Graham Flying Service v. Commr.*, 8 TC 557, Dec. 15,674 (1947), aff'd, CA-8, 48-1 USTC ¶ 5921, 167 F2d 91, cert. denied, 335 US 817, 69 SCt 38 (1948); *Gus Grissman Co., Inc. v. Commr.*, 10 TC 499, Dec. 16,308 (1948); *Fairfax Mutual Wood Products Co. v. Commr.*, 5 TC 1279, Dec. 14,881 (1945), Acq.; *L.L. Tweedy v. Commr.*, 47 BTA 341, Dec. 12,588 (1942), appeal dismissed (CA-2, 1945); *I. Garnets v. Commr.*, 26 BTA 384, Dec. 7624 (1932); Mim. 3802, 1930-1 CB 121. Compare the rulings issued under Section 209 of the Revenue Act of 1917 (P.L. 50) and subsequent similar provisions relating to businesses with no more than nominal capital. See also ¶ 1902.01.

in the case of limited partnerships, the risk to which a general partner's credit is subject.[176]

.03 Donee's Status as the Owner of the Partnership Interest

The Commissioner is still free to question the "reality" of the donee's ownership of his or her interest in the partnership.[177] Where such ownership is derived from a gift, the regulations provide that the execution of legally sufficient deeds under state law is a factor to be taken into account, but is not determinative.[178] The Tax Court has interpreted this to mean that unless there has been compliance with all state law formalities required to evidence a completed gift, no valid gift of a capital interest in the partnership has been consummated for tax purposes.[179] In addition, the donee must be granted an interest in the partnership capital as such, including accretions thereto, which interest must be distributable to him or her upon withdrawal or upon dissolution or liquidation of the partnership.[180] An assignment of the economic rights to a partnership interest should be recognized as a transfer of a partnership interest for purposes of Code Sec. 704(e)(1).[181] The regulations define a "capital interest in a partnership" as "an interest in the assets of the partnership, which is distributable to the owner of the capital interest upon his or her withdrawal from the partnership or upon liquidation of the partnership.[182]

As a result of the Commissioner's right to question the "reality" of the donee's ownership of his or her interest in the partnership, many of the issues involved in pre-1951 cases continue.[183] For example, where the donor retains substantial incidents of ownership, he or she may continue to be recognized as the true owner of the interest purportedly transferred.[184] In this respect, however, the Committee Report on the Revenue Act of

---

[176] Reg. § 1.704-1(e)(3)(i)(*c*) and (ii)(*c*).

[177] H.R. Rep. No. 586, 82d Cong., 1st Sess., 331 (1951); *Bayou Verret Land Co v. Commr.*, CA-5, 71-2 USTC ¶ 9713, 450 F2d 850; *J.D. Ballou v. U.S.*, CA-6, 67-1 USTC ¶ 9141, 370 F2d 659, cert. denied, 338 US 911, 87 SCt 2114 (1967); *F. Occhipinti v. Commr.*, 28 TCM 968, Dec. 29,746(M), TC Memo. 1969-190; cf. *M.J. Spiesman, Jr. v. Commr.*, 28 TC 567, Dec. 22,411 (1957), aff'd, CA-9, 58-2 USTC ¶ 411, 260 F2d 940.

[178] Reg. § 1.704-1(e)(2); see *Driscoll v. U.S.*, DC Cal., 69-2 USTC ¶ 9536.

[179] *L.A. Woodbury v. Commr.*, 49 TC 180, Dec. 28,696 (1967); cf. *L.E. Tennyson, Jr. v. U.S.*, DC Ark., 76-1 USTC ¶ 9597 (gift not complete until satisfaction of conditions precedent).

[180] Reg. § 1.704-1(e)(1)(v). If these requirements are satisfied, the assignee of a partner's entire interest in a partnership will be treated for these purposes as a donee partner, even though such assignee is not a substituted partner for purposes of local law. *Evans v. Commr.*, 50 TC 40, Dec. 29,915 (1970), aff'd, CA-7, 71-2 USTC ¶ 9597, 447 F2d 547.

[181] *Evans v. Commr.*, 71-2 USTC ¶ 9597, 447 F2d 547.

[182] Reg. § 1.704-1(e)(1)(v).

[183] Among the previous sources of litigation eliminated by the Internal Revenue Code of 1954 (P.L. 591) were the presence or absence of a business purpose or a tax-avoidance motive. See, *e.g.*, *E.A. Ardolina v. Commr.*, CA-3, 51-1 USTC ¶ 9133, 186 F2d 176 (prior law); *J. Maiatico v. Commr.*, CA-DC, 50-1 USTC ¶ 9343, 183 F2d 836; *S.H. Miller v. Commr.*, CA-6, 50-1 USTC ¶ 9327, 183 F2d 246; *A. Slifka v. Commr.*, CA-2, 50-1 USTC ¶ 9314, 182 F2d 345. But see Reg. § 1.704-1(e)(2)(x) (". . . the presence or absence of a tax-avoidance motive is one of many factors to be considered in determining the reality of the ownership of a capital interest acquired by gift"); *J.T. Finlen v. F.J. Healy*, DC Mont., 60-2 USTC ¶ 9688, 187 FSupp 434.

[184] *G.T. Helvering v. G.B. Clifford, Jr.*, SCt, 40-1 USTC ¶ 9265, 309 US 331, 60 SCt 554; *R.G. Hornback v. U.S.*, DC Mo., 69-1 USTC ¶ 9377, 298 FSupp 977. Prior to the Revenue Act of 1951 (P.L. 183), and subsequent to the *Culbertson* (49-1 USTC ¶ 9323) decision, most family-partnership litigation was directed toward determining the reality of the parties' intention to participate in a joint enterprise. In making this determination, some courts considered the question of "control" over donated capital, and the use to which the partnership income was put. See, *e.g.*, *W.M. Lamb v. F.R. Smith*, CA-3, 50-2 USTC ¶ 9418, 183 F2d 938; *T.M. Stanback v. C.H. Robertson*, CA-4, 50-2 USTC ¶ 9414, 183 F2d 889, cert. denied, 340 US 904, 71 SCt 280. Under the Internal Revenue Code, these factors continue to be of major importance.

1951 [185] states that a distinction should be made between retained powers vested in the donor for his or her own benefit and those exercisable for the benefit of others. The retention of substantial powers by the donor "as a managing partner or in any other fiduciary capacity" will not, according to the Committee, necessarily taint the gift as a sham transaction.[186]

The regulations [187] indicate continued suspicion of family partnerships, particularly those which include minor children.[188] Unless it can be shown that a minor child is competent to manage his or her own property and participate in partnership activities,[189] the child's interest in any family partnership will be recognized only if it is controlled for his or her sole benefit by a judicially supervised fiduciary [190] or is placed in trust. An independent trustee is ordinarily recognized as the true owner of the partnership interest.[191]

The regulations state that if a trustee is made a partner, the trustee-partner will ordinarily be recognized as the owner of the partnership interest which he or she holds for the trust, provided that the trustee-partner is unrelated to and independent of the grantor, participates as a partner and receives distribution of the income distributable to the trust, and that the grantor retains no controls inconsistent with such ownership.[192]

If the trustee is the donor or a person amenable to his or her will, the regulations add scrutiny. The trustee must demonstrate that he or she is acting in the donee's best interest, the trust is visibly part of the partnership's activities, and there is no excess retention of profits.[193] Where the grantor or a person "amenable to his or her will" is trustee, special scrutiny of the trustee's responsibilities as a fiduciary and of his or her activities will follow, with particular attention to whether the trust is recognized as a partner in business dealings and to the use of the trust income for the sole benefit of the trust beneficiaries.[194] Exculpatory clauses for the trustee are frowned upon.[195] In this context, both the extent of the trustee's powers

---

[185] P.L. 183.

[186] H.R. Rep. No. 586, 82d Cong., 1st Sess., 33 (1951). The regulations caution, however, that retention of management powers "inconsistent with normal relationships among partners" will negate the reality of any purported gift. Reg. § 1.704-1(e)(2)(ii)(*d*).

[187] Reg. § 1.704-1(e).

[188] "The use of the child's property or income for support for which a parent is legally responsible will be considered use for the parent's benefit." Reg. § 1.704-1(e)(2)(viii); *C.T. Olson v. U.S.*, DC Cal., 67-1 USTC ¶ 9239, appeal dismissed (CA-9, 1967). Where the wife is the donor of the interest, note Reg. § 1.704-1(e)(3)(ii)(*a*), Ex. 2.

[189] *J.T. Finlen v. F.J. Healy*, DC Mont., 60-2 USTC ¶ 9688, 187 FSupp 434.

[190] Judicial supervision "includes filing of such accounts and reports as are required by law." Reg. § 1.704-1(e)(2)(viii); *A. Pflugradt v. U.S.*, CA-7, 63-1 USTC ¶ 9112, 310 F2d 412; *M.J. Spiesman, Jr.*, 28 TC 567, Dec. 22,411 (1957), aff'd, CA-9, 58-2 USTC ¶ 9890, 260 F2d 940.

[191] Reg. § 1.704-1(e)(2).

[192] Reg. § 1.704-1(e)(2)(vii). See *J. Smith*, 32 TC 1261, Dec. 23,764 (1959), Acq.; *S.H. Hartman v. Commr*, 43 TC 105, Dec. 27,022 (1964); cf. *J.D. Ballou v. U.S.*, CA-6, 67-1 USTC ¶ 9141, 370 F2d 659, cert. denied, 338 US 911, 87 SCt 2114 (1967); *Carriage Square, Inc. v. Commr.*, 69 TC 119, Dec. 34,710(1977).

[193] Reg. § 1.704-1(e)(2)(vii).

[194] *Id.*; *M. Kuney, Jr. v. W.E. Frank*, CA-9, 62-2 USTC ¶ 9769, 308 F2d 719; *H.S. Reddig*, 30 TC 1382, Dec. 23,195 (1958), appeal dismissed (CA-6, 1960); *A.K. Krause v. Commr.*, 57 TC 890, Dec. 31,322 (1972), aff'd, CA-6, 74-1 USTC ¶ 9470, 497 F2d 1109.

[195] See Mim. 6767,1952-1 CB 111 (declared obsolete, Rev. Rul. 69-31, 1969-1 CB 307).

under the terms of the trust instruments and the actual pattern of exercise of these powers by the trustee pursuant to such instruments are relevant.[196]

The donee's right to sell or liquidate his or her interest without financial penalty is another factor relating to "real ownership" which is given considerable emphasis in the regulations.[197] Any restriction on such rights of the donee will be considered by the Treasury as a particularly significant factor indicative of the donor's real ownership and control. This factor is especially troublesome if either the donee is a limited partner [198] or the donor of a general partnership interest has otherwise retained control of business management.[199]

> ***LLC Observation.*** In the context of an LLC, for purposes of Code Sec. 704(e), a donee non-manager member's ownership of the interest will probably be treated as ownership by a limited partner for purposes of Code Sec. 704(e). Therefore, the ownership may be disregarded if he or she has no right to liquidate the interest. Code Sec. 704(e) is a safe harbor. This would still leave the donor and donee free to treat the donee as a member for income tax purposes. However, the IRS is free to disagree.

Of course, if the donee actually participates substantially in formulating the management policies of the business and is otherwise actively engaged in the venture, the evidence of the donee's ownership is greatly strengthened.[200] Actual distribution to the donee of all or most of his or her distributive share of the partnership's income coupled with independent control of the use and enjoyment of such funds is also strong evidence of the donee's real ownership.[201]

.04 Purchasing Family Member's Status as a Partner

The regulations provide that where a partnership interest has been acquired by purchase from a family member, or by or through a loan from such a person, the purchase will be recognized as bona fide if:

---

[196] Compare *M.J. Kuney, Jr. v. U.S.*, CA-9, 71-2 USTC ¶ 9646, 448 F2d 22, on remand, DC Wash., 72-1 USTC ¶ 9385, with *M.J. Kuney, Jr. v. W.E. Frank*, CA-9, 62-2 USTC ¶ 9769, 308 F2d 719. In a 1971 decision, the Ninth Circuit held that a taxpayer should be given an opportunity to show that changes in subsequent years (1958-1963) in prior practices (1952-54) of which the court had been critical in its 1962 decision warranted different determination as to ultimate question of ownership of corpus for tax purposes, despite absence of any amendments to trust instruments limiting powers vested in trustee thereunder; a difference in facts as shown by record thus necessitated remand. On remand, the District Court found that the trustee had not properly acted in a fiduciary capacity, but this finding was reversed by the Ninth Circuit on appeal. *M.J. Kuney, Jr. v. U.S.*, CA-9, 75-2 USTC ¶ 9767, 524 F2d 795.

[197] Reg. § 1.704-1(e)(2)(ii)(*b*).

[198] Reg. § 1.704-1(e)(2)(ix). Provisions in the partnership agreement restricting the assignability of a limited partner's interest, and permitting withdrawal of a limited partner's contribution only upon the expiration of an extended term, are not, however, unusual in normal limited partnership agreements.

[199] Reg. § 1.704-1(e)(2)(ii)(*d*). A donee will not be considered free to withdraw his or her interest unless he or she "is independent of the donor and has such maturity and understanding of his rights as to be capable of deciding to exercise, and capable of exercising, his right to withdraw."

[200] "Such participation presupposes sufficient maturity and experience. . . to deal with the business." Reg. § 1.704-1(e)(2)(iv).

[201] Reg. § 1.704-1(e)(2)(v). Income may be retained by the partnership "for the reasonable needs of the business." Reg. § 1.704-1(e)(2)(ii)(*a*).

- The terms of the purchase are similar to those that would be expected in an arm's length transaction; or
- The purchase is genuinely intended to promote the success of the partnership business.[202]

In addition, the "purchase" qualifies as a transfer by satisfying the rules as to whether a gift is a transfer of a partnership interest.

If payment of the purchase price is made out of partnership earnings, the transaction may be regarded as a gift subject to deferred enjoyment of the income and, therefore, lacking in reality either as a gift or a purchase.[203]

.05 *Gifts of Partnership Interest When Partnership Capital Is Not a Material Income-Producing Factor*

In those family partnerships in which capital is not a material income-producing factor, the recognition of a donee partner's interest continues to depend upon the previous judicial standards, and it will undoubtedly be difficult to sustain the validity of a donee's interest unless he or she performs some substantial services.[204]

.06 *Nonpartner Family Member Performs Services for the Partnership*

Code Sec. 704(e) applies only if there is a transfer of a partnership interest. If a partnership is formed and one who is never a member of the partnership is employed by the partnership and is paid less than the partnership is paid for the services, net income may be shifted to the partners.

> ***Observation.*** A variant to the family partnership is the partnership consisting entirely of relatives of the prime earner—a partnership in which the prime earner is never a member at all even though he or she may make substantial contributions to the success of the partnership's business. The family partnership provisions discussed here have no application to such a partnership, and, so long as the partnership's income is actually earned by it, the fact that a related individual, not a member of the partnership, may control the source of the partnership's business is not likely to result in the imputation of partnership income to such individual under Code Sec. 704(e).[205] However, the

---

[202] Reg. § 1.704-1(e)(4). See, *e.g.*, *F. Occhipinti v. Commr.*, 28 TCM 968, Dec. 29,746(M), TC Memo. 1969-190; *Carriage Square, Inc. v. Commr.*, 69 TC 119, Dec. 34,710 (1977). The mimeograph relation to pre-1951 family partnerships included a much more stringent test. Mim. 6767, 1952-1 CB 111 (declared obsolete, Rev. Rul. 69-31, 1969-1 CB 307); Code Sec. 191 (purchase from family member treated as a gift).

[203] Reg. § 1.704-1(e)(4)(i).

[204] *B.H. Nichols v. Commr*, 32 TC 1322, Dec. 23,773 (1959), Acq. (wife performed substantial services). Compare *Teitelbaum v. Commr.*, CA-7, 65-1 USTC ¶ 9440, 346 F2d 266.

[205] *R.P. Crowley v. Commr.*, 34 TC 333, Dec. 24,198 (1960), Acq.; cf. *Nat Harrison Associates, Inc. v. Commr.*, 42 TC 6011, 621, Dec. 26,858 (1964), appeal dismissed (CA-5, 1964); *Alabama-Geogia Syrup Co. v. Commr.*, 36 TC 747, 767, Dec. 24,957 (1961), Acq. But cf. *Carriage Square, Inc. v. Commr.*, 69 TC 119, Dec. 34,710 (1977).

application of Code Sec. 482 could result in a reallocation of the income from the partnership to a nonpractitioner (*e.g.* family member) who is performing services for the partnership.

An interesting illustration of this principle is furnished by the case of *Robert P. Crowley v. Commissioner.*[206] In this case a partnership consisting of the mother as a trustee for each of four minor children was created to engage in the insurance and real estate loan business. The father, who was the chief executive officer and the controlling stockholder of a federal savings and loan association, thereupon directed a substantial number of appraisal and inspection fees, insurance commissions, and abstract and title policy commissions to the partnership through his control of the savings and loan association. The services performed by the partnership to earn these fees and commissions were performed by the eldest son. In addition, the partnership made loans on which it received interest. Most of the funds for these loans were derived from advances made by the parents to the partnership in return for demand promissory notes bearing interest at 2-1/2% per annum. The partnership lent these funds out at 6% per annum.

The Commissioner argued that all the partnership's income was in essence due to the activity of the father and should therefore be taxable to him. A majority of the Tax Court, with four judges dissenting, held that all of the partnership income, other than the income resulting from the loans made by the partnership, should be taxed to the partnership members and not to either of the parents. The majority determined that the partnership's noninterest income was in fact due to the personal services rendered by the eldest son and with respect to the father drew a distinction between "being in a position to control who shall perform the activities which produce the income and being in a position to control either the use of income-producing capital or who shall receive income after it is produced."[207]

The court, however, took a different view of the interest income earned by the partnership from the use of capital loaned by the parents to the partnership. With one judge dissenting, the court determined that the parents had not fully relinquished ownership or control over the capital used by the partnership in the loan business.[208]

¶ 906 Depreciation Recapture

A partner's share of depreciation recapture income is equal to the lesser of:

1. That partner's share of the total gain realized by the partnership on the disposition of the property generating the recapture income; or

[206] *R.P. Crowley v. Commr.*, 34 TC 333, Dec. 24,198 (1960), Acq.

[207] *Id.*

[208] *Id.*

2. That partner's share of the depreciation or amortization claimed by the partnership with respect to the property.[209]

A partner's share of the recapture income with respect to property contributed to the partnership includes depreciation allowed to the partner before the contribution. A transferee of a partnership interest steps into the shoes of the transferor. Finally, a partner's share of the recapture is adjusted for curative or remedial allocations under Reg. § 1.704-3(c) and (d).

¶ 907 Credits

Allocation of a credit must be made in the same manner as losses or deductions arising from the same expenditure.[210]

¶ 908 Income Allocation Recharacterized as Payment for Capital Expenditure

Some payments a partnership makes are nondeductible and must instead be capitalized. One example is payments for land and legal fees that are incurred in connection with the acquisition of land, which would be capitalized under Code Sec. 263 as part of the land's basis. Such payments can be made to an existing partner or an outside party. If the payments are made to an existing partner and are properly categorized as Code Sec. 707(a)(1) or (c) payments, they are capitalized under Code Sec. 263 as though made to an outside party. On the other hand, if a partner is allocated income for services to the partnership, the partner's income allocation is effectively a deduction with respect to the remaining partners. Prior to the Deficit Reduction Act of 1984, the technique used to avoid the capitalization was to structure the payment as a distributive share of partnership income. If the person performing services or "contributing property" was not already a partner, he or she would be made a partner for purposes of the arrangement. If the payment is considered the partner's distributive share of partnership income, the payment simply reduced the income taxed to the other partners—effectively allowing them to deduct the payment and avoid the capitalization requirements of Code Sec. 263. This approach was used when the tax effect to the service or "contributing" partner was the same whether it was a payment for services or a share of the partnership's income.

Code Sec. 707(a)(2)(A) and (B) state that if a transaction appears to be properly characterized as one between a nonpartner and the partnership, the transaction will be governed by Code Sec. 707(a)(1). The Senate Finance Committee report [211] lists six factors that are important in determining whether the allocation/distribution arrangement is in reality a payment for capitalizable services or property:

---

[209] Reg. § 1.1245-1(e)(2).

[210] Reg. § 1.704-1(b)(4)(ii) and (5), Ex. 11.

[211] S. Rep. No. 169, 98th Cong., 2d Sess., 226-30 (1984).

1. A partner must bear the risk of failure of the business venture.

2. The duration of the partner's interest in the partnership should not be merely transitory.

3. A short time period between the performance of services or transfer of property and the "allocation and distribution" is viewed as a payment rather than a distributive income share.

4. If under all the facts and circumstances, it appears that the recipient became a partner primarily to obtain tax benefits for himself or for the partnership, which would not have been available had the recipient rendered services to the partnership in a third-party capacity, he or she will be disregarded as a partner.

5. A relatively small size of continuing partnership interest after a major allocation/distribution is viewed as a payment.

6. If, in the case of a sale disguised as a property contribution, after an income allocation equal to the property's value, the "partner" will no longer be entitled to future allocations and distributions the partnership interest will be disregarded.

The report directs the Secretary to outline other relevant factors in regulations and states:

> In applying these various factors, the Treasury and courts should be careful not to be misled by possibly self-serving assertions in the partnership agreement as to the duties of a partner in his partner capacity, but should instead seek the substance of the transaction.

On September 25, 1992, the IRS finalized the regulations under Code Sec. 707(a)(2)(B) for disguised sales of property, but not under Code Sec. 707(a)(2)(A) for disguised payments for services. Reg. § 1.707-2, "Disguised payments for services," remains "reserved." Until regulations are issued, some guidance may perhaps be gleaned from the general concepts of the disguised sale rules. Under the disguised sale regulations, a transfer of property (excluding money or an obligation to contribute money) by a partner to a partnership and a transfer of money or other consideration by the partnership to the partner is a sale of property only if, based on all the facts and circumstances:

- The transfer of money would not have been made but for the transfer of property; and

- In cases in which the transfers are not made simultaneously, the later transfer is not dependent on the entrepreneurial risks of partnership operations.[212]

[212] Reg. § 1.707-3(b)(1).

Transfers between a partnership and a partner that are made within two years of each other are presumed to be a sale, and transfers made more than two years apart are presumed not to be a sale. Each of these presumptions may be rebutted with facts and circumstances that clearly establish to the contrary.[213] The regulations provide for exceptions for guaranteed payments for capital, reasonable preferred returns, or when operating cash flow distributions applies.[214]

¶ 909 Effect of Partnership Operations on Basis

A partner is required each year to adjust his or her basis in the partnership interest for the partner's distributive share of the partnership's income or loss.[215] These adjustments are required to ensure that the partnership remains a conduit for tax purposes. Income and deductions are to be taxed only once. Tax-exempt income, nondeductible expenditures, and distributions made from previously taxed income and contributions are not to be taken into account by the partner in computing tax liability at all.

.01 *Taxable Income and Loss*

The basis of a partnership interest is increased by both the taxable and tax-exempt income allocated to the partner. Absent this basis increase, undistributed, previously taxed income could be taxed again as gain from the sale of the partnership interest. A partner who sells his or her partnership interest before the retained taxed income is distributed will likely receive a purchase price that will reflect his or her share of the retained income. A basis increase for the same amount is necessary to avoid gain for this increase in value that has already been taxed. The same considerations require the partner to reduce his or her partnership interest adjusted basis for his or her share of the partnership's losses. The after-tax investment in the partnership interest, its basis, is decreased by the loss's amount. If the partner's basis in his or her interest is not reduced, he or she will be allowed a second loss, or at least a reduced gain, for amounts previously deducted.

.02 *Contributions and Distributions*

Contributions and distributions are increases and decreases in basis, respectively, so that the changed after tax investment will not result in taxable income or loss if the partnership interest is sold. For example, if money is contributed, the value of the partnership interest is increased by a like amount. If a corresponding basis increase is not made, a subsequent sale of the partnership interest will produce gain derived from the contribution.

.03 *Tax Exempt Income and Nondeductible Expenditures*

A partner's share of tax-exempt income increases his or her basis so that the retained tax-exempt income is not taxed upon a liquidating

---

[213] Reg. § 1.707-3(c)(1) and (d).

[214] See Reg. § 1.707-4.

[215] Code Sec. 705(a).

distribution or on a sale of the partnership interest. Finally, nondeductible expenditures which are not capital expenditures reduce basis so that the reduced value of the partnership interest after the nondeductible expenditure is not reflected as a loss or reduced gain on a liquidating distribution or sale of the interest.

> ***Comment.*** In all cases when downward adjustments to basis are required, the statute expressly provides that basis is not to be reduced below zero. A basis in a partnership interest *never* has a value below zero. While a negative *capital account* is very common, a negative basis is impossible.

The above-described adjustments to the basis of a partnership interest are intended to ensure that (1) a partner's share of taxable income and deductions is taken into account only once, (2) nondeductible expenditures and tax-exempt income remain characterized as such, and (3) distributions of previous contributions and previously taxed income are not taxed. The necessary adjustments are relatively simple to perform, and if they are made on a yearly basis, a partner's basis in his or her interest is normally easy to maintain. Each year's adjustments can be made to the previous year's ending basis. Thus, a partner's basis reflects the cumulative effect of all prior required adjustments. Unfortunately, in a situation when necessary adjustments from one or more years are unavailable, this historical method of maintaining basis is useless. When the chain of adjustments is broken, another approach is necessary.

Code Sec. 705(b) provides an alternative rule for determining a partner's basis in his or her partnership interest if it is impractical or impossible to apply the foregoing rules, or if the Commissioner reasonably concludes that the result under the alternative rule will not produce a substantially different result.[216] The alternative rule initially consists of determining the partner's basis by reference to the adjusted basis of his or her pro rata share of the partnership property. After making certain necessary adjustments,[217] this is the partner's basis for his or her partnership interest. The regulations add that a partner may also determine his or her basis by making certain adjustments to the sum of his or her tax basis capital account and share of the partnership's liabilities.[218] As a general observation on the usefulness of these alternative methods of finding the basis of a partner's interest, note that while they at first appear an attractive theoretical option, they are in practice difficult to use in anything other than a very simple setting. The necessary adjustments can become unmanageable and a tax-basis capital account difficult to compute. See ¶ 1103 for a complete discussion.

---

[216] Reg. § 1.705-1(b).

[217] Necessitated, for example, by contributions of appreciated or depreciated property, partnership interest transfers, and property distributions. Reg. § 1.705-1(b).

[218] Reg. § 1.705-1(b), Ex. 3.

¶ 910 Loss Limitations

There are three commonly encountered limitations on a partner's ability to take into account the partner's share of a partnership's loss in computing his or her individual tax liability. A partner is entitled to deduct his or her share of the partnership's loss only after satisfying all three of these rules. First, since the adoption of the Internal Revenue Code of 1954,[219] the partnership taxation rules have limited a partner's deductible share of losses to the partner's basis in his or her partnership interest. Second, since 1976,[220] the at-risk rules have limited a partner's deduction for his or her share of losses to the amount the partner is considered to have economically at-risk in the venture. Third, beginning with the effective date of the Tax Reform Act of 1986,[221] if the partner's share of the partnership's losses are considered "passive losses," the partner must combine them with his or her passive losses from other sources and is allowed to deduct the total only to the extent of the partner's passive income from all sources. These three limits are applied in the order mentioned. If the partner is to be allowed to take a share of partnership loss into account in determining taxable income at the partner level:

1. There must be partnership interest adjusted basis equal to or more than the loss;

2. If there is sufficient basis in the partnership interest, the partner must be at risk for the amount of the deduction; and

3. If the partner has sufficient basis and at-risk amount if the loss is a passive loss the partner must either have an equal amount of passive income or must have disposed of the activity generating the loss.

.01 Basis

If a partner's loss allocation exceeds the adjusted basis of his or her partnership interest, the excess must be carried forward.[222] If the total loss is comprised of different types of deductions, a proportionate share of each deduction is carried forward.[223] The parties are not allowed to choose which items will and will not be deducted. The carry-forward has no time limitation and the loss is combined with the succeeding year's deductions and allowed to the extent of the partner's basis at that year's end after the annual adjustment to basis is made for income, distributions, and contributions. In effect, the entire carryover will be allowed in the year in which subsequent positive basis adjustments are large enough to absorb the current year distributions and deductions plus the carryover losses. The carry-forward is personal to the partner and cannot be claimed by a purchaser if a partner sells his or her partnership interest.

---

[219] P.L. 591.

[220] Tax Reform Act of 1976, P.L. 94-455.

[221] P.L. 99-514.

[222] Code Sec. 704(d).

[223] Reg. § 1.704-1(d)(4), Ex. 3.

Any disallowed losses caused by the basis limit can be carried forward indefinitely during the period the partnership retains partnership status, and used when the partner has additional basis in his or her partnership interest.[224] If the partner sells his or her zero basis partnership interest at a gain, the partner is not allowed to offset the gain with the carryover loss. The sale of the partnership interest does not result in a basis increase for the partnership interest. When a partner has sufficient basis to deduct his or her share of losses, but insufficient at-risk amount or passive income if the loss is passive, the partner is disallowed the loss but must reduce his or her basis. This basis reduction can increase future gain on the partnership interest's sale. Under these circumstances the losses carried over solely because of the at-risk or passive rules may be used as a gain offset.

> ***S Corporation Observation.*** The application of this loss limitation mechanism demonstrates another distinction between S corporations and partnerships. An S corporation's shareholder's deductible share of losses is allowed only to the extent of his or her basis in the stock plus the basis and debt the corporation owes to the shareholder. Specifically, the fact that an S corporation shareholder cannot include a proportionate share of corporate liabilities in his or her stock basis is a factor that must be considered in making the choice of entity decision. A partner is also allowed to deduct his or her share of the partnership's losses only to the extent of the partner's basis for his or her partnership interest, but Code Sec. 752(a) generally allows partners to increase their bases in their partnership interests by the amount of any increases in their shares of partnership liabilities. Although a shareholder loan to an S corporation will always provide more basis for purposes of the loss limitations applied to shareholders.[225] In contrast, a partner's loan to the partnership may not increase his or her basis in the partnership interest by the entire amount of the loan. See Chapter 10.

.02 At Risk

At risk limitations apply to most business activities carried on by partnerships and individuals, and to some corporate operations.[226] If the activity is carried on by a partnership, however, the limit is applied at the partner level, rather than the partnership level.[227] Therefore, a partner who is not subject to the at-risk rules will not have losses disallowed by Code Sec. 465.

---

[224] Technically, the disallowed loss is treated as incurred in the succeeding taxable year with respect to the *partner*. If the partner should terminate his or her interest in the partnership, his or her ability to use the previously disallowed loss will apparently be lost since he or she will no longer be a partner.

[225] Because merely guaranteeing a loan to the corporation is insufficient to create basis for a shareholder, shareholders should consider the alternative of borrowing funds directly, and then loaning the proceeds to the corporation in their individual capacities. *W.H. Perry v. Commr.*, CA-8, 68-1 USTC ¶ 9297, 392 F2d 458. Compare *E.M. Selfe v. U.S.*, CA-11, 86-1 USTC ¶ 9115, 778 F2d 769 (basis increase allowable if shareholder could prove that loan was in fact made to her).

[226] See Code Sec. 465(a)(1).

[227] See, for example, Prop. Reg. § 1.465-41, Ex. 1.

A partner is allowed to currently deduct his or her share of losses only to the extent the partner has amounts at risk in the activity. As in the case for deductions in excess of the partner's basis in his or her partnership interest, to the extent the partner's allocated loss exceeds the amount at risk in the partnership investment, the excess may be indefinitely carried forward and allowed in a year in which the partner is considered to be at risk for the total of the deductions generated in the carry-forward year and the amount carried over from prior years.[228] Calculating the amount for which a partner is considered to be at risk is very similar to the computations required in determining his or her basis in his or her partnership interest. The amount at-risk is increased by cash contributions, the basis of property contributions, and the partner's share of the partnership's taxable and tax-exempt income. It is decreased by cash distributions, the basis of property distributions, nondeductible noncapitalized expenditures and the partner's share of the partnership's losses.[229]

The major difference between the calculation of a partner's basis in his or her partnership interest and at-risk amount is the manner in which partnership debt is taken into account. All nonrecourse debt is taken into account in determining the various partners' bases in their partnership interests; however, nonrecourse debt is taken into account in calculating the partners' at-risk amount only if it meets the requirements of "qualified nonrecourse financing." This is nonrecourse debt that is secured by real property and which was borrowed to hold the property. It does not include amounts borrowed from persons related to the borrower or borrowed from the seller.[230] Recourse debts shared by the partners for both basis and at-risk purposes is shared among the partners who bear the economic risk of repayment. For Code Sec. 465 purposes, debt secured by property contributed to the partnership and used in the at-risk activity is disregarded.[231]

LLC Observation. An LLC's recourse debt is considered to be nonrecourse debt for purposes of the at-risk limitation because no member is personally responsible for the debt's repayment. It is considered qualified nonrecourse debt if:

1. It is borrowed with respect to holding real property;

2. Is borrowed from a qualified person; and

3. Is effectively nonrecourse because of the state's limited liability statute.[232]

See ¶ 103 for more details.

Other than "qualified nonrecourse financing," a partner may take indebtedness into account only to the extent that the partner risks personal

---

[228] Code Sec. 465(a)(2).
[229] Prop. Reg. § 1.465-22(c).
[230] Code Sec. 465(b)(3)(C).
[231] Code Sec. 465(b)(2).
[232] Reg. § 1.465-27.

liability for repayment, or secures the debt with his or her own property rather than that of the partnership. In the case of "qualified nonrecourse financing," each partner's at risk amount includes his or her share of each debt as determined under Code Sec. 752(a).[233] There is no official guidance specifying a partner's share of other debt for purposes of the at-risk rules. It is common practice to also use the Code Sec. 752 rules for purposes of determining each partner's share of recourse debt and nonrecourse debt other than qualified nonrecourse debt. An entry on the partner's K-1 showing a share of the partnership's nonrecourse debt (other than qualified nonrecourse debt) alerts him or her to a potential at-risk limitation situation arising. As a consequence of these rules, a partner's at-risk amount will either be equal to or less than his or her basis in the partnership interest. Thus, when the at-risk rules apply, it is more likely that the at-risk limitations, rather than the basis limitation, will disallow the loss. Although a partner may have basis sufficient to be allowed the deduction, he or she will be required to generate an additional at-risk amount to be entitled to use it. It should be noted that when a partner is disallowed a loss due to insufficient at-risk amount, the partner is nevertheless required to reduce his or her basis by the full amount of the loss. This potential inequity of this requirement is alleviated by another major difference between the computation of the at-risk amount and basis: gain from the disposition of the partnership interest is considered to generate an additional at-risk amount.[234] Thus, a carryover loss resulting from an insufficient amount at risk can be offset with gain from the sale of the partnership interest, while carryovers of disallowed losses resulting from insufficient basis may not be used to offset gain. Often, however, both limitations will apply equally in disallowing the same loss. In this situation, the partner will be required to generate both additional basis and at-risk amounts in order to claim the deduction.

.03 *Passive Activity*

The at-risk and basis limitations were designed to restrict deductions to roughly the amounts "invested" in the venture. In contrast, Code Sec. 469 was enacted to restrict taxpayers from using deductions from losses generated by certain passive investment activities to offset or "shelter" income from other sources.

Operating rules. The income and losses from each of the taxpayer's passive activities are first computed and then combined. In any one taxable year, passive activity losses can be deducted only to the extent of the taxpayer's income from passive activities for that year. To the extent that total losses from passive activities for the taxable year exceed the taxpayer's passive income, the excess losses are carried forward and deducted (subject to the same limitation) against future net income from passive activities. Although the passive activity rules limit the taxpayer's deduc-

[233] Code Sec. 465(b)(6)(C).

[234] Prop. Reg. § 1.465-66(a).

tion for *total* passive losses to the amount of his or her *total* passive income from all sources, any excess loss is considered to consist of a pro rata portion of each activity's loss.[235] Disallowed losses from a particular activity (but not credits) may be deducted in full upon a taxable disposition of the entire activity.[236] These rules apply to individuals (including partners), estates, trusts, personal service corporations, and in a modified form to closely held corporations.[237] As in the case of the at-risk rules, the passive loss limitations are applied on a partner-by-partner basis, not at the partnership level. The limitations are applied only after application of the basis and at-risk limitations.[238] As with the at-risk limitations, a partner's basis in his or her partnership interest is reduced for losses, but cannot go below zero, even though they are disallowed by the passive loss limitations.

Passive activity defined. The passive loss limitations are imposed only on losses from passive activities. A "passive activity" is any activity[239] involving the conduct of any trade or business[240] in which the taxpayer does not "materially participate."[241] A taxpayer materially participates in an activity only if he or she is involved on a regular, continuous, and substantial basis in the operation of the activity.[242] With one exception, Code Sec. 469 sweeps all rental activities within the definition of "passive activity," even if the taxpayer manages the property.[243] Some relief is provided for moderate-income taxpayers who "actively participate" in rental real estate activities. The rental losses are passive, but up to $25,000 of net passive losses attributable to rental real estate activities can be used against income from nonpassive activities if the individual owns at least a 10 percent interest in the property.[244] This relief, however, is generally phased out for adjusted gross income in excess of $100,000.

Starting in 1994, taxpayers who have more than 50 percent of their hours of personal services performed in a real estate trade or business, if these services exceed 750 hours, are exempted from the presumption that rental realty is a passive activity.[245] Taxpayers who are engaged in a real property trade or business are entitled to the only possible exception to the presumption that rental income and loss are considered passive.[246] If a taxpayer performs more than 750 hours and more than half of his or her time is engaged in a real property trade or business, the taxpayer is allowed to prove that he or she materially participates. When a real estate trade or

---

[235] Temp. Reg. § 1.469-1T(f)(2).

[236] Code Sec. 469(g).

[237] Code Sec. 469(a)(2).

[238] Temp. Reg. § 1.469-2T(d)(6); General Explanation of the Tax Reform Act of 1986 (P.L. 99-514), Joint Committee on Taxation, p. 223, fn. 17.

[239] Other than working interest in oil and gas properties.

[240] Including nonbusiness, profit-motivated activities within the ambit of Code Sec. 212.

[241] Code Sec. 469(c).

[242] Code Sec. 469(h)(1); see Temp. Reg. § 1.469-5T.

[243] Code Sec. 469(c)(2). The temporary regulations have taken the liberty of reclassifying various types of rental income and gains from the sale of rental property as nonpassive income. Temp. Reg. § 1.469-2T(f). In addition, short term rentals may not be considered passive. Temp. Reg. § 1.469-1T(e). rental income which is small in relationship to the basis or value of the property may be nonpassive. Temp. Reg. § 1.469-1T(e). the rental of property consisting mainly of nondepreciable property may be treated as nonpassive activity. Temp. Reg. § 1.469-2T(f).

[244] Code Sec. 469(i)(1), (2), and (6).

[245] Code Sec. 469(c)(7).

[246] *Id.*

business taxpayer materially participates in a real estate rental activity, he or she generates nonpassive income and loss.[247]

The definition of passive income excludes interest, dividends, annuities, and royalties not derived in the ordinary course of a trade or business, as well as gains from the disposition (other than in the ordinary course of a trade or business) of assets producing such types of income.[248] The definition of passive deductions also excludes expenses incurred in producing these types of income; and it excludes losses from the disposition of assets producing such income. These types of investment income and deductions are referred to by the legislative history of the Tax Reform Act of 1986 [249] and regulations as "portfolio" income and expenses. If the partner itemizes his or her deductions rather than uses the standard deduction, the deductions other than interest directly connected with the production of portfolio income are deductible to the extent that they, together with the other miscellaneous itemized deductions, exceed 2 percent of the taxpayer's adjusted gross income.[250] In addition, interest incurred in producing this type of income is subject to investment interest limitations.[251]

Many of the difficult questions arising in this area involve the application of the material participation standard to partners. Through a separate analysis of each partner and of each separate activity in which the partnership engages, it is determined whether or not a partner's share of income or loss is derived from a passive activity. The activities of the partnership must be examined to determine which of these activities are classified as separate "activities," and the degree of the partner's participation in each activity must be examined to determine whether it is "material."

Code Sec. 469 conclusively presumes, except as otherwise provided in regulations, that all limited partnership interests are activities in which the taxpayer does not materially or actively participate.[252] Limited partners are not eligible for the rental real estate exception for active participation.[253] However, any payment received by a partner, whether a limited or general partner, for the performance of services (for example, by way of a fee or a guaranteed payment) is not treated as income from a passive activity.[254]

.04 What Is an Activity?

With reference to what constitutes a separate activity, the legislative history provides that: "[t]he determination of what constitutes a separate activity is intended to be made in a realistic economic sense" by looking to whether the "undertakings consist of an integrated and interrelated eco-

[247] Code Sec. 469(c)(7) is effective for years beginning after 1993.

[248] Code Sec. 469(e)(1)(A).

[249] P.L. 99-514.

[250] Code Secs. 212 and 67.

[251] Code Sec. 163(d)

[252] Code Sec. 469(h)(2); Temp. Reg. § 1.469-5T(e).

[253] Code Sec. 469(i)(6)(C).

[254] Reg. § 1.469-2(e).

nomic unit, conducted in coordination with or reliance upon each other, and constituting an appropriate unit for the measurement of gain or loss."[255]

Under regulations effective for tax years ending after May 11, 1992, taxpayers have a great deal of flexibility in designating the groups of endeavors that they consider a single activity. One or more trade or business activities or rental activities are treated as a single activity if the activities are an appropriate economic unit for the measurement of gain or loss for purposes of the passive loss rules.[256] A taxpayer can use any reasonable method of applying the relevant facts and circumstances in grouping activities. Factors that are given the greatest weight in determining whether a group of activities should be treated as one for purposes of the passive loss rules are:

- Similarities and differences in types of business;
- The extent of common control;
- The extent of common ownership;
- Geographical location; and
- Interdependencies between the activities.[257]

.05 Material Participation

Assuming that the partnership's separate activities can be identified, the partner's participation in each activity must be analyzed to determine whether or not it is "material." General partner status does not automatically guarantee material participation. The legislative history suggests that the following factors be taken into account:[258]

1. The involvement must relate to operations as opposed to support functions. For example, the services of accountants and lawyers as independent contractors provided to a hotel would likely not constitute material participation.

2. When the activity is the taxpayer's principal business, material participation is likely present. However, the fact that an activity is or is not an individual's principal business is not conclusive—a taxpayer is likely to materially participate in an activity if he or she does everything that is required to be done to conduct the activity, even though the actual amount of work

[255] The General Explanation of the Tax Reform Act of 1986 (P.L. 99-514), Joint Committee on Taxation, pp. 245-246. In addition to the legislative history, Temp. Reg. § 1.469-4T devoted approximately 25 pages to determining separate activities. Generally, each location of realty that can be separately conveyed qualifies as a different activity. The regulations, however, allowed the taxpayer a one-time election to combine any number of these realty activities and treat them as a single activity. These temporary regulations were replaced by Reg. § 1.469-4. These regulations are two pages long and grant much more flexibility to the taxpayers in designating the groups of endeavors that they would consider a single activity. The final regulations are generally effective for taxable years ending after May 10, 1992.

[256] Reg. § 1.469-4(c)(1).

[257] Reg. § 1.469-4(c)(2).

[258] General Explanation of the Tax Reform Act of 1986 (P.L. 99-514), Joint Committee on Taxation, pp. 237-242.

to be done to conduct the activity is low in comparison to other activities.

3. The regularity of the person's presence at the place of principal operations of the activity is highly relevant, although not conclusive. The taxpayer's purpose for being present would also be examined.

4. Bona fide performance of management functions is taken into account in determining the extent of the taxpayer's involvement. It is not the right to direct the business but the exercise of that right which indicates material participation.

5. The taxpayer's expertise and knowledge of the activity are highly significant.

The regulations provide that an individual is a material participant if he or she satisfies any of seven tests.[259] Under the regulations these tests are exclusive—material participation may not be met under any other standard, including any standard set forth under other provisions of the Internal Revenue Code, such as Code Secs. 1402 and 2032A. Under the temporary regulations, a taxpayer is considered to be a material participant in an activity for a taxable year if:

1. The taxpayer participates for more than 500 hours in the activity for the year;

2. The taxpayer's participation in the activity for the taxable year constitutes substantially all of the participation of all individuals in the activity for the year;

3. The taxpayer participates for more than 100 hours, and this is more than the participation of all other individuals;

4. The taxpayer's participation is "significant," and his or her "significant" participation in all activities exceeds a total of 500 hours for the year—significant participation requires more than 100 hours of participation during the year;

5. The taxpayer materially participated in the activity for any five taxable years during the last ten taxable years;

6. In the case of a personal service activity (such as health, law, engineering, accounting, and the performing arts), the taxpayer materially participated in the activity during only three prior years; and

[259] Temp. Reg. § 1.469-5T, adopted 2/19/88 by T.D. 8175, 1988-1 CB 191, amended 5/11/89 by T.D. 8253, 1989-1 CB 121; Reg. § 1.469-5, adopted 5/12/92 by T.D. 8417, 1992-1 CB 173.

7. The taxpayer, based on all the facts and circumstances, participates in the activity on a regular, continuous and substantial basis, as described by the factors listed in the legislative history.

The regulations list situations when a limited partner is considered to materially participate. The partner is considered to materially participate if he or she satisfies either rules 1, 5, or 6 above, or if he or she has a general partnership interest in addition to his or her limited interest and is a material participant.[260] In addition, a limited partner is not entitled to the $25,000 active participation exception even if the limited partner has 500 hours of participation.

LLC Observation. The regulations define a limited partner to include any participant whose liability is limited under state law.[261] A limited interpretation of the regulation would cause LLC members to be considered limited partners. The result is that unless requirements 1, 5 or 6 above are satisfied, income and loss are passive. This will result in passive income to the LLC member who is relatively active in the LLC's activities, but does not participate 500 hours.

¶ 911 Preparation of Form 1065, Schedules K and K-1

Some degree of confusion and misunderstanding is often involved in the preparation of the partners' Schedules K-1.

- The Treasury's instructions for preparations of the Form 1065 and Schedules K and K-1 leave some questions unanswered, and the regulations do not offer much guidance.
- Moreover, *where* an item of income, deduction, gain or loss is entered on the schedule is far less important that the *accuracy* of the number accompanied by an *indication* of which item the number represents.

Thus, it is understandable that many practitioners vary on the manner in which items are reported.

Nevertheless, the purpose of this section on reporting partners' distributive shares is to summarize the rules regarding where various items should appear on the schedule.

.01 Reconciling Partners' Capital Account Balances

One main section of Schedule K-1 is box N, which reconciles the partners' capital account balances.

The aggregate of the partners' items in box N should agree with the accounting methods employed in the preparation of the Schedule L balance sheets and the reconciliation of the total partnership capital in Schedule M-2.

The other main section is the 20 boxes of distributive share information.

---

[260] Temp. Reg. § 1.469-5T(e)(2) and (3)(ii).

[261] Temp. Reg. § 1.469-5T(e)(3).

.02 *Schedules M-1 and M-2*

Commencing with 1991 forms, partnership returns include Schedule M-1 and M-2, in a fashion similar to C corporations.

Schedule M-1, Reconciliation of Income Per Books With Income Per Return:

1. Starts with book income.
2. Adds income items reflected on the partners' K-1s but not on the books (line 2), Guaranteed Payments (line 3), and expenses per books not on the K-1s (line 4).
3. Subtracts income items on the books but not reflected on the K-1s, including tax exempt interest (line 6), and items of deductions on the K-1s not on the books (line 7).
4. Ends with the total of the income and deduction items distributable to the partners on their K-1s (this ties with the net income on Schedule K, Partnership Income or Loss).

Schedule M-2, Analysis of Partners' Capital Accounts:

1. Starts with the capital account balances at the beginning of the year.
2. Adds capital contributed during year (line 2).
3. Adds net income per books (line 3) and other increases (line 4).
4. Subtracts distributions to partners (line 6).
5. Subtracts other decreases (line 7).
6. Equals the capital account balances at the end of the year.

Partners' individual capital accounts are reconciled in box N of Schedule K-1. Prior to the 1991 forms, the amounts of income and deductions on Schedule K-1 could be traced to the capital account reconciliation. Now, however, all the income and deduction effects on the capital accounts are combined and appear in "Current year increase (decrease)" line of box N.

Thus, it is very *important* that the amount in the "Current year increase (decrease)" line of box N, which is *not* always explained on Schedule K-1, be reported to the partners. It appears that the appropriate place to make such reporting is in the other information box of the K-1. Such items are:

- Variances between book income and K-1 line items of distributable income and deductions (Schedule M-1, lines 2, 4, 6 and 7); and
- Other increases and decreases to the capital account balance.

.03 *Separately Stated Items*

There are two dimensions to the separately stated requirement of Code Sec. 702(a):

1. *Items having a special tax characteristic.* Items of income, gain, loss, or deduction having a distinctive tax characteristic are separately reported on boxes 1 through 13 of Schedule K-1. Except for boxes 1 and 2, the lines can contain regularly allocated as well as specially-allocated items.

2. *Items receiving a special allocation.*

   - Line 1, "Ordinary income (loss) from trade or business activities" represents the partner's share of the "bottom line" on page 1 (see Schedule K).
   - Similarly, line 2, "Net Income (loss) from rental real estate activities" represents the partner's share of the "bottom line" on Form 8825.
   - These two amounts should be allocated to the partners according to their respective "regular" profit and loss ratios and should not include any item that is specially allocated.
   - All specially allocated items of ordinary income or loss should be reported on *line 11* (or income items on line 11 and loss items on line 13e).

.04 Separate Reporting

Reg. § 1.702-1(a)(8)(i) requires the separate reporting of any item subject to a special allocation "under the partnership agreement." Does this apply to the *mandatory* special allocations under Code Sec. 704(c)(1)(A)? Most likely, yes. Recall that Code Sec. 704(c) was amended in 1984 [262] to make the previous optional-by-agreement adjustment regarding contributed property a mandatory one. Reg. § 1.702-1(a)(8)(i) predates the 1984 amendment and thus refers to the pre-1984 Code Sec. 704(c) provision. Similarly, any "curative allocations" should be separately reported.

[262] Deficit Reduction Act of 1984, P.L. 98-369.

PART IV

PARTNER'S SHARE OF PARTNERSHIP DEBT

Chapter 10

Partner's Share of Partnership Debt

¶ 1001 Introduction

In keeping with an aggregate approach to partnership taxation, the partners are allowed to include the partnership's liabilities in the basis of their partnership interests. This chapter discusses the importance of including debt in a partner's partnership interest basis, what debts are included in basis and how a partner determines his or her share of the debt to be included in the basis of a partnership interest.

¶ 1002 Importance of Partner's Share of Partnership Debt

.01 Adjustments to Basis for Changes in Partner's Share of Liabilities

A partner must know his or her share of the partnership's debt to determine his or her basis in his or her interest whether the partner is using the historical approach to keeping track of the basis under Code Sec. 705(a) or the alternative method under Code Sec. 705(b) of adding his or her tax basis capital account to his or her share of debt. The preparer of the partnership's K-1s must disclose each partner's share of:

1. Nonrecourse debt other than that considered qualified nonrecourse debt under Code Sec. 465(b)(6).[1]

2. Qualified nonrecourse financing.

3. Other. This last category will consist of each partner's share of the partnership's recourse debt. Recourse debt is a liability for which any partner or party related to a partner bears the economic risk of loss.[2]

---

[1] The partnership should include in this category debt secured by real estate even though the property was placed in service before the December 31, 1986, effective date of applying the at-risk rules to real estate. The at-risk rules will apply to partners who acquire their interests after December 31, 1986, regardless of when the partnership placed the realty in service. See Act § 503(c)(2) of the Tax Reform Act of 1986, P.L. 99-514, 99th Cong., 2d Sess. The partner's K-1 should include an attachment explaining the nature of the debt, the date it was borrowed and when the recurring property was placed in service.

[2] Reg. § 1.752-1(a)(1).

Code Sec. 752 treats an increase or a decrease in a partner's share of partnership liabilities as a deemed money contribution or distribution, respectively. Deemed money contributions increase a partner's basis in his or her interest.[3] Deemed distributions decrease a partner's basis in his or her interest, but not below zero; distributions in excess of basis trigger recognition of gain.[4] It is a *change* in the share of the partnership's liabilities which generates the deemed money contribution or distribution. A deemed contribution or distribution will arise only if one or both of the following events occurs:

1. The total partnership debt changes; and/or
2. The method for sharing partnership debt changes.

The partner's debt share is calculated twice. First before and then after any event that alters his dollar share of the partnership debt. The change is a deemed money contribution if it is an increased share. It is a deemed money distribution if it is a decreased share of the partnership's debt. A partner's share of debt is calculated as of the last day of the partnership year. A partner, therefore, can easily find whether there has been a deemed money contribution or distribution due to a change in debt share by comparing his or her total share of the partnership debt appearing in Item F of Schedule K-1, Form 1065, at the end of the current year to his share of the debt at the end of the previous year. Although the partner's deemed money contribution or distribution is relatively simple to determine at the partner level from the partnership's K-1, the partnership's preparation of Item F, Schedule K-1, Form 1065, can be much more involved and is discussed at ¶ 1004.

.02 Contributions and Distributions of Encumbered Property

Code Sec. 752 treats a partner who assumes a partnership liability or takes property subject to it as contributing money to the partnership. This is the case, for example, when a partnership distributes encumbered property. If the partner assumes the debt or takes the property subject to the debt he or she is treated as having contributed money to the partnership equal to the debt assumed or encumbering the property.[5] When a partnership assumes a partner's liability or takes property subject to a partner's liability in a contribution, the partner is treated as if he or she received a money distribution equal to the amount of the debt. The debt calculation for distributions and contributions of encumbered property requires a two part analysis:

1. The distributee or contributing partner has an assumption or relief of debt which is a deemed money contribution or distribution.

---

[3] Code Sec. 722.

[4] Code Secs. 733(1) and 731(a)(1). Deemed money distributions as well as actual money distributions can generate ordinary income to the partner even in the absence of a distribution in excess of basis if the partnership holds substantially appreciated inventory as defined by Code Sec. 751(d). See Code Sec. 751(b).

[5] Code Sec. 752(c).

2. The partnership has more or less debt. This will affect some or all of the partner's dollar shares of the partnership's debt when compared to the case immediately before the distribution or contribution of encumbered property.

Contributions. In the case of a contribution of encumbered property, both the contributing partner and the other partners should treat the contribution of encumbered property as consisting of two transactions:

1. The existence of the debt is ignored and the results of the contribution are analyzed as described in Chapter 3—the effect to the contributing partner is an increased basis for his or her partnership interest in the amount of the contributed property's basis. This will have no effect on the outside bases of the other partners.

2. The effect of the debt is then taken into account after the effect of the above property contribution: each partner has a deemed cash contribution or distribution depending upon whether the total of the liabilities transferred to the partnership results in a net increase or decrease in his or her liabilities.[6] This calculation is made for all partners regardless of whether or not only an individual partner is contributing encumbered property to the partnership or more than one partner is doing so; partners with deemed cash contributions will increase their basis by this amount [7] and partners with deemed cash distributions will reduce their basis by the amount of this distribution.[8] If any partner has a deemed distribution in excess of his or her basis, as determined in step one above, such excess is reported as gain [9] and it is treated as gain from the sale of a partnership interest (capital gain in most instances). The crux of the analysis is determining how the contribution of encumbered property affects each partner's share of partnership liabilities.

Before a partnership takes over a partner's liabilities, each partner's total liabilities can be categorized as consisting of his or her share of the partnership's liabilities, for which the partner is indirectly responsible, plus his or her own separate nonpartnership liabilities connected to the contributed property, for which the partner is directly responsible. When encumbered property is contributed to a partnership and the partnership agrees to become primarily liable for paying the debt, the contributing partner's nonpartnership-related liabilities connected to the contributed property for which the partner is directly responsible decrease by the amount of such debt. This debt relief is treated as a cash distribution from the partnership. In taking over the liability related to the property, however, the partnership has a simultaneous increase in its total indebtedness by the same amount. When a partnership's total debt increases, then each partner is

[6] See Code Sec. 752.
[7] See Code Sec. 722.
[8] Code Secs. 705(a) and 733.
[9] Code Sec. 731(a).

treated as if he or she made a cash contribution to the partnership for his or her share of that new debt. This is because each partner, including the partner contributing the encumbered property, is treated as if he or she is responsible for a portion of partnership debt.

A contribution of encumbered property by one of the partners, therefore, causes each of the other partners to be treated as if he or she had made a cash contribution to the partnership equal to his or her share of the increased partnership debt. This increases his or her basis by that amount. The contributor of the encumbered property is also treated as having made a cash contribution for his or her new share of the increased partnership indebtedness, but he or she is simultaneously considered to have received an offsetting cash distribution for the amount of the debt related to the property for which the partner is no longer primarily responsible. When the partnership has no other indebtedness, the partner contributing encumbered property will always have a net deemed distribution of money equal to the debt shifted from himself to the other partners. The net distribution is first applied to reduce his or her basis in the partnership, and any excess over this amount is treated as gain. In short, the contributor of the encumbered property is treated as receiving a cash distribution in the amount of his or her net debt relief and the other partners are each treated as having made a cash contribution for their share of the same amount.

Example 10-1. Claire is invited to join the AB equal general partnership, made up of Alison and Blythe. Before she is admitted, the partnership balance sheet is as follows:

AB Partnership

Assets	***FMV***	***Tax Basis***
Cash	$500	$500
Stock	50	50
Greenacre	550	550
	$1,100	*$1,100*
Liabilities	$ 0	$ 0
Capital Accounts		
Alison	$550	$550
Blythe	550	550
	$1,100	*$1,100*

Alison and Blythe each have a basis in their partnership interests of $550. Claire contributes Purpleacre to the partnership, which has a basis and value of $850, and is made an equal one-third partner in capital, profits, and losses. The property is encumbered by a recourse indebtedness of $300, which the partnership assumes. When analyzing the tax consequences of this contribution of encumbered property, the first step is to account for the property contribution as if the property were unencumbered. The results are as follows:

ABC Partnership

Assets	*FMV*	*Tax Basis*
Cash	$500	$500
Stock	50	50
Greenacre	550	550
Purpleacre	850	850
	$1,950	*$1,950*
Liabilities	$ 0	$ 0
Capital Accounts		
Alison	$550	$550
Blythe	550	550
Claire	850	850
	$1,950	*$1,950*

Alison and Blythe continue to have a $550 basis in their partnership interests and Claire's basis is $850. The debt is then taken into account in the second step as follows:

ABC Partnership

Assets	*FMV*	*Tax Basis*
Cash	$500	$500
Stock	50	50
Greenacre	550	550
Purpleacre	850	850
	$1,950	*$1,950*
Liabilities	$300	$300
Capital Accounts		
Alison	$550	$550
Blythe	550	550
Claire	550	550
	$1,950	*$1,950*

For purposes of basis but not capital accounts, Alison and Blythe are each treated as if they made a $100 cash contribution and their bases are each increased from $550 to $650. For basis purposes, Claire is treated as if she received a $300 cash distribution and made a $100 cash contribution, for a net cash distribution of $200; her basis in her partnership interest is reduced from $850 to $650. For capital account purposes, her capital account is reduced by the full amount of the debt.[10] Her capital account now reflects the $550 net value of her contribution.

Computing the amount of the contributing partner's deemed cash distribution is relatively straightforward. It is the gross amount of debt shifted from the partner to the partnership. It is immaterial whether the contributing partner remains personally liable for repayment on the partnership's default or whether the partnership itself becomes personally

[10] Reg. § 1.704-1(b)(2)(iv).

liable. Secured debt is treated as the obligation of the securing property's owner.[11]

Computing the offsetting deemed cash contribution is more involved. An increase in a partner's share of partnership liabilities is treated as a cash contribution. This requires a comparison of the partner's share of partnership liabilities before the partnership acquired the new indebtedness to his or her share afterward. Naturally, if the contributing partner was not a member of the partnership before the contribution of the encumbered property, his or her share of the partnership's debt was zero. From the partner's point of view, the calculations are relatively easy. The partners examine their most recent Schedule K-1s after the encumbered property has been contributed and compare it to the Schedule K-1 of the prior year end. Any increase in a partner's share of the total partnership debt is a deemed money contribution. This usually results in a basis increase for any partner not contributing encumbered property. For partners contributing encumbered property, the debt taken over by the partnership is a deemed money distribution. The money distribution is netted with the deemed money contribution found by comparing the partner's current debt share shown on Schedule K-1 with the prior year's debt share shown on Schedule K-1. This usually results in a net distribution which is a reduction to basis. If the net money distribution exceeds basis, the excess is gain and the contributor of the encumbered property has a zero basis in his or her interest.

Distributions. When there is a distribution of encumbered property by the partnership, calculations which are similar to contributions of encumbered property are necessary. There are three steps:

1. Each partner's share of the new amount of partnership debt is determined—this is a deemed distribution to all of the partners who include any portion of the debt in their partnership interest adjusted basis before the distribution;

2. The distributee partner has a deemed money contribution for the amount of partnership debt related to the property. This is netted with any deemed money distribution from Step 1. The distributee generally has a net deemed money contribution which increases his or her partnership interest adjusted basis by the same amount; and

3. The effects of a distribution of unencumbered property are taken into account as discussed in Chapters 15 through 19.

¶ 1003 What Is a "Liability" for Purposes of Code Sec. 752?

.01 Debt vs. Equity

Many issues involved in identifying a debt are essentially the same as those involved in determining whether the "lender" is really an equity

[11] Code Sec. 752(c).

partner. It is a factual determination. Given the facts of this particular transaction, is it more properly characterized as a debt or something else—such as a contribution to the partnership's equity? The essential question is whether or not the "lender" was participating in the enterprise as (1) an entrepreneur providing risk capital, or (2) a creditor seeking a *return on capital independent of the success or failure of the venture.*[12]

Debt factors. The following factors are among those that have been used in determining whether the transaction was a bona fide "debt":

1. Fixed payment date in the not-too-distant future.[13]
2. Loan is secured by property with a value in excess of the loan principal.[14]
3. The extent to which the loan is subordinated to other liabilities of the business.[15]
4. Return on the loan is fixed and not dependent on profit from the enterprise.[16]
5. Borrower is not too thinly capitalized.[17]
6. Control over daily business decisions is a partner characteristic. Excessive powers of this type vested in the "lender" would, along with other factors, add to a finding of partner status.
7. Expectation of repayment and presence of security.[18]

Contingent interest. Although there has been some dissent on the issue (notably the *Farley* decision [19]), the courts have generally disregarded the fact that the lender received some form of contingent interest in the venture's profits as additional interest in ruling on the validity of purported debt instruments.[20]

.02 Additional Code Sec. 752 Requirements

Under the principles of balancing inside and outside basis, a "liability" is any "obligation" that either creates/increases basis in a partnership asset (including cash), is generated as part of a deduction taken into account in

[12] See, *e.g.*, *U.S. v. Title Guarantee & Trust Co.*, CA-6, 43-1 USTC ¶ 9293, 133 F2d 990 (stockholder intends to take corporate risk and chance of profit, creditor does not); *Commr. v. O.P.P. Holding Corp.*, CA-2, 35-1 USTC ¶ 9179, 76 F2d 11 (repayment of shareholder capital contingent; repayment of debt not contingent); *J.W. Hambuechen v. Commr.*, 43 TC 90, Dec. 27,018 (1964); Rev. Rul. 72-350, 1972 CB 394 (convertible "loan" to partnership held to be capital placed at risk in the venture).

[13] *Wood Preserving Corp. of Baltimore, Inc. v. U.S.*, CA-4, 65-2 USTC ¶ 9509, 347 F2d 117.

[14] *Ambassador Apartments, Inc. v. Commr.*, 50 TC 236, Dec. 28,945 (1968), aff'd, CA-2, 69-1 USTC ¶ 9164, 406 F2d 288.

[15] *P.M. Finance Corp. v. Commr.*, CA-3, 62-1 USTC ¶ 9465, 302 F2d 786.

[16] *Farley Realty Corp. v. Commr.*, CA-2, 60-2 USTC ¶ 9525, 279 F2d 701.

[17] *Fin Hay Realty Co. v. U.S.*, CA-3, 68-2 USTC ¶ 9438, 398 F2d 694.

[18] *Gibson Products Co. v. U.S.*, CA-5, 81-1 USTC ¶ 9213, 637 F2d 1041 (note given by partnership not true loan—no expectation of repayment, absence of security).

[19] *Farley Realty Corp. v. Commr.*, CA-2, 60-2 USTC ¶ 9525, 279 F2d 701.

[20] See *e.g.*, *K.D. Dorzback v. N. Collison*, CA-3, 52-1 USTC ¶ 9263, 195 F2d 69; *Wynnefield Heights, Inc. v. Commr.*, 25 TCM 953, Dec. 28,070(M), TC Memo. 1966-185; Rev. Rul. 76-413, 1976-2 CB 214; Rev. Rul. 72-2, 1972-1 CB 19.

computing the taxable income of the obligor, or is an expenditure that is not deductible in computing the obligor's taxable income and is not properly capitalized.[21]

> ***Example 10-2.*** Based upon the above reasoning, it is the IRS's opinion that a cash-method taxpayer's trade payables do not create basis under Code Sec. 752(a), not withstanding that the obligation is clear and would be fully "accruable" if the partnership was an accrual basis partnership. Thus, the same "obligation" may or may not be a "liability" for Code Sec. 752 purposes depending on the accounting method of the partnership.[22]

> ***Observation.*** The preparer of Form 1065 in most instances will ignore cash basis accounts payable in calculating partnership debt. This is because booking the debt to the balance sheet on Schedule L will cause capital plus debt to exceed assets unless there is a balancing amount added to assets.

For the same reasons, contingent liabilities do not affect basis until they create an asset or are the source of a deduction.[23] Under the principles of balancing inside and outside basis, a nonrecourse obligation is treated as a "liability" for Code Sec. 752 purposes to the same extent that it is treated as a liability for purposes of basis of property or deduction. If the nonrecourse liability is not recognized as a liability for basis or deduction purposes, it should not be recognized as a liability for Code Sec. 752 purposes.[24]

Technically, under a strict reading of Code Sec. 752(a) and (b), while debt of a "top tier" partnership increases basis under Code Sec. 752(a) to any partnership holding an interest in the top-tier partnership, there is nothing in the language of Code Sec. 752(a) that would treat that basis as a "liability" to the bottom-tier partnership, so that Code Sec. 752(a) could be reapplied to increase the basis of the partners of the bottom-tier partnership. However, the IRS has applied the "aggregate" theory of partnerships and held that the top-tier-partnership liabilities would be considered liabilities of lower tiers for purpose of reapplication of the debt basis to partners of such lower tiers.[25] This approach, consistent with the "balance inside and outside basis" approach to partnerships, has been adopted in the regulations.[26]

---

[21] See former Temp. Reg. § 1.752-1T(g). The final regulations do not contain the same language, but there is no reason to think this indicates a change in the IRS's position.

[22] See former Temp. Reg. § 1.752-1T(k), Ex. 2; see also Rev. Rul. 88-77, 1988-2 CB.

[23] See *M. Long v. Commr.*, 71 TC 1, Dec. 35,449 (1978), motion for reconsideration denied, 71 TC 724, Dec. 35,868 (1979), rem'd, aff'd in part, rev'd in part on other issues, CA-10, 81-2 USTC ¶ 9668, 660 F2d 416 (for an accrual-basis taxpayer contingent or contested liabilities are not "liabilities" for Code Sec. 752 purposes until they have become fixed or liquidated). But see Proposed Reg. § 1.752-7 for rules under which partners must reduce their bases in their partnership interests to reflect contingent liabilities transferred to the partnership.

[24] See *Est. of C.T. Franklin v. Commr.*, 64 TC 752, Dec. 33,359 (1975), aff'd, CA-9, 76-2 USTC ¶ 9773, 544 F2d 1045.

[25] Rev. Rul. 77-309, 1977-2 CB 216.

[26] Reg. § 1.752-4(a).

¶ 1004 Partner's Share of Partnership Recourse Debt

A partnership liability is considered recourse to the extent that any partner bears the economic risk of loss for that liability.[27] A partner's share of a recourse liability is the amount for which he or she bears the economic risk of loss.[28]

> ***LLC Observation.*** Debt which is recourse under debtor/creditor laws will normally be considered nonrecourse for tax purposes except to the extent the members become personally liable for the LLC's debt through a guarantee or similar arrangement.

A partner bears the economic risk of loss for a partnership liability to the extent that, if the partnership's assets became completely worthless and it liquidated, the partner or a person related to that partner would be obligated to make a payment to any person (or a contribution to the partnership) because that liability becomes due and payable and the partner or related person would not be entitled to reimbursement from another partner or a person who is related to the partnership.[29] The constructive liquidation test for allocation of partnership recourse liabilities involves the following hypothetical events:

1. All of the partnership's liabilities become payable in full;
2. With the exception of property contributed solely to secure a partnership liability, all of the partnership's assets, including cash, have a zero value;
3. The partnership disposes of all of its properties for no consideration (except relief from nonrecourse liabilities);
4. All items of partnership income, gain, loss, and deduction are allocated among the partners; and
5. The partnership liquidates.

> ***Observation.*** One effect of the zero value liquidation calculation is the allocation of debt based upon ending capital accounts after a hypothetical loss is allocated among the partners. Therefore, the smaller the partner's capital account before the hypothetical loss on the zero value liquidation, the greater the share of debt. Therefore, distributions and loss allocations will have the effect of shifting basis to that partner receiving the distribution or loss allocation.

Under the recourse debt rules a limited or general partner bears the economic risk of loss for a partnership liability only if that partner (or person related to that partner) can be required to make a capital contribution to the partnership, restore a capital account deficit, pay a creditor directly, or reimburse another partner for a contribution or payment made by the other partner. In general, the partner's or related party's obligation

[27] Reg. § 1.752-1(a)(1).
[28] Reg. § 1.752-2(a).
[29] Reg. § 1.752-2(b)(1).

to make these payments takes into account all statutory and contractual obligations. A partner who has a greater than 10 percent interest in the partnership is also deemed to bear the economic risk of loss for any loan that the partner or person related to that partner makes to the partnership, assuming the loan is nonrecourse to the partnership and the other partners.[30]

The finding of an obligation by a partner (or related person) concerning a liability is based on the "facts and circumstances at the time of the determination."[31] Statutory and contractual obligations taken into consideration include:

1. Contractual obligations outside the partnership agreement, such as guarantees, indemnifications, reimbursement agreements, and other obligations owed directly to creditors or to other persons, or to the partnership;[32]

2. Obligations to the partnership that are imposed by the partnership agreement, including the obligation to make a capital contribution and to restore a deficit capital account upon liquidation of the partnership; and

3. Payment obligations imposed by state law, including the governing state partnership statute.

Reimbursement rights. An obligation is reduced to the extent that the partner is entitled to reimbursement from another partner or a person who is related to another partner. Generally, all general partners are liable for all liabilities of a partnership. However, a general partner has a right of recovery against the other general partners to the extent he or she is required to pay more than his or her loss share of any liability.

Assumed liability to pay. The regulations presume that the partner who has an obligation in fact discharges the obligation on the constructive liquidation of the partnership, notwithstanding that the partner may not in fact possess sufficient assets to do so.[33]

Plan to avoid. An obligation will be disregarded if the facts and circumstances indicate a plan to circumvent or avoid such obligation.[34]

Tantamount to a guarantee. An arrangement need not actually be a "guarantee" under non-tax rules to be considered one for purposes of treating it as a guarantee. If one or more partners or related persons undertake contractual obligations that substantially eliminate a creditor's risk on an otherwise nonrecourse loan, the arrangement may be considered tantamount to a guarantee and treated for all purposes under the regulations as a guarantee.[35]

---

[30] Reg. § 1.752-2(c)(1) and (d).

[31] Reg. § 1.752-2(b)(3).

[32] *Id.*

[33] Reg. § 1.752-2(b)(6).

[34] Reg. § 1.752-2(j).

[35] Reg. § 1.752-2(j)(2).

Example 10-3. Assume that partnership ABC has purchased property from *X*, where *X* has provided 100% financing on a nonrecourse basis. Assume that partner *A* has also agreed to lease the property from partnership ABC for an amount that will pay the interest. *A*'s lease may be "tantamount to a guarantee."

Time of satisfaction. The extent to which a partner or related person bears the economic risk of loss for a partnership obligation is determined by taking into account any delay in the time when an obligation is to be satisfied. If a payment obligation to a third party is taken into account at its face amount, it must be payable within a *reasonable time* after the liability becomes due. An obligation to make a contribution to the partnership must be payable before the later of the end of the year in which the partner's interest is liquidated or 90 days after the liquidation. Otherwise, the obligation is recognized only to the extent of its *value*.[36] The obligation's value equals its face value if the interest rate is equal to the applicable federal rate under Code Sec. 1274(d). Otherwise, it is discounted to present value as calculated under Code Sec. 1274(b).[37] An obligation under local law is deemed to meet the payment time requirements of the regulations.

Assumption. An assuming person is considered liable, provided that:

1. The assuming person is subject to personal liability with respect to such liability; and

2. In case of assumption by the partner, the creditor is aware of the assumption and can directly enforce the partner's obligation.[38]

Guarantees. The partners who bear the economic risk of loss are deemed to bear the risk of loss constituting the obligation. If a partner is only secondarily liable, the person with the primary liability will be considered the party with the risk of loss. A guarantor generally has a "reimbursement right" and is therefore not the person with the ultimate risk of loss.[39]

Interest guarantees. If a liability would otherwise be a nonrecourse liability except that one or more partners (or persons related to a partner) are obligated to pay more than 25 percent of the total interest that will accrue on the liability if the partnership fails to pay such interest, and it is "*reasonable to expect*" that the guarantor will be required to pay "*substantially all*" of the future interest if the partnership fails to do so, then the guarantor partners (or partners related to the guarantors) will be treated as having an economic risk of loss with respect to the liability to the extent of the present value of the guaranteed interest payments, with the balance of the liability being treated as nonrecourse.[40]

[36] Reg. § 1.752-2(g)(1).
[37] Reg. § 1.752-2(g)(2).
[38] Reg. § 1.752-1(d).
[39] Reg. § 1.752-2(b)(5).
[40] Reg. § 1.752-2(e)(1).

Generally, it is "reasonable to expect" that the guarantor will be required to pay substantially all of the guaranteed interest if, upon default by the partnership, the lender can enforce the interest guaranty without foreclosing on the property and extinguishing the underlying debt. The assumption is that the lender would assert the foreclosure remedy before a significant portion of the interest guaranty accrued.[41]

The partner's risk of loss is deemed to be equal to the present value of the unpaid guaranteed interest, valued as of the date of determination. The present value determination is made by using the interest rate stated in the liability or, if none is stated, the applicable federal rate compounded semi-annually.[42]

The interest guarantee rules do not apply if the guaranty is for a period not greater than the lesser of five years or one-third of the period of the loan.[43] Interest that has already accrued but is unpaid is treated as a separate liability.

Example 10-4. In the SL partnership, Sylvia and Lewis have equal capital accounts, but share profits and losses 60% to Sylvia and 40% to Lewis. In addition, Sylvia "guarantees" to Lewis that on liquidation of the partnership, Lewis will receive no less than $1,000.

The partnership balance sheet is as follows:

Cash and other assets	*$10,000*
Recourse liabilities	$8,000
Capital—Sylvia	1,000
Capital—Lewis	1,000
	$10,000

The allocation of the $8,000 liability is as follows:

	Sylvia	*Lewis*
Capital accounts	$1,000	$1,000
Hypothetical loss	6,000	4,000
Preliminary balances	(5,000)	(3,000)
Guarantee	(4,000)	4,000
Final balances	*$(9,000)*	*$1,000*

Thus, as Lewis has no net liability obligation, the entire $8,000 liability should be allocated to Sylvia under Code Sec. 752 in order to determine the basis of her partnership interest under Code Sec. 705.

Without the guarantee from Sylvia to Lewis, the $8,000 liability would be allocated $5,000 to Sylvia and $3,000 to Lewis.

---

[41] *Id.*

[42] Reg. § 1.752-2(e)(2).

[43] Reg. § 1.752-2(e)(3).

Worksheets. The following worksheets and examples illustrate a mechanical approach to allocating recourse debt among partners.

WORKSHEET 1—SHARING OF LIABILITIES: ECONOMIC RISK OF LOSS

Partner:	A	B	C	Total
Limited Partner Contribution Requirement:				
Profit Percentage:				
Loss Percentage:				
Opening CAPITAL ACCOUNT:				

Liabilities	List Assets	Amount Realized	Book Basis	Gain (Loss)				
R/N								
R/N								
R/N								
R/N								
R/N								
	SUBTOTAL [1]							

Reallocations:				
1. Limited partners ≯ contribution obligation				
SUBTOTAL [2]				
2. Partner-to-Partner Obligations (allocate per Subtotal 2)				
3. Special Obligations and Reimbursement Rights				
TOTAL (Grand Total = Liability Total)				

Rules:

1. If multiple liabilities are secured by one property, treat as separate assets, with book basis assigned to asset by security priority, allocating for liabilities of equal priority.
2. Amount Realized:
   a. Recourse Liability—0
   b. Nonrecourse Liability—Amount of Liability
3. Special Obligations are such things as a partner being specifically allocated a liability obligation.

4. Partner-to-Partner Obligations: If a partner has a positive Subtotal 2 capital account, *increase* other partners' capital accounts by a proportional share of that amount, and *reduce* the positive capital account to zero. This removes the cross-partner obligations from the capital accounts.

5. Totals equal economic risk of loss for each partner, and equals share of liabilities for basis purposes. Carry totals as positive numbers (absolute value) to Worksheet 2.

WORKSHEET 2—LIABILITY SHIFT

Liability Shift :

	Worksheet 1 After Transaction
–	Worksheet 1 Before Transaction
=	Liability Shift

	A	B	C
Worksheet 1 After =			
Worksheet 1 Before =	( )	( )	( )
Liability Shift =			

WORKSHEET 3—CALCULATION OF BASIS

Partners	A	B	C
Basis Preliability Analysis			
Less Partner Liabilities Assumed by Partnership			
Plus Partnership Liabilities Assumed by Partner			
Plus Liability Shift / Share			
Ending Basis If less than zero, Basis = 0 plus gain			

Example 10-5. ABC is a general partnership. *A* contributes a property he purchased for $1,000, by paying $200 in cash and obtaining a recourse mortgage for $800, secured by the property. At the time of the contribution the property's basis and value are still $1,000. The partnership does not have any other debt. *B* contributes $120 in cash and *C* contributes $80 in cash. Their interests in the partnership

profits and losses are: *A*—50%; *B*—30%; *C*—20%. What is the basis of each of the partners in their partnership interests?

WORKSHEET 1—SHARING OF LIABILITIES: ECONOMIC RISK OF LOSS

Partner:	A	B	C	Total
Limited Partner Contribution Requirement:				
Profit Percentage:	50	30	20	
Loss Percentage:	50	30	20	
Opening CAPITAL ACCOUNT:	200	120	80	

Liabilities	List Assets	Amount Realized	Book Basis	Gain (Loss)				
800 R/N	Build	0	1,000	(1,000)	(500)	(300)	(200)	
R/N	Cash	0	200	(200)	(100)	(60)	(40)	
R/N								
R/N								
R/N								
800	SUBTOTAL [1]		1,200		(400)	(240)	(160)	

Reallocations:				
1. Limited partners ≯ contribution obligation	---	---	---	
SUBTOTAL [2]	(400)	(240)	(160)	
2. Partner-to-Partner Obligations (allocate per Subtotal 2)	---	---	---	
3. Special Obligations and Reimbursement Rights	---	---	---	
TOTAL (Grand Total = Liability Total)	(400)	(240)	(160)	(800)

Rules:

1. If multiple liabilities are secured by one property, treated as separate assets, with book basis assigned to asset by security priority, allocating for liabilities of equal priority.
2. Amount Realized:
   a. Recourse Liability—0
   b. Nonrecourse Liability—Amount of Liability
3. Special Obligations are such things as a partner being specifically allocated a liability obligation.

4. Partner-to-Partner Obligations: If a partner has a positive Subtotal 2 capital account, ***increase*** the partners' capital accounts, who will reimburse him or her by a proportional share of that amount, and ***reduce*** the positive capital account of the partner who will be reimbursed to zero. This removes the cross-partner obligations from the capital accounts.

5. Totals equal economic risk of loss for each partner, and equals share of liabilities for basis purposes. Carry totals as positive numbers (absolute value) to Worksheet 2.

WORKSHEET 2—LIABILITY SHIFT

Liability Shift :

Worksheet 1 After Transaction

− Worksheet 1 Before Transaction

= Liability Shift

	A	B	C
Worksheet 1 After =	400	240	160
Worksheet 1 Before =	(0)	(0)	(0)
Liability Shift =	400	240	160

WORKSHEET 3—CALCULATION OF BASIS

Partners	A	B	C
Basis Preliability Analysis	1,000	120	80
Less Partner Liabilities Assumed by Partnership	(800)	0	0
Plus Partnership Liabilities Assumed by Partner	0	0	0
Plus Liability Shift / Share	400	240	160
Ending Basis If less than zero, Basis = 0 plus gain	600	360	240

Balance Sheet

Assets	*FMV*	*Tax Basis*
Building	$1,000	$1,000
Building	—	—
Cash	200	200
	$1,200	*$1,200*

Liabilities	$800	$800
Capital Accounts		
A	$200	$200
B	120	120
C	80	80
	$1,200	*$1,200*

Example 10-6. Assume in the previous example that prior to his contribution of the property, *A* had deducted $400 depreciation, such that the basis of the property was $600 (but value is still $1,000). Worksheet 1 is identical to that of the previous example.

WORKSHEET 2—LIABILITY SHIFT

Liability Shift :

Worksheet 1 After Transaction

− Worksheet 1 Before Transaction

= Liability Shift

	A	B	C
Worksheet 1 After =	400	240	160
Worksheet 1 Before =	(0)	(0)	(0)
Liability Shift =	400	240	160

WORKSHEET 3—CALCULATION OF BASIS

Partners	A	B	C
Basis Preliability Analysis	600	120	80
Less Partner Liabilities Assumed by Partnership	(800)	0	0
Plus Partnership Liabilities Assumed by Partner	0	0	0
Plus Liability Shift / Share	400	240	160
Ending Basis If less than zero, Basis = 0 plus gain	200	360	240

Balance Sheet

Assets	***FMV***	***Tax Basis***
Building.	$1,000	$600
Building.	—	—
Cash.	200	200
	$1,200	*$800*

Liabilities	$800	$800
Capital Accounts		
A	$200	$(200)
B	120	120
C	80	80
	$400	*$ 0*

Example 10-7. Assume, in the previous example, that *A* had taken $700 depreciation concerning the property prior to contribution. What is *A*'s basis in his partnership interest? Worksheet 1 is identical to that of the previous example.

WORKSHEET 2—LIABILITY SHIFT

Liability Shift :

Worksheet 1 After Transaction

− Worksheet 1 Before Transaction

= Liability Shift

	A	B	C
Worksheet 1 After =	400	240	160
Worksheet 1 Before =	(0)	(0)	(0)
Liability Shift =	400	240	160

WORKSHEET 3—CALCULATION OF BASIS

Partners	A	B	C
Basis Preliability Analysis	300	120	80
Less Partner Liabilities Assumed by Partnership	(800)	0	0
Plus Partnership Liabilities Assumed by Partner	0	0	0
Plus Liability Shift / Share	400	240	160
Ending Basis If less than zero, Basis = 0 plus gain	(100) Basis=0 Gain=100	360	240

Balance Sheet

Assets	***FMV***	***Tax Basis***
Building	$1,000	$300
Building	—	—
Cash	200	200
	$1,200	*$500*

Liabilities	$800	$800
Capital Accounts		
A	$200	$(500)
B	120	120
C	80	80
	$400	*$(300)*

Example 10-8. What if in the previous examples, instead of cash, *B* contributed property with a value and basis of $720, for which *B* paid $120 in cash and had a $600 recourse mortgage. What are the bases of *A*, *B*, and *C*?

WORKSHEET 1—SHARING OF LIABILITIES: ECONOMIC RISK OF LOSS

Partner:	A	B	C	Total
Limited Partner Contribution Requirement:				
Profit Percentage:	50	30	20	
Loss Percentage:	50	30	20	
Opening CAPITAL ACCOUNT:	200	120	80	

Liabilities	List Assets	Amount Realized	Book Basis	Gain (Loss)				
800 R/N	Build	0	1,000	(1,000)	(500)	(300)	(200)	
600 R/N	Build	0	720	(720)	(360)	(216)	(144)	
R/N	Cash	0	80	(80)	(40)	(24)	(16)	
R/N								
R/N								
1,400	SUBTOTAL [1]		1,800		(700)	(420)	(280)	

Reallocations:				
1. Limited partners ≯ contribution obligation	---	---	---	
SUBTOTAL [2]	(700)	(420)	(280)	
2. Partner-to-Partner Obligations (allocate per Subtotal 2)	---	---	---	
3. Special Obligations and Reimbursement Rights	---	---	---	
TOTAL (Grand Total = Liability Total)	(700)	(420)	(280)	(1400)

Rules:

1. If multiple liabilities are secured by one property, treated as separate assets, with book basis assigned to asset by security priority, allocating for liabilities of equal priority.
2. Amount Realized:
   a. Recourse Liability—0
   b. Nonrecourse Liability—Amount of Liability
3. Special Obligations are such things as a partner being specifically allocated a liability obligation.
4. Partner-to-Partner Obligations: If a partner has a positive Subtotal 2 capital account, ***increase*** other partners' capital accounts by a proportional share of that amount, and ***reduce*** the positive capital account to zero. This removes the cross-partner obligations from the capital accounts.
5. Totals equal economic risk of loss for each partner, and equals share of liabilities for basis purposes. Carry totals as positive numbers (absolute value) to Worksheet 2.

WORKSHEET 2—LIABILITY SHIFT

Liability Shift :

Worksheet 1 After Transaction

− Worksheet 1 Before Transaction

= Liability Shift

	A	B	C
Worksheet 1 After =	700	420	280
Worksheet 1 Before =	(0)	(0)	(0)
Liability Shift =	700	420	280

WORKSHEET 3—CALCULATION OF BASIS

Partners	A	B	C
Basis Preliability Analysis	300	720	80
Less Partner Liabilities Assumed by Partnership	(800)	(600)	0
Plus Partnership Liabilities Assumed by Partner	0	0	0
Plus Liability Shift / Share	700	420	280
Ending Basis If less than zero, Basis = 0 plus gain	200	540	360

Balance Sheet

Assets	*FMV*	*Tax Basis*
Building	$1,000	$300
Building	720	720
Cash	80	80
	$1,800	*$1,100*
Liabilities	$1,400	$1,400
Capital Accounts		
A	$200	$(500)
B	120	120
C	80	80
	$400	*$300*

¶ 1005 Partner's Share of Partnership Nonrecourse Debt

Nonrecourse liabilities are those liabilities for which *no partner (or related person)* bears personal risk of loss.[44] In the event that the partnership defaults on the loan, the lender can foreclose upon any property serving as collateral for the loan, but has no further recourse against any partner in the partnership.

If the loan is obtained from a partner, or from a related party to a partner, then the lender, who is a partner in the partnership, bears personal risk of loss and the liability will be treated as a recourse loan for purposes of Code Sec. 752, even if it is structured as a nonrecourse loan.[45] Similar consequences apply if the loan is guaranteed by one or more partners. Because the guaranty will require the guarantor(s) to make payment in the event of partnership default, one or more partners (the guarantors) bear personal risk of loss for the loan and it is not classified as a nonrecourse loan.[46]

---

[44] Reg. § 1.752-1(a)(2).
[45] Reg. § 1.752-2(c)(1).
[46] Reg. § 1.752-2(c)(2).

Nonrecourse liabilities create unique problems from a tax policy standpoint. Although none of the partners have any personal obligation for repayment, no lender would make a loan if it did not expect to be repaid, so the debt is real. It therefore is included in basis. The question then becomes how to allocate the debt (and the related tax basis) among the partners. An evaluation of the partners' economic risks is irrelevant to the question—none of them have any economic risk. Thus, the question becomes how the partners will share in the repayment of the loan. Historically, Code Sec. 752 has looked to the partners' interests in partnership profits to answer this question.

.01 Nonrecourse Liabilities Allocated by Reference to Partners' Profits Interests

Prior to January 30, 1990, nonrecourse liabilities were allocated in accordance with the partners' interests in partnership profits. Because no partner bears personal liability with respect to such debts, the only way these liabilities will be repaid is from partnership profits. Thus, every partner's share of profits will be reduced by payments on the nonrecourse debt, and the partners can be viewed as sharing such debt in the same ratios in which they share partnership profits. Unfortunately, these allocation rules created problems in partnerships where deductions, such as depreciation associated with the property encumbered by the nonrecourse liabilities, were allocated in a manner different than the allocation of partnership profits. In such cases, many partners receiving special allocations of depreciation found themselves with insufficient tax basis in their partnership interests to deduct the specially allocated depreciation. New rules proposed in 1990 (and finalized on December 28, 1991) alleviate this problem.

The current regulations address this problem by creating a hierarchy of profits interests to which the partnership must look in allocating nonrecourse debts among the partners. Specifically, they divide the partners' interests in partnership profits into three categories: (1) "book" minimum gain; (2) Code Sec. 704(c) minimum gain; and (3) other profits. Under the general rule of the regulations, a partner's share of partnership nonrecourse liabilities equals the sum of:

1. The partner's share of "book" minimum gain determined in accordance with the rules of Code Sec. 704(b);

2. The amount of taxable gain that would be allocated to the partner under Code Sec. 704(c) (or in the same manner as Code Sec. 704(c) in connection with a revaluation of partnership property) if the partnership disposed of (in a taxable transaction) all partnership property subject to one or more nonrecourse liabilities of the partnership in full satisfaction of its liabilities and for no other consideration; and

3. The partner's share of the excess nonrecourse liabilities (those not allocated under 1 and 2 above) of the partnership as determined in accordance with the partner's share of partnership profits.

To provide the maximum amount of flexibility, the regulations provide two alternatives to the allocation in step 3. First, they expressly give the partnership the option to allocate nonrecourse liabilities in excess of the two categories of minimum gain (*i.e.*, excess nonrecourse liabilities) "in accordance with the manner in which it is reasonably expected that the deductions attributable to those nonrecourse liabilities will be allocated."[47] Thus, for example, if the partnership agreement allocates depreciation attributable to properties encumbered by nonrecourse liabilities differently than it allocates profits, excess nonrecourse liabilities may be allocated in accordance with the partners' shares of such depreciation.

Additionally, the partnership may first allocate an excess nonrecourse liability to a partner "up to the amount of built-in gain that is allocable to the partner on section 704(c) property (as defined under § 1.704-3(a)(3)(ii)) or property for which reverse section 704(c) allocations are applicable (as described in § 1.704-3(a)(6)(i)) where such property is subject to the nonrecourse liability to the extent that such built-in gain exceeds the gain described" in step 2 above.[48] Thus, the regulations give the partnership sufficient flexibility to ensure that partners with special allocations of depreciation, and partners who contribute property with fair market values well in excess of tax basis, can be allocated sufficient liabilities to prevent them from having to recognize gain which would otherwise be triggered to prohibit them from having negative basis in their partnership interests (*i.e.*, Code Sec. 731(a) gain).

.02 Minimum Gain

Partnership "minimum gain" is the amount of gain which would be recognized by the partnership if it surrendered the property to the nonrecourse lender in satisfaction of the outstanding balance of the debt (*e.g.*, as in a foreclosure). Because such a transaction is treated as a sale or exchange, the partnership will realize gain in an amount equal to the excess of the outstanding balance of the loan over the book value (adjusted for depreciation deductions) of the property. The partnership could realize more gain on disposition of the property (if its fair value exceeds its book value, adjusted for depreciation), but never less.

Example 10-9. Partnership Alpha owns real estate with a book value (net of accumulated depreciation) of $250,000. The property is encumbered by a $375,000 nonrecourse mortgage incurred to finance acquisition of the property. No partner or related person has any personal risk of loss with respect to the loan. Thus, default by the partnership will effectively result in the transfer of the property to the

[47] Reg. § 1.752-3(a)(3).

[48] *Id.*

lender in full satisfaction of the $375,000 remaining principal balance of the note. A sale at this price would generate a gain of $125,000.[49] Since default and foreclosure is the worst-case scenario for the partnership with respect to this property, this is the "minimum gain" that will be realized by the partnership with respect to this property.

Under the section 704(b) regulations, the existence of partnership minimum gain allows partners' capital accounts to fall below zero even in the absence of any requirement on their parts to make additional capital contributions to "restore" these deficit balances. As long as the deficits do not exceed the partners' shares of partnership minimum gain, any deficit in their capital accounts can be made up—restored—with an allocation of minimum gain. This allocation has tax consequences in that it increases the partners' taxable income. These consequences give the underlying loss allocations economic effect under the section 704(b) regulations. Following the same rationale, the regulations under section 752 look to the allocation of minimum gain to support the allocation of the underlying nonrecourse debt associated with that minimum gain.

Example 10-10. *L* and *M* form a limited partnership to acquire a hotel. *L*, the general partner, contributes $80,000 cash, and *M*, the limited partner, contributes $320,000 cash to the partnership. The partnership issues a $3,600,000 nonrecourse note to an unrelated lender and purchases the hotel for $4,000,000. The partners agree to share losses 20% to *L* and 80% to *M*. Partnership income is to be shared equally. These allocations are recognized by the IRS under Code Sec. 704(b). Minimum gain is to be shared 20/80 in order to substantiate the loss-sharing arrangement. In each of its first three years, the partnership's revenues just offset its operating expenses giving it net income of $0 before depreciation. Assume an annual depreciation deduction of $100,000, resulting in a ($100,000) annual tax loss, which will impact the partners' capital accounts as follows:

	L	*M*
Beginning Capital	$ 80,000	$ 320,000
Loss in years 1-4	(80,000)	(320,000)
Capital, end of year 4	0	0
Year 5 loss	(20,000)	(80,000)
Capital, end of year 5	(20,000)	(80,000)

At the end of year 4, there is no partnership minimum gain so the nonrecourse liability is allocated equally between the partners in accordance with their general profit-sharing ratios. At the end of year 5, however, partnership minimum gain is $100,000 (basis = 4,000,000 − 500,000 depreciation = 3,500,000 vs. principal amount of loan = $3,600,000). Thus, the first $100,000 of the nonrecourse loan is allocated 20% to *L* and 80% to *M* in accordance with their interests in partnership minimum gain. The remaining nonrecourse liability of

[49] See Reg. § 1.1001-2(c), Examples (7) and (8).

$3,500,000 is allocated equally. Thus, at the end of year 5, *L*'s share of partnership nonrecourse debt is $1,770,000 ($20,000 share of partnership minimum gain plus $1,750,000 share of the excess) and *M*'s share is $1,830,000 ($80,000 + $1,750,000).

.03 Code Sec. 704(c) Minimum Gain

Code Sec. 704(c) minimum gain arises when a partnership owns property encumbered by nonrecourse debt which has a book value in excess of its tax basis. In such cases, the total amount of "minimum gain" which would be recognized by the partnership in the event of default and foreclosure by the nonrecourse lender is equal to the excess of the principal amount of the note over the tax basis of the property. This total minimum gain is divided into two parts. "Book" minimum gain is equal to the excess of the nonrecourse debt balance over the book value of the property; the remainder of the minimum gain will be allocated under Code Sec. 704(c). It is possible to have Code Sec. 704(c) minimum gain, but no "book" minimum gain. Indeed, this is common—since the book value of contributed property is equal to its fair value at the date of contribution (subsequently adjusted for book depreciation), any minimum gain with respect to such property in the years immediately following contribution will generally consist solely of Code Sec. 704(c) minimum gain. Similarly, it is possible to have "book" minimum gain, but no Code Sec. 704(c) minimum gain. Again, this is common—for example, for property acquired by the partnership via purchase or self-construction, as opposed to contribution from a partner, book value will generally equal tax basis unless the partnership has revalued its properties under Reg. § 1.704-1(b)(2)(iv)(f).

Where minimum gain would be allocated under Code Sec. 704(c) to one or more partners, the allocation of the nonrecourse liability follows the allocations of the minimum gain, to the extent of the minimum gain.

Example 10-11. *G* and *H* form a general partnership to acquire and manage residential properties. *G* contributes $250,000 to the partnership that it uses to acquire an apartment complex. *H* contributes a second apartment building valued at $425,000. The basis of the property contributed by H is $150,000 and it is subject to a nonrecourse debt of $175,000. The two partners share all profits and losses equally. The $175,000 nonrecourse loan, however, is not shared equally by the partners. The first $25,000 of such loan is allocated to *H* because *H* would be allocated $25,000 of partnership gain under Code Sec. 704(c) if the partnership disposed of the apartment building in full satisfaction of the nonrecourse liability. The remainder of the nonrecourse liability is allocated between the partners in proportion to their equal interests in partnership profits. Thus, *G*'s share of the $175,000 nonrecourse liability is $75,000 (1/2 of $150,000) and *H*'s share is $100,000 ($25,000 + 1/2 of $150,000).

Example 10-12. CDE Partnership owns depreciable realty with a book value of $250,000 and a tax basis of $140,000. The property is encumbered by a nonrecourse liability of $300,000. (Assume the market value of the property exceeds this amount). Thus, the total minimum gain with respect to this property is $160,000 (the $300,000 balance of the nonrecourse note over its tax basis of $140,000). Of this amount, $50,000 is "book" minimum gain (the $300,000 balance of the nonrecourse mortgage over its $250,000 book value), and the remainder is Code Sec. 704(c) minimum gain. The book minimum gain will be allocated among the partners in accordance with the manner in which they have shared the book depreciation deductions. The Code Sec. 704(c) minimum gain will be allocated to the partner who contributed the property to the partnership. The allocation of the first $160,000 of the nonrecourse mortgage will follow these allocations of minimum gain. The remainder will be allocated in accordance with the partners' shares of partnership profits. Alternatively, the partnership may choose to allocate the remainder of the nonrecourse note in accordance with the manner in which it expects to allocate future depreciation deductions.

.04 *"Excess" Nonrecourse Liabilities*

Under the general rule, partnership nonrecourse liabilities in excess of the partnership's book and Code Sec. 704(c) minimum gain (*i.e.*, "excess" liabilities) are allocated in accordance with the partners' interests in general partnership profits. However, rather than base this allocation on the partners' general profits interests, the regulations provide that a partnership *may choose* to allocate *excess* nonrecourse liabilities first to the contributing partner to the extent of built-in gain allocable to that partner under Code Sec. 704(c) which exceeds the amount of Code Sec. 704(c) minimum gain as determined under step 2. Alternatively, it *may choose* to allocate *excess* nonrecourse liabilities among the partners in accordance with the manner in which it expects to allocate depreciation deductions attributable to the properties encumbered by the nonrecourse liabilities.

> ***Observation.*** The regulations state explicitly that a partnership is not required to use the same method to allocate its excess nonrecourse deductions every year.[50] Thus a partnership that apportions excess nonrecourse liabilities by reference to its partners' general profits interests may choose to change to an allocation based on the partners' interests in depreciation in a year in which a reduction in the principal balance of the nonrecourse debt is reduced.

Nonrecourse liabilities are generally allocated on a liability-by-liability basis, so that accurate measures of book and tax minimum gain, and the partners' interests therein, can be determined.[51] The separately computed amounts are then added together to determine each partner's aggregate share of partnership nonrecourse liabilities.

---

[50] Reg. § 1.752-3(a)(3), last sentence.

[51] Reg. § 1.704-2(d)(1).

Example 10-13. Mockingbird Partners was formed several years ago by three partners, *H*, *L* and *G*. *H* contributed depreciable property with a tax basis of $450,000 and a fair market value of $750,000. The property was encumbered by a $600,000 nonrecourse debt. *L* contributed $150,000 cash and *G* contributed $200,000 cash. The partnership agreement allocates partnership profits 30% to *H*, 30% to *L* and 40% to *G*. Depreciation is allocated equally among the partners. For simplicity, assume that each property is depreciated using the straight line method over 15 years.

Shortly after formation, the partnership borrowed $550,000 on a nonrecourse mortgage and began development of a large real estate project at a total cost of $900,000. At the end of its first year, the book and tax bases of the partnership's assets were as follows:

	Book Value	*Tax Basis*
Property contributed by H	$ 750,000	$ 450,000
Accumulated depreciation	(50,000)	(30,000)
	700,000	420,000
Property acquired by Partnership	900,000	900,000
Accumulated depreciation	(60,000)	(60,000)
	840,000	840,000
Total Assets	$ 1,540,000	$ 1,260,000

Assume the partnership has made no payments against the principal balances of the nonrecourse mortgages. The nonrecourse liabilities would be allocated as follows:

	H	*L*	*G*
Mortgage on property contributed by *H*:			
Book minimum gain	0	0	0
Tax minimum gain	180,000	0	0
General profits	126,000	126,000	168,000
Mortgage on acquired property:			
Book minimum gain	0	0	0
Tax minimum gain	0	0	0
General profits	165,000	165,000	220,000
Totals	471,000	291,000	388,000

As an alternative to the third step above, the partnership could allocate its "excess" nonrecourse liabilities equally, in accordance with its allocations of depreciation. (If and when the partnership has book minimum gain, that portion of the nonrecourse liabilities will be allocated equally since book minimum gain will be created as a result of depreciation allocations.)

.05 *Multiple Properties Secured by Single Nonrecourse Liability*

In cases where a single nonrecourse loan is secured by multiple properties, measurement of minimum gain is problematic. The regulations give partnerships almost complete flexibility in making this determination.

Partnerships may use any "reasonable" method to apportion the liability among the different properties securing it, so long as the apportionment does *not* result in the allocation of debt to any property in excess of its fair market value.[52] However, once the liability has been allocated among the various properties securing the loan, it may *not* be reallocated among those properties using a different method.

The only exception to this prohibition against reallocating the liability among the properties securing that liability arises when the lender releases a property from the debt. If a property to which a portion of the nonrecourse liability has been allocated subsequently becomes no longer subject to the liability, the portion of the nonrecourse debt allocated to that property must be reallocated to the other properties still subject to that debt. The reallocation is still subject to the limitation against allocating debt to a property in excess of its fair value.

Finally, the regulations provide that where the outstanding principal balance of the liability is reduced, the reduction must be allocated among multiple properties in the same proportion as the liability was allocated to those properties.[53] This requirement is consistent with the prohibition described above against changing the method of allocation of the nonrecourse liability among multiple properties securing it.

¶ 1006 Proposed Reg. § 1.752-7 Liabilities (Contingent Liabilities)

.01 General

Proposed regulations issued in the summer of 2003 prescribe new rules for so-called "§ 1.752-7 liabilities."[54] Although the regulations do not really define these liabilities, it appears that a § 1.752-7 liability is essentially a contingent liability which, due to the uncertainty of either the amount of the debt or the likelihood of repayment, is not treated as a liability for purposes of Code Secs. 752(a) or (b). For example, the transfer to a partnership of property encumbered by potential environmental liabilities would trigger these provisions.

The purpose of the proposed regulations is to prevent partners from transferring the tax deductions associated with these contingent liabilities to the other partners in the partnership, or to accelerate his or her own loss by selling the partnership interest prior to the partnership's disposal of the property subject to the contingent liability. Accordingly, the new rules apply the principles of Code Sec. 704(c) (relating to built-in gains or losses inherent in contributed property) to transfers of property encumbered by contingent debts by a partner to a partnership.

---

52 Reg. § 1.752-3(b)(1).

53 Reg. § 1.752-3(b)(2).

54 Proposed Reg. § 1.752-7, effective June 24, 2003. These regulations effectively replace Temporary Reg. § 1.752-6 which applied to assumptions of partnership liabilities after October 18, 1999 and before June 24, 2003.

.02 Mechanics

Under the proposed regulations, when a partner transfers property to a partnership subject to a § 1.752-7 liability, the liability is not treated as a liability for purposes of Code Sec. 752, but instead is treated as built-in loss under Code Sec. 704(c). At a later date, when the partnership satisfies all or part of a contingent liability, any resulting tax deduction or loss must be allocated to the contributing partner to the extent of the built-in loss at the date of contribution.[55]

> ***Example 10-14.*** *J*, *F* and *K* form DumpStation, Ltd. to develop and operate a landfill. *J* contributes vacant land with a fair market value and tax basis of $600,000. The land is subject to potential environmental liabilities in the amount of $150,000. In exchange, *J* receives a 20% interest in the partnership. *F* contributes $675,000 cash in exchange for a 30% interest in the partnership, and *K* contributes $1,125,000 cash in exchange for a 50% interest. The partnership subsequently pays $250,000 to satisfy the environmental liability on the property contributed by *J*. Assume that the $250,000 payment is deductible by the partnership. The first $150,000 of this deduction must be allocated to *J*. The remainder will be allocated in accordance with the partners' loss-sharing ratios (presumably 20:30:50, although a different sharing ratio will be acceptable so long as the requirements of Code Sec. 704(b) are satisfied).

> ***Observation.*** The proposed regulations imply that § 1.752-7 liabilities are treated as liabilities for "book" (*i.e.*, Code Sec. 704(b)) purposes, but not for tax purposes. Thus, a partner/member's Code Sec. 704(b) capital account must be reduced by the "value" of the contingent liability, while his or her capital account on the entity's tax balance sheet will not be affected.

> ***Caution.*** The proposed regulations do not explain how to value a § 1.752-7 liability. The regulations provide that the value of such a liability is equal to "the amount of cash that a willing assignor would pay to a willing assignee to assume the § 1.752-7 liability in an arm's length transaction."[56] Thus, at this point, practitioners are on their own for purposes of attempting to measure such liabilities.

.03 Sale or Transfer of an Interest in a Partnership with § 1.752-7 Liabilities

When a partner sells his or her interest in the partnership before the § 1.752-7 liability has been satisfied, the proposed regulations require that the basis of the partnership interest be reduced by the remaining § 1.752-7 liability amount.[57] The basis reduction is triggered immediately before the sale, exchange or other disposition of the interest, thus increasing the selling

[55] Proposed Reg. § 1.752-7(c)(1).

[56] Proposed Reg. § 1.752-7(b)(2)(ii).

[57] Proposed Reg. § 1.752-7(e)(1).

partner's gain (or reducing his or her loss) on the disposition. Note that in such cases, the partnership retains the § 1.752-7 liability. Under the proposed regulations, if it subsequently makes a payment in partial or full satisfaction of that liability, it is allowed a deduction or capital expense *only* to the extent that the payment exceeds the remaining built-in loss associated with liability immediately prior to the payment. Moreover, the capital accounts of the remaining partners are adjusted only to the extent such payment is deductible (or capitalizable). If the partnership notifies the original contributing partner that the § 1.752-7 liability has been satisfied, the partner will be allowed a loss or deduction to the extent of the lesser of the built-in loss (the reduction in basis) or the amount paid to satisfy the liability.

Example 10-15. Assume the same facts as in Example 10-14. *J* contributes raw land with a tax basis and fair market value of $600,000 to DumpStation, Ltd. in exchange for a 20% interest therein. *J*'s tax basis in her partnership interest will be $600,000. However, due to a contingent environmental liability of $150,000, her interest is worth only $450,000. Assume that *J* later sells her partnership interest for $450,000. Under Reg. § 1.752-7(e)(1), *J* must reduce her tax basis in the partnership interest by the $150,000 potential environment liability. Thus, she will recognize no gain or loss on the sale. If the partnership subsequently satisfies the obligation for $250,000, it will be entitled to a $100,000 deduction (the amount paid to satisfy the obligation over the estimated amount of the liability at the date of *J*'s contribution to the partnership). If the partnership contacts *J*, she will be entitled to a $150,000 deduction for the built-in loss inherent in the property attributable to the environmental liability.

Caution. Nothing in the regulations obligates the partnership or LLC to notify the former partner that the § 1.752-7 liability has been satisfied. Departing partners should be counseled to obtain a commitment from the partnership that it will provide notification in the event that the § 1.752-7 liability is subsequently paid in a future year. The § 1.752-7 partner must attach a copy of the notification received from the partnership to his or her tax return in the year a deduction is claimed. The notification must include the following information:[58]

- The amount paid in satisfaction of the liability;
- Whether the amount(s) paid was in partial or complete satisfaction of such liability;
- The name and address of the person satisfying the liability;
- The date of payment of such liability; and
- The character of the loss triggered by payment of the liability.

[58] Proposed Reg. § 1.752-7(h).

.04 *Liquidating Distribution to § 1.752-7 Partner or Distribution of Property Secured by § 1.752-7 Liability to Another Partner*

Two other types of transactions also trigger the application of the basis adjustment rules described above:

1. Receipt of a liquidating distribution by a § 1.752-7 partner from the partnership;[59] or
2. Assumption of the § 1.752-7 liability by *another partner* of the partnership[60] (*e.g.*, as when the property encumbered by the § 1.752-7 liability is distributed to another partner).

In either of the above circumstances, the partner who contributed the property subject to the contingent liability (the § 1.752-7 partner) is required to reduce his or her basis in the partnership interest by the remaining built-in loss associated with the § 1.752-7 liability. If and when the § 1.752-7 liability is later satisfied, the payor is entitled to a deduction *only to the extent that the amount paid in satisfaction of the liability exceeds the value of the liability (the built-in loss) at the date of the distribution or assumption.*[61] If the partnership notifies the § 1.752-7 partner that the liability has been discharged (fully or partially), the partner will be entitled to a deduction in an amount equal to the lesser of the built-in loss associated with the liability or the amount paid in satisfaction thereof.

Special rules apply where another partner assumes the contributor's responsibility for the § 1.752-7 liability. First, immediately following the assumption of the § 1.752-7 liability from the partnership by a partner other than the § 1.752-7 liability partner, the partnership must reduce its basis in its assets by the remaining built-in loss associated with the liability. The basis adjustment is allocated among the partnership's assets following the rules of Code Sec. 734(b).

The assuming partner, on the other hand, is not allowed to account for the § 1.752-7 liability until such time as the liability is satisfied. At that time, the assuming partner adjusts his or her basis in the partnership interest, any assets distributed by the partnership to such partner, or gain or loss on disposition of the partnership interest as if a recognized liability had been assumed. The amount of the adjustment is equal to the lesser of the amount paid in satisfaction of the debt or the remaining built-in loss associated with the debt. Any amounts paid in excess of such amount are deductible or treated as a capital expenditure by the assuming partner.[62]

> ***Example 10-16.*** *Q*, *L* and *R* form the QLR Partnership. *Q* contributes property 1 with a tax basis and fair market value of

---

[59] Proposed Reg. § 1.752-7(f)(1).

[60] Proposed Reg. § 1.752-7(g)(1).

[61] As indicated in Example 22, a deduction is allowed in the event that the liability is satisfied in exchange for a payment that exceeds the built-in loss inherent in the liability at the date of the distribution or assumption of such liability by another partner/member. See Proposed Reg. §§ 1.752-7(f)(2) and 1.752-7(g)(4).

[62] Similar rules apply when the encumbered property is contributed by the partnership to another partnership or corporation. See Proposed Reg. § 1.752-7(i).

$3,000,000. The property is subject to a contingent liability valued at $1,200,000. In return, she receives a 25% interest in the partnership. *L* contributes $1,800,000 in cash in exchange for a 25% interest, and *R* contributes $3,600,000 cash in exchange for a 50% interest. The partnership uses the cash provided by *L* and *R* to purchase additional property.

Two years later, the partnership distributes Property 1 to *R* in partial liquidation of *R*'s interest in the partnership. *R* took the property subject to the $1,200,000 § 1.752-7 liability. Upon the distribution of Property 1 to *R*, *Q* is required to reduce her basis in her partnership interest by $1,200,000 (to $1,800,000). Similarly, the QLR Partnership is required to reduce its tax basis in its other properties by $1,200,000. *R* takes a $3,000,000 carryover basis in Property 1, equal to its tax basis in the hands of the partnership. Assuming that *R*'s tax basis in the partnership interest remained $3,600,000 prior to receipt of the distribution, her remaining tax basis in the interest will be reduced to $600,000.

Assume that *R* subsequently pays $900,000 to satisfy the § 1.752-7 liability. *R* will not be entitled to a tax deduction for the payment. Instead, *R* will increase the tax basis of the encumbered property (Property 1) by the $900,000 payment. If *R* notifies *Q* that the debt has been satisfied, *Q* will be allowed a $900,000 ordinary loss for the amount paid by *R* in satisfaction of the debt, and a $300,000 capital loss deduction for the excess of the built-in loss over the amount paid in satisfaction of the § 1.752-7 liability.

.05 Exceptions

The provisions of Proposed Reg. § 1.752-7 do not apply to contingent liabilities transferred in the following situations:

- The partnership assumes the liability in connection with a contribution by the partner of the trade or business with which such liability is associated and the entity continues to carry on that trade or business after the contribution; or
- Just prior to the contribution, the remaining built-in loss associated with the § 1.752-7 liability is less than the lesser of 10 percent of the gross value of all partnership assets or $1,000,000; or
- The § 1.752-7 partner transfers his or her interest in the partnership (in whole or in part) in a nonrecognition transaction (*e.g.*, under Code Sec. 351 or 721).

PART V

DISPOSITION OF A PARTNERSHIP INTEREST

Chapter 11

Amount and Character of Seller's Gain or Loss: Basic Rules

¶ 1101 Introduction

As is the case when any asset is sold, the amount of the transferor partner's gain or loss on the transfer of that partner's partnership interest is determined in accordance with Code Sec. 1001. Gain or loss realized is equal to the amount realized by the transferor partner for the transfer of the partner's partnership interest less adjusted basis in his or her partnership interest ("outside basis"). In keeping with the entity approach to the taxation of transfers of partnership interests, this gain or loss is considered to be gain or loss from the sale or exchange of a capital asset except as otherwise provided.[1] Code Sec. 751(a) provides an important statutory exception to this general rule which, as a practical matter, applies to many sales of partnership interests. Under this exception, the amount of the seller's gain or loss allocable to the seller's share of the net appreciation or depreciation in the partnership's ordinary income assets is taxed as ordinary income or loss on the sale of the partnership interest. Only the remaining gain is capital. This chapter covers the rules governing the amount and timing of gain or loss from the sale of a partnership interest. Chapter 12 covers the rules related to the character of gain or loss.

> ***S Corporation Observation.*** Unless Code Sec. 341's collapsible corporation rules apply, all gain from the sale of S corporation stock is capital gain.[2]

Long term gain from the sale of a partnership interest attributable to the appreciation of collectibles is not ordinary income, but it is taxed at a

---

[1] Code Sec. 741.

[2] See ¶ 1206 for a discussion of Code Sec. 341.

28 percent rate, not the usual 20 percent rate that generally applies to long term capital gains.[3] In addition, a 25 percent rate applies to the long-term gain attributable to the partner's share of the partnership's unrecaptured depreciation.[4] The selling partner is required to submit with his or her income tax return for the taxable year a statement setting forth:

- The date of sale;
- The amount of any gain attributable to collectibles and partnership unrecaptured Code Sec. 1250 gain; and
- The gain or loss on the sale of the partnership interest.[5]

S Corporation Observation. Gain from the sale of S corporation stock is subject to the same rule for the shareholder's share of collectibles but not for unrecaptured depreciation.[6]

As a statutory starting point, the general rule is that the partnership provisions in Subchapter K of the Internal Revenue Code adopt an "entity approach" in dealing with the tax consequences when partnership interests are transferred. The transferred interest is treated like corporate stock and is considered to be a separate intangible asset rather than an undivided tenancy-in-common interest in the partnership assets, as it would be treated under an "aggregate approach" to partnership taxation. Section 751(a), however, carves out an important exception to this principle, as is discussed in Chapter 12.

LLC Observation. The rules discussed in this chapter apply equally to state law partnerships and LLCs taxed as partnerships.

¶ 1102 Amount Realized

As is the situation with most sales of property, the amount realized by the transferor partner equals the amount of cash and the fair market value of any property received by the transferor partner, plus debt relief.[7] In the case of sales of partnership interests, debt relief takes the form of a decreased share of partnership liabilities.[8]

¶ 1103 Partnership Interest Adjusted Basis

The transferor partner's adjusted basis in his or her partnership interest at the time of transfer is the sum of the transferor partner's basis on the day he or she acquired an interest plus adjustments reflecting operations during the transferor partner's holding period. The calculation of a partner's initial basis varies according to whether the partner acquired his or her interest through a contribution to the partnership or from another

[3] Code Sec. 1(h)(6)(B); Prop. Reg. § 1.1(h)-1.

[4] Code Sec. 1(h)(7)(A); Prop. Reg. § 1.1(h)-1.

[5] Prop. Reg. § 1.1(h)-1(e); Reg. § 1.751-1(a)(3). The proposed regulations refer to unrecaptured Code Sec. 1250 gain as "Section 1250 gain."

[6] Code Sec. 1(h)(5)(B).

[7] Reg. § 1.1001-2(a)(1); Code Sec. 752(d).

[8] Code Secs. 1001(b) and 752(b). Debt relief is determined in accordance with the provisions of Reg. § 1.752-1(e) if the debt was incurred before February 1, 1989, or Reg. §§ 1.752-1 through -4 if incurred on or after December 28, 1992. See Reg. § 1.752-5 for effective dates and transitional rules.

partner and whether the partner is using the statutory general rule for calculating basis or the statutory alternative method.[9]

.01 General Rule

The initial basis in a partnership interest obtained in exchange for the contribution of cash or property is generally equal to the amount of cash plus the tax basis of any property contributed.[10] The initial adjusted basis of the *transferee* partner in his or her partnership interest is determined under the rules generally applicable to acquisition of other types of property.[11] Thus, if a partner purchases a partnership interest, the partner takes a cost basis in that interest.[12] Similarly, a partner who acquires his or her partnership interest by inheritance gets a stepped-up (or stepped-down) basis in the partnership interest equal to its fair market value at the date of the testator's death or at the alternative valuation date, increased by his or her share of the partnership's debt.[13]

The beginning adjusted basis is then increased by the partner's share of partnership taxable income and tax exempt income. Adjustments are made for income reported for the taxable year of transfer as well as for prior years.[14] The partners' contributions made either in the transfer year or any prior taxable year are added to that amount. The beginning adjusted basis is decreased by the transferor partner's distributive share of partnership losses and expenses incurred in producing tax-exempt income, and other nondeductible/noncapitalized expenditures for the taxable year of transfer and for prior years,[15] and by any partnership distributions.[16] For purposes of calculating gain or loss on sale, the regulations require the seller's basis to reflect these adjustments as of the date of sale whether the seller is selling all of his or her partnership interest or just a part of that interest.[17] These increases and decreases to basis include deemed money contributions and distributions for increases and decreases in the partner's share of partnership debt.[18] The effect of the statutory general rule is that the partner must keep a running tally of the cumulative adjustments to the basis of his or her partnership interest after its acquisition. As a practical matter, the partner may not have retained the records needed to make these calculations. Code Sec. 705(b) provides an alternative approach which may be used in the absence of the partner having information necessary to comply with the approach of Code Sec. 705(a).

---

[9] Code Secs. 722 or 742 govern, depending on whether the partner acquired his or her interest by contribution to the partnership or by the transfer to the partner of an existing partnership interest.

[10] See Chapter 3.

[11] Code Sec. 742.

[12] Code Sec. 1012. The transferee partner's cost includes his or her share of the partnership's liabilities. Code Sec. 752(d). This is determined under Reg. § 1.752-1(e) if the debt was incurred before February 1, 1989, or Reg. § § 1.752-1 through -4 if incurred on or after December 28, 1992. See Reg. § 1.752-5 for effective dates and transitional rules.

[13] Code Sec. 1014. The basis of the partnership interest may not include the value of the partnership interest attributable to "income in respect of a decedent" (IRD) assets under Code Sec. 691. Code Sec. 1014(c).

[14] Code Secs. 705(a)(1) and 722. See Chapter 9.

[15] Code Sec. 705(a)(2) and (3).

[16] Code Sec. 733.

[17] Reg. § 1.705-1(a)(1).

[18] Code Sec. 752(a) and (b).

.02 Alternate Rule

In addition to the Code Sec. 705(a) "historical approach" to maintaining a partner's basis in that partner's partnership interest, a partner is allowed to treat his or her share of the partnership's basis in its assets as his or her basis in the interest. This alternative appears inviting at first blush when compared to accounting for yearly adjustments to basis as described above. However, as a practical matter, the necessary calculations and adjustments may make it an unappealing—but perhaps necessary—choice for a typical partnership when there have been property contributions and distributions and/or transfers of partnership interests.

The regulations provide that a partner may use the alternative rule of Code Sec. 705(b) to determine the tax basis of his or her partnership interest by reference to the total adjusted basis of partnership property in two circumstances:

1 Where the partner "cannot practicably apply the general rule set forth in Code Sec. 705(a)"; or

2. If, in the opinion of the IRS Commissioner, the result would be the same under the general rule.[19]

Example 11-1. Individuals Charlie Cook, Dawn Danforth and Ed Eng formed the equal CDE Partnership in 1946. Charlie is selling his partnership interest in the current year, but does not have the necessary information to establish his tax basis. The adjusted basis of all partnership property is $300,000. The partnership has liabilities totalling $100,000. What is the tax basis of Charlie's partnership interest?

The partnership has been in existence for 55 years. Apparently the language of the regulation is satisfied if a partnership has been in existence for many years. Charlie would be entitled to one-third of the partnership property on liquidation and therefore has a basis for his interest equal to one-third of the partnership's basis in its assets, $100,000.

The examples in the regulations involve two approaches to finding a partner's share of the partnership's property basis. The first approach, which is the least appealing of the two, is to determine the partner's share of the value of the partnership's assets; this is his or her tentative share of the partnership's basis in its assets. The resulting amount is the partner's tentative basis in his or her interest. This tentative basis is, as discussed further below, adjusted to take into account (1) inside/outside basis inequalities generated, for example, because the partner purchased his or her

[19] Reg. § 1.705-1(b).

interest, and (2) disproportionate sharing of the basis of the partnership's assets. This can happen, for example, when a partner contributes appreciated or depreciated assets and when a partner joins the partnership at a time when the partnership holds appreciated assets.

Adjustments arise from contributions of property, as well as from transfers of a partnership interest or distributions of property to the partners. The regulation requires that adjustments be made to take this discrepancy into account.[20] In general, adjustments are necessary because:

1. The general application of the alternate rule assumes that aggregate inside and outside basis are equal. They may not be equal.

2. Even though aggregate inside and outside basis may be equal, each partner's share of that basis may not equal his or her share of the value of the partnership's assets because of the operation of Code Sec. 704(c) or the lack of a Code Sec. 754 election.

3. The Code Sec. 752 regulations may allocate debt differently than the partner's share of the assets.

Example 11-2. Individuals *C*, *D*, and *E* formed the equal CDE Partnership in 1946. *C* is selling his partnership interest in the current year, but does not have the necessary information to establish his tax basis. The adjusted basis of all partnership property is $300,000. The partnership has liabilities totalling $100,000. Land and a building still owned by the partnership were contributed by *C* with a value on contribution of $30,000 and an adjusted basis of $10,000. *D* and *E* each contributed $30,000 as their initial and only capital contributions to the partnership.

Here, *C* contributed property with a basis of $10,000 in exchange for a one-third interest, while *D* and *E* contributed property with a basis of $30,000 for a one-third interest. Thus, the aggregate of the initial bases of partnership assets was $70,000. The partnership assets now have an aggregated basis of $300,000. *C*'s initial one-third share of $70,000 is $23,333, or $13,333 more than the $10,000 basis of property contributed by *C*. Thus, a *permanent* reduction of $13,333 is necessary to compute *C*'s basis under the alternative rule. On the other hand, a permanent increase of $6,667 (*i.e.*, $30,000 – $23,333) is necessary to compute *D* or *E*'s basis under the alternative rule.

[20] *Id.*

C's FMV share of bases of partnership assets (1/3 × $300,000)	$100,000
C's basis adjustment	(13,333)
C's adjusted basis in his partnership interest (Code Sec. 705(b))	*$86,667*
D's and *E*'s FMV share of basis of partnership assets (1/3 × $300,000)	$100,000
D's or *E*'s basis adjustment	6,667
D's or *E*'s adjusted basis of his partnership interest (Code Sec. 705(b))	*$106,667*

When working under Code Sec. 705(b) with the concept of the equality of the total adjusted basis of partnership property and the total adjusted bases of partnership interests, the presence of liabilities generally is neutral because the debt has been taken into account in the basis of each, having been included in the adjusted bases of assets created or purchased with cash from the debt and also included in the bases of the partners' interests in the partnership. Alternatively, if cash had been dispersed for expenses, the increase in adjusted basis by reason of the debt would have been offset by an equal deduction for the expenditures. The presence or absence of liabilities is, in essence, irrelevant under this alternative approach to figuring the basis of a partnership interest. However, even though, in the aggregate, the increase and the decrease are theoretically equal, in reality the debt may be allocable in a different manner than the expenses paid with the debt or the partners' shares of the adjusted basis of partnership assets (their prorated claim on the assets divided by total assets times total adjusted bases of the property to the partnership).

The first alternate method of computing a partner's basis in his or her partnership interest described above focuses on finding the partner's share of the basis of the partnership's assets. This requires that the partner have access to the partnership's books and records or that the partnership does the calculations necessary to find the partner's basis in his or her interest. However, if the partner had inherited or purchased the interest, the partnership may not be able to figure the partner's basis for his or her partnership interest either. This is because the partnership would need to be aware of the partner's original basis to use the alternative rule described immediately above. The partner may not have access to the partnership's books and records, the partnership may be unwilling to do the necessary work, and a partner who was not one of the original partners may not be willing to reveal the beginning basis for his or her interest.

Fortunately, the regulations include a second approach under Code Sec. 705(b). This method helps to obviate most of the adjustments necessary to avoid a significant discrepancy which may result from simply dividing inside basis by a partner's share of the partnership. The second approach to the alternative method focuses on the liability and equity section of the partnership's balance sheet. This approach is based upon the accounting principle that the assets on the partnership's balance sheet equal the liabilities plus equity. This variation in the alternative method provides that a partner's share of equity plus liabilities equals his or her share of the assets' bases. This information is often readily available to the partners if the partnership uses tax accounting principles for preparing the Form 1065. It is found on the Schedule K-1 issued each year by the partnership. The partner's capital account is found in Item J, column (e), and the partner's share of debt is contained in Item F.

Example 11-3. The ABC equal general partnership has the following tax basis balance sheet:

ABC Partnership

Assets	*Tax Basis*
Land	$100
Building	200
	$300
Liabilities	
(recourse)	$900
Capital	
A	$(200)
B	(200)
C	(200)
	$(600)

Partner *A* receives the partnership Schedule K-1, which shows his ending capital account of $(200) (item J column (e)) and his debt share of $300 (Item F). His basis under Code Sec. 705(b) is $100. Note, however, that this approach only works when using tax basis capital accounts.

Observation. The modified alternative should be used with care, especially when the partner has a negative capital account.

Example 11-4. *Alternative method and negative capital account.* The ABC general partnership was formed by *A*, *B*, and *C* with cash contributions of $200 each. The partnership purchased land for $300 and borrowed an additional $600 of recourse debt to build a $900 improvement. The ABC partnership's gross income has equaled nondepreciation expenses and all $900 of depreciation from the building has been specially allocated to Partner *C*. Its current tax basis balance sheet is as follows:

ABC Partnership

Assets	*Tax Basis*
Land	$300
Building	0
	$300

Liabilities	
(recourse)	$600
Capital	
A	$200
B	200
C	(700)
	$*(300)*

Partner *C* receives the partnership Schedule K-1, which shows his ending capital account of ($700) (Item J, column (e)) and his share of debt of $600 (Item F). His partnership interest basis is not $(100). It is zero and there is a $100 carryover loss at Partner *C*'s level because he has been allocated $100 of partnership losses in excess of his basis in his partnership interest of zero.

Partner *C*'s original basis in his partnership interest ($200 cash contribution plus one-third of the partnership debt of $600)	$400
Deemed money contribution for Partner *C*'s increased share of debt as a result of the Code Sec. 752(a) debt shift	400
Partnership losses allocated to Partner *C*	(900)
Partner *C*'s ending basis	$*0*
Partner *C*'s carryover loss	$100

Code Sec. 752(a) Debt Shift [*]

	Initial Debt Share	***Ending Debt Share***
Amount realized	$ 0	$ 0
Land's basis/book value	(300)	(300)
Building's basis/book value	(900)	0
Loss	$*(1,200)*	$*(300)*
C's share of loss	$(400)	$(100)
C's capital account before loss	200	(700)
C's capital account after loss	$*(200)*	$*(800)*
C's share of debt	$200	$600
C's increased share of debt		$400

[*] *Zero value liquidation test per Reg. § 1.752-2(b)(1).*

The regulations attempt to be more accurate under this modified alternative approach to funding a partner's share of the basis of partnership assets than simply taking into account the asset section of the partnership's balance sheet. In reality, a partner's basis in his or her interest includes the partner's share of the debt. The first approach of the alternative method ignores debt. This second approach to the alternative method takes into account the possibility that debt is shared differently under Code Sec. 752 than the partner's share of partnership assets by first removing all debt and then reallocating it pursuant to the normal sharing rules.

The regulations then treat each partner's tax basis capital account plus each partner's debt share as equaling his or her share of the assets' basis. This figure would then be modified by any relevant inside/outside basis inequalities. For example, a partner who purchased or inherited an interest would add to this figure any difference between the original basis in the partner's partnership interest and his or her original capital account plus debt share. This method of finding a partner's share of the partnership's assets basis naturally presumes that the partner has access to his or her correct tax basis capital account.

If a portion of a partnership interest is sold, only that portion of the partnership interest is taken into account for purposes of calculating gain or loss. Because a partner has only a single basis for the entire partnership interest, an allocation of basis is necessary. The partner first determines his or her basis in the interest before taking his or her share of debt into account. The partner allocates a portion of this basis to the portion sold based upon its fraction of the total value of the partnership interest. To this amount is added the partner's share of any remaining basis in the entire partnership interest generated by debt which is transferred in the sale. Naturally, the sales price will also include the net debt relief created by the sale as amounts realized offsetting any remaining basis generated by debt. If the partner's share of partnership liabilities exceeds his or her basis in the partnership interest, basis is allocated to that portion of the interest that is transferred in the same proportion as the partnership. The holding period of a partnership interest is also divided, for example, if a partner acquires his or her interest at different times.[21]

.03 Adjustments to Basis for Changes in Partner's Share of Liabilities

A partner must have access to his or her share of the partnership's debt to determine his or her basis in the interest, whether the partner is using the Code Sec. 705(a) "historical approach" to keep track of the basis or the partner is using the alternative method. The preparer of the partnership's Schedule K-1 must separately disclose in Item F each partner's share of:

1. Nonrecourse debt other than that considered qualified nonrecourse debt under Code Sec. 465(b)(6);[22]

2. Qualified nonrecourse financing; and

3. Other—this last category consists of each partner's share of the partnership's recourse debt. Recourse debt is a liability for

[21] Code Sec. 1223(1).

[22] The partnership should include in this category debt secured by real estate even though the property was placed in service before the December 31, 1986, effective date of applying the at-risk rules to real estate. The at-risk rules will apply to partners who acquire their interests after December 31, 1986, regardless of when the partnership placed the realty in service. See Act § 503(c)(2) of the Tax Reform Act of 1986, P.L. 99-514, 99th Cong., 2d Sess. The partner's Schedule K-1 should include an attachment explaining the nature of the debt, the date it was borrowed, and when the recurring property was placed in service.

which any partner or party related to a partner bears the economic risk of loss.[23]

When a partner is using the historical method of keeping track of the basis of his or her partnership interest, any increase or decrease in his or her total share of partnership debt is a deemed money contribution or distribution. The partner can simply compare the prior year's total of the three types of debt on Schedule K-1, Item F, to the current year-end's total. If the total has increased, the partner has a deemed money contribution. If the total has decreased, there is a deemed money distribution.

When the partner is using the first alternative approach under Code Sec. 705(b) to determine his or her basis in the partnership interest, the partner's share of debt is disregarded.

When the partner is using the modified alternative approach, basis in the partnership interest is equal to his or her tax basis capital account plus the total debt shown in Schedule K-1, Item F, and then modified as described above. Modifications are generally necessary when the partner was not one of the original partners.

Observation. The foregoing paragraphs describe how a partner's share of partnership debt is taken into account in both the amount realized and adjusted basis. It is useful sometimes to simplify the gain or loss calculations to eliminate debt from both amounts.

Amount Realized	=	(Money + Debt Relief)	to	Money
(Adjusted Basis)	=	(Capital Account + Debt Share)	to	(Capital Account)
gain/loss		gain/loss		gain/loss

Naturally, because this shortcut uses the alternative method of funding a partner's basis in the partnership interest, the modifications described above may be necessary.

¶ 1104 Installment Sale of a Partnership Interest

A partner who sells a partnership interest at a gain for consideration that includes the buyer's note must report the sale on the installment method unless he or she elects to report the gain in the year of sale. The gross profit, total contract price, gross profit reporting ratio, and yearly payments are based upon the same principles as installment sales of other property. The selling partner's share of partnership liabilities are taken into account as part of the total contract price and as year-of-sale payments only to the extent they exceed the selling partner's basis in his or her interest.[24]

[23] Reg. § 1.752-1(a)(1).

[24] Rev. Rul. 76-483, 1976-2 CB 131.

If the partnership interest sold represents the selling partner's interest in both ordinary income and capital assets, as discussed in Chapter 12, Code Sec. 751(a) will result in some of the gain being characterized as ordinary income rather than capital gain. In the case of installment method reporting, the income portion of installment payments received by the partner will be treated pro rata as capital gains and ordinary income.[25] In addition, when the partner is reporting the sale on the installment method and the partnership owns appreciated depreciable property subject to depreciation recapture, then the selling partner must report his or her share of such Code Sec. 751(a) ordinary income in the year of sale.[26]

The partner's share of Code Secs. 1245 and 1250 depreciation recapture income may not, as mentioned, be reported under the installment method.[27] Also, the general rule is that the installment method is not available for the sale of inventory.[28] The IRS's position is that the portion of any gain from the sale of a partnership interest attributable to the partner's share of the partnership inventory is not reportable under the installment method.[29] The Treasury Department is authorized to prescribe regulations which treat the role of a partnership interest as a "proportionate share of the assets of the partnership" for purposes of Code Sec. 453A.[30] Code Sec. 453A contains restrictions on pledges of installment notes and provides for interest on deferred tax liability under some circumstances. Code Sec. 453(k)(2) authorizes the Treasury Department to prescribe regulations which deny the installment sale method to the sale of a partnership interest when it is an indirect sale of publicly traded stocks and securities. Such regulations have not been issued.

Example 11-5. The equal ABC general partnership has the following tax basis balance sheet:

ABC Partnership

Assets	***Tax Basis***	***FMV***
Land	$300	$1,200
Liabilities	$ 0	$ 0
Capital		
A	$100	$400
B	100	400
C	100	400
	$300	$1,200

Partner *A*, who has a $100 basis in his partnership interest, sells his interest to *D* for a $100 cash payment and a note for $300. His gross profit reporting ratio of 75% is calculated as follows:

---

25 See *B.A. VeenKant v. Commr.*, CA-6, 69-2 USTC ¶ 9634, 416 F2d 93; Rev. Rul. 68-13, 1968-1 CB 195.

26 Code Sec. 453(i)(2).

27 Code Sec. 453(i)(2).

28 Code Sec. 453(b)(2).

29 Rev. Rul. 89-108, 1989-2 CB 100.

30 Code Sec. 453(e).

Selling Price (SP) . . .	$400	($100 cash + $300 note)
Basis.	(100)	
Gross Profit (GP) . . .	*$300*	

The gross profit reporting ratio is equal to the gross profit (GP) divided by the total contract price (TKP). The TKP in the absence of debt relief exceeding basis is merely the face of the note plus cash received in the year of sale.

$$\text{Gross Profit Reporting Ratio} = \frac{GP}{TKP} = \frac{\$300}{\$400} = 75\%$$

Partner *A* must report gain of $75 in the year of sale and 75% of each principal payment when received.

Gross Profit Reporting Ratio (75%) × Payment ($100) = $75

Example 11-6. *Partner's debt share exceeds basis.* The ABC equal general partnership has the following balance sheet:

ABC Partnership

Assets	***Tax Basis***	***FMV***
Land	$300	$900
Building.	0	900
	$300	*$1,800*
Liabilities	$600	$600
Capital Accounts		
A	$(100)	$400
B	(100)	400
C	(100)	400
	$300	*$1,200*

Partner *A*, who has a $100 basis in his partnership interest, sells his interest to *D* for a $100 cash payment and a note for $300. His gross profit reporting ratio is 100% and he has a deemed $100 payment in the year of sale.

Selling Price (SP) . . .	$600	($100 cash + $200 debt relief + $300 note)
Basis.	(100)	
Gross Profit (GP) . . .	*$500*	

Note: *The SP includes Partner A*'s former $200 share of the partnership debt.

The gross profit reporting ratio is defined as:

$$\frac{\text{Gross Profit} \qquad (GP)}{\text{Total Contract Price} \qquad (TKP)}$$

Total contract price (TKP) is equal to the cash purchase price received in the year of sale plus the principal amount of the note received, plus debt relief in excess of the basis of the partnership interest, and is equal to:

Down Payment	$100
Note's face value	300
Debt in excess of basis	100
Total Contract Price	*$500*

The gross profit reporting ratio (GPRR) is equal to:

$$GPRR = \frac{GP}{TKP} = \frac{\$500}{\$500} = 100\%$$

Partner *A*'s gain reportable in the year of sale is equal to the product of the gross profit reporting ratio times the year of sale payments. For this purpose, the $100 debt relief in excess of basis is a deemed cash payment in the year of sale.

$$GPRR\ (100\%) \times \text{Payments } (\$100 + \$100) = \$200$$

Two hundred dollars is reported as gain in the year partner *A* sells his interest.

Example 11-7. *Code Sec. 1245 recapture.* The ABC equal general partnership has the following balance sheet. The partnership's equipment had originally been purchased for $1,000 and any gain on its sale would be ordinary income under Code Sec. 1245:

ABC Partnership

Assets	***Tax Basis***	***FMV***
Land	$300	$900
Equipment	0	900
	$300	*$1,800*
Liabilities	$600	$600
Capital Accounts		
A	$(100)	$400
B	(100)	400
C	(100)	400
	$300	*$1,200*

Partner *A*, who has a $100 basis in his partnership interest, sells his interest to *D* for a $100 cash payment and a note for $300. His gross profit reporting ratio is 100%, he has a deemed $100 payment in the year of sale, and he reports $300 of ordinary income for his share of the gain attributable to his share of the partnership's depreciation recapture income which cannot be deferred under the installment method of accounting.

Selling Price (SP) . . .	$600	($100 cash + $200 debt relief + $300 note)
Basis	(100)	
Gross Profit (GP) . . .	*$500*	

Note: *The SP includes Partner A*'s former $200 share of the partnership debt.

The portion of the gain attributable to Partner *A*'s $300 share of the Code Sec. 1245 depreciation recapture related to the equipment is not deferred under the installment method; therefore, the gross profit reportable under the installment method is $200.

The gross profit reporting ratio (GPRR) is the gross profit (GP) divided by the total contract price (TKP). The TKP is equal to any purchase price received in the year of sale, plus the note's principal amount, plus debt relief in excess of basis. Partner *A*'s total contract price is equal to:

Cash down payment	$100
Note's face value	300
Debt in excess of basis	100
Total Contract Price	$*500*

Partner *A*'s gross profit reporting ratio is:

$$GPRR = \frac{GP}{TKP} = \frac{\$200}{\$500} = 40\%$$

Partner *A*'s gain reportable in the year of sale is equal to this gross profit reporting ratio (GPRR) times payments received in the year of sale. For this purpose, Partner *A*'s debt relief in excess of basis of $100 is a deemed principal payment for the sale year. Partner *A*'s capital gain reported under the installment method is as follows:

Year of Sale	=	$80	= 40% × $200 *
Future Years	=	120	= 40% × $300 **
		$*200*	Total Capital Gain
		300	Ordinary income in the year of sale
		$*500*	Total gain from Partner *A*'s sale of his partnership interest

* *GPRR: 40%; Principal Payments: $100 cash + $100 debt over basis.*
** *GPRR: 40%; Principal Payments: $300 note paid after sale year.*

¶ 1105 Abandonments and Gifts of a Partnership Interest

The abandonment, forfeiture, or similar disposition of a partnership interest is treated in a manner similar to the taxation of an abandonment, foreclosure, or deed-in-lieu of other property. The same is true of the worthlessness of a partnership interest. If there is no debt relief connected with those types of dispositions, there is no sale or exchange under Code Sec. 1222 and any loss is ordinary in character.[31] The partner establishes worthlessness by showing the partnership interest has no value.[32] Establishing the abandonment or worthlessness of a partnership interest is a question of fact. The partner can establish abandonment by proving that he or she intends to discontinue all investment and other involvement with the partnership.[33]

[31] *G.G. Gannon v. Commr.*, 16 TC 1134, Dec. 18,304 (1951), Acq.; *P. Hutcheson v. Commr.*, 17 TC 14, Dec. 18,430 (1951), Acq.; *J.C. Echols v. Commr.*, CA-5, 91-2 USTC ¶ 50,360, 935 F2d 703; Rev. Rul. 93-80, 1993-2 CB 230.

[32] *E.g., Tejon Ranch Co. v. Commr.*, 49 TCM 1357, Dec. 42,058(M), TC Memo. 1995-207.

[33] *E.g., S. Pallan v. Commr.*, 51 TCM 497, Dec. 42,891(M), TC Memo. 1986-76.

Example 11-8. Partner *A* is an equal member of the ABC general partnership. At a meeting of the partners he announces that he will no longer make contributions to the partnership as required by the partnership agreement. He also offers to transfer his interest to anyone interested in acquiring it in exchange for assuming his obligations under the agreement. The Tax Court held that this did not establish abandonment of his interest.[34] The Fifth Circuit Court of Appeals held that it did.[35]

When a partner abandons or otherwise disposes of a partnership interest and is relieved of a share of partnership debt, the transaction is treated as a sale for the amount of the debt relief.[36] Although there is no authority directly on point, the retention by a taxpayer of an interest in a worthless partnership may generate an ordinary loss even though there is partnership debt. So long as he or she remains a partner there is no deemed money payment for debt relief under Code Sec. 752(b).

In the case of a gift of a partnership interest when the partner does not have a deemed cash payment for a decrease in his or her share of liabilities, there is no amount realized upon a disposition of property and therefore there can be no gain [37] or loss.[38] Gain, but not loss, can be incurred when the gift of a partnership interest results in a reduction in the donor's share of the partnership debt. As in the case of an abandonment, this deemed money distribution under Code Sec. 752(b) is treated as an amount realized in a bargain sale transaction. The transaction will be recharacterized as a partial sale and gain will be recognized to the extent the debt relief exceeds the partner's tax basis of the interest deemed sold.[39] Any loss is disallowed.[40] If the gift is to a charity, the IRS has taken the position that the amount of the charitable contribution deduction is based upon the type of property held by the partnership.[41] For example, the amount of the charitable contribution is reduced to the extent that the partner would recognize ordinary income had he or she sold the partnership interest (*i.e.*, under Code Sec. 751(a)).[42]

¶ 1106 Like-Kind Exchanges of Partnership Interests

Before the Tax Reform Act of 1984,[43] the tax law surrounding the exchange of a partnership interest in one partnership for an interest in another partnership was uncertain. Although this clearly amounts to an "exchange" for the purposes of realizing gain or loss under Code Sec. 741, the uncertainty arose out of whether or not Code Sec. 1031, which provides for the nonrecognition of gain or loss on certain like-kind exchanges of property held for productive use in trade, business, or investment, applied

---

[34] *J.C. Echols v. Commr.*, 93 TC 533, Dec. 46,141 (1989).

[35] *J.C. Echols v. Commr.*, CA-5, 91-2 USTC ¶ 50,360, 935 F2d 703.

[36] *E.g.*, *N.J. O'Brien v. Commr.*, 77 TC 113, Dec. 38,076 (1981); Rev. Rul. 93-80, 1993-2 CB 239.

[37] Code Sec. 1001(a).

[38] Code Sec. 262.

[39] Code Sec. 1011(b).

[40] Reg. § 1.1001-1(e).

[41] Rev. Rul. 60-352, 1960-2 CB 208.

[42] Code Sec. 170(e)(1).

[43] P.L. 98-369.

to an exchange of partnership interests. The IRS had ruled that partnership interests did not qualify as like-kind property that could be exchanged tax-free under Code Sec. 1031.[44] The Tax Court, however, held that exchanges of partnership interests might qualify for tax-free, like-kind exchange treatment under Code Sec. 1031 if the underlying assets of both partnerships were "substantially similar in nature."[45] It was held, however, that an exchange of a general partnership interest for a limited partnership interest could *not* meet the requirements of Code Sec. 1031 because general and limited partnership interests are not like-kind property.[46] Code Sec. 1031(a)(2)(D) now explicitly provides that a partnership interest exchanged for a partnership interest in the same or another partnership does not qualify for nonrecognition under that section. This is true even though the underlying properties may be identical.

.01 Code Sec. 1031(a)(2)(D)

The exchange of an interest in one partnership for an interest in another is expressly excluded from treatment as a tax-free, like-kind exchange by the Tax Reform Act of 1984,[47] which provides that the nonrecognition provisions would not apply to "any exchange of . . . interests in a partnership."[48] The legislative history of this provision, however, contained in the Deficit Reduction Act of 1984 [49] indicates that exchanges of interests in *different* partnerships were prohibited. The IRS has indicated that a change in status from a limited partner to a general partner in the same partnership was not an exchange. After the change in status the partner would be required to redetermine his or her share of the partnership's liabilities.[50] If the partner's share increased, he or she had a deemed money contribution for that increase and the partner's basis was increased. If the change in status resulted in a decreased share of the partnership's liabilities, the decrease was treated as a distribution of money. The deemed money distribution is first a recovery of his or her basis in the partnership interest and gain for any excess. Oddly, five years later in a private letter ruling [51] the IRS applied Code Sec. 1031 concepts to the exchange of a limited partnership interest for a general partnership interest in the same partnership. The IRS clarified its position in the regulations, which provide that Code Sec. 1031 does *not* apply to any exchange of partnership interests in a partnership regardless of whether the interests exchanged are general or limited partnership interests in the same partnership or in different partnerships.[52] As a result, exchanges of interests in different partnerships are taxable. Exchanges of interests in the same partnerships are taxable,

---

[44] Rev. Rul. 78-135, 1978-1 CB 256.

[45] *Est. of R.E. Meyer, Sr. v. Commr.*, 58 TC 311, Dec. 31,390 (1972), aff'd per curiam, CA-9, 74-2 USTC ¶ 9676, 503 F2d 556; *Gulfstream Land and Development Co. v. Commr.*, 71 TC 587, Dec. 35,838 (1979).

[46] *Est. of R.E. Meyer, Sr. v. Commr.*, 58 TC 311, Dec. 31,390 (1972), aff'd per curiam, CA-9, 74-2 USTC ¶ 9676, 503 F2d 556.

[47] P.L. 98-369.

[48] Code Sec. 1031(a)(2)(D).

[49] P.L. 98-369.

[50] Rev. Rul. 84-52, 1984-1 CB 157.

[51] See IRS Letter Ruling 8912023 (12-22-88) (Code Sec. 1031 applies), and IRS Letter Ruling 8944043 (8-8-89) (revocation of the earlier private ruling applying Code Sec. 1031).

[52] Reg. § 1.1031(a)-1(a)(1).

but changes in states are not taxable unless collateral rules apply to cause a taxable event. For example, a change in status could trigger income by creating a negative at-risk amount [53] or cause a deemed money distribution in excess of basis on account of a decrease in a partner's share of liabilities.[54]

LLC Observation. When a partnership is converted to an LLC or an LLP, the same concepts apply. For federal income tax purposes, the new LLC partnership is a continuation of the old partnership. The new liability limitations may, however, affect the continuing partner's shares of the partnership debt.

The Joint Committee Report accompanying the Deficit Reduction Act of 1984 [55] indicates that the amendment excluding the exchange of different partnership interests from Code Sec. 1031 treatment was brought about by abuses in the tax shelter area when partnership interests in tax shelter limited partnership investments were being exchanged in like-kind exchanges for interests in other partnerships.[56] The Senate Report commented that:

> Under this arrangement, taxation of the gain inherent in an interest in a "burned-out" tax shelter partnership—*i.e.*, a partnership which has taken substantial deductions for nonrecourse liabilities without actually paying off such liabilities, and hence without the partners' suffering real economic loss, may be able to be avoided if the interest is exchanged, tax-free, for an interest in another partnership, provided the old partnership has a section 754 election in effect and the new partnership does not. While court decisions have limited like-kind exchange treatment to partnerships holding similar underlying assets, this rule may be inadequate to deal with the burned-out tax shelter abuses and the administrative hardships. The committee believes that such abuses and hardships are best prevented by specifically excluding partnership interests from the like-kind exchange rule.

The House Committee Report questions whether the like-kind exchange provisions were originally intended to apply to exchanges of partnership interests since Code Sec. 1031 does not apply to exchanges of stock, certificates of trust, beneficial interests, or other securities or evidences of indebtedness or interest. These exclusions, the House Report suggests, were intended to prevent taxpayers from taking advantage of tax-free, like-kind exchange treatment by trading interests in appreciated investment property. The report, referring specifically to interests in tax shelter investments, stated that under "current conditions," partnership interests represent investment interests similar to those already explicitly excluded.[57]

---

[53] Code Sec. 465(e).

[54] Code Sec. 752(b)

[55] P.L. 98-369.

[56] General Explanation of the Revenue Provisions of the Tax Reform Act of 1984 (P.L. 98-369), staff of the Joint Committee on Taxation (1985).

[57] H.R. Rep. No. 432, 98th Cong., 2d Sess. (1984).

.02 Planning for Exchanges of Some Partnership Property and Sale of Other Partnership Property

The Tax Reform Act of 1984 [58] appeared to have delivered a knockout blow to an attempt to exchange, as like-kind, an interest in a partnership that contains inherent gain. This might have occurred, for example, when the partner had received the benefit of substantial depreciation deductions by virtue of having his or her basis in the partnership interest increased by a significant amount of real estate nonrecourse indebtedness incurred by the partnership, and by the partner not being subject to the "at-risk" rules of Code Sec. 465. This is exemplified by the activity of the partnership that consists of "holding real property" when "qualified nonrecourse financing" has been used. Once the partner's outside basis has been depreciated to zero, the partner might have attempted to avoid the gain inherent in his or her "burned-out" partnership interest by affecting a like-kind exchange of his or her interest for an interest in another partnership holding similar underlying assets, and by making sure that his or her share of the new partnership's liabilities was in excess of his or her share of the liabilities in the burned-out partnership. The increased share of liabilities would, in effect, give the partner more depreciable basis under Code Sec. 1031(d). Thus, the partner's basis in his or her new partnership interest would equal the basis of zero in the partner's old partnership interest increased by the amount of the increase in his or her share of liabilities.[59] Furthermore, since at least a portion of the avoided gain may have been ordinary income under Code Sec. 1250, arguably this would remain with the old partnership if the new partnership held sufficient Code Sec. 1250 property. Code Sec. 1245 recapture may not have been so easily avoided.[60]

Co-ownership. Although a direct exchange of partnership interests is no longer directly possible, a similar result might be obtained by using the concept of co-ownership. Often the partners will agree that the partnership should dispose of its property but will disagree as to the form of the disposition. Some will prefer a cash sale, others an installment sale, and some will want a tax-free exchange into like-kind property under Code Sec. 1031. One commonly encountered solution to this dilemma is for the partnership to distribute a tenancy-in-common interest in its property to partners who want to custom tailor the tax results of their disposition. Under the current regulations and the case law applicable to Code Sec. 1031, it is possible to exchange a co-ownership interest in property for a co-ownership interest in other property. Many practitioners have advised that a partnership may make a distribution to a partner of a co-ownership interest in the partnership's property. This co-ownership interest may, in turn, be used for a like-kind exchange, perhaps for a similarly distributed undivided interest in another partnership's property.[61] This maneuver,

[58] P.L. 98-369.

[59] Code Sec. 752(a).

[60] Code Sec. 1245(b)(4)(B).

[61] At a minimum, the transaction's legal form must track its intended tax treatment. *D.G. Chase v. Commr.*, 92 TC 874, Dec. 45,634 (1989) (Code Sec. 1031 treatment denied when the taxpayer did not record the deed from the partnership until shortly before the sale, did not directly pay his or

while apparently skirting the 1984 amendments in an efficient manner, may nonetheless fall afoul of the regulations that provide that:

> [M]ere co-ownership of property which is maintained, kept in repair, and rented or leased does not constitute a partnership (what might be called "passive co-ownership"). Tenants in common, however, may be partners if they actively carry on a trade, business, financial operation, or venture and divide the profits thereof. For example, a partnership exists if co-owners of an apartment building lease space and in addition provide services to the occupants either directly or through an agent[.][62]

Relevant cases such as *McManus v. Commissioner*[63] and *Allison v. Commissioner*[64] indicate that it is the degree of business activity that determines whether what the parties thought was a co-tenancy is taxed as a partnership. It is thus possible, despite the distribution of a co-ownership interest in the partnership property, that the distributee and the partnership will be taxed as partners and not as co-tenants should they continue to generate sufficient business activity together with regard to the property after the Code Sec. 1031 exchange.[65] Naturally, if the property distributed is being used in the active conduct of a trade or business, as discussed above, co-ownership of the property with the partnership is by definition a partnership. An equal ten-person partnership operating a hardware business could not effectively distribute to one of its partners a one-tenth tenancy-in-common interest in the business. The purported distribution would not cause nine-tenths of the operations to be reported on the partnership's Form 1065 and one-tenth on the partner's Form 1040 Schedule C. Creating a co-tenancy with the partnership through a distribution of an undivided interest in partnership property will require that the property distributed not be used in the active conduct of the partnership's trade or business.[66]

In the event that the distribution and the exchange occur simultaneously, or as one uninterrupted chain of events, it is possible that the "step-transaction doctrine" or "form over substance doctrine" will apply, and the transactions will be telescoped into one transaction comprising an attempt at a like-kind exchange of interests in different partnerships or a partnership interest for a direct interest in property.[67] Under these circumstances, Code Sec. 1031 treatment would be disallowed.

Furthermore, since Code Sec. 1031 requires both the exchanged property and the property received to be held for productive use in a trade or business, or for investment, it is possible that the transactions would be denied Code Sec. 1031 treatment on the ground that the distributed co-ownership interest was not held for this use, but held merely to be ex-

(Footnote Continued)

her share of the property's operating expenses, nor receive the property's rental income).

[62] Reg. § 1.761-1(a).

[63] *T.K. McManus v. Commr.*, 65 TC 197, Dec. 33,483 (1975), aff'd, CA-9, 78-2 USTC ¶ 9748, 583 F2d 443.

[64] *I.T. Allison v. Commr.*, 35 TCM 1069, Dec. 33,968(M), TC Memo. 1976-248.

[65] See also Rev. Rul. 75-374, 1975-2 CB 261.

[66] See ¶ 105 for a discussion of the creation of a co-tenancy interest in partnership property not integrally related to the active conduct of a partnership's trade or business.

[67] *D.G. Chase v. Commr.*, 92 TC 874, Dec. 45,634 (1989) (the Tax Court's denial of Code Sec. 1031 treatment, partially due to the application of the substance over form doctrine).

changed for the new tenancy-in-common interest. If the partnership exchanges part of its property on behalf of the partners who want exchange treatment and then distributes the replacement property to those partners, a similar Code Sec. 1031 issue arises. Code Sec. 1031 requires that both the relinquished and replacement properties be held for investment or business purposes. If the partnership immediately distributes the replacement property, the IRS may claim that the partnership did not receive property which is partnership investment or business property. In addition, the property received may not be qualified investment or trade or business property if it is to be immediately contributed to another partnership, perhaps one which owns the remaining tenancy-in-common interest.[68]

> ***Comment.*** If a partnership has a buyer for its property and some of the partners wish to cash out and others wish to exchange into replacement property under Code Sec. 1031, the partnership should distribute the portion of property to be sold, not the portion of the property to be exchanged. Then the partnership makes the Code Sec. 1031 exchange. Structuring the transaction in this way avoids the above Code Sec. 1031 issues which arise when it is the distributed property which will be exchanged.

Since the Tax Reform Act of 1984[69] made partnership interests somewhat less attractive forms of investment from the standpoint of Code Sec. 1031 exchanges, it is likely that taxpayers may now attempt to make greater use of the co-ownership form of investment. It is important to remember that property which is co-owned and generates sufficient joint business activity may result in the co-tenancy being treated as a partnership for tax purposes. Accordingly, the co-ownership tactic may not free the co-owners from the restrictions that apply to partnership interests, and the co-owners, if taxed as partners, may not avail themselves of tax-free, like-kind exchange treatment under Code Sec. 1031.[70]

The Revenue Reconciliation Act of 1990[71] amended Code Sec. 1031(a)(2) of the Internal Revenue Code to clarify the effect of an election for exclusion from Subchapter K in qualifying for like-kind exchange treatment under that section. An interest in such a partnership will be treated as an interest in each of the assets of the partnership and not as an interest in a partnership. The amendment is effective for transfers after July 18, 1984. Thus, each partner will be treated as a tenant in common for purposes of providing the partners with an opportunity to, in effect, exchange partnership interest for property of like kind to the partnership's property. This may provide a useful alternative for dispositions of jointly held investments that the owners have treated as a partnership for tax

[68] See *T.J. Starker v. U.S.*, 79-2 USTC ¶ 9541, 602 F2d 1341; *F.B. Biggs v. Commr.*, 69 TC 905, Dec. 35,035 (1978), aff'd, CA-5, 81-1 USTC ¶ 9114, 632 F2d 1171. But see Rev. Rul. 79-44, 1979-2 CB 304; *N.J. Magneson v. Commr.*, 81 TC 767, Dec. 40,557 (1983), aff'd, CA-9, 85-1 USTC ¶ 9205, 753 F2d 1490; *J.R. Bolker v. Commr.*, 81 TC 782, Dec. 40,558 (1983), aff'd, CA-9, 85-1 USTC ¶ 9400, 760 F2d 1039.

[69] P.L. 98-369.

[70] See discussion in Chapter 1 distinguishing co-owners from partners.

[71] P.L. 101-508.

purposes. After a Code Sec. 761(a) election each member can choose whether to sell or exchange his or her share of the property without a formal liquidation of the partnership.

Partnership level combined exchange and installment sale. If a partnership wishes to dispose of partnership property and some of the partners want to cash out while others prefer to roll over their investments in a Code Sec. 1031 exchange, a Code Sec. 1031 exchange combined with a receipt of an installment note should be considered. The note is boot for Code Sec. 1031 purposes, but gain is not recognized until it is paid. The partnership then distributes the note in liquidation of the interest of a partner who wishes to cash out. The distribution of the note is not taxable [72] and the note receives a basis equal to the partner's basis in his or her partnership interest. If it is a current distribution, the note's basis will be the lesser of the partnership basis in the note (likely zero) or the basis of the distributee's partnership interest.[73] When the note is paid, the partner will have capital gain to the extent the partnership would have had capital gain. In effect, the partner will be reporting his or her share of the property's appreciation and, in addition, all or a portion of the other partners' shares of the partnership built-in gain. In the case of a liquidating distribution, the note's basis in the hands of the partnership (normally zero) is replaced by the basis the partner has in his or her partnership interest. The partner's basis in the partnership interest normally is equal to his or her share of the partnership's basis in its assets. If the partnership has only one asset, the note's basis will then equal the partner's share of the basis of that asset and the partner will report gain on the installment method equal to his or her share of that property's appreciation. If the partnership has more than one property and only one property is exchanged, the liquidated partner will recover his or her share of the basis for all the partnership's property under the installment method. Therefore, the partner's total gain reported under the installment method will not normally exceed his or her aggregate share of the appreciation in the partnership's property. If the partnership does not have a Code Sec. 754 election in effect, the partnership has the added benefit of transferring the entire basis of its relinquished property to the replacement property, increased by any liabilities that exceed the liabilities of the relinquished property under Code Sec. 1031(d). The result is that the inside basis of the replacement property will exceed the aggregate outside basis of the partnership interests. The remaining partners will in effect continue to have the liquidated partner's share of the property's basis available to the partnership.

[72] Reg. § 1.453-9(c)(2).

[73] Code Sec. 732. The note is likely to have a zero basis because the gross profit to be reported is equal to the cash boot which would be reportable if cash in the amount of the face value of the note had been received by the partnership. Cash boot is not taxable only to the extent it exceeds the gain realized from the exchange. This basis of the note is equal to 100% minus the gross profit reporting ratio multiplied by the ratio's principal amount. A zero basis in such a note distributed in a current distribution would normally be unappealing to the partner.

Example 11-9. The equal Alvin Jones, Ken Grabes and Cynthia Mallow general partnership has the following balance sheet:

Assets	*Tax Basis*	*FMV*
Investment Land	$18,000	$30,000
Liabilities	$ 0	$ 0
Capital Accounts		
Alvin	$6,000	$10,000
Ken	6,000	10,000
Cynthia	6,000	10,000
	$18,000	*$30,000*

A developer has offered the partnership $30,000 for the property, but is willing to participate in a Code Sec. 1031 exchange. Alvin and Ken want to continue as partners and roll over their shares of the assets into new property. Cynthia wants to cash-out. The developer transfers $20,000 of like-kind replacement property and a $10,000 one-year note to the partnership. The exchange is not taxable. The replacement property has a basis to the partnership of $18,000 and the note has a basis to the partnership of $0.

When the note is distributed to Cynthia in liquidation of her interest, her basis in the note will be $6,000. When its face value of $10,000 is paid, Cynthia incurs $4,000 of capital gain. This is her share of the partnership's built-in gain of $12,000. The partnership's balance sheet is now as follows:

Assets	*Tax Basis*	*FMV*
New Investment Land	$18,000	$20,000
Liabilities	$ 0	$ 0
Capital Accounts		
Alvin	$6,000	$10,000
Ken	6,000	10,000
	$12,000	*$20,000*

Sale followed by exchange. The partnership may also consider selling a portion of the assets for cash and distributing the cash to the partner who wishes to be cashed out in a liquidating distribution. The partnership year closes with respect to the retiring partner and his or her share of the partnership's income for the portion of the year for which he or she was a partner would include a special allocation of gain from the asset sold. The partnership would then later exchange the remaining assets.

Debt financed liquidation. If the partnership has the ability to borrow enough cash to liquidate interests of the partners who want to cash out, a liquidating cash distribution is a simple solution to the problem.

Code Sec. 1031 exchange with boot—Special allocation of boot gain. Finally, the partnership could consider a Code Sec. 1031 exchange with cash boot. The exchange is taxable to the extent of the cash boot received. The partnership would specially allocate the gain to the partners who wish to cash out. The special allocation must have substantial economic effect under Code Sec. 704(b) to be effective. There are some issues relating to the requirement of "substantial" which must be addressed. An allocation is not substantial if:[74]

1. There is not a "reasonable possibility that the allocation will affect substantially the dollar amounts to be received by the partners from the partnership, independent of tax consequences";[75] and

2. The total tax liability of the partners for the year to which the allocation relates will be less than if the special allocation were not taken into account.

The first condition is satisfied. The distributee and remaining partners' rights to money if the partnership liquidated immediately after the exchange are not changed by the special allocation of boot gain. The capital account of the distributee partner who is specially allocated the boot gain would be increased by the entire gain. But the amount distributed would be his or her share of the value of the partnership assets. The amount distributed will not match his or her ending capital account unless it is adjusted. The capital account revaluation rules of Reg. § 1.704-1(b)(2)(iv)(*f*) remedy the problem by revaluing the distributee partner's capital account to fair market value on a liquidating distribution. A literal interpretation of the regulations would imply that such a revaluation is required. However, if a special allocation were not invoked and the gain were allocated equally, a capital account revaluation would also be required. Therefore, with or without the special allocation, the distributee's capital account after adjustments is equal to the value of the distributee's partnership interest. The same analysis applies to the dollar amounts to be received by the continuing partners if the partnership liquidated immediately after the exchange. The special allocation of the boot gain would not affect the net amount distributed to them on liquidation of the partnership immediately after the exchange. They would receive the fair market value of their interests in the partnership whether or not there was a special allocation of the boot gain to the same partners.

However, is the total tax liability of the partners reduced because of the allocation? Initially, absent special circumstances, the same tax will be paid whether all the gain is taxed to one partner or the gain is allocated among all the partners. However, if the allocation is coupled with a

[74] See ¶ 1109.02 for a discussion of "substantial economic effect."

[75] Reg. § 1.704-1(b)(2)(iii)(*a*).

liquidating distribution, the distributee partner is likely to have an offsetting loss generated by the liquidating distribution. This is because the partner has added more than his or her share of the gain to his or her basis. This gain includes the other partner's share of the partnership's built-in gain, not just the distributee partner's share of the property's appreciation. This is because Code Sec. 1031 requires that boot (the cash received by the partnership) is recognized gain to the extent of the partnership's built-in gain. When the liquidated partner adds this gain to the basis of his or her partnership interest, absent special circumstances, it will exceed that partner's share of the property's value. Therefore, a liquidating cash distribution generates a loss. The combination of the loss on the liquidating distribution and the inflated allocation of gain results in the partner reporting the correct net gain. However, after the special allocation of all the gain to the liquidated partner, the remaining partners have no gain to report. The aggregate basis of the partnership property exceeds the aggregate basis of the remaining partners. The partnership has the same basis in the replacement property as the relinquished property, but the continuing partners' bases in their interests is unchanged and the liquidated partner is gone. This will reduce their future tax liability.

In addition, if a special allocation were not invoked in the year of the Code Sec. 1031 exchange, the aggregate tax liability would exceed the liability if no special allocation were used. This is because if the gain were allocated equally, the entire gain would be taxed; but if the gain is specially allocated to one partner who is liquidated, the gain is offset with the loss on the liquidating distribution. Therefore, it can be argued under these circumstances that the effect of the allocation is to reduce the aggregate tax liability of the partners. Naturally, if the liquidating distribution did not result in a loss, the aggregate tax liability of the group would not be reduced—for example, if property other than cash were distributed as part of the liquidation distribution, or if the distribution were not a liquidating distribution. However, if the partner who is specially allocated all of the boot gain is not entitled to a loss, the partner will have reported some portion of the other partner's shares of the gain.

¶ 1107 Change in Status

The IRS's position is that a conversion of a limited partnership interest into a general partnership interest or the reverse is not a disposition.[76] The change in status may result in an increase or decrease in the partner's debt share, which will be treated as a deemed distribution or a contribution of property. A deemed distribution of money in excess of basis is taxed under Code Sec. 731. If the conversion results in a negative amount at risk in the activity, it is taxable under Code Sec. 465(e).

[76] Rev. Rul. 84-52, 1984-1 CB 157.

¶ 1108 Miscellaneous Partnership Interest Transfers

The following is a brief list and description of some additional less commonly encountered exchanges:

- *Contribution of Partnership Interest to a Corporation or Partnership.* In the unlikely event that the partner has no share of the partnership debt, or if the partner's share of debt does not exceed his or her partnership interest adjusted basis, Code Sec. 351 (contribution to a corporation) or Code Sec. 721 (contribution to a partnership) will apply and the contribution will not be taxable. When there is a contribution of a partnership interest with liabilities in excess of the basis of the interest to a corporation, application of Code Sec. 357(c) will result in gain.[77] If the partnership interest (Partnership 1) is contributed to another partnership (Partnership 2), the partner's share of Partnership 1's debt is considered a deemed money distribution from Partnership 2. This deemed money distribution is in turn netted with any deemed money contribution to Partnership 2 under Code Sec. 752(a) for the partner's share of Partnership 2's debt.[78] There is gain if and only if the net debt relief is in excess of the basis the partner had in Partnership 1.

- *Distribution of a Partnership Interest by a Corporation.* If an appreciated partnership interest is distributed by a corporation it is treated as if it were sold.[79] If this deemed sale results in a loss, the loss is not allowed.

- *Distribution of a Partnership Interest by a Partnership.* Given the absence of any direct authority governing the results of a partnership (Partnership 1) distributing an interest it owns in another partnership (Partnership 2), the general rules of property distributions should apply. If the distributed partnership interest (Partnership 2) has no share of Partnership 2's debt, it is merely treated as a distribution of unencumbered property. If the distributed partnership interest (Partnership 2) shares in that Partnership 2's debt, it is treated as a distribution of encumbered property. The distributee partner has a deemed money contribution to Partnership 1 for his or her share of Partnership 2's debt. The distributee partner has a deemed money distribution for his or her reduced share of Partnership 1's debt, which no longer includes its share of Partnership 2's debt. Any excess of the deemed money contribution over the money distribution is a deemed money contribution to Partnership 1. The partner's share in Partnership 1 is increased

[77] See Rev. Rul. 81-38, 1981-1 CB 386.

[78] Rev. Rul. 79-205, 1979-2 CB 255; Rev. Rul. 77-309, 1977-2 CB 216.

[79] Code Sec. 311(b).

by this amount and then reduced by Partnership 1's basis in Partnership 2. In a current distribution, the partner's basis in Partnership 2 is the lesser of what was Partnership 1's basis or the partner's basis in Partnership 1 after the deemed money contribution. In a liquidating distribution, the distributee's basis in Partnership 1 becomes his basis in Partnership 2.

Chapter 12

Sales of Partnership Interest When the Partnership Holds Ordinary Income Property

---

¶ 1201 Introduction

As a statutory starting point, the general rule is that the partnership provisions in Subchapter K of the Internal Revenue Code adopt an "entity approach" in dealing with the tax consequences when partnership interests are transferred. The transferred interest is treated like corporate stock and is considered to be a separate intangible asset rather than an undivided tenancy-in-common interest in the partnership assets, as it would be treated under an "aggregate approach" to partnership taxation.

Code Sec. 751(a) provides the major exception to the statutory general rule under Code Sec. 741—gain or loss from the sale of a partnership interest is treated as capital gain or loss. It provides that any amount realized on the sale of a partnership interest which is attributable to unrealized receivables or inventory is treated as an amount realized from the sale of a noncapital asset. Unrealized receivables and inventory are commonly referred to as "Code Sec. 751" or "hot" assets. They are generally property other than Code Sec. 1231 and capital assets. They are the partnership's assets with built-in ordinary income or loss. A partnership which holds these assets is sometimes referred to as a "collapsible" partnership.

LLC Observation. The rules discussed in this chapter apply equally to state law partnerships and LLCs taxed as partnerships.

¶ 1202 Historical Background

The pre-1954 Internal Revenue Code judicial doctrines give some insight into the current rules. The 1939 Internal Revenue Code had no counterpart to either Code Sec. 741 or Code Sec. 751, and consequently, case law provided the only guidance as to the character of gain or loss from selling a partnership interest. Generally, the IRS was in favor of an aggregate concept and attempted to fragment the gain on the interest's sale into its constituent parts by treating it as a sale of the partner's share of the assets.[1] The IRS's concern was that the allowance of capital gain treatment upon the sale of a partnership interest might convert ordinary income into long-term capital gain if the purchasing partners "collapsed" the partnership after the sale. Collapsing the partnership consisted of immediately liquidating it. In a liquidating distribution, the purchasers generally obtain bases in the former partnership assets equal to their bases in their partnership interests and would therefore have no gain on the immediate sale of the assets.[2] The sellers, in turn, would have received capital gain treatment on the appreciation in value of the partnership interest. This appreciation might have been partially due to the appreciation of noncapital assets, and ordinary income might thus have been converted into capital gain by the use of the collapsible partnership.

After losing most of the cases, however, the IRS finally conceded that "the sale of a partnership interest should be treated as the sale of a capital asset."[3] This concession did not, however, apply to sales that were not, in "substance and effect" (as distinguished from "form and appearance"), sales, exchanges, and other transfers of partnership interests. Prior to the enactment of the 1954 Internal Revenue Code, the judiciary began to develop the following principles:

1. A partner could not escape his or her share of partnership income simply by selling the partnership interest before the end of the partnership year.[4]

2. The "assignment of income" rules operated to prevent a cash-basis partnership from converting accounts receivable and work-in-process (and inventory) to long-term capital gain.[5]

3. A partner who sold his or her partnership interest in light of substantially completed partnership business activities was taxed as if the activities were completed.[6]

---

[1] See, for example, *A.F. Williams v. G.T. McGowen*, CA-2, 46-1 USTC ¶ 9120, 153 F2d 570, in which the court held that the gain on the sale of a partnership interest was determined according to the nature of the underlying assets.

[2] Code Sec. 732. Under the current rules, however, "hot" assets cannot receive basis increases on distribution. Code Sec. 732(c).

[3] GCM 26379, 1950-1 CB 58, declared obsolete by Rev. Rul. 67-406, 1967-1 CB 420.

[4] Later codified in Code Sec. 706.

[5] This is now codified in Code Sec. 751.

[6] This is now considered an unrealized receivable. Reg. § 1.751-1(c)(ii).

While these judicial doctrines were being developed, Congress developed its own solution by creating a general rule in Code Sec. 741, and an exception to it in Code Sec. 751(a), to prevent "converting rights to income into capital gain by virtue of transfers of partnership interests."[7]

> ***Observation.*** Under the current Code Sec. 751(a) rules, absent a Code Sec. 754 election, the seller's share of the ordinary income is taxed twice: first, in the sale of the partnership interest under Code Sec. 751(a); second, when the partnership itself recognizes the built-in ordinary income.

¶ 1203 Mechanics of Code Sec. 751(a) for Sales of Partnership Interests After December 14, 1999

Code Sec. 751(a) basically applies only to sales or exchanges of a partnership interest. The section itself does not expressly create a sale or exchange limitation, but the legislative history indicates that it is intended to have coverage identical to Code Sec. 741. Code Sec. 751(a), furthermore, is not applicable to amounts received as distributions from the partnership, since these are taxed under Code Sec. 751(b). Code Sec. 751(a) applies equally, whether the transfer is of all, or part, of an interest or is to another partner or to an outsider.

The amount of money or the fair market value of any property a selling partner receives in exchange for all or part of his or her interest in the partnership attributable to "unrealized receivables" or to "inventory" items is treated as an amount realized from the sale or exchange of property that is not a capital asset.[8]

The ordinary income or loss realized by a partner upon the sale or exchange of a partnership interest is the amount of ordinary income or loss that would have been allocated to that partner if the partnership sold all its assets, including its Code Sec. 751 property (ordinary income assets).[9] The partnership's hypothetical sale of its Code Sec. 751 assets is deemed to be part of a fair market value sale of all its property immediately before the transfer of the partnership interest. The regulations are silent as to the effect of an arm's length agreement allocating the purchase price among the partnership's underlying assets. The preamble to Reg. § 1.751-1 indicates that this would be "inconsistent with the hypothetical sale approach of the regulations."[10] When capital gains are taxed at a preferred rate, the seller clearly wants to allocate as little as possible to Code Sec. 751 assets in order to minimize his or her ordinary income. The buyer, however, will have tax consequences only if a Code Sec. 743(b) adjustment of the basis of the

[7] House Ways and Means Committee Report, H.R. Rep. No. 1337, 83rd Cong., 2d Sess., 70.

[8] Code Sec. 751(a); Reg. § 1.751-1(a)(1). For sales or exchanges of partnership interests prior to August 5, 1997, the provision applies only to "substantially appreciated inventory." The Taxpayer Relief Act of 1997, P.L. 105-34, Act § 1062(a).

[9] Reg. § 1.751-1(a)(2). Note: these regulations were amended by T.D. 8847, 1999-52 IRB 701, effective for transfers of partnership interests occurring after December 15, 1999. This citation refers to the amended regulations.

[10] Preamble, T.D. 8847, 1999-52 IRB 701.

partnership property is to be made, or if the buyer receives a Code Sec. 732(d) distribution.[11] In other situations the IRS should not be bound by the "agreement" that affects only one party. However, most circuit courts have taken the position that a party to the agreement (as opposed to the IRS) must have strong proof to upset it.

> ***Observation.*** If the partnership has a Code Sec. 754 election in effect and there is an adverse bargaining position due to the buyer's Code Sec. 743(b) adjustments and the character of the seller's gain, an agreement would have some evidentiary weight as to the relative values of the partnership assets.

.01 Definition of Unrealized Receivables

Generally, Code Sec. 751(c) defines unrealized receivables for all purposes of partnership taxation (Subchapter K of the Internal Revenue Code). References to "unrealized receivables" may be found in the following sections in Subchapter K:

1. Code Sec. 731(a)(2), which provides for the recognition of loss upon certain distributions in liquidation of a partner's partnership interest;
2. Code Sec. 732(c), which provides for an allocation of adjusted basis to distributed property to be made first to Code Sec. 751 assets;
3. Code Sec. 735(a), which provides that the character of gain or loss realized on a subsequent sale of unrealized receivables received in a distribution is ordinary income; and
4. Code Sec. 724, which provides that the character of partnership gain or loss realized on a subsequent sale of unrealized receivables contributed by a partner is ordinary income.

As originally enacted, Code Sec. 751(c) included only a single sentence dealing with rights to receive payments for goods and services provided or to be provided. Currently, however, the last two sentences of the section are a history of Congressional exceptions to capital gain treatment enacted over the years. Since the last sentence was added by the Tax Reform Act of 1984,[12] other than for purposes of Code Secs. 724(a), 735(a)(1) and 736(a), the term "unrealized receivables" now includes the following items:

1. Depreciation recapture under Code Sec. 1245.
2. Excess depreciation under Code Sec. 1250.
3. Mining exploration expenses recapture under Code Sec. 617(d).

---

[11] This is a distribution that occurs within two years of the purchase when a Code Sec. 754 election has not been made.

[12] P.L. 98-369.

4. Stock in a D.I.S.C. [13] or certain foreign corporations.[14]

5. Franchises, trademarks, etc.[15]

6. Oil, gas or geothermal property.[16]

7. Excess farm loss recapture under Code Sec. 1252.

8. Market discount bonds [17] and short-term obligations.[18]

Code Sec. 751(c) does not purport to be an exhaustive list of "unrealized receivables" but merely indicates that the term "includes" the items listed. To date, the IRS has not argued for any other inclusion, but the language to support such an argument is in the section.

As indicated, the term "unrealized receivables" includes the rights to payments for services rendered or to be rendered to the extent not already reported. The sources for this part of the definition are the pre-1954 cases in which a cash-method partnership with zero basis accounts receivable had partners sell their partnership interest for long-term capital gain. The provisions of the 1954 Internal Revenue Code went far beyond merely remedying this abuse.

The term "rights . . . to payment for" is construed liberally, including a noncontractual or equitable right (*quantum meruit*) to payment, whether it is partially or fully earned, and when there is a noncancellable future contract to perform services or deliver goods. However, if the agreement is cancellable at will by the buyer-customer, it is not an unrealized receivable to the seller. Thus, general expectations of profit are likened to goodwill, which is not a Code Sec. 751 asset. Even though goodwill represents future profits to which the purchaser has assigned economic value, the seller will have capital gain on its disposition.

Unrealized receivables include the right to receive payments for goods delivered or to be delivered. The right to be paid for "goods" is defined as the right to receive payment for property other than a capital asset.[19] However, to the extent these constitute accounts receivable for financial accounting purposes, they most likely will have been recognized by the partnership because taxpayers selling inventoried goods generally must use the accrual method of accounting for sale of goods. Accrual method partnerships will often have a right to be paid for goods that have been ordered but not yet delivered.

The recapture items referred to in the last two sentences of Code Sec. 751(c) are different from the right to receive payments for goods or services in that they do not involve any type of contractual right to receive payments. They are, in effect, the current unrealized potential ordinary

[13] Code Sec. 992(a).
[14] Code Sec. 1248.
[15] Code Sec. 1253.
[16] Code Sec. 1254.
[17] As defined in Code Sec. 1278.
[18] As defined in Code Sec. 1283.
[19] Reg. § 1.751-1(c)(1)(i).

income inherent in the property if it were sold at its current fair market value. This unrealized receivable is an amount of ordinary income determined by referring to the fair market value of the asset, its adjusted basis, and the type of gain, ordinary or capital, which would be reported if it were sold.

Since Code Sec. 751 assets include only assets that represent potential ordinary income; assets with short-term capital gain potential are not Code Sec. 751 assets, and gain from the sale of the partnership interest attributable to such items will receive long-term capital gain treatment if the partnership interest has been held long term.

.02 *Definition of Inventory Items*

The second category of Code Sec. 751 assets consists of inventory items. Code Sec. 751(d) sets out four categories of inventory items.[20]

The first of the four categories of inventory items is true inventory in terms of Code Sec. 1221(1), and dealer property held primarily for sale to customers in the ordinary course of the partnership's business.[21]

The second category comprises other property which, when sold or exchanged by the partnership, would be considered property other than a capital asset in terms of Code Sec. 1221 and other than a Code Sec. 1231(b) asset.[22] This category is so broad as to apparently encompass all the other categories and specifically includes the accounts receivable of a cash-basis taxpayer,[23] realized account receivables of an accrual-basis taxpayer, depreciation recapture, and all unrealized receivables. When a partnership interest is sold, the fact that an asset is an unrealized receivable will alone result in characterizing gain equal to its appreciation as ordinary income. Classifying this same asset as an inventory item does not result in more ordinary income. This overlapping definition of inventory and unrealized receivables creates confusion in applying other provisions of Subchapter K which provide special separate treatment for inventory and unrealized receivables.[24]

The fact that Code Sec. 751(d)(2) refers to noncapital assets and not to noncapital gains potentially means that Code Sec. 306 stock, Code Sec. 341 gains, gains from original issue discount, and other gains which are from capital assets but are taxed as ordinary income are excluded from the definition of inventory under Code Sec. 751(d)(2). If this were the case, most recapture items would not be inventory items. Code Sec. 64, however, appears to classify these assets as other than Code Sec. 1231(b) or capital

[20] Prior to August 5, 1997, the effective date of Act § 1062(a) of the Taxpayer Relief Act of 1997 (P.L. 105-34), the second category of Code Sec. 751 assets was "substantially appreciated" inventory. If the inventory items were, in the aggregate sense, "substantially appreciated" within the guidelines of Code Sec. 751(d)(1), then "substantially appreciated" inventory existed.

[21] Code Sec. 751(d)(1).

[22] Code Sec. 751(d)(2).

[23] Although this would seem unwarranted, the regulations specifically provide for this result. Reg. § 1.751-1(d)(2)(ii).

[24] Code Secs. 724 and 735.

assets, and therefore these assets are unlikely to be excluded from statutes as inventory.

The third category of inventory items comprises the potential gain from the sale of Code Sec. 1246 stock.[25]

The fourth category is any other partnership property that would be either Code Sec. 1221(1) property, other noncapital assets or non-Code Sec. 1231(b) property, or property giving rise to potential gain from the sale of Code Sec. 1246 stock if it were held by the selling partner.[26] Therefore, if the property falls into one of the first three categories "if held by the selling . . . partner," it is considered to be inventory for the purposes of Code Sec. 751(a). The legislative history does not indicate the purpose for this provision which, in effect, requires the property to be tested at two levels.

Whether or not property is "held primarily for sale" under Code Sec. 1221(1) is a factual test focusing on the taxpayer's intent with regard to the property in question. In the context of Code Sec. 751(d)(4), this test is difficult to apply since the partner does not actually own the property. It could be argued that a selling partner, who is otherwise a dealer in the type of assets the partnership owns, can have investment accounts, and that this particular property would be such an investment. A trader or dealer in certain types of property may invest in that property if he or she shows an intent. One method of showing this intent is to set the property aside from other similar property that he or she deals in. Ownership through a partnership that is not controlled by the partner would help show investment motive. However, with respect to a similar provision, Code Sec. 341(e) provides that, if the taxpayer has similar inventory, this is enough to create a presumption that it would be held for sale.[27]

> ***Observation.*** This rule treating partnership property as inventory if it would be inventory in the hands of the selling partner could have some surprising and unwelcome results. For example, a dealer in unimproved land who is a partner in a partnership which invests in the same type of land will report as capital gain his or her share of the partnership's capital gain when the property is sold. However, under the Code Sec. 751(d)(4) definition of inventory, the IRS can take the position that ordinary income is generated on the sale of his or her partnership interest if the partner sells the interest rather than waiting for the partnership to sell the investment land.

---

[25] Foreign investment company stock. Code Sec. 751(d)(3).

[26] Code Sec. 751(d)(4).

[27] Code Sec. 341(b)(1) refers to the purchase of property described in Code Sec. 341(b)(3), which defines "Section 341 assets." See Rep. No. 781, 82d Cong., 1st Sess. (1951), reprinted in 1951-2 CB 458, 481. See also *Jacobs v. Commr.*, CA-9, 55-2 USTC ¶ 9555, 224 F2d 412. Reg. § 1.341-6(b)(4). This issue potentially causes additional problems when Code Sec. 751(b) is applicable as it may give ordinary income to the other nondealer partners upon a deemed property distribution to the dealer. The regulations cure this by limiting Code Sec. 751(d)(4) to property retained by the partnership. Reg. § 1.751-1(d)(2)(iii). See further discussion of Code Sec. 751(b) under distributions in Chapter 18.

For sales and exchanges prior to August 5, 1997, partnership inventory items were not Code Sec. 751 assets unless they were "substantially appreciated" in the aggregate. Code Sec. 751(d)(1) laid down a mechanical test for determining whether inventory was substantially appreciated. The total fair market value of the inventory must exceed 120 percent of the total adjusted basis of all the inventory items to the partnership.[28] Prior to the August 5, 1997, effective date of the Taxpayer Relief Act of 1997 amendments, Code Sec. 751(d)(1) was, in effect, a *de minimis* rule allowing the partnership to avoid the complexities of Code Sec. 751 if the potential conversion from ordinary income to capital gain is small. The *de minimis* tests focused on whether the assets themselves had significant net appreciation. However, since the rule was not applicable to unrealized receivables, most partners still risked having to recognize ordinary gain under Code Sec. 751(a). This mechanical test could be avoided by using cash to buy inventory that is not appreciated.

In addition to forcing partners to treat immaterial amounts of appreciation in the partnership inventory as ordinary income on a sale of their partnership interest, the repeal of this *de minimis* test also has the effect of allowing the potential for an ordinary loss on the sale of a partnership interest if, in the aggregate, the unrealized receivables and inventory have a net built-in loss.

Example 12-1. Alice and Barbara Smale are equal partners in personal service AB Partnership. Barbara transfers her interest in the AB Partnership to Ted Gibbons for $15,000 when the AB Partnership's balance sheet (reflecting a cash receipts and disbursements method of accounting) is as follows:

AB Partnership

Assets	***Adjusted Basis***	***FMV***
Cash	$3,000	$3,000
Loans Receivable	10,000	10,000
Capital Assets	7,000	5,000
Unrealized Receivables	0	14,000
Total	*$20,000*	*$32,000*
Liabilities and Capital		
Liabilities	$2,000	$2,000
Capital		
Alice	9,000	15,000
Barbara	9,000	15,000
Total	*$20,000*	*$32,000*

None of the assets owned by the AB Partnership is Code Sec. 704(c) property, and the capital assets are nondepreciable. The total amount realized by Barbara is $16,000, consisting of:

---

[28] The Taxpayer Relief Act of 1997, P.L. 105-34, Act § 1062(a). Special basis adjustments under Code Secs. 743(b) and 732(d) were excluded. Reg. § 1.751-1(d)(1).

Amount Realized

Cash	$15,000
Debt Relief	1,000
	$16,000

Barbara's Adjusted Basis in Her Partnership Interest [29]

Tax Basis Capital Account	$9,000
Debt Share	1,000
	$10,000

If Code Sec. 751(a) did not apply to the sale, Barbara would recognize $6,000 of capital gain from the sale of the interest in the AB Partnership. However, Code Sec. 751(a) does apply to the sale because Barbara's undivided half-interest in the partnership property includes a half-interest in the partnership's unrealized receivables. Barbara's basis in her partnership interest is $10,000.

If the AB Partnership sold all of its Code Sec. 751 property in a fully taxable transaction immediately prior to the transfer of Barbara's partnership interest to Ted, Barbara would have been allocated $7,000 of ordinary income from the sale of the ABC Partnership's unrealized receivables. Therefore, Barbara will recognize $7,000 of ordinary income with respect to the unrealized receivables. The difference between the amount of capital gain or loss that the partner would realize in the absence of Code Sec. 751 ($6,000) and the amount of ordinary income or loss ($7,000) is the transferor's capital gain or loss on the sale of its partnership interest. In this case, Barbara will recognize a $1,000 capital loss.

Barbara's Character of Gain

Amount Realized	$16,000
Partnership Interest Adjusted Basis	(10,000)
Total Gain	*$6,000*
Less Ordinary Income Share	(7,000)
Capital Gain (Loss)	*$(1,000)*

Example 12-2. *A, B, C,* and *D* formed the calendar-year ABCD Partnership, each with a one-fourth interest in the capital, profits, and losses of the partnership. The original contributions to ABCD were $10 in cash from each partner. The partnership has neither earned any income nor received additional contributions. The partnership uses for financial accounting purposes and for tax purposes the accrual method of accounting for the purchase and sale of inventory that it sells on a C.O.D. basis and the cash method for all other purposes. In addition to producing inventory assets for sale, the partnership renders consulting services related to the use of its products to some of its customers. *A, B,*

[29] Code Sec. 705(b).

C, and *D* derive their income exclusively from the partnership. The current balance sheet is as follows:

ABCD Balance Sheet (12/31/Y1)

Assets	*Book Value*	*FMV*
Cash	$2,000	$2,000
Accounts Receivable (from services)	0	2,500
Inventory	2,000	2,500
Stock Investment	16,000	16,000
Land Investment	2,000	5,000
Total Assets	*$22,000*	*$28,000*
Liabilities and Capital		
Liabilities (Nonrecourse)		
Mortgages	$18,000	$18,000
Capital		
A	800	2,300
B	1,200	2,700
C	1,000	2,500
D	1,000	2,500
Total Liabilities and Capital Accounts	*$22,000*	*$28,000*

On January 1 of Year 2, the first day of the next year, *E* purchases Partner *A*'s interest in ABCD for $3,800 cash, which represents a one-fourth interest in profits and losses, and a 20% interest in total capital accounts. Partner *A*'s basis in his partnership interest is $5,300.

$8,300	Amount Realized—$3,800 cash plus *A*'s $4,500 share of the liabilities (25%).
(5,300)	Adjusted Basis—Stipulated by facts. Normally in the absence of a Code Sec. 754 election, basis equals a partner's tax basis capital account plus his share of the debt.[30]
$3,000	Total—*A*'s total gain on the sale of the partnership interest.

If the ABCD Partnership sold its business for its $28,000 fair market value, Partner *A*'s $750 share of ordinary income for the sale of Code Sec. 751 assets is calculated as follows:

	Unrealized Receivables	*Inventory*
Amount realized	$2,500	$2,500
Adjusted basis	(0)	(2,000)
	$2,500	*$500*
Partner *A*'s share	$625	$125

The character of Partner *A*'s $3,000 total gain from the sale of his partnership interest is as follows:

[30] Reg. § 1.705-1(b), Ex. 3.

Total gain..........................	$3,000
Gain from sale of ordinary income property..........................	(750)
Capital gain	$2,250

.03 Tiered Partnerships

Prior to the Tax Reform Act of 1984,[31] it was uncertain whether or not the ordinary income treatment that applied to unrealized receivables and substantially appreciated inventory under Code Sec. 751 also applied when these assets were held in a lower-tier partnership. Taxpayers attempted to avoid the provisions of Code Sec. 751 by holding all the Code Sec. 751 assets in a lower-tier partnership and by arguing that when an interest in the upper-tier partnership was sold, the portion of the upper-tier partner's partnership interest consisting of his or her proportionate interest in the lower-tier partnership constituted the sale of a capital asset and not a Code Sec. 751 asset.

Code Sec. 751(f), added by the Tax Reform Act of 1984, is intended to eliminate this argument. It provides that, in determining whether partnership property is an unrealized receivable or an inventory item, a partnership will be treated as owning its proportionate share of the property held by any other partnership in which it is a partner. The purpose of this provision is to assure that the collapsible partnership rules will be applied evenly without regard to whether property is held directly by a partnership or indirectly through another partnership.

The application of Code Sec. 751(f) to the simple situation in which a parent partnership's only significant asset is its interest in a subsidiary is straight forward. For example, the subsidiary partnership's activities, trade or business, intent, and so forth, are attributed directly to the parent partnership along with the ownership of the parent's share of the subsidiary partnership's assets.

However, if the parent partnership is engaged in a separate trade or business, should the character of the subsidiary partnership's assets be determined in its hands and then attributed to the parent partnership along with the ownership of its share of the subsidiary's assets? Should the assets be tested by treating the parent partnership as owning them directly? In keeping with the apparent legislative purpose to neutralize the significance of tiered partnership agreements, most—if not all—of these and similar questions should be resolved by completely ignoring the separate existence of subsidiary partnerships. Accordingly, Code Sec. 751(d) should be applied on a "consolidated" basis, and the parent partnership should be viewed as owning a share of the subsidiary's assets and engaging directly in the subsidiary's business and its own business for purposes of

[31] P.L. 98-369.

determining the character of its share of the subsidiary's assets. Neither the statute nor the legislative history resolve questions of this type.

¶ 1204 Mechanics of Code Sec. 751(a) for Sales of Partnership Interests Before December 15, 1999

The amount of money or the fair market value of any property a selling partner receives in exchange for all or part of his or her interest in the partnership attributable to "unrealized receivables" or to "appreciated inventory" items is treated as an amount realized from the sale or exchange of property that is not a capital asset.[32]

The ordinary income realized by a partner is the difference between (1) the portion of the total amount realized allocated to Code Sec. 751 assets, and (2) the portion of the selling partner's basis for his or her entire interest allocated to Code Sec. 751 assets. Generally, the portion of the total amount realized which the seller and the purchaser allocate to Code Sec. 751 assets in an arm's-length transaction will be regarded as correct.[33]

The portion of the partner's adjusted basis for his or her partnership interest allocated to Code Sec. 751 property is an amount equal to the basis such property would have had under Code Sec. 732 if the selling partner had received his or her share of such properties in a current distribution made immediately before the sale.[34] Generally, the distributee will take the adjusted basis that the partnership had in the asset immediately before the deemed distribution if it does not exceed his or her predistribution adjusted basis in his or her partnership interest.[35] When the partnership's adjusted basis in the property deemed distributed exceeds the partner's adjusted basis in his or her partnership interest, the entire adjusted basis (limited to the partner's basis in his or her partnership interest) is allocated to the Code Sec. 751 assets in proportion to their adjusted bases to the partnership.[36]

The following five steps must be taken to determine the consequences under Code Sec. 751(a):

1. Determine the portion of the amount realized by the transferor of a partnership interest that is attributable to Code Sec. 751 property;

2. Determine the adjusted basis that the selling partner would have had in the partnership's Code Sec. 751 property if he or she had received his or her share in a "current distribution" immediately prior to the transfer of the interest;

---

[32] Code Sec. 751(a); Reg. § 1.751-1(a)(1). For sales or exchanges of partnership interests prior to August 5, 1997, the provision applies only to "substantially appreciated inventory." The Taxpayer Relief Act of 1997, P.L. 105-34, Act § 1062(a).

[33] Reg. § 1.751-1(a)(2), prior to amendment by T.D. 8847, 1999-52 IRB 701.

[34] *Id.*

[35] Code Sec. 732(a)(1) and (2).

[36] Code Sec. 732(c).

3. Reduce his or her partnership interest adjusted basis by the amount in Step 2;

4. Compute the ordinary income or loss under Code Sec. 751(a) as the difference between Step 1 and Step 2; and

5. Compute Code Sec. 741 capital gain or loss as the remaining amount realized less the remaining adjusted basis of the partnership interest after taking into account Steps 1 and 2.

It is apparent from the above analysis that a selling partner may have ordinary income on his or her portion of Code Sec. 751 assets and a capital loss on the rest of the sale. The following example illustrates this point. This would be the case when the partnership's capital and Code Sec. 1231 assets are depreciated but there is some ordinary income potential.

Example 12-3. Partner *A* sells his partnership interest with an adjusted basis of $110 for $100. The value of *A*'s share of unrealized receivables and inventory items is $80; his adjusted basis for these assets is $20. If Code Sec. 751(a) were not applicable, the consequences of the sale to *A* would be as follows:

Amount realized	$100
Adjusted basis	(110)
Capital loss realized . . .	$*(10)*

By applying the provisions of Code Sec. 751(a) to these facts, however, *A* would realize and recognize $20 of ordinary income and a $30 capital loss computed as follows:

Portion of amount realized attributable to Code Sec. 751 assets			$80
Basis would take on a current distribution			(20)
Amount of ordinary income realized			$*60*
Remainder of amount realized . . .	($100 − $80)	$20	
Remainder of adjusted basis	($110 − $20)	(90)	
Capital loss under Code Sec. 741		$*(70)*	

The first of the above steps requires *A* to allocate a portion of the amount realized on the sale of the partnership interest to Code Sec. 751 assets. While the regulations do not specify how the allocation is to be made, the general treatment is to allocate an amount equal to the seller's share of the fair market value of the Code Sec. 751 assets to those assets and the remainder of the amount realized to the "other assets." If the buyer and seller agree to allocate a portion of the total amount realized to the Code Sec. 751 assets, then their allocation will be respected if it is made at arm's length.[37] As discussed later, it is difficult to imagine an arm's-length bargaining position if there is no Code Sec. 754 election in effect, unless the

[37] Reg. § 1.751-1(a)(2), prior to amendment by T.D. 8847, 1999-52 IRB 701. Note that T.D. 8847 specifically rejects this approach in determining the selling partner's ordinary gain under amended Reg. § 1.751-1(a)(2).

purchasing partner expects a property distribution to take place within two years, and he or she plans to make an election under Code Sec. 732(d).

A theoretically acceptable method of allocating a portion of the amount realized to Code Sec. 751 assets comprises the following three steps:

Step 1—Determine the selling partner's share of the fair market value of each Code Sec. 751 asset and each "other asset" by referring to his or her interest in capital, profits, and losses—this step encompasses finding the selling partner's share of the fair market value of unrealized receivables [38] and the fair market value of inventory.

Step 2—Allocate the aggregate amount realized to each asset based on its share of the total fair market value.

Step 3—Allocate the selling price of the partnership interest to specific assets, which is relatively easy if the amount realized for the interest equals the seller's share of the fair market value of all the partnership assets, and if each partner's share of capital, profits, and losses is equal.

Example 12-4. Partner *A* sells his one-third interest in the ABC Partnership for a cash payment of $100. The balance sheet of the ABC partnership (indicating the adjusted basis of its assets) is as follows:

ABC Partnership

Assets	***Adjusted Basis***	***FMV***
Cash	$100	$100
Unrealized Receivables	0	200
Capital Assets	100	100
Total	*$200*	*$400*
Liabilities and Capital		
Liabilities	$100	$100
Capital		
A	33-1/3	100
B	33-1/3	100
C	33-1/3	100
Total	*$200*	*$400*

The total amount realized for *A*'s partnership interest is $133.33, consisting of $100 in cash and a $33.33 reduction in *A*'s share of the partnership liabilities.[39] The amount realized on Code Sec. 751 assets is $66.66, determined as follows:

$$\frac{\text{Fair market value of Code Sec. 751 assets}}{\text{Fair market value of all assets}} = \frac{\$200}{\$400} = 50\%$$

[38] This includes the value of expected payments for the delivery of agreed-upon future services and goods less the expected cost of providing the service. Code Sec. 751(c); Reg. § 1.751-1(c)(3), prior to amendment by T.D. 8847, 1999-52 IRB 701.

[39] This is one-third of $100.

Thus 50%, or $66.66, of the total amount realized from the sale of the interest is allocable to Code Sec. 751 assets.

If a seller has different interests in capital, profits, and losses, the determination of his or her share of Code Sec. 751(a) and (b) assets, "hot assets," is more difficult. The proper method of allocation under these circumstances is unclear, and the regulations and case law provide no light. A seller's share of Code Sec. 751 assets should be equal to the sum of:

[seller's % interest in capital]	×	*[book-value of Code Sec. 751 assets]*
	+	
[seller's interest in profits]	×	*[appreciation of appreciated Code Sec. 751 assets]*
	or	
	−	
[seller's interest in losses]	×	*[depreciation of depreciated Code Sec. 751 assets]*

Although there appears to be an item-by-item requirement, an allocation agreement between the buyer and the seller can allocate the purchase price to specific partnership assets in addition to making overall allocations between categories of assets.[40] A specific amount can then be allocated to the fair market value of unrealized receivables for goods and/or services [41] and to depreciated recapture property.[42] However, an allocation of purchase price to inventory has not been specifically sanctioned, possibly because the Treasury was concerned with the avoidance of the substantial appreciation test that applied to inventory prior to the August 5, 1997, effective date of the Taxpayer Relief Act of 1997.[43] Other allocations are also required, but if there is an allocation to inventory and unrealized receivables, other allocations are less important.

The position taken in the regulations that an arm's-length allocation to the total amounts of Code Sec. 751 assets between buyer and seller will be respected seems to be based upon the assumption that the parties have contrary bargaining positions.[44] When capital gains are taxed at a preferred rate, the seller clearly wants to allocate as little as possible to Code Sec. 751 assets in order to minimize his or her ordinary income. The buyer, however, will have tax consequences only if a Code Sec. 743(b) adjustment of the basis of the partnership property is to be made, or if the buyer receives a Code Sec. 732(d) distribution.[45] In other situations the IRS should not be bound by the "agreement" that affects only one party. However, most circuit courts have taken the position that a party to the agreement (as opposed to the IRS) must have strong proof to upset it.

---

[40] Reg. § 1.1245-1(a)(2).

[41] Reg. § 1.751-1(c)(3), prior to amendment by T.D. 8847, 1999-52 IRB 701.

[42] Reg. § 1.751-1(c)(4)(iii), prior to amendment by T.D. 8847, 1999-52 IRB 701.

[43] P.L. 105-34.

[44] Reg. § 1.751-1(a)(2), prior to amendment by T.D. 8847, 1999-52 IRB 701.

[45] This is a distribution that occurs within two years of the purchase when a Code Sec. 754 election has not been made.

The second step is an allocation of a portion of the seller's basis in his or her partnership interest to Code Sec. 751 property. Here the regulations provide that the adjusted basis allocated to the Code Sec. 751 assets is to be the adjusted basis which these assets would have had in the hands of a distributee partner if they had been received by him or her in a current distribution immediately before the sale.[46] Generally, the distributee will take the adjusted basis that the partnership had in the asset immediately before the deemed distribution if it does not exceed his or her predistribution adjusted basis in his or her partnership interest.[47] When the partnership's adjusted basis in the property deemed distributed exceeds the distributee partner's adjusted basis in his or her partnership interest, the entire adjusted basis (limited to the distributee partner's basis in his or her partnership interest) is allocated to the Code Sec. 751 assets in proportion to their adjusted bases to the partnership.[48]

In Step 3, the partner's remaining adjusted basis in his or her partnership interest is reduced by the adjusted basis attributed to his or her share of Code Sec. 751 assets. The final steps in computing the Code Sec. 751 ordinary gain and Code Sec. 741 capital gain or loss are arithmetical and can be tabulated as follows:

Total amount realized	–	Amount realized on Code Sec. 751 property	=	Remaining amount realized
Total partnership interest basis	–	Adjusted basis of the seller's share of Code Sec. 751 basis property	=	Remaining adjusted basis
		Ordinary income per Code Sec. 751		Capital gain per Code Sec. 741

The transferor is required to file a statement with his or her tax return for the year of sale.[49] The statement is to provide the following information:

1. The date of the transfer;
2. The adjusted basis of the partnership interest and the share attributable to the Code Sec. 751 assets;
3. The total amount realized;
4. In a case when Code Sec. 732(d) is involved, the basis information required by Reg. § 1.732-1(d)(3); and
5. The amount of the adjustment if a special adjustment has been made to basis under Code Sec. 743(b).

[46] Reg. § 1.751-1(a)(2), prior to amendment by T.D. 8847, 1999-52 IRB 701.
[47] Code Sec. 732(a)(1) and (2).
[48] Code Sec. 732(c).
[49] Reg. § 1.751-1(a)(3), prior to amendment by T.D. 8847, 1999-52 IRB 701.

.01 *Definition of Unrealized Receivables*

For a discussion of the definition of unrealized receivables, see ¶ 1203.01. This definition was not changed by the August 1997 and December 1999 changes in Section 751 and the regulations thereunder.

.02 *Definition of Appreciated Inventory Items*

The second category of Code Sec. 751 assets consists of appreciated inventory items. Former Code Sec. 751(d)(2) sets out four categories of inventory items. Prior to the August 5, 1997, effective date of Act § 1062(a) of the Taxpayer Relief Act of 1997,[50] the second category of Code Sec. 751 assets was "substantially appreciated" inventory. If the inventory items were, in the aggregate sense, "substantially appreciated" within the guidelines of former Code Sec. 751(d)(1), then "substantially appreciated" inventory existed.

The first of the four categories of inventory items is true inventory in terms of Code Sec. 1221(1) and dealer property held primarily for sale to customers in the ordinary course of the partnership's business.[51]

The second category comprises other property which, when sold or exchanged by the partnership, would be considered property other than a capital asset in terms of Code Sec. 1221 and other than a Code Sec. 1231(b) asset.[52] This category is so broad as to apparently encompass all the other categories and specifically includes the accounts receivable of a cash-basis taxpayer,[53] realized account receivables of an accrual-basis taxpayer, depreciation recapture, and all unrealized receivables. When a partnership interest is sold, the fact that an asset is an unrealized receivable will alone result in characterizing gain equal to its appreciation as ordinary income. Classifying this same asset as an inventory item does not result in more ordinary income.

The inclusion of unrealized receivables as inventory (in this second category) has an effect on only the "substantial appreciation test." The result is that, in the case of a cash-basis partnership, it is more likely that the traditional category of inventory will be appreciated, while the opposite is often true of an accrual-basis partnership.

The fact that former Code Sec. 751(d)(2)(B) refers to noncapital assets and not to noncapital gains could potentially mean that Code Sec. 306 stock, Code Sec. 341 gains, gains from original issue discount, and other gains which are from capital assets but are taxed as ordinary income are excluded from the definition of inventory under former Code Sec. 751(d)(2)(B). If this were the case, most recapture items would not be inventory items. Code Sec. 64, however, appears to classify these assets as

[50] P.L. 105-34.
[51] Code Sec. 751(d)(2)(A).
[52] Code Sec. 751(d)(2)(B).
[53] Although this would seem unwarranted, the regulations specifically provide for this result. Reg. § 1.751-1(d)(2)(ii).

other than Code Sec. 1231(b) or capital assets, and therefore these assets are unlikely to be excluded from status as inventory.

The third category of inventory items comprises the potential gain from the sale of Code Sec. 1246 stock.[54]

The fourth category is any other partnership property that would be either Code Sec. 1221(1) property, other noncapital assets or non-Code Sec. 1231(b) property, or property giving rise to potential gain from the sale of Code Sec. 1246 stock if it were held by the selling or distributee partner.[55] Therefore, if the property falls into one of the first three categories "if held by the selling or distributee partner," it is considered to be inventory for the purposes of Code Sec. 751. The legislative history does not indicate the purpose for this provision which, in effect, requires the property to be tested at two levels.

Whether or not property is "held primarily for sale" under Code Sec. 1221(1) is a factual test focusing on the taxpayer's intent with regard to the property in question. In the context of former Code Sec. 751(d)(2)(D), this test is difficult to apply since the partner does not actually own the property. It could be argued that a selling partner, who is otherwise a dealer in the type of assets the partnership owns, can have investment accounts, and that this particular property would be such an investment. A trader or dealer in certain types of property may invest in that property if he or she shows an intent. One method of showing this intent is to set the property aside from other similar property that he or she deals in. Ownership through a partnership that is not controlled by the partner would help show investment motive. However, with respect to a similar provision, the Code Sec. 341(e) regulations provide that, if the taxpayer has similar inventory, this is enough to create a presumption that it would be held for sale.[56]

For sales and exchanges prior to August 6, 1997, partnership inventory items are not Code Sec. 751 assets unless they are "substantially appreciated" in the aggregate. Former Code Sec. 751(d)(1) lays down a mechanical test for determining whether inventory is substantially appreciated. The total fair market value of the inventory must exceed 120 percent of the total adjusted basis of all the inventory items to the partnership.[57]

---

[54] Foreign investment company stock. Former Code Sec. 751(d)(2)(C).

[55] Former Code Sec. 751(d)(2)(D).

[56] This issue potentially causes additional problems when Code Sec. 751(b) is applicable, as it may give ordinary income to the other nondealer partners upon a deemed property distribution to the dealer. The regulations cure this by limiting former Code Sec. 751(d)(2)(D) to property retained by the partnership. Reg. § 1.751-1(d)(2)(iii), prior to amendment by T.D. 8847, 1999-52 IRB 701. See further discussion of Code Sec. 751(b) under distributions.

[57] Special basis adjustments under Code Secs. 743(b) and 732(d) are excluded. Reg. § 1.751-1(d)(1), prior to amendment by T.D. 8847, 1999-52 IRB 701. The Taxpayer Relief Act of 1997, P.L. 105-34, Act § 1062(a).

Prior to the August 5, 1997, effective date of the Taxpayer Relief Act of 1997 amendments,[58] former Code Sec. 751(d)(1) was, in effect, a *de minimis* rule allowing the partnership to avoid the complexities of Code Sec. 751 if the potential conversion from ordinary income to capital gain is small. The *de minimis* tests focused on whether the assets themselves had significant appreciation. However, since the rule was not applicable to unrealized receivables, most partners still risked having to recognize ordinary gain under Code Sec. 751(a). This mechanical test could be avoided by using cash to buy inventory that is not appreciated.

Example 12-5. *A, B, C,* and *D* formed the calendar-year ABCD Partnership, each with a one-fourth interest in the capital, profits and losses of the partnership. The original contributions to ABCD were $10 in cash from each partner. The partnership has neither earned any income nor received additional contributions. The partnership uses for financial accounting purposes and for tax purposes the accrual method for the purchase and sale of inventory that it sells on a C.O.D. basis, and the cash method for all other purposes. In addition to producing inventory assets for sale, the partnership renders consulting services to some of its customers. *A, B, C,* and *D* derive their income exclusively from the partnership. The current balance sheet is as follows:

ABCD BALANCE SHEET (12/31/Y1)

Assets	*Book Value*	*FMV*
Cash	$2,000	$2,000
Accounts Receivable (from services)	0	2,500
Inventory	2,000	2,500
Stock Investment	16,000	16,000
Land (Investment)	2,000	5,000
Total Assets	*$22,000*	*$28,000*
Liabilities and Capital		
Liabilities		
Mortgages	$18,000	$18,000
Capital		
A	800	2,300
B	1,200	2,700
C	1,000	2,500
D	1,000	2,500
Total Liabilities and Capital Accounts	*$22,000*	*$28,000*

On January 1, Year 2, the first day of the next year, *E* offers *A* $2,300 cash for *A*'s interest in ABCD. If *A* accepts *E*'s offer, what is the amount (and character) of *A*'s gain or loss?

[58] P.L. 105-34.

$6,800	Amount Realized—$2,300 cash plus *A*'s $4,500 share of the liabilities (1/4 × $1,800).
(5,300)	Adjusted Basis—Normally in the absence of a Code Sec. 754 election, basis equals a partner's tax basis capital account plus his share of the debt.[59]
$1,500	Total—*A*'s total gain on the sale of the partnership interest.

Example 12-6. Gain allocated to Code Sec. 751 assets. Following the facts of the example above, the Code Sec. 751 assets are the accounts receivable and the inventory. A problem arises in allocating the amount realized to Code Sec. 751 assets when *A* has a different interest in the capital of the partnership than his interest in profits and losses.

A formula used to allocate the amount realized to Code Sec. 751 assets when the selling partner has a different interest in capital and profits/losses can be expressed as follows:

[A's percentage interest in partnership capital]	×	*[book-value of the assets]*
	+	
[A's percentage interest in ABCD's profits]	×	*[appreciation of the assets]*
	or	
	−	
[A's percentage interest in ABCD's losses]	×	*[depreciation of the assets]*

This formula must be applied to each Code Sec. 751 asset. Here, *A* has a 20% interest in capital ($800 divided by $4,000) and a 25% interest in profits and losses.

Under this approach, *A* is considered to have a 20% interest in $4,000 of the basis of particular partnership assets attributable to the original contributions and a 20% interest in $18,000 of the basis of other partnership property. The latter figure is attributable to his share of the basis of the assets acquired with the funds from the partnership liability, which depending upon its nature (recourse or nonrecourse) is shared according to his loss or profit ratio of 25%. Whether it is assumed that he has a 20% or 25% portion of the basis for the inventory, the same amount of Code Sec. 751 income will arise as the basis and amount realized will bear a fixed relationship to each other.

Amount realized allocated to:

Accounts Receivable

(20% × $0) + (25% × $2,500)	=	$0	+	$625	=	$625

Inventory

(20% × $2,000) + (25% × $500)	=	$400	+	$125	=	$525

[59] Reg. § 1.705-1(b), Ex. 3.

A's amount realized allocated to the Code Sec. 751 assets is $625 plus $525, or $1,150. This represents his economic ownership in these assets determined on an aggregate approach.

Former Reg. § 1.751-1(a)(2) states that the portion of the partner's basis for his partnership interest to be allocated to Code Sec. 751 property shall be an amount equal to the basis such property would have had under Code Sec. 732 if the selling partner had received his share of such properties in a current distribution made immediately before the sale. Pursuant to Code Sec. 732(a), generally, *A*'s basis in the Code Sec. 751 assets would be his share of the bases of the assets in the hands of the partnership ($2,000). *A* is treated as if he were distributed his share of the Code Sec. 751 assets. (If *A*'s basis in his partnership interest were less than $400, for example $300, then his basis in the hot assets would be limited to that basis, *i.e.*, $300, because of the Code Sec. 732(a)(2) limitation.)

The bases of Code Sec. 751 assets on a distribution to *A* would be *A*'s share of their total bases of $2,000. The regulations dictate that this basis is the basis the assets would have under Code Sec. 732 if distributed.[60] Under one approach to finding *A*'s share of the Code Sec. 751 assets book value/basis, he would treat his share of total capital as his share of the book value/basis of each asset. As the partnership is deemed to distribute the assets as determined above, *A* is considered to have the same basis on distribution (20% × ($0 + $2,000) = $400) subject to the Code Sec. 732(a)(2) limitation.

A's Code Sec. 751 gain

$1,150	Amount realized allocated to Code Sec. 751 assets
(400)	Basis allocated to Code Sec. 751 assets
$750	

A's Code Sec. 741 gain

$5,650	Amount Realized—*A*'s total amount realized minus the amount realized allocated to Code Sec. 751 assets ($6,800 minus $1,150)
4,900	Adjusted Basis—*A*'s total basis minus basis allocated to Code Sec. 751 assets ($5,300 minus $400)
$750	Total—Code Sec. 741 Capital gain

Example 12-7. *Alternative approach to finding* A*'s share of the basis of hot assets.* Review Examples 12-6 and -7 above. The rule is that *A*'s basis to be used in the Code Sec. 751(a) computation is the adjusted basis of the property which he would take on a current distribution of his share of the property. Here, we have determined that his share of the value of accounts receivable is 25%, with a basis

[60] Reg. § 1.751-1(a)(2), prior to amendment by T.D. 8847, 1999-52 IRB 701.

of zero. His share of the inventory's value is 21% ($525 ÷ 2,500), and 21% of their basis is $420 (21% × $2,000). Thus, upon a current distribution of a tenancy in common interest of *A*'s share of the hot assets he would take a basis equal to 23% of the partnership's basis.

Code Sec. 751(a)

$1,150	Amount realized
(420)	Adjusted basis
$730	Ordinary income Code Sec. 751(a)

Code Sec. 741

$5,650	Amount realized (see above)
(4,880)	Adjusted basis (*A*'s total basis less *A*'s basis allocated to Code Sec. 751 assets ($5,300 − $420))
$770	Long-term capital gain Sec. 741

In practice, taxpayers often approximate the Code Sec. 751 gain on the sale of a partnership interest by calculating how much ordinary income would have been realized if they had remained in the partnership (in the example above, ordinary gain potential of $3,000 ÷ 4 = $750). This comports with the underlying rationale of Code Sec. 751. However, it will not necessarily produce the same result as a mechanical application of the regulations in all cases. The regulations, however, lack guidance on how Code Sec. 751(a) applies when percentage interests in capital vary from profit and loss sharing. Where the partner's basis for his partnership interest is less than the *distributed* Code Sec. 751 assets' bases to the partnership, Code Sec. 732(a)(2) limits the basis allocated to the Code Sec. 751 assets to the lower basis of the partnership interest. In this case, the Code Sec. 751(a) gain may exceed that which would have been realized by continuing in the partnership. Other variations arise where the value and the face amount of an item (accounts receivable) differ and where the gain is tainted under Code Sec. 751(d)(2)(D) because of the partner's status.

¶ 1205 Enforcement

As part of the Tax Reform Act of 1984,[61] Congress focused on—and attempted to remedy—the problem of noncompliance with the requirements of Code Sec. 751. The Congressional "solution" to this problem is in Code Sec. 6050K, which imposes reporting requirements in connection with transfers of partnership interests after December 31, 1984. Code Sec. 6050K(a) generally requires partnerships to file information returns with the Form 1065, U.S. Partnership Return of Income, for any transfers described in Code Sec. 751(a) for the tax year in which the calendar year of the exchange takes place.[62] These returns must identify the transferor and transferee involved in the exchange and provide such other information as the regulations require. Code Sec. 6050K(b) also requires that the informa-

[61] P.L. 98-369.

[62] Form 8308, Report of a Sale or Exchange of Certain Partnership Interests.

tion in the return be disclosed to the transferor and transferee "before January 31 following the calendar year for which the return . . . was made."[63]

Code Sec. 6050K(c)(1) requires that any transferor of a partnership interest give prompt notice of the transfer to the partnership,[64] and Code Sec. 6050K(c)(2) delays the partnership's required filing date until after it is "notified of such exchange." Thus, the burden of triggering the entire reporting process falls on the transferor.

Even though the clear intent of Code Sec. 6050K is to force compliance with Code Sec. 751(a), neither the section itself nor the Form 8308, Report of a Sale or Exchange of Certain Partnership Interests, or its instructions, or Reg. § 1.6050K-1, require the partnership to notify the partner of the information necessary to calculate the seller's ordinary income under Code Sec. 751(a). The partner is merely informed of the requirement to treat a portion of gain or loss from the sale of his or her partnership interest as ordinary in character.[65]

The collapsible partnership rules in Code Sec. 751 are very complex and are frequently overlooked (or ignored) by both practitioners and revenue agents. However, the Code Sec. 751(a) rules are extremely broad and are potentially applicable to a wide variety of common situations. In part, the wide applicability of these rules is a direct consequence of the definition of "unrealized receivables." Thus, any partner who transfers his or her partnership interest is likely to be subject to Code Sec. 751(a) if the partnership owns depreciable personal property or uses the cash method of accounting.

¶ 1206 Comparison with Code Sec. 341

The above provisions are comparable to those applicable to collapsible corporations and Code Sec. 751 is similar, in effect, to Code Sec. 341 since both have the same purpose—namely, to preclude the conversion of ordinary income into capital gains. Code Sec. 341, however, has many important differences from Code Sec. 751; for example, it adopts an "all-or-nothing" approach because the shareholder's gain is all ordinary income or all long-term capital gain. Furthermore, unlike Code Sec. 751, which is completely mechanical, Code Sec. 341 is triggered only if a shareholder has the requisite subjective intent described in Code Sec. 341(a). Finally, Code Sec. 751(a) prevents shifting of ordinary income between partners, whereas Code Sec. 341 is aimed mainly at the complete avoidance of ordinary

[63] Pub. 541, Tax Information on Partnerships, indicates that "The partnership must also provide a copy of the Form 8308 (or a written statement with the same information) to each transferee and transferor, by the later of January 31, following the end of the calendar year or 30 days after it receives notice of the exchange."

[64] Within 30 days of the transfer or by January 15 of the year following the year of transfer if earlier.

[65] Reg. § 1.6050K-1(c).

income. If the partnership does not have a Code Sec. 754 election in effect, the selling partner's share of ordinary income is reported twice—first by him, and then by the purchaser.

> ***S Corporation Observation.*** Code Sec. 341 applies to S corporations as well as C corporations, but Code Sec. 751(a) does not apply to S or C corporations.

Chapter 13

Sale of a Partnership Interest—Effect on the Partnership

¶ 1301 Introduction

The sale by a partner of his or her partnership interest will affect the partnership only if: (1) it causes a partnership termination, (2) the partnership has a Code Sec. 754 election in effect, or (3) the partnership has a "substantial built-in loss" immediately after the sale.

As a statutory starting point, the general rule is that the partnership provisions in Subchapter K of the Internal Revenue Code adopt an "entity approach" in dealing with the tax consequences when partnership interests are transferred. The transferred interest is treated like corporate stock and is considered to be a separate intangible asset rather than an undivided tenancy-in-common interest in the partnership assets, as it would be treated under an "aggregate approach" to partnership taxation.

> ***LLC Observation.*** The rules discussed in this chapter apply equally to state law partnerships and LLCs taxed as partnerships.

¶ 1302 Technical Terminations

The continuing partners, those partners who remain members of the partnership after the transferor partner has transferred his or her interest in the partnership to the transferee partner, are generally not affected by the transfer even when there is a substantial built-in loss or a Code Sec. 754 election in effect. However, the transfer of a partnership interest can have a significant tax impact on the continuing partners if the transfer causes the "termination" of the partnership under Code Sec. 708(b). Assuming that the business and financial operations of the partnership continue to be carried on by the partnership, a termination occurs only when 50 percent or more of the total interest in the partnership's capital and profits is sold or exchanged within a 12-month period. Thus, the partnership will not be terminated provided the partnership interest sold or exchanged together with any other partnership interests sold or exchanged within a 12-month period constitutes less than a 50 percent interest in partnership capital and profits, or the transfer does not constitute a "sale or exchange." There is no guidance in the Internal Revenue Code or Treasury regulations as to the definitions of capital account and profits interest. Percent of capital is probably the percent of the value of the assets the partner would be entitled to receive upon a liquidating distribution. It is not clear how different profits interests in various aspects of the partnership's operations should be taken into account. However, if capital accounts are taken into account at their fair market values, a profits interest in existing built-in gain would be part of the capital account test of Code Sec. 708(b). There is no guidance as to how various interests in future appreciation in the partnership's properties and operating profits can combine into one overall interest in partnership profits.

A sale or exchange includes:

1. Sales violating an anti-assignment agreement;[1]
2. Taxable and tax-free exchanges;[2]
3. Distributions of partnership interests from a partnership or a corporation;[3]
4. Contributions of partnership interests to a corporation;[4]
5. Contributions of partnership interests to another partnership;[5]
6. Abandonment of a partnership interest when the partner is relieved of a share of partnership debt under Code Sec. 752(b) in excess of his or her basis in his or her interest; and
7. Sales to existing partners.[6]

A sale or exchange does not include:

1. Bequests and inheritances;[7]
2. Gifts when the donor has no debt relief under Code Sec. 752(b).[8] Debt relief suggests a part gift/part sale analysis; and
3. Entry of a new partner.[9]

For sales and exchanges on or after May 9, 1997, if a partnership is terminated by a sale or exchange of an interest, the following is deemed to occur:

---

[1] *D.L. Evans v. Commr.*, 54 TC 40, Dec. 29,915 (1970), aff'd, CA-7, 71-2 USTC ¶ 9597, 447 F2d 547.

[2] *A.E. Long v. Commr.*, 77 TC 1045, Dec. 38,402 (1981) (taxable exchange of partnership interests); *D.L. Evans v. Commr.*, 54 TC 40, Dec. 29,915 (1970) (contribution under Code Sec. 351 to a corporation).

[3] Code Sec. 761(e). However, a partnership interest deemed distributed by a partnership terminated under Code Sec. 708(b) is not treated as a sale or exchange for purposes of terminating the subsidiary partnership. Reg. § 1.761-1(e).

[4] Rev. Rul. 81-38, 1981-1 CB 386; *D.L. Evans v. Commr.*, 54 TC 40, Dec. 29,915 (1970), aff'd CA-7, 447 F2d 547.

[5] IRS Letter Rulings 8929003, 8229034.

[6] Reg. § 1.708-1(b)(1)(ii).

[7] *Id.*

[8] *Id.*

[9] *Id.*

1. The partnership contributes all of its assets and liabilities to a new partnership in exchange for an interest in the new partnership; and,

2. Immediately thereafter, the terminated partnership distributes interests in the new partnership to the purchasing partner and the other remaining partners in proportion to their respective interests in the terminated partnership in liquidation of the terminated partnership, either for the continuation of the business by the new partnership or for its dissolution and winding up.

Example 13-1. *A* and *B* each contribute $10,000 cash to form AB, a general partnership, as equal partners. AB purchases depreciable Property *X* for $20,000. Property *X* increases in value to $30,000, at which time *A* sells her entire 50% interest to *C* for $15,000 in a transfer that terminates the partnership under Code Sec. 708(b)(1)(B). At the time of the sale, Property *X* had an adjusted tax basis of $16,000 and a book value of $16,000 (original $20,000 tax basis and book value reduced by $4,000 of depreciation). In addition, *A* and *B* each had a capital account balance of $8,000 (original $10,000 capital account reduced by $2,000 of depreciation allocations with respect to Property *X*).

Following the deemed contribution of assets and liabilities by the terminated AB partnership to a new partnership (new BC) and the liquidation of the terminated AB partnership, the adjusted tax basis of Property *X* in the hands of new BC is $16,000.[10] The book value of Property *X* in the hands of new partnership AB is also $16,000 (the book value of Property *X* immediately before the termination), and *B* and *C* each have a capital account of $8,000 in new AB (the balance of their capital accounts in AB prior to the termination).[11]

Property *X* was not Code Sec. 704(c) property in the hands of terminated AB and is therefore not treated as Code Sec. 704(c) property in the hands of new AB, even though Property *X* is deemed contributed to new AB at a time when the fair market value of Property *X* ($30,000) was different from its adjusted tax basis ($16,000).[12]

If a partnership is terminated by a sale or exchange of an interest in the partnership, a Code Sec. 754 election by the new partnership on its

[10] Code Sec. 723.

[11] See Reg. § 1.704-1(b)(2)(iv)(*l*) (providing that the deemed contribution and liquidation with regard to the terminated partnership are disregarded in determining the capital accounts of the partners and the books of the new partnership). Additionally, under Reg. § 301.6109-1(d)(2)(iii), new BC partnership retains the taxpayer identification number of the terminated AB partnership.

[12] See Reg. § 1.704-3(a)(3)(i) (providing that property contributed to a new partnership under Reg. § 1.708-1(b)(1)(iv) is treated as Code Sec. 704(c) property only to the extent that the property was Code Sec. 704(c) property in the hands of the terminated partnership immediately prior to the termination).

initial return, or a Code Sec. 754 election made by the terminated partnership on its final return that is in effect for the taxable year of the new or terminated partnership in which the sale occurs, applies with respect to the incoming partner. Therefore, the bases of partnership assets are adjusted pursuant to Code Secs. 743 and 755 prior to their deemed contribution to the new partnership.[13] If the terminated partnership has made Code Sec. 743(b) adjustments to its property, these carry over to the new partnership.[14]

In summary:

1. The termination does not require that the new partnership get a new taxpayer identification number.[15]

2. The termination requires the terminated partnership to file a "Final Return" for the short year ending with the date of sale.

3. The termination requires the new partnership to file an initial short year partnership tax return.

4. The termination continues any remaining Code Sec. 704(c) gain for the continuing partners.[16]

5. The old partnership's taxable year, accounting method, and other elections do *not* carry over to the new partnership.

6. The termination is disregarded in determining the capital accounts of the partners.[17]

7. The holding period of the new partnership is the same as the terminated partnership.[18]

8. Code Sec. 724 taint. It is unclear whether the new partnership retains the Code Sec. 724 taint. This code provision simply provides that the character of gain from the sale of contributed assets, which are ordinary income assets to the contributing partner, will be ordinary income to the old partnership. Code Sec. 724 does not treat these assets as inventory or unrealized receivables to the old partnership. These contributions to the new partnership by the old partnership are not literally subject to Code Sec. 724. Absent this, Code Sec. 724 does not cause the

---

[13] Reg. § 1.708-(b)(1)(v). For sales and exchanges on or before May 9, 1997, if the sale does cause a termination to occur, the result is that the partnership is deemed to make a pro rata liquidating distribution of an undivided tenancy-in-common interest in its property to the new purchasing partners and the continuing partners who are treated as if they immediately contributed their interests to a new partnership. For sales and exchanges on or before May 9, 1997, the "new" partnership's basis for its assets will equal the basis the partners received in the deemed liquidating distribution. This basis is equal to the partners' basis in their partnership interests. Therefore an unintended termination normally results in the partnership having a new basis for its Code Secs. 1221 and 1231 assets reflecting any appreciation in the buyer's share of all partnership assets. The basis step up or down is only for the buyer under the rules of Code Sec. 704(c).

[14] Reg. § 1.743-1(h)(1).

[15] Reg. § 1.708-1(b)(1)(iv), Ex.

[16] Reg. § 1.704-3(a)(3)(i).

[17] Reg. § § 1.704-1(b)(2)(iv)(*l*), and 1.708-1(b)(1)(iv), Ex. (ii).

[18] Code Secs. 722 and 1223.

new partnership's disposition to be affected by its provisions. However, application of Code Sec. 64 may result in all the old partnership's hot assets being treated as subject to Code Sec. 724.

9. Any Code Sec. 465, at-risk loss carryover, and Code Sec. 469, passive activity loss carryover, continues if the activity continues.

10. Code Sec. 704(d) carryover losses are probably lost because the partner will never have basis in the partnership which generated the loss.[19]

11. The terminated partnership is entitled to make a Code Sec. 754 election in its final return which applies with respect to the incoming partner.[20]

12. The new partnership is entitled to make a Code Sec. 754 election in its initial return which applies to the incoming partner.[21]

13. It is the Treasury Department's opinion that the "property deemed contributed to the new partnership will continue to be subject to the anti-churning provisions of Code Sec. 168(f)(5), which will generally require the new partnership to depreciate the property as if it were newly acquired property under the same depreciation system used by the terminated partnership."[22] However, the new partnership steps into the shoes of the terminated partnership's amortization of Code Sec. 197 assets.[23]

14. The tax basis of the assets in the hands of the new partnership is the same as the basis to the terminated partnership.[24]

15. There is no guidance on the treatment of unamortized Code Sec. 709 costs. The organization costs of the terminated partnership may be considered an interest of the new partnership.

16. Depreciation recapture under Code Secs. 1245 and 1250 is not triggered by a termination.

¶ 1303 Basis Adjustment for Partnership Property—Code Sec. 743(b) Basis Adjustments

Under an aggregate approach to partnership taxation, a partner who acquires his or her partnership interest by purchase would receive a cost

[19] Cf. *W. Sennett v. Commr.*, 80 TC 825, Dec. 40,077 (1983), aff'd, CA-9, 85-1 USTC ¶ 9153, 752 F2d 428.

[20] Reg. § 1.708-1(b)(1)(v). The basis of the assets are adjusted prior to their deemed contribution to the new partnership.

[21] Reg. § 1.761-1(e).

[22] Preamble to Prop. Reg. § 1.708-1(b), adopted by T.D. 8717, 1996-1 CB 877, 878.

[23] Code Sec. 197(f)(2)(B).

[24] Reg. § 1.708-1(b)(1)(iv), Ex. (ii).

basis in his or her share of the partnership assets. The partner's position would be similar to that of a tenant-in-common.

Under an entity approach to partnership taxation, however, the price paid by the purchasing partner affects only the partner's adjusted basis in his or her partnership interest, not the basis of his or her share of the partnership assets. A shareholder's acquisition of corporate stock is an example of the operation of the entity approach.

Prior to 1954, neither the aggregate nor the entity approach had been completely accepted by the courts, but the weight of authority came down on the side of the entity approach. The rationale for not allowing a change in the adjusted basis of the partnership assets on the transfer of a partnership interest was that the purchasing partner had not acquired an interest in the partnership property itself, but only in the partnership as an entity. Code Sec. 743(a) codified this approach.

Code Sec. 743(b), however, provides that if an election under Code Sec. 754 is in effect for the year of sale or if the partnership has a substantial built-in loss (as defined in Code Sec. 743(d)) immediately after the transfer, the entity rules of Code Sec. 743(a) give way to the modified aggregate rules of Code Sec. 743(b). In such cases, the transfer of a partnership interest will trigger a required adjustment to the basis of partnership assets. This adjustment affects the transferee partner only. The purchasing partner's treatment is similar to an acquisition of a tenancy-in-common interest in the partnership's assets.

.01 Code Sec. 743(b) Transfers

Code Sec. 743(b) is applicable only to certain transfers of partnership interests. It applies to sales, exchanges, and transfers of partnership interests upon death. It applies to any transfer considered a sale or exchange. For example, Code Sec. 743(b) applies to distributions of a partnership interest by a corporation or a partnership.[25] It does not apply to gifts or to contributions to a partnership in exchange for an interest in that partnership.

Partner dies with community property partnership interest. When property is held as community property and either the husband or wife dies, the decedent's share of the partnership interest is includable in his or her gross estate at its value on the applicable valuation date.[26] The devisee will take a tax basis for the partnership interest equal to its value plus his or her share of the partnership's debt.[27] The surviving spouse's community property portion of the partnership interest is not included in the decedent's gross estate and is not transferred to the surviving spouse by reason of the decedent's death. The surviving spouse's share of the partnership interest, however, also receives a basis equal to its value at the

[25] Code Sec. 761(e). H.R. Rep. No. 801, 98th Cong., 2d Sess., 863-865 (1984).

[26] Code Sec. 2031 or 2032.

[27] Code Secs. 1014(a), 642, and 752.

appropriate valuation date.[28] The IRS has ruled that in spite of the absence of a partnership interest being transferred, the surviving spouse's share of the assets is adjusted if the partnership has a Code Sec. 754 election in effect for the partnership year in which the decedent's death occurred.[29]

Purchase of economic rights only. With respect to a transfer of the economic rights to a partnership interest when the new owner of the economic rights is not formally admitted to the partnership, the IRS has ruled that the economic owner is the partner for tax purposes.[30] Although there is no authority directly on this point, such a transfer should qualify as a sale of a partnership interest for Code Sec. 743(b) purposes.

.02 Code Sec. 743(b) Adjustments—Overview

In order to obtain a result for the purchasing partner which is similar to the acquisition of a tenancy-in-common interest, an adjustment is computed for the acquiring partner under Code Sec. 743(b) and then allocated to the respective partnership assets under Code Sec. 755. The partnership will then compute gain, loss on disposition or depreciation, etc., with reference to the basis of its property as adjusted in this manner for the incoming partner.

The total amount of the adjustment to all the partnership property is the difference between the incoming partner's basis for his or her partnership interest and that partner's share of the adjusted basis of the partnership property at the time of purchase. If the purchasing partner's initial adjusted basis in the partnership interest is greater than his or her share of the adjusted basis of partnership assets, the total basis adjustment to the partnership assets is upward in an amount equal to the excess. Conversely, the adjustment is downward where the reverse is true. The adjustment thus results in the partner's adjusted basis in his or her partnership interest being equal to the adjusted basis of his or her share of the partnership assets. The total adjustment is then allocated among the partnership properties in accordance with rules contained in Code Sec. 755.

While the total net adjustment under Code Sec. 743(b) reflects a literal aggregate approach, the allocation of this adjustment under Code Sec. 755 does not always precisely produce this result. Accordingly, a partner's adjusted basis in specific partnership assets, derived by applying a Code Sec. 743(b) adjustment allocated to the specific assets according to the terms of Code Sec. 755, does not always equal the cost basis in the purchaser's share of specific assets that would have resulted from assuming that the acquiring partner had purchased a tenancy-in-common interest in the assets.

Code Sec. 743(b) adjustments usually affect the timing of income, sometimes affect the character of income, but rarely affect the amount of

---

[28] Code Sec. 1014(b)(6).

[29] Rev. Rul. 79-124, 1979-1 CB 224.

[30] Rev. Rul. 77-137, 1977-1 CB 178.

income ultimately reported by the purchasing partner. An upward adjustment to a partner's share of the adjusted basis of partnership assets may affect the timing of that partner's receipt of income since he or she may receive less income during partnership operations, but because the partner will then have a lower basis in his or her partnership interest the partner will be obliged to recognize more gain or less loss on the disposition of his or her partnership interest. This may be simply illustrated by the example of an upward adjustment under Code Sec. 743(b), causing an increase in the partner's share of the partnership's adjusted basis in depreciable assets. The partner concerned would accordingly be entitled to more depreciation deductions, whereas, without the adjustment, the partner would be getting the lower depreciation deductions to which the former partner was entitled. Because the partner's increased basis in depreciable assets causes him or her to have an increased share of partnership deductions, the partner reduces his or her partnership interest adjusted basis more quickly. The partner will ultimately recognize more gain or less loss when he or she sells the partnership interest than if there had been no Code Sec. 743(b) adjustment. The partner has thus deferred the recognition of income as a result of the partnership's election of Code Sec. 754.

The previous example also illustrates the effect that a Code Sec. 743(b) adjustment may have on the character of the partner's income. When the partner's share of the partnership's adjusted basis in depreciable assets is adjusted upward, the partner normally recognizes less ordinary income from partnership operations during the time he or she remains a partner. The partner does so usually at the expense of having to realize and recognize more capital gain when the partner sells his or her partnership interest. Thus, assuming Code Sec. 751(a) is not applicable, the adjustment may result in the conversion of ordinary income into capital gain.

The amount of income the partner ultimately receives is usually affected only if the partner dies before selling his or her partnership interest. In such an event, the partner's heirs may receive a "stepped-up" basis in the partnership interest under Code Sec. 1014 that is equal to the fair market value of the partnership interest at the date of the partner's death, or at the alternative valuation date plus his or her share of the partnership's debt. Nobody is required to include in income the additional amount by which the partnership interest adjusted basis would have been reduced, owing to the Code Sec. 743(b) adjustment.

.03 Partnerships with "Substantial Built-in Loss" Immediately Following Transfer of an Interest

Basis adjustments under Code Sec. 743(b) are triggered by the sale or transfer of an interest in a partnership in two circumstances:

1. The partnership makes an election under Code Sec. 754 (or has such an election in effect at the date of the transfer); or

2. The partnership has a "substantial built-in loss" immediately following the transfer.

A partnership has a substantial built-in loss if, immediately following the transfer of an interest in the partnership, the adjusted basis of partnership property exceeds by more than $250,000 the fair market value of such property.[31]

Exception for "securitization" partnerships. Code Sec. 743(f) provides that the built-in loss rules do not apply to "securitization partnerships." Thus, unless these partnerships have a Code Sec. 754 election in effect (or make one), no adjustment to the basis of partnership assets is required under Code Sec. 743(b) following the sale or transfer of a partnership interest.

A "securitization partnership" is defined as any partnership whose sole business activity "is to issue securities which provide for a fixed principal (or similar) amount and which are primarily serviced by the cash flows of a discrete pool (either fixed or revolving) of receivables or other financial assets that by their terms convert into cash in a finite period, but only if the sponsor of the pool reasonably believes that the receivables and other financial assets comprising the pool are not acquired so as to be disposed of."[32]

Special rules for electing investment partnerships. Eligible investment partnerships can elect to be treated as if they do not have substantial built-in losses following the sale or transfer of a partnership interest. If an eligible partnership so elects, it will not be required to adjust its basis in partnership property following the sale of an interest.[33] However, when the partnership subsequently disposes of depreciated securities, the transferee partner (the purchaser) will only be allowed to deduct his or her share of such losses to the extent that they exceed the loss recognized by the transferor, including any prior transferor, on the sale or transfer of the partnership interest.[34] Disallowed losses under this provision do not reduce the transferee partner's basis in his or her partnership interest.[35] These provisions apply without regard to whether or not the sale or transfer of the partnership interest results in a technical termination of the partnership under Code Sec. 708(b)(1)(B).

In computing the amount of the loss recognized by the transferor partner, and thus the amount of the transferee partner's share of subsequent partnership losses which is disallowed, Code Sec. 743(e)(5) allows adjustment for "step-downs" in basis under Code Sec. 732(a)(2) on property distributed to the transferee partner following his or her acquisition of the partnership interest. To the extent that the transferee partner's basis in property distributed to him or her by the partnership is lower than the

[31] Code Sec. 743(d).
[32] Code Sec. 743(f)(2).
[33] Code Sec. 743(e)(1).
[34] Code Sec. 743(e)(2).
[35] Code Sec. 743(e)(3).

basis of such property in the partnership's hands, the "built-in" loss associated with the earlier acquisition of the partnership interest is reduced.

> ***Example 13-2.*** GDF Partners is an investment partnership with a depreciated portfolio. *G*, a one-fifth partner, has a tax basis in his partnership interest of $250,000. He sells it to *K* for $175,000, recognizing a ($75,000) capital loss. This loss represents 20% of the partnership's $350,000 unrealized loss inherent in its investment portfolio. The partnership does not have a Code Sec. 754 election in effect, and elects under Code Sec. 743(e)(5) not to adjust its basis in its assets to reflect the loss recognized by *G*. *K* will take a $175,000 tax basis in the newly acquired partnership interest. Assume that the partnership subsequently sells securities with a tax basis of $500,000 for $300,000, recognizing a ($200,000) loss on the transaction. *K*'s 20% share of this loss is ($40,000). This loss is not deductible by *K*, and does not reduce her basis in the partnership interest.

> ***Comment.*** The limitation of Code Sec. 743(e) is applied to the transferee partner's share of the gross amount of loss recognized by the partnership on any subsequent sale of depreciated assets (to the extent of the loss previously recognized by the transferor partner on sale of the partnership interest). If the partnership sells some assets for a loss, and other assets for a gain, the transferee partner must report his or her share of the gain, but cannot deduct his or her share of the loss.[36]

Only eligible investment partnerships may make the election under Code Sec. 743(e). To be eligible, a partnership must satisfy the following criteria:

- The partnership would be an investment company under section 3(a)(1)(A) of the Investment Company Act of 1940 but for an exemption under paragraph (1) or (7) of section 3(c) of such Act;
- The partnership has never been engaged in a trade or business;
- The partnership holds substantially all of its assets for investment;
- At least 95 percent of the assets contributed to such partnership consist of money;
- No assets contributed to such partnership had an adjusted basis in excess of fair market value at the time of contribution;
- All partnership interests of such partnership are issued by such partnership pursuant to a private offering before the date

[36] Code Sec. 743(e)(2).

which is 24 months after the date of the first capital contribution to such partnership;

- The partnership agreement of such partnership has substantive restrictions on each partner's ability to cause a redemption of the partner's interest; and
- The partnership agreement of such partnership provides for a term that is not in excess of 15 years.

Once made, an election under Code Sec. 743(e) is irrevocable except with the consent of the Secretary.

.04 Partnerships Without Substantial Built-in Losses

If the partnership does not have a substantial built-in loss immediately after the sale or transfer of a partnership interest, no basis adjustment is required or allowed unless the partnership has a Code Sec. 754 election in effect or chooses to make one effective for the year of the transfer.

It is important to note that both basis adjustments required by Code Sec. 743(b) and Code Sec. 734(b) are activated by a single Code Sec. 754 election, and that the taxpayer cannot limit his or her election to one section or the other.[37]

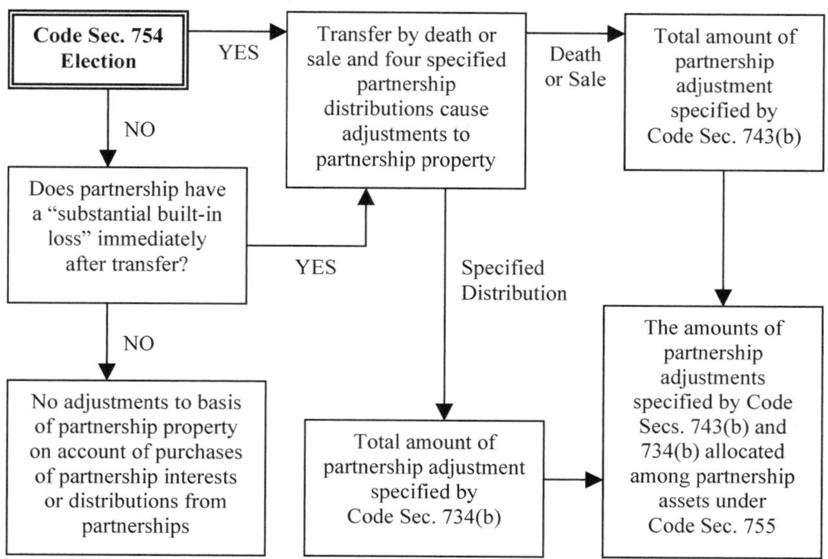

> ***Comment.*** The election can only be made in a year in which a Code Sec. 743(b) transfer or a Code Sec. 734(b) distribution is made.

[37] Code Sec. 734(b) adjustments are discussed in Chapter 16.

The election cannot be made in contemplation of such a transfer or distribution in a future year.[38]

Making the election. The election is made by attaching a statement to the partnership's Form 1065, U.S. Partnership Return of Income, declaring a Code Sec. 754 election which includes the partnership's name, address and taxpayer identification number and is signed by any partner.[39] The election applies to all sales, exchanges, transfers upon death, and the four distributions listed in Code Sec. 734(b) until it is terminated. Since it is the partnership that makes the election, any purchasing partner, in order to ensure the benefits of the Code Sec. 743(b) adjustment, should have the partnership amend its partnership agreement to include an obligation to make such an election. It may be prudent to require the partnership to allow the affected partner to mail the partnership's Form 1065 after inspecting the election and getting a power of attorney to make the election on behalf of the partnership if it is not properly executed. However, the other partners should obtain an agreement on the part of the new partner to bear any additional accounting expenses.

> ***Observation.*** This could provide for some lively negotiation as the new partner may then be obligated to pay the extra expenses to account for all future Code Sec. 743(b) and 734(b) adjustments. This is because future adjustments are required for most transfers of partnership interests and some distributions. When a Code Sec. 754 election is the result of the demands of an incoming partner, that partner is the cause of all future adjustments the partnership is required to make. A new incoming partner may not be willing to accept responsibility for paying for the partnership's accounting for the new adjustments required by his or her purchase. This would be especially true if the adjustment is negative or immaterial in amount. Of course, the continuing partners receive no tax benefit or detriment derived from a Code Sec. 743(b) adjustment. It may be a reasonable compromise to require that the incoming partner who initiates the Code Sec. 754 election pay for the accounting for his adjustment, negative adjustments and *de minimis* adjustments.

Deadline for election. As to the timing of the Code Sec. 754 election, the regulations require that it be made with a "timely return for the taxable year during which the distribution or transfer occurs."[40] This is interpreted to include extensions. An application for revocation of an election must be filed no later than 30 days after the close of the partnership's taxable year with respect to which the election is intended to take effect.

The IRS has the general power to grant an extension beyond the deadline for filing elections when:[41]

---

[38] Reg. § 1.754-1(b)(1).
[39] Reg. § 1.754-1(b).
[40] Reg. § 1.754-1(b)(1).
[41] Reg. § 301.9100-1(a).

- The filing deadline is not expressly provided by statute;[42]
- The request for extension is filed before the time fixed by regulations or within such time after the time fixed by regulations that the IRS considers reasonable under the circumstances;[43] and
- It is shown to the IRS's satisfaction that granting the extension would not jeopardize the interests of the government.[44]

The factors which the IRS will take into account in whether to grant an extension of time to make the Code Sec. 754 election include:[45]

- The taxpayer's due diligence despite missing the election's due date.
- Prompt action once the error is discovered.
- The taxpayer's showing of an intent to have made the election.
- No prejudice to the interests of the Treasury.

The time for filing the basis adjustment election qualifies for an automatic 12-month extension if the proper procedure is followed and all affected taxpayers report their income (in an original or amended tax return) consistent with the results if a timely election had been made.[46] Any filing that must be made to obtain an automatic extension must provide the following statement at the top of the document: "FILED PURSUANT TO REV. PROC. 92-85." No request for a private letter ruling is required to obtain the extension. Accordingly, taxpayers don't have to pay user fees.[47]

Permission to make the election may be granted even after the partnership terminates under Code Sec. 708. Thus, where an equal partner of a two-man partnership died on January 1, and no election was filed on the partnership's return for the year ending on December 31 of the same year, the election could be filed for the January 1 transfer, even though the estate of the deceased partner sold its interest to the other partner, thereby terminating the partnership.[48]

Revoking the election. An application for revocation of a Code Sec. 754 election must, as previously stated, be filed no later than 30 days after the close of the partnership's taxable year with respect to which the election is intended to take effect. The approval of a District Director of the IRS is needed for a revocation of the Code Sec. 754 election.[49] The regulations suggest the following acceptable reasons for revocation:

[42] Reg. § 301.9100-1(a)(1).
[43] Reg. § 301.9100-1(a)(2).
[44] Reg. § 301.9100-1(a)(3).
[45] Rev. Proc. 79-63, 1979-2 CB 578.
[46] Rev. Proc. 92-85, Appendix A, 1992-2 CB 490, amended by Rev. Proc. 93-28, 1993-1 CB 344.
[47] Rev. Proc. 92-85, § 4.03, 1992-2 CB 490.
[48] Rev. Rul. 86-139, 1986-2 CB 95.
[49] Reg. § 1.754-1(c).

1. A change in the nature of partnership trade or business.
2. A substantial increase in assets.
3. A change in the nature of assets.
4. An increasing administrative burden.

A potential decrease in the basis of partnership assets, owing to the effect of the Code Sec. 754 election, is not a sufficient reason for permission for a revocation to be granted.

Termination of the partnership under Code Sec. 708 eliminates the election since there is then a new partnership which is separate and distinct for tax purposes from the partnership that made the election.

In light of the nature of the Code Sec. 743 and 734 adjustments, it is important, before the election is made, to consider the cost of accounting for the adjustment and the possibility that the continued existence of a Code Sec. 754 election may require a future downward adjustment in basis. Furthermore, record keeping problems can be significant.

.05 Code Sec. 743(b) Adjustments for Sales of Partnership Interests After December 14, 1999

Total amount of Code Sec. 743(b) adjustment. The total basis adjustment which must be made by the partnership equals the initial adjusted basis [50] of the incoming partner's interest in the partnership less that partner's proportionate share of the adjusted basis to the partnership of the partnership's property.[51]

The incoming partner's share of the adjusted basis to the partnership of partnership property is equal to the sum of that partner's interest as a partner in the partnership's previously taxed capital, plus his or her share of partnership liabilities. Generally, an incoming partner's interest in the partnership's previously taxed capital [52] is equal to:

1. The amount of cash that the incoming partner would receive on a liquidation of the partnership following the disposition of the partnership of all its assets immediately after the transfer of the partnership interest in a fully taxable transaction for cash equal to the fair market value of the assets. The regulations refer to this deemed asset sale followed by a liquidation as "the hypothetical transaction;"[53] increased by
2. The amount of tax loss [54] that would be allocated to the transferee from the hypothetical transaction; or decreased by

[50] Determined by applying the rules of Code Sec. 742.

[51] Reg. § 1.743-1(b).

[52] To the extent attributable to the acquired partnership interest.

[53] Reg. § 1.743-1(d)(2).

[54] Including any remedial allocations under Reg. § 1.704-3(d).

3. The amount of tax gain[55] that would be allocated to the transferee from the hypothetical transaction.

Example 13-3. *A* is a member of the ABC Partnership in which the partners have equal interests in capital and profits. The partnership has made an election under Code Sec. 754. *A* sells her interest to *T* for $22,000. The balance sheet of the partnership at the date of sale shows the following:

Assets	*Adjusted Basis*	*FMV*
Cash	$5,000	$5,000
Accounts receivable	10,000	10,000
Inventory	20,000	21,000
Depreciable assets	20,000	40,000
Total	*$55,000*	*$76,000*
Liabilities and Capital		
Liabilities	$10,000	$10,000
Capital		
A	15,000	22,000
B	15,000	22,000
C	15,000	22,000
Total	*$55,000*	*$76,000*

The amount of the basis adjustment under Code Sec. 743(b) is the difference between the basis of *T*'s interest in the partnership and *T*'s share of the adjusted basis to the partnership of the partnership's property. Under Code Sec. 742, assume the basis of *T*'s interest is $25,333.[56] *T*'s interest in the partnership's previously taxed capital is $15,000, calculated as follows.

ABT Liquidation Schedule

Cash received from sale of partnership assets	$76,000	
Less liabilities paid	(10,000)	
Partnership cash remaining	*$66,000*	
Cash paid to *T*		$22,000

T's Gain from Liquidation

Amount realized from deemed sale of assets	$76,000	
Adjusted basis	(55,000)	
Partnership gain	*$21,000*	
Gain to *T*		(7,000)
T's interest in previously taxed capital		*$15,000*

T's share of the adjusted basis to the partnership of the partnership's property is $18,333.

T's share of previously taxed capital	$15,000
T's share of partnership liabilities	3,333
T's share of the partnership's basis in its property	*$18,333*

[55] *Id.*

[56] $22,000 (cash paid by income Partner *T* to outgoing Partner *A*) plus $3,333 (Partner *T*'s share of partnership liabilities).

The amount of the basis adjustment under Code Sec. 743(b) to partnership property, therefore, is $7,000. Note that this is also equal to the gain recognized by partner *A* on the sale.

T's basis in his partnership interest	$25,333
T's share of the adjusted basis of the partnership property	(18,333)
T's total Code Sec. 743(b) adjustment	*$7,000*

Example 13-4. *S*, *B*, and *C* form the SBC Partnership, to which *S* contributes land with a fair market value of $1,000 and an adjusted basis to *S* of $400, and *B* and *C* each contribute $1,000 cash. Each partner has $1,000 credited to him on the books of the partnership as his capital contribution. The partners share in profits equally.

The SBC Partnership has the following initial balance sheets:

Assets	***Basis***	***FMV***
Cash	$2,000	$2,000
Land	400	1,000
	$2,400	*$3,000*
Liabilities	$ 0	$ 0
Capital		
S	$400	$1,000
B	1,000	1,000
C	1,000	1,000
Total	*$2,400*	*$3,000*

During the partnership's first taxable year, the land appreciates in value to $1,300. *S* sells her one-third interest in the partnership to *P* for $1,100 when an election under Code Sec. 754 is in effect. The amount of tax gain that would be allocated to *S* from a cash sale of the partnership's assets is $700 ($600 Code Sec. 704(c) built-in gain plus one-third of the additional gain). Thus, *P*'s interest in the partnership's previously taxed capital is $400 ($1,100, the amount of cash *P* would receive if ABC liquidated immediately after the cash sale of its assets, decreased by $700, *P*'s share of gain from a cash sale of the partnership's assets). The amount of *P*'s basis adjustment under Code Sec. 743(b) to partnership property is $700 (the excess of $1,100, *P*'s cost basis for the interest, over $400, *P*'s share of the adjusted basis to the partnership of partnership property).

PBC Liquidation Schedule

Cash received from sale of partnership assets	$3,300	
Less liabilities paid	0	
Partnership cash remaining	*$3,300*	
Cash paid to *P*		$1,100

P's Gain from Liquidation

Amount realized from deemed sale of assets .	$3,300	
Adjusted basis	2,400	
Partnership gain	*$1,300*	
Gain to *P* [1/3 ($300) + $600]		(700)
P's interest in previously taxed capital		*$400*
Plus *P*'s share of partnership liabilities		0
P's share of the partnership's basis in its property		*$400*

P's Code Sec. 743(b) Basis Adjustment

P's basis in his partnership interest	$1,100
P's share of the partnership's basis in its property	(400)
P's total Code Sec. 743(b) adjustment	*$700*

Where there has been more than one transfer of a partnership interest, a transferee's basis adjustment is determined without regard to any prior transferee's basis adjustment. In the case of a gift of an interest in a partnership, the donor is treated as transferring, and the donee as receiving, that portion of the basis adjustment attributable to the gifted partnership interest.

Example 13-5. *A*, *B*, and *C* form the ABC Partnership. *A* and *B* each contribute $1,000 cash, and *C* contributes land with a basis and fair market value of $1,000.

The ABC Partnership has the following initial balance sheet:

Assets	***Basis***	***FMV***
Cash.	$2,000	$2,000
Land	1,000	1,000
	$3,000	*$3,000*
Liabilities	$ 0	$ 0
Capital		
A	1,000	1,000
B	1,000	1,000
C	1,000	1,000
Total	*$3,000*	*$3,000*

When the land has appreciated in value to $1,300, *C* sells her interest to *D* for $1,100 (one-third of $3,300, the fair market value of the partnership property). An election under Code Sec. 754 is in effect; therefore, *D* has a basis adjustment under Code Sec. 743(b) of $100.

After the land has further appreciated in value to $1,600, *D* sells his interest to *E* for $1,200 (one-third of $3,600, the fair market value of the partnership property). *E* has a basis adjustment under Code Sec. 743(b) of $200. This amount is determined without regard to any basis adjustment under Code Sec. 743(b) that *D* may have had in the partnership assets.

During the following year, *E* makes a gift to *F* of 50% of *E*'s interest in ABC. At the time of the transfer, *E* has a $200 basis adjustment under Code Sec. 743(b). *E* is treated as transferring $100 of the basis adjustment to *F* with the gift of the partnership interest.

Allocating the Code Sec. 743(b) adjustment between Code Sec. 1221/1231 assets and ordinary income assets. The total basis adjustment determined under Code Sec. 743(b) is allocated among the partnership assets under Code Sec. 755. The regulations, effective for transfers of partnership interests on or after December 15, 1999, first allocate the total Code Sec. 743(b) adjustment between the two classes of property described in Code Sec. 755(b). These classes of partnership property are:[57]

1. Capital gain property;[58] and
2. Ordinary income property.[59]

The basis adjustment allocated to each class is then allocated among the items within each class. The portion of the basis adjustment allocated to ordinary income property would be equal to the total income, gain and loss (including remedial allocations) that would be allocated to the transferee upon the sale of the partnership's ordinary income property if the partnership sold all its assets in a fully taxable transaction.[60] The basis adjustment to capital gain property is equal to the total adjustment less the amount allocated to ordinary income property. If the basis adjustment to capital gain property is a decrease, it cannot exceed the partnership's basis [61] in capital gain property.[62] Any excess is applied to reduce the basis of ordinary income property. This allocation method has the effect of treating the capital asset class as the spillover category that absorbs basis adjustments required for a purchase price of a partnership interest greater or less than the purchaser's share of the value of the assets.

Example 13-6. *A* and *B* form equal AB Partnership. *A* and *B* each contribute $1,000 cash which the partnership uses to purchase land and a building which are Code Sec. 1231 assets and wine and cheese which are inventory assets. After one year, *A* sells its partnership interest to *T* for $1,000. *T*'s basis adjustment under Code Sec. 743(b) is zero.

Immediately after the transfer of the partnership interest to *T*, the adjusted basis and fair market value of AB Partnership's assets are as follows:

---

[57] Reg. § 1.755-1(a).

[58] Capital assets and Code Sec. 1231(b) property.

[59] All property which is not capital gain property or Code Sec. 1231(b) property. Unrealized receivables as defined by Code Sec. 751(c) are considered separate ordinary income property. For this purpose, depreciation recapture under Code Secs. 1245 and 1250 is considered to be a zero basis unrealized receivable with a value equal to the built-in gain.

[60] Reg. § 1.755-1(b)(2). The regulations refer to this deemed sale of all partnership assets as the "hypothetical transaction." Reg. § 1.755-1(b)(1)(ii).

[61] Or in the case of property subject to the remedial allocation method, the transferee's share of any remedial loss from the hypothetical transaction under Reg. § 1.704-3(d).

[62] Reg. § 1.755-1(b)(2)(i).

Assets	Adjusted Basis	FMV	*Built-in* Gain/ (Loss)	*T*'s Share of Gain/ (Loss)
Capital Gain Property:				
Building	$500	$750	$250	$125
Land	500	500	0	0
	$1,000	*$1,250*	*$250*	*$125*
Ordinary Income Property:				
Wine	$500	$250	$(250)	$(125)
Cheese	500	500	0	0
	$1,000	*$750*	*$(250)*	*$(125)*
Total	*$2,000*	*$2,000*	*$ 0*	*$ 0*

If, immediately after the transfer of the partnership interest to *T*, the ABC Partnership sold all of its assets in a fully taxable transaction at fair market value, *T* would be allocated a loss of $125 from the sale of the ordinary income property. Thus, the amount of the basis adjustment to ordinary income property is $(125). The amount of the basis adjustment to capital gain property is $125 (zero, the amount of the basis adjustment under Code Sec. 743(b), less $(125), amount of the basis adjustment allocated to ordinary income property).

Allocating the adjustment among ordinary income assets. Among ordinary income assets, the amount of the basis adjustment to each item of property within the class of ordinary income property is equal to:[63]

1. The amount of income, gain or loss (including any remedial allocations) [64] that would be allocated to the transferee from the hypothetical sale of the item; reduced by

2. The product of:

   a. Any decrease to the amount of the basis adjustment to ordinary income property because a negative adjustment allocated to capital assets exceeds their basis;

   b. A fraction, the numerator of which is the fair market value of the item of property to the partnership and the denominator of which is the total fair market value of all the partnership's items of ordinary income property.[65]

Within the class of ordinary income property, the basis of the purchaser's share of each property is therefore generally equal to its fair market value. However, this basis adjustment to fair market value may be reduced by negative adjustments to capital gain property exceeding the basis of the capital gain property. These negative amounts are "allocated back" to the ordinary income class and allocated based upon relative values as indicated in adjustment (2) immediately above.

[63] To the extent attributable to the acquired partnership interest.

[64] Reg. § 1.704-3(d).

[65] Reg. § 1.755-1(b)(3)(i).

Allocating the adjustment among Code Sec. 1221/1231 assets. The amount of the basis adjustment to each item of property within the class of capital gain property is equal to:[66]

1. The amount of income, gain, or loss (including any remedial allocations)[67] that would be allocated to the transferee from the hypothetical sale of the item; reduced by

2. The product of:

   a. The total amount of gain or loss (including any remedial allocations)[68] that would be allocated to the transferee from the hypothetical sale of all items of capital gain property, minus the amount of the positive basis adjustment to all items of capital gain property, or plus the amount of the negative basis adjustment to capital gain property; multiplied by

   b. A fraction, the numerator of which is the fair market value of the item of property to the partnership, and the denominator of which is the fair market value of all of the partnership's items of capital gain property.[69]

Example 13-7. *A* and *B* form equal AB Partnership. *A* contributes $50,000 cash and Blackacre, a capital asset with a fair market value of $50,000 and an adjusted tax basis of $25,000. *B* contributes $100,000. The AB Partnership uses the cash to purchase Whiteacre, which is a capital asset, and wine and cheese, which are inventory assets. After a year, *A* sells her interest in the AB Partnership to *T* for $120,000. At the time of the transfer, *A*'s share of the partnership's basis in partnership assets is $75,000. Therefore, *T* receives a $45,000 basis adjustment.

Immediately after the transfer of the partnership interest to *T*, the adjusted basis and fair market value of the AB Partnership's assets are as follows:

Assets	Adjusted Basis	FMV	*Built-in* Gain/ (Loss)	*T's* Share of Gain/ (Loss)
Capital Gain Property:				
Blackacre	$25,000	$75,000	$50,000	$37,500[70]
Whiteacre	100,000	117,500	17,500	8,750
	$125,000	*$192,500*	*$67,500*	*$46,250*
Ordinary Income Property:				
Wine	$40,000	$45,000	$5,000	$2,500
Cheese	10,000	2,500	(7,500)	(3,750)
	$50,000	*$47,500*	*$2,500*	*($1,250)*
Total	*$175,000*	*$240,000*	*$65,000*	*$45,000*

[66] To the extent attributable to the acquired partnership interest.
[67] Reg. § 1.704-3(d).
[68] *Id.*
[69] Reg. § 1.755-1(b)(3)(ii).
[70] $25,000 + $12,500.

Allocating the $45,000 Code Sec. 743(b) Adjustment Between Classes of Partnership Property—Hypothetical Transaction[71]

Ordinary Income Assets:		
Wine		
Amount Realized	$45,000	
Adjusted basis	(40,000)	
Gain		*$5,000*
Cheese		
Amount Realized	$2,500	
Adjusted Basis	(10,000)	
Loss		*$(7,500)*
Net loss from sale of the ordinary income property		*$(2,500)*
T's share of ordinary loss (50%)		$(1,250)
Capital Gain Property:		
Blackacre		
Amount Realized	$75,000	
Adjusted basis	(25,000)	
Gain		*$50,000*
Whiteacre		
Amount Realized	$117,500	
Adjusted Basis	(100,000)	
Gain		*$17,500*
Net gain from sale of the capital gain property		*$67,500*
T's share of Code Sec. 704(c) built-in gain		$25,000
Fifty percent of the remainder [50% × ($67,500 − $25,000)]		21,250
T's share of capital gain		*$46,250*

The amount of the basis adjustment that is allocated to ordinary income property is equal to $(1,250) (the amount of the loss allocated to *T* from the hypothetical sale of the ordinary income property).

The amount of the basis adjustment that is allocated to capital gain property is equal to $46,250 (the amount of the basis adjustment, $45,000, less $(1,250), the amount of loss allocated to *T* from the hypothetical sale of the ordinary income property).

Example 13-8. Assume the same facts as Example 13-7 above. Of the $45,000 basis adjustment, $46,250 was allocated to capital gain property. The amount allocated to ordinary income property was $(1,250).

Blackacre is a capital gain asset, and *T* would be allocated $37,500 from the sale of land in the hypothetical transaction. Therefore, the amount of the adjustment to land is $37,500.

[71] Deemed fair market value sale of all partnership assets.

Whiteacre is a capital gain asset, and *T* would be allocated $8,750 from the sale of Whiteacre in the hypothetical transaction. Therefore, the amount of the adjustment to Whiteacre is $8,750.

The wine is ordinary income property, and *T* would be allocated $2,500 from the sale of the wine in the hypothetical transaction. Therefore, the amount of the adjustment to the wine is $2,500.

The cheese is ordinary income property, and *T* would be allocated $(3,750) from the sale of the cheese in the hypothetical transaction. Therefore, the amount of the adjustment to the cheese is $(3,750).

Example 13-9. Assume the same facts as Example 13-8 above, except that *A* sold her interest in the AB Partnership to *T* for $110,000 rather than $120,000. *T*, therefore, receives a basis adjustment under Code Sec. 743(b) of $35,000, rather than $45,000. Of the $35,000 basis adjustment, $(1,250) is allocated to ordinary income property, and $36,250 is allocated to capital gain property.

The wine is ordinary income property, and *T* would be allocated $2,500 from the sale of the wine in the hypothetical transaction. Therefore, the amount of the adjustment to the wine is $2,500.

The cheese is ordinary income property, and *T* would be allocated $(3,750) from the sale of the cheese in the hypothetical transaction. Therefore, the amount of the adjustment to the cheese is $(3,750).

Blackacre is a capital gain asset, and *T* would be allocated $37,500 from the sale of Blackacre in the hypothetical transaction. Whiteacre is a capital gain asset, and *T* would be allocated $8,750 from the sale of Whiteacre in the hypothetical transaction. The total amount of gain that would be allocated to *T* from the sale of the capital gain assets in the hypothetical transaction is $46,250, which exceeds the amount of the basis adjustment allocated to capital gain property by $10,000. The amount of the adjustment to Blackacre is $33,604 ($37,500 – ($10,000 × $75,000/$192,500)). The amount of the basis adjustment to Whiteacre is $2,646 ($8,750 – ($10,000 × $117,500/$192,500)).

The AB Partnership allocates the total Code Sec. 743(b) adjustments of $37,500 to all capital gain property among this class as follows:

	To Blackacre
$37,500	Partner *T*'s share of Blackacre's built-in gain before the adjustment
(3,896)	[$10,000 × $75,000 ÷ $192,500]*
$33,602	Adjustment to Blackacre

* *The total gain built into all capital gain property after the adjustment ($10,000), multiplied by the value of Blackacre ($75,000) divided by the value of all capital gain property ($192,500).*

To Whiteacre

$8,750	Partner *T*'s share of Whiteacre's gain before the adjustment
(6,104)	[$10,000 × $117,500 ÷ $192,500]**
$2,646	Adjustment to Whiteacre

** *The total gain built into all capital gain property after the adjustment ($10,000), multiplied by the value of Whiteacre ($117,500) divided by the value of all capital gain property ($192,500).*

Effect of assets on the adjustment's allocation. Where a partnership interest is transferred as a result of the death of a partner, under Code Sec. 1014(c) the transferee's basis in its partnership interest is not adjusted for that portion of the interest, if any, which is attributable to items representing income in respect of a decedent under Code Sec. 691.[72] If a partnership interest is transferred as a result of the death of a partner, and the partnership holds assets representing income in respect of a decedent, no part of the basis adjustment under Code Sec. 743(b) is allocated to these assets.[73]

Example 13-10. *A* and *B* are equal partners in personal service AB Partnership. As a result of *B*'s death, *B*'s partnership interest is transferred to *T* when the AB Partnership's balance sheet (reflecting a cash receipts and disbursements method of accounting) is as follows:

Assets	***Basis***	***FMV***
Capital Asset	$2,000	$5,000
Unrealized Receivables	0	15,000
	$2,000	*$20,000*
Capital		
A	$1,000	$10,000
B	1,000	10,000
	$2,000	*$20,000*

None of the assets owned by the AB Partnership is Code Sec. 704(c) property, and the capital asset is nondepreciable. The fair market value of *T*'s partnership interest on the applicable date of valuation set forth in Code Sec. 1014 is $10,000. Of this amount, $2,500 is attributable to *T*'s 50% share of the partnership's capital asset, and $7,500 is attributable to *T*'s 50% share of the partnership's unrealized receivables. The partnership's unrealized receivables represent income in respect of a decedent. Accordingly, under Code Sec. 1014(c), *T*'s basis in its partnership interest is not adjusted for that portion of the interest which is attributable to the unrealized receivables. Therefore, *T*'s basis in her partnership interest is $2,500.

---

[72] Reg. § 1.742-1.

[73] See Reg. § 1.743-1(b).

At the time of the transfer, *B*'s share of the partnership's basis in partnership assets is $1,000. Accordingly, *T* receives a $1,500 basis adjustment under Code Sec. 743(b). The entire basis adjustment is allocated to the partnership's capital asset.

Special rules for miscellaneous transfers. Special rules apply to the allocation of Code Sec. 743(b) adjustments resulting from transferred basis exchanges, such as partnership interests contributed to corporations and other partnerships.[74] The special rules generally are modeled on the rules for allocating basis adjustments under Code Sec. 734(b). The regulations do not contain a specific anti-abuse rule regarding the special basis allocation rules which are applicable to such transfers. However, there may be situations where taxpayers will attempt to undertake abusive transactions using these special rules. For instance, a partner could acquire a partnership interest during a year in which no Code Sec. 754 election is in effect, and then (in a related transaction) contribute the property to a wholly-owned corporation in order to take advantage of the basis allocation rules applicable to transferred basis exchanges. In appropriate situations, the IRS may attack such abusive transactions under a variety of judicial doctrines, including substance over form or step transactions, or under Reg. § 1.701-2.

Effects of Code Sec. 743(b) adjustments. The basis adjustment constitutes an adjustment to the basis of partnership property with respect to the transferee only. No adjustment is made to the common basis of partnership property. Thus, for purposes of calculating income, deduction, gain, and loss, the transferee will have a special basis for those partnership properties, the bases of which are adjusted under Code Sec. 743(b). The adjustment to the basis of partnership property under Code Sec. 743(b) has no effect on the partnership's computation of any partnership item under Code Sec. 703.

The partnership first computes its partnership items of income, deduction, gain or loss at the partnership level under Code Sec. 703. It then allocates these items among the partners, including the transferee, in accordance with Code Sec. 704, and adjusts the partners' capital accounts accordingly. The partnership then adjusts the transferee's distributive share of the items of partnership income, deduction, gain, or loss to reflect the effects of the transferee's basis adjustment under Code Sec. 743(b). These adjustments to the transferee's distributive shares must be reflected on Schedules K and K-1 of the partnership tax return (Form 1065, U.S. Partnership Return of Income). These adjustments to the transferee's distributive shares do not affect the transferee's book capital [75] account.[76]

[74] Reg. § 1.755-1(b)(5).

[75] For this purpose, book capital accounts are those maintained under Reg. § 1.704-1(b)(2)(iv).

[76] Reg. § 1.743-1(j)(2). See also Reg. § 1.704-1(b)(2)(iv)(*m*)(*2*).

Comment. The Code Sec. 743 regulations state that the Code Sec. 743(b) adjustments "do not affect the transferee's capital account."[77] This is consistent with the Code Sec. 704 regulations,[78] and presumably refers to a book and not tax basis balance sheet.

Sale of property with Code Sec. 743(b) basis adjustment. The amount of a transferee's income, gain, or loss from the sale or exchange of a partnership asset in which the transferee has a basis adjustment is equal to:

- The transferee's share of the partnership's common gain or loss from the sale of the asset;[79]
- Minus the amount of the transferee's positive basis adjustment for the partnership asset (determined by taking into account the recovery of the basis adjustment); or
- Plus the amount of the transferee's negative basis adjustment for the partnership asset.[80]

Example 13-11. *Negative Code Sec. 743(b) adjustments—Code Sec. 704(c) property sold for a tax loss. A* and *B* form the equal AB Partnership. *A* contributes nondepreciable property with a fair market value of $50 and an adjusted tax basis of $100. The AB Partnership will use the traditional allocation method under Reg. § 1.704-3(b). *B* contributes $50 cash.

Assets	***Basis***	***FMV***
Cash	$50	$50
Property	100	50
	$150	*$100*
Liabilities	$ 0	$ 0
Capital		
A	100	50
B	50	50
	$150	*$100*

A sells his interest to *T* for $50. The AB Partnership has an election in effect to adjust the basis of partnership property under Code Sec. 754. *T* receives a negative $50 basis adjustment under Code Sec. 743(b) that, under Code Sec. 755, is allocated to the nondepreciable property. The AB Partnership then sells the property for $60. The AB Partnership recognizes a book gain of $10 (allocated equally between *T* and *B*) and a tax loss of $40. Because Partner *T* steps into the shoes of Partner *A* who contributed the built-in loss property, Partner *T* will receive an allocation of $40 of tax loss under the

[77] Reg. § 1.743-1(j)(2) (last sentence).

[78] Reg. § 1.704-1(b)(2)(iv)(*m*)(*2*).

[79] Including any remedial allocations under Reg. § 1.704-3(d).

[80] Determined by taking into the account the recovery of the basis adjustment under Reg. § 1.743-1(j)(4)(ii)(B).

principles of Code Sec. 704(c). However, because *T* has a negative $50 basis adjustment in the nondepreciable property, *T* recognizes a $10 gain from the sale of the partnership's property. The calculations are as follows:

Partnership's Gain on Sale of Property

	Tax	*Book*
Amount realized	$60	$60
Adjusted basis	(100)	(50)
The AB Partnership's Gain/(Loss)	*$(40)*	*$10*
Partner T*'s share of tax loss:*		
Before Code Sec. 743(b) adjustment	$40	
Code Sec. 743(b) adjustment	(50)	
Partner *T*'s recognized Gain/(Loss)	*$10*	

Comment. It may at first appear unfair that Partner *T* in the previous example reports a $10 gain. Partner *T* is a 50% owner and the property has increased $10 in value to $60 since *T*'s purchase of a half interest. One might expect that Partner *T*'s share of the taxable gain is $5, which is equal to 50% of the book gain. Presumably, Partner *B*'s taxable gain is $5. Therefore, a net $15 gain is generated by a sale that would have produced a net $40 loss if *A* had not sold his partnership interest to *T*. Recall, however, that the selling partner, *A*, has already recognized a $50 loss related to this share of the property which ultimately was sold for a $40 overall loss. In effect, *T* is also taking into income *A*'s over-reported $10 loss.

Example 13-12. *Positive Code Sec. 743(b) adjustments—Code Sec. 704(c) property sold for a tax gain.* *A* and *B* form the equal AB Partnership. *A* contributes nondepreciable property with a fair market value of $100 and an adjusted tax basis of $50. *B* contributes $100 cash. The AB Partnership will use the traditional allocation method under Reg. § 1.704-3(b).

Assets	***Basis***	***FMV***
Cash	$100	$100
Property	50	100
	$150	*$200*
Liabilities	$ 0	$ 0
Capital		
A	100	100
B	50	100
	$150	*$200*

A sells his interest to *T* for $100. The AB Partnership has an election in effect to adjust the basis of partnership property under Code Sec. 754. Therefore, *T* receives a $50 basis adjustment under Code Sec. 743(b) that, under Code Sec. 755, is allocated to the nondepreciable property. The AB Partnership then sells the nondepreciable property for $90. The AB Partnership recognizes a book loss of $10 (allocated equally between *T* and *B*) and a tax gain of $40. Because Partner *T* steps into the shoes of Partner *A* who contributed the built-in gain property, Partner *T* will receive an allocation of the entire $40 of tax gain under the principles of Code Sec. 704(c). However, because *T* has a $50 basis adjustment in the property, *T* recognizes a $10 loss from the partnership's sale of the property.

Gain on Sale of Property

	Tax	***Book***
Amount realized	$90	$90
Adjusted basis	(50)	(100)
The AB Partnership's Gain/(Loss)	*$(40)*	*$10*
Partner T*'s share of tax loss:*		
Before Code Sec. 743(b) adjustment	$40	
Code Sec. 743(b) adjustment	(50)	
Partner *T*'s Gain/(Loss)	*$(10)*	

Example 13-13. *Negative Code Sec. 743(b) adjustment and Code Sec. 704(c) property sold for a tax loss.* *A* and *B* form the equal AB Partnership. The AB Partnership will make allocations under Code Sec. 704(c) using the remedial allocation method.[81] *A* contributes nondepreciable property with a fair market value of $100 and an adjusted tax basis of $150. *B* contributes $100 cash.

Assets	***Basis***	***FMV***
Cash	$100	$100
Property	150	100
	$250	*$200*
Liabilities	$ 0	$ 0
Capital		
A	150	100
B	100	100
	$250	*$200*

A sells his partnership interest to *T* for $100. The AB Partnership has an election in effect to adjust the basis of partnership property under Code Sec. 754. *T* receives a negative $50 basis adjustment under Code Sec. 743(b) that, under Code Sec. 755, is allocated to the property. The partnership then sells the property for $120. The partnership recognizes a $20 book gain and a $30 tax loss. The book gain will be allocated equally between the partners. The entire $30 tax loss will be allocated to *T* under the principles of Code Sec. 704(c) because Partner *T* steps into the shoes of Partner *A* who contributed the built-in loss property. To match his $10 share of book gain, *B* will be

[81] Described in Reg. § 1.704-3(d).

allocated $10 of remedial gain, and *T* will be allocated an offsetting $10 of remedial loss. *T* was allocated a total of $40 of tax loss with respect to the property. However, because *T* has a negative $50 basis adjustment to the property, *T* recognizes a $10 gain from the partnership's sale of the property.

Gain on Sale of Property

	Tax	*Book*
Amount realized	$120	$120
Adjusted basis	(150)	(100)
The AB Partnership's Gain/(Loss)	$*(30)*	$*20*
Partner T*'s share of tax loss:*	$(30)	
Remedial Allocation	(10)	
Code Sec. 743(b) adjustment	50	
Partner *T*'s Gain/(Loss)	$*10*	

The amount of any positive basis adjustment that is recovered by the transferee in any year is added to the transferee's distributive share of the partnership's depreciation or amortization deductions for the year. The basis adjustment is adjusted under Code Sec. 1016(a)(2) to reflect depreciation or other cost recovery.

Depreciation of Code Sec. 743(b) adjustments. With one exception for purposes of depreciation, if the basis of a partnership's recovery property is increased as a result of the transfer of a partnership interest, then the increased portion of the basis is taken into account as if it were newly-purchased recovery property placed in service when the transfer occurs. Consequently, any applicable recovery period and method may be used to determine the recovery allowance with respect to the increased portion of the basis. However, no change is made for purposes of determining the recovery allowance under Code Sec. 168 for the portion of the basis for which there is no increase.[82]

The one exception to the described rule above applies when a partnership elects to use the remedial allocation method [83] with respect to an item of the partnership's recovery property; in such cases, the portion of any increase in the basis of the item of the partnership's recovery property under Code Sec. 743(b) that is attributable to Code Sec. 704(c) built-in gain is recovered over the remaining recovery period for the partnership's excess book basis in the property.[84] Any remaining portion of the basis increase is recovered as described above.

Example 13-14. *A, B,* and *C* are equal partners in the ABC Partnership, which owns equipment, an item of depreciable property that has a fair market value in excess of its adjusted tax basis. *C* sells her interest in the ABC Partnership to *T* while the ABC Partnership

[82] Reg. § 1.743-1(j)(4)(i).

[83] Reg. § 1.704-3(d).

[84] Determined in the final sentence of Reg. § 1.704-3(d)(2).

has an election in effect under Code Sec. 754. The ABC Partnership, therefore, increases the basis of the equipment with respect to *T*.

In the year following the transfer of the partnership interest to *T*, *T*'s distributive share of the partnership's common basis depreciation deductions from the equipment is $1,000. Also assume that the amount of the basis adjustment under Code Sec. 743(b) that *T* recovers during the year is $500. The total amount of depreciation deductions from the equipment reported by *T* is equal to $1,500.

Example 13-15. *Positive Code Sec. 743(b) adjustment to Code Sec. 704(c) property with remedial allocation.* *A* and *B* form the equal AB Partnership. *A* contributes property with an adjusted basis of $100,000 and a fair market value of $500,000. *B* contributes $500,000 cash. When the AB Partnership is formed, the property has five years remaining in its recovery period. The partnership's adjusted basis of $100,000 will, therefore, be recovered over the five years remaining in the property's recovery period. The AB Partnership elects to use the remedial allocation method [85] with respect to the property. If the AB Partnership had purchased the property at the time of the partnership's formation, the basis of the property would have been recovered over a 10-year period. The $400,000 of Code Sec. 704(c) built-in gain will, therefore, be amortized [86] over a 10-year period beginning at the time of the partnership's formation.

The AB Partnership's depreciation deductions attributable to the contributed property are as follows:

	Years 1-5	*Years 6-10*
Carryover basis	$20,000	$ 0
Built-in gain excess book basis	40,000	40,000
Total partnership depreciation	*$60,000*	*$40,000*
Book depreciation allocated to each of *A* and *B*	$30,000	$20,000
Partner *A*'s remedial income	40,000	40,000
Partner *A*'s reported net income from property . . . . (essentially negative depreciation)	*$10,000*	*$20,000*

Except for the depreciation deductions, the AB Partnership's expenses equal its income in each year of the first two years commencing with the year the partnership is formed. After two years, *A*'s share of the adjusted basis of partnership property is $120,000, while *B*'s is $440,000:

[85] Under Reg. § 1.704-3(d).

[86] *Id.*

Capital Accounts

	A		B	
	Book	*Tax*	*Book*	*Tax*
Initial Contribution . . .	$500,000	$100,000	$500,000	$500,000
Depreciation:				
Year 1	(30,000)		(30,000)	(20,000)
Remedial		10,000		(10,000)
	$470,000	*$110,000*	*$470,000*	*$470,000*
Depreciation:				
Year 2	(30,000)		(30,000)	(20,000)
Remedial		10,000		(10,000)
	$440,000	*$120,000*	*$440,000*	*$440,000*

A sells his interest in the AB Partnership to *T* for its fair market value of $440,000. A valid election under Code Sec. 754 is in effect with respect to the sale of the partnership interest. Accordingly, the AB Partnership makes an adjustment, pursuant to Code Sec. 743(b), to increase the basis of partnership property. Under Code Sec. 743(b), the amount of the basis adjustment is equal to $320,000. Under Code Sec. 755, the entire basis adjustment is allocated to the property.

The amount of *T*'s $320,000 Code Sec. 743(b) basis adjustment is calculated as follows:

$440,000	Partner *T*'s basis for the partnership interest
(120,000)	Partner *T*'s share of the adjusted basis to the partnership of the partnership property
$320,000	

$440,000	Partner *T*'s share of the value of partnership assets
(320,000)	Taxable gain Partner *T* would recognize on a sale of partnership assets with no Partner *T*'s share of the partnership's basis
$120,000	Partner *T*'s share of the adjusted basis to the partnership of the partnership property

At the time of the transfer, $320,000 of Code Sec. 704(c) built-in gain from the property was still reflected on the partnership's books, and all of the basis adjustment is attributable to Code Sec. 704(c) built-in gain. Therefore, the basis adjustment will be recovered over the remaining recovery period for the Code Sec. 704(c) built-in gain under Reg. § 1.704-3(d).

For purposes of Code Sec. 168, if the basis of an item of a partnership's recovery property is decreased as the result of the transfer of an interest in the partnership, then the decrease is recovered over the remaining useful life of the item of the partnership's recovery property. The portion of the decrease that is recovered in any year during the recovery period is equal to the product of:

1. The amount of the decrease to the item's adjusted basis (determined as of the date of the transfer); multiplied by

2. A fraction, the numerator of which is the portion of the adjusted basis of the item recovered by the partnership in that year, and the denominator of which is the adjusted basis of the item on the date of the transfer (determined prior to any basis adjustments).[87]

The amount of any negative basis adjustment allocated to an item of depreciable or amortizable property that is recovered in any year first decreases the transferee's distributive share of the partnership's depreciation or amortization deductions from that item of property for the year. If the amount of the basis adjustment recovered in any year exceeds the transferee's distributive share of the partnership's depreciation or amortization deductions from the item of property, then the transferee's distributive share of the partnership's depreciation or amortization deductions from other items of partnership property is decreased. The transferee then recognizes ordinary income to the extent of the excess, if any, of the amount of the basis adjustment recovered in any year over the transferee's distributive share of the partnership's depreciation or amortization deductions from all items of property.[88]

Example 13-16. *A*, *B*, and *C* are equal partners in the ABC Partnership, which owns equipment, an item of depreciable property that has a fair market value that is less than its adjusted tax basis. *C* sells its interest in the ABC Partnership to *T* while the ABC Partnership has an election in effect under Code Sec. 754. The ABC Partnership, therefore, decreases the basis of the equipment with respect to *T*.

In the year following the transfer of the partnership interest to *T*, *T*'s distributive share of the partnership's common basis depreciation deductions from the equipment is $1,000. Assume that the amount of the basis adjustment under Code Sec. 743(b) that *T* recovers during the year is $500. The total amount of depreciation deductions from the equipment reported by *T* is equal to $500.

Example 13-17. *Negative Code Sec. 743(b) adjustment to Code Sec. 704(c) property with traditional allocation.* *A* and *B* form the equal AB Partnership. *A* contributes property with an adjusted basis of $100,000 and a fair market value of $50,000. *B* contributes $50,000 cash. When the AB Partnership is formed, the property has five years remaining in its recovery period. The partnership's adjusted basis of $100,000 will, therefore, be recovered over the five years remaining in the property's recovery period. The ABC Partnership uses the traditional allocation method under Reg. § 1.704-3(b) with respect to the property. As a result, *B* will receive $5,000 of depreciation deductions from the property in each of Years 1 through 5. This is equal to his

[87] Reg. § 1.743-1(j)(4)(ii)(B).

[88] Reg. § 1.743-1(j)(4)(ii).

share of the book depreciation ($50,000 book value/5 years). *A*, as the contributing partner, will receive $15,000 of depreciation deductions in each of these years. This is equal to the total tax depreciation in excess of *B*'s share ($100,000 tax basis/5years, less $5,000).

Except for the depreciation deductions, the AB Partnership's expenses equal its income in each of the first two years commencing with the year the partnership is formed. After two years, *A*'s share of the adjusted basis of partnership property is $70,000, while *B*'s is $40,000. *A* sells his interest in the AB Partnership to *T* for its fair market value of $40,000. A valid election under Code Sec. 754 is in effect with respect to the sale of the partnership interest. Accordingly, the ABC Partnership makes an adjustment, pursuant to Code Sec. 743(b), to decrease the basis of partnership property. Under Code Sec. 743(b), the amount of the adjustment is equal to $(30,000). Under Code Sec. 755, the entire adjustment is allocated to the property. The calculations are as follows:

Amount of Partner* T*'s Code Sec. 743(b) Adjustment

$40,000	Partner *T*'s basis in the partnership interest
(70,000)	Partner *T*'s share of the partnership's basis in its property
$*(30,000)*	T's Code Sec. 743(b) basis adjustment

Partner* T*'s Share of the Basis of Partnership Property

$40,000	Cash value of *T*'s partnership interest
30,000	Plus *T*'s share of partnership loss if it sold its assets before a Code Sec. 743(b) adjustment
$*70,000*	

T*'s Depreciation*

$15,000	Share of partnership's depreciation
(10,000)	Amortization of negative Code Sec. 743(b) basis adjustment
$*5,000*	T's net depreciation deduction in Years 3 through 5

Example 13-18. *Negative Code Sec. 743(b) adjustment exceeds depreciation. A*, *B*, and *C* are equal partners in the ABC Partnership, which owns equipment, an item of depreciable property that has a fair market value that is less than its adjusted tax basis. *C* sells its interest in the ABC Partnership to *T* while the ABC Partnership has an election in effect under Code Sec. 754. The ABC Partnership, therefore, decreases the basis of the equipment with respect to *T*.

Assume that in the year following the transfer of the partnership interest to *T*, *T*'s distributive share of the partnership's common basis depreciation deductions from the equipment is $500. The ABC Partnership allocates no other depreciation to *T*. Also assume that the amount of the negative basis adjustment that *T* recovers during the year is $1,000. *T* will report $500 of ordinary income because the amount of the negative basis adjustment recovered during the year exceeds *T*'s distributive share of the partnership's common basis depreciation deductions from the equipment.

.06 *Distribution of Property with Code Sec. 743(b) Adjustments*

The consequences of distributing partnership property that is subject to a Code Sec. 743(b) basis adjustment depend partly upon to which partner the property is distributed. If the property is distributed to the partner for whom the special basis adjustment was made, that partner's basis under Code Sec. 732 will take into account the special basis adjustment.[89] If, however, the property subject to a special basis adjustment is distributed to a partner(s) other than the one for whom the adjustment was made, the special basis adjustment is shifted to property of like kind still remaining in the partnership but continues to affect only the same partner.[90] When the interest of a partner with respect to whom a special basis adjustment is in effect is completely liquidated, the partner's entire remaining adjustments in all partnership property must be allocated to the distributed property.[91] However, the partner will have a total adjusted basis in the distributed property equal to the adjusted basis of his or her partnership interest. The total basis of the distributed property is not affected by the Code Sec. 743(b) adjustment. The Code Sec. 743(b) adjustment probably will change the allocation of the adjusted basis of the partnership interest among the respective distributed assets but not the total basis of the distributed property. Property distributed in complete liquidation of a partnership interest has a total basis equal to the partner's pre-distribution basis in his or her partnership interest. This total amount is allocated among the distributed properties in a manner which takes into account their bases to the partnership, including special basis adjustments due to the Code Sec. 754 election.

> ***Example 13-19.*** *A*, *B*, and *C* are equal partners in the ABC Partnership. Each partner originally contributed $10,000 in cash, and the ABC Partnership used the contributions to purchase five nondepreciable capital assets. The ABC Partnership has no liabilities. After five years, the ABC Partnership's balance sheet appears as follows:

Assets	***Basis***	***FMV***
Land	$10,000	$10,000
Stock	4,000	6,000
Roman Coins	6,000	6,000
Paintings	7,000	4,000
Stamps	3,000	13,000
Total	*$30,000*	*$39,000*
Capital		
A	10,000	13,000
B	10,000	13,000
C	10,000	13,000
Total	*$30,000*	*$39,000*

[89] Reg. § 1.743-1(g)(1)(i).
[90] Reg. § 1.743-1(g)(2).
[91] Reg. § 1.743-1(g)(3).

Partner *A* sells his interest to *T* for $13,000 when the ABC Partnership has an election in effect under Code Sec. 754. *T* receives a basis adjustment under Code Sec. 743(b) in the partnership property that is equal to $3,000 (the excess of *T*'s basis in the partnership interest, $13,000, over *T*'s share of the adjusted basis to the partnership of partnership property, $10,000). The basis adjustment is allocated under Code Sec. 755, and the partnership's balance sheet appears as follows:

Assets	*Adjusted Basis*	*FMV*	*Basis Adjustment*
Land	$10,000	$10,000	$ 0.00
Stock	4,000	6,000	666.67
Roman Coins	6,000	6,000	0.00
Paintings	7,000	4,000	(1,000.00)
Stamps	3,000	13,000	3,333.33
Total	*$30,000*	*$39,000*	*$3,000.00*

Capital	*Adjusted Per Books*	*FMV*	*Special Basis Adjustment*
T	$10,000	$13,000	$3,000
B	10,000	13,000	0
C	10,000	13,000	0
Total	*$30,000*	*$39,000*	*$3,000*

Current distribution to T. Assume that the ABC Partnership distributes the stock to *T* in partial liquidation of *T*'s interest in the partnership. *T* has a basis adjustment under Code Sec. 743(b) of $666.67 in the stock. *T* takes the basis adjustment into account under Code Sec. 732. Therefore, *T* will have a basis in the stock of $4,666.67 following the distribution.

Distribution not to T. Assume instead that the ABC Partnership distributes the stamps to *C* in complete liquidation of *C*'s interest in the ABC Partnership. *T* has a basis adjustment under Code Sec. 743(b) of $3,333.33 in the stamps. *C* does not take *T*'s basis adjustment into account under Code Sec. 732. Therefore, the partnership's basis for purposes of Code Secs. 732 and 734 is $3,000. *T*'s $3,333.33 basis adjustment is reallocated among the remaining partnership assets under Reg. § 1.755-1(c).

Liquidating distributions to T. Assume instead that the ABC Partnership distributes the stamps to *T* in complete liquidation of her interest in the ABC Partnership. Immediately prior to the distribution of the stamps to *T*, the ABC Partnership must adjust the basis of the stamps. Therefore, immediately prior to the distribution, ABC Partnership's basis in the stamps is equal to $6,000, which is the sum of:

1. $3,000, the ABC Partnership's common basis in the stamps, plus
2. $3,333.33, *T*'s basis adjustment to the stamps, plus
3. $(333.33), the sum of *T*'s basis adjustments in the stock and paintings.

For purposes of Code Secs. 732 and 734, therefore, the ABC Partnership will be treated as having a basis in the stamps equal to $6,000.

When the partner who has a special basis adjustment in partnership property receives a liquidating distribution entirely in cash, the partnership succeeds to the special basis adjustment as part of its common basis.[92] Also, where a distribution gives rise to a Code Sec. 734(b) adjustment, the Code Sec. 743(b) adjustment is used in calculating the amount of the adjustment.

.07 Transfer of Partnership Interests with Existing Code Sec. 743(b) Adjustments

Transfers by sale. A new partner who acquires his or her partnership interest from an outgoing partner, in respect of whom a Code Sec. 743(b) adjustment was in effect, does not succeed to the selling partner's basis adjustment because it does not carry over to him or her on the transfer of the partnership interest. However, unless the Code Sec. 754 election has been terminated, a new basis adjustment is calculated with reference to the new partner's purchase price for the partnership interest and the new partner's share of the partnership's common basis for its assets. A partner who sells a part of his or her partnership interest will be required to eliminate the special basis adjustment proportionately.

Contribution of partnership with existing Code Sec. 743(b) adjustment to another partnership. If a partnership contributes to another partnership property with respect to which a basis adjustment has been made, the basis adjustment is treated as contributed to the lower-tier partnership, regardless of whether the lower-tier partnership makes a Code Sec. 754 election. The lower tier partnership's basis in the contributed assets and the upper tier partnership's basis in the partnership interest received in the transaction are determined with reference to the basis adjustment. However, that portion of the basis of the upper tier partnership's interest in the lower tier partnership attributable to the basis adjustment must be segregated and allocated solely to the transferee partner for whom the basis adjustment was made. Similarly, that portion of the lower tier partnership's basis in its assets attributable to the basis adjustment must be segregated and allocated solely to the upper tier partnership and the transferee. A partner with a basis adjustment in property held by a partnership that terminates

[92] Reg. § 1.734-2(b)(1).

under Code Sec. 708(b)(1)(B) will continue to have the same basis adjustment with respect to property deemed contributed by the terminated partnership to the new partnership, regardless of whether the new partnership makes a Code Sec. 754 election.[93]

Contribution of partnership interest with existing Code Sec. 743(b) adjustment to a corporation. A corporation's adjusted tax basis in property transferred to it by a partnership in a transaction described in Code Sec. 351 is determined with reference to any basis adjustments to the property under Code Sec. 743(b).[94]

The amount of gain, if any, recognized by the partnership on a transfer of property by the partnership to a corporation in a transfer described in Code Sec. 351 is determined without reference to any basis adjustment to the transferred property under Code Sec. 743(b). The amount of gain, if any, recognized by the partnership on the transfer that is allocated to a partner with a basis adjustment in the transferred property is adjusted to reflect the partner's basis adjustment in the transferred property.[95]

The partnership's adjusted tax basis in stock received from a corporation in a transfer described in Code Sec. 351 is determined without reference to the basis adjustment in property transferred to the corporation in the Code Sec. 351 exchange. A partner with a basis adjustment in property transferred to the corporation, however, has a basis adjustment in the stock received by the partnership in the Code Sec. 351 exchange in an amount equal to the partner's basis adjustment in the transferred property, reduced by any basis adjustment that reduced the partner's gain.[96]

> ***Example 13-20.*** *A*, *B*, and *C* are equal partners in the ABC Partnership. The partnership's only asset, investment land, has an adjusted tax basis of $60 and a fair market value of $120. The land is a nondepreciable capital asset and is not Code Sec. 704(c) property. *A* has a basis in his partnership interest of $40, and a positive Code Sec. 743(b) adjustment of $20 in the land. In a transaction to which Code Sec. 351 applies, the ABC Partnership contributes the land to *X*, a corporation, in exchange for $15 in cash and *X* stock with a fair market value of $105.
>
> The ABC Partnership realizes $60 of gain on the transfer of the land to *X*. It recognizes only $15 of that gain under Code Sec. 351(b)(1). Of this amount, $5 is allocated to each partner. *A* must use $5 of the basis adjustment in the land to offset his share of the ABC Partnership's gain.

[93] Reg. §§ 1.743-1(h)(1) and 1.708-1(b)(1)(iv).

[94] Other than any basis adjustment that reduces a partner's gain under Reg. § 1.743-1(h)(2)(ii).

[95] Reg. § 1.743-1(h)(2)(ii).

[96] Reg. § 1.743-1(h)(2)(iii).

The ABC Partnership's basis in the stock received from *X* is $60. However, *A* has a basis adjustment in the stock received by the ABC Partnership equal to $15 (his basis adjustment in the land, $20, reduced by the portion of the adjustment which reduced *A*'s gain, $5).

X's basis in the land equals $90.

$60	Partnership ABC's common basis in the land
15	Gain recognized by ABC under Code Sec. 351(b)(1)
20	*A*'s Code Sec. 743(b) adjustment
(5)	Portion of *A*'s adjustment which reduced *A*'s share of the Code Sec. 351(b)(1) gain
$*90*	

.08 Compliance Requirements Under Code Sec. 754

A partnership that adjusts the bases of partnership properties under Code Sec. 743(b) must attach a statement to the partnership return for the year of the transfer setting forth the name and taxpayer identification number of the transferee, as well as the computation of the adjustment and the partnership properties to which the adjustment has been allocated.

A transferee that acquires, by sale or exchange, an interest in a partnership with an election under Code Sec. 754 in effect for the taxable year of the transfer must notify the partnership, in writing, within 30 days of the sale or exchange. The written notice to the partnership must be signed under penalties of perjury and must include:

- The names and addresses of the transferee and (if ascertainable) of the transferor;
- The taxpayer identification numbers of the transferee and (if ascertainable) of the transferor;
- The relationship (if any) between the transferee and the transferor;
- The date of the transfer;
- The amount of any liabilities assumed or taken subject to by the transferee;
- The amount of any money, the fair market value of any other property delivered or to be delivered for the transferred interest in the partnership; and
- Any other information necessary for the partnership to compute the transferee's basis.

A transferee that acquires, on the death of a partner, an interest in a partnership with an election under Code Sec. 754 in effect for the taxable year of the transfer must notify the partnership, in writing, within one year of the death of the deceased partner. The written notice to the partnership must be signed under penalties of perjury and must include:

- The names and addresses of the deceased partner and the transferee;
- The taxpayer identification numbers of the deceased partner and the transferee;
- The relationship (if any) between the transferee and the transferor, the deceased partner's date of death;
- The date on which the transferee became the owner of the partnership interest;
- The fair market value of the partnership interest on the applicable date of valuation set forth in Code Sec. 1014; and
- The manner in which the fair market value of the partnership interest was determined.

In making the adjustments under Code Sec. 743(b) and filing any statement or return relating to such adjustments under this section, a partnership may rely on the written notice provided by a transferee to determine the transferee's basis in a partnership interest, unless any partner who has responsibility for federal income tax reporting by the partnership has knowledge of facts indicating that the statement is clearly erroneous.

A partnership is not required to make the adjustments under Code Sec. 743(b) (or any statement or return relating to those adjustments) with respect to any transfer until it has been notified of the transfer. For purposes of this section, a partnership is notified of a transfer when either:

1. The partnership receives the required written notice from the transferee; or
2. Any partner who has responsibility for federal income tax reporting by the partnership has knowledge that there has been a transfer of a partnership interest.

> ***Comment.*** The current regulations make it clear that it is the partnership and not the partners who takes the Code Sec. 743 (b) adjustments into account.[97] The prior regulations were ambiguous in this respect and it was common practice for the partnership to prepare Form 1065 and Schedules K-1 without the Code Sec. 743(b) adjustment and the various partners would make the adjustments for purposes of reporting their shares of the partnership income.

If the transferee fails to provide the partnership with written notice of the transfer, the partnership must attach a statement to its return in the year that the partnership is otherwise notified of the transfer. This statement must set forth the name and taxpayer identification number (if

[97] Reg. § 1.743-1(j)(2).

ascertainable) of the transferee. In addition, the following statement must be prominently displayed in capital letters on the first page of the partnership's return for such year, and on the first page of any schedule or information statement relating to such transferee's share of income, credits, deductions, etc.: "RETURN FILED PURSUANT TO SECTION 1.743-1(k)(5)." The partnership is then entitled to report the transferee's share of partnership items without adjustment to reflect the transferee's basis adjustment in partnership property. If, following the filing of a return, the transferee provides the applicable written notice to the partnership, the partnership must make the adjustments necessary to adjust the basis of partnership property (as of the date of the transfer) in any amended return otherwise to be filed by the partnership or in the next annual partnership return of income to be regularly filed by the partnership. At such time, the partnership must also provide the transferee with such information as is necessary for the transferee to amend its prior returns to properly reflect the adjustment under Code Sec. 743(b).

.09 Partner-Level Code Sec. 743(b) Adjustments—Code Sec. 732(d)

Although it is the partnership that must invoke Code Secs. 743 and 734 by making a Code Sec. 754 election, Code Sec. 732(d) provides that a transferee partner, to whom a distribution of partnership property (other than money) is made within two years of the date the transferee partner acquired his or her partnership interest, can make an election to treat the adjusted basis of the distributed partnership property as if a Code Sec. 743(b) adjustment were in effect with respect to the partnership property. This adjustment is allocated among the distributed properties under the provisions of Code Sec. 755. Code Sec. 732(d), however, unlike Code Secs. 754 and 743(b), does not require the partnership to make further basis adjustments for subsequent transfers and distributions. If at the time of the purchase there would have been a positive adjustment to the partnership's property basis on behalf of the purchasing partner, the Code Sec. 732(d) election has the effect of providing the purchasing partner with a higher basis in the distributed property and a lower basis in his or her partnership interest.

> ***Example 13-21.*** *D* has a basis in his one-third interest in the profits, losses, and capital account of the ABD Partnership of $40,000. He bought his interest in the prior year from retiring Partner *C*. The partnership decided not to elect Code Sec. 754. ABD makes a current distribution to *D* of an asset with a basis of $10,000. *D*'s capital account is appropriately reduced, but his interest in all items of partnership profit and loss is unchanged. At the time *D* bought his interest, the asset was worth $45,000 (his share was $15,000) and *D* would have been entitled to a $5,000 basis adjustment if Code Sec. 754

were in effect. What are the tax consequences to *D* on a current distribution of the asset?

The Code Sec. 732(d) election is applicable to current and liquidating distributions.[98] Thus, *D* can elect to have Code Sec. 732(d) apply and receive a special basis adjustment for the distributed asset which is equal to the adjusted basis the asset would have had if the Code Sec. 754 election were in effect with respect to the partnership property when *D* bought his interest. *D* received the distribution within two years after the transfer as required. Therefore, *D*'s basis for the asset is $15,000 ($10,000 basis to the partnership plus the $5,000 special basis adjustment under Code Sec. 732(d)). *D*'s basis for his partnership interest is reduced by $15,000 after the distribution to $25,000.

An additional discussion of Code Sec. 732(d) can be found at ¶ 1602.04.

.10 Code Sec. 743(b) Adjustments for Sales of Partnership Interests Before December 15, 1999

Total amount of Code Sec. 743(b) adjustment. The total basis adjustment equals the initial adjusted basis (determined by applying the rules of Code Sec. 742) of the partner's interest in the partnership less that partner's proportionate share of the common adjusted basis of the partnership assets.

A partner's proportionate share of the common basis of partnership assets "is equal to the sum of his interest as a partner in partnership capital and surplus, plus his share of partnership liabilities."[99] In other words, a partner's proportionate share of the aggregate adjusted basis of partnership assets is determined with reference to the partner's share of the aggregate adjusted basis of partnership tax basis capital accounts,[100] together with his or her share of the aggregate of the partnership's liabilities. The aggregate "adjusted basis" of partnership capital accounts may not be clearly evident from partnership records and, therefore, sometimes must be derived from its operating history.

Examples 1 and 2 of former Reg. § 1.743-1(b) indicate that a partner's interest in "partnership capital and surplus" is merely the partner's share of the partnership's total "adjusted basis-per-book" of its assets (presumably the adjusted basis of its assets), less the partner's share of the partnership's liabilities. The buying partner's share of the aggregate partnership capital and surplus computed in this manner is determined with reference to the basis of his or her predecessor's contributions and distributions, his or her share of taxable and tax-exempt income, and his or her share of deductible and nondeductible expenditures. The partner's share of partner-

[98] Reg. § 1.732-1(d)(4), Ex. 2.

[99] Reg. § 1.743-1(b)(1) prior to amendment by T.D. 8847, 1999-52 IRB 701.

[100] The partner's tax basis capital account.

ship liabilities is determined in accordance with the provisions of the Code Sec. 752 regulations.

Once the partner's share of "adjusted basis" partnership capital and surplus has been determined, his or her proportionate share of the adjusted basis of partnership assets may be derived simply by adding to the former his or her share of partnership liabilities. Thus, although the aggregate adjusted basis of partnership assets may be determined from the partnership's books, in order to derive the partner's share of the basis of these assets it is necessary to determine the adjusted basis of his or her interest in partnership capital and surplus.

Example 13-22. *A* sells his interest in the equal-interest partnership ABC to *D* for cash of $2,600. Prior to the sale, ABC's balance sheet reflects its adjusted basis in its assets as follows:

Assets	*Adjusted Basis*	*FMV*
Cash	$6,000	$6,000
Capital asset	800	2,600
Total	*$6,800*	*$8,600*
Liabilities and Capital Accounts [101]		
Liabilities	$2,000	$2,000
Capital		
A	2,000	2,750
B	800	1,100
C	2,000	2,750
	$6,800	*$8,600*

Since *D* paid $2,600 cash and assumed one-third of the partnership's liabilities, $666, his initial basis in his partnership interest under Code Sec. 742 is $3,266. *D*'s share of the adjusted basis of the partnership's assets in the absence of a Code Sec. 754 election is, in terms of Code Sec. 743(a), the same as selling partner's *A*'s share of the adjusted basis of partnership assets. This is determined by first deriving *A*'s interest in partnership capital and surplus. The aggregate adjusted basis of partnership capital and surplus is first determined by subtracting from the aggregate book value of the partnership's assets ($6,800) the aggregate partnership liabilities of $2,000. *A*'s share of the aggregate partnership capital and surplus of $4,800 is $2,000. Having determined *A*'s (adjusted basis) interest in partnership capital and surplus, his proportionate share of the common basis of partnership assets may be determined by adding to this figure his share of partnership liabilities.[102] Thus, the share of the partnership's inside basis for *A*, as well as *D*, is $2,666. *D*'s basis adjustment is therefore

[101] The total adjusted basis of $6,800, less the adjusted basis of the liabilities, may be independent of the ratio that the fair market value of each individual financial capital account bears to the total of the financial capital accounts. Reg. § 1.743-1(b)(1), Ex. 2, prior to amendment by T.D. 8847, 1999-52 IRB 701.

[102] Reg. § 1.743-1(b)(1) prior to amendment by T.D. 8847, 1999-52 IRB 701.

$600 (his $3,266 basis for his partnership interest less his $2,666 share of the partnership's common basis). It may seem odd that the calculations involve first subtracting the debt and then adding it back in. This is done so that the rules of Code Sec. 752 may be applied in determining *D*'s share of the partnership's basis in the assets in the same manner as the partner determines his basis in his partnership interest.

Separate records must be kept by the partnership or *D* in order to keep track of the partnership's common adjusted basis and of *D*'s special basis adjustment. This onus may militate against a partnership's making a Code Sec. 754 adjustment. In addition, the regulations require that *D* attach a statement to his tax return (Form 1040, U.S. Individual Income Tax Return) showing the above computation for the first year in which a Code Sec. 754 election affects his tax.[103]

Allocating the Code Sec. 743(b) adjustment among the partnership assets. Prior to December 15, 1999, the allocation rules of Code Sec. 755 provided that the total Code Sec. 743(b) adjustment is to be allocated among all the partnership's assets in any manner that has the effect of reducing the difference between the fair market value of the assets and their respective adjusted bases. Although Code Sec. 755(a) provided for allocation "in any other manner permitted by the regulations," the regulations provided a detailed example of only one method and stipulated that any increases or decreases in the bases of assets must reduce or eliminate the difference between the respective basis and the value of the assets.[104]

The method described by the regulations separated the partnership assets into two classes. The total Code Sec. 743(b) basis adjustment is allocated between these two classes of assets based upon the relative net appreciation or depreciation of each class. The portion of the total adjustment allocated to each class is then allocated to the assets within that class based on the relative appreciation or depreciation of each asset. Thus, Examples 1 through 3 in former Reg. § 1.755-1(c) espouse the following steps:

1. Partnership assets are divided into "class I" assets comprising capital assets and Code Sec. 1231 property, and into "class II" assets comprising all other assets.

2. The Code Sec. 743(b) adjustment is allocated between the two classes. If the adjustment is positive, the amount allocable to each class is determined by calculating the net appreciation of each class and then by apportioning the total adjustment be-

[103] Reg. § 1.743-1(b)(1) and (3) prior to amendment by T.D. 8847, 1999-52 IRB 701.

[104] Reg. § 1.755-1(a)(2), prior to amendment by T.D. 8847, 1999-52 IRB 701, provides that if a partnership wishes to adjust the basis of its assets under Code Sec. 743(b) in another manner, it must file an application for permission to use a different method with the District Director no less than 30 days after the close of the partnership's taxable year in which the proposed adjustment is to be made.

tween the classes based upon their relative net appreciations. But if one class has declined in value, the whole positive adjustment is allocated to the appreciated class. Where the adjustment is negative, it is allocated between the classes on the basis of their relative net depreciations. If one class is appreciated, no part of the adjustment is allocated to it.

3. The adjustment to each class is allocated within the class among the assets of that class so as to minimize the difference between their fair market values and their adjusted bases.[105] Accordingly, the regulations suggest an allocation based upon the relative appreciation or depreciation of the respective assets within each class. Thus, where there is a net positive adjustment within a class, depreciated assets within that class are not included in the allocation,[106] and, conversely, in the case of a net negative adjustment allocated to a class of assets, appreciated assets within that class are ignored in making the allocation among the assets within that class.[107]

Example 13-23. Partner *C* sells to *D* his one-third interest in the equal-interest partnership ABC for $6,000 in cash.[108]

Balance Sheet of ABC Partnership

Assets	*Adjusted Basis*	*FMV*
Cash	$3,000	$3,000
Unrealized receivables	0	6,000
Land	6,000	9,000
Total	*$9,000*	*$18,000*
C's one-third share	$3,000	$6,000

Since the aggregate of the adjusted basis of partnership assets prior to the sale was $9,000 and, as there are no partnership liabilities reflected in the balance sheet, the aggregate adjusted basis of the partnership's capital accounts is also $9,000. Assuming that the partners' financial capital accounts and tax basis capital accounts are equal in value, the book value of *C*'s interest in partnership capital is $3,000. As there are no partnership liabilities, his share of the common basis of partnership assets is $3,000.[109] Incoming partner *D*'s share of the basis of the partnership assets is the same as *C*'s, namely $3,000, whereas his basis for his interest is $6,000. Hence, the total Code Sec. 743(b) adjustment is $3,000, the difference between his basis in the partnership interest (equal to fair market value) and his share of the partnership's basis in its assets.

[105] Code Sec. 755(a); Reg. § 1.755-1(a)(1) prior to amendment by T.D. 8847, 1999-52 IRB 701.

[106] Reg. § 1.755-1(a)(1)(ii) prior to amendment by T.D. 8847, 1999-52 IRB 701.

[107] Reg. § 1.755-1(a)(1)(iii) prior to amendment by T.D. 8847, 1999-52 IRB 701.

[108] Under the facts of this example, Code Sec. 751(a) would apply to the *seller*.

[109] Reg. § 1.743-1(b)(1) prior to amendment by T.D. 8847, 1999-52 IRB 701.

Having ascertained the total $3,000 Code Sec. 743(b) adjustment, this adjustment must be allocated according to the three steps provided in the regulations under Code Sec. 755, and referred to above.

First, the total appreciation in partnership assets is allocated between class I ("capital gain assets") and class II ("ordinary income assets") assets as follows:

Assets	*FMV*	*Adjusted Basis*	*Appreciation*	*Percentage of Total Appreciation*
Class I	$9,000	$6,000	$3,000	33-1/3
Class II	6,000	0	6,000	66-2/3
	$15,000	*$6,000*	*$9,000*	*100%*

The Code Sec. 743(b) adjustment of $3,000 is allocated on the basis of net appreciation or depreciation only. Cash will have no effect on the allocation and may accordingly be omitted from the above table.

Second, a determination is made as to how the $3,000 Code Sec. 743(b) adjustment is to be allocated between the two classes:

Assets	*Proportion of Total Appreciation*		*Total of Code Sec. 743(b) Adjustment*		*Allocation to Each Class*
Class I	33-1/3%	×	$3,000	=	$1,000
Class II	66-2/3%	×	$3,000	=	$2,000

Third, the amount of the adjustment allocated to each class is, in turn, allocated within each class among the specific assets in that class in order to minimize the difference between the fair market values and the adjusted bases of those assets. In this example, each class of assets contains only one asset and, therefore, the entire adjustment allocated to that class will be added to that asset's basis. In order to determine *D*'s share of the partnership's income or loss, *D*'s share of the partnership's basis in the unrealized receivables is $2,000 and, for the land, is $3,000.

As a matter of first impression, it appears a useless step to first break the total adjustment into the parts allocated to class I assets and class II assets. A straightforward allocation of a total Code Sec. 743(b) adjustment among all the assets without first allocating between two classes will produce the same result only when all the assets are either appreciated or depreciated. When some assets are appreciated and others depreciated, one class of assets has net appreciation and the other net depreciation, and each class has both appreciated and depreciated assets, the two-step approach will produce a result different than a simple one-step allocation among all assets.

Code Sec. 743(b) adjustments are allocated to all types of assets, both tangible and intangible, including goodwill,[110] unamortized prepaid interest,[111] unrealized receivables, and substantially appreciated inventory.[112]

Example 13-24. ABC Factory Company is a calendar-year accrual method partnership in which each partner has a one-third interest in capital and profits. Each partner has a basis of $73,333 for his partnership interest.

A sells his partnership interest to *D* for $95,000 cash. Immediately prior to the sale, the balance sheet of the partnership was as follows:

Assets	*Book Value and Adjusted Basis*	*FMV*
Cash	$75,000	$75,000
Accounts Receivable	30,000	30,000
Inventory	10,000	15,000
Building (assume no Code Sec. 1245 recapture potential)	55,000	70,000
Investment Land		
Parcel *X*	40,000	90,000
Parcel *Y*	10,000	45,000
	$220,000	*$325,000*

Liabilities and Capital		
Liabilities	$40,000	$40,000
Capital		
A	60,000	95,000
B	60,000	95,000
C	60,000	95,000
	$220,000	*$325,000*

Code Sec. 743(a) reflects the entity theory of partnership taxation, providing that the basis of partnership property is not adjusted as a result of a transfer of an interest in a partnership by sale or exchange or death of a partner unless a Code Sec. 754 election is in effect. If such an election is not in effect in this case, *D*'s share of the adjusted basis of the partnership assets would total $73,333 (1/3 of $220,000), which is less than his initial basis for his partnership interest of $108,333 ($95,000 cash plus $13,333 share of liabilities).[113]

Code Sec. 743(b) reflects the aggregate theory of partnership taxation, providing that on a transfer of a partnership interest by sale or exchange (or death) when the Code Sec. 754 election is in effect, the partnership shall (1) increase the adjusted basis of the partnership

[110] Reg. § 1.755-1(a)(1)(iv) prior to amendment by T.D. 8847, 1999-52 IRB 701.

[111] *G.R. Bartolme v. Commr.*, 62 TC 821, Dec. 32,774 (1974).

[112] Reg. § 1.751-1(g), Exs. 3 and 4, prior to amendment by T.D. 8847, 1999-52 IRB 701.

[113] See Code Sec. 742.

property by the excess of the basis to the transferee partner of his interest in the partnership over his proportionate share of the adjusted basis of the partnership property, or (2) decrease the adjusted basis of the partnership property by the excess of the transferee partner's proportionate share of the adjusted basis of the partnership property over the basis of his interest in the partnership.

Assume the partnership has a Code Sec. 754 election in effect. *D*'s special basis adjustment under Code Sec. 743(b) is the difference between his initial basis in his partnership interest ($108,333) and his share of the adjusted basis in the partnership assets ($73,333), or $35,000.

Where the partners have the same share of both capital and profits, as here, it is easy to determine *D*'s share of the common basis. However, in other situations, that determination will involve adding *D*'s capital account to his share of liabilities.[114]

Prior to December 15, 1999, the general rule of Code Sec. 755(a) required allocation of any increase or decrease in the adjusted basis of partnership property under Code Sec. 743(b) in a manner that reduces the difference between the fair market value and the adjusted basis of partnership properties. Code Sec. 755(b) provides a special rule which requires that increases or decreases in the adjusted basis of partnership property attributable to capital assets and Code Sec. 1231(b) property, and those which are attributable to all other partnership property be allocated to partnership property of the same class (provided the basis of any such partnership property is not reduced below zero).

Application of the Code Sec. 755 allocation rules to this example is summarized as follows:

The adjustment under Code Sec. 743(b) is $35,000. The total appreciation attributable to the class of Code Sec. 1221/1231(b) assets (the building and Parcels *X* and *Y*) is $100,000. The total appreciation attributable to other property is $5,000. The total appreciation for all partnership assets is $105,000.

[114] Reg. § 1.743-1(b)(1), fifth sentence, prior to amendment by T.D. 8847, 1999-52 IRB 701, which is similar to the concept of Reg. § 1.705-1(b), Ex. 3.

Total Allocation of Code Sec. 743(b) Amount

$$\textbf{To Code Sec. 1221/1231(b) assets} = \frac{\text{Sec. 1221/1231 net appreciation}}{\text{Total appreciation}}$$

$$\$35{,}000 \text{ (Code Sec. 743(b) amount)} \times \frac{\$100{,}000}{\$105{,}000} = \$33{,}333$$

$$\textbf{To other assets} = \frac{\text{Other assets' net appreciation}}{\text{Total appreciation}}$$

$$\$35{,}000 \text{ (Code Sec. 743(b) amount)} \times \frac{\$5{,}000}{\$105{,}000} = \$1{,}667$$

Allocation of Adjustment Within Each Class

Within Code Sec. 1221/1231 class

To Building:

$$\$33{,}333 \times \frac{\text{Building appreciation}}{\text{Total appreciation of appreciated assets in Code Sec. 1221/1231 class}}$$

$$\$33{,}333 \times \frac{\$15{,}000}{\$100{,}000} = \$5{,}000$$

To Parcel X:

$$\$33{,}333 \times \frac{\text{Parcel } X \text{ appreciation}}{\text{Total appreciation of appreciation in assets Code Sec. 1221/1231 class}}$$

$$\$33{,}333 \times \frac{\$50{,}000}{\$100{,}000} = \$16{,}666$$

To Parcel Y:

$$\$33{,}333 \times \frac{\text{Parcel } Y \text{ appreciation}}{\text{Total appreciation of appreciation in assets Code Sec. 1221/1231 class}}$$

$$\$33{,}333 \times \frac{\$35{,}000}{\$100{,}000} = \$11{,}667$$

Within other asset class

To Inventory:

$$\$1{,}667 \times \frac{\text{Inventory appreciation}}{\text{Total appreciation in other asset class}}$$

$$\$1{,}667 \times \frac{\$5{,}000}{\$5{,}000} = \$1{,}667$$

Assets	1/3 Common Basis	Market Value 1/3 FMV	(Appreciation)
Code Sec. 1221/1231 Assets			
Building	$18,333	$23,333	$5,000
Land			
Parcel *A*	13,334	30,000	16,666
Parcel *B*	3,333	15,000	11,667
	$35,000	*$68,333*	*$33,333*
Ordinary Income Assets			
Cash	$25,000	$25,000	$ 0
Accounts Receivable . .	10,000	10,000	0
Inventory	3,334	5,000	1,667
	$38,334	*$40,000*	*$1,667*

PART VI

DISTRIBUTIONS

Chapter 14

Partnership Distributions—The Tax Definition

¶ 1401 Introduction

Before a partner applies the distribution rules to money or property received from a partnership, the taxpayer must determine whether there has been a distribution, when it occurred, and what was distributed. Although one would assume that there should normally be an obvious answer, in some cases it will not be so clear. Transfers from the partnership to partners which would clearly be distributions for nontax purposes can be treated as something else for tax purposes. On the other hand, the partnership tax rules often create deemed distributions of property and/or money when nothing has been actually distributed by the partnership.

> ***LLC Observation.*** The distribution rules discussed in this chapter apply equally to state law partnerships and LLCs taxed as partnerships.

¶ 1402 Distributions Deemed Sales for Purposes of Partnership Taxation

To the extent that a distribution changes the distributee's share of the value of the partnership's ordinary income assets, the amount of the distribution equal to the value of that shift is recharacterized as a purchase/sale transaction between the partnership and the distributee-partner.[1] This is discussed in more detail in Chapter 18. However, a simple example of such a distribution is appropriate at this point to convey the general concept for those who are unfamiliar with these rules.

[1] Code Sec. 751(b).

Example 14-1. The ABC equal, calendar-year, cash-basis partnership owns commercial realty which it leases to retail merchants. Yearly rental payments are based upon a specified percentage of the tenant's gross receipts and are payable on January 30 of the following calendar year. As of December 31, $300 is estimated to be the partnership's rent to be received the following month. Partner *A*'s distributive share would be $100. The partnership agrees to liquidate Partner *A*'s interest for $200.

The partnership is in substance paying Partner *A* for his share of its earned but uncollected rental income, plus $100 for his share of remaining partnership assets. Under Code Sec. 751(b), the transaction will be divided into these two parts. The payment to *A* for his share of the rent receivable will be treated as a fully taxable payment—effectively a sale from *A* to the partnership of *A*'s interest in the receivable. The remaining $100 distributed to *A* will be treated as a liquidating distribution.

In other cases, distributions received by a partner within two years of a contribution of property by such partner to the partnership may be recharacterized as sale proceeds.[2] The unexpected "innocent" applicability of these deemed sale rules to distributions may appear to be an unlikely theoretical abstraction. However, the application of these rules is not unlikely, given their nonintuitive complexity. This is especially true because the partners may trigger these rules before seeking tax advice. For example, a distribution to any partner who has at anytime in the past contributed property *may* be recast as an installment sale payment for the previously contributed property under Code Sec. 707(a)(2)(B). Any partner who has contributed appreciated property to the partnership and receives a distribution of other non like-kind property within seven years *will* receive sale treatment for the contributed property under Code Sec. 737. If property is contributed to a partnership and later is distributed to another partner within seven years of its contribution, the *contributing* partner, rather than the distributee partner, *will* have gain or loss under Code Sec. 707(c)(1)(b) even though he or she receives no actual distribution. These provisions are discussed in detail in Chapter 5.

¶ 1403 Deemed Distributions

Partnership payments made on behalf of a partner are not deductible by the partnership, but are treated as if the partnership distributed the amounts paid on behalf of the partner to that partner who then paid the amount directly.[3] Examples of these deemed distributions include:

- Charitable contributions.
- Medical expenses of a partner.

[2] See Chapter 5.

[3] See Chapter 8 for further discussion.

- Foreign taxes paid on a partner's share of income.
- Alimony.
- Cooperative housing corporation payments on behalf of a partner.
- Medical insurance covering a partner.
- Personal expenses of a partner.[4]

Reductions in a partner's share of partnership debt are treated as deemed money distributions for tax purposes, although they do not affect the partners' capital accounts. In applying the tax rules governing partnership distributions, reductions in debt share are equivalent in all respects to an actual cash distribution on the last day of the partnership's taxable year.[5]

Loans from the partnership to a partner can be recharacterized as distributions if the surrounding facts and circumstances indicate that a true debtor/creditor relationship does not exist. The test which is applied is generally the same as that applied in the context of distinguishing purported loans from corporations to shareholders from dividends, and in distinguishing loans to family members from gifts. The IRS has ruled that "an unconditional and legally enforceable obligation to repay a sum certain at a determinable date" is required for treatment as a loan.[6] The ruling specifically provides that a provision in the partnership agreement requiring partners with deficit capital balances to restore those balances to zero is not a loan between the partnership and those partners with capital account deficiencies.

> ***Example 14-2.*** *Partnership loan.* Samantha Each, a one-third partner in a law firm, wanted to take a vacation, but since she received an enormous cash distribution in the previous year to pay for her last vacation, her basis for her partnership interest was now very low: $5. She wanted to avoid paying any unnecessary tax, so she suggested that she "borrow" $100 from the partnership.
>
> A loan from the partnership to Samantha will be treated as a disguised distribution unless there is "an unconditional and legally enforceable obligation to repay a sum certain at a determinable date."[7] If this requirement is met, the loan will be treated like any other loan between the partnership and a nonpartner under Code Sec. 707(a).

---

[4] See, for example, *M.R. White v. Commr.*, CA-10, 93-1 USTC ¶ 50,273, 991 F2d 657, in which payments made by a partnership for construction of a vacation home on property owned by a partner were deemed distributions.

[5] Rev. Rul. 94-4, 1994-1 CB 195. See Chapter 10 for a complete discussion of a partner's share of partnership debt.

[6] Rev. Rul. 73-301, 1973-2 CB 216.

[7] *Id.* If the partnership cancels the loan it is considered to be a distribution at that time and not as cancelled debt income to the partner.

Samantha could also argue that this was merely an advance or draw against her distributive share of the current year's income.[8] However, such an advance would be considered a distribution at year-end. Possibly, the advance classification would require the partnership to be producing profits.

If a partnership cancels a bona fide loan of money to a partner, the obligor-partner is treated as receiving a distribution of money when the debt is cancelled.[9] If a partnership cancels a partner's debt to the partnership which arose on account of the partner's installment purchase of a partnership asset, the partner is treated as receiving a distribution of property. When there is a distribution to a partner of his or her own indebtedness acquired by the partnership from a third party so that the debt is extinguished, the partner recognizes capital gain or loss to the extent the fair market value of the debt differs from its basis.[10] If the partner's debt to the partnership is not based upon a loan from the partnership, but is evidence of his or her obligation to contribute funds in the future, it is likely not to be treated as a distribution. Although there is no authority directly on point, it is likely to be treated as a release from his or her obligation to make further contributions to the partnership.

¶ 1404 Distributions Recharacterized as Guaranteed Payments or Shares of Income

Under Code Sec. 736, when liquidating distributions are made to a general partner retired from a continuing service partnership (or the partner's representative if he or she has died, such as an accounting or law firm), some of the distributions are likely to be treated as if they are not distributions. The distributions to the retired partner or the representative that are equal to the partner's share of the unrealized receivables, such as cash-basis accounts receivable, are not treated as distributions. They are treated as either Code Sec. 707(c) guaranteed payments or shares of partnership income, depending upon whether the amount is fixed or contingent. Distributions from a service partnership representing the retired or deceased general partner's share of the partnership's goodwill may be treated as Code Sec. 707(c) guaranteed payments or as a distribution at the election of the partnership. The subject is discussed in detail in Chapter 19.

¶ 1405 Distributions Disregarded

Actual distributions of money or property during the partnership taxable year may be treated as "advances or drawings of money or property against a partner's distributive share of income."[11] The distribution rules do not apply to payments of money or property to a partner which are considered "draws" against future profits. During the year, "draws" appear as memo accounts on the partnership's books. For tax purposes, they are

[8] Reg. § 1.731-1(a)(1)(ii).
[9] Reg. § 1.731-1(c)(2).
[10] Rev. Rul. 93-7, 1993-1 CB 125.
[11] Reg. § 1.731-1(a)(1)(ii).

treated as distributions on the last day of the partnership's year.[12] This rule probably is inapplicable to the extent the draw exceeds the partner's distributive share of the partnership's income.[13]

Example 14-3. *Income draw.* On January 1 of Year 1, Austin Hall's basis for his partnership interest in the ABC partnership is $50. Austin draws $10 each month from the partnership during Year 1. The partnership is on a calendar year. All distributions are in cash. ABC has no profits from January to November, but has profits of $400 for December. Austin's share of the profits is 40%.

For purposes of Code Secs. 731 and 705, "advances or drawings of money or property against a partner's distributive share of income" are not treated as immediate distributions but are deemed to be current distributions made on the last day of the partnership's taxable year.[14] Austin, therefore, has no gain from the drawings because his basis would be determined after including his distributive share of income which would increase his basis. If the drawings were immediate distributions, then, after May, Austin would have a zero basis and any further distributions would result in income to Austin under Code Sec. 731. In addition, he would have to report his share of partnership income at the end of the year.

Deemed money distributions caused by a reduction in a partner's share of partnership liabilities receive draw treatment, assuming they meet the other requirements.[15]

A partner who receives a distribution of a note evidencing the partnership's obligation to pay money has not received either a property or money distribution until the note is paid.

Example 14-4. Hank Stelman wanted a distribution, but he didn't want the adjusted basis of his partnership interest of $100 to be decreased. He suggested the partnership make a current distribution to him of a note from the partnership to himself of $100. They would then pay this note next year.

This would be a useful exercise if Hank could discount the note or borrow money against it. It would appear that the closer the note came to being a cash equivalent, the better argument could be made to treat it as cash. But the note will have zero basis, and when paid by the partnership it will result in more gain than a distribution of cash now.

Under the "substance over form" doctrine, the "assignment of income" doctrine, or the "reallocation of income between related parties" rules of Code Sec. 482, distributions of property to a partner may sometimes be

[12] *Id.*

[13] See Rev. Rul. 81-241, 1981-2 CB 146; Rev. Rul. 81-242, 1981-2 CB 147.

[14] Reg. § 1.731-1(a)(1)(ii). See also Reg. § 1.705-1(a)(1), whereunder its reference to complete liquidations requiring a basis determination at other than year-end suggests that current distributions should be grouped and applied at year-end for gain determination.

[15] Rev. Rul. 99-4, 1994-1 CB 195.

disregarded. For example, if the partnership negotiates a Code Sec. 1031 like-kind exchange, but distributes the property to the partners who execute the exchange, the IRS may contend that the distribution occurred after the exchange.[16]

¶ 1406 Distributions of Encumbered Property

When there is a distribution of encumbered property, partnership debt is shifted to the distributee partner. For tax purposes such a transfer is treated as a concurrent property distribution, cash contribution, and cash distribution. The tax analysis is the same as the previously discussed contribution of encumbered property. In the case of a distribution, the total partnership debt is reduced and, therefore, all the partners, including the distributee partner, have a deemed cash distribution for their reduced shares of that debt.[17] This is true even if the partnership remains jointly liable for the debt.[18] In addition, the distributee has a deemed money contribution for the debt to which the property is subject.[19]

An ordering problem exists if a partnership distributes encumbered property to a partner so that the single distribution results both in a decrease of the distributee's share of partnership liabilities under Code Sec. 752(b) and the assumption by the distributee partner of partnership liabilities under Code Sec. 752(a). The question is whether the deemed money contribution or the distribution is taken into account first for purposes of Code Sec. 752. If the reduction of a partner's share of partnership liabilities is a prior and separate transaction, the amount of money considered to have been distributed under Code Sec. 752(b) may exceed the adjusted basis for the partner's partnership interest and thereby create taxable gain under Code Sec. 731(a)(1).

> ***Example 14-5.*** Austin Hall, who is a 50% partner with a basis for his partnership interest of $1,000, receives a distribution of property from the partnership with a value of $6,000 and subject to a recourse liability of $4,000. Because the partnership liabilities were reduced by $4,000, Austin was relieved of his 50% share, $2,000. This is a deemed money distribution under Code Sec. 752(b) of $2,000. Because he is responsible for the full $4,000 in his personal capacity, however, this is a deemed money contribution under Code Sec. 752(a). If Code Sec. 752(b) is applied first, the partner would recognize gain of $1,000 ($2,000 liability relief less basis for his partnership interest of $1,000) under Code Sec. 731(a).

The IRS considered this issue in Revenue Ruling 79-205 [20] and concluded that the reduction in the distributee partner's share of

[16] *Commr. v. Coast Holding Co.*, SCt, 45-1 USTC ¶ 9215, 324 US 331, 65 SCt 707; Rev. Rul. 75-113, 1975-1 CB 19.

[17] Code Sec. 752(b).

[18] *J.W. LaRue v. Commr.*, 90 TC 465, Dec. 44,652 (1998).

[19] Code Sec. 752(a).

[20] 1979-2 CB 255. This position is adopted in Reg. § 1.752-1(f) and -1(g). See also Rev. Rul. 87-120, 1987-2 CB 161, extending the simultaneity rationale of Rev. Rul. 79-205 for Code Sec. 752(a) and (b) liability adjustments to liquidating distribu-

partnership liabilities and the increase in his or her individual liabilities by the assumption of partnership liabilities are deemed to have occurred at the same time. Only the excess, if any, of the reduction of the distributee partner's share of partnership liabilities over the amount of his or her assumption of partnership liabilities is treated as money distributed for purposes of Code Sec. 731(a)(1). Thus, in this example, Austin would be viewed for purposes of Code Sec. 752 as making a net cash contribution since his debt assumption under Code Sec. 752(b) of $4,000 more than offsets the Code Sec. 752(a) liability relief of $2,000. Austin is treated as having made a $2,000 net cash contribution to the partnership.

As described in the previous example, deemed money contributions and distributions created by a distribution of encumbered property are netted. There is normally a deemed net money contribution. What has not been directly addressed is whether the property distribution or the net money contribution is accounted for first when encumbered property is distributed.

Example 14-6. *Encumbered property distribution.* Carl McMullen has a 10% interest in the equal 10 person Deca Partnership. Carl received a distribution consisting of a downtown San Francisco lot, fair market value $150, with a recourse encumbrance of $100 (which was the only debt the partnership had) and a basis to the partnership of $60. Carl's basis in his partnership interest was $5.

Gain computation. Carl has a 10% interest in partnership capital, profit, and loss. Liabilities total $100. Carl's deemed money contribution from net debt increase is:

Liabilities assumed treated as a contribution of cash [21] ..	$100.00
Relief from his share of liabilities, treated as a distribution of cash.[22] These computations are done simultaneously[23]	(10.00)
Net contribution of cash	*$90.00*

Carl recognizes no gain:

Beginning basis [24]	$5.00
Net cash distribution	(0.00)
Gain recognized [25]	*$0.00*

(Footnote Continued)

tions (actual as well as constructive under Reg. § 1.708-1(b)(1)(iv)) to a partner. Reg. § 1.752-12(f).

[21] Code Sec. 752(a).

[22] Code Sec. 752(b).

[23] Rev. Rul. 79-205, 1979-2 CB 255.

[24] Code Sec. 705.

[25] Code Sec. 731(a).

Carl's postdistribution basis in his partnership interest is:

Original basis (given)		$5.00
Liabilities assumed [26]	$100.00	
Liabilities relieved [27]	(10.00)	
Net deemed cash contribution		90.00
		$95.00
Less partnership's basis in lot [28]		(60.00)
Final postdistribution basis in his partnership interest . . .		*$35.00*

The ordering of the liability adjustments is significant. Carl may prefer that the limitation of Code Sec. 732(a)(2) be applied before Code Sec. 752 is taken into account. In that case, Carl would take a basis of $5 in the property distributed and the deemed contribution to the partnership under Code Sec. 752 will increase the basis in the partnership interest to $90. The example in the 1956 regulations seems to call for giving the lot a basis of $5.[29]

There is little or no direct statutory authority for or against such an approach. Results differ markedly in the gain computation if the liabilities treated as a distribution of cash are given effect prior to the liabilities treated as a contribution of cash. Gain would be recognized in the amount of $5. Results also differ as to the postdistribution basis of the lot. If the basis of the partnership interest is not adjusted for liabilities before the basis of the lot is computed, the basis of the lot is limited by Code Sec. 732(a)(2) to 5$! The Internal Revenue Code at Code Sec. 732(a)(2) and (b) appears to require that the effects of concurrent *cash distributions* be taken into account before the consequence of property distributions are determined. Also, the IRS has ruled and the regulations state that the Code Sec. 752(a) and (b) computations are to be netted.[30] If cash distributions are required to be accounted for before concurrent property distributions, and deemed cash distributions and contributions are to be netted, it is reasonable to assume that the net deemed cash contribution is accounted for before the concurrent property distribution. This is the reverse of the accounting for a contribution of encumbered property. In that case, the deemed cash distribution is accounted for after the concurrent property contribution.

Can the taxpayer structure the distribution as a part sale to him or her because the taxpayer is taking over the debt of $100? He or she is paying $100 for a two-thirds interest in the property by assuming debt of $100 and the taxpayer is receiving a distribution of a one-third interest in the property. There would be an entirely different analysis. The taxpayer would receive a higher basis in the asset.

[26] Code Secs. 752(a) and 723.

[27] Code Secs. 752(b) and 733.

[28] Code Sec. 733.

[29] Reg. § 1.752-1(a)(2).

[30] Rev. Rul. 79-205, 1979-2 CB 255; compare Rev. Rul. 81-242, 1981-2 CB 147. Reg. § 1.752-1(f) and (g).

Example 14-7. *Part sale/ part distribution.* Gina Young, an equal one-tenth partner in the Commune Partnership, was worried about her pet project, the new solar greenhouse the Commune Partnership owned. She drew up the plans and supervised the construction. It was expensive to build and had an outstanding construction loan against it for $80. The Commune would be hard pressed to find permanent financing. Gina, who was a one-tenth partner, was independently wealthy. She offered to *buy* the greenhouse for $20 cash (it had a fair market value of $150 and adjusted basis of $25) and to assume the $80 liability. This is the partnership's only debt and her share of the debt is $8. She would lease it back to the Commune at fair rental. The Commune agreed to this plan; what choice did it have? But the other partners insisted that Gina's interest in the partnership capital be reduced by $50. The basis in her partnership interest was $50.

Transaction treated as part distribution and part purchase. A possible characterization of this transaction would be a one-third distribution and a two-thirds purchase since she paid only two-thirds of the property's fair market value and received the entire property, and her capital account is reduced by the equity not paid for by her cash payment and debt assumption.

Result at Partnership Level

	Sale	*Distribution*
FMV	$100.00	$50.00
Adjusted Basis	(16.67)	$8.33
Partnership gain	*$83.33*	

$100.00	Adjusted basis in the property to Gina obtained on purchase portion of transfer
8.33	Basis to Gina on distribution portion
$108.33	

Gina has a total basis of $108.33 in the property, $100 from her purchase, and $8.33 from the partnership. She would have $8.33 from the partnership because this portion of the partnership's basis for the asset has been allocated to the distribution. The partnership's basis allocated to the distribution would be $8.33.[31] Her basis in her partnership interest would be reduced from $50 by her share of the partnership debt relief of $8 and increased by her share of the income by $8.33. It would be further reduced by the basis of the property distributed. Gina's ending basis in her partnership interest is:

Partnership interest beginning basis	$50.00
Less net debt relief	(8.00)
Plus gain share	8.33
Partnership interest basis before property distribution	*$50.33*
Basis of property distributed	(8.33)
Ending basis of partnership interest	*$42.00*

[31] Code Sec. 732(a)(1).

¶ 1407 Distribution of Securities

For purposes of Code Secs. 731(a)(1) and 737, after December 8, 1994, the term "money" generally includes "marketable securities."[32] As a result, a partner generally recognizes gain to the extent the value of the distributed securities exceeds the partner's basis in his or her partnership interest.

However, the provision permits a partner to receive marketable securities attributable to *his or her share* of the net appreciation of the partnership's marketable securities without recognizing gain. This is done by reducing the amount of marketable securities treated as money by:

1. The excess of the partner's share of net gain that would be recognized if all securities of the type distributed held by the partnership immediately *before* the transaction were sold for fair market value, over

2. The partner's share of gain that would be taken into account if the securities held by the partnership immediately *after* the transaction had been sold.

As a result, Code Sec. 731(c) generally applies only when a partner receives a distribution of marketable securities in exchange for the partner's share of appreciated assets other than marketable securities—*i.e.*, a distribution consisting of more than his or her share of marketable securities from the partnership.

The total value of marketable securities distributed is entered on Form 1065, Schedule K, line 19a, "Distributions of Cash and Marketable Securities," and each partner's share of the value of marketable securities distributed is reported on Schedule K-1, box 19, "Distributions." The amount of the cash distribution shown on line 19a on the Schedule K, Form 1065, and box 19 on Schedule K-1, "does not include the distributee partner's share of the gain on the securities distributed to that partner."

In conformance with legislative intent, all marketable securities retained by the partnership are considered to be of the same type as the distributed securities.[33] A simple example adapted from the legislative history of Code Sec. 731(c) illustrates the general concept.

> ***Example 14-8.*** ABC Partnership holds 300 shares of publicly traded stock; it also owns other assets. Each share has a basis of $10 and a value of $100. *A*'s adjusted basis in his partnership interest is $5,000. *A*'s 1/3 interest in the partnership is liquidated in exchange for the 300 shares of stock worth $30,000.

---

[32] Code Sec. 731(c). Code Sec. 731(c) was enacted as part of the Uruguay Round Agreements Act, P.L. 103-465. This provision does not apply to securities distributed before January 1, 1995, if held by the partnership on July 27, 1994. P.L. 103-465, Act § 741(c)(2).

[33] Reg. § 1.731-2(b)(1); Code Sec. 731(c)(3)(B).

The $30,000 of stock treated as money is reduced by $9,000. This is the excess of (1) *A*'s $9,000 share of the net gain in the partnership's securities before the distribution, over (2) *A*'s $0 share of the net gain in partnership securities after the distribution. It is the amount of gain that would have been allocated to *A* if the partnership sold the shares. Consequently, *A* recognizes a gain of $16,000 which is the amount of stock treated as money ($21,000) reduced by *A*'s $5,000 basis in the partnership. This reduction of gain equals the reduced share of partnership gain which is built into the basis of the distributed securities.

If ABC's share of *X* stock had a fair market value and tax basis of $100 per share, all of the $30,000 value of *X* stock distributed to *A* would be treated as cash. Because the stock would have no built-in gain, *A* would not derive any benefit from this gain limitation despite the fact that *A* may have owned his interest in ABC, and ABC may have owned its *X* stock for several years.

Code Sec. 731(c) provides no relief with respect to a distribution to a partner of his or her pro rata share of that partnership's marketable securities if such securities are not appreciated. Code Sec. 731(c) was amended, in part, to address the deficiencies in Code Sec. 751(b) since the latter provision does not apply to intra-character exchanges of assets in partnership solution.[34] If Code Sec. 731(c) was meant only to tax an exchange by a partner of his or her interest in other appreciated partnership assets for an increased interest in marketable securities, however, it would seem logical for the statute to exclude from the provision a partner's pro rata share of the distributed securities (regardless of whether appreciated) to which he or she would have been entitled absent any shifting of ownership in other partnership assets. However, the approach taken in this limitation on recognized gain seems to indicate that Congress felt that Code Secs. 704(c)(1)(B), 707(a)(2)(B), 737, and 751(b) did not adequately prevent a distributee partner from shifting the economic appreciation in his or her partnership interest into a highly liquid, easily valued security that provided such partners with much potential for realizing value on a tax deferred (or tax eliminated) basis. Only to the extent that the existing appreciation in a distributee partner's partnership interest reflected such partner's share of appreciation in marketable securities already owned by the partnership did Congress apparently believe the distributee partner deserved relief from gain recognition under Code Sec. 731(c). Only in this case can it be assured that no appreciation attributable to other assets (other than appreciation already inherent in marketable securities) is shifted from those assets to highly liquid marketable securities.

As long as a partner's inside basis in the assets of a partnership are in parity with the partner's outside basis in his or her partnership interest, a partner should be able to withdraw his or her full distributive share of

[34] S. Rep. No. 103d Cong., 2d Sess., 155 (1994).

marketable securities without recognizing any gain under Code Sec. 731. If such partner is foregoing a nonappreciated interest in other partnership assets in return for the distribution of marketable securities, the partner should still not recognize gain under Code Sec. 731(a) to the extent the partner has outside basis in the partnership interest that matches his or her share of inside basis in such other assets. The built-in gain limitation is designed to result in gain recognition under Code Sec. 731(a) only when the distributee partner is distributed marketable securities in return for his or her share of unrealized appreciation in such other assets (*i.e.*, shifting built-in gain attributable to those other assets into the marketable securities).

Problems arise, however, under this approach when an inside-outside basis disparity exists with respect to a distributee partner's interest. For example, a partner may have purchased an interest in a partnership at a time when the value of marketable securities held by the partnership was well below their original cost (*i.e.*, reflecting a built-in loss). Later, at a time when the securities had substantially appreciated in value to their original cost, the partnership distributes to such partner his or her pro rata share of such securities. Assuming the partnership had not made a Code Sec. 754 election, the Code Sec. 731(c)(3)(B) limitation would provide the distributee partner with no protection from gain recognition. This would be true even if there were no appreciation in other assets being shifted to the marketable securities (or even if there were no other assets owned by the partnership). These same inequities can arise in any other situation in which an inside-outside basis disparity exists.

Under the statute, the reduction in marketable securities treated as money provided by Code Sec. 731(c)(3)(B) turned on a partner's share of appreciation in marketable securities of the same *class* and *issuer* as the distributed securities. This would severely restrict the application of this limitation on gain somewhat unfairly because part of the reason for the enactment of Code Sec. 731(c) was the view that all marketable securities were cash equivalents. The regulations provide that for purposes of Code Sec. 731(c)(3)(B), all marketable securities held by a partnership are treated as marketable securities of the same class and issuer as the distributed securities.[35] The IRS and Treasury proposed this rule because "treating all marketable securities as a single asset for this purpose is consistent with the basic rationale of Code Sec. 731(c) that marketable securities are the economic equivalent of money. As a result, the amount of the distribution that is not treated as money will depend on the partner's share of the net appreciation in all partnership securities, not on the partner's share of the appreciation in the type of securities distributed."[36]

The effect of the final regulations' expansive definition of the "same class and issuer" rule in the statute is illustrated in the following example.

[35] Reg. § 1.731-2(b)(1).

[36] Preamble to Prop. Reg. § 1.732-2.

Example 14-9. *One class rule.* Assume that Partnership ABC owns securities issued by two different companies. One block of securities issued by *X* Co. has a fair market value of $400 and a tax basis of $400. The other block of securities issued by *Y* Co. has a fair market value of $400 and a tax basis of $100. ABC has liabilities of $500 that had originally been used to purchase the securities (in other words, the securities were 100% debt financed).

ABC distributes to *A*, in liquidation of its one-third interest, $100 of the securities issued by *Y* Co. *A*'s one-third share of ABC's $300 built-in gain in the *Y* Co. securities before the distribution is $100. Since this distribution will completely retire *A*'s interest in ABC, *A*'s share of ABC's built-in gain in the *Y* Co. securities after the distribution is zero. Thus, *A*'s reduction in his share of built-in gain in the *Y* Co. securities is $100. As a result, no portion of the value of the *Y* Co. securities distributed to *A* is characterized as cash under Code Sec. 731(c)(3)(B).

If, instead, ABC distributes $100 of *X* Co. securities (*i.e.*, the nonappreciated securities) in liquidation of *A*'s interest in ABC, the same result should follow. Even though the *X* Co. securities are of a different class and issuer from the *Y* Co. securities that reflect all of ABC's built-in gain, the regulations require that the *X* Co. securities and *Y* Co. securities be treated as securities of the same class and issuer as the distributed securities.[37] Thus, no portion of the distributed *X* Co. securities (up to $100 in value) should be characterized as cash under Code Sec. 731(c).

The single-class-of-stock rule is almost always favorable to taxpayers. However, it does have an adverse result when built-in-loss securities are aggregated with built-in-gain securities to reduce or eliminate the net built-in gain for purposes of the reduction in cash distribution rule.

.01 Definition of Marketable Securities [38]

The term "marketable securities" is very broad; it generally means financial instruments and foreign currencies which are actively traded within the meaning of the straddle provisions of Code Sec. 1092(d)(1). The term "financial instrument" means stocks, other equity interests, debt, options, forward or futures contracts, notional principal contracts, and derivatives. Marketable securities also include interests in actively traded precious metals and other financial instruments specified in the Internal Revenue Code and Treasury regulations.[39] There are four exceptions to the general rule that distributions of marketable securities are treated as money distributions:

---

[37] Reg. § 1.731-2(b)(1).

[38] Code Sec. 731(c)(2).

[39] Code Sec. 731(c)(3)(A) and (C).

1. The provision does not apply if the security was contributed to the partnership by the distributee-partner.

2. To the extent provided in regulations, the provision does not apply if the property distributed was not a marketable security when acquired by the partnership.[40]

3. This provision does not apply to distributions of marketable securities received in a nonrecognition provision such as a Code Sec. 351 contribution or a Code Sec. 368 reorganization if additional requirements are met.[41]

4. Finally, the provision is inapplicable if the partnership is an investment partnership and the partner is an eligible partner. Look-through rules are provided for tiered partnerships.[42]

An investment partnership is a partnership that has never been engaged in a trade or business and substantially all of the assets of which have always consisted of investment assets specified in the Internal Revenue Code and Treasury regulations.[43] A partnership is not treated as engaged in a trade or business by reason of activity as an investor, trader, or dealer in an investment asset.

The term eligible partner is defined in the negative. An eligible partner is any partner who did not contribute any property other than the specified investment asset before the date of distribution.[44] However, a transferee in a nonrecognition transfer is not an eligible partner if the transferor was not an eligible partner.

.02 Basis in Securities Distributed, Partnership Interest and Assets Remaining in the Partnership

The basis to the partner of the distributed securities is increased by the amount of gain recognized under this provision. The basis increase is allocated to individual securities received in proportion to the amounts of unrealized appreciation inherent in each. Neither the deemed money distribution nor the gain recognized under this provision affect the distributee's basis in his or her partnership interest. In addition, Code Sec. 734(b) is applied as if no gain were recognized.

> ***Example 14-10.*** ABC Partnership holds 300 shares of publicly traded stock; it also owns other assets which are not marketable securities. Each share has a basis of $10 and a value of $100. *A*'s adjusted basis in his partnership interest is $5,000. *A*'s one-third interest in the partnership is liquidated in exchange for the 300 shares of stock worth $30,000.

[40] Reg. § 1.731-2(d)(1)(iii).
[41] See Reg. § 1.731-2(d)(1)(ii) and (3).
[42] Code Sec. 731(c)(3)(C)(iv).
[43] Code Sec. 731(c)(3)(C)(i).
[44] Code Sec. 731(c)(3)(C)(iii).

The $30,000 of stock treated as money is reduced by $9,000, the amount of gain that would have been allocated to *A* if the partnership sold the shares. Consequently, *A* recognizes a gain of $16,000 which is the amount of stock treated as money ($21,000) reduced by *A*'s $5,000 basis in the partnership.

A's basis in the stock is $21,000. This is the $5,000 basis he would have in the stock without Code Sec. 731(c) plus the $16,000 gain he recognized because of Code Sec. 731(c). His basis in his partnership interest is his beginning basis of $5,000 and is not adjusted for the deemed money distribution of $21,000, but is adjusted for a distribution of property with a basis of $3,000. This is a liquidating distribution and therefore his basis in his partnership becomes the basis in the securities which is then increased by the $16,000 gain recognized under Code Sec. 731(c).[45] Had this been a current distribution, his partnership interest basis would have been reduced from $5,000 by the partnership's $3,000 basis for the securities to $2,000, and the securities would have a basis equal to the partnership basis of $3,000 plus the Code Sec. 731(c) gain of $16,000, or $19,000.

If *A* sold the shares for their value his gain would be:

Shares Received in a Liquidating Distribution		***Shares Received in a Current Distribution***
$30,000	Sales price	$30,000
(21,000)	Basis	(19,000)
$9,000	Gain from sale of shares	*$11,000*
16,000	Gain on stock distribution	16,000
$25,000	Total	*$27,000*

$25,000 is equal to the gain *A* would have had if the partnership distributed $30,000 cash to him in a liquidating distribution with or without selling the stock.

.03 Coordination with Other Provisions

Code Sec. 731(c) is not the only provision that applies when a partnership distributes marketable securities to a partner. In addition to Code Sec. 731, the partnership must consider the following provisions:

- Code Sec. 704(c)(1)(B) may simultaneously apply if another partner contributed the marketable securities. If so, any basis increase generated by Code Sec. 704(c)(1)(B) is taken into account before Code Sec. 731(c) is applied.[46]

- The Internal Revenue Code and the legislative history are silent on the application of the provision to a termination under Code

[45] If the partnership has a Code Sec. 754 election in effect, it will be required to reduce its basis in remaining assets by the $2,000 step-up in the basis of the securities received by *A*.

[46] Reg. § 1.731-2(g)(1).

Sec. 708(b)(1)(B). However, the regulations treat the newly reconstituted partnership as if it were the terminated partnership for purposes of Code Sec. 731(c).[47]

- The disguised sale rules of Code Sec. 707(a)(2)(B) take precedence over the new provision.

- To the extent that marketable securities are treated as money, that amount also is treated as money for purposes of Code Sec. 737. This reduces the amount of gain recognized under Code Sec. 737. In addition, the portion of the marketable securities not treated as money is treated as property for purposes of Code Sec. 737.[48]

- Code Sec. 751(b) takes precedence over the provisions of Code Sec. 731(c).

The regulations contain several examples of the application of the rules, some of which are analyzed below.[49] In these examples, it is assumed that the deemed sale rules of Code Secs. 707(a)(2)(B), 704(c)(1)(B), 737, and 751(b) do not apply unless otherwise provided. It is further assumed that none of the exceptions to Code Sec. 731(c) apply to the distributed securities, unless otherwise provided.

Example 14-11. *Recognition of gain.* *A* and *B* form partnership AB as equal partners. *A* contributes property with a fair market value of $1,000 and an adjusted tax basis of $250. *B* contributes $1,000 cash. AB subsequently purchases Security *X* for $500 and immediately distributes the security to *A* in a current distribution. *A*'s basis in her partnership interest at the time of distribution is $250.

The distribution of Security *X* is treated as a distribution of money in an amount equal to the fair market value of Security *X* on the date of distribution ($500). As a result, *A* recognizes $250 of gain under Code Sec. 731(a)(1) on the distribution ($500 distribution of money less $250 adjusted tax basis in *A*'s partnership interest).

Because there was no built-in gain or loss inherent in Security *X* at the date of distribution, the amount of the distribution that is treated as money is not reduced under Code Sec. 731(c)(3)(B). The transaction is treated as a cash distribution in its entirety.

Example 14-12. *Reduction in amount treated as money.* *A* and *B* form partnership AB as equal partners. AB subsequently distributes Security *X* to *A* in a current distribution. Immediately before the distribution, AB held securities with the following fair market values, adjusted tax bases, and unrecognized gain or loss:

---

[47] Reg. § 1.731-2(g)(2).

[48] Code Sec. 731(c)(1); Reg. §§ 1.731-2(g)(1)(ii) and 1.704-4(e)(1).

[49] Reg. § 1.731-2(j).

	FMV	*Tax Basis*	*Gain (Loss)*
Security *X* (distributed)	$100	$70	$30
Security *Y*	$100	$80	$20
Security *Z*.	$100	$110	$(10)

If AB had sold the securities for fair market value immediately before the distribution to *A*, the partnership would have recognized $40 of net gain ($30 gain on Security *X* plus $20 gain on Security *Y*, minus $10 loss on Security *Z*). *A*'s distributive share of this gain would have been $20 (one-half of $40 net gain). If AB had sold the remaining securities immediately after the distribution of Security *X* to *A*, the partnership would have $10 of net gain ($20 of gain on Security *Y* minus $10 loss on Security *Z*). *A*'s distributive share of this gain would have been $5 (one-half of $10 net gain). As a result, the distribution resulted in a decrease of $15 in *A*'s distributive share of the net gain in AB's securities ($20 net gain before distribution minus $5 net gain after distribution).

The amount of the distribution of Security *X* that is treated as a distribution of money is reduced by $15. The distribution of Security *X* is therefore treated as a distribution of $85 of money to *A* ($100 fair market value of Security *X* minus $15 reduction).

Example 14-13. *Reduction in amount treated as money—Change in partnership allocations.* *A* is admitted to partnership ABC as a partner with a 1% interest in partnership profits. At the time of *A*'s admission, ABC held no securities. ABC subsequently acquires Security *X*. *A*'s interest in partnership profits is subsequently increased to 2% for securities acquired after the increase in *A*'s profits interest. *A* retains a 1% interest in all securities acquired before the increase. ABC then acquires Securities *Y* and *Z* and later distributes Security *X* to *A* in a current distribution. Immediately before the distribution, the securities held by ABC had the following fair market values, adjusted tax bases, and unrecognized gain or loss:

	FMV	*Tax Basis*	*Gain (Loss)*
Security *X*	$1,000	$500	$500
Security *Y*	$1,000	$800	$200
Security *Z*.	$1,000	$1,100	$(100)

If ABC had sold the securities for fair market value immediately before the distribution to *A*, the partnership would have recognized $600 of net gain ($500 gain on Security *X* plus $200 gain on Security *Y*, minus $100 loss on Security *Z*). *A*'s distributive share of this gain would have been $7 (1% of $500 gain on Security *X* plus 2% of $200 gain on Security *Y*, minus 2% of $100 loss on Security *Z*).

If ABC had sold the remaining securities immediately after the distribution of Security *X* to *A*, the partnership would have $100 of net gain ($200 gain on Security *Y* minus $200 loss on Security *Z*). *A*'s distributive share of this gain would have been $2 (2% of $200 gain on Security *Y* minus 2% of $200 loss on Security *Z*). As a result, the distribution resulted in a decrease of $5 in *A*'s distributive share of the net gain in ABC's securities ($7 net gain before distribution minus $2 net gain after distribution).

The amount of the distribution of Security *X* that is treated as a distribution of money is reduced by $5. The distribution of Security *X* is therefore treated as a distribution of $995 of money to *A* ($1,000 fair market value of Security *X* minus $5 reduction).

Example 14-14. *Basis consequences—Distribution of marketable security. A* and *B* form partnership AB as equal partners. *A* contributes nondepreciable real property with a fair market value and adjusted tax basis of $100.

AB subsequently distributes Security *X* with a fair market value of $120 and an adjusted tax basis of $90 to *A* in a current distribution. At the time of distribution, *A*'s basis in her partnership interest is $100. The amount of the distribution that is treated as money is reduced under Code Sec. 731(c)(3)(B) by $15 (one-half of $30 net gain in Security *X*). As a result, *A* recognizes $5 of gain under Code Sec. 731(a) on the distribution (excess of $105 distribution of money over $100 adjusted tax basis in *A*'s partnership interest).

A's adjusted tax basis in Security *X* is $95 ($90 adjusted basis of Security *X* determined under Code Sec. 732(a)(1) plus $5 of gain recognized by *A* by reason of Code Sec. 731(c)). The basis in *A*'s interest in the partnership is $10 as determined under Code Sec. 733 ($100 predistribution basis minus $90 basis allocated to Security *X* under Code Sec. 732(a)(1)).

Example 14-15. *Basis consequences—Distribution of marketable security and other property. A* and *B* form partnership AB as equal partners. *A* contributes nondepreciable real property, with a fair market value of $100 and an adjusted tax basis of $10.

AB subsequently distributes Security *X* with a fair market value and adjusted tax basis of $40 to *A* in a current distribution *not subject to Code Sec. 737* and, as part of the same distribution, AB distributes Property *Z* to *A* with an adjusted tax basis and fair market value of $40. At the time of distribution, *A*'s basis in her partnership interest is $10. *A* recognizes $30 of gain under Code Sec. 731(a) on the distribution (excess of $40 distribution of money over $10 adjusted tax basis in *A*'s partnership interest).

A's adjusted tax basis in Security *X* is $35 ($5 adjusted basis determined under Code Sec. 732(a)(2) and (c)(2), plus $30 of gain recognized by *A* by reason of Code Sec. 731(c)). *A*'s basis in Property *Z* is $5, as determined under Code Sec. 732(a)(2) and (c)(2).

The basis in *A*'s interest in the partnership is $0 as determined under Code Sec. 733 ($10 predistribution basis minus $10 basis allocated between Security *X* and Property *Z* under Code Sec. 732). Code Sec. 731(c)(5) provides that Code Sec. 733 is applied in determining a distributee's basis in its partnership interest following a distribution of marketable securities as if no gain was recognized under Code Sec. 731(c) and as if the basis of the distributed securities had not been adjusted for any such gain recognition.

AB's adjusted tax basis in the remaining partnership assets is unchanged unless the partnership has a Code Sec. 754 election in effect. If AB made such an election, the aggregate basis of AB's assets would be increased by $70 (the difference between the $80 combined basis of Security *X* and Property *Z* in the hands of the partnership before the distribution and the $10 combined basis of the distributed property in the hands of *A* under Code Sec. 732 after the distribution, but before the basis increase under Code Sec. 731(c)(4)). Under Code Sec. 731(c)(5), Code Sec. 734 (like Code Sec. 733) shall be applied as if no gain had been recognized by *A* by reason of Code Sec. 731(c), and as if no step-up in basis in the distributed marketable securities in the hands of *A* had occurred by reason of Code Sec. 731(c).

Determination of basis when both marketable securities and other property are distributed is not as simple as this example indicates. In Example 14-15, it is assumed that Code Sec. 737 does not apply. Example 14-16, set forth below, illustrates the interaction of Code Secs. 731(c) and 737 in a situation in which the other property distributed has no basis to the partnership.

If the other property has a positive basis, it is not possible to allocate the basis of both properties under Code Sec. 732(a)(2) and (c)(2) because Code Sec. 737(c)(1) (second sentence) states that the basis of the distributed Code Sec. 737 property reflects the increase in the basis of the partnership interest because of gain recognized under Code Sec. 737(a). As a result of this basis increase, neither Code Sec. 732(a)(2) nor (b) will apply to the distributed Code Sec. 737 property. As a result, it is necessary to first apply Code Sec. 732 to the distributed marketable security and then apply Code Secs. 737(c)(1) (second sentence) and 732 to the distributed Code Sec. 737 property. This computation may be illustrated as follows:

Security *X* FMV = $40			Property *Z* FMV = $40	
Tax Basis = $40			Tax Basis = $40	

Partnership interest basis	=	$10	
Security *X* basis	=	$10	(Code Sec. 732(a)(2))
		+ 30	(Code Sec. 731(c)(4))
		$40	
Property *Y* basis	=	$40	(Code Sec. 737(c)(1) increases the adjusted tax basis of *A*'s partnership interest by $40 of Code Sec. 737(a) gain)

Example 14-16. *Coordination with Code Sec. 737. A* and *B* form partnership AB. *A* contributes Property *A*, nondepreciable real property with a fair market value of $200 and an adjusted basis of $100, in exchange for a 25% interest in partnership capital and profits. AB owns marketable Security *X*.

Within seven years of the contribution of Property *A*, AB subsequently distributes Security *X*, with a fair market value of $120 and an adjusted tax basis of $100 to *A* in a current distribution that is subject to Code Sec. 737. As part of the same distribution, AB distributes Property *Y* to *A* with a fair market value of $20 and an adjusted tax basis of $0. At the time of distribution, there has been no change in the fair market value of Property *A* or the adjusted tax basis in *A*'s interest in the partnership.

If AB had sold Security *X* for fair market value immediately before the distribution to *A*, the partnership would have recognized $20 of gain. *A*'s distributive share of this gain would have been $5 (25% of $20 gain). Because AB has no other marketable securities, *A*'s distributive share of gain in partnership securities after the distribution would have been $0. As a result, the distribution resulted in a decrease of $5 in *A*'s share of the net gain in AB's securities ($5 net gain before distribution minus $0 net gain after distribution). The amount of the distribution of Security *X* that is treated as a distribution of money is reduced by $5. The distribution of Security *X* is therefore treated as a distribution of $115 of money to *A* ($120 fair market value of Security *X* minus $5 reduction). The portion of the distribution of the marketable security that is not treated as a distribution of money ($5) is treated as other property for purposes of Code Sec. 737.

A recognizes total gain of $40 on the distribution. *A* recognizes $15 of gain under Code Sec. 731(a)(1) on the distribution of the portion of Security *X* treated as money ($115 distribution of money less $100 adjusted tax basis in *A*'s partnership interest). *A* recognizes $25 of gain under Code Sec. 737 on the distribution of Property *Y* (FMV $20) and the portion of Security *X* that is not treated as money ($5). *A*'s Code

Sec. 737 gain is equal to the lesser of (1) *A*'s precontribution gain ($100), or (2) the excess of the fair market value of property received ($20 fair market value of Property *Y* plus $5 portion of Security *X* not treated as money) over the adjusted basis in *A*'s interest in the partnership immediately before the distribution ($100) reduced (but not below zero) by the amount of money received in the distribution ($115).

A's adjusted tax basis in Security *X* is $115 ($100 basis of Security *X* determined under Code Sec. 732(a)(2) plus $15 of gain recognized by reason of Code Sec. 731(c)). *A*'s adjusted tax basis in Property *Y* is $0 under Code Sec. 732(a)(2). The basis in *A*'s interest in the partnership is $25 ($100 basis before distribution minus $100 basis allocated to Security *X* under Code Sec. 732(a) (and Code Sec. 733), plus $25 gain recognized under Code Sec. 737(a) and (c)(1)).

This example, taken from the regulations, illustrates the interaction between Code Secs. 731(c) and 737, but only in the context where the basis of the other property in the hands of the partnership was zero. In Example 14-15, if Property *Y* had a basis greater than zero (*e.g.* $20) and $25 of gain was recognized under Code Sec. 737(a), does the $5 of securities treated as property for purposes of Code Sec. 737 obtain a basis step-up to $120 pursuant to the operation of Code Secs. 737(c)(1) and 732? Presumably yes, although this situation should be made clear.

Example 14-17. *Comprehensive.* Equal ABC Partnership has 600 shares of *X* stock (per-share FMV = $100, Adjusted Basis = $10). *A*'s basis for his partnership interest is $5,000. The partnership distributes 300 shares to *A* with a fair market value equal to $30,000. *A* remains an equal profits and loss member of the partnership.

General rule of Code Sec. 731(c)(1).

$30,000	Stock's value
(5,000)	Basis of *A*'s partnership interest
$25,000	Gain

Gain is reduced under Code Sec. 731(c)(3)(B).

$18,000	*A*'s share of appreciation before	($600 × $90/3)
(9,000)	*A*'s share of appreciation after	($300 × $90/3)
$9,000	Gain reduction	
$25,000	Gain under Code Sec. 731(c)(1)	
(9,000)	Reduced under Code Sec. 731(c)(3)(B)	
$16,000	Gain	

Basis of distributed stock. Add gain to what the basis would have been under Code Sec. 732:

$3,000	Carryover basis for current distribution [50]
16,000	Plus gain under Code Sec. 731(c)
$19,000	Stock's basis

Note: Allocate basis increase according to relative appreciation if shares are not identical.[51]

Partnership interest adjusted basis. Apply Code Sec. 733 only—*i.e.*, partnership interest adjusted basis is decreased by basis of stock, but not deemed money distribution under Code Sec. 731(c) (FMV Securities). *A*'s partnership interest adjusted basis is:

$5,000	Adjusted basis before distribution
(3,000)	Basis reduction for current distribution disregarding *Code Sec. 731(c)*
$2,000	Ending basis

Basis in remaining property. The gain does not generate a Code Sec. 754/734(b) adjustment.

Coordination with Code Sec. 737. To the extent securities are considered money under Code Sec. 731(c), they are not property under Code Sec. 737 and any basis step-up under Code Sec. 737(c) is not allocated to the securities.

[50] Code Sec. 733.

[51] Code Sec. 731(c)(4); see Reg. § 1.731-2(f)(1).

Chapter 15

Partner Results—Proportionate Nonliquidating Distributions

¶ 1501 Introduction

Nonliquidating distributions, often referred to as current distributions, are distributions of money or other property that are not intended, either alone or in conjunction with other planned distributions, to terminate the partner's interest in the partnership.[1] Although the tax rules governing nonliquidating and liquidating distributions from partnerships are contained in the same sections of the Internal Revenue Code and are very similar in many respects, the differences between them are sufficiently significant to warrant separate discussion. The current chapter focuses on nonliquidating distributions. Chapter 16 discusses the consequences associated with liquidating distributions.

In addition to the distinction between current and liquidating distributions, the law also imposes different consequences for distributions that alter the recipient partner's economic interest in any partnership ordinary income assets (so-called "disproportionate" distributions). These provisions, which recharacterize a portion of the distribution as a taxable exchange between the partner and the partnership, apply to both current and nonliquidating distributions, and are discussed in Chapter 18.

> ***LLC Observation:*** The distribution rules discussed in this chapter apply equally to state law partnerships and LLCs taxed as partnerships.

¶ 1502 Partner Gain

Whether the distribution is liquidating or current, a partner has gain only if that partner receives money in excess of the partner's basis in his or her partnership interest.

---

[1] Code Sec. 761(d).

A cash distribution is first treated as a return of the partner's adjusted basis in the partnership interest. It results in gain only if the distribution exceeds the partner's basis in his or her partnership interest immediately before the distribution.[2] If both cash and property are distributed simultaneously, the cash is treated as being distributed first.[3] Gains are generally taxed as capital gains.[4] A partner is never allowed to recognize a loss on a nonliquidating distribution.[5]

Unless a distribution is a "disproportionate distribution" from a partnership having both ordinary income and capital gain assets, or part of a disguised sale or a distribution of 704(c) property or to a 704(c) partner,[6] there is no other circumstance when a distribution can result in a gain to the partner.[7] However, it must be remembered that, for purposes of this rule, (1) whether a cash distribution has occurred, (2) how much cash has been distributed, and (3) when the distribution occurs, is subject to the rules discussed in Chapter 14.

> ***Example 15-1.*** Angie Lee is a one-third partner in the ABC partnership. Her basis in her partnership interest at year-end is $5,000. At that date, the partnership distributed $30,000 cash to Angie. The distribution was not part of a disguised sale and was not subject to Code Secs. 704(c)(2), 707(a)(2)(b), 737 or 751. Under Code Sec. 731(a), Angie must recognize a $25,000 gain. Under Code Sec. 741, the gain has the same character as if Angie had sold her partnership interest. Thus, assuming Angie has held the partnership interest for more than 12 months, the gain will be a long-term capital gain. Her remaining post-distribution basis in the partnership interest will be zero.

¶ 1503 Partner Loss from Current Distributions

A partner is not allowed a loss as a result of a current distribution. This is because the partner's continuing investment in the partnership precludes a realized loss from the activity.

¶ 1504 Current Distributions—Effect on Basis

In the absence of a cash distribution exceeding the partner's basis in his or her interest, no gain or loss is recognized by a partner on receipt of cash or property in a proportionate nonliquidating distribution. The tax effect of distributions that don't result in gain or loss to the partner require only that the partner and partnership account for the basis of the partner's partnership interest, the basis of any property distributed and the basis of property retained by the partnership.

---

[2] Code Sec. 731(a). A cash distribution for this purpose includes a "deemed" money distribution under Code Sec. 752(b).

[3] Code Sec. 732(d)(2).

[4] Code Sec. 741.

[5] Code Sec. 731(a)(2).

[6] Code Secs. 704(c)(1)(B) and 737.

[7] Disproportionate distributions are discussed in Chapter 17.

.01 *Money Distribution*

The partner must reduce the basis in his or her partnership interest by the amount of money distributed to the partner.[8] If money and property are distributed together, the money distribution is taken into account first.[9] As previously stated, money distributions in excess of the partner's basis result in capital gain to the partner who will then have a zero basis in his or her partnership interest.

.02 *Property Distributions*

A property distribution is generally treated as a nontaxable withdrawal of the property from the partnership. When determining the partner's basis in distributed property and the effect of the distribution on remaining basis in the partnership interest, the focus is first on the adjusted basis of the distributee's partnership interest and then on the partnership's basis in the distributed property.

The basis of property received in a nonliquidating distribution is the basis it had in the partnership immediately before the distribution.[10] The partnership's basis is transferred to the partner. The adjusted basis of the partner's partnership interest is then reduced by the same amount.[11] When there is a Code Sec. 754 election in effect, the property's basis for this purpose includes any Code Sec. 743(b) adjustments related to the distributee partner.[12] Code Sec. 743(b) adjustments to the property's basis which are personal to other partners are reallocated to the partnership's remaining like-kind property. Any Code Sec. 743(b) adjustments which are personal to the distributee partner are included in his or her basis for the property.[13] The partnership's basis also includes Code Sec. 734(b) adjustments made as a result of earlier distributions enumerated in Code Sec. 734(b) when there was a Code Sec. 754 election in effect.[14] These adjustments pass through to the distributee partner and are included in his or her basis in the distributed property, subject to the limitations of Sec. 732.

If a single property is distributed and its basis to the partnership exceeds the partner's basis in his or her partnership interest, then the partner's adjusted basis in the partnership interest will, in effect, become the substituted basis of the property. This will result in a zero basis in his or her partnership interest and a step down in the property's basis.[15]

Example 15-2. Jed Mooney has a basis in his partnership interest of $18,000. In a nonliquidating distribution, he receives a tract of raw land worth $60,000. Its basis in the partnership's hands prior to the distribution was $25,000. Jed will recognize no gain on receipt of the distribution and will take an $18,000 basis in the property (the lesser

[8] Code Sec. 733(1).
[9] Code Sec. 732(d)(2).
[10] Code Sec. 732(a)(1).
[11] Code Sec. 733.
[12] Reg. §§ 1.743-1(g)(1) and 1.732-2(b).
[13] Reg. § 1.743-1(b)(2)(ii).
[14] Reg. § 1.732-2(g).
[15] Code Secs. 732(a)(2) and 733(2).

of $18,000 basis in his partnership interest or $25,000 basis of the property).

If more than one property is distributed in a single distribution and the partnership's total basis for these assets exceeds the partner's basis in his or her interest, an allocation of that basis to the distributed property is necessary. The partnership interest's adjusted basis, once reduced by concurrent cash distributions, is first allocated to any unrealized receivables,[16] and inventory is distributed up to the partnership's predistribution basis in these assets.[17]

Example 15-3. Susan Timmons has a tax basis in her partnership interest of $20,000. In a nonliquidating distribution, she receives the following assets:

Assets	*Tax Basis*	*FMV*
Cash	$10,000	$10,000
Accounts Receivable	0	15,000
Inventory	7,500	17,500
Capital Asset	12,000	20,000
	$29,500	*$62,500*

She recognizes no gain on the distribution. The cash reduces her basis in the partnership interest to $10,000. She then allocates zero basis to the receivables and $7,500 to the inventory. Her remaining $2,500 of basis is allocated to the capital asset.

If the partner does not have enough available basis to cover the full amount of the partnership's basis in unrealized receivables and inventory, the shortfall in available basis must be allocated among the unrealized receivables and inventory. The difference between (1) the partnership's basis in the unrealized receivables and inventory, and (2) the partner's substituted basis available for allocation is treated as a basis "decrease." The decrease is allocated first to properties with unrealized depreciation.[18] Any remaining decrease is allocated in proportion to the respective bases of the unrealized receivables and inventory.[19] This formula is designed to reduce the partner's basis in depreciated property, and will reduce loss when the property is disposed of.

Example 15-4. Assume the same facts as in the previous example, except that Susan's tax basis in her partnership interest prior to the distribution was only $15,000. Thus, the basis of the properties received from the partnership must be reduced by $14,500 ($29,500 − $15,000). As before, she will allocate basis to the assets received in the following order: (1) cash; (2) receivables and inventory; (3) other assets. The cash will reduce the basis of her partnership to $5,000. This basis will be allocated to the receivables and inventory, which have a

[16] Except for the accounts receivable of an accrual-basis partnership, this basis is normally zero.

[17] Code Sec. 732(c).

[18] Code Sec. 732(c)(3)(A).

[19] Code Sec. 732(c)(1)(A)(ii) and (3)(B).

basis to the partnership of $7,500. Since neither asset has declined in value, the $2,500 basis decrease is allocated to the two assets in this category in proportion to their respective bases. Thus, the inventory will receive the full $2,500 basis decrease attributable to this category of assets, leaving her with a basis in the inventory of $5,000. The remaining $12,000 decrease in basis will be applied to the capital asset, giving her a basis of zero in that asset.

Basis remaining after allocations to inventory and unrealized receivables is allocated to other properties (Code Sec. 1221/1231 property) to the extent of the partnership's basis in those properties. A decrease in the basis of Code Sec. 1221/1231 property is required if the partner does not have sufficient basis to allocate the partnership's full basis in these properties.[20] The basis decrease is first allocated to property with unrealized depreciation to the extent of the unrealized depreciation in each property.[21] If insufficient basis is available to decrease the partner's basis by the full amount of depreciation in each property, the available basis decrease is allocated to the properties in proportion to their respective amounts of unrealized depreciation. Any remaining decrease is allocated to the properties in proportion to their respective adjusted bases.[22] The decrease made in proportion to the bases of the properties is calculated taking into account any basis decreases made to depreciated property.

Example 15-5. Blum Partnership, which has two assets, *C* and *D*, distributes them both to a partner, Sabina Lowe, whose basis in her partnership interest is $2,000. Neither asset is inventory or an unrealized receivable. Asset *C* has a basis to the partnership of $1,500 and a fair market value of $1,500, and Asset *D* has a basis to the partnership of $1,500 and a fair market value of $500.

Sabina's basis is first allocated to the extent of the partnership's basis in each distributed property—$1,500 to each distributed property—for a total of $3,000. However, since Sabina's basis in her interest is only $2,000, a downward adjustment of $1,000 ($3,000 – $2,000) is required. The entire amount of the $1,000 downward adjustment is allocated to Asset *D* due to its unrealized depreciation, reducing its basis to $500. Thus, the basis of Asset *C* is $1,500 in Sabina's hands, and the basis of Asset *D* is $500 in Sabina's hands. Her remaining basis in her interest is zero.

A special election applies to property distributions that occur within two years of a partner's acquisition of his or her partnership interest. Even though a Code Sec. 754 election is not in effect for the year the partnership interest is acquired, the partner may treat the partnership's basis in the

[20] For distributions prior to the August 5, 1997, effective date of the Taxpayer Relief Act of 1997 (P.L. 105-34), if the partner's basis in his or her interest was less than the basis to the partnership, the basis of his or her interest was allocated to the distributed assets according to their relative basis.

[21] Code Sec. 732(c)(3)(A).

[22] Code Sec. 732(c)(3)(B).

distributed property as if it included any adjustment that would have been made under Code Sec. 743(b) if such an election was in effect.[23]

As a result of these modified carryover basis rules, the partnership's unrealized appreciation or depreciation will be taxed to the partner when he or she makes a taxable disposition of the property. The partner's holding period in the property includes the partnership's holding period. The character of the gain or loss as capital or ordinary is generally determined by reference to the nature of the partner's post-distribution use. There are two circumstances, however, when a later taxable disposition will result in ordinary gain or loss to the distributee partner without regard to his or her personal use of the property: (1) sales of distributed partnership unrealized receivables,[24] and (2) sales of distributed partnership inventory within five years of the distribution.[25] These rules are discussed in the next section.

.03 Subsequent Sale of Distributed Property

The characterization of gain or loss on the disposition of property is generally determined by the character of the asset in the hands of the taxpayer who disposes of the property. But property acquired in a nonrecognition transaction is often subject to special rules that govern not only its basis and holding period, but also the tax character of the asset.[26] So it is with property received by a partner in a distribution from a partnership. The basis rules of Code Sec. 732 limit the basis of ordinary income assets received by a partner to the partnership's basis in those assets. To complete the grand design and prevent the conversion of partnership ordinary income into partner capital gain, Code Sec. 735 provides additional rules to govern the character of gain or loss on the subsequent disposition of ordinary income property received by the partner in a distribution. In this respect, Code Sec. 735 is similar to Code Sec. 724, covering property contributions to a partnership, which preserves the ordinary income character of certain property contributed to a partnership in appropriate cases. Code Sec. 735 also provides for the tacking of the partnership's holding period in the distributed property.

Characterization. Under Code Sec. 735(a), gains or losses recognized by a distributee partner on the disposition of what were partnership "unrealized receivables" received in a distribution are treated as ordinary income or loss,[27] and gains or losses on the sale or exchange of distributed partnership inventory items (whether or not substantially appreciated) suffer a similar character taint if they are sold or exchanged by the partner within five years from the date of distribution.[28] In the case of unrealized

[23] Code Sec. 732(d). A discussion of this adjustment appears at ¶ 1602.04.

[24] Code Sec. 735(a)(1)(A).

[25] Code Sec. 735(a)(1)(B).

[26] See, *e.g.*, Code Secs. 351, 358, 362(a), 1032, 1223(1), (2), 1245(a)(2) and (b)(3).

[27] Code Sec. 735(a)(1). "Unrealized receivables" are as defined in Code Sec. 751(c), except that recapture items are not included in the definition for purposes of Code Sec. 735(a).

[28] Code Sec. 735(a)(2). In defining inventory items under Code Sec. 735(a)(2), the long-term holding period requirement for Code Sec. 1231 property is disregarded. Code Sec. 735(c)(1). Thus, if property would be Code Sec. 1231 property except for the fact that the partnership did not hold it

receivables, the character taint remains with the assets as long as they are held by the distributee partner. Since the taint is not permanent with inventory, a patient partner who holds these items as capital assets may avoid ordinary income characterization on the sale or exchange of the inventory by delaying any disposition until the expiration of five years from the date of distribution.[29] If an item is both an unrealized receivable and an inventory item, the more stringent rules governing unrealized receivables are applicable. The Code Sec. 735 taint cannot be removed in a nonrecognition transaction or a series of such transactions.[30] Except in the case of C corporation stock received in a Code Sec. 351 corporate formation, the taint carries over to the exchanged basis property received in the transaction.[31]

Example 15-6. *Income character.* The ABC partnership is a land dealership. *B*, an attorney, receives a current distribution of land from ABC on June 1 of Year 1. The basis of the land to the partnership is $20 and its fair market value at the date of distribution is $21. *B*'s basis in his partnership interest prior to the distribution is $50. On July 1 of Year 4, *B* sells the land for $30.

Amount realized	$30
Basis [32]	(20)
Gain	$*10*

The land was partnership inventory when distributed as defined in Code Sec. 751(d)(2)(A). When sold by *B*, it would produce ordinary income even though it may be a capital asset in *B*'s hands because Code Sec. 735(a)(2) preserves the ordinary character of the gain until five years after distribution.

Example 15-7. *Alternative 1.* In Example 15-6 above, assume that *B* sold the land on July 1 of Year 6. If the property is a Code Sec. 1231 or a capital asset in *B*'s hands, the character of this gain is capital because *B* held the land for more than five years and Code Sec. 735(a)(2) would no longer taint the property.

Example 15-8. *Alternative 2.* Assume the same facts as above, except that ABC purchased the land on June 1 of Year 1, for $20, distributed it to *B* on June 1 of Year 2, and *B* sold it on July 1, Year 6, for $30. What is the amount and character of *B*'s gain? *B*'s gain is $10. The character of the gain is ordinary since *B* sold it before he held it for five years.[33] Code Sec. 735(b) does not allow *B* to tack the holding period of the partnership for purposes of Code Sec. 735(a)(2).

(Footnote Continued)

long-term, it nonetheless is treated as Code Sec. 1231 property and not as an inventory item. Code Sec. 751(d)(2)(B).

[29] For purposes of measuring this period, the holding period in the hands of the partnership does not tack. Code Sec. 735(b), parenthetical clause.

[30] Code Sec. 735(c)(2)(A).

[31] Code Sec. 735(c)(2)(B).

[32] Code Sec. 732(a)(1).

[33] Code Sec. 735(a)(2).

Example 15-9. *Income character.* ABC partnership was formed in October of Year 1. Prior to formation, *A* had, as a sole proprietor, been in the business of building and selling single family homes as a developer; he contributed to the partnership a number of single family homes held for sale to customers. *B* contributed a shopping center adjacent to *A*'s subdivision. *C* contributed cash. The business of the partnership was holding the contributed property for rental purposes. On December 31 of Year 4, ABC liquidated and distributed to *C* the single family homes originally contributed by *A*. *C* continued to hold the homes as rental property until July 30 of Year 9, when he sold them to one buyer in one transaction at a substantial gain. The gain is ordinary income.

Because the single family homes were inventory items to *A*, any gain or loss on their disposition by the partnership within five years after receipt will be treated as ordinary income or loss under Code Sec. 724(b). Code Sec. 724(b) does not carryover to the partnership the character of *the property* but only the character of the gain or loss; these homes are not inventory to the partnership, but they remain inventory items under Code Sec. 751(d)(2). Code Sec. 64 provides that gain from the sale of property treated as ordinary income will be treated as gain from the sale of property that is neither a capital asset nor Code Sec. 1231(b) property. Code Sec. 751(d)(2)(B) defines as an inventory item property that on sale is considered other than a capital asset or Code Sec. 1231 property. Thus, these single family homes from *A* are inventory items to the partnership although not held for sale. When the partnership distributes them to *C* they are therefore inventory items and because *C* sold them within five years of distribution, the gain is ordinary income under Code Sec. 735(a)(2).

Example 15-10. Assume the same facts as above, except that rather than selling the property in Year 9, *C* exchanged it for like-kind property on June 30 of Year 8, and sold the like-kind property on September 30 of Year 9. The gain to *C* on the sale of the property received in the like-kind exchange is also ordinary income property under Code Sec. 735(c)(2)(A) because it is "substituted basis property" to which the same tax treatment applies.

Example 15-11. Assume the same facts as in Example 15-9, except that rather than selling the property, *C* contributed it to a corporation under Code Sec. 351 on June 30 of Year 8, and sold the stock at a gain on September 30 of Year 9. *C*'s gain would now be capital. Although the corporate stock has a substituted basis, the "substituted basis property" rule of Code Sec. 735(c)(2)(A) does not apply to corporate stock in a C corporation received in a Code Sec. 351 exchange for the inventory items.[34] *C* has not disposed of the inventory

[34] Code Sec. 735(c)(2)(B).

items by sale or exchange or of any covered substituted basis property, so Code Sec. 735(a)(2) does not apply.

Code Sec. 735(a) does not apply to recapture property.[35] But the recapture gain which the partnership would have recognized on a sale of the property carries over to the distributee partner, who recognizes ordinary income (to the extent thereof) on a subsequent sale or exchange. This is accomplished through the definitions of "recomputed basis" and "additional depreciation" in the applicable recapture provisions. For example, where Code Sec. 1245 property is distributed by a partnership to a partner, the amount of Code Sec. 1245(a) ordinary income which the partnership would have recognized had it sold the recapture property at its fair market value on the date of the distribution is generally added to the distributee's recomputed adjusted basis in the property in determining his or her ordinary income.[36] The Senate Report accompanying the passage of Code Sec. 1245 provides an example of a distribution of property subject to Code Sec. 1245 recapture. The example would also apply if it were a current distribution. It illustrates the rule as follows:[37]

> The application of this provision is illustrated as follows: A, B, and C are equal partners in a partnership whose assets consist of three pieces of Code Sec. 1245 property, assets X, Y, and Z, each with a fair market value of $100,000. Asset X has an adjusted basis of $60,000 and a recomputed basis of $85,000; Asset Y has an adjusted basis of $85,000 and a recomputed basis of $110,000; and Asset Z has an adjusted basis of $95,000 and a recomputed basis of $100,000. Asset Y is distributed to B in complete liquidation of his partnership interest. B's basis in his partnership interest is $75,000, and under Code Sec. 732 this basis is allocated to Asset Y. If B later sells Asset Y for $103,000 at a time when the adjusted basis is still $75,000 and if B has not taken any depreciation deductions with respect to Asset Y since the distribution, the gain to which Code Sec. 1245(a) applies would be $15,000, since the recomputed basis of the property is only $90,000, that is, the adjusted basis of the property ($75,000) increased by the amount of gain ($15,000) which would have been recognized to the partnership if the asset had been sold for its fair market value at the time of distribution ($100,000 minus $85,000).[38]

Tacked holding periods. Code Sec. 735(b) requires the distributee partner to take the partnership's holding period [39] with respect to property with a transferred basis from the partnership.[40] Tacking is not permitted, however, in measuring the five year taint applicable to distributed "inventory items."[41] This tacking rule applies regardless of whether the property is received in a current or a liquidating distribution, and consequently the distributee may be required to take the partnership's holding period (rather than the holding period of his or her partnership interest) even though the basis of the distributed property is computed with reference to the basis of

[35] *Id.*

[36] Code Sec. 1245(b)(6)(B)(i). See Code Sec. 1245(a)(2) for the definition of "recomputed basis." Code Sec. 1245(a)(1)(A). The recomputed basis must be reduced by any Code Sec. 751(b) gain recognized with respect to the property on the distribution.

[37] S. Rep. No. 1881, 87th Cong., 2d Sess. (1962), reprinted in 1962-3 CB 984.

[38] Similar rules apply to other types of recapture property. See, *e.g.*, Code Sec. 1250(d)(6).

[39] Tacking is not permitted, however, on property received in a Code Sec. 751(b) deemed purchase rather than a Code Sec. 731 distribution.

[40] Code Sec. 1223(2). This rule also applies when the partner would take a transferred basis from the partnership but for the limitations of Code Sec. 732(a)(2), (c) and (d).

[41] Code Sec. 735(b), parenthetical clause.

his or her partnership interest.[42] If the partnership acquired the distributed property by contribution from a partner, the distributee is also required to include the period for which the property was held by the contributing partner.[43]

Example 15-12. *Holding period.* The ABC partnership has many assets, one of which is land with an adjusted basis of $18 and a fair market value of $20. ABC purchased this land on September 30 of Year 2. *C* receives this land as a current distribution on January 1 of Year 3. Prior to the distribution, *C*'s basis in his partnership interest, which he purchased on December 29 of Year 2, was $100. On February 1 of Year 3, *C* sells the land at a gain. Assuming the land is a capital asset to *C*, the gain is short term capital gain. Code Sec. 735(b) allows *C* to tack the holding period of the partnership under Code Sec. 1223. Even with tacking, however, the holding period is not in excess of one year.

Example 15-13. *Alternative 1—Long term.* Assume the same facts as in Example 15-12. *C* sells the land on October 1 of Year 3. With Code Sec. 735(b) and Code Sec. 1223 tacking, *C*'s holding period is more than one year.

Example 15-14. *Alternative 2—Distribution of contributed property.* Assume the land in Example 15-12 was purchased by *A* on September 1 of Year 2. *A* contributed the land to ABC on September 30 of Year 2. On January 1 of Year 3, the land is distributed to *C*, who sells it at a gain on September 15 of Year 3. When ABC received the land, it was able to tack the holding period of *A*. When the land is distributed to *C*, Code Sec. 735(b) and Code Sec. 1223 allow *C* to tack the holding period of ABC, which includes *A*'s holding period.[44] *C*'s gain is long-term.

Example 15-15. *Alternative 3—Character of income.* Assume that, instead of land, the asset distributed to *C* in Example 15-12 on January 1 of Year 2, was partnership inventory. If *C* sells the land on June 1 of Year 2, for $20, *C*'s gain is $2. *C*'s gain is ordinary.[45] This is true even if the inventory is not substantially appreciated. Any gain on resale of the partnership's inventory within five years of the distribution is ordinary income. The recharacterization is not limited to the potential ordinary income in the hands of the partnership at time of distribution.

---

[42] Code Sec. 732(a)(2) or (b).

[43] Code Sec. 1223(2); Reg. § 1.735-1(b).

[44] Reg. § 1.735-1(b).

[45] Code Sec. 735(a)(2).

Chapter 16

Partner Results—Liquidating Distributions

¶ 1601 Introduction

A partner's interest in a partnership may be liquidated either as part of the liquidation of the entire partnership or merely the termination of a specific partner's interest in an ongoing partnership. In the case of a liquidating partnership, a relatively simple set of rules governs the distributee's gain, loss and basis in distributed assets if there is not a disproportionate distribution involving unrealized receivables and substantially appreciated inventory items. There are no tax consequences to the partnership; it simply ceases to exist.[1] However, in the case of a liquidating distribution, it is especially likely that the distributee partner will receive property that does not represent his or her pro rata share of the ordinary income and capital gain assets and, therefore, the provisions of Code Sec. 751(b) governing disproportionate distributions will often apply (see Chapter 18). When a service partnership continues and a general partner's interest is terminated by a distribution, both the partnership and the distributee general partner's results are governed by a combination of the provisions governing liquidating distributions and operating distributions.[2] In such cases, some portion of the liquidating distribution to the general partner is generally treated as either a guaranteed payment under Code Sec. 707(c) or as a share of income.

If the special rules applying to the liquidation of a general partner's interest in a continuing service partnership do not apply, the liquidated partner's tax consequences are the same whether the partnership is liquidated or continues with only the partner's elimination.

Even though the economic result may be similar, the distribution rules do not apply when a partner's interest is reduced or terminated by a sale to

[1] Code Sec. 731(b).

[2] Code Sec. 736. A detailed discussion of this topic is contained in Chapter 19.

the other partners. In a liquidating distribution, the remaining partners buy out a partner with partnership assets, but in a cross-purchase the other partners use their personal assets.

This chapter addresses the basic rules applying to partnership distributions in complete liquidation of a partner's interest. After the basic rules are described, the effects of Code Sec. 751(b) on disproportionate liquidating distributions are outlined in Chapter 18. Distributions to a general partner which are in liquidation of an interest in a service partnership are discussed in Chapter 19.

> ***LLC Observation.*** The liquidating distribution rules discussed in the chapter apply equally to state law partnerships and LLCs taxed as partnerships.

¶ 1602 Distributee Partner Gain or Loss

As with operating distributions, also known as current or nonliquidating distributions, a retiring partner recognizes gain on a liquidating distribution only to the extent that the cash received exceeds the partner's outside basis in the partnership interest. If both cash (which is not in excess of basis) and other property are distributed, Code Secs. 731 and 732 work in tandem to treat the distribution as a nonrecognition transaction. First, the partner reduces basis in the partnership interest by the cash received and then, in effect, exchanges his or her remaining partnership interest for the other assets received in the distribution. Code Sec. 731 affords nonrecognition treatment to the partner and the partnership on the distribution, and Code Sec. 732(b) provides the partner with an aggregate basis in the distributed property equal to his or her predistribution outside basis in the partnership interest less any cash received in the liquidation. This exchanged basis mechanism preserves any gain or loss inherent in the partner's interest for recognition when the partner subsequently disposes of the distributed assets. If more than one asset is received, Code Sec. 732(c) once again prescribes the method for allocating the aggregate exchanged basis.[3]

Liquidating distributions usually involve a complete termination of liability for any share of partnership debt because either the partnership ceases to exist or the partner is no longer responsible for its debts. This reduced share of partnership debt is netted with any liabilities the partner takes over from the partnership. Net debt relief is treated as additional money received.[4] If the partner takes over more than his or her share of partnership liabilities, the partner's basis in the partnership will be increased by the net increase and will be allocated among the distributed assets as described below. If the partner takes over his or her pro rata share of the partnership debt, there will be no deemed cash receipt or payment.

---

[3] If the retiring partner received cash in excess of his or her outside basis, the partner would recognize capital gain to the extent of the excess and any distributed assets would take a zero basis in the partner's hands.

[4] Code Sec. 752(a) and (b). See Chapter 10.

But consider the partner who receives solely cash, unrealized receivables and inventory items in a liquidating distribution.[5] In that event, unlike the case with operating distributions, Code Sec. 731(a)(2) provides that the partner recognizes a loss to the extent that his or her outside basis exceeds the sum of the cash distributed plus the partner's Code Sec. 732 transferred basis in the receivables and inventory items. The loss is considered as incurred on the sale or exchange of a partnership interest and thus is a capital loss under Code Sec. 741. Where a partner receives only cash, any realized loss must be recognized because the partner may not defer recognition by way of an exchanged basis for cash. If the partner also receives ordinary income assets, the basis of these assets cannot be increased.[6] The excess of the partner's former basis in his or her partnership interest in excess of the basis allocated among the ordinary income assets is recovered as loss. The immediate recognition of loss is required to prevent the partner from converting a capital loss into an ordinary loss on the sale of the distributed assets.

The converse, however, is not true. If the partner's basis in his partnership interest is less than the partnership's basis in the ordinary income assets, the distributee partner's basis in them will be less than the partnership's basis. In that case, the ordinary income reported from the sale of these assets by the partner will exceed the amount of ordinary income that would have been reported by the partnership.

To illustrate, assume that a retiring partner with an outside basis of $60 receives $20 cash and ordinary income assets with an inside basis of $25 in a liquidating distribution to which Code Sec. 751(b) does not apply.[7] The partner first reduces his or her outside basis by the $20 cash received and, without more, the partner would be left with a $40 exchanged basis to spread among the ordinary income assets, which would result in less ordinary income or more ordinary loss when the partner sells those assets. But recall that Code Sec. 732(c)(1) limits the partner's basis in ordinary income assets to the partnership's predistribution inside basis—$25 in this example. As a corollary to this rule, Code Sec. 731(a)(2) provides that the partner recognizes a $15 capital loss—the excess of his or her $60 outside basis over the sum of the $20 cash received and the $25 transferred basis in the ordinary income assets.

Example 16-1. Richard Hall is a partner in the equal ABC Partnership. His basis in his partnership interest is $9,000. Richard receives a distribution of the following assets in liquidation of his entire partnership interest:

Assets	*Adjusted Basis*
Cash	$1,000
Inventory	$6,000

[5] This assumes no application of Code Sec. 736(a) or 751(b).

[6] Code Sec. 732(c)(1)(A)(i).

[7] Code Secs. 736(a) and 751(b) are both inapplicable if the retiring partner receives a pro rata distribution of partnership properties.

The cash distribution reduces Richard's basis to $8,000, which can be allocated only to the extent of $6,000 to the inventory items. The remaining $2,000 basis, not allocable to the distributed property, is deductible as a capital loss to Richard under Code Sec. 731(a)(2).[8]

Observation. When a liquidating distribution will cause a capital loss to the partner, the parties should consider distributing low value Code Sec. 1231 property in addition to cash and ordinary income assets. The capital loss is converted to basis in the Code Sec. 1231 property. Assuming the property remains Code Sec. 1231 property to the partner, its sale at a loss is an ordinary loss.

¶ 1603 Former Partner's Basis in the Distributed Assets

A liquidating distribution generally results in the partner's basis in his or her partnership interest being transferred to the distributed property.[9] It is allocated as previously noted first to cash and then to inventory and unrealized receivables.[10] The maximum basis that can be allocated to these assets is their former basis to the distributing partnership. Any remaining basis in the partnership interest is allocated to any other property received in the distribution. The amount of the liquidated partner's basis in his or her partnership interest allocated to capital asset/Code Sec. 1231 property is a substituted basis. This allocation is identical to that required when there is a nonliquidating distribution, if the partnership's basis in the distributed property exceeds the distributee's basis in his or her partnership interest. In the substituted basis transaction, distributed properties assume the same total basis as the partner's basis in his or her partnership interest.[11]

.01 Basis of Distributed Property Decreased

Allocate first to unrealized receivables and inventory. A distributee partner's substituted basis is first allocated to any unrealized receivables or inventory items that were distributed as part of the transaction.[12] Basis is allocated to unrealized receivables and inventory to the extent of the partnership's basis in these items.[13] Unrealized receivables and inventory are defined in Code Sec. 751(c) and Code Sec. 751(d), respectively.

Insufficient basis to cover unrealized receivables and inventory. If the partner does not have enough available basis to cover the full amount of the partnership's basis in unrealized receivables and inventory, the shortfall in available basis must be allocated among the unrealized receivables and inventory. The difference between the partnership's basis in the

[8] If the election under Code Sec. 754 is in effect, see Code Sec. 734(b) for adjustment of the basis of undistributed partnership property.

[9] Code Sec. 732(b).

[10] Code Sec. 732(c).

[11] Substituted basis is used when the partner's interest is liquidated. Substituted basis also applies when a partner receiving a nonliquidating distribution cannot carry over the partnership's basis in the property because the carryover basis exceeds the partner's basis in the partnership.

[12] Note that basis is first reduced by any cash received.

[13] Code Sec. 732(c)(1)(A).

unrealized receivables and inventory, and the partner's substituted basis available for allocation is treated as a basis "decrease." The decrease is allocated first to properties with unrealized depreciation.[14] This formula is designed to reduce the partner's basis in depreciated property, and will prevent excessive losses when the property is disposed of. Any remaining decrease is allocated based upon the relative basis of the unrealized receivables and inventory as adjusted.

Example 16-2. Roberta Gahl, a partner in the equal ABC Partnership, receives a distribution in liquidation of her entire partnership interest. Roberta's basis in her partnership interest is $9,000. She receives the following assets:

Assets	*Adjusted Basis*
Cash	$6,000
Inventory	6,000
Real Property	4,000
	$16,000

The cash distribution reduces Roberta's basis to $3,000, which is allocated entirely to the inventory items. The real property has a zero basis in Roberta's hands. The partnership bases not carried over to Roberta for the distributed properties are lost unless an election under Code Sec. 754 is in effect requiring the partnership to adjust the bases of remaining partnership properties under Code Sec. 734(b).

Other distributed properties. Any basis remaining after allocations to inventory and unrealized receivables is allocated to other properties to the extent of the partnership's basis in those properties. After this amount, basis increases are allocated first to properties with unrealized appreciation. Any additional increase is allocated in proportion to the relative values of the properties. A decrease in basis is required if the partner does not have sufficient basis to allocate the partnership's full basis in the properties.[15] The basis decrease is first allocated to property with unrealized depreciation to the extent of the unrealized depreciation in each property.[16] If insufficient decrease is available to decrease the partner's basis by the full amount of depreciation in each property, the available decrease is allocated to the properties in proportion to their respective amounts of unrealized deprecation. Any remaining decrease is allocated to the properties in proportion to their respective adjusted bases.[17] The decrease made in proportion to the properties' bases is calculated after taking into account any basis decreases made to depreciated property.

Example 16-3. Pear Partnership distributes Assets *C* and *D* in liquidation to a partner, Sabrina Yeltsin, whose basis in her partner-

[14] Code Sec. 732(c)(3)(A).

[15] For distributions prior to the August 5, 1997, the effective date of the Taxpayer Relief Act of 1997 (P.L. 105-34), if the partner's basis in his or her interest was less than the basis to the partnership, the basis of his or her interest was allocated to the distributed assets according to their relative basis.

[16] Code Sec. 732(c)(3)(A).

[17] Code Sec. 732(c)(3)(B).

ship interest is $2,000. Neither asset is inventory or an unrealized receivable. Asset *C* has a basis to the partnership of $1,500 and a fair market value of $1,500, and Asset *D* has a basis to the partnership of $1,500 and a fair market value of $500.

Sabrina's basis is first allocated to the extent of the partnership's basis in each distributed property, or $1,500 to each distributed property, for a total of $3,000. However, since Sabrina's basis in her interest is only $2,000, a downward adjustment of $1,000 ($3,000 – $2,000) is required. The entire amount of the $1,000 downward adjustment is allocated to Asset *D* due to its unrealized depreciation, reducing its basis to $500. Thus, the basis of Asset *C* is $1,500 in Sabrina's hands, and the basis of Property *D* is $500.

Example 16-4. Leopold Zahn is a one-fourth equal partner in Partnership ABCD and has an adjusted basis in his partnership interest of $200. The ABCD Partnership distributes Asset *X* and Asset *Y* to Leopold in liquidation of his entire partnership interest.

Asset	*Adjusted Basis*	*FMV*
X	$150	$200
Y	$150	$50

Neither of the assets consists of inventory items or unrealized receivables. Leopold's basis is first assigned to the distributed property to the extent of the partnership's basis in each distributed property. Thus, Asset *X* and Asset *Y* are each assigned $150. Because the aggregate adjusted basis of the distributed property, $300, exceeds the basis to be allocated, $200, a decrease of $100 in the basis of the distributed property is required. Assets *X* and *Y* have unrealized depreciation of $50 and $100, respectively. Thus, one-third of the decrease is allocated to Asset *X* and two-thirds to Asset *Y*. After the distribution, Leopold has an adjusted basis of $116.67 in Asset *X* and $83.33 in Asset *Y*.

.02 *Basis of Distributed Property Increased*

The partner's basis in his or her partnership interest is first allocated to unrealized receivables and inventory to the extent of these assets' basis to the partnership. Any remaining basis is next allocated to Code Sec. 1221/1231 assets to the extent of the partnership's basis in these assets prior to the distribution. Remaining basis is also allocated to these assets, to the extent of the unrealized appreciation inherent in each. If the basis increase is less than the total unrealized appreciation inherent in the Code Sec. 1221/1231 assets, it is allocated in proportion to the relative appreciation inherent in each. If the remaining basis increase exceeds the aggregate unrealized appreciation inherent in these assets, the excess is allocated to the Code Sec. 1221/1231 assets in proportion to their relative fair market values.[18]

[18] Code Sec. 732(c)(2).

Example 16-5. Star Partnership makes a liquidating distribution of Asset *A* and Asset *B* to a partner, Sean Blough. Sean's basis in his partnership interest is $5,500. Neither asset is inventory or unrealized receivables. Asset *A* has a basis to the partnership of $500 and a fair market value of $4,000, and Asset *B* has a basis to the partnership of $1,000 and a fair market value of $1,000.

Sean's basis is first allocated to Asset *A* in the amount of $500 and to Asset *B* in the amount of $1,000 (each asset's adjusted basis to the partnership).

The remaining basis adjustment is an increase of $4,000 (that is, Sean's $5,500 basis minus the partnership's total basis in the distributed assets of $1,500). Sean's remaining basis is next allocated to Asset *A* in the amount of $3,500, its unrealized appreciation. However, there is no basis allocation to Asset *B* attributable to unrealized appreciation because its fair market value equals the partnership's adjusted basis. The final basis adjustment of $500 (that is, $4,000 − $3,500) is allocated in the ratio of the two assets' fair market values—$400 to Asset *A* (for a total basis of $4,400), and $100 to Asset *B* (for a total basis of $1,100).

Example 16-6. George Daog is a one-fourth partner in the equal ABCD Partnership and has an adjusted basis in his partnership interest of $850. The ABCD Partnership distributes inventory items and Assets *X* and *Y* to George in liquidation of George's entire partnership interest.

	Adjusted Basis	*FMV*
Inventory	$100	$200
Asset *X*	100	400
Asset *Y*	100	200
	$300	$800

Neither Asset *X* nor Asset *Y* consists of inventory items or unrealized receivables. George's basis in his partnership interest is allocated first to the inventory items in an amount equal to their adjusted basis to the partnership. George, therefore, has an adjusted basis in the inventory items of $100. The remaining basis, $750, is allocated to Assets *X* and *Y* in an amount equal to each property's adjusted basis to the partnership. Thus, Asset *X* and Asset *Y* are each allocated $100. Asset *X* is then allocated $300, and Asset *Y* $100, the amount of appreciation inherent in each. Finally, the remaining basis, $50, is allocated to Assets *X* and *Y* in proportion to their fair market values—$33.33 to Asset *X* (400/600 × $50), and $16.67 to Asset *Y* (200/600 × $50). Therefore, after the distribution, George has an adjusted basis of $433.33 in Asset *X* and $116.67 in Asset *Y*.

George's basis in his partnership interest	$850
Allocated to Inventory	(100)
Basis of Both Assets *X* and *Y*	*$750*

	Basis to Partnership	***Appreciation***	***Relative FMV***	
Asset *X*	$100	$300	$33.33	(400/600 × $50)
Asset *Y*	100	100	16.67	(200/600 × $50)
	$200	*$400*	*$50.00*	

Prior to its amendment by Act § 1061 of the Taxpayer Relief Act of 1997,[19] Code Sec. 732(c) apportioned a partner's basis in his or her partnership interest among assets received by that partner in liquidation of the partnership interest in proportion to the adjusted bases of such assets. This apportionment did not take the fair market value of the distributed assets into account. The liquidation of a partnership with a relatively small amount of tangible assets and a large amount of zero basis goodwill could create large bases in low value assets. Upon the purchase of a partnership interest followed by liquidation, former Code Sec. 732(c) apportioned the bulk of the purchase price to the tangible assets, which could then either be recovered through depreciation or sold for a taxable loss.

However, even as amended, Code Sec. 732(c) does not apportion basis solely with respect to relative appreciation or depreciation. The practical result is that the distributed assets may have highly disproportionate built-in gains or losses.

Example 16-7. Betty Mueller has an $1,800 basis in her partnership interest and received a liquidating distribution from the partnership consisting of investment Property *A*, with a basis in the hands of the partnership of $300, and a fair market value of $1,200, and investment Property *B*, with a basis in the hands of the partnership of $700 and a fair market value of $800. Under old law, Investment Properties *A* and *B* would take a basis in the hands of the distributee of $540 and $1,260, respectively (*i.e.*, based upon their respective 30% and 70% relative adjusted bases in the hands of the partnership, multiplied by the partner's $1,800 basis for her partnership interest). Under current law, the basis allocation would be made as follows:

	Investment Property A	**Investment Property *B***
First $1,000 of basis—equal to partnership's adjusted basis	$300	$700
Remaining $800 of basis—based upon relative unrealized appreciation in the distributed properties ($900 vs. $100)	720	80
Betty's basis	*$1,020*	*$780*
FMV	$1,200	$800

[19] P.L. 105-34.

.03 *Multiple Year Liquidating Distributions*

The basis rules applicable to liquidating distributions are difficult to apply if a series of distributions spanning more than one partnership taxable year is treated as a single liquidating distribution.[20] These rules depend on both the distributee's basis in his or her partnership interest and the partnership's basis in the properties at the time of distribution. The partner's basis in his or her interest may change during the liquidation period, as well as the bases of the various properties involved. If the statutory provisions are applied with their literal meaning, the distributee's basis at the time of the final distribution, unadjusted for the previous liquidating distributions, should be allocated among all distributed properties according to the ratio of the bases of these properties to the partnership at the times of their actual distributions. Since, under this approach, the basis of property distributed early in the "series" cannot be determined until the liquidation is complete, it is impossible to currently calculate depreciation deductions or gain and loss on resale of the property by the distributee. Accordingly, it would be necessary for the distributee to file amended returns if the regulations were followed precisely.

Example 16-8. *Multiple-year liquidating distributions.* Kay Harrah was tired of the frenetic energy at the partnership. She was considering a withdrawal. She wanted to start a spiritual retreat at the hot springs the partnership purchased the previous year. She requested a distribution of the hot springs and the land surrounding it. Although she definitely wanted out of the partnership, she had an unfounded fear that she would have an earlier tax obligation if the property were distributed to her all at once in a liquidating distribution. Therefore, she insisted upon a distribution of a one-fourth undivided interest in the property each year over a four-year period. Her basis in her partnership interest was $20. The basis of the hot springs in the hands of the partnership was $15. The tax consequences at the end of four years are summarized below.

Comparison of potential tax treatment:

	Current	*Liquidating*
Basis of her partnership interest	$20.00	$20.00
Basis of the hot springs in the hands of the partnership	$15.00	$15.00
Gain recognized	$ 0.00	$ 0.00
Postdistribution basis in the hot springs	$15.00 [21]	$20.00 [22]
Postdistribution basis in partnership interest	$5.00	$ 0.00

Thus, Kay pays no tax whether she receives a current distribution or a liquidating distribution. In a liquidating distribution, she ends up with a higher basis in the hot springs, which is desirable upon resale.

[20] See Reg. § 1.761-1(d).
[21] Code Sec. 732(a)(1).
[22] Code Sec. 732(b).

However, she does not have the choice as to whether this is a current or liquidating distribution if the distributions were considered a series of liquidating distributions.

Liquidating distributions are defined as made in termination of a partner's entire interest "by means of a distribution or a series of distributions."[23]

The series of distributions in liquidation can extend over more than one year. In such a case, the interest is not considered liquidated until the final distribution has been made. It is arguable that where a series of distributions spanning more than one taxable year is treated as a single liquidating distribution, the partner's basis in his or her partnership interest will change, and the basis of the assets in the hands of the partnership will change during the liquidation period.

Also, it will be impossible to determine the basis of assets distributed because in liquidating distributions these assets have a basis determined with reference to the basis of the partner in his or her interest, not their basis to the partnership (except for unrealized receivables and inventory items). However, in a prolonged liquidating distribution scheme, when is this calculation done? It is impossible to do it in the first year because it is not known what basis increase or decrease the partner will have over the liquidating year, nor is it known what assets will be distributed in future years or what their basis will be.

A problem with such an approach is that it would be difficult to calculate depreciation deductions or gain on resale of property that is distributed early in the series of distributions. Amended returns might be an appropriate solution. However, an alternative approach would be to make the calculations as described above. As the partner derives additional income with its accompanying basis adjustment, that basis will attach to subsequent distributions.

.04 Partner's Election to Adjust Basis of Distributed Partnership Assets

The basis rules discussed immediately above govern how a partner determines the basis of distributed property. The distributing partnership's basis in the property is the beginning part of these rules. The partnership's basis in its property is affected by whether or not the partnership has a Code Sec. 754 election in effect and whether or not the property's basis to the partnership includes a Code Sec. 743(b) adjustment related to the distributee partner. When the partnership does not have a Code Sec. 754 election in effect, Code Sec. 732(d) allows a distributee partner who receives a distribution within two years of purchasing or inheriting the partnership interest to elect to determine his or her basis in distributed property as if

[23] Reg. § 1.761-1(d).

there were a Code Sec. 754 election in effect when the partner purchased or inherited the partnership interest.

The Treasury Department issued revised regulations affecting the calculation of the Code Sec. 743(b) adjustment effective for transfers of partnership interests that occur on or after December 15, 1999.[24] The following discussion covers Code Sec. 743(b) adjustments for transfers after December 14, 1999, and then before December 15, 1999.[25]

Partner's election to adjust basis of distributed assets distributed after December 14, 1999. A partnership's basis in its assets is not adjusted on the transfer of a partnership interest absent a Code Sec. 754 election.[26] There is an exception for partnerships that do not have a basis adjustment election in effect, allowing a partner who receives a nonliquidating or liquidating distribution of property (other than money) within two years after the partner acquired his or her interest, in whole or in part, by transfer or by the death of a partner to elect the same basis treatment on the distributed property the partner would have been entitled to if the partnership had a basis adjustment election in effect when the partner acquired his or her interest.[27] For example, a person who inherits a partnership interest may be able to use the above rule to receive a fair market value basis in the assets received in a distribution made within two years of the inheritance, whether or not the partnership has a Code Sec. 754 election in effect.

The partner's election to make this adjustment applies only for purposes of determining the basis of distributed property (other than money) in the partner's hands. It does not enable the electing partner to amend prior income tax returns to recompute income based on this adjustment.[28] Accordingly, in computing the adjustment, no reduction is made for any depletion or depreciation of that portion of the basis of partnership property which arises from the basis adjustment, since no depletion or depreciation of the basis adjustment for the period before the distribution is allowed or allowable unless the partnership had an election in effect.[29]

The basis adjustments are calculated in the same manner as those for transferees where the partnership has a basis adjustment election in effect. If the distribution occurs after December 14, 1999, the Code Sec. 743(b) adjustment is computed and allocated among the partnership's assets under the rules applicable to sales of partnership interests after December 14, 1999, even if the interest was purchased or inherited before that date. For

---

[24] Reg. § 1.743-1(l).

[25] In order to allow a partnership which made Code Sec. 754 elections based upon the allocation provisions contained in the previous regulation, a partnership with a Code Sec. 754 election is given permission to revoke its election by attaching a statement to Form 1065, U.S. Partnership Return of Income, for its taxable year end which includes December 15, 1999. Reg. § 1.754-1(c)(2).

[26] A partnership with or without a Code Sec. 754 election in effect adjusts the basis of its assets to the extent the distribution is a deemed sale under Code Secs. 704(c)(2), 707(a)(2)(B), 737 and 751(b).

[27] Code Sec. 732(d).

[28] *Id.*

[29] Reg. § 1.732-1(d)(1)(iv).

instance, a portion of a transferee partner's basis will be attributed to goodwill and going concern value.

If a partner who makes this election receives property in a liquidating or current distribution that is not the same property that would have had a basis adjustment, the partner can apply the adjustment to any like-kind property received in the distribution provided that, in exchange for the property distributed, the partner has given up his or her interest in the property to which the partner would have had a basis adjustment. Although the regulations allow this transfer of an adjustment to property distributed in either a current or liquidating distribution, the requirement that the distributee give up his or her interest in the asset to which the adjustment would have applied is normally satisfied in a liquidating distribution. In the case of a current distribution, the partners would have to agree to segregate the partnership's remaining assets among partners. This rule applies whether the property in which the transferee gave up his or her interest is retained or disposed of by the partnership.[30]

The election to have the basis of distributed assets computed as if a basis adjustment election had been in effect when a partnership interest was acquired must be made by the affected partner.[31] A transferee partner who wishes to make the special basis adjustment election must make it with the tax return:

1. For the year of the distribution if the distribution includes any property subject to depreciation, depletion, or amortization,[32] or

2. For any taxable year no later than the first year in which the basis of any of the distributed property is pertinent in determining his or her income tax, if the distribution does not include any property subject to depreciation, depletion, or amortization.[33]

The partner must submit with the return in which the election is made a schedule setting forth:

1. That, under Code Sec. 732(d), the partner elects to adjust the basis of property received in a distribution,[34] and

2. The computation of the basis adjustment and the properties to which the adjustment has been allocated.[35]

Example 16-9. As a transferee partner, Terry Kline purchased a one-fourth interest in the Apple Partnership for $62,500. At the time of the purchase the partnership's assets were as follows:

---

[30] Reg. § 1.732-1(d)(1)(v).

[31] Code Sec. 732(d).

[32] Reg. § 1.732-1(d)(2)(i).

[33] Reg. § 1.732-1(d)(2)(ii).

[34] Reg. § 1.732-1(d)(3)(i).

[35] Reg. § 1.732-1(d)(3)(ii).

Assets	*Basis*	*FMV*
Cash	$20,000	$20,000
Inventory	10,000	20,000
Blackacre	40,000	100,000
Whiteacre	90,000	110,000
	$160,000	*$250,000*

Apple Partnership has never made a Code Sec. 754 election. Within two years of Terry's purchase of his interest he receives Blackacre from the partnership and remains a one-fourth profits and losses partner, but his capital account is reduced for the distribution. Terry's basis in Blackacre is $55,000. This is the partnership's common basis of $40,000 plus the $15,000 Code Sec. 743(b) adjustment which would be credited to Terry if there had been a Code Sec. 754 election in effect when he purchased his partnership interest. If Terry relinquishes his interest in Whiteacre, his basis in Blackacre is $60,000—this is the partnership's common basis of $40,000 plus what the Code Sec. 743(b) adjustment would have been to both Blackacre and Whiteacre of $15,000 and $5,000.[36]

Example 16-10. As a transferee partner, Tina Vij purchased a one-fourth interest in ABCT Partnership for $17,000. At the time Tina purchased the partnership interest, the election under Code Sec. 754 was not in effect and the partnership owned only cash and inventory with a basis of $14,000 and a fair market value of $16,000. Tina's purchase price reflected $500 of this difference. Thus, $4,000 of the $17,000 paid by Tina for the partnership interest was attributable to Tina's share of partnership inventory with a basis of $3,500. After Tina purchased her partnership interest, the partnership purchased Assets *X* and *Y*. Within two years after Tina acquired the partnership interest, Tina retired from the partnership and received in complete liquidation the following property:

Assets	*Adjusted Basis to ABC*	*FMV*
Cash	$1,500	$1,500
Inventory	3,500	4,000
Asset *X*	2,000	4,000
Asset *Y*	4,000	5,000
	$10,500	*$10,500*

The amount to be allocated among the properties received by Tina in the liquidating distribution is $15,500 ($17,000, Tina's basis for the partnership interest, reduced by the amount of cash received, $1,500). The fair market value of the inventory received by Tina was one-fourth of the fair market value of all partnership inventory and represented Tina's share of such property. This is true whether or not

[36] Note that if Terry receives Blackacre in a liquidating distribution, his basis will be $62,500 (his basis in the partnership interest), making a 732(d) election unnecessary.

the inventory Tina received was on hand when Tina acquired the interest. In accordance with Tina's election under Code Sec. 732(d), the amount of Tina's share of partnership basis that is attributable to partnership inventory is increased by $500 (one-fourth of the $2,000 difference between the fair market value of the property, $16,000, and its $14,000 basis to the partnership at the time Tina purchased its interest). This adjustment under Code Sec. 732(d) applies only for purposes of distributions to Tina, and not for purposes of partnership depreciation, depletion, or gain or loss on disposition.

The remaining $15,500 is allocated as follows: (1) the basis of the inventory items received is $4,000, consisting of the $3,500 common partnership basis, plus (2) the basis adjustment of $500 which Tina would have had under Code Sec. 743(b). The remaining basis of $11,500 ($15,500 − $4,000) is allocated among the remaining property distributed to Tina by assigning to each property the adjusted basis to the partnership of such property and adjusting that basis by any required increase or decrease. Thus, the adjusted basis to Tina of Asset *X* is $5,111 ($2,000, the adjusted basis of Asset *X* to the partnership, plus $2,000, the amount of unrealized appreciation in Asset *X*, plus $1,111 ($4,000/$9,000 × $2,500)). Similarly, the adjusted basis of Asset *Y* to Tina is $6,389 ($4,000, the adjusted basis of Asset *Y* to the partnership, plus $1,000, the amount of unrealized appreciation in Asset *Y*, plus $1,389 ($5,000/$9,000 × $2,500)).

Inventory

$3,500	Partnership's common basis
500	Code Sec. 743(b) adjustment
$4,000	Inventory

Asset X

$2,000	Partnership's common basis
2,000	Unrealized built-in gain
1,111	Asset *X*'s share of the FMV of Code Sec. 1221/1231 assets *
$5,111	Asset *X*

* $\frac{X\text{'s FMV}}{X + Y\text{'s FMV}}$ × (Adjustment) = ($4,000 ÷ $9,000) × $2,500

Note: $2,500 is the excess of Tina's partnership interest basis over partnership's basis in inventory Assets *X* and *Y*

	Asset Y
$4,000	Partnership's common basis
1,000	Unrealized appreciation
1,389	Asset *Y*'s share of the FMV of Code Sec. 1221/1231 assets *
$6,389	Asset *Y*

* $\frac{Y\text{'s FMV}}{X + Y\text{'s FMV}}$ × (Adjustment) = ($5,000 ÷ $9,000) × $2,500

Note: $2,500 is the excess of Tina's partnership interest basis over partnership's basis in inventory Assets *X* and *Y*

Total basis of assets distributed	$15,500
Cash	1,500
Tina's basis in the partnership before liquidation	*$17,000*

Code Sec. 743(b) adjustments for transfers before December 15, 1999. In the case of distribution before December 15, 1999, the Code Sec. 732(d) adjustments are figured using the Code Secs. 743(b)/755 rules which were in effect for sales and deaths before December 15, 1999. The remainder of the Code Sec. 732(d) rules are described in the previous section.

Partners required to adjust basis of distributed partnership assets. One obscure and ignored provision of Code Sec. 732(d) requires an adjustment to distributed property in some circumstances. If a partner acquired his or her interest by a transfer to which the Code Sec. 754 election was not in effect, the partner is required to apply the Code Sec. 732(d) adjustments to a distribution made to him or her at any time (not only within two years) if at the time the partner acquired his or her interest:

1. The fair market value of all partnership property (other than money) exceeds 100 percent of its adjusted basis to the partnership;

2. An allocation of basis under Code Sec. 732(c), if his or her interest had been liquidated immediately after the transfer, would have shifted basis from property not subject to an allowance for depreciation, depletion, or amortization to property subject to such allowance; and

3. A special basis adjustment under Code Sec. 743(b) would change the basis to the distributee of the property actually distributed.[37]

The apparent purpose of the requirement is to prevent income distortions beneficial to the taxpayer resulting from shifting increases in value of nondepreciable property to the basis of depreciable property through the medium of a distribution of the property. Such a shift could be possible because the allocation under Code Sec. 732(c) is partially made with

[37] Reg. § 1.732-1(d)(4).

reference to basis and value of the properties and not only with regard to their appreciation.

The mandatory application of Code Sec. 732(d) was enacted prior to the effective date of the Taxpayer Relief Act of 1997.[38] Before that date, the distributee's basis in distributed property was determined under Code Sec 732(c) entirely by reference to the partnership's basis in the property. The value of the property and appreciation were irrelevant. Under the current rules of Code Sec. 732(c) there is much less possibility of shifting basis to low value. Unappreciated depreciable property and the mandatory application of Code Sec. 732(d) should become an even more remote possibility. The regulations in this area have not been updated to reflect the new Code Sec. 732(c) distribution rules.[39]

¶ 1604 Subsequent Sale of Distributed Property

The subsequent sale of some distributions is governed by Code Sec. 735. The application of this provision is not affected by whether the property is received in a current or liquidating distribution and is discussed in ¶ 1504.03.

[38] P.L. 105-34.

[39] Reg. § 1.732-1(d)(4).

Chapter 17

Partnership Results of Distributions to Partners

¶ 1701 Introduction

The impact, or lack thereof, that a distribution has on the partnership is largely determined by whether a Code Sec. 754 election is in effect for the year of the distribution. If there is not a disproportionate distribution, a partnership incurs neither gain nor loss because of a cash distribution.[1] In addition, without a Code Sec. 754 election, and assuming no disproportionate distribution or other deemed sale event, there is no effect on the basis of the partnership's remaining property.[2] Therefore, as long as Code Secs. 704(c)(2), 707(a)(2)(B), 737, 751(b) and 754 do not apply, a cash distribution is treated by the partnership in much the same manner as a Subchapter C or S corporation treats a cash distribution. There is no partnership gain or loss and there is no basis adjustment to the partnership's remaining property.

An exception to the general rule that no basis adjustments are allowed or required absent a Code Sec. 754 election by the partnership applies when a distribution results in a "substantial basis reduction" as defined in Code Sec. 734(d). Under this statute, added by the American Jobs Creation Act of 2004, a "substantial basis reduction" exists when the sum of:

i. The amount of loss recognized by the distributee partner under Code Sec. 731(a) on receipt of the distribution; and

ii. The step-up in basis of distributed property in the distributee partner's hands under Code Sec. 732

exceeds $250,000. In such cases, the partnership is required to adjust its basis in remaining partnership properties under Code Sec. 734(b) whether or not the partnership has a Code Sec. 754 election in effect.[3] Note,

---

[1] Code Sec. 731(b).

[2] Code Sec. 734(a).

[3] Code Sec. 734(d).

however, that this exception does not apply to "securitization partnerships" as defined in Code Sec. 743(f).[4]

For example, if there is no Code Sec. 754 election in effect for the year of the distribution, the partnership is not allowed to increase its basis in its remaining property for any gain a distributee partner reports as a result of the distribution.[5] In the case of a partner who receives a liquidating cash distribution resulting in a gain, it is readily apparent that economically the gain (the excess of the cash distributed over the partner's outside basis) represents the distributee partner's share of the appreciation in value of the assets which the partnership retains. The partner has "cashed out" all or a portion of his or her share of the value of the partnership assets. Because the basis in his or her partnership interest is generally equal to the partner's share of the costs of the partnership's assets, the gain on liquidation is equal to the gain on the indirect sale of his or her share of the assets. However, the partnership's adjusted basis in the assets remains the same (because there is no Code Sec. 754 election in effect). This is true even though the remaining partners have in effect used their share of the partnership's cash to purchase the liquidated partner's share of the assets. If the partnership sells its remaining assets, the gain will be taxed again when the property is sold. This double reporting of gain will be rectified later because the increase in the adjusted bases of the partners in their partnership interests will cause a reduction in the gain on the ultimate sale or liquidation of their partnership interests. However, a timing difference will exist without a Code Sec. 734 adjustment. Thus, although the overall taxable income will ultimately be the same, tax by the remaining partners may be paid considerably sooner should the partnership sell the appreciated assets a long time before the remaining partners sell their partnership interests. The Code Sec. 734(b) adjustment in effect gives the partnership a cost basis in the liquidated partner's share of partnership assets purchased by the remaining partners.

> ***C and S Corporation Observation.*** When a corporation distributes appreciated property to a shareholder, the corporation recognizes gain (but not loss) as if the corporation sold the property to the shareholder and distributed the cash.[6]

> ***LLC Observation.*** The distribution rules discussed in this chapter apply equally to state law partnerships and LLCs taxed as partnerships.

¶ 1702 No Code Sec. 754 Election in Effect

If there is no Code Sec. 754 election in effect and the distribution does not trigger a substantial basis reduction, absent a disproportionate distribution within the meaning of Code Sec. 751(b) or a deemed sale transaction

[4] Code Sec. 734(e). See ¶ 1303 for definition of securitization partnerships.

[5] Code Secs. 311(b) and 1239.

[6] Code Sec. 734(b)(1).

under Code Secs. 704(c)(2), 707(a)(2)(B), or 737, a distribution of money and/or property does not affect the partnership.[7] Money or property is removed from its books of account and the liquidated partner's capital account is appropriately adjusted. Partnership distributions generally are not treated as taxable events to the partnership.[8]

¶ 1703 Code Sec. 754 Election in Effect or Substantial Basis Reduction

The mechanics of making the Code Sec. 754 election are not affected by whether adjustments result because of a transfer of a partnership interest or a distribution. The mechanics of making the Code Sec. 754 election are discussed in ¶ 1303.03.

Similar to the provisions of Code Sec. 743 which provide that there is no change in the basis of partnership assets on a sale of a partnership interest, Code Sec. 734(a) provides the general rule that the basis of retained partnership property will not be adjusted following a distribution to a partner unless the partnership makes a Code Sec. 754 election or unless there is a substantial basis reduction; in that event, a Code Sec. 734(b) basis adjustment will be made to the retained partnership property. The adjustment process has two steps:

- Computing the total adjustment, and
- Allocating the total adjustment to the partnership assets.

.01 Amount of the Adjustment

The amount of the required Code Sec. 734(b) basis adjustment to partnership property is determined as follows:

1. In the case of a distribution to a partner of money that is greater than the adjusted basis the partner has in his or her partnership interest, the partnership will increase the adjusted basis of its assets ("partnership property") by the amount of gain recognized by the distributee partner under Code Sec. 731(a).[9]

2. In the case of a distribution to a partner consisting solely of money, unrealized receivables, and/or inventory in complete liquidation of his or her partnership interest when the distributee partner recognizes a loss under Code Sec. 731(a)(2), the partnership will reduce the adjusted basis of its undistributed assets by the amount of the loss.[10]

3. Code Sec. 732(b) provides that the adjusted basis of property distributed in complete liquidation of the partnership's interest equals the partner's outside basis reduced by any money dis-

[7] Code Sec. 734(a).
[8] Code Sec. 731(b).
[9] Code Sec. 734(b)(1)(A).
[10] Code Sec. 734(b)(2)(A).

tributed in the same transaction. If the total adjusted basis of the distributed assets was greater in the hands of the partnership than in the hands of the distributee partner, owing to the application of Code Sec. 732(b), the partnership will increase the basis of the retained assets ("partnership property") by the amount of this excess.[11]

4. The converse situation to that outlined in (3) above occurs when, upon the complete liquidation of a partner's interest, the total adjusted basis of the assets in the distributee partner's hands is greater than it was in the hands of the partnership immediately before the distribution. The partnership must decrease the adjusted basis of its retained partnership property by the amount of this difference.[12]

If there is a Code Sec. 754 election in effect, the partnership adjusts its basis in its assets to allow its remaining members to avoid any distortion in reporting their future shares of partnership taxable income. In the case of a purchase or inheritance of a partnership interest, the Code Sec. 743(b) adjustment attempts to ensure that inside and outside basis run in tandem and that a purchaser or successor in interest of a partnership interest does not recognize gain or loss built into the partnership assets before his or her tenure. Its companion adjustment, that of Code Sec. 734(b), attempts to effectuate the same policy in the context of partnership distributions. In contrast to the Code Sec. 743(b) adjustment which is personal to the new partner who acquires his or her interest by purchase, bequest, or devise, the Code Sec. 734(b) adjustment is available to the partnership as a whole. This includes the distributee if he or she remains a partner. A distribution of partnership assets, unless pro rata among the members, often reflects an exchange or purchase of some share of the non-distributed assets by the remaining partners for the relinquishment of their share of the distributed assets.[13] The Code Sec. 734(b) adjustment attempts to treat such a transaction accordingly. For example, when a partner receives a cash distribution resulting in a gain, the gain (the excess of the cash distributed over the partner's outside basis) represents the distributee partner's share of the appreciation in value of the assets that the partnership retains.

Example 17-1. In a partnership that possesses two assets—cash of $11,000, and a Code Sec. 1221 asset with a basis of $19,000 and a fair market value of $22,000—a complete liquidation for cash of a partner with a basis of $10,000 and a value of $11,000 will produce a $1,000 gain to the distributee. A partnership with a Code Sec. 754 election would be entitled to a $1,000 positive basis adjustment to the Code Sec. 1221 asset. The asset would take a $20,000 basis; consequently, the partnership would recognize only $2,000 of gain on a

[11] Code Sec. 734(b)(1)(B).

[12] Code Sec. 734(b)(2)(B).

[13] This is similar to the treatment of Code Sec. 751(b) distributions.

subsequent disposition of the Code Sec. 1221 asset. In essence, the adjustment remedies the fact that the partnership did not distribute to the distributee his pro rata share of each asset ($6,333 cash and one-third of the Code Sec. 1221 asset with a basis of $6,333 and value of $7,333) which would preserve the $1,000 gain potential for the distributee and retain for the partnership only a $2,000 gain (basis for the remaining two thirds interest in the Code Sec. 1221 asset of $12,666 and a value of $14,666) in undistributed assets.

When a partnership makes a liquidating cash distribution under circumstances resulting in a loss to the distributee, that loss represents the difference between the distributee's share of the fair market value of the partnership property and the distributee's share of its basis, which in turn is equal to the adjusted basis of his or her partnership interest. If the distributee partner can deduct the loss, and if the partnership is also able to recognize a loss on the sale of the partnership assets (since the fair market value of the assets will have depreciated below the partnership's adjusted basis in the assets), a temporary double reporting of the loss will occur. This is later rectified through adjustments to the partners' outside bases, but it may cause a significant timing difference without a Code Sec. 734(b) adjustment.

Example 17-2. The RHC Communities Partnership has the following balance sheet:

Assets	*Adjusted Basis*	*FMV*
Greenacre	$ 500,000	$ 100,000
Blackacre	400,000	250,000
Whiteacre	600,000	300,000
Redacre	500,000	350,000
	$2,000,000	$1,000,000
Liabilities	0	0
Capital Accounts		
Richard	$ 600,000	250,000
Helen	400,000	250,000
Cassandra	1,000,000	500,000
	$2,000,000	$1,000,000

Richard's tax basis in his partnership interest is $600,000. It is worth only $250,000. The partnership borrows $250,000, giving the bank a lien against Redacre, and distributes the money to Richard in liquidation of his partnership interest. (His share of the $250,000 debt will increase his basis, but this increase will be only temporary as he is leaving the partnership immediately.) Richard will recognize a $350,000 loss on the distribution under Code Sec. 731(a). Assume the partnership does not have a Code Sec. 754 election in effect, and that it chooses not to make one for the year of the liquidating distribution. Because Richard's loss exceeded $250,000, the distribution created a "substantial basis reduction" as defined in Code Sec. 734(d). Thus, under Code Sec. 734(b), the partnership will still be required to reduce its basis in Greenacre, Blackacre, Whiteacre and Redacre by $350,000 to reflect the loss recognized by Richard on receipt of the liquidating distribution. Note that had Helen received the liquidating distribution, rather than Richard, she would have recognized a loss of only $150,000 ($400,000 tax basis in her partnership interest less the $250,000 cash distribution), and the partnership would not be required to adjust its basis in its assets under Code Sec. 734(b) (because no Code Sec. 754 election is in effect). Likewise, no basis adjustment would be required under Code Sec. 734(b) had the partnership distributed Blackacre to Richard rather than cash—his basis in the property, $600,000, would not have been more than $250,000 greater than the partnership's basis in that property ($400,000), and thus the step-up in basis would not constitute a "substantial basis reduction" under Code Sec. 734(d).

.02 *Allocation of Total Adjustment Among Partnership Property*

The total Code Sec. 734(b) adjustment must be allocated among the undistributed partnership assets according to the rules of Code Sec. 755. Although Code Sec. 755 provides rules for allocating Code Sec. 743(b) adjustments, it also contains different rules for Code Sec. 734(b) adjustments.[14] But the underlying rationale of both sets of rules is that the total basis adjustments are allocated among the assets in a way that eliminates or reduces the difference between the fair market value and the adjusted basis of partnership properties. Code Sec. 734(b) adjustments are not made with respect to any particular partner or partners, but apply to the common basis of partnership assets.

Allocation of total adjustment between the Code Sec. 1221/1231 and ordinary income classes of partnership property. The allocation rules first apportion the total Code Sec. 734(b) adjustment between two classes of partnership property: ordinary income property and Code Sec. 1221/1231 "capital gains" property. After this bifurcation of the total adjustment, the amount of the adjustment allocated to each class is further allocated among the assets within each class.

The allocations are made according to the following rules:[15]

1. If a positive Code Sec. 734(b)(1)(A) adjustment arises when the distributee partner recognizes gain under Code Sec. 731(a)(1), or negative adjustment under Code Sec. 734(b)(2)(A) if he or she recognizes a loss under Code Sec. 731(a)(2), then the upward or downward adjustment is to be allocated *only* to "capital gains assets."[16] The adjustment is allocated in such a way as to

[14] Reg. § 1.755-1(b)(1).
[15] Reg. § 1.755-1(c).
[16] Code Secs. 1221 and 1231 property; Reg. § 1.755-1(c)(1)(ii).

reduce the difference between the fair market values and the adjusted bases of the assets of that class that have appreciated in value, in the case of an upward basis adjustment, or have depreciated in value, for a downward basis adjustment.[17] In applying these rules, the basis of an asset may not be reduced below zero,[18] and, if the partnership either has no retained capital gain property, or has insufficient basis in the property in the class to fully absorb a negative adjustment allocated to that class, the balance of the adjustment is to be applied to subsequently acquired capital gain property.[19]

2. If the Code Sec. 734(b) adjustment is caused by the distributee partner's adjusted basis in the distributed property being less than or greater than the partnership's adjusted basis in that property immediately before the distribution, then the increase or decrease is allocated to the remaining partnership assets that are of a character similar to that of the distributed property. For example, when the partnership's adjusted basis in distributed "capital assets" immediately before the distribution exceeds that of the distributee partner after the distribution, the upward adjustment in undistributed partnership assets will be allocated entirely to the undistributed "capital assets" of the partnership. If the distributed assets that produced the upward Code Sec. 734(b) adjustment were "inventory," the adjustment would be allocated to the partnership's remaining inventory.[20] In applying these rules, the basis of an asset may not be reduced below zero,[21] and, if an adjustment is allocated to a class in which the partnership either has no retained property or has insufficient basis in the property in the class to fully absorb a negative adjustment allocated to that class, the balance of the adjustment is to be applied to subsequently acquired property of that class.[22]

Allocation of adjustment among partnership property within a class. If there is an increase in basis to be allocated to a group of properties within a class, the increase must be allocated first to properties with unrealized appreciation in proportion to their respective amounts of unrealized appreciation before such increase (but only to the extent of each property's unrealized appreciation). Any remaining increase must be allocated among the properties within the class in proportion to their fair market values.[23]

---

[17] Code Sec. 755(a).

[18] Reg. § 1.704-1(c)(3).

[19] Reg. § 1.755-1(c)(4).

[20] Reg. § 1.755-1(c)(1)(i).

[21] Reg. § 1.704-1(c)(3).

[22] Reg. § 1.755-1(c)(4).

[23] Reg. § 1.755-1(c)(2)(i). The regulations governing distributions prior to December 15, 1999, had no provision for handling positive adjustments which created basis in excess of value.

If there is a decrease in basis to be allocated to a group of properties within a class, the decrease must be allocated first to properties with unrealized depreciation in proportion to their respective amounts of unrealized depreciation before such decrease (but only to the extent of each property's unrealized depreciation). Any remaining decrease must be allocated among the properties within the class in proportion to their adjusted bases (as adjusted under the preceding sentence).[24] Where a decrease in the basis of partnership assets is required under Code Sec. 734(b)(2) and the amount of the decrease exceeds the adjusted basis to the partnership of property of the required character, the basis of such property is reduced to zero (but not below zero).[25]

Where, in the case of a distribution, an increase or a decrease in the basis of undistributed property cannot be made because the partnership owns no property of the character required to be adjusted, or because the basis of all the property of a like character has been reduced to zero, the adjustment is made when the partnership subsequently acquires property of a like character to which an adjustment can be made.

Example 17-3. *A*, *B*, and *C* form equal ABC Partnership. Partner *A* contributes $50,000 and Asset 1—capital gain property with a fair market value of $50,000 and an adjusted tax basis of $25,000. Partners *B* and *C* each contribute $100,000. The ABC Partnership uses the cash to purchase Assets 2, 3, 4, 5, and 6. Assets 4, 5, and 6 are the only ordinary income assets held by the partnership which are subject to Code Sec. 751. The partnership has an election in effect under Code Sec. 754. After seven years, the adjusted basis and fair market value of ABC Partnership's assets are as follows:

Assets	*Adjusted Basis*	*FMV*
Capital Gain Property:		
Asset 1	$25,000	$75,000
Asset 2	100,000	117,500
Asset 3	50,000	60,000
Ordinary Income Property:		
Asset 4	40,000	45,000
Asset 5	50,000	60,000
Asset 6	10,000	2,500
Total	$275,000	$360,000

Assume that the ABC Partnership distributes Assets 3 and 5 to *A* in complete liquidation of Partner *A*'s interest in the partnership. Partner *A*'s basis in the partnership interest was $75,000. The partnership's basis in Assets 3 and 5 was $50,000 each. Partner *A*'s $75,000 basis in his partnership interest is allocated between Assets 3 and 5 under Code Secs. 732(b) and (c). Partner *A* will, therefore, have a basis of $25,000 in Asset 3 (capital gain property), and a basis of $50,000 in

[24] Reg. § 1.755-1(c)(2)(ii).

[25] Reg. § 1.755-1(c)(3).

Asset 5 (ordinary income property). The distribution results in a $25,000 decrease in the basis of capital gain property. There is no change in the basis of ordinary income property. Therefore, the partnership is required to increase the basis of its remaining property by $25,000. This increase is allocated to the partnership's remaining Code Sec. 1221/1231 property and must be allocated among partnership property within that class.

The amount of the basis increase to capital gain property is $25,000 and must be allocated among the remaining capital gain assets in proportion to the difference between the fair market value and basis of each. The fair market value of Asset 1 exceeds its basis by $50,000. The fair market value of Asset 2 exceeds its basis by $17,500. Therefore, the basis of Asset 1 will be increased by $18,519 ($25,000 × $50,000 ÷ $67,500), and the basis of Asset 2 will be increased by $6,481 ($25,000 × $17,500 ÷ $67,500).

Example 17-4. The ABC partnership is a cash-method, calendar-year partnership that has made the Code Sec. 754 election. The profit and loss ratios of the partners are not equal. It has the following balance sheet:

Assets	*Book Value and Adjusted Basis*	*FMV*	*Appreciation (Depreciation)*
Cash	$18,000	$18,000	$ 0
Parcel *X*	23,000	22,000	(1,000)
Parcel *Y*	19,000	29,000	10,000
	$60,000	*$69,000*	*$9,000*
Capital Accounts			
A	$20,000	$18,000	$(2,000)
B	20,000	22,000	2,000
C	20,000	29,000	(9,000)
	$60,000	*$69,000*	*$9,000*

What are the tax consequences to the partners and the partnership if Partner *A* receives the cash in complete liquidation of his partnership interest which has an adjusted basis of $20,000?

A partner recognizes loss if the partnership distributes only money in liquidation of the partner's interest in the partnership to the extent that the partner's adjusted basis in his partnership interest exceeds the sum of money distributed.[26] *A* received $18,000 and had an adjusted basis of $20,000. He therefore recognizes a $2,000 loss. Partner *A*'s $2,000 loss creates a negative $2,000 partnership adjustment.

Code Sec. 734(b)(2)(A) is applicable when the Code Sec. 754 election is in effect and provides that the amount of loss recognized to

[26] Code Sec. 731(a)(2)(A).

a distributee partner with respect to distributions under Code Sec. 731(a)(2) must be reflected by a decrease in the adjusted basis of partnership property in accordance with the rules provided in Code Sec. 755.[27] A decrease in basis must first be allocated to the assets whose bases exceed their value and in proportion to the difference between the basis and value of each.[28]

Parcel *X*'s basis is first reduced from $23,000 to $22,000. The $1,000 of remaining basis reduction is then allocated between Parcel *X* and Parcel *Y* based on their relative adjusted bases.

Adjustment Allocation	*Parcel X*	Parcel *Y*
Per relative depreciation	$1,000	$ 0
Per relative basis	537	436
Total negative adjustment	*$1,537*	*$436*

Nonliquidating property distributions can often result in the distributed property taking a basis to the distributee partner which is less than the partnership's former basis. This occurs whenever the distributed property's basis to the partnership exceeds the partner's basis in his or her partnership interest. If there is no Code Sec. 754 election in effect for the year of the distribution, this basis is lost. If there is an effective Code Sec. 754 election, the basis step-down becomes an upward adjustment to the partnership's remaining property.[29] The basis step-down to distributed property which includes capital and Code Sec. 1231 assets is added to the basis of capital and Code Sec. 1231 assets remaining with the partnership.[30] It is allocated first according to such assets' relative appreciation.[31] Any remaining increase is allocated among the Code Sec. 1221/1231 assets in proportion to their respective values.[32] The basis step-down in distributed ordinary income assets is added to the basis of ordinary income assets still held by the partnership and is allocated in the same manner.[33]

Usually, a partner who receives a liquidating property distribution takes a basis in that property either above or below that of the partnership since Code Sec. 732(b) provides that the partner's basis in the distributed property is determined with reference to the adjusted basis of the partner's interest in the partnership reduced by any money distributed in the same transaction. Even where the partner's outside basis is equal to his or her pro rata share of the partnership's basis for its assets, it is unlikely the partner will receive a distribution of a pro rata cross section of the assets. The partnership will merely choose assets that have a value equal to the partner's partnership interest. This step down in basis represents unrealized appreciation or depreciation that will never be recognized if a Code

[27] Code Sec. 734(c).

[28] The former regulation apparently did not intend that decreases be made if the fair market value of any asset will equal or exceed the resulting adjusted basis. Reg. § 1.755-1(a)(1)(i). Thus, the basis of Parcel *X* was reduced by only $1,000 to $22,000. See Code Sec. 755(b) for the special rule when decreases in adjusted basis are prevented. Former Reg. § 1.755-1(a)(1)(iii).

[29] Code Sec. 734(b)(1)(B).

[30] Reg. § 1.755-1(c)(1)(i).

[31] Reg. § 1.755-1(c)(2)(i).

[32] *Id.*

[33] Reg. § 1.755-1(c)(2)(ii).

Sec. 754 election is not in effect, since the gain or loss inherent in the distributed property escapes taxation, owing to the tax-free step-up or step-down basis. Also note that, without this adjustment, inside and outside bases will be out of alignment.

Example 17-5. The ABC partnership is a cash-method, calendar-year partnership that has made the Code Sec. 754 election. The profit and loss ratios of the partners are not equal. It has the following balance sheet:

Assets	*Book Value and Adjusted Basis*	*FMV*	*Appreciation (Depreciation)*
Cash	$18,000	$18,000	$ 0
Parcel *X*	23,000	22,000	(1,000)
Parcel *Y*	19,000	29,000	10,000
	$60,000	*$69,000*	*$9,000*
Capital Accounts			
A	$20,000	$18,000	$(2,000)
B	20,000	22,000	2,000
C	20,000	29,000	9,000
	$60,000	*$69,000*	*$9,000*

Partner *B* receives Parcel *X* in complete liquidation of his partnership interest.

Code Sec. 732(b) provides that the basis of property distributed by a partnership to a partner in liquidation of the partner's interest shall be an amount equal to the adjusted basis of such partner's interest in the partnership reduced by any money distributed in the same transaction. Since *B* received no cash in the transaction, his adjusted basis in Parcel *X* is equal to his adjusted basis in his partnership interest of $20,000.

The consequences to the partnership are governed by Code Sec. 734(b)(1)(B), which provides that when Code Sec. 732(b) applies to a distribution of property, there will be an increase in the adjusted basis of the partnership property to the extent of the excess of the adjusted basis of the partnership property to the partnership immediately before the distribution over the partner's basis in such property immediately after the distribution. In this case, the excess is $3,000. Therefore, the partnership will increase its basis in Parcel *Y* (the only like-kind asset) by $3,000 in accordance with the rule set forth in Code Sec. 755.[34] If there were appreciated like-kind assets other than Parcel *Y*, in that class, the adjustments would be allocated first in proportion to their relative appreciation and then any excess positive adjustment is allocated based on their relative values.[35]

[34] Code Sec. 734(c).

[35] Reg. § 1.755-1(c).

Example 17-6. Assume the same facts as above, except that Partner *C* receives Parcel *Y*, rather than Parcel *X*, in complete liquidation of his partnership interest. Partner *C*'s basis in Parcel *Y* is $20,000. The $1,000 increase in the basis of Parcel *Y* over the partnership's pre-distribution basis in that asset precipitates the application of Code Sec. 734(b). The partnership will reduce its basis in Parcel *X* by $1,000 to $22,000.[36]

Example 17-7. Assume the pre-distribution balance sheet of the Ed, Frank and George Partnership is as follows:

Assets	*Book Value and Adjusted Basis*	*FMV*	*Appreciation (Depreciation)*
Accounts Receivable . . .	$50,000	$50,000	$ 0
Cash	$50,000	$50,000	$ 0
Inventory	20,000	30,000	10,000
Investment Stock	20,000	60,000	40,000
Business Automobiles . .	60,000	30,000	(30,000)
Land	30,000	40,000	10,000
Building *	70,000	160,000	90,000
	$300,000	*$420,000*	*$120,000*

* No Code Sec. 1250 recapture.

Capital Accounts			
Ed	$100,000	$140,000	$40,000
Frank	100,000	140,000	40,000
George	100,000	140,000	40,000
	$300,000	*$420,000*	*$120,000*

Assume that each of the partners has an adjusted basis in his partnership interest of $100,000. In complete liquidation of his partnership interest, Ed receives the inventory, the investment stock, the business automobiles and $20,000. Assume that a Code Sec. 754 election is in effect.

Ed's basis in his partnership interest prior to distribution is $100,000.[37] Code Sec. 732(b) provides that the basis of property distributed by a partnership to a partner in liquidation of a partner's interest shall be an amount equal to the adjusted basis of such partner's interest in the partnership reduced by any money distributed in the same transaction. Ed received $20,000 in the transaction. Therefore, the $80,000 remaining basis will be allocated pursuant to Code Sec. 732(c)—$20,000 will be allocated first to the inventory items in an amount equal to the adjusted basis of those assets to the partnership.[38] Under Code Sec. 732(c)(2), the balance of Ed's basis in

[36] Code Sec. 734(b)(2)(B); Reg. § 1.755-1(a)(1)(iii).

[37] Code Sec. 751 does not apply because the inventory (accounts receivable and inventory) is not substantially appreciated.

[38] Code Sec. 732(c)(1).

his partnership interest, $60,000, will be allocated to the investment stock and the business automobiles.

The $60,000 total basis to be allocated to the assets is $20,000 less than the pre-distribution basis of the assets to the partnership. This is a basis decrease. The $20,000 decrease is allocated to the only depreciated asset, the business automobile.

Ed's basis in each asset is:

Assets	*Basis*	*FMV*
Stock	$20,000	$60,000
Automobiles	40,000	30,000
	$60,000	*$90,000*

The Code Sec. 734 adjustment is computed by comparing any increase or decrease in the respective Code Sec. 755 classes. Here the distributed property class consists of capital assets and Code Sec. 1231 property. The partnership has a Code Sec. 734(b)(1)(B) upward adjustment of $20,000, since this is the excess of the adjusted basis of distributed property to the partnership immediately before the distribution ($100,000) over the basis of the distributed property to the distributee partner ($80,000). The entire Code Sec. 734(b) increase is allocated only to the retained capital and Code Sec. 1231(b) assets.[39] This increase is allocated between the land and building as follows:[40]

Assets	*Adjusted Basis*	*FMV*	*Excess of Value over Basis*
Land	$30,000	$40,000	$10,000
Building	70,000	160,000	90,000
	$100,000	*$200,000*	*$100,000*

To Land = 10% × $20,000 = $2,000 Adjustment
To Building = 90% × $20,000 = $18,000 Adjustment

[39] Code Sec. 755(b); Reg. § 1.755-1(c)(1)(ii).

[40] Code Sec. 755(a)(2); Reg. § 1.755-1(c)(2)(i).

Chapter 18

Disproportionate Distributions—Results to Partner and Partnership When the Partner's Share of Ordinary Income Assets Is Affected

---

¶ 1801 Introduction

Code Sec. 751(b) is intended to preclude a partner from obtaining the potential tax benefits of distribution treatment when the partner has received in distribution all or a portion of the value of his or her partnership if, in reality, the economic effect is trading of the partner's share of the ordinary income assets to the other partners in exchange for a distribution of cash or capital gain property. It also applies when the distributee is, in effect, trading to the other partners his or her share of the capital gain property in exchange for a distribution of ordinary income property.

Rules similar to Code Sec. 751(a) require that a liquidating distribution does not change the partner's proportionate share of "unrealized receivables" and "substantially appreciated inventory," as defined in Code Secs. 751(b)(3), (c) and (d). These ordinary income assets are sometimes referred to as Code Sec. 751 assets or hot assets. When a partner receives more or less than his or her share in value of these ordinary income assets in a distribution in exchange for an increased or decreased interest in capital, Code Sec. 1231 assets, or cash, the distribution is partially recast as a taxable exchange. Thus, for example, a partner is required to report his or her share of the potential ordinary income from this portion of the substantially appreciated inventory and unrealized receivables when the partner receives a liquidating cash distribution. The partnership obtains a fair market value basis in the partner's preliquidation share of these assets. When a partner receives more than his or her share of the ordinary income assets, the partner is treated as receiving the excess through a sale to the partnership of his or her share of the nonordinary income assets for the excess ordinary income assets the partner received. The partner will report capital gains for his or her share of the appreciation in capital gain assets relinquished to the other partners. The portion of the ordinary income assets received in the deemed exchange will have a cost basis to the distributee equal to their fair market value.

Code Sec. 751(b) is activated if a distribution results in an exchange of capital gains property for ordinary income property or the reverse. The exchange is measured in terms of a partner's interest in the *values* of these assets before and after the distribution disregarding their respective bases. For example, a distributee partner is allowed to receive a depreciated asset in exchange for giving up his or her share in an appreciated asset of the same class, and it remains possible, therefore, to shift gain among partners through distributions of disproportionately appreciated assets of the same class. It also remains possible to shift gain among partners through distributions of disproportionately appreciated assets of a different class if they have equal values.

> ***Comment.*** From the distributee's point of view, if he or she receives a liquidating distribution, Code Sec. 751(b) produces a result which is similar to the Code Sec. 751(a) result to a selling partner. Each partner will have ordinary income in an amount equal to their share of the partnership's ordinary income appreciation. However, from the standpoint of the partnership, the result is very different. Under Code Sec. 751(b), the partnership, consisting of the remaining partners who have purchased the liquidated partner's share of the ordinary income assets, will have a fair market value cash basis in these assets. Under Code Sec. 751(a), the partnership receives a fair market value cash basis for the purchaser's share of the assets only if there is a Code Sec. 754 election in effect.

> ***LLC Observation.*** The disproportionate distribution rules discussed in this chapter apply equally to state law partnerships and LLCs taxed as partnerships.

¶ 1802 Definition of Unrealized Receivables

Generally, Code Sec. 751(c) defines unrealized receivables for all purposes of partnership taxation (Subchapter K of the Internal Revenue Code). References to "unrealized receivables" may be found in the following sections in Subchapter K:

1. Code Sec. 731(a)(2), which provides for the recognition of loss upon certain distributions in liquidation of a partner's partnership interest;

2. Code Sec. 732(c), which provides for an allocation of adjusted basis to distributed property to be made first to Code Sec. 751 assets; and

3. Code Sec. 735(a), which provides that the character of gain or loss realized on a subsequent sale of unrealized receivables received in a distribution is ordinary income.

As originally enacted, Code Sec. 751(c) included only a single sentence dealing with rights to receive payments for goods and services provided or to be provided. Currently, however, the last two sentences of the section are representative of Congressional exceptions to capital gain treatment enacted over the years. Other than for purposes of Code Sec. 736(a), the term "unrealized receivables" now includes the following items:

1. Depreciation recapture under Code Sec. 1245.
2. Excess depreciation under Code Sec. 1250.
3. Mining exploration expenses recapture under Code Sec. 617(d).
4. Stock in a D.I.S.C.[1] or certain foreign corporations.[2]
5. Franchises, trademarks, etc.[3]
6. Oil, gas or geothermal property.[4]
7. Excess farm loss recapture under Code Sec. 1252.
8. Market discount bonds [5] and short-term obligations.[6]

Code Sec. 751(c) does not purport to be an exhaustive list of "unrealized receivables" but merely indicates that the term "includes" the items listed. To date, the IRS has not argued for any other inclusion, but the language to support such an argument is in the section.

As indicated, the term "unrealized receivables" includes the rights to payments for services rendered or to be rendered to the extent not already reported. The term "rights . . . to payment for" is construed liberally, including a noncontractual or equitable right (*quantum meruit*) to payment, whether it is partially or fully earned, and when there is a noncancellable future contract to perform services or deliver goods. However, if the agreement is cancellable at will by the buyer-customer, it is not an unrealized receivable to the seller. Thus, general expectations of profit are likened to goodwill, which is not a Code Sec. 751 asset. Even though goodwill represents future profits on which the purchaser has put economic value, the seller will have capital gain on its disposition.

Unrealized receivables include the right to receive payments for goods delivered or to be delivered. However, to the extent these constitute accounts receivable for financial accounting purposes, they most likely will have been recognized by the partnership because taxpayers selling inventoried goods generally must use the accrual method of accounting for sale of goods. Accrual method partnerships will often have a right to be paid for goods that have been ordered but not yet delivered.

---

[1] Code Sec. 992(a).
[2] Code Sec. 1248.
[3] Code Sec. 1253.
[4] Code Sec. 1254.
[5] As defined in Code Sec. 1278.
[6] As defined in Code Sec. 1283.

The recapture items referred to in the last two sentences of Code Sec. 751(c) are different from the right to receive payments for goods or services in that they do not involve any type of contractual right to receive payments. They are, in effect, the current, unrealized, potential ordinary income inherent in the property if it were sold at its current fair market value. This unrealized receivable is an amount determined by referring to the fair market value of the asset, its adjusted basis, and the type of gain, ordinary or capital, which would be reported if it were sold. The unrealized receivable is the ordinary income the partnership would realize if it sold the asset. An arm's-length agreement between the partnership and the distributee may be used in certain circumstances to establish what is exchanged.[7]

> ***Observation.*** It must be remembered that it is the ordinary income asset's value and basis that controls the results to the distributee partner and distributing partnership. For example, a cash basis partnership's accounts receivable are an unrealized receivable to the extent of the value the buyer and seller of the partnership's business would agree upon. This amount could very likely be less than the receivables' face value. In the case of an accrual basis partnership, that value is likely to be less than the basis of the receivables.

Since Code Sec. 751 assets include only assets that represent potential ordinary income, assets with short-term capital gain potential are not Code Sec. 751 assets, and gain from the sale of the partnership interest attributable to such items may receive long-term capital gain treatment.

¶ 1803 Definition of Substantially Appreciated Inventory Items

The second category of Code Sec. 751 assets consists of substantially appreciated inventory items. This requires a two part analysis: first, the asset must be inventory—Code Sec. 751(d) sets out four categories of inventory items; second, the inventory must be substantially appreciated.

The first of the four categories of inventory items is true inventory in terms of Code Sec. 1221(1) and dealer property held primarily for sale to customers in the ordinary course of the partnership's business.[8]

The second category comprises other property which, when sold or exchanged by the partnership, would be considered property other than a capital asset in terms of Code Sec. 1221 and other than a Code Sec. 1231(b) asset.[9] This category is so broad as to apparently encompass all the other categories and specifically includes the accounts receivable of a cash-basis taxpayer,[10] realized accounts receivable of an accrual-basis taxpayer, depreciation recapture, and all other unrealized receivables. When there is a

[7] Reg. § 1.751-1(g), Exs. (3)(c), (3)(d)(1) and (5)(c).

[8] Code Sec. 751(d)(1).

[9] Code Sec. 751(d)(2).

[10] Although this would seem unwarranted, the regulations specifically provide for this result. Reg. § 1.751-1(d)(2)(ii).

disproportionate distribution involving unrealized receivables, the fact that an asset is an unrealized receivable will alone result in characterizing a part of the distribution as a sale of these unrealized receivables. In addition, however, classifying this same asset as an inventory item may result in the partnership's other inventory being deemed substantially appreciated when they otherwise might not have been, or not substantially appreciated when it otherwise would have been.

> ***Observation.*** The inclusion of unrealized receivables as inventory (in this second category) has an effect on only the "substantial appreciation test." The result is that, in the case of a cash-basis partnership, it is more likely that the traditional category of inventory will be appreciated, while the opposite is often true of an accrual-basis partnership.

The fact that Code Sec. 751(d)(2) refers to noncapital assets and not to noncapital gains could potentially mean that Code Sec. 306 stock, Code Sec. 341 gains, gains from original issue discount, and other gains which are from capital assets but are taxed as ordinary income, are excluded from the definition of inventory under Code Sec. 751(d)(2). Recapture items would not be inventory items. Code Sec. 64, however, appears to classify recapture items as other than Code Sec. 1231(b) or capital assets, and therefore these assets are unlikely to be excluded from status as inventory.

The third category of inventory items comprises the potential gain from the sale of Code Sec. 1246 stock.[11]

The fourth category is any other partnership property that would be either Code Sec. 1221(1) property, other noncapital assets or non-Code Sec. 1231(b) property, or property giving rise to potential gain from the sale of Code Sec. 1246 stock if it were held by the distributee partner.[12] Therefore, if the property would fall into one of the first three categories "if held by the selling or distributee partner," it will be considered to be inventory for the purposes of Code Sec. 751. The legislative history does not indicate the purpose for this provision which, in effect, requires the property to be tested at two levels.

> ***Observation.*** This fourth category of inventory has the potential to produce unexpected tax consequences. For example, it is clear that a dealer in real estate who is a limited partner in a partnership which invests in real estate incurs capital gains for his share of the profits if the partnership produces capital gains from the sale of its real estate investments. However, under the Code Secs. 751(b)/751(d)(4) rules, if the limited partner receives a liquidating cash distribution from the partnership, the IRS could recharacterize some or all of the distribution as ordinary income.

---

[11] Foreign investment company stock. Code Sec. 751(d)(3).

[12] Code Sec. 751(d)(4).

Whether or not property is "held primarily for sale" in terms of Code Sec. 1221(1) is a factual test focusing on the taxpayer's intent with regard to the property in question. In the context of Code Sec. 751(d)(4), this test is difficult to apply since the partner does not actually own the property. It could be argued that a selling partner, who is otherwise a dealer in the type of assets the partnership owns, can have investment accounts, and that this particular property would be such an investment. A trader or dealer in certain types of property may invest in that type of property if he or she shows such an intent. One method of showing investment intent is to set the property aside from other similar property that he or she does deal in. Ownership through a partnership that is not controlled by the partner would help show investment motive. However, with respect to a similar provision, the Code Sec. 341(e) rules provide that, if the taxpayer has similar inventory, this is enough to create a presumption that it would be held for sale.[13]

For distributions, partnership inventory items are not Code Sec. 751 assets unless they are "substantially appreciated" in the aggregate. Code Sec. 751(b)(3) lays down a mechanical test for determining whether inventory is substantially appreciated. The total fair market value of the inventory must exceed 120 percent of the total adjusted basis of all the inventory items to the partnership.[14]

Before the August 5, 1997, effective date of Act § 1062(a) of the Taxpayer Relief Act of 1997,[15] only substantially appreciated inventory could generate ordinary income on both sales of partnership interests under Code Sec. 751(a) and disproportionate distributions under Code Sec. 752(b). Since that date, the substantial appreciation requirement affects only disproportionate distributions. Inventory is considered substantially appreciated for this purpose only if the aggregate fair market value of these assets exceeds their aggregate basis by 120 percent.[16] For this purpose, inventory is disregarded if a principle purpose for acquiring it was to prevent the partnership's inventory items from being substantially appreciated (*e.g.*, if it was depreciated at the date of acquisition or contribution by a partner).[17]

Example 18-1. *Liquidating cash distribution. A, B, C,* and *D* formed the calendar year ABCD partnership, each with a one-fourth interest in the capital, profits, and losses of the partnership. The original contributions to ABCD were $100 in cash from each partner.

---

[13] Code Sec. 341(b) refers to the purchase of property described in Code Sec. 341(b)(3) which defines "Section 341 assets." See also S. Rep. No. 781, 82d Cong., 1st Sess. (1951), reprinted in 1951-2 CB 458, 481. This issue potentially causes additional problems when Code Sec. 751(b) is applicable, as it may give ordinary income to the other nondealer partners upon a deemed property distribution to the dealer. The regulations cure this by limiting Code Sec. 751(d)(2)(D) to property retained by the partnership. Reg. § 1.751(d)(2)(iii). See further discussion of Code Sec. 751(b) under distributions.

[14] Special basis adjustments under Code Secs. 743(b) and 732(d) are excluded. Reg. § 1.751-1(d)(1). The Taxpayer Relief Act of 1997, P.L. 105-34, Act § 1062(a).

[15] P.L. 105-34.

[16] Code Sec. 751(b)(3); Reg. § 1.751-1(d)(1).

[17] Code Sec. 751(b)(3)(B).

For financial accounting purposes and for tax purposes the partnership uses the accrual method for the purchase and sale of inventory that it sells on a C.O.D. basis, and the cash method for all other purposes. In addition to producing inventory assets for sale, the partnership renders consulting services to some of its customers. *A, B, C,* and *D* derive their income exclusively from the partnership. The current balance sheet is as follows:

Assets	*Book Value and Adjusted Basis*	*FMV*
Cash	$240	$240
Inventory	60	100
Capital Asset *X*	100	260
	$400	*$600*
Capital		
A	$100	$150
B	100	150
C	100	150
D	100	150
	$400	*$600*

The adjusted basis of each partner's partnership interest is $100. The partnership distributes $150 in liquidation of Partner *A*'s interest.

The distribution of the cash to *A* results in a Code Sec. 751(b) distribution because *A* is exchanging part of his interest in Code Sec. 751 property (the inventory) for cash, a non-Code Sec. 751 asset. In order to determine the amount of the exchange and the amount of the distribution, it is helpful to proceed as follows.

Initially, one must classify the assets. The cash and Capital Asset *X* are not Code Sec. 751 property because neither is within the definition of Code Sec. 751(c) or (d). The inventory is Code Sec. 751 property because it is inventory within the definition of Code Sec. 751(d), and meets the substantial appreciation test of Code Sec. 751(b)(3)(A).

Next, one must determine *A*'s interest in the respective assets before and after the distribution in order to determine which assets are being exchanged:

1. *A's predistribution* interest in:

Cash	=	1/4	×	$240	=	$60
Inventory	=	1/4	×	$100	=	$25
Asset *X*	=	1/4	×	$260	=	$65

2. *A*'s *postdistribution* interest in each asset retained by the partnership is $0 because *A* is no longer a partner.

3. Property distributed to *A* is cash of $150.

As *A* receives only cash, he has relinquished his interest in Capital Asset *X* worth $65 and his interest in inventory worth $25 for cash of $90. Only the relinquishment of the inventory for cash is a Code Sec. 751(b) exchange. *A* has relinquished an interest in inventory worth $25 for cash of $25. The exchange of an interest in a capital asset for cash is irrelevant as the statutory focus is on a relinquishment of his share of Code Sec. 751 property.[18]

The basis of the *hot assets* (the inventory) deemed exchanged for the cash is determined under Code Sec. 732(a) as if *A* had received the assets in a current distribution immediately before the exchange. *A* exchanged an interest in inventory worth $25 for cash of that amount. The basis of the inventory to *A* is $25/$100 × $60 or $15, *i.e.*, *A*'s one-fourth interest in the inventory. *A* has gain equal to the difference between the cash he received in the exchange and his basis in the relinquished *hot assets*.

Amount realized	$25	Cash received in exchange for the inventory
Basis.	(15)	Basis of the inventory exchanged by *A*
	$*10*	*A*'s gain on the Code Sec. 751(b) exchange

The partnership does not have gain because it is deemed to have purchased the inventory assets with cash. The character of *A*'s gain is ordinary since he is deemed to have sold to the partnership the inventory deemed distributed to him. Sale of the inventory immediately after a distribution results in ordinary income.[19]

The remaining cash distributed to *A* is treated as a distribution to which Code Secs. 731 through 735 apply. *A* has gain under Code Sec. 731(a)(1) because he received cash in excess of his basis in his partnership interest. The amount of the distribution is $125 (the total of $150 minus the amount allocated ($25) to the sale of inventory). *A*'s basis in his partnership interest at the time of the cash distribution ($100) must be reduced by *A*'s share of the basis for the inventory ($15) which was deemed to have been distributed to him immediately before the Code Sec. 751(b) exchange. This reduction occurs under Code Sec. 733 and reduces *A*'s basis in his partnership interest to $85. *A* has a capital gain on the distribution of $125 minus $85, or $40.

1. *A*'s taxable gain on the distribution is $50. Ten dollars of the gain is ordinary from the deemed sale of the inventory and $40 of it is capital gain from the cash distribution in excess of basis.

[18] The exchange of *A*'s $65 share of Capital Asset *X* for cash is accounted for under Code Sec. 734(b)(1)(A) if the partnership has a Code Sec. 754 election in effect. See Chapter 16.

[19] Code Sec. 735(a)(2).

2. The partnership has no gain on the distribution. It did not *sell* Code Sec. 751(b) property, but only *bought* the inventory from *A* with cash.

3. The partnership's adjusted basis in the inventory is $60 (its beginning basis) minus the adjusted basis of the portion of the inventory that was deemed to be distributed to *A* ($15), plus the purchase price of that same portion of the inventory that it bought from *A* for $25. The total thus is $70 ($60 − $15 + $25).

4. Assuming the partnership does not have a Code Sec. 754 election in effect, its post-distribution balance sheet is as follows:

Assets	*Basis*	*FMV*
Cash	$90	$90
Inventory	70	100
Capital Asset *X*	100	260
	$260	*$450*
Capital		
B	100	150
C	100	150
D	100	150
	$300	*$450*

Inside and outside adjusted bases, if computed on a tax basis, are not equal. The difference between the bases of the assets and the capital accounts results from *A* recognizing a gain of $40 on the distribution. The discrepancy of $40 is equal to the amount the Code Sec. 734(b) adjustment and the Code Sec. 743(b) adjustment that would be made if *A* had sold his partnership interest to the other partners and there was a Code Sec. 754 election in effect. This adjustment would have been added to the partnership's basis for Capital Asset *X*. This would bring one-fourth of its basis to fair market value.

A's Share of *X*'s value	(25% × $260)	=	$65
A's share of *X*'s basis	(25% × $100)	=	25
Adjustment necessary to bring to value			*$40*

If the partnership liquidates, *B*, *C*, and *D* each will have a $23.33 basis for their share of the inventory (1/3 of $70). Their basis for their shares of the capital asset is $46.67. This is equal to:

$100.00	Beginning partnership interest basis
(30.00)	Cash
(23.33)	Basis allocated to inventory
$46.67	

Comment. The preceding example is the clearest application of Code Sec. 751(b). The partner leaves the partnership with a liquidating distribution of cash and gives up his interest in all other assets. The liquidated partner has received his share of the cash and the other partners have also given a portion of their shares of the partnership's cash for the liquidated partner's share of the noncash assets. This is a clear case of the other partners purchasing the liquidated partner's share of the noncash assets.

Example 18-2. *Non-liquidating hot asset distribution. A, B, C,* and *D* are equal partners of the ABCD Partnership. At the present time, ABCD's balance sheet is as follows:

Assets	***Basis***	***FMV***
Inventory	$40	$150
Capital Asset *X*	360	650
	$400	*$800*
Capital		
A	$100	$200
B	100	200
C	100	200
D	100	200
	$400	*$800*

The adjusted basis of each partner's partnership interest is $100.

It is agreed that the partnership will distribute the inventory to *A*. Following the distribution, *A*'s overall interest in profits and capital will be reduced from one-fourth to one-thirteenth. The interests of *B*, *C*, and *D* each will be increased from one-fourth to four-thirteenths.

The distribution of the inventory to *A* is a Code Sec. 751(b) distribution because *A* is exchanging part of his interest in the non-Code Sec. 751 property (Capital Asset *X*) for Code Sec. 751 property (inventory). To determine the amount of the exchange and the amount of the distribution, one should proceed as follows.

Initially, one must classify the assets. The inventory is Code Sec. 751 property because it is inventory within the definition of Code Sec. 751(d) and meets the substantial appreciation test of Code Sec. 751(b)(3). Capital Asset *X* is not Code Sec. 751 property because it is a capital asset.

Next, one must determine *A*'s interests in the respective assets before and after the transaction in order to determine which assets are being exchanged.

1. *A*'s predistribution interest in:

   Inventory = 1/4 × $150 = $37.50
   Asset *X* = 1/4 × $650 = $162.50

2. *A*'s postdistribution interest in each asset retained by ABCD:

   Asset *X* = 1/13 × $650 = $50

3. Property distributed to *A* is inventory of $150

As *A* received only inventory, he has relinquished an interest in Capital Asset *X* worth $112.50 for an interest in the inventory worth $112.50. The remaining $37.50 of inventory *A* received was a distribution of his share of that inventory and is not subject to the provisions of Code Sec. 751(b).

The basis of the asset exchanged is determined under Code Sec. 732(a) as if *A* had received the asset in a current distribution immediately before the exchange. *A* exchanged an interest in Asset *X* worth $112.50. The basis of the asset is $112.50/$650 × $360 or $62.30 (fair market value of the exchanged asset deemed distributed over the total value of the asset times the basis of the asset).

A recognizes taxable gain in an amount equal to the difference between the value of the property received by him in the exchange, the inventory, and his basis in the relinquished asset, Capital Asset *X*.

Amount realized	$112.50	Value of inventory received in the exchange
Basis.	62.30	Basis of the portion of Asset *X* deemed exchanged by *A*
	$50.20	*A*'s gain on the Code Sec. 751(b) exchange is characterized as capital since *A* is treated has having disposed of a portion of a capital asset for the inventory. Whether the gain should be long-term or short-term depends upon the asset's holding period.

The partnership has gain equal to the difference between the value of the property received (Capital Asset *X*) and the basis of the property exchanged (the inventory).

Amount realized	$112.50	Value of Asset *X* "purchased" in the exchange
Basis.	30.00	Basis of the portion of inventory exchanged*
	$82.50	ABCD's ordinary income on the Code Sec. 751(b) exchange

*The adjusted basis is the remaining share (3/4) of the basis ($40) of the inventory after reduction by A's share of the inventory distributed to him.

The character of ABCD's gain is ordinary since it is deemed to have "exchanged" inventory. ABCD's gain on this transaction will be allocated to *B*, *C*, and *D* on the basis of each partner's postdistribution interest in profits and loss.[20]

The remaining portion of the inventory is treated as a distribution to which Code Secs. 731 through 735 apply. *A* has no gain on the

[20] Reg. § 1.751-1(b)(2)(ii) and (3)(ii).

distribution of inventory worth $37.50 (1/4 of the inventory which was his portion before the distribution) under Code Sec. 731(a). His basis in this portion of the inventory is $10.

Comment. Code Sec. 751(b) applies only if the distributee is both (1) receiving a distribution of one class of assets, and (2) relinquishing a share in the value of the other class of assets. In Example 18-2, Partner *A*'s share of capital and profits was reduced by the distribution. In some cases, receipt of a nonliquidating distribution may reduce the distributee's capital account, but have no impact on his or her interest in profits and losses. In such cases, the distribution may not affect the distributee's future share of income. The regulations are silent on how a distributee partner determines his or her pre- and post-distribution share of partnership assets when that partner's profit/loss sharing ratios are not the same as his or her share of capital. However, a theoretical case can be argued for the application of Code Sec. 751(b) when a distribution doesn't result in a reduced profit sharing ratio, but the potential distortion addressed by Code Sec. 751(b) is not present. Unless the regulations are amended to clearly apply in such a case, arguably Code Sec. 751(b) might not apply.

Example 18-3. *Nonliquidating cold asset property distribution.* Partner *A* of the equal AB Partnership has a $95 basis in his partnership interest. The partnership has $300 of ordinary income property and $100 of capital gain property, with bases of $150 and $40, respectively. *A* receives a distribution of the capital gain property in a nonliquidating distribution, reducing his interest in partnership profits, losses and capital to one-third. Before the distribution, *A* had an indirect $150 interest in the ordinary income property and a $50 interest in the capital gain property for a total interest valued at $200. After the distribution, the value of *A*'s interest is $100 and is comprised entirely of a reduced interest in the ordinary income property. The distribution results not only in *A*'s obtaining an undivided direct interest in *his* share of the capital gain property, but also in his receiving a direct undivided ownership in the *other* partner's share of the capital gain property in exchange for giving the other partner $50 in value of his indirect interest in the ordinary income property.

If the rate of tax imposed upon capital gains is lower than that imposed upon ordinary income, *A*'s motivation for the distribution in the previous example is obvious. Before the distribution, his share of the partnership's potential taxable income consists of $30 of capital gains and $75 of ordinary income. In the absence of Code Sec. 751(b), he will, after distribution, have a $60 interest in the unrealized capital gain and a $50 share of the partnership's ordinary income. Thus, *A* exchanged an ordinary income potential of $25 for an additional $30 of potential capital gains. In addition, if the ordinary income assets are sold, and *A* receives $100 as a liquidating distribution, he will be entitled to a $5 loss after adjusting his basis for his share of the gain and distributions.[21] With a long-term capital gain rate of 15%, and ordinary tax rates up to 35%, this is a good trade.

In this example, Code Sec. 751(b) treats the disproportionate distribution as the distributee partner's sale of his reduced share of the ordinary income assets to the other partners. Technically, he is treated as if he received the other partners' shares of capital gains property by purchasing it with the share of inventory he relinquished to them. The regulations specify the mechanics of this exchange.[22] He is treated as if he receives, in a current distribution, the share of ordinary income assets given up and immediately sells them to the partnership. He has ordinary income for the appreciation of his relinquished share of ordinary income assets and a fair market value basis for the disproportionate segment of the capital asset received in the exchange. The remaining portion of the distribution, the distribution of his prorated share of capital assets, is taken into account under the normal distribution rules. *A*'s deemed distribution of ordinary income property is as follows:

$50 Value ($150.00 share before distribution less $100.00 share after)
$25 Basis (Basis to the partnership of 1/6 of the inventory)

His basis in his interest is reduced by $25 to $70.

A's deemed exchange of this inventory with the partnership for $50 of capital gain property results in $25 of ordinary income and a basis of $50 in that portion of the asset. The partnership's basis in this portion of the inventory is increased by $25 to $50. The $25 increase is for *B*'s benefit only.

The $50 remaining portion of the capital asset distribution is governed by the normal distribution rules. *A*'s basis in this portion is $20. His ending basis in the $100 capital asset is $70. His ending basis in his partnership interest is $50. *A*'s predistribution ordinary income share was $75. He has recognized $25. If the partnership sells the ordinary income asset, his share of the gain is $50 (1/3 of $150) and *B*'s share is $75 (2/3 of $150 less $25).

The partnership is, in turn, treated as if it used a share of the capital gain property to purchase the ordinary income property. AB

[21] First, the nonliquidating property distribution reduces *A*'s initial basis in his partnership interest ($95) by the partnership's basis in the distributed property ($40) to $55. Second, his share of the income resulting from a liquidation of the partnership's assets (ordinary income of $50) increases his basis to $105. Last, upon a liquidation of the partnership *A* is entitled to a $100 cash distribution (1/3 of the partnership assets). A $100 liquidating cash distribution to a partner with a $105 basis in his interest results in a $5 loss. Code Sec. 731(a)(2).

[22] Reg. § 1.751-1(b)(2).

incurs capital gains to the extent of the appreciated portion of the capital asset considered to be disproportionately distributed. The partnership receives a fair market value basis in the ordinary income assets deemed acquired in the exchange. The basis increase to the ordinary income asset is normally equal to the amount of ordinary gain the distributee reports. The basis increase to the distributed capital assets is normally equal to the capital gain the partnership recognizes.

Chapter 19

Service Partnerships—Death or Retirement of a General Partner

---

¶ 1901 Introduction

When a partner is to discontinue his or her participation in a partnership, there are several available alternatives that put the partner in substantially the same economic position but have different tax consequences:

1. The partner can sell his or her interest to the remaining partners and/or to an unrelated party;

2. The partnership can continue but the partner's interest can be liquidated by the partnership redeeming his or her interest; or

3. The partnership can itself liquidate.

Tax planning most often involves a choice between the first and second alternatives if the business is to be continued without interruption. The tax consequences of selling a partnership interest are discussed in Chapters 11 and 12. The consequences of liquidating the partnership are discussed in Chapter 16. This chapter covers the tax consequences when a service partnership continues but a general partner's interest is terminated not by sale but by the partnership's liquidating payment. Chapter 16 covers the tax consequences when a general partner retires from a nonservice partnership and when a nongeneral partner retires from a service partnership. The following table contains a brief comparison of the tax consequences of a general partner's retirement by a continuing service partnership through a liquidation versus a cross-purchase.

Liquidation by Partnership	Sale to Other Partner(s)
1. Partnership makes payments to retiring partner (or deceased partner's successor in interest.	1. Partner(s) make payments to retiring partner.
2. Difference between tax basis and FMV of distributed property (other than cash) not taxed until sold by distributee partner.	2. Cash and FMV of property received treated as sales proceeds. Difference between proceeds and partnership interest tax basis is realized gain.
3. Installment payments for share of partnership property not taxed until proceeds exceed outside basis (however, may elect to prorate basis).	3. All installment payments taxed. Outside basis is prorated and applied against each payment.
4. Can produce both capital gain and ordinary income for retiring partner.	4. Usually produces capital gain for retiring partner—unless collapsible partnership rules apply (Code Sec. 751(a)).
5. Can often be structured so some of the payments are deductible by the partnership.	5. Payments increase purchasing partner's basis in his or her interest and may result in a Code Sec. 754 step-up, but payments are usually not immediately deductible by the purchasing partner.
6. Not considered to be a sale or exchange that can terminate the partnership under Code Sec. 708.	6. The sale of 50% or more of the partnership's capital and profits interests within a 12-month period terminates the partnership under Code Sec. 708.
7. Installment payments are not subject to the OID rules (*i.e.*, the payments can include no interest or below-market interest).	7. Any deferred payments must provide for "adequate" interest or interest will be imputed under the OID rules.

LLC Observation. The statute, legislative history and regulations are silent with respect to which members, if any, of an LLC are considered general partners for Code Sec. 736 purposes.[1]

Some partnership payments in liquidation of a partner's entire interest in a continuing partnership are treated differently from payments to a partner when the partnership itself liquidates. The reason for the different treatment results from the differences in the nature of the payments to the partner. When a partnership itself liquidates, each partner receives his or

[1] In 1997, the IRS issued proposed regulations addressing the classification of LLC members as limited vs. general partners for purposes of the self-employment tax (Prop. Reg. § 1.1402(a)-2). Congress reacted by prohibiting the IRS from issuing further regulations on this subject before July 1, 1998. No further regulations have yet been issued.

her share of the value of the partnership's net assets. Normally, this share is distributed in a lump-sum payment and the partnership ends its business activity. Alternatively, when a partnership continues its activity after a partner's interest is liquidated, the amount of the liquidation payment often exceeds the retiring partner's share of the value of the partnership's existing tangible assets. This difference represents a payment to the retiring partner for a share of the partnership's future earning capacity, *i.e.*, a payment for partnership "goodwill."

Unlike partnership liquidation payments, payments liquidating only a particular partner's interest often span more than one tax accounting period. Without specific guidance, it is often difficult to distinguish continuing profit-share payments to an inactive partner from installment liquidating distributions that are contingent upon future partnership earnings. Code Sec. 736 governs the treatment of payments made to a retiring or deceased general partner when the service partnership continues. Code Sec. 736 directs whether the tax rules governing liquidating distributions apply solely or whether the tax rules governing normal operating income allocations and guaranteed payments will also apply along with the liquidating distribution rules. Code Sec. 736 can apply only when a general partner (or the successor to a deceased general partner) receives a distribution or distributions in complete liquidation of the partner's interest from a continuing service partnership.[2] It does not apply when the continuing partners purchase the interest of the retiring or deceased partners. It also does not apply to distributions when the partnership itself liquidates even though the economic consequences may be similar whether the withdrawing partner is bought out by the partnership or by all the remaining partners.[3]

The Code Sec. 736 rules do apply when there is a complete liquidation of one general partner's interest in a two-partner service partnership.[4] With respect to the withdrawal of one member of a two-person partnership, the parties should be particularly careful in the manner in which payments to the withdrawing partner are made to ensure that the intended tax consequences result. If Code Sec. 736 treatment is desired, the partnership agreement should clearly provide that the payments will be made from funds of the business rather than from the separate funds of the remaining partner. In addition, the Code Sec. 736 payments to the withdrawing partner should be reflected in the books of the continuing business. These precautions are suggested because, upon the withdrawal of one of two partners, the "partnership" continues as a federal income tax entity as long as Code Sec. 736 payments are made to the withdrawing partner by the partnership. If the payments are considered to come from the remaining partner, the IRS could claim that, rather than a liquidation of the withdrawing partner's interest by the partnership, the remaining partner actually purchased the withdrawing partner's interest. If such a

[2] Reg. § § 1.736-1(a)(1)(i) and 1.761-1(d).

[3] Reg. § 1.736-1(a)(1)(i).

[4] Reg. § 1.736-1(a)(6).

recharacterization were successful, Code Sec. 736 would not apply to the payments and the partnership would terminate for federal income tax purposes at the time of the "purchase" (*i.e.*, when the partner withdraws).

After the effective date of the Revenue Reconciliation Act of 1993,[5] Code Sec. 736 does not apply to distributions to limited partners. Code Sec. 736 also does not apply to any distributions, whether or not made to limited partners, if capital is a material income-producing factor for the partnership. Therefore, the Revenue Reconciliation Act of 1993 limited the significance of Code Sec. 736 primarily to service-oriented partnerships (*e.g.*, such as general partnerships involved in the practice of medicine, dentistry, law, architecture, and accounting).

> ***LLC Comment.*** In the case of a service-oriented LLC there is no guidance that identifies which members are considered general or limited partners for purposes of Code Sec. 736. Until the IRS or the Treasury issues guidance, it would be reasonable to treat members who act as general partners as such for Code Sec. 736 purposes. For example, member managers who have the authority to operate the LLC's business and are actively involved in its business should be treated as general partners for Code Sec. 736 purposes.

The purpose of Code Sec. 736 is to classify payments to a withdrawing partner. Code Sec. 736 does not determine the tax consequences that follow from that classification. Once the classification of liquidating payments to a withdrawing partner is made, other provisions of Subchapter K determine the tax consequences to the withdrawing and continuing partners.

Code Sec. 736 generally classifies payments from a partnership to a withdrawing partner into one of three categories. Liquidating payments may be classified as (1) distributions,[6] (2) a distributive share of partnership income,[7] or (3) a guaranteed payment.[8] Amounts received by a partner may be classified into one category of Code Sec. 736,[9] or may be comprised of two, or all three, categories.

The characterization of payments from a partnership to a withdrawing partner is significant because it determines:

1. Whether the withdrawing partner recognizes capital gain or loss or ordinary income with respect to the payments;
2. The timing of the gain, loss, or income recognition by the withdrawing partner;
3. Whether the partnership is entitled to a deduction with respect to the payments; and

---

[5] P.L. 103-66, Act § 13262(b). The general effective date is for partners dying on or after January 5, 1993.

[6] Code Sec. 736(b).

[7] Code Sec. 736(a)(1).

[8] Code Sec. 736(a)(2).

[9] Code Sec. 736(a)(1), (2), or (b).

4. Whether the remaining partners are entitled to exclude from their own share of partnership income amounts paid to the retiring partner.

In addition, classification under Code Sec. 736 determines whether the amounts paid to the successors of a deceased partner constitute income in respect of a decedent.[10]

Overview of Code Sec. 736's Designation of Liquidating Distributions

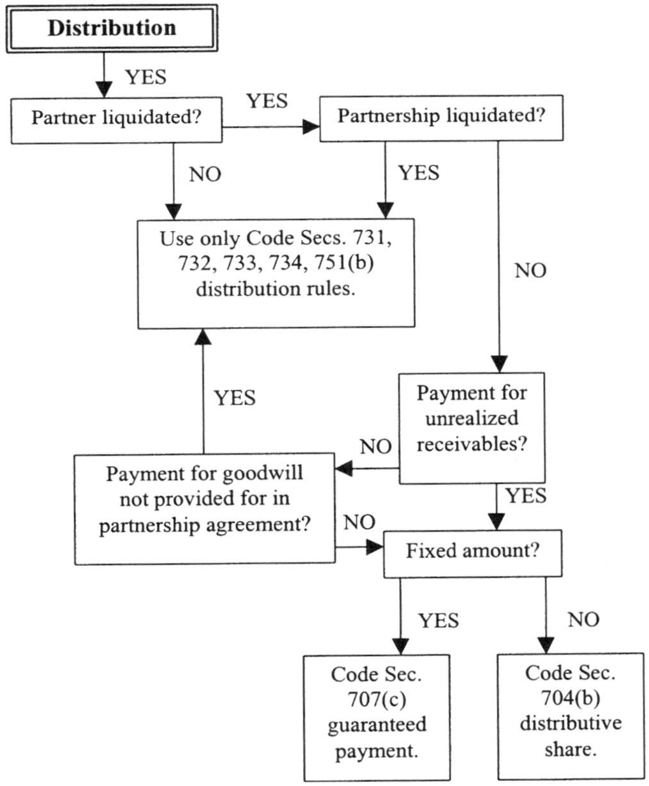

¶ 1902 Payment for Retiring General Partner's Interest in a Partnership When Capital Is Not a Material Income-Producing Factor

In the case of liquidating payments to general partners in a partnership in which capital is not a material income-producing factor, the provisions of Code Sec. 736 are most easily understood by viewing a retiring

[10] Code Secs. 691 and 753.

partner's partnership interest as representing an indirect ownership in three types of assets.

1. Unrealized receivables.[11]

2. Goodwill.

3. Everything else.

.01 *When Is Capital a Material Income-Producing Factor?*

The legislative history of the Revenue Reconciliation Act of 1993 provides that capital is not a material income-producing factor when substantially all of the gross income of the partnership business consists of fees, commissions or other compensation for personal services performed by an individual. The practice of a doctor, dentist, lawyer, architect, or accountant will not, as such, be treated as a trade or business in which capital is a "material income-producing factor" although a partnership may have made substantial capital investments incidental to the professional practice. The legislative history of the Revenue Reconciliation Act of 1993 states that the determination of whether capital is a material income-producing factor will be made under principles of present and prior law (under Code Secs. 401(c)(2), 911(d), and former Code Sec. 1348(b)(1)(A)).[12]

Code Sec. 401(c)(2) defines "earned income" for purposes of determining whether a self-employed person may make a contribution to a qualified plan. Code Sec. 401(c)(2) provides that the term "earned income" means net earnings from self-employment, but that such net earnings shall be determined only with respect to a trade or business in which personal services of the taxpayer are a material income-producing factor.[13]

Code Sec. 911(d) defines "earned income" for purposes of deciding what income of a U.S. citizen or resident living abroad can be excluded from gross income. Code Sec. 911(d)(2)(A) provides that earned income includes amounts received as compensation for personal services actually rendered. Code Sec. 911(d)(2)(B) provides special treatment for income earned in connection with a trade or business in which both personal services and capital are material income-producing factors.

Former Code Sec. 1348 (repealed by the Economic Recovery Tax Act of 1981 [14]) imposed a maximum tax of 50 percent on "personal service income." Code Sec. 1348(b)(1) provided that the term "personal service income" meant any income that was earned income within the meaning of Code Sec. 401(c)(2)(C) or Code Sec. 911(b). As with Code Sec. 911, Code Sec. 1348 afforded special treatment if an individual was engaged in a

[11] Defined in Code Sec. 751(c).

[12] H. Rept. No. 103-111 (P.L. 103-66), p. 782.

[13] Code Sec. 401(c)(2)(A)(i).

[14] P.L. 97-34.

trade or business in which both personal services and capital were "material income-producing factors."[15]

Under former Code Sec. 1348, capital was a material income-producing factor if a "substantial portion" of the gross income of the business was attributable to the employment of capital in the business, as reflected, for example, by a substantial investment in inventories, plant, machinery or other equipment.[16] In general, capital was not deemed a material income-producing factor where the gross income of the business consisted principally of fees, commissions, or other compensation for personal services performed by an individual.[17]

The key issue in determining whether Code Sec. 736 will apply is whether a capital investment is merely incidental to a business or whether a substantial portion of the gross income of a business is produced from capital. Such determination must be decided by reference to all the facts of each case. The cases under Code Sec. 1348 typically looked at such facts as: (1) the amount of capital investment in the business; (2) its relation to the amount of personal services performed; (3) how the capital was used; (4) how critical it was to the business; and (5) for what (*i.e.*, providing services or capital) the business received gross income.[18]

The outcome of cases tended to be fairly predictable. In the majority of cases involving businesses that used capital of any sort (such as inventories, equipment, or buildings) in a nontrivial and nonincidental way (rather than providing little beyond services), capital was held a material income-producing factor. Perhaps the key point was that, under the standard, the use of capital did not have to be more significant than the use of labor but merely of some significance.

Examples of situations where capital has been found to be a material income-producing factor include the funeral services business, contracting business, wholesale distribution of jewelry business, development business, wholesale and retail bowling supply business, grocery store business, and auto repair facility business.[19]

---

[15] Reg. § 1.1348-3(a)(3)(i).

[16] Reg. § 1.1348-3(a)(3)(ii).

[17] *Id.*

[18] See, *e.g.*, *Curry v. U.S.*, CA-FC, 86-2 USTC ¶ 9744, 804 F2d 647.

[19] Among the businesses that were held, under the facts of the particular cases, to use capital as a material income-producing factor, were *Parker v. Commr.*, CA-9, 87-2 USTC ¶ 9441, 822 F2d 905 (designing, producing and using slot machines); *Hicks v. U.S.*, CA-5, 86-1 USTC ¶ 9355, 787 F2d 1018 (general contracting); *Holland v. Commr.*, CA-4, 80-2 USTC ¶ 9469, 622 F2d 95 (maintenance contracting); *Gullion v. Commr.*, TC Memo. 1982-106 (concrete flatwork); *McGowan v. Commr.*, TC Memo. 1982-65 (making landfill); *Hardy v. U.S.*, 589 FSupp 330 (E.D. Wis. 1984) (estate development); *Nelson v. Commr.*, CA-10, 85-2 USTC ¶ 9504, 767 F2d 667 (painting business); *Treatman v. Commr.*, TC Memo. 1981-74 (mail order business); *Friedlander v. U.S.*, CA-9, 83-2 USTC ¶ 9632, 718 F2d 294 (jewelry store); *Whaley v. U.S.*, 84-1 USTC ¶ 9395 (W.D. Miss. 1984) (pharmacy); *Moore v. Commr.*, 71 TC 533, Dec. 35,823 (1979) (retail grocery store); *Block v. U.S.*, 569 FSupp 981 (W.D. Tenn. 1983) (cotton merchant); *Weiss v. U.S.*, 78-2 USTC ¶ 9734 (N.D. Ohio 1978) (metal treating); *Thomas v. Commr.*, 92 TC 206, Dec. 45,460 (1989) (book publishing); *Harris v. Commr.*, TC Memo. 1984-189 (publishing cookbooks); *Wilson v. Commr.*, TC Memo. 1982-289 (eggs); *Gaudern v. Commr.*, 77 TC 1305, Dec. 38,504 (1981) (selling bowling supplies); *Crowell v. Commr.*, TC Memo. 1988-305 (securities brokerage); *Herman v. Commr.*, TC Memo. 1985-396 (operating motels); *Curry v. U.S.*, CA-FC, 86-2 USTC ¶ 9744, 804 F2d 647 (funeral home); *Pilkington v. Commr.*, TC Memo. 1983-111 (bars and lounges); *Novikoff v. Commr.*, TC Memo. 1980-330 (movie theaters); and *Bender v. Commr.*, TC Memo. 1985-375.

Examples of situations where capital has been found to be incidental include construction and design of wrought-iron rails, manufacture and sale of taxidermy supplies, investment brokerage business, bail bondsmen, and a real estate brokerage firm.[20]

Capital does not have to be directly invested in a business to be a material income-producing factor (*e.g.*, capital lent to a business).[21]

Assuming that the legal standard of whether capital is a material income-producing factor in a business is exactly the same under Code Sec. 736 as under former Code Sec. 1348, these cases are not firm precedent regarding the same types of businesses today, since each was decided under its particular facts. Nonetheless, the cases as a whole support two conclusions. First, relatively few activities, outside those specifically listed in the material participation regulations (*i.e.*, health, law, engineering, architecture, accounting, actuarial science, performing arts, and consulting) are likely to be treated as personal service activities. A business's deployment of significant capital (such as buildings, inventory, or equipment) tends to establish that capital is a material income-producing factor and, thus, that it is not a personal service activity for purposes of the regulations. Second, while a wide range of taxpayers are entitled to be fairly certain that they are not engaged in personal services activities, complete certainty about this (or even sufficient certainty for a cautious practitioner to issue an opinion letter) is hard to come by. The standard remains too amorphous and case-specific to support certainty in cases that are close to the line.

.02 Retired Partner Defined

A partner is treated as a "retired" partner when such partner ceases to be a partner under local law.[22] It is not clear from the wording of Code Sec. 736 or the corresponding regulations whether the partner must have actually ceased to be a partner for local law purposes at the time of a payment in order for Code Sec. 736 to apply, or, alternatively, whether the payment must only be in contemplation that the withdrawing partner will cease to be a partner for local law purposes. The statute refers to a "retiring" rather than a "retired" partner. However, the regulations state that Code Sec. 736 does not apply to the successor of a deceased partner that "continues to be a partner in its own right under local law."[23] The implication may be that a "retiring" partner similarly may not continue to be a partner for local law purposes, since there is no justification for distinguishing the successors of a deceased partner from another retiring partner in this context. The wording of the statute (and the regulations in the case of a "retiring" partner) could

---

[20] Capital was not held a material income-producing factor for particular businesses involved in *Van Dyke v. U.S.*, CA-FC, 696 F2d 9057 (taxidermy supply); *Bruno v. Commr.*, 71 TC 191, Dec. 35,529 (1978) (bail bonding); *Fried v. Commr.*, TC Memo. 1989-430 (promoting tax shelters); *Barnes v. Commr.*, TC Memo. 1987-544 (securities brokerage); *Roselle v. Commr.*, TC Memo. 1981-394 (providing management services); and *Van Kalker v. Commr.*, CA-7, 84-2 USTC ¶9727, 804 F2d 967 (fabricating and installing ornamental iron railings).

[21] Rev. Rul. 78-306, 1978-2 CB 218.

[22] Reg. § 1.736-1(a)(1)(ii).

[23] Reg. § 1.736-1(a)(1)(i).

be interpreted as not requiring that the withdrawing partner cease his or her status as a partner for local law purposes in order for Code Sec. 736 to apply (if, for example, the partner were under a binding contract to withdraw under local law in the future). However, if Code Sec. 736 treatment is desired, it would be advisable for the partner to withdraw from the partnership under local law at or before the time the partner receives his or her first liquidation payment.

If a general partner ceases to be a partner under local law and receives payments from the service partnership in liquidation of his or her partnership interest, Code Sec. 736 applies regardless of the reason for the partner's ceasing to be a partner.[24] The regulations under Code Sec. 736 are not concerned with the reasons or the circumstances surrounding a partner's ceasing to be a member of the partnership and the courts have concluded that Code Sec. 736 applies whether the withdrawal is voluntary or involuntary. Code Sec. 736 does not apply to any distributions made to a continuing partner (*e.g.*, distributions that only partially liquidate a partner's interest).[25]

.03 *Payments for Retiring Partner's Share of Unrealized Receivables—Code Sec. 736(a)*

The tax treatment of payments received by a retired partner (or his or her successor in interest) for that retired partner's share of partnership unrealized receivables depends upon whether the payments to be received are fixed in amount or whether they are instead contingent upon future partnership income. Where the payments are fixed in amount, the portion of each payment attributable to the retired partner's share of partnership unrealized receivables (*e.g.*, accounts receivable and unbilled work in process) is treated as a Code Sec. 707(c) guaranteed payment, deductible by the partnership and taxed as ordinary income to the recipient.[26] Note that total payments received by the retired partner (or his or her successor in interest) include deemed payments from a reduction in the partner's share of partnership debt.[27] Because this deemed payment is fixed in amount it is a guaranteed payment if it is for the retired partner's share of unrealized receivables. Amounts treated as guaranteed payments under these rules are taxable to the recipient in his or her taxable year "within or with which ends the partnership year in which the partnership deducted such payment."[28]

If the amount of the payments to be received by the withdrawing partner is contingent on future partnership income, the parties treat the portion of the payments attributable to unrealized receivables as a continu-

[24] Reg. § 1.736-1(a)(1)(ii).

[25] Reg. § 1.736-1(a)(1)(i).

[26] If a partnership terminates before all guaranteed payments have been made, successors to the partnership who continue to make such payments are entitled to a deduction for such payments. See Rev. Rul. 75-154, 1975-1 CB 186; Rev. Rul. 83-155, 1983-2 CB 38; IRS Letter Ruling 7939099 (6-28-79) (undivided shareholders entitled to the deduction for their payments after partnership incorporated).

[27] Code Sec. 752(b).

[28] Reg. § § 1.736-1(a)(5) and 1.707-1(c).

ing profit share.[29] Partnership income, up to the amount of such payments, is allocated to the retired partner, and the continuing partners exclude the payments from their share of the partnership's income. The retired partner is, for tax purposes, treated as a continuing member of the partnership while such payments continue. Therefore, the character (*e.g.*, ordinary income versus capital gain) of the payments representing a continuing profit share are treated the same as under the normal distributive share rules of Code Sec. 702. It may be more beneficial for a withdrawing partner to receive a distributive share of partnership items that may include capital gain rather than to receive a guaranteed payment that will represent ordinary income.

The regulations create some confusion about when the withdrawing partner includes a distributive share of income under Code Sec. 736(a)(1). The withdrawing partner is required to include a "payment" as a distributive share.[30] It therefore could be argued that the implication of the regulation is that a Code Sec. 736(a)(1) payment must be included only when paid by the partnership. The regulations further provide that the withdrawing partner is to claim the payments as income "for his taxable year with or within which ends the partnership taxable year for which the *payment* is a distributive share."[31] This regulation could be read to mean that it is the partnership's taxable year in which the payment is actually made that determines the year of inclusion for the withdrawing partner. However, the accepted practice is to treat the timing of Code Sec. 736(a)(1) payments the same as the payment of any other share of partnership income and require inclusion in the partner's year with or within which the partnership year ends.[32]

After the effective date of the Revenue Reconciliation Act of 1993, for purposes of Code Sec. 736 the term "unrealized receivables" is limited to rights to be paid for services rendered or to be rendered and goods delivered or to be delivered not previously includible in the partnership's income.[33] As a practical matter, this will include mainly cash basis accounts receivable and unbilled work in process.[34] Partnership payments for the retiring partner's share of depreciation recapture will be treated under Code Sec. 736(b) as a distribution for the retiring partner's interest in partnership property. In a liquidating cash distribution, payments for the retired partner's share of recapture will generally cause a disproportionate distribution within the meaning of Code Sec. 751(b). Therefore, that portion of the Code Sec. 736(b) payments representing depreciation recapture will trigger ordinary income for the retired partner and a basis step-up for the partnership under the rules of Code Sec. 751(b).

---

[29] Code Sec. 736(a)(1).

[30] Reg. § 1.736-1(a)(4).

[31] Reg. § 1.736-1(a)(5) (emphasis added).

[32] Code Sec. 706(a).

[33] Code Sec. 751(c), second sentence.

[34] P.L. 103-66, Act § 13262(b); Code Sec. 751(c).

.04 Payments for Retiring Service Partner's Share of Goodwill—Code Sec. 736(a) or (b)

Code Sec. 736 settles the tax treatment of the departing service partner's payment for his or her share of the goodwill. Judicial decisions prior to the addition of Code Sec. 736 by the Internal Revenue Code of 1954 [35] are in conflict about whether such payments should be considered as a continuing share of the partnership's income, and thus treated by the retiring partner as ordinary income, or should be considered as a sale of goodwill and therefore capital gain. The resolution of this conflict is also important to the continuing partners. If the distribution by the partnership is considered a purchase of the departing partner's share of goodwill and there is a Code Sec. 754 election in effect, the basis of acquired goodwill can be amortized over 15 years. However, amounts paid by the partnership for the retired partner's share of goodwill reduce the current year's income allocated to the continuing partners if they are treated as guaranteed payments or distributive shares of income.

Under Code Sec. 736, a partnership in which capital is *not* a material income-producing factor has the discretion to treat a payment to a general partner for goodwill as either:

1. A Code Sec. 736(a) payment (*i.e.*, a distributive income share or guaranteed payment depending upon whether the amount is fixed or contingent), or

2. A Code Sec. 736(b) payment (*i.e.*, a distribution).[36]

The partnership and the retiring partner may "elect" to treat the payment as a distribution by simply providing in the partnership agreement that a retiring partner is to be paid for goodwill.[37] If such a provision is absent and the partnership pays a fixed sum, it is considered a guaranteed payment under Code Sec. 707(c). If the amount is contingent on partnership income, the absence of such a provision in the partnership agreement results in the payment being considered a distributive share of the partnership's income.

Code Sec. 707(a) specifically provides that the deduction by a partnership of a guaranteed payment under Code Sec. 162(a) is subject to Code Sec. 263 (which disallows a current deduction with respect to capital expenditures). The purchase of goodwill is a capital expenditure; however, the limitation on deductions set forth in Code Sec. 263 does not apply to Code Sec. 707(c) payments that are treated as such by Code Sec. 736(a)(2).[38] Therefore, Code Sec. 736(a)(2) payments are always deductible by a partnership under Code Sec. 162(a).[39] Guaranteed payments made to a withdrawing partner under Code Sec. 736(a)(2) are deductible by the

[35] P.L. 591.

[36] Code Sec. 736(b)(2)(B).

[37] *Id.*

[38] Reg. § 1.707-1(c).

[39] The Tax Reform Act of 1976, P.L. 94-455, Act § 213(b)(3), amended Code Sec. 707(c) and clarified that deductibility of Code Sec. 707(c) payments under Code Sec. 162(a) is subject to the capitaliza-

paying party when the partnership terminates for a reason other than the withdrawal of the partner, and the former partners, or a successor to the partnership, continue payment to the withdrawing partner.[40]

Classifying the payments as expressly for goodwill or not need not affect the amount that the retiring partner receives. The parties are free to negotiate the amount of the retirement payments by considering or disregarding goodwill. Whether payments for goodwill to a retiring partner in a "service partnership" will be treated as a Code Sec. 736(a) payment or a Code Sec. 736(b) payment depends entirely on whether the "partnership agreement" specifically allocates liquidation payments to goodwill. If it does, the payments will be treated as Code Sec. 736(b) payments. The courts have shown a tendency to strictly apply Code Sec. 736 (*i.e.*, the partners can decide the classification of distributions, apart from the "true" nature of the distribution payments).[41] However, if a written allocation is ambiguous, the courts will look beyond the partnership agreement to find out the intent of the partners.[42] Frequently, partnership agreements do not address the issue of the character of payments to be made to a retiring partner in liquidation of the partner's interest in the partnership (*i.e.*, Code Sec. 736(a) verses Code Sec. 736(b)). Instead, the parties will often negotiate a liquidation agreement that specifies amounts and timing. It is important that such agreements expressly provide how much, if any, of the agreed upon amount is paid for goodwill.[43] If the agreement clearly includes or omits payments for goodwill, the underlying intentions of the partners are not controlling.[44] Goodwill payments for which the partners desire Code Sec. 736(a) treatment should not mention the words "goodwill" and such payments will be classified as "Code Sec. 736(a) payments."

The "partnership agreement" must specify a payment for goodwill if it is to qualify as a Code Sec. 736(b) payment. The term "partnership agreement" includes "any modifications of the partnership agreement made prior to, or at, the time prescribed by law for the filing of the partnership return for the taxable year (not including extension . . .)."[45] Therefore, an amendment to the partnership agreement providing for

(Footnote Continued)

tion mandate of Code Sec. 263. Prior to that amendment, taxpayers argued that a Code Sec. 707(c) guaranteed payment was deductible even if the expenditure was capital in nature. See, *e.g.*, *J.E. Cagle, Jr. v. Commr.*, 63 TC 86, Dec. 32,828 (1974), aff'd, CA-5, 76-2 USTC ¶ 9672, 539 F2d 409. The legislative history of the 1976 amendment to Code Sec. 707(c) states that the amendment "is not intended to affect adversely the deductibility to the partnership of a payment described in Code Sec. 736(a)(2) to a retiring partner." S. Rep. No. 938, 94th Cong., 1st Sess., 94, n. 7 (1976). This concept of continuing to allow a partnership deduction for a Code Sec. 736(a)(2) payment, notwithstanding the 1976 amendment to Code Sec. 707(c), is reflected in Reg. § 1.707-1(c).

[40] Rev. Rul. 75-154, 1975-1 CB 186; IRS Letter Ruling 7939099 (6-28-79).

[41] *V.Z. Smith v. Commr.*, 37 TC 1033, Dec. 25,383 (1962), aff'd, CA-10, 63-1 USTC ¶ 9211, 313 F2d 16; *Miller v. U.S.*, CtCls, 67-2 USTC ¶ 9685, 181 CtCls 331.

[42] *Jackson Investment Co. v. Commr.*, 41 TC 675, Dec. 26,664 (1964), rev'd on other grounds, CA-9, 65-2 USTC ¶ 9451, 346 F2d 187; *Julian E. Jacobs v. Commr.*, 33 TCM 848, Dec. 32,702(M), TC Memo. 1974-196.

[43] *Id.*

[44] Is a partnership agreement amendment on this point effective which is entered into after the death of a withdrawing partner? There is little guidance on this issue. However, Code Sec. 761(c) does provide that the partnership agreement includes any amendments adopted on or before the filing date of the partnership tax return.

[45] Code Sec. 761(c).

goodwill payments to a withdrawing partner should be effective as long as the amendment is entered into on or before the earlier of the due date (without extensions) of the partnership tax return for the year in which the partner withdraws for purposes of local law or in which the partner receives the first potential Code Sec. 736(b) payment.[46] If, for example, a partner withdraws from a calendar year partnership (or receives the first Code Sec. 736(b) payment) in Year 1, an amendment providing for goodwill payments must be entered into no later than April 15, Year 2, in order to be effective.[47]

Certainly the original partnership agreement as amended will qualify as the agreement which must specify for a payment for goodwill. It has also been held that a collateral agreement between the withdrawing partner and the remaining partner specifying a payment for goodwill is effective to qualify the payment as a Code Sec. 736(a) payment.[48] For purposes of Subchapter K of the Internal Revenue Code, the term "partnership agreement" includes modifications to the agreement "which are agreed to by all of the partners, or which are adopted in such other manner as may be provided by the partnership agreement."[49] However, in view of the controversy as to what is considered as part of the partnership amendment for Code Sec. 736 purposes, any collateral agreement between the partners regarding goodwill payments to a withdrawing partner should be signed by all partners or otherwise comply strictly with the terms of the partnership agreement relating to amendments, even if the collateral agreement does not strictly constitute an amendment to the partnership agreement for state law purposes.

The regulations indicate that a modification to the partnership agreement may be written or oral.[50] Therefore, if applicable law allows for oral modifications to a written agreement, if the partnership agreement is itself oral, or if the partnership agreement provides for oral modifications, an oral agreement providing for goodwill payments should be respected.

If a partnership has a tax basis in capitalized goodwill (*e.g.*, because of a business purchased by the partnership or a prior basis adjustment pursuant to Code Sec. 743(b)) payments to the extent of such basis are Code Sec. 736(b) payments, regardless of the language in the partnership agreement.[51]

Goodwill payments treated as Code Sec. 736(b) payments will be treated under the normal partnership distribution rules. The partnership is not entitled to a deduction for any Code Sec. 736(b) payment made to a withdrawing partner. Such a distribution will trigger an adjustment to the

---

[46] It is unclear whether an amendment to the agreement in a year subsequent to the retirement year is effective.

[47] Code Sec. 6072.

[48] *Jackson Investment Company v. Commr.*, CA-9, 65-2 USTC ¶ 9451, 346 F2d 187, rev'g, 41 TC 675, Dec. 26,664 (1964).

[49] Code Sec. 761(c).

[50] Reg. § 1.761-1(c).

[51] Reg. § 1.736-1(b)(3).

partnership's basis in goodwill under Code Sec. 734(b) only if there is a Code Sec. 754 election in effect. In the absence of an election under Code Sec. 754 by the partnership, a Code Sec. 736(b) payment to a withdrawing partner has no tax effect on the remaining partners if the partnership does not have substantially appreciated inventory. However, if a Code Sec. 754 election applies to the Code Sec. 736(b) payment and gain is recognized by the withdrawing partner, the partnership is entitled to increase the basis of its remaining property to the extent of the withdrawing partner's gain.[52]

.05 *Payments for Property Other Than Unrealized Receivables and Goodwill—Code Sec. 736(b)*

Payments for a partner's share of partnership property other than unrealized receivables and goodwill are always classified by Code Sec. 736 as distributions. As a rule, if cash distributions are made to a partner for an interest in partnership property, the partner is normally allowed to recover his or her basis in the partnership free of tax, and any payments over such basis result in capital gain.[53] There are exceptions to this general rule. One exception applies when a partnership has substantially appreciated inventory or items of recapture (*e.g.*, depreciation recapture); in such cases, the retiring or deceased partner will be required to recognize ordinary income from the constructive sale of his or her interest in such substantially appreciated inventory or recapture items.[54] Under these circumstances the continuing partnership will receive a fair market value basis for the departing partner's share of these assets. A second exception involves an election that is available to apportion payments made over several years between the recovery of partnership interest basis and gain recognition.[55] A partner is allowed a capital loss if the partner's basis in the partnership interest is not recovered by such payments.[56]

The partnership is not entitled to a deduction for any Code Sec. 736(b) payment made to a withdrawing partner. In the absence of an election under Code Sec. 754 by the partnership, a Code Sec. 736(b) payment to a withdrawing partner has no tax effect on the remaining partners if the partnership does not have substantially appreciated inventory or assets subject to recapture. However, if the partnership has a Code Sec. 754 election in effect and gain is recognized by the withdrawing partner, the partnership is entitled to increase the basis of its remaining property to the extent of the withdrawing partner's gain.[57]

Property distributions are governed by the normal rules applicable to liquidating property distributions. The partnership can be adversely affected by Code Sec. 736(b) liquidation payments if a retiring partner originally acquired the partnership interest by purchase or inheritance and

[52] Code Sec. 734(b).

[53] The provisions of Code Sec. 751(b) will apply if a portion of the cash distribution is payment for the retiring partner's share of the partnership's substantially appreciated inventory.

[54] Reg. § 1.736-1(b)(6); Code Sec. 751(b).

[55] Reg. § 1.736-1(b)(6).

[56] *Id.*

[57] Code Sec. 734(b).

a Code Sec. 754 election was not made in connection with the original acquisition of such interest. If a Code Sec. 754 election is made in connection with Code Sec. 736(b) liquidating property distributions, the partnership could be required to reduce the basis of its assets pursuant to Code Sec. 734(b)(2) to the extent the retiring partner takes a stepped-up basis in distributed property.

.06 Allocating the Payment Among Code Sec. 736 Categories

Typically, liquidating distributions include payments for all three categories of property (unrealized receivables, goodwill, and other property). If there is one lump-sum payment, it is allocated to the different categories of payments based upon their relative values.

While the IRS should ordinarily respect the partners' determination of the value of the withdrawing partner's share of partnership property because of the competing interests of the withdrawing partner and the continuing partners, it will not necessarily respect the valuation in every case. Generally, the valuation the partners place upon a partner's interest in partnership property in an arm's-length agreement will be regarded as correct.[58] If the partners are not dealing at arm's length (for example, if the withdrawing partner and the continuing partners are members of the same family), the IRS may question the value of the withdrawing partner's interest in partnership property agreed to by the parties. If the partners do not attempt to value the withdrawing partner's interest in the partnership property, however, the courts may do so.[59] It is therefore advisable to agree to a value and to formalize the agreement in a written document.

A partner increases his or her basis in the partnership interest by increases in his or her share of partnership indebtedness [60] and is required to decrease his or her basis to the extent that the partner's share of partnership indebtedness is reduced.[61] The valuation of a partner's interest in partnership property should be on a gross, rather than a net, basis (*i.e.*, total value without reduction for liabilities), because the reduction in the partner's share of liabilities will itself be treated as part of the liquidating payment(s) received by the partner.

.07 Accounting for a Series of Payments

When there is an installment liquidation, the partner treats part of each payment as a distributive share of partnership income, and/or a guaranteed payment (depending upon whether the amount was fixed or

[58] Reg. § 1.736-1(b)(1).

[59] The Tax Court valued a withdrawing partner's interest in partnership property where the partners failed to allocate liquidation payments between Code Sec. 736(a) and (b) payments in *A.O. Champlin v. Commr.*, 36 TCM 802, Dec. 34,476(M), TC Memo. 1977-196. The determination by the court was based on a "careful examination of the record and all the factors affecting the negotiations between the parties." See also *Est. of T.P. Quirk v. Commr.*, 55 TCM 1188, Dec. 44,870(M), TC Memo. 1988-286, aff'd, CA-6, 91-1 USTC ¶ 50,148, 928 F2d 751. Value and character of retiring partner's interest determined even though such issues were the subject of litigation in state court; values on partnership's financial statements adopted because taxpayer failed to produce contrary evidence.

[60] Code Sec. 752(a).

[61] Code Sec. 752(b).

contingent),[62] and any remainder as a liquidating distribution.[63] The retiring partner and the partnership may agree upon an allocation of each payment between Code Sec. 736(a) and Code Sec. 736(b) amounts.[64] Lacking such an agreement, the ordering depends upon whether the amount of the total payments is fixed or contingent upon future partnership income. If the amount is contingent, the payments treated as distributions are accounted for first.[65] The remainder of the fixed payments are accounted for as a share of partnership income. If the amount is fixed, the portion of each payment treated as a distribution is the amount that the total of the Code Sec. 736(b) payments bears to the total of all payments. The remainder of each payment is treated as a Code Sec. 707(c) guaranteed payment.[66] If the withdrawing partner receives less than the amount the parties had agreed would be the fixed amount to be paid as a Code Sec. 736(b) payment in any year, the deficit amount is carried over to the next year and added to the fixed amounts paid in the succeeding year in determining the Code Sec. 736(b) amount in the later year.[67]

If a withdrawing partner receives both fixed and contingent payments over time in liquidation of his or her interest in the partnership and the fixed amounts to be received over the entire payout period (whether or not supplemented by any additional amounts) equal or exceed the value of the withdrawing partner's interest in partnership properties, a proportionate share of each fixed payment is considered to be a Code Sec. 736(b) amount in the manner described above. The balance of each fixed payment and the entire amount of each contingent payment will constitute Code Sec. 736(a) amounts.[68] If the total amount of the fixed payments a withdrawing partner is to receive over the payout period is less than the value of the partner's interest in partnership property, the entire amount of each fixed payment is considered to be a Code Sec. 736(b) amount. In addition, each contingent payment is considered to be a Code Sec. 736(b) amount until the full amount of fixed payments to be received plus the contingent amounts allocated to Code Sec. 736(b) equal the value of the withdrawing partner's interest in partnership property.[69]

When a withdrawing partner receives a series of Code Sec. 736(b) cash distributions in the absence of a contrary election, he or she recognizes gain or loss and reports it in accordance with a cash basis, cost recovery method of accounting.[70] The partner recovers his or her entire basis in his or her partnership interest before recognizing any gain, and a loss is not recognized until the final Code Sec. 736(b) distribution is made to the withdrawing partner.[71] As an alternative, the regulations allow a withdrawing partner to elect to include the total gain or loss to be recognized ratably

[62] Code Sec. 736(a).
[63] Code Sec. 736(b).
[64] Reg. § 1.736-1(b)(5)(iii).
[65] Reg. § 1.736-1(b)(5)(ii).
[66] Reg. § 1.736-1(b)(5)(i).
[67] *Id.*
[68] *Id.*
[69] *Id.*
[70] Reg. §§ 1.736-1(b)(6), 1.731-1(a)(1) and (2).
[71] Reg. § 1.731-1(a)(2).

over all Code Sec. 736(b) distributions if the total amount of Code Sec. 736(b) distributions to be received is fixed.[72]

A withdrawing partner who elects to apportion the gain or loss attributable to Code Sec. 736(b) must attach a statement to his or her tax return for the first taxable year he or she receives a Code Sec. 736(b) distribution, indicating his or her election and showing the computation of the gain or loss included in or deducted from gross income.[73]

Example 19-1. *A* is a general partner in the equal ABCDE Partnership. He is retiring on June 15, Year 1. In liquidation of his interest he is to receive $4,000 per year for the next eight years. The partnership agreement does not provide for a payment to a retiring partner for goodwill. The partnership does not have a Code Sec. 754 election in effect and uses the cash method of accounting. *A*'s basis for his interest is $9,400.[74]

ABCDE Balance Sheet 6/15/Year 1

Assets	*Tax Basis*	*FMV*
Cash	$17,000	$17,000
Accounts Receivable	0	80,000
Building (No Recapture)	16,000	25,000
Land	14,000	24,000
Goodwill	0	55,000
	$47,000	*$201,000*
Liabilities and Capital		
Mortgage (Recourse)	$41,000	$41,000
Capital—*A*	1,200	32,000
Capital—Other Partners	4,800	128,000
Total Liabilities and Capital	*$47,000*	*$201,000*

The total payments to be received by *A* must be increased by the deemed payment for liability relief. Thus, in determining the consequences under Code Sec. 736, *A* is treated as liquidating his partnership interest for a total of $40,200 ($32,000 cash payments over eight years, plus $8,200 debt relief). The debt relief occurs at the time of *A*'s withdrawal from the partnership. Thus, his Year 1 payments total $12,200 ($4,000 cash payment, plus $8,200 debt relief). Each subsequent year's payment will be $4,000.

Of the total payments to be received, $13,200 will be treated as Code Sec. 736(b) payments (*A*'s 20% share of the value of the cash, building and land). The remainder will be governed by Code Sec. 736(a). Thus, $4,006 of the first year's total payments will be classified under 736(b) (13,200/40,200 × 12,200), and $8,194 under Code Sec. 736(a) (27,000/40,200 × 12,200). Of the $4,000 payment received in

[72] Reg. § 1.736-1(b)(6).
[73] *Id.*
[74] $1,200 tax basis capital account plus *A*'s $8,200 debt share.

each subsequent year, $1,313 will be classified as a Code Sec. 736(b) payment and $2,687 as a Code Sec. 736(a) payment.

Assume that in Years 3, 4, and 5 the partnership is unable to make the agreed upon $4,000 payments, but it catches up with additional payments of $4,000 in Years 6, 7, and 8. Classification of the payments received by *A* would be as follows:[75]

Year	*Code Sec. 736(b)*	*Code Sec. 736(a)*	*Total*
1	$4,006	$8,194	$12,200
2	1,313	2,687	4,000
3	0	0	0
4	0	0	0
5	0	0	0
6	5,252	2,748	8,000
7	1,313	6,687	8,000
8	1,313	6,687	8,000
	*$13,200**	*$27,000**	*$40,200*

* Note: slight difference due to rounding.

A's Code Sec. 736(b) payments are first recovery of his $9,400 basis in his partnership interest. Starting in Year 6, *A* will recognize capital gain. With the sixth payment he will have recovered his $9,400 basis and have received $1,171 in excess of that basis. During Years 7 and 8, *A* will have $1,313 capital gain each year.

Had *A* been a partner in a partnership in which capital was a material income-producing factor, all retirement payments would have been treated as Code Sec. 736(b) payments for partnership property (which would include the unrealized receivables and goodwill). To the extent the payments are deemed to be for unrealized receivables, *A* would recognize ordinary income under the Code Sec. 751(b) hot asset rules. To the extent the Code Sec. 754 election results in an increase in the partnership's goodwill, an amortizable asset would be created.

Because *A* continues to be treated as a partner until his liquidation payments cease, he will continue to receive Schedules K-1 through Year 8. For each year, the Code Sec. 736(b) payment should be shown on A's Schedule K-1 as a cash distribution in the capital account reconciliation. The Code Sec. 736(a) payments should be treated as guaranteed payments—*i.e.*, deducted on Form 1065, U.S. Partnership Return of Income, Page 1, line 10, and reported as income on box 4 of A's Schedule K-1.

Example 19-2. *A* is a general partner in the equal ABCDE Partnership. He is retiring on June 15, Year 1. In liquidation of his interest he is to receive 20% of the partnership's net income per year for the next eight years. The partnership agreement does not provide for a payment to a retiring partner for goodwill. The partnership does

[75] Reg. § 1.736-1(b)(5)(i).

not have a Code Sec. 754 election in effect and uses the cash method of accounting. *A*'s basis for his interest is $9,400.[76]

ABCDE Balance Sheet 6/15/Year 1

Assets	Tax Basis	FMV
Cash	$17,000	$17,000
Accounts Receivable	0	80,000
Building (No Recapture)	16,000	25,000
Land	14,000	24,000
Goodwill	0	55,000
	$47,000	$201,000
Liabilities and Capital		
Mortgage (Recourse)	$41,000	$41,000
Capital—*A*	1,200	32,000
Capital—Other Partners	4,800	128,000
Total Liabilities and Capital	$47,000	$201,000

As before, $13,200 of *A*'s retirement payments will be classified as Code Sec. 736(b) payments. *A* must treat all of the payments as Code Sec. 736(b) payments until he has received $13,200. Assuming partnership net income of $20,000 per year, *A* accounts for the payments as follows:

Year	Code Sec. 736(b)	Code Sec. 736(a)	Total
1	$12,200	$ 0	$12,200
2	1,000	3,000	4,000
3	0	4,000	4,000
4	0	4,000	4,000
5	0	4,000	4,000
6	0	4,000	4,000
7	0	4,000	4,000
8	0	4,000	4,000
	$13,200	$27,000	$40,200

.08 Allocating Property Distributions Between Code Sec. 736(a) Payments and Code Sec. 736(b) Payments

There is no guidance in the Internal Revenue Code or the Treasury regulations on how to account for distributions that are all or partly property. The method of allocation between Code Sec. 736(a) and (b) payments (*e.g.*, pro rata, property distribution first treated as Code Sec. 736(b) distributions, etc.) is important because treating a distribution of appreciated property as a Code Sec. 736(a) payment will seemingly require the partnership to recognize the appreciation as gain. Arguably, the partners can, and should, allocate each distribution, whether in cash or property, between Code Sec. 736(a) and Code Sec. 736(b).[77]

[76] $1,200 tax basis capital account plus *A*'s $8,200 debt share.

[77] Reg. § 1.736-1(b)(5)(iii).

Since Code Sec. 736 applies to "payments," the implication of the provision as well as the implication of the regulations [78] is that Code Sec. 736 applies to cash payments. It is not clear whether Code Sec. 736 also applies to a partnership distribution of property, however. While Code Sec. 736 uses the term "payment," the provision is not specifically limited to a distribution of cash. Neither the legislative history of Code Sec. 736 nor the regulations provides any guidance as to whether Code Sec. 736 applies to in-kind distributions. On the other hand, the Code Sec. 736 regulations as originally proposed specifically provided that Code Sec. 736 applied only to cash payments and not to property distributions.[79] While there is no explanation set forth in the Treasury Decision that adopted the final regulations [80] for the deletion of the language in the proposed regulations limiting the application of Code Sec. 736 to cash payments, the deletion provides at least an inference that Code Sec. 736 applies to both property and cash distributions.[81]

.09 *Passive Gain or Loss*

The portion of the Code Sec. 736(a) payments that are allocable to unrealized receivables (as defined in Code Sec. 751(c)) and goodwill that is treated as passive activity gross income may not exceed the percentage of the passive activity gross income that would be included in the gross income that the retiring partner or deceased partner would have recognized if the unrealized receivables and goodwill had been sold when the liquidation of the interest commenced.[82] Gain or loss because of a Code Sec. 736(b) payment is treated as passive activity gross income or a passive activity deduction to the extent that the gain or loss would have been passive activity gross income or a passive activity deduction of the retiring or deceased partner if it had been recognized when the liquidation of the interest commenced.[83]

.10 *Effect of Code Sec. 754 Election*

A Code Sec. 754 election generally has no effect when the partnership itself is liquidating.[84] But when partnership operations continue and a particular partner's interest is liquidated, there is often an effect. The portion of the payments to the retiring partner treated as distributions

---

[78] Only cash payments are used as examples in the Code Sec. 736 regulations, which arguably could be read to mean that Code Sec. 736 applies only to cash payments and not to distributions of other property.

[79] Prop. Reg. § 1.736-1(a)(2), NPRM (1954), 20 FR 5854 (August 12, 1955).

[80] T.D. 6175, 1956-1 CB 211.

[81] An additional indication that the IRS believes that Code Sec. 736 applies to property distributions is provided by IRS Letter Ruling 8538094 (6-27-85), which discusses the tax consequences of the incorporation of a general partnership. Some of the partners withdrew from the partnership as part of the same transaction which culminated in incorporation. Property was distributed to the withdrawing partner in kind. The ruling recognizes that Code Sec. 736 may apply to the property distributions but sidesteps the issue by excepting from the ruling the tax consequences to the extent that the property distributions to the withdrawing partners constituted payments under Code Sec. 736.

[82] Reg. § 1.469-2(e)(2)(iii)(B).

[83] Reg. § 1.469-2(e)(2)(iii)(A).

[84] In the case of a technical termination under Code Sec. 708 caused by a sale of 50% or more of the partnership interests in a 12-month time period, the adjustments under Code Sec. 743(b) may affect the way basis is allocated to the distributed property in the deemed liquidating distribution.

under Code Sec. 736(b) can be the source of a Code Sec. 734(b) adjustment to remaining partnership property.

1. The retired partner's gain from a cash distribution in excess of his or her basis in the partnership interest generates an increase in the partnership's basis for its capital and Code Sec. 1231 assets in a like amount.[85]

2. Any loss recognized by the retiring partner causes the partnership to reduce its basis in its remaining capital and Code Sec. 1231 assets.[86]

3. If a retired partner's basis in distributed property after the distribution exceeds the partnership's former basis, the partnership decreases its basis in remaining similar property by the same amount.[87]

4. If a retired partner's basis in distributed property after the distribution is less than the partnership's former basis, the partnership increases its basis in remaining similar property by the same amount.[88]

When a partner receives a liquidating cash distribution resulting in a gain, the gain (the excess of the cash distributed over the partner's outside basis) represents the distributee partner's share of the appreciation in value of the assets that the partnership retains. However, if the partnership's adjusted basis in the assets remains the same, (*i.e.*, there is no Code Sec. 754 election in effect), at the time the partnership sells them, the gain will be taxed again when the property is sold. This double reporting of gain will be rectified later by the increase in the adjusted bases of the partners in their partnership interests. That increase will cause a reduction in the gain on the ultimate sale of their partnership interests. However, a timing difference will exist without a Code Sec. 734(b) adjustment. Thus, although the total taxable income will ultimately be the same, tax may be paid considerably sooner should the partnership sell the appreciated assets a long time before the partners sell their partnership interests. The Code Sec. 734(b) adjustment in effect gives the partnership a cost basis in the share of partnership assets that have essentially been purchased from the distributee.

Conversely, when a partnership makes a liquidating cash distribution under circumstances resulting in recognition of loss by the distributee, that loss represents a decrease in the distributee's share of the fair market value of the partnership property below his or her share of its basis, which in turn is equal to his or her partnership interest adjusted basis. If the distributee partner can deduct the loss, and if the partnership is also able to recognize

[85] Code Sec. 734(b)(1)(A).
[86] Code Sec. 734(b)(2)(A).
[87] Code Sec. 734(b)(2)(B).
[88] Code Sec. 734(b)(2)(A).

a loss on the sale of the partnership assets (since the fair market value of the assets will have depreciated below the partnership's adjusted basis in the assets), a temporary double reporting of the loss will occur. This is later rectified through adjustments to the partners' outside bases, but it may cause a significant timing difference without a Code Sec. 734(b) adjustment.

Usually, a partner who receives a liquidating property distribution takes a basis in that property either above or below that of the partnership since Code Sec. 732(b) provides that the partner's basis in the distributed property is determined by reference to the adjusted basis of the partner's interest in the partnership reduced by any money distributed in the same transaction. Even where the partner's outside basis is equal to his or her pro rata share of the partnership's basis for its assets, it is unlikely he or she will receive a distribution of a pro rata cross section of the assets. The partnership will merely choose assets that have a value equal to his or her partnership interest. This step-up or step-down in basis represents unrealized appreciation or depreciation that may never be recognized if a Code Sec. 754 election is not in effect, since the gain or loss inherent in the distributed property escapes taxation, owing to the tax-free step-up or step-down basis. Also, note that, without this adjustment, inside and outside bases will be out of alignment.

Similar to the provisions of Code Sec. 743(a), Code Sec. 734(a) provides the general rule that the basis of retained partnership property will not be adjusted following the distribution of property to a partner unless a Code Sec. 754 election is made by the partnership; in that event, a Code Sec. 734(b) basis adjustment will be made to the retained partnership property.

The amount of the required Code Sec. 734(b) basis adjustment to partnership property where a Code Sec. 754 election is in effect is as follows:[89]

1. In the case of a distribution of money to a partner that is greater than the adjusted basis the partner has in his or her partnership interest, the partnership will increase the adjusted basis of its assets ("partnership property") by the amount of gain recognized to the distributee partner under Code Sec. 731(a).[90]

2. In the case of a distribution to a partner consisting solely of money, unrealized receivables, and/or inventory in complete liquidation of his or her partnership interest when the distributee partner recognizes a loss under Code Sec. 731(a)(2), then the partnership will reduce the adjusted basis of its undistributed assets by the amount of the loss.[91]

[89] A complete discussion of these rules is contained in Chapter 16.

[90] Code Sec. 734(b)(1)(A).

[91] Code Sec. 734(b)(2)(A).

3. Code Sec. 732(b) provides that the adjusted basis of property distributed in complete liquidation of the partnership's interest equals the partner's outside basis reduced by any money distributed in the same transaction. Code Sec. 734(b)(1)(B) provides that if the adjusted basis of the distributed assets was greater in the hands of the partnership than in the hands of the distributee partner, owing to the application of these sections, the partnership will increase the basis of the retained assets ("partnership property") by the amount of this excess.

4. The converse situation to that outlined in (3) above occurs when, upon the complete liquidation of a partner's interest, the adjusted basis of the assets in the distributee partner's hands is greater than it was in the hands of the partnership immediately before the distribution owing to the distributee partner's receiving a total basis in the distributed assets equal to his or her basis in his or her partnership interest. The partnership will accordingly decrease the adjusted basis of its retained partnership property by the amount of this difference.[92]

The Code Sec. 734(b) adjustments are not made with respect to any particular partner or partners but apply to the common basis of partnership assets. The total Code Sec. 734(b) adjustment must be allocated among the undistributed partnership assets according to the rules of Code Sec. 755. Although Code Sec. 755 provides rules for allocating Code Sec. 743(b) adjustments which arise on the purchase of a partnership interest or a transfer at death, it also contains different rules for Code Sec. 734(b) adjustments.[93] But the underlying rationale of both sets of rules is that the total basis adjustments are allocated among the assets in a way that eliminates or reduces the difference between the fair market value and the adjusted basis of partnership properties.

The allocations are made according to the following rules in Reg. § 1.755-1(b)(1):[94]

1. If the Code Sec. 734(b) adjustment is triggered by the distributee partner recognizing gain under Code Sec. 731(a)(1), then the upward or downward adjustment is to be allocated *only* to "capital gains assets."[95] The adjustment is allocated in order to reduce the difference between the fair market values and the adjusted bases of the assets of that class that have appreciated in value (or have depreciated in value, for a downward basis adjustment).[96]

---

[92] Code Sec. 734(b)(2)(B).

[93] Reg. § 1.755-1(b)(1).

[94] A complete discussion of these rules is contained in Chapter 16.

[95] Reg. § 1.755-1(b)(1)(ii).

[96] Code Sec. 755(a).

Reg. § 1.755-1(b)(3) provides that in applying these rules, the basis of an asset may not be reduced below zero and, if an adjustment is allocated to a class in which the partnership either has no retained property, or has insufficient basis in the property in the class to fully absorb a negative adjustment allocated to that class, the balance of the adjustment is to be applied to subsequently acquired property of that class.

2. If the Code Sec. 734(b) adjustment is caused by the distributee partner's adjusted basis in the distributed property being less than or greater than the partnership's adjusted basis in that property immediately before the distribution, then the increase or decrease in question is to be allocated to the remaining partnership assets that are of a character similar to that of the distributed property.

For example, when the partnership's adjusted basis in distributed "capital assets" immediately before the distribution exceeds that of the distributee partner after the distribution, the upward adjustment in undistributed partnership assets will be allocated to the undistributed "capital assets" of the partnership to the extent of the difference. If the distributed assets that produced the upward Code Sec. 734(b) adjustment were "inventory," the adjustment would be allocated to the partnership's remaining inventory.[97]

The adjustment to the basis of the partnership property allowed under Code Sec. 734(b) should correspond in both timing and amount with the recognition of gain or loss by a retiring partner with respect to payments that are treated as a distribution under Code Sec. 731 by Code Sec. 736(b).[98]

.11 *Classification of Retirement Payments as Self-Employment Income*

Code Sec. 1402(a), which defines net earnings from self-employment, specifically excludes retirement payments to a partner if the following requirements are satisfied:

1. The payments must be made on a periodic basis by the partnership pursuant to a written plan that provides for payments on account of retirement to partners generally or to a class or classes of partners to continue at least until the partner's death;[99]

2. The retired partner to whom the payments are made must not render services with respect to any trade or business carried on

[97] Reg. § 1.755-1(b)(1)(i).
[98] Rev. Rul. 93-13, 1993-1 CB 126.
[99] Code Sec. 1402(a)(10) and Reg. § 1.1402(a)-17.

by the partnership (or its successors) during the taxable year of the partnership (or its successors), which ends within or with the taxable year of the partner and in which the payment was received;

3. No obligation exists (as of the close of the partnership year referred to in item 2 above) from the other partners to the retired partner except with respect to retirement payments under the plan or rights such as benefits payable on account of sickness, accident, hospitalization, medical expenses, or death; and

4. The retired partner's share of the capital of the partnership has been paid to him in full before the close of the partnership's taxable year referred to in item 2 above.

Under the regulations, if the above requirements are satisfied, all payments received by the partner on account of retirement are excluded from the partner's self-employment income. If any of the above requirements are not satisfied, none of the payments will be excluded. The regulations further provide that the effect of the conditions set forth in items 3 and 4 above is that the exclusion may apply with respect to such payments received by the retired partner during the taxable year only if at the close of the partnership taxable year the retired partner has no financial interest in the partnership except for the right to retirement payments.

¶ 1903 Payment for Retiring Partner's Interest When Capital Is a Material Income-Producing Factor or Partner Is a Limited Partner

Code Sec. 736(a) is inapplicable for post-1992 liquidating payments made to limited partners and general partners of partnerships having capital as a material income-producing factor.[100] All payments are governed by the distribution rules described immediately above in connection with Code Sec. 736(b) payments for other than unrealized receivables and goodwill.

The Revenue Reconciliation Act of 1993 amendments to Code Sec. 736 generally apply to partners retiring or dying on or after January 5, 1993.[101] However, if a written contract to purchase a partner's interest was binding on January 4, 1993, and at all times after that, the 1993 Act amendments are not applicable.[102] The legislative history adds that a written contract is to be considered binding only if the contract specifies the amount to be paid for the partnership interest and the timing of any such payments.[103] Many partnership agreements provide for the partnership to purchase a deceased

[100] Specifically, Code Sec. 736(a) is inapplicable to payments made to these types of partners retiring after January 15, 1993, the effective date of the Revenue Reconciliation Act of 1993, P.L. 103-66, Act § 13262(b).

[101] P.L. 103-66, Act § 13262(b).

[102] The Revenue Reconciliation Act of 1993, P.L. 103-66, Act § 13262(c)(2).

[103] H.R. Rep. N. 102-11, 103rd Cong., 1st Sess. (1993).

partner's interest based on a formula price. It is unclear if a formula price will be deemed to represent a "specified amount." It seems that such a formula price buy-out should qualify the parties to use Code Sec. 736 as it existed before the 1993 Act. This is because informed partnerships have based their formulas, in part, upon the tax laws in existence when the agreement was reached. A change in the tax laws doesn't automatically grant any partner a right to change the agreement.

The House Committee Report to the Revenue Reconciliation Act of 1993 states that the changes to Code Sec. 736 are not intended to affect the deductibility of compensation to a retiring partner for past services. Therefore, legitimate and reasonable compensation for past services paid to a retiring partner whose interest is being liquidated in a partnership in which capital is a material income-producing factor will be governed by the principles of Code Sec. 707 (*e.g.*, as a deductible guaranteed payment under Code Sec. 707(c) or (a)). Therefore, though Code Sec. 736 will no longer permit capital-intensive partnerships the right to classify retirement payments as deductible guaranteed payments; the partnership may still obtain a deduction for payments to the extent they represent reasonable compensation for past services.

¶ 1904 Partnership Interest Sale Compared to Liquidation

	Liquidation Approach	*Sale Approach*
Depreciation recapture		
All partners	736(b), 751(b)	751(a)
Unrealized receivables (other than depreciation recapture)		
Service partner	736(a)	751(a)
Other partner	736(b), 751(b)	751(a)
Substantially appreciated inventory (other than unrealized receivables)		
All partners	736(b), 751(b)	751(a)

Appendix

Caution: Before using any of these appendices, consult the laws in the jurisdiction where the material will be used.

¶ 2501 Form 1065, U.S. Partnership Return of Income

Form **1065** Department of the Treasury Internal Revenue Service

U.S. Return of Partnership Income

For calendar year 2004, or tax year beginning ...., 2004, and ending ...., 20....

▶ See separate instructions.

OMB No. 1545-0099

2004

A Principal business activity	Use the IRS label. Otherwise, print or type.	Name of partnership	D Employer identification number
B Principal product or service		Number, street, and room or suite no. If a P.O. box, see page 14 of the instructions.	E Date business started
C Business code number		City or town, state, and ZIP code	F Total assets (see page 14 of the instructions) $

G Check applicable boxes: (1) ☐ Initial return (2) ☐ Final return (3) ☐ Name change (4) ☐ Address change (5) ☐ Amended return

H Check accounting method: (1) ☐ Cash (2) ☐ Accrual (3) ☐ Other (specify) ▶

I Number of Schedules K-1. Attach one for each person who was a partner at any time during the tax year ▶

Caution: *Include **only** trade or business income and expenses on lines 1a through 22 below. See the instructions for more information.*

Income	1a Gross receipts or sales	1a		
	b Less returns and allowances	1b		1c
	2 Cost of goods sold (Schedule A, line 8)			2
	3 Gross profit. Subtract line 2 from line 1c			3
	4 Ordinary income (loss) from other partnerships, estates, and trusts *(attach schedule)*			4
	5 Net farm profit (loss) *(attach Schedule F (Form 1040))*			5
	6 Net gain (loss) from Form 4797, Part II, line 17			6
	7 Other income (loss) *(attach statement)*			7
	8 **Total income (loss).** Combine lines 3 through 7			8
Deductions (see page 16 of the instructions for limitations)	9 Salaries and wages (other than to partners) (less employment credits)			9
	10 Guaranteed payments to partners			10
	11 Repairs and maintenance			11
	12 Bad debts			12
	13 Rent			13
	14 Taxes and licenses			14
	15 Interest			15
	16a Depreciation *(if required, attach Form 4562)*	16a		
	b Less depreciation reported on Schedule A and elsewhere on return	16b		16c
	17 Depletion **(Do not deduct oil and gas depletion.)**			17
	18 Retirement plans, etc.			18
	19 Employee benefit programs			19
	20 Other deductions *(attach statement)*			20
	21 **Total deductions.** Add the amounts shown in the far right column for lines 9 through 20			21
	22 **Ordinary business income (loss).** Subtract line 21 from line 8			22

Sign Here

Under penalties of perjury, I declare that I have examined this return, including accompanying schedules and statements, and to the best of my knowledge and belief, it is true, correct, and complete. Declaration of preparer (other than general partner or limited liability company member) is based on all information of which preparer has any knowledge.

▶ Signature of general partner or limited liability company member manager ▶ Date

May the IRS discuss this return with the preparer shown below (see instructions)? ☐ Yes ☐ No

Paid Preparer's Use Only

Preparer's signature	Date	Check if self-employed ▶ ☐	Preparer's SSN or PTIN
Firm's name (or yours if self-employed), address, and ZIP code ▶		EIN ▶	
		Phone no. ( )	

For Privacy Act and Paperwork Reduction Act Notice, see separate instructions. Cat. No. 11390Z Form **1065** (2004)

Form 1065 (2004) Page **2**

Schedule A **Cost of Goods Sold** (see page 19 of the instructions)

1	Inventory at beginning of year	1	
2	Purchases less cost of items withdrawn for personal use	2	
3	Cost of labor	3	
4	Additional section 263A costs *(attach statement)*	4	
5	Other costs *(attach statement)*	5	
6	**Total.** Add lines 1 through 5	6	
7	Inventory at end of year	7	
8	**Cost of goods sold.** Subtract line 7 from line 6. Enter here and on page 1, line 2	8	

9a Check all methods used for valuing closing inventory:
- **(i)** ☐ Cost as described in Regulations section 1.471-3
- **(ii)** ☐ Lower of cost or market as described in Regulations section 1.471-4
- **(iii)** ☐ Other (specify method used and attach explanation) ▶

b Check this box if there was a writedown of "subnormal" goods as described in Regulations section 1.471-2(c) ▶ ☐

c Check this box if the LIFO inventory method was adopted this tax year for any goods *(if checked, attach Form 970)*. ▶ ☐

d Do the rules of section 263A (for property produced or acquired for resale) apply to the partnership? ☐ **Yes** ☐ **No**

e Was there any change in determining quantities, cost, or valuations between opening and closing inventory? ☐ **Yes** ☐ **No** If "Yes," attach explanation.

Schedule B **Other Information**

		Yes	No
1	What type of entity is filing this return? Check the applicable box: **a** ☐ Domestic general partnership **b** ☐ Domestic limited partnership **c** ☐ Domestic limited liability company **d** ☐ Domestic limited liability partnership **e** ☐ Foreign partnership **f** ☐ Other ▶		
2	Are any partners in this partnership also partnerships?		
3	During the partnership's tax year, did the partnership own any interest in another partnership or in any foreign entity that was disregarded as an entity separate from its owner under Regulations sections 301.7701-2 and 301.7701-3? If yes, see instructions for required attachment		
4	Did the partnership file Form 8893, Election of Partnership Level Tax Treatment, or an election statement under section 6231(a)(1)(B)(ii) for partnership-level tax treatment, that is in effect for this tax year? See Form 8893 for more details		
5	Does this partnership meet all three of the following requirements? **a** The partnership's total receipts for the tax year were less than $250,000; **b** The partnership's total assets at the end of the tax year were less than $600,000; and **c** Schedules K-1 are filed with the return and furnished to the partners on or before the due date (including extensions) for the partnership return. If "Yes," the partnership is not required to complete Schedules L, M-1, and M-2; Item F on page 1 of Form 1065; or Item N on Schedule K-1		
6	Does this partnership have any foreign partners? If "Yes," the partnership may have to file Forms 8804, 8805 and 8813. See page 20 of the instructions		
7	Is this partnership a publicly traded partnership as defined in section 469(k)(2)?		
8	Has this partnership filed, or is it required to file, Form 8264, Application for Registration of a Tax Shelter?		
9	At any time during calendar year 2004, did the partnership have an interest in or a signature or other authority over a financial account in a foreign country (such as a bank account, securities account, or other financial account)? See page 20 of the instructions for exceptions and filing requirements for Form TD F 90-22.1. If "Yes," enter the name of the foreign country. ▶		
10	During the tax year, did the partnership receive a distribution from, or was it the grantor of, or transferor to, a foreign trust? If "Yes," the partnership may have to file Form 3520. See page 21 of the instructions		
11	Was there a distribution of property or a transfer (e.g., by sale or death) of a partnership interest during the tax year? If "Yes," you may elect to adjust the basis of the partnership's assets under section 754 by attaching the statement described under *Elections Made By the Partnership* on page 9 of the instructions		
12	Enter the number of Forms 8865, Return of U.S. Persons With Respect to Certain Foreign Partnerships, attached to this return ▶		

Designation of Tax Matters Partner (see page 21 of the instructions)

Enter below the general partner designated as the tax matters partner (TMP) for the tax year of this return:

Name of designated TMP ▶ Identifying number of TMP ▶

Address of designated TMP ▶

Form **1065** (2004)

Form 1065 (2004) Page 3

Schedule K Partners' Distributive Share Items

Section	Line	Item		Line	Total amount
Income (Loss)	1	Ordinary business income (loss) (page 1, line 22)		1	
	2	Net rental real estate income (loss) *(attach Form 8825)*		2	
	3a	Other gross rental income (loss)	3a		
	b	Expenses from other rental activities *(attach statement)*	3b		
	c	Other net rental income (loss). Subtract line 3b from line 3a		3c	
	4	Guaranteed payments		4	
	5	Interest income		5	
	6	Dividends: a Ordinary dividends		6a	
		b Qualified dividends	6b		
	7	Royalties		7	
	8	Net short-term capital gain (loss) *(attach Schedule D (Form 1065))*		8	
	9a	Net long-term capital gain (loss) *(attach Schedule D (Form 1065))*		9a	
	b	Collectibles (28%) gain (loss)	9b		
	c	Unrecaptured section 1250 gain *(attach statement)*	9c		
	10	Net section 1231 gain (loss) *(attach Form 4797)*		10	
	11	Other income (loss) *(attach statement)*		11	
Deductions	12	Section 179 deduction *(attach Form 4562)*		12	
	13a	Contributions		13a	
	b	Deductions related to portfolio income *(attach statement)*		13b	
	c	Investment interest expense		13c	
	d	Section 59(e)(2) expenditures: (1) Type ▶ (2) Amount ▶		13d(2)	
	e	Other deductions *(attach statement)*		13e	
Self-Employment	14a	Net earnings (loss) from self-employment		14a	
	b	Gross farming or fishing income		14b	
	c	Gross nonfarm income		14c	
Credits & Credit Recapture	15a	Low-income housing credit (section 42(j)(5))		15a	
	b	Low-income housing credit (other)		15b	
	c	Qualified rehabilitation expenditures (rental real estate) *(attach Form 3468)*		15c	
	d	Other rental real estate credits		15d	
	e	Other rental credits		15e	
	f	Other credits and credit recapture *(attach statement)*		15f	
Foreign Transactions	16a	Name of country or U.S. possession ▶			
	b	Gross income from all sources		16b	
	c	Gross income sourced at partner level		16c	
		Foreign gross income sourced at partnership level			
	d	Passive ▶ e Listed categories *(attach statement)* ▶ f General limitation ▶		16f	
		Deductions allocated and apportioned at partner level			
	g	Interest expense ▶ h Other ▶		16h	
		Deductions allocated and apportioned at partnership level to foreign source income			
	i	Passive ▶ j Listed categories *(attach statement)* ▶ k General limitation ▶		16k	
	l	Foreign taxes: (1) Paid ▶ (2) Accrued ▶		16l(2)	
	m	Reduction in taxes available for credit *(attach statement)*		16m	
Alternative Minimum Tax (AMT) Items	17a	Post-1986 depreciation adjustment		17a	
	b	Adjusted gain or loss		17b	
	c	Depletion (other than oil and gas)		17c	
	d	Oil, gas, and geothermal properties—gross income		17d	
	e	Oil, gas, and geothermal properties—deductions		17e	
	f	Other AMT items *(attach statement)*		17f	
Other Information	18a	Tax-exempt interest income		18a	
	b	Other tax-exempt income		18b	
	c	Nondeductible expenses		18c	
	19a	Distributions of cash and marketable securities		19a	
	b	Distributions of other property		19b	
	20a	Investment income		20a	
	b	Investment expenses		20b	
	c	Other items and amounts *(attach statement)*			

Form **1065** (2004)

Form 1065 (2004) Page 4

Analysis of Net Income (Loss)

1 Net income (loss). Combine Schedule K, lines 1 through 11. From the result, subtract the sum of Schedule K, lines 12 through 13e, 16l(1), and 16l(2) . . . 1

2 Analysis by partner type:	(i) Corporate	(ii) Individual (active)	(iii) Individual (passive)	(iv) Partnership	(v) Exempt organization	(vi) Nominee/Other
a General partners						
b Limited partners						

Note: Schedules L, M-1, and M-2 are not required if Question 5 of Schedule B is answered "Yes."

Schedule L Balance Sheets per Books	Beginning of tax year		End of tax year	
Assets	(a)	(b)	(c)	(d)
1 Cash				
2a Trade notes and accounts receivable				
b Less allowance for bad debts				
3 Inventories				
4 U.S. government obligations				
5 Tax-exempt securities				
6 Other current assets *(attach statement)*				
7 Mortgage and real estate loans				
8 Other investments *(attach statement)*				
9a Buildings and other depreciable assets				
b Less accumulated depreciation				
10a Depletable assets				
b Less accumulated depletion				
11 Land (net of any amortization)				
12a Intangible assets (amortizable only)				
b Less accumulated amortization				
13 Other assets *(attach statement)*				
14 Total assets				
Liabilities and Capital				
15 Accounts payable				
16 Mortgages, notes, bonds payable in less than 1 year				
17 Other current liabilities *(attach statement)*				
18 All nonrecourse loans				
19 Mortgages, notes, bonds payable in 1 year or more				
20 Other liabilities *(attach statement)*				
21 Partners' capital accounts				
22 Total liabilities and capital				

Schedule M-1 **Reconciliation of Income (Loss) per Books With Income (Loss) per Return**

1 Net income (loss) per books		6 Income recorded on books this year not included on Schedule K, lines 1 through 11 (itemize):	
2 Income included on Schedule K, lines 1, 2, 3c, 5, 6a, 7, 8, 9a, 10, and 11, not recorded on books this year (itemize):		a Tax-exempt interest $	
3 Guaranteed payments (other than health insurance)		7 Deductions included on Schedule K, lines 1 through 13e, 16l(1), and 16l(2), not charged against book income this year (itemize):	
4 Expenses recorded on books this year not included on Schedule K, lines 1 through 13e, 16l(1), and 16l(2) (itemize):		a Depreciation $	
a Depreciation $			
b Travel and entertainment $		8 Add lines 6 and 7	
		9 Income (loss) (Analysis of Net Income (Loss), line 1). Subtract line 8 from line 5	
5 Add lines 1 through 4			

Schedule M-2 **Analysis of Partners' Capital Accounts**

1 Balance at beginning of year		6 Distributions: a Cash	
2 Capital contributed: a Cash		b Property	
b Property		7 Other decreases (itemize):	
3 Net income (loss) per books			
4 Other increases (itemize):			
		8 Add lines 6 and 7	
5 Add lines 1 through 4		9 Balance at end of year. Subtract line 8 from line 5	

Form **1065** (2004)

¶ 2502 Schedule K-1 (Form 1065), Partner's Share of Income, Credits, Deductions, etc.

6511

☐ Final K-1 ☐ Amended K-1 OMB No. 1545-0099

Schedule K-1 (Form 1065) **2004**

Department of the Treasury
Internal Revenue Service

Tax year beginning ____________, 2004
and ending ____________, 20__

Partner's Share of Income, Deductions, Credits, etc. ▶ See back of form and separate instructions.

Part I Information About the Partnership

A Partnership's employer identification number

B Partnership's name, address, city, state, and ZIP code

C IRS Center where partnership filed return

D ☐ Check if this is a publicly traded partnership (PTP)
E ☐ Tax shelter registration number, if any ____________
F ☐ Check if Form 8271 is attached

Part II Information About the Partner

G Partner's identifying number

H Partner's name, address, city, state, and ZIP code

I ☐ General partner or LLC member-manager ☐ Limited partner or other LLC member

J ☐ Domestic partner ☐ Foreign partner

K What type of entity is this partner? ____________

L Partner's share of profit, loss, and capital:

	Beginning	Ending
Profit	%	%
Loss	%	%
Capital	%	%

M Partner's share of liabilities at year end:
Nonrecourse . . . . $____________
Qualified nonrecourse financing . . $____________
Recourse . . . . $____________

N Partner's capital account analysis:
Beginning capital account . . . . $____________
Capital contributed during the year . $____________
Current year increase (decrease) . . $____________
Withdrawals & distributions . . . $(____________)
Ending capital account . . . . $____________

☐ Tax basis ☐ GAAP ☐ Section 704(b) book
☐ Other (explain)

Part III Partner's Share of Current Year Income, Deductions, Credits, and Other Items

1 Ordinary business income (loss)
2 Net rental real estate income (loss)
3 Other net rental income (loss)
4 Guaranteed payments
5 Interest income
6a Ordinary dividends
6b Qualified dividends
7 Royalties
8 Net short-term capital gain (loss)
9a Net long-term capital gain (loss)
9b Collectibles (28%) gain (loss)
9c Unrecaptured section 1250 gain
10 Net section 1231 gain (loss)
11 Other income (loss)
12 Section 179 deduction
13 Other deductions
14 Self-employment earnings (loss)
15 Credits & credit recapture
16 Foreign transactions
17 Alternative minimum tax (AMT) items
18 Tax-exempt income and nondeductible expenses
19 Distributions
20 Other information

*See attached statement for additional information.

For IRS Use Only

For Privacy Act and Paperwork Reduction Act Notice, see Instructions for Form 1065. Cat. No. 11394R **Schedule K-1 (Form 1065) 2004**

This list identifies the codes used on Schedule K-1 for all partners and provides summarized reporting information for partners who file Form 1040. For detailed reporting and filing information, see the separate Partner's Instructions for Schedule K-1 and the instructions for your income tax return.

1. Ordinary business income (loss). You must first determine whether the income (loss) is passive or nonpassive. Then enter on your return as follows:

	Enter on
Passive loss	See the Partner's Instructions
Passive income	Schedule E, line 28, column (g)
Nonpassive loss	Schedule E, line 28, column (h)
Nonpassive income	Schedule E, line 28, column (j)
2. Net rental real estate income (loss)	See the Partner's Instructions
3. Other net rental income (loss)	
Net income	Schedule E, line 28, column (g)
Net loss	See the Partner's Instructions
4. Guaranteed payments	Schedule E, line 28, column (j)
5. Interest income	Form 1040, line 8a
6a. Ordinary dividends	Form 1040, line 9a
6b. Qualified dividends	Form 1040, line 9b
7. Royalties	Schedule E, line 4
8. Net short-term capital gain (loss)	Schedule D, line 5, column (f)
9a. Net long-term capital gain (loss)	Schedule D, line 12, column (f)
9b. Collectibles (28%) gain (loss)	28% Rate Gain Worksheet, line 4 (Schedule D Instructions)
9c. Unrecaptured section 1250 gain	See the Partner's Instructions
10. Net section 1231 gain (loss)	See the Partner's Instructions

11. Other income (loss)

Code	
A Other portfolio income (loss)	See the Partner's Instructions
B Involuntary conversions	See the Partner's Instructions
C Sec. 1256 contracts & straddles	Form 6781, line 1
D Mining exploration costs recapture	See Pub. 535
E Cancellation of debt	Form 1040, line 21 or Form 982
F Other income (loss)	See the Partner's Instructions
12. Section 179 deduction	See the Partner's Instructions

13. Other deductions

A Cash contributions (50%)	Schedule A, line 15
B Cash contributions (30%)	Schedule A, line 15
C Noncash contributions (50%)	Schedule A, line 16
D Noncash contributions (30%)	Schedule A, line 16
E Capital gain property to a 50% organization (30%)	Schedule A, line 16
F Capital gain property (20%)	Schedule A, line 16
G Deductions—portfolio (2% floor)	Schedule A, line 22
H Deductions—portfolio (other)	Schedule A, line 27
I Investment interest expense	Form 4952, line 1
J Deductions—royalty income	Schedule E, line 18
K Section 59(e)(2) expenditures	See Partner's Instructions
L Amounts paid for medical insurance	Schedule A, line 1 or Form 1040, line 31
M Educational assistance benefits	See the Partner's Instructions
N Dependent care benefits	Form 2441, line 12
O Preproductive period expenses	See the Partner's Instructions
P Commercial revitalization deduction from rental real estate activities	See Form 8582 Instructions
Q Penalty on early withdrawal of savings	Form 1040, line 33
R Pensions and IRAs	See the Partner's Instructions
S Reforestation expense deduction	See the Partner's Instructions
T Other deductions	See the Partner's Instructions

14. Self-employment earnings (loss)

Note. *If you have a section 179 deduction or any partner-level deductions, see the Partner's Instructions before completing Schedule SE.*

A Net earnings (loss) from self-employment	Schedule SE, Section A or B
B Gross farming or fishing income	See the Partner's Instructions
C Gross non-farm income	See the Partner's Instructions

15. Credits & credit recapture

A Low-income housing credit (section 42(j)(5))	Form 8586, line 5
B Low-income housing credit (other)	Form 8586, line 5
C Qualified rehabilitation expenditures (rental real estate)	Form 3468, line 1
D Qualified rehabilitation expenditures (other than rental real estate)	Form 3468, line 1
E Basis of energy property	Form 3468, line 2
F Qualified timber property	Form 3468, line 3
G Other rental real estate credits	See the Partner's Instructions
H Other rental credits	See the Partner's Instructions

Code	*Enter on*
I Undistributed capital gains credit	Form 1040, line 69, box a
J Work opportunity credit	Form 5884, line 3
K Welfare-to-work credit	Form 8861, line 3
L Disabled access credit	Form 8826, line 7
M Empowerment zone and renewal community employment credit	Form 8844, line 3
N New York Liberty Zone business employee credit	Form 8884, line 3
O New markets credit	Form 8874, line 2
P Credit for employer social security and Medicare taxes	Form 8846, line 5
Q Backup withholding	Form 1040, line 63
R Recapture of low-income housing credit (section 42(j)(5))	Form 8611, line 8
S Recapture of low-income housing credit (other)	Form 8611, line 8
T Recapture of investment credit	See Form 4255
U Other credits	See the Partner's Instructions
V Recapture of other credits	See the Partner's Instructions

16. Foreign transactions

A Name of country or U.S. possession	Form 1116, Part I
B Gross income from all sources	Form 1116, Part I
C Gross income sourced at partner level	Form 1116, Part I
Foreign gross income sourced at partnership level	
D Passive	Form 1116, Part I
E Listed categories	Form 1116, Part I
F General limitation	Form 1116, Part I
Deductions allocated and apportioned at partner level	
G Interest expense	Form 1116, Part I
H Other	Form 1116, Part I
Deductions allocated and apportioned at partnership level to foreign source income	
I Passive	Form 1116, Part I
J Listed categories	Form 1116, Part I
K General limitation	Form 1116, Part I
Other information	
L Total foreign taxes paid	Form 1116, Part II
M Total foreign taxes accrued	Form 1116, Part II
N Reduction in taxes available for credit	Form 1116, line 12
O Foreign trading gross receipts	Form 8873
P Extraterritorial income exclusion	Form 8873
Q Other foreign transactions	See the Partner's Instructions

17. Alternative minimum tax (AMT) items

A Post-1986 depreciation adjustment
B Adjusted gain or loss
C Depletion (other than oil & gas)
D Oil, gas, & geothermal—gross income
E Oil, gas, & geothermal—deductions
F Other AMT items

} See the Partner's Instructions and the Instructions for Form 6251

18. Tax-exempt income and nondeductible expenses

A Tax-exempt interest income	Form 1040, line 8b
B Other tax-exempt income	See the Partner's Instructions
C Nondeductible expenses	See the Partner's Instructions

19. Distributions

A Cash and marketable securities	See the Partner's Instructions
B Other property	See the Partner's Instructions

20. Other information

A Investment income	Form 4952, line 4a
B Investment expenses	Form 4952, line 5
C Fuel tax credit information	Form 4136
D Look-back interest—completed long-term contracts	Form 8697
E Look-back interest—income forecast method	Form 8866

F Dispositions of property with section 179 deductions
G Recapture of section 179 deduction
H Special basis adjustments
I Section 453(l)(3) information
J Section 453A(c) information
K Section 1260(b) information
L Interest allocable to production expenditures
M CCF nonqualified withdrawals
N Information needed to figure depletion—oil and gas
O Amortization of reforestation costs
P Unrelated business taxable income
Q Other information

} See the Partner's Instructions

¶ 2503 Form 1128, Application To Adopt, Change, or Retain a Tax Year

Form **1128** (Rev. September 2003) Department of the Treasury Internal Revenue Service

Application To Adopt, Change, or Retain a Tax Year

► See separate instructions.

OMB No. 1545-0134

Part I General Information

Important: *All applicants must complete Part I and sign below. See page 2 of the instructions.*

Type or Print

Name of applicant (if a joint return is filed, also enter spouse's name)	**Applicant's identifying no.** (see page 3 of instructions)
Number, street, and room or suite no. (if a P.O. box, see page 3 of the instructions)	Service Center where income tax return will be filed
City or town, state, and ZIP code	Applicant's area code and telephone number/Fax number ( ) / ( )
Name of filer, if different than the applicant (see instructions)	Filer's identifying number
Name of person to contact (if not the applicant or filer, attach a power of attorney)	Contact person's area code and telephone number/Fax number ( ) / ( )

1 Check the appropriate box(es) to indicate the type of applicant (see page 3 of the instructions).

- ☐ Individual
- ☐ Partnership
- ☐ Estate
- ☐ Domestic corporation
- ☐ S corporation
- ☐ Personal service corporation (PSC)
- ☐ Cooperative (sec. 1381(a))
- ☐ Possession corporation (secs. 936 and 30A)
- ☐ Controlled foreign corporation (CFC) (sec. 957)
- ☐ Foreign personal holding company (sec. 552)
- ☐ Foreign sales corporation (FSC) or Interest-charge domestic international sales corporation (IC-DISC)
- ☐ Specified foreign corporation (SFC) (sec. 898)
- ☐ Passive foreign investment company (PFIC) (sec. 1297)
- ☐ Other foreign corporation
- ☐ Tax-exempt organization
- ☐ Homeowners Association (sec. 528)
- ☐ Other .... (Specify entity and applicable Code section)

2a Approval is requested to (check one) (see page 3 of the instructions):

☐ Adopt a tax year ending ►.................. (Partnerships and PSCs: Go to Part III after completing Part I.)

☐ Change to a tax year ending ►.................. ☐ Retain a tax year ending ►..................

b If changing a tax year, indicate the date the present tax year ends. ►..................

c If adopting or changing a tax year, the first return or short period return will be filed for the tax year beginning ► , 20 , and ending ► , 20 .

3 Is the applicant's present tax year, as stated on line 2b above, also its current financial reporting year? ► ☐ **Yes** ☐ **No**

If "No," attach an explanation.

4 Indicate the applicant's present overall method of accounting.

☐ Cash receipts and disbursements method ☐ Accrual method

☐ Other method (specify) ►..................

5 State the nature of the applicant's business or principal source of income.

Signature—All Applicants (See **Who Must Sign** on page 2 of the instructions.)

Under penalties of perjury, I declare that I have examined this application, including accompanying schedules and statements, and to the best of my knowledge and belief it is true, correct, and complete. Declaration of preparer (other than applicant) is based on all information of which preparer has any knowledge.

Applicant*	**Preparer (other than applicant)**
Applicant or officer's signature and date	Signature of individual preparing the application and date
Name and title (print or type)	Name of individual preparing the application
	Name of firm preparing the application

*If the application is filed by one or more U.S. shareholders of a controlled foreign corporation or foreign personal holding company, the U.S. shareholders must sign (see instructions).

For Privacy Act and Paperwork Reduction Act Notice, see separate instructions. Cat. No. 21115C Form **1128** (Rev. 9-2003)

Form 1128 (Rev. 9-2003) Page 2

Part II **Automatic Approval Request** (If the answer to any of the questions below is "Yes," sign Form 1128 and see the instructions for **Where To File. Do not** file with the National Office. **Do not** include a user fee. **Do not** complete Part III. See page 3 of the instructions.)

Section A—Corporations (Other Than S Corporations or Personal Service Corporations) (Rev. Proc. 2002-37)	**Yes**	**No**
1 Is the applicant a corporation (including a homeowners association (section 528)) that is requesting a change in tax year **and** is not precluded from using the automatic approval rules under section 4 of Rev. Proc. 2002-37?		
2 Does the corporation intend to elect to be an S corporation for the tax year immediately following the short period? If "Yes" and the corporation is electing to change to a permitted tax year, file Form 1128 as an attachment to Form 2553.		
3 Is the applicant a CFC requesting a revocation of its 1-month deferral election that was made under section 898(c)(1)(B) **and** to change its tax year to the majority U.S. shareholder year (as defined in section 898(c)(1)(C))?		
4 Is the applicant a corporation requesting a concurrent change for a CFC, FSC or IC-DISC? (see page 4 of the instructions) . . . ▶		
Section B—Partnerships, S Corporations, and Personal Service Corporations (PCSs) (Rev. Proc. 2002-38)		
5 Is the applicant a partnership, S corporation, or PSC that is requesting a tax year **and** is not precluded from using the automatic approval rules under section 4 of Rev. Proc. 2002-38? (see page 4 of the instructions) ▶		
6 Is the partnership, S corporation, or PSC requesting to change to its required tax year or a 52-53 week tax year ending with reference to such tax year? . . . ▶		
7 Is the partnership, S corporation, or PSC (other than a member of a tiered structure) requesting a tax year that coincides with its natural business year described in section 4.01(2) of Rev. Proc. 2002-38? (see page 4 of the instructions for information required to be submitted) . . . ▶		
8 Is the S corporation requesting an ownership tax year? (see page 4 of the instructions) . . . ▶		
9 Is the applicant a partnership requesting a concurrent change pursuant to section 6.10 of Rev. Proc. 2002-37 or section 5.04(8) of Rev. Proc. 2002-39? (see page 4 of the instructions) . . . ▶		
Section C—Individuals (Rev. Proc. 2003-62) (see page 5 of the instructions)		
10 Is the applicant an individual requesting a change from a fiscal year to a calendar year? . . . ▶		
Section D—Tax-Exempt Organizations (Rev. Proc. 76-10 or 85-58) (see page 5 of the instructions)		
11 Is the applicant a tax-exempt organization requesting a change? . . . ▶		

Part III **Ruling Request** (All applicants requesting a ruling must complete Section A and any other section that applies to the entity. See page 5 of the instructions.)

Section A—General Information	**Yes**	**No**
1 Is the applicant under examination by the IRS, before an appeals office, or a Federal court? . . . ▶ If "Yes," see the instructions on page 5 for information that must be included on an attached explanation.		
2 Has the applicant changed its annual accounting period at any time within the most recent 48-month period ending with the last month of the requested tax year? . . . ▶ If "Yes" and a letter ruling was issued granting approval to make the change, attach a copy of the letter ruling, or if not available, an explanation including the date approval was granted. If a letter ruling was not issued, indicate when and explain how the change was implemented.		
3 Within the most recent 48-month period, has any accounting period application been withdrawn, not perfected, denied, or not implemented? . . . ▶ If "Yes," attach an explanation.		
4a Is the applicant requesting to establish a business purpose under section 5.02(1) of Rev. Proc. 2002-39? . ▶ If "Yes," attach an explanation of the legal basis supporting the requested tax year (see page 5 of the instructions). **b** If your business purpose is based on one of the natural business year tests under section 5.03, check the applicable box. ☐ Annual business cycle test ☐ Seasonal business test ☐ 25-percent gross receipts test Attach a statement showing gross receipts from sales and services (and inventory cost if applicable) for the test period. (See page 5 of the instructions)		
5 Enter the taxable income or (loss) for the 3 tax years immediately preceding the year of change and for the short period. If necessary, estimate the amount for the short period. Short period $ .... First preceding year $ .... Second preceding year $ .... Third preceding year $ .... **Note:** *Individuals, enter adjusted gross income. Partnerships and S corporations, enter ordinary income. Section 501(c) organizations, enter unrelated business taxable income. Estates, enter adjusted total income. All other applicants, enter taxable income before net operating loss deduction and special deductions.*		

Form **1128** (Rev. 9-2003)

Form 1128 (Rev. 9-2003) Page 3

		Yes	No
6	Corporations only, enter the losses or credits, if any, that were generated or that expired in the short period: Generated / Expiring Net operating loss . . . . $ ______ $ ______ Capital loss . . . . $ ______ $ ______ Unused credits . . . . $ ______ $ ______		
7	Enter the amount of deferral, if any, resulting from the change (see section 5.05(1), (2), (3) and 6.01(7) of Rev. Proc. 2002-39) . . . . ▶ $ ______		
8a	Is the applicant a U.S. shareholder in a CFC? . . . . ▶		
	If "Yes," attach a statement for each CFC providing the name, address, identifying number, tax year, the percentage of total combined voting power of the applicant, and the amount of income included in the gross income of the applicant under section 951 for the 3 tax years immediately before the short period and for the short period.		
b	Will each CFC concurrently change its tax year? . . . . ▶		
	If "Yes" to line 8b, go to Part II, line 3. If "No," attach a statement explaining why the CFC will not be conforming to the tax year requested by the U.S. shareholder.		
9a	Is the applicant a U.S. shareholder in a PFIC as defined in section 1297? . . . . ▶		
	If "Yes," attach a statement providing the name, address, identifying number, and tax year of the PFIC, the percentage of interest owned by the applicant, and the amount of distributions or ordinary earnings and net capital gain from the PFIC included in the income of the applicant.		
b	Did the applicant elect under section 1295 to treat the PFIC as a qualified electing fund? . . . . . ▶		
10a	Is the applicant a member of a partnership, a beneficiary of a trust or estate, a shareholder of an S corporation, a shareholder of an IC-DISC, or a shareholder of an FSC? . . . . ▶		
	If "Yes," attach a statement providing the name, address, identifying number, type of entity (partnership, trust, estate, S corporation, IC-DISC, or FSC), tax year, percentage of interest in capital and profits, or percentage of interest of each IC-DISC or FSC and the amount of income received from each entity for the first preceding year and for the short period. Indicate the percentage of gross income of the applicant represented by each amount.		
b	Will any partnership concurrently change its tax year to conform with the tax year requested? . . . . ▶		
c	If "Yes" to line 10b, has any Form 1128 been filed for such partnership? . . . . ▶		
11	Does the applicant or any related entity currently have any accounting method, tax year, ruling, or technical advice request pending with the IRS National Office? . . . . ▶		
	If "Yes," attach a statement explaining the type of request (method, tax year, etc.) and the specific issues involved in each request.		
12	Is **Form 2848,** Power of Attorney and Declaration of Representative, attached to this application? . . . . ▶		
13	Does the applicant request a conference of right (in person or by telephone) with the IRS National Office, if the IRS proposes to disapprove the application? . . . . ▶		
14	Enter amount of **user fee** attached to this application (see page 6 of the instructions) . . . . . . ▶ $		

Section B—Corporations (other than S corporations and controlled foreign corporations) (see page 6 of instructions)

15 Enter the date of incorporation. ▶

		Yes	No
16a	Does the corporation intend to elect to be an S corporation for the tax year immediately following the short period? . . . . ▶		
b	If "Yes," will the corporation be going to a permitted S corporation tax year? . . . . ▶ If "No" to line 16b, attach an explanation.		
17	Is the corporation a member of an affiliated group filing a consolidated return? . . . . ▶		
	If "Yes," attach a statement providing **(a)** the name, address, identifiying number used on the consolidated return, tax year, and Service Center where the applicant files the return; **(b)** the name, address, and identifying number of each member of the affiliated group; **(c)** the taxable income (loss) of each member for the 3 years immediately before the short period and for the short period; and **(d)** the name of the parent corporation.		
18a	Personal service corporations (PSCs): Attach a statement providing each shareholder's name, type of entity (individual, partnership, corporation, etc.), address, identifying number, tax year, percentage of ownership, and amount of income received from the PSC for the first preceding year and the short period.		
b	If the PSC is using a tax year other than the required tax year, indicate how it obtained its tax year. ☐ Grandfathered (attach copy of letter ruling) ☐ Section 444 election (date of election ______) ☐ Letter ruling (date of letter ruling ______ (attach copy))		

Form **1128** (Rev. 9-2003)

Form 1128 (Rev. 9-2003) Page **4**

Section C—S Corporations (See page 6 of the instructions)

		Yes	No
19	Enter the date of the S corporation election. ▶		
20	Is any shareholder applying for a corresponding change in tax year? . . . . ▶ If "Yes," each shareholder requesting a corresponding change in tax year must file a separate Form 1128 to get advance approval to change its tax year.		
21	If the corporation is using a tax year other than the required tax year, indicate how it obtained its tax year. ☐ Grandfathered (attach copy of letter ruling) ☐ Section 444 election (date of election ____________) ☐ Letter ruling (date of letter ruling ____________(attach copy))		
22	Attach a statement providing each shareholder's name, type of shareholder (individual, estate, qualified subchapter S Trust, electing small business trust, other trust, or exempt organization), address, identifying number, tax year, percentage of ownership, and the amount of income each shareholder received from the S corporation for the first preceding year and for the short period.		

Section D—Partnerships (see page 6 of instructions)

		Yes	No
23	Enter the date the partnership's business began. ▶		
24	Is any partner applying for a corresponding change in tax year? . . . . ▶		
25	Attach a statement providing each partner's name, type of partner (individual, partnership, estate, trust, corporation, S corporation, IC-DISC, etc.), address, identifying number, tax year, and the percentage of interest in capital and profits.		
26	Is any partner a shareholder of a PSC as defined in Regulations section 1.441-3(c)? . . . . ▶ If "Yes," attach a statement providing the name, address, identifiying number, tax year, percentage of interest in capital and profits, and the amount of income received from each PSC for the first preceding year and for the short period.		
27	If the partnership is using a tax year other than the required tax year, indicate how it obtained its tax year. ☐ Grandfathered (attach copy of letter ruling) ☐ Section 444 election (date of election ____________) ☐ Letter ruling (date of letter ruling ____________ (attach copy))		

Section E—Controlled Foreign Corporations (CFC)

28	Attach a statement for each U.S. shareholder (as defined in section 951(b)) providing the name, address, identifying number, tax year, percentage of total value and percentage of total voting power, and the amount of income included in gross income under section 951 for the 3 tax years immediately before the short period and for the short period.		

Section F—Tax-Exempt Organizations

		Yes	No
29	Type of organization: ☐ Corporation ☐ Trust ☐ Other (specify) ▶		
30	Date of organization. ▶		
31	Code section under which the organization is exempt. ▶		
32	Is the organization required to file an annual return on Form 990, 990-C, 990-PF, 990-T, 1120-H, or 1120-POL? ▶		
33	Enter the date the tax exemption was granted. ▶........................ Attach a copy of the letter ruling granting exemption. If a copy of the letter ruling is not available, attach an explanation.		
34	If the organization is a private foundation, is the foundation terminating its status under section 507? . . ▶		

Section G—Estates

35 Enter the date the estate was created. ▶

36a Attach a statement providing the name, identifying number, address, and tax year of each beneficiary and each person who is an interested party of any portion of the estate.

b Based on the adjusted total income of the estate entered in Part III, Section A, line 5, attach a statement showing the distribution deduction and the taxable amounts distributed to each beneficiary for the 2 tax years immediately before the short period and for the short period.

Section H—Certain Foreign Corporations

37 If the applicant is a passive foreign investment company or foreign personal holding company, attach a statement providing each U.S. shareholder's name, address, identifying number, and percentage of interest owned.

Form **1128** (Rev. 9-2003)

¶ 2504 Instructions for Form 1128

Instructions for Form 1128

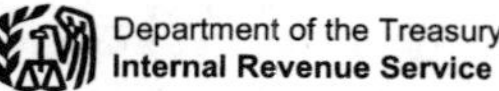

(Rev. September 2003)

Application To Adopt, Change, or Retain a Tax Year

Section references are to the Internal Revenue Code unless otherwise noted.

Changes To Note

- Partnerships must now file Form 1128 to change to a required tax year.
- A taxpayer that wants to change from a 52-53-week tax year that references a particular month to a non-52-53-week tax year that ends on the last day of that month, or vice versa, must file Form 1128.

Note: *If the applicant qualifies, the above changes must be made using the automatic approval procedures. See the instructions for Part II on page 3 for details.*

General Instructions

Purpose of Form

File Form 1128 to request a change in tax year. Partnerships, S corporations, or personal service corporations (PSCs) may be required to file the form to adopt or retain a certain tax year. For more information, see **Pub. 538,** Accounting Periods and Methods.

Who Must File

Generally, all taxpayers must file Form 1128 to adopt, change, or retain a tax year. However, see **Exceptions** below.

The common parent of a consolidated group that files a consolidated return files one Form 1128 for the consolidated group. In addition, the common parent corporation must **(a)** indicate that the Form 1128 is for the common parent corporation and all its subsidiaries and **(b)** answer all relevant questions on the application for each member of the consolidated group.

If a consolidated group filing a consolidated return wants to change its tax year by using Rev. Proc. 2002-37, 2002-1 C.B. 1030, every member of the group must meet the revenue procedure requirements.

If a controlled foreign corporation (CFC) or a foreign personal holding company (FPHC) does not have a U.S. trade or business, then the CFC's controlling U.S. shareholder(s) or the FPHC's U.S. shareholders must file Form 1128 on behalf of such foreign corporation to change its tax year (except as provided above with respect to a controlling U.S. shareholder that is a member of a consolidated group). See Regulations section 1.964-1(c)(5) for the definition of controlling U.S. shareholders of a CFC.

Exceptions

Do not file Form 1128 in the following circumstances.

Corporations

- A corporation adopting its first tax year.
- A corporation required to change its tax year to file a consolidated return with its new common parent (see Regulations sections 1.442-1(c) and 1.1502-76(a)).
- A foreign sales corporation (FSC) or an interest charge domestic international sales corporation (IC-DISC) changing to the tax year of the U.S. shareholder with the highest percentage of voting power (see section 441(h)). Also see Temporary Regulations section 1.921-1T(b)(4). However, a FSC or IC-DISC must file Form 1128 to change its tax year concurrently, if a tax year change has been made by the U.S. shareholder.

Partnerships, S Corporations, and Personal Service Corporations

- A newly formed partnership adopting a required tax year or a 52-53 week tax year with reference to such required tax year.
- A partnership, S corporation, or PSC terminating its section 444 election (see Temporary Regulations section 1.444-1T(a)(5)).
- A newly formed partnership, an electing S corporation, or a newly formed PSC that elects under section 444 a tax year other than the required tax year by filing **Form 8716,** Election To Have a Tax Year Other Than a Required Tax Year.
- A corporation electing to be treated as an S corporation and filing **Form 2553,** Election by a Small Business Corporation.

Individuals

Newly married individuals changing to the tax year of the other spouse in order to file a joint return (Regulations section 1.442-1(d) must be followed).

Exempt Organizations

An organization exempt under section 501(a) does not file Form 1128 unless the organization has changed its tax year at any time within a 10-calendar-year period, and the organization has had an annual filing requirement during that 10-year period (see Rev. Proc. 85-58, 1985-2 C.B. 740). This exception does not apply to organizations exempt from tax under section 521, 526, 527, or 528; organizations described in section 401(a); and organizations involved in a group change in tax year for all its subordinate organizations.

Trusts

- A trust (other than a tax-exempt trust or a grantor trust under Rev. Rul. 90-55, 1990-2 C.B. 161) that adopts the calendar year as required by section 645.
- Certain revocable trusts electing to be treated as part of an estate.
- An employee plan or trust filing **Form 5308,** Request for Change in Plan/Trust Year, to change its plan or trust year.

When To File

Tax Year Adoption, Change, or Retention

- To request a ruling to adopt, change, or retain a tax year, file by the due date (not including extensions) of the Federal income tax return for the first effective year. **Do not** file earlier than the day following the end of the first effective year.
- To request automatic approval to change a tax year under Rev. Proc. 2002-37 (Part II, Section A) or Rev. Proc. 2002-38 (Part II, Section B), file by the due date of the return (including extensions) for the first effective year required by the change.

Cat. No. 61752V

• For an individual filing to change to a calendar year under Rev. Proc. 2003-62, 2003-32 I.R.B. 299 (Part II, Section C), Form 1128 must be filed on or before the due date (including extensions) for filing the Federal income tax return for the short period required to effect the change.
• To change a tax year under Rev. Proc. 85-58 (Part II, Section D), file by the 15th day of the 5th calendar month after the first effective year ends.

Late Applications

Generally, an application filed after the appropriate due date stated above is considered late.

However, applications filed within 90 days after the due date may be considered as timely filed under Regulations section 301.9100-1 when the applicant establishes that:

1. The taxpayer acted reasonably and in good faith and

2. Granting relief will not prejudice the interests of the government.

Applications that are filed more than 90 days after the due date are presumed to jeopardize the interests of the Government, and will be approved only in unusual and compelling circumstances.

Under either circumstance an extension request must be filed under Procedure and Administration Regulations section 301.9100-3 and is a ruling request under Rev. Proc. 2003-1, 2003-1 I.R.B. 1 (updated annually), and is subject to public inspection under section 6110. See section 8 of Rev. Proc. 2003-1 for information on requesting a ruling.

Note: *An extension request under Rev. Proc. 2003-1 (or its successor), requires payment of a user fee.*

Early Applications

Generally, an application to adopt or change a tax year will not be considered if it is submitted before the close of the first effective year.

Where To File

Part II—Automatic Approval Request

If the applicant completes Part II (automatic approval request), file Form 1128 with the Internal Revenue Service Center, Attention: Entity Control, where the applicant's income tax return is filed. The applicant also must attach a copy of Form 1128 to the Federal income tax return filed for the short period required to effect the change. A shareholder filing the form on behalf of an applicant that is a CFC or FPHC should file the form with the service center where the shareholder's income tax return is filed.

Applications prior to an election to become an S corporation. If a corporation is requesting to change its tax year prior to making an election to become an S corporation, it may be necessary to file Form 1128 with Form 2553 to ensure that the S corporation is permitted the tax year requested on Form 2553. See line 2 of Part II on Form 1128. Form 1128 must be filed with Form 2553 instead of the above address for automatic approval requests if:
• The corporation is requesting to change its tax year under the automatic approval request procedures,
• The corporation intends to elect to be an S corporation for the tax year immediately following the short period, **and**
• The requested tax year is a permitted tax year for S corporations (e.g., a calendar tax year).

Do not file a request for automatic approval with either address below. Doing so will result in a significant delay in the processing of your request.

Part III—Ruling Request

If the applicant completes Part III (ruling request), file Form 1128 and the appropriate user fee with the IRS National Office. Mail Form 1128 to:

Internal Revenue Service,
Associate Chief Counsel (Income Tax and Accounting)
Attention: CC:PA:T:CRU,
P.O. Box 7604, Ben Franklin Station,
Washington DC 20044-7604.

The IRS will acknowledge receipt of the application within 45 days. You can inquire about the status of the application by writing to:

Control Clerk, CC:ITA,
Internal Revenue Service, Room 4516,
1111 Constitution Ave., NW,
Washington DC 20224-0002.

The applicant will receive notification of its approval or denial. If no communication is received from the IRS regarding the application within 90 days, contact the Control Clerk.

Exempt organizations requesting a ruling should send Form 1128 and the application user fee to:

Internal Revenue Service
Commissioner, Tax Exempt and Government Entities
Attention: T:EO
P.O. Box 27720
McPherson Station
Washington DC 20038

You can inquire about the status of an application for exempt organizations by calling 202-283-2300.

Who Must Sign

Except as discussed below (regarding certain foreign corporations), Form 1128 **must** be signed by the applicant as discussed below. A valid signature by the individual or an officer of the organization is required on Form 1128. If the form does not have a valid signature, it will not be considered.

Individuals

If this application is for a husband and wife, enter both names on the line "Name of applicant." Both husband and wife must sign the application on the line "Applicant or officer's signature and date."

Partnerships

Show the partnership name, followed by the signature of a general partner on behalf of a state law partnership, or a member-manager on behalf of a limited liability company.

Estates

Show the name of the estate and the signature and title of the fiduciary or other person legally authorized to sign.

Tax-Exempt Organizations

Show the name of the organization and the signature of a principal officer or other person authorized to sign, followed by his or her title.

All Other Applicants

The application must show the name of the company and the signature of the president, vice president, treasurer, assistant treasurer, or chief accounting officer (such as tax officer) authorized to sign, and their official title. Receivers, trustees, or assignees must sign any application they are required to file. For a consolidated group filing a consolidated return with its common parent, the form should be signed by an authorized officer of the common parent corporation.

An application that is filed on behalf of a CFC must be signed by an authorized officer of each of its controlling U.S. shareholder(s). An application that is filed on behalf of a FPHC must be signed by an authorized officer of each of its U.S. shareholder(s). If any such shareholder is a member of a consolidated group, then an authorized officer of the common parent must sign. If multiple signatures are required, the signatures must be provided on a "SIGNATURE ATTACHMENT" to the form under the "declaration under penalties of perjury" (this is the statement that appears on Form 1128 immediately above the relevant signature line). Write "see attached" in the signature area of Form 1128.

Preparer Other Than Applicant

The preparer cannot sign on behalf of the applicant. Unless you are self-employed, show the name of the firm that employs you. If you file on an applicant's behalf, include a power of attorney. Show any specific acts the power of attorney grants, such as representation before the IRS.

Note: *The individual preparing the application must also sign it.*

Specific Instructions

Part I–General Information

All applicants must complete Part I. Attachments to Form 1128 must show the applicant's name, identifying number, and address. Also indicate that the statement is an attachment to Form 1128.

Name

If the application is filed for a husband and wife who file a joint income tax return, the names of both should appear in the heading.

Identifying Number

Individuals enter their social security number (SSN). If the application is for a husband and wife who file a joint return, enter both SSNs. However, if one or both are engaged in a trade or business, enter the employer identification number (EIN) instead of the SSNs. All other applicants enter their EIN.

Except as discussed below (regarding foreign corporations), if the applicant does not have an EIN or SSN, it must apply for one. An EIN may be applied for:

- Online—Click on the EIN link at **www.irs.gov/business/small**. The EIN is issued immediately once the application information is validated.
- By telephone at 1-800-829-4933 from 7:30 am to 5:30 pm in the corporation's local time zone.
- By mailing or faxing **Form SS-4,** Application for Employer Identification Number.

A limited liability company must determine which type of federal tax entity it will be (i.e., partnership, corporation, or disregarded entity) before applying for an EIN (see **Form 8832,** Entity Classification Election, for details).

Note: *The online application process is not yet available for the following types of entities: Entities with addresses in foreign countries or Puerto Rico, REMICs, state and local governments, Federal government/military entities, and Indian Tribal Government/Enterprise entities. Please call the toll-free Business and Specialty Tax Line at 1-800-829-4933 for assistance in applying for an EIN.*

An SSN must be applied for on **Form SS-5,** Application for a Social Security Card. Form SS-5 can be obtained at SSA offices or by calling the SSA at 1-800-772-1213.

If the applicant has not received its EIN or SSN by the time the application is due, write "Applied for" in the space for the EIN/SSN . See **Pub. 583,** Starting a Business and Keeping Records.

Note: *If the applicant is a foreign corporation that is not otherwise required to have or obtain an EIN, enter "Not applicable" in the space provided for the EIN/SSN.*

Address

Include the suite, room, or other unit number after the street address.

If the Post Office does not deliver mail to the street address and the applicant has a P.O. box, show the box number instead.

Person To Contact

The person to contact must be the person authorized to sign the Form 1128, or the applicant's authorized representative. If the person to contact is not the applicant or the filer, attach **Form 2848,** Power of Attorney and Declaration of Representative.

Line 1. Check all applicable boxes to indicate the type of entity filing this application. For example, an entity that is a domestic corporation may also be a regulated investment company (RIC). That entity would check both the "Domestic corporation" box and the "Other" box, and write, "RIC under sec. 851" on the dotted line.

Lines 2a and 2b. If the requested year is a 52-53-week tax year, describe the year (e.g., last Saturday in December or Saturday nearest to December 31). A 52-53-week tax year must end on the date a specified day of the week last occurs in a particular month or on the date that day of the week occurs nearest to the last day of a particular calendar month.

Line 2c. The required short period return must begin on the day following the close of the old tax year and end on the day before the first day of the new tax year. An applicant's first tax year generally starts when business operations begin.

A corporation's tax year begins at the earliest date it first:

- Has shareholders,
- Has assets, or
- Begins doing business. The initial year ends on the day before the first day of the new tax year.

Part II—Automatic Approval Request

Part II is completed by applicants requesting automatic approval of a change in tax year under:

- Rev. Proc. 2002-37 (corporations),
- Rev. Proc. 2002-38 (pass-through entities),
- Rev. Proc. 2003-62 (individuals),
- Rev. Proc. 76-10, 1976-1 C.B. 548 and Rev. Proc. 85-58 (exempt organizations), and
- Rev. Proc. 85-15, 1985-1 C.B. 516 (all filers), to correct an improper tax year.

Note: *Applicants requesting an automatic approval, complete Parts I and II only.*

Note: *A user fee is not required if requesting an automatic approval under any of the sections of Part II listed below.*

Complete Part II if the applicant can use the automatic approval rules under one of the sections listed below and the application is filed on time.

-3-

If the applicant is:	Complete only
A corporation (other than an S corporation or a PSC)	Section A
A partnership, S corporation, or a PSC	Section B
An individual	Section C
A tax-exempt organization.	Section D

If the applicant does not qualify for automatic approval, a ruling must be requested. See Part III for more information.

If the Service Center denies approval because Form 1128 was not filed on time, the applicant may request relief under Regulations section 301.9100-3, discussed earlier under **Late Applications** on page 2, by completing Part III, as discussed on page 5, and sending Form 1128 to the IRS National Office for consideration.

Section A—Corporations (Other than S Corporations or Personal Service Corporations)

Rev. Proc 2002-37 provides exclusive procedures for certain corporations to obtain automatic approval to change their annual accounting period under section 442 and Regulations section 1.442-1(b). A corporation complying with all the applicable provisions of this revenue procedure will be deemed to have established a business purpose and obtained the approval of the IRS to change its accounting period. See Rev. Proc. 2002-37 for more information.

A corporation is not eligible to make an automatic approval request if it:

1. Has changed its annual accounting period at any time within the most recent 48-month period ending with the last month of the requested tax year. For exceptions, see section 4.02(1) of Rev. Proc. 2002-37.

2. Has an interest in a pass-through entity as of the end of the short period. For exceptions, see section 4.02(2) of Rev. Proc. 2002-37.

3. Is a shareholder of a FSC or IC-DISC, as of the end of the short period. For exceptions, see section 4.02(3) of Rev. Proc. 2002-37.

4. Is a FSC or an IC-DISC.

5. Is an S corporation.

6. Attempts to make an S corporation election for the tax year immediately following the short period, unless the change is to a permitted tax year.

7. Is a PSC.

8. Is a CFC or a foreign personal holding company (FPHC). For exceptions, see sections 4.01(4) and 4.02(8) of Rev. Proc. 2002-37.

9. Is a tax-exempt organization, other than an organization exempt from tax under section 521, 526, 527, or 528.

10. Has in effect a possessions corporation election under section 936.

11. Is a cooperative association (within the meaning of section 1381(a)) with a loss in the short period required to effect the change of annual accounting period, unless the patrons of the cooperative association are substantially the same in the year before the change of annual accounting period, in the first effective year required to effect the change, and in the year following the change.

12. Has a required tax year (e.g., a real estate investment trust), unless the corporation is changing to its required tax year and is not described in 1 through 11 above.

Line 3. If the answer to question 3 is "Yes," attach a statement providing the names, addresses, and identifying numbers for each U.S. shareholder of the foreign corporation.

Line 4. If a corporation's interest in a pass-through entity, CFC, FSC, or IC-DISC (related entity) is disregarded under section 4.02(2) or 4.02(3) of Rev. Proc. 2002-37 because the related entity is required to change its tax year to the corporation's new tax year (or, in the case of a CFC, to a tax year beginning one month earlier than the corporation's new tax year), the related entity must change its tax year concurrently with the corporation's change in tax year, either under Rev. Proc. 2002-37 or 2002-38. This related party change is required notwithstanding the testing date provisions in section 706(b)(4)(A)(ii), section 898(c)(1)(C)(ii), Temporary Regulations section 1.921-1T(b)(6), and the special provision in section 706(b)(4)(B).

Section B—Partnerships, S Corporations, or Personal Service Corporations

A partnership, S corporation, or PSC may be able to adopt, change, or retain its tax year by following Rev. Proc. 2002-38.

Line 5. A partnership, S corporation, or PSC is not eligible to make an automatic approval request if any of the following apply:

1. It is under examination, unless it obtains consent of the appropriate director as provided in section 7.03(1) of Rev. Proc. 2002-38.

2. It is before an appeals office with respect to any income tax issue and its annual accounting period is an issue under consideration by the appeals office.

3. It is before a Federal court with respect to any income tax issue and its annual accounting period is an issue under consideration by the Federal court.

4. On the date the partnership or S corporation would otherwise file its application, the partnership's or S corporation's annual accounting period is an issue under consideration in the examination of a partner's or shareholders's Federal income tax return or an issue under consideration by an area office or by a Federal court with respect to a partner's or shareholder's Federal income tax return.

5. It is requesting a change to, or retention of, a natural business year as described in section 4.01(2) of Rev. Proc. 2002-38 if the entity has changed its annual accounting period at any time in the most recent 48-month period ending with the last month of the requested tax year. For this purpose, the following changes are not considered prior changes in annual accounting period: **(a)** a change to a required tax year or ownership tax year; **(b)** a change from a 52-53 week tax year to a non-52-53 week tax year that ends with reference to the same calendar month, and vice versa; or **(c)** a change in accounting period by a S corporation or PSC, in order to comply with the common tax year requirements of Regulations sections 1.1502-75(d)(3)(v) and 1.1502-76(a)(1).

Line 7. A partnership, S corporation, electing S corporation, or PSC establishes a "natural business year" under Rev. Proc. 2002-38 by satisfying the following "25-percent gross receipts test:"

1. Prior three years gross receipts.

a. Gross receipts from sales and services for the most recent 12-month period that ends with the last month of the requested annual accounting period are totaled and then divided into the amount of gross receipts from sales and services for the last 2 months of this 12-month period.

b. The same computation as in **a** above is made for the two preceding 12-month periods ending with the last month of the requested annual accounting period.

2. Natural business year:

a. Except as provided in **b** below, if each of the three results described in **1** equals or exceeds 25 percent, then the requested annual accounting period is deemed to be the taxpayer's natural business year.

b. The taxpayer must determine whether any annual accounting period other than the requested annual accounting period also meets the 25-percent test described in **a.** If one or more other annual accounting periods produce higher averages of the three percentages (rounded to 1/100 of a percent) described in **1** than the requested annual accounting period, then the requested annual accounting period will not qualify as the taxpayer's natural business year.

3. Special rules:

a. To apply the 25-percent gross receipts test for any particular year, the taxpayer must compute its gross receipts under the method of accounting used to prepare its federal income tax returns for such tax year.

b. If the taxpayer has a predecessor organization and is continuing the same business as its predecessor, the taxpayer must use the gross receipts of its predecessor for purposes of computing the 25-percent gross receipts test.

c. If the taxpayer (including any predecessor organization) does not have a 47-month period of gross receipts (36-month period for the requested tax year plus an additional 11-month period for comparing the requested tax year with other potential tax years), then it cannot establish a natural business year under this revenue procedure.

d. If the requested tax year is a 52-53-week tax year, the calendar month ending nearest to the last day of the 52-53-week tax year is treated as the last month of the requested tax year for purposes of computing the 25-percent gross receipts test.

Line 8. For an S corporation, an "ownership tax year" is the tax year (if any) that, as of the first day of the first effective year, constitutes the tax year of one or more shareholders (including any shareholder that concurrently changes to such tax year) holding more than 50 percent of the corporation's issued and outstanding shares of stock. For this purpose, a shareholder that is tax-exempt under section 501(a) is disregarded if such shareholder is not subject to tax on any income attributable to the S corporation. Tax-exempt shareholders are not disregarded, however, if the S corporation is wholly-owned by such tax-exempt entities. A shareholder in an S corporation that wants to concurrently change its tax year must follow the instructions generally applicable to taxpayers changing their tax years contained in Regulations section 1.442-1(b), Rev. Proc. 2002-39, or any other applicable administrative procedure published by the IRS.

Line 9. The partnership must concurrently change its tax year as a term and condition of a related entity change in tax year.

Section C—Individuals

An individual is eligible for automatic approval if:

• The individual is changing from a fiscal year to a calendar year and
• The individual ia not subject to the restrictions of section 4.02 of Rev. Proc. 2003-62 (or its successor).

Section D—Tax-Exempt Organizations

A tax-exempt organization may request a change to its tax year under the simplified method of either Rev. Proc. 85-58 or Rev. Proc. 76-10.

Under Rev. Proc. 85-58, an organization exempt under section 501(a) does not have to file Form 1128 unless:

1. The organization was required to file an annual information return or **Form 990-T,** Exempt Organization Business Income Tax Return, at any time during the last 10 calendar years, and

2. The organization has changed its tax year at any time within the last 10 calendar years ending with the calendar year that includes the beginning of the first effective year resulting from the change of tax year.

An organization described in section 501(c) or (d) is exempt from tax under section 501(a) unless the exemption is denied under section 502 or 503.

Rev. Proc. 85-58 does **not** apply to:

• Farmers' cooperatives exempt from Federal income tax under section 521,
• Organizations described in sections 526, 527, and 528,
• Organizations described in section 401(a), and
• Organizations requesting a change in a tax year on a group basis.

A central organization should follow Rev. Proc. 76-10 to apply for a group change in tax year for all its subordinate organizations.

Rev. Proc. 76-10 does **not** apply to:

• Farmers' cooperatives exempt from Federal income tax under section 521,
• Certain organizations that have unrelated business taxable income defined in section 512(a), and
• Organizations that are private foundations defined in section 509(a).

Part III—Ruling Request

Part III is completed only by applicants requesting to adopt, change, or retain a tax year that cannot use the automatic procedures listed in Part II.

Also, the applicant must complete the specific section(s) in Part III that applies to that particular applicant.

If the applicant is:	Complete only
A corporation (other than an S corporation or CFC)	Sections A and B, plus any other applicable section in Part III
An S corporation	Sections A and C
A Partnership	Sections A and D
A Controlled Foreign Corporation	Sections A and E

Do not file a tax return using the requested tax year until this application is approved.

Rev. Proc. 2002-39 provides the general procedures for obtaining approval to adopt, change, or retain a tax year for taxpayers not qualifying under the automatic approval rules or if the application is late.

-5-

Section A—General Information

All applicants must complete this section to request a ruling on an adoption, change to, or retention of a tax year.

Line 1. If the applicant is:

- **Under examination.** Attach to the application a statement from the director consenting to the change or retention. The applicant must also attach to the application a statement indicating if a copy of the application has been given to the examination agent as required by section 6.06(1)(b) of Rev. Proc. 2002-39, as well as the name and telephone number of the examination agent.
- **Before an appeals (area) office.** Attach to the application a statement signed by an appropriate person certifying that, to the best of that person's knowledge, the entity's annual accounting period is not an issue under consideration by the appeals (area) office. The applicant must also attach to the application a statement indicating if a copy of the application has been given to the appeals officer as required by section 6.06(2) of Rev. Proc. 2002-39, as well as the name and telephone number of the appeals officer.
- **Before a Federal court.** Attach to the application a statement signed by an appropriate person certifying that, to the best of that person's knowledge, the entity's annual accounting period is not an issue under consideration by the Federal court. The applicant must also attach to the application a statement indicating if a copy of the application has been given to the government counsel as required by section 6.06(3) of Rev. Proc. 2002-39, as well as the name and telephone number of the government counsel.

Line 4a. Attach an explanation of the legal basis supporting the requested tax year. Include all authority (statutes, regulations, etc.) supporting the requested year. The applicant is encouraged to include all relevant facts and circumstances that may establish a business purpose.

Line 4b. If the applicant requests to establish a natural business year under the annual business cycle test or seasonal business test of sections 5.03(1) and 5.03(2) of Rev. Proc. 2002-39, it must provide its gross receipts from sales or services and approximate inventory costs (where applicable) for each month in the requested short period and for each month of the three immediately preceding tax years.

If the applicant is requesting to change to a natural business year that satisfies the 25-percent gross receipts test described in section 5.03(3) of Rev. Proc. 2002-39, the applicant must supply the gross receipts for the most recent 47 months for itself (or any predecessor).

Line 14. Applicants filing to request an automatic approval for a change in tax year under Rev. Procs. 2002-37, 2002-38, 2003-62, 85-58, or 76-10 (Part II) are **not** required to pay a **user fee** when Form 1128 is filed on time.

Applicants filing to request a letter ruling on a change in tax year under Rev. Proc. 2003-1 and Rev. Proc. 2002-39 must pay a $1,000 user fee. A request for an exempt organization letter ruling on a change in tax year under Rev. Proc. 2003-8, 2003-1 I.R.B. 236, requires payment of a $150 user fee.

A separate $1,200 user fee is also required for applicants filing a letter ruling request for an extension of time to file under Regulations section 301.9100-3 (including requests under Rev. Procs. 2002-37, 2002-38, and 2003-62 (Part II, Sections A, B, and C)).

Note: *The user fees referred to in the above paragraphs are published in Rev. Proc. 2003-1 (exempt organizations, see Rev. Proc. 2003-8), or an annual update. The annual updates are published as revenue procedures in the Internal Revenue Bulletin. The Internal Revenue Bulletins can be accessed on the IRS web site, www.irs.gov.*

Payment of the user fee (check or money order made payable to the United States Treasury) must be attached to Form 1128 at the time the form is filed. See Rev. Proc. 2003-1 for more information.

Section B—Corporations (Other Than S Corporations and Controlled Foreign Corporations)

Corporations must complete this section and any other section in Part III that applies to that particular entity. For example, a PFIC completes Section B and attaches the statement required by Section H. Complete Sections B and F for a tax-exempt organization that is a corporation.

Section C—S Corporations

An S corporation must have a permitted tax year unless it has elected under section 444 to have a tax year other than the required tax year. A "permitted tax year" is:

1. A tax year that ends on December 31 or

2. Any other tax year if the corporation can establish a business purpose to the satisfaction of the IRS.

For purposes of **2,** any deferral of income to shareholders will not be treated as a business purpose. For more information, see Rev. Proc. 2002-38

If any shareholder is applying for a corresponding change in tax year, that shareholder must file a separate Form 1128 to get advance approval to change its tax year.

Section D—Partnerships

A partnership must obtain advance approval from the IRS to adopt, change, or retain a tax year unless it is not required to file Form 1128, or it meets one of the automatic approval rules discussed in Part II, Section B on page 4. See **Exceptions** on page 1.

Partners **must** also get separate advance approval to change their tax years.

Line 23. Enter the first date a business transaction resulted in a tax consequence, such as receiving income or incurring an expense.

Privacy Act and Paperwork Reduction Act Notice. We ask for the information on this form to carry out the Internal Revenue laws of the United States. Section 442 says that you must obtain IRS approval if you want to adopt, change, or retain a tax year. To obtain approval, you are required to file an application to adopt, change, or retain a tax year. Section 6109 requires that you disclose your taxpayer identification number (SSN or EIN). Routine uses of this information include giving it to the Department of Justice for civil and criminal litigation, and to cities, states, and the District of Columbia for use in administering their tax laws. Failure to provide this information in a timely manner could result in approval of your application being delayed or withheld.

In addition, the Privacy Act requires that when we ask you for information we must first tell you our legal right to ask for the information, why we are asking for it, and what could happen if we do not receive it and whether your response is voluntary, required to obtain a benefit, or mandatory under the law.

Our authority to ask for information is sections 6001, 6011, and 6012(a) and their regulations, which require you to file a return or statement with us for any tax for which you are liable. Your response is mandatory under these sections. Section 6109 requires that you provide your SSN or EIN on what you file. This is so we know who you are, and can process your return and other papers. You must fill in all parts of the form that apply to you.

You are not required to provide the information requested on a form that is subject to the Paperwork Reduction Act unless the form displays a valid OMB control number. Books or records relating to a form or its instructions must be retained as long as their contents may become material in the administration of any Internal Revenue law. Generally, tax returns and return information are confidential, as required by section 6103.

However, section 6103 allows or requires the Internal Revenue Service to disclose or give the information shown on your application to others as described in the Code. For example, we may disclose your tax information to the Department of Justice to enforce the tax laws, both civil and criminal, and to cities, states, the District of Columbia, U.S. commonwealths or possessions, and certain foreign governments to carry out their laws. We may also disclose this information to Federal and state or local agencies to enforce Federal nontax criminal laws and to combat terrorism.

Keep this notice with your records. It may help you if we ask you for other information. If you have any questions about the rules for filing and giving information, call or visit any Internal Revenue Service office.

The time needed to complete and file this form will vary depending on individual circumstances. The estimated average times are:

	Recordkeeping	**Learning about the law or the form**	**Preparing and sending the form to the IRS**
Parts I and II	8 hr., 36 min.	5 hr., 51 min.	6 hr., 15 min.
Parts I and III	22 hr., 14 min.	5 hr., 37 min.	7 hr., 26 min.

If you have comments concerning the accuracy of these time estimates or suggestions for making this form simpler, we would be happy to hear from you. You can write to the Tax Products Coordinating Committee, Western Area Distribution Center, Rancho Cordova, CA 95743-0001. **Do not** send the tax form to this office. Instead, see **Where To File** on page 2.

-7-

¶ 2505 Form 8275, Disclosure Statement

Form **8275**
(Rev. May 2001)
Department of the Treasury
Internal Revenue Service

Disclosure Statement

Do not use this form to disclose items or positions that are contrary to Treasury regulations. Instead, use Form 8275-R, Regulation Disclosure Statement.
See separate instructions.
▶ **Attach to your tax return.**

OMB No. 1545-0889
Attachment Sequence No. **92**

Name(s) shown on return	**Identifying number shown on return**

Part I **General Information** (see instructions)

	(a) Rev. Rul., Rev. Proc., etc.	(b) Item or Group of Items	(c) Detailed Description of Items	(d) Form or Schedule	(e) Line No.	(f) Amount
1						
2						
3						

Part II **Detailed Explanation** (see instructions)

1

2

3

Part III **Information About Pass-Through Entity.** To be completed by partners, shareholders, beneficiaries, or residual interest holders.

Complete this part only if you are making adequate disclosure for a pass-through item.

Note: *A pass-through entity is a partnership, S corporation, estate, trust, regulated investment company (RIC), real estate investment trust (REIT), or real estate mortgage investment conduit (REMIC).*

1 Name, address, and ZIP code of pass-through entity	2 Identifying number of pass-through entity
	3 Tax year of pass-through entity / / to / /
	4 Internal Revenue Service Center where the pass-through entity filed its return

For Paperwork Reduction Act Notice, see separate instructions. Cat. No. 61935M Form **8275** (Rev. 5-2001)

Form 8275 (Rev. 5-2001) Page 2

Part IV **Explanations** *(continued from Parts I and/or II)*

Form **8275** (Rev. 5-2001)

¶ 2506 Instructions for Form 8275

Instructions for Form 8275

Department of the Treasury
Internal Revenue Service

(Rev. May 2001)

Disclosure Statement

General Instructions

Section references are to the Internal Revenue Code unless otherwise noted.

Purpose of Form

Form 8275 is used by taxpayers and income tax return preparers to disclose items or positions, except those taken contrary to a regulation, that are not otherwise adequately disclosed on a tax return to avoid certain penalties. The form is filed to avoid the portions of the accuracy-related penalty due to disregard of rules or a substantial understatement of income tax if the return position has a reasonable basis. It can also be used for disclosures relating to preparer penalties for understatements due to unrealistic positions or disregard of rules.

Caution. *The portion of the accuracy-related penalty attributable to the following types of misconduct cannot be avoided by disclosure on Form 8275:*
- *Negligence*
- *Substantial understatement of tax on a tax shelter item.*
- *Substantial valuation misstatement under chapter 1.*
- *Substantial overstatement of pension liabilities.*
- *Substantial estate or gift tax valuation understatements.*

Who Should File

Form 8275 is filed by individuals, corporations, pass-through entities, and income tax return preparers. If you are disclosing a position taken contrary to a regulation, use **Form 8275-R, Regulation Disclosure Statement,** instead of Form 8275.

For items attributable to a pass-through entity, disclosure should be made on the tax return of the entity. If the entity does not make the disclosure, the partner (or shareholder, etc.) may make adequate disclosure of these items.

Exception to filing Form 8275. Guidance is published annually in a revenue procedure in the Internal Revenue Bulletin that identifies circumstances when an item reported on a return is considered adequate disclosure for purposes of the substantial understatement aspect of the accuracy-related penalty and for avoiding the preparer's penalty relating to understatements due to unrealistic positions. See the example. You do not have to file Form 8275 for items that meet the requirements listed in this revenue procedure.

Example. Generally, you will have met the requirements for adequate disclosure of a charitable contribution deduction, if you complete the contributions section of Schedule A (Form 1040) and supply all the required information. If you make a contribution of property other than cash that is over $500, the form required by the Schedule A instructions must be attached to your return.

How To File

File Form 8275 with your original tax return. Keep a copy for your records. You may be able to file Form 8275 with an amended return. See Regulations sections 1.6662-4(f) and 1.6664-2(c)(3) for more information.

To make adequate disclosure for items reported by a pass-through entity, you must complete and file a separate Form 8275 for items reported by each entity.

Carrybacks, carryovers, and recurring items. If you disclose **carryover** items on a return in the year they originated, you do not have to file another Form 8275 for those items for the carryover tax years.

If you disclose **carryback** items on a return in the year they originated, you do not have to file another Form 8275 for those items for the carryback years.

However, if you disclose items of a **recurring nature** (such as depreciation expense), you must file Form 8275 for each tax year in which the item occurs.

Accuracy-Related Penalty

Generally, the accuracy-related penalty is 20% of any portion of a tax underpayment attributable to:

1. Negligence or disregard of rules or regulations.
2. Substantial understatement of income tax.
3. Any substantial valuation misstatement under chapter 1.
4. Any substantial overstatement of pension liabilities.

However, the penalty is 40% of any portion of a tax underpayment attributable to one or more gross valuation misstatements in 3 and 4 above if the applicable dollar limitation under section 6662(e)(2) is met.

Generally, you can avoid the disregard of rules and substantial understatement portions of the accuracy-related penalty if the position is adequately disclosed and the position has at least a reasonable basis. Reasonable basis is a significantly higher standard than the *not frivolous* standard applicable to preparers. See Regulations section 1.6694-2(c)(2).

The penalty will not be imposed on any part of an underpayment if there was reasonable cause for your position and you acted in good faith in taking that position.

If you failed to keep proper books and records to substantiate items properly, you cannot avoid the penalty by disclosure. Also, you cannot avoid the penalty by disclosure if the position is frivolous.

Substantial Understatement

An **understatement** is the excess of:
- The amount of tax required to be shown on the return for the tax year **over**
- The amount of tax shown on the return for the tax year, reduced by any rebates.

There is a **substantial understatement** of income tax if the amount of the understatement for any tax year exceeds the greater of:

1. 10% of the tax required to be shown on the return for the tax year or
2. $5,000 ($10,000 for a corporation other than an S corporation or a personal holding company as defined in section 542).

For purposes of the substantial understatement portion of the accuracy-related penalty, the amount of the understatement will be reduced by the part that is attributable to:
- An item (other than a tax shelter item), for which there was substantial authority for the treatment claimed at the time the return was filed or on the last day of the tax year to which the return relates.
- An item (other than a tax shelter item) that is adequately disclosed on this form **and** there is a reasonable basis for the tax treatment of the item.

Note. *In no event will a corporation be treated as having a reasonable basis for its tax treatment of an item attributable to a multi-party financing transaction entered into after August 5, 1997, if the treatment does not clearly reflect the income of the corporation.*
- A tax shelter item (other than a corporate tax shelter item) if **(a)** there was substantial authority for the treatment at the time the return was filed or on the last day of the tax year to which the return relates, and **(b)** you reasonably believed that the tax treatment of the item was more likely than not the proper tax treatment.

Note. *For corporate tax shelter transactions, the only exception to the substantial understatement portion of the*

Cat. No. 62063F

accuracy-related penalty is the reasonable cause exception. For more details, see section 1.6664-4(e).

Tax shelter items. A tax shelter, for purposes of the substantial understatement portion of the accuracy-related penalty, is a partnership or other entity, plan, or arrangement, whose principal purpose is to avoid or evade Federal income tax. For transactions after August 5, 1997, a tax shelter is a partnership or other entity, plan, or arrangement, with a *significant purpose* to avoid or evade Federal income tax.

A tax shelter item is any item of income, gain, loss, deduction, or credit that is directly or indirectly attributable to the principal or significant purpose of the tax shelter to avoid or evade Federal income tax.

Income Tax Return Preparer Penalties

A preparer who files an income tax return or claim for refund is subject to a $250 penalty for taking a position which understates any part of the liability if:

- The position has no realistic possibility of being sustained on its merits, and
- The preparer knew or reasonably should have known of the position, and
- The position is frivolous or not adequately disclosed on the return or on the appropriate disclosure statement.

The penalty will not apply if it can be shown that there was reasonable cause for the understatement and that the preparer acted in good faith.

In cases where any part of the understatement of the liability is due to a willful attempt by the return preparer to understate the liability, or if the understatement is due to reckless or intentional disregard of rules or regulations by the preparer, the preparer is subject to a $1,000 penalty.

The preparer penalties generally may be avoided if a position is sufficiently disclosed and is not frivolous.

Note. *For more information about the accuracy-related penalty and preparer penalties, and the means of avoiding these penalties, see Regulations sections 1.6662, 1.6664, and 1.6694.*

Specific Instructions

Be sure to supply all the information for Parts I, II and, if applicable, Part III. Your disclosure will be considered adequate if you file Form 8275 and supply the information requested in detail.

Use Part IV on Page 2 if you need more space for Part I or II. Indicate the corresponding part and line number from page 1. You may use a continuation sheet(s) if you need additional space. Be sure to put your name and identifying number on each sheet.

Part I

Column (a). If you are disclosing a position contrary to a rule (such as a statutory position or IRS revenue ruling), you must identify the rule in column (a).

Column (b). Identify the item by name.

If any item you disclose is from a pass-through entity, you must identify the item as such. If you disclose items from more than one pass-through entity, you must complete a separate Form 8275 for each entity. Also, see **How To File** on page 1.

Column (c). Enter a complete description of the item(s) you are disclosing.

Example. If entertainment expenses were reported in **column (b),** then list in **column (c)** "theater tickets, catering expenses, and banquet hall rentals."

If you claim the same tax treatment for a group of similar items in the same tax year, enter a description identifying the group of items you are disclosing rather than a separate description of each item within the group.

Columns (d) through (f). Enter the location of the item(s) by identifying the form number or schedule and the line number in **columns (d)** and **(e)** and the amount of the item(s) in **column (f)**.

Part II

Your disclosure must include:

1. A description of the relevant facts and the nature of the controversy affecting the tax treatment of the item **or**

2. A concise description of the legal issues presented by these facts.

Note. *Disclosure will not be considered adequate unless **1** and **2** above are provided using Form 8275. For example, your disclosure will not be considered adequate if you attach a copy of an acquisition agreement to your tax return to disclose the issues involved in determining the basis of certain acquired assets. Also, If Form 8275 is not completed and attached to the return, the disclosure will not be considered valid even if the information in **1** and **2** above is provided.*

Part III

Line 4. Contact your pass-through entity if you do not know where its return was filed. However, for partners and S corporation shareholders, information for line 4 can be found on the Schedule K-1 that you received from the partnership or S corporation.

Paperwork Reduction Act Notice. We ask for the information on this form to carry out the Internal Revenue laws of the United States. You are required to give us the information if you wish to use this form to make adequate disclosure to avoid the portion of the accuracy-related penalty due to a substantial understatement of income tax or disregard of rules, or to avoid certain preparer penalties. We need it to ensure that you are complying with these laws and to allow us to figure and collect the right amount of tax.

You are not required to provide the information requested on a form that is subject to the Paperwork Reduction Act unless the form displays a valid OMB control number. Books or records relating to a form or its instructions must be retained as long as their contents may become material in the administration of any Internal Revenue law. Generally, tax returns and return information are confidential, as required by section 6103.

The time needed to complete and file this form will vary depending on individual circumstances. The estimated average time is:

Recordkeeping	3 hr., 35 min.
Learning about the law or the form	1 hr.
Preparing and sending the form to the IRS . . .	1 hr., 6 min.

If you have comments concerning the accuracy of these time estimates or suggestions for making this form simpler, we would be happy to hear from you. See the instructions for the tax return with which this form is filed.

-2-

¶ 2507 Form 8832, Entity Classification Election

Form **8832** (Rev. September 2002) Department of the Treasury Internal Revenue Service

Entity Classification Election

OMB No. 1545-1516

Type or Print	Name of entity	EIN ▶
	Number, street, and room or suite no. If a P.O. box, see instructions.	
	City or town, state, and ZIP code. If a foreign address, enter city, province or state, postal code and country.	

1 Type of election (see instructions):

a ☐ Initial classification by a newly-formed entity.

b ☐ Change in current classification.

2 Form of entity (see instructions):

a ☐ A domestic eligible entity electing to be classified as an association taxable as a corporation.

b ☐ A domestic eligible entity electing to be classified as a partnership.

c ☐ A domestic eligible entity with a single owner electing to be disregarded as a separate entity.

d ☐ A foreign eligible entity electing to be classified as an association taxable as a corporation.

e ☐ A foreign eligible entity electing to be classified as a partnership.

f ☐ A foreign eligible entity with a single owner electing to be disregarded as a separate entity.

3 Disregarded entity information (see instructions):

a Name of owner ▶ ....

b Identifying number of owner ▶ ....

c Country of organization of entity electing to be disregarded (if foreign) ▶ ....

4 Election is to be effective beginning (month, day, year) (see instructions) . . . . ▶ ___/___/___

5 Name and title of person whom the IRS may call for more information	6 That person's telephone number ( )

Consent Statement and Signature(s) (see instructions)

Under penalties of perjury, I (we) declare that I (we) consent to the election of the above-named entity to be classified as indicated above, and that I (we) have examined this consent statement, and to the best of my (our) knowledge and belief, it is true, correct, and complete. If I am an officer, manager, or member signing for all members of the entity, I further declare that I am authorized to execute this consent statement on their behalf.

Signature(s)	Date	Title

For Paperwork Reduction Act Notice, see page 4. Cat. No. 22598R Form **8832** (Rev. 9-2002)

¶ 2508 Instructions for Form 8832

General Instructions

Section references are to the Internal Revenue Code unless otherwise noted.

Purpose of Form

For Federal tax purposes, certain business entities automatically are classified as corporations. See items **1** and **3** through **8** under the definition of **corporation** on this page. Other business entities may choose how they are classified for Federal tax purposes. Except for a business entity automatically classified as a corporation, a business entity with at least two members can choose to be classified as either an association taxable as a corporation or a partnership, and a business entity with a single member can choose to be classified as either an association taxable as a corporation or disregarded as an entity separate from its owner.

Generally, an eligible entity that does not file this form will be classified under the default rules described below. An eligible entity that chooses not to be classified under the default rules or that wishes to change its current classification must file Form 8832 to elect a classification. The IRS will use the information entered on this form to establish the entity's filing and reporting requirements for Federal tax purposes.

60-month limitation rule. Once an eligible entity makes an election to change its classification, the entity generally cannot change its classification by election again during the 60 months after the effective date of the election. However, the IRS may (**by private letter ruling**) permit the entity to change its classification by election within the 60-month period if more than 50% of the ownership interests in the entity as of the effective date of the election are owned by persons that did not own any interests in the entity on the effective date of the entity's prior election. See Regulations section 301.7701-3(c)(1)(iv) for more details.

Note: *The 60-month limitation does not apply if the previous election was made by a newly formed eligible entity and was effective on the date of formation.*

Default Rules

Existing entity default rule. Certain domestic and foreign entities that were in existence before January 1, 1997, and have an established Federal tax classification generally do not need to make an election to continue that classification. If an existing entity decides to change its classification, it may do so subject to the 60-month limitation rule. See Regulations sections 301.7701-3(b)(3) and 301.7701-3(h)(2) for more details.

Domestic default rule. Unless an election is made on Form 8832, a domestic eligible entity is:

1. A partnership if it has two or more members.

2. Disregarded as an entity separate from its owner if it has a single owner.

A change in the number of members of an eligible entity classified as an association does not affect the entity's classification. However, an eligible entity classified as a partnership will become a disregarded entity when the entity's membership is reduced to one member and a disregarded entity will be classified as a partnership when the entity has more than one member.

Foreign default rule. Unless an election is made on Form 8832, a foreign eligible entity is:

1. A partnership if it has two or more members and **at least** one member does not have limited liability.

2. An association taxable as a corporation if all members have limited liability.

3. Disregarded as an entity separate from its owner if it has a single owner that does not have limited liability.

Definitions

Association. For purposes of this form, an association is an eligible entity that is taxable as a corporation by election or, for foreign eligible entities, under the default rules (see Regulations section 301.7701-3).

Business entity. A business entity is any entity recognized for Federal tax purposes that is not properly classified as a trust under Regulations section 301.7701-4 or otherwise subject to special treatment under the Code. See Regulations section 301.7701-2(a).

Corporation. For Federal tax purposes, a corporation is any of the following:

1. A business entity organized under a Federal or state statute, or under a statute of a federally recognized Indian tribe, if the statute describes or refers to the entity as incorporated or as a corporation, body corporate, or body politic.

2. An association (as determined under Regulations section 301.7701-3).

3. A business entity organized under a state statute, if the statute describes or refers to the entity as a joint-stock company or joint-stock association.

4. An insurance company.

5. A state-chartered business entity conducting banking activities, if any of its deposits are insured under the Federal Deposit Insurance Act, as amended, 12 U.S.C. 1811 et seq., or a similar Federal statute.

6. A business entity wholly owned by a state or any political subdivision thereof, or a business entity wholly owned by a foreign government or any other entity described in Regulations section 1.892-2T.

7. A business entity that is taxable as a corporation under a provision of the Code other than section 7701(a)(3).

8. A foreign business entity listed on page 5. See Regulations section 301.7701-2(b)(8) for any exceptions and inclusions to items on this list and for any revisions made to this list since these instructions were printed.

Disregarded entity. A disregarded entity is an eligible entity that is treated as an entity that is not separate from its single owner. Its separate existence will be ignored for Federal tax purposes unless it elects corporate tax treatment.

Eligible entity. An eligible entity is a business entity that is not included in items **1** or **3** through **8** under the definition of corporation above.

Limited liability. A member of a foreign eligible entity has limited liability if the member has no personal liability for any debts of or claims against the entity by reason of being a member. This determination is based solely on the statute or law under which the entity is organized (and, if relevant, the entity's organizational documents). A member has personal liability if the creditors of the entity may seek satisfaction of all or any part of the debts or claims against the entity from the member as such. A member has personal liability even if the member makes an agreement under which another person (whether or not a member of the entity) assumes that liability or agrees to indemnify that member for that liability.

Partnership. A partnership is a business entity that has **at least** two members and is not a corporation as defined on page 2.

Who Must File

File this form for an **eligible entity** that is one of the following:

- A domestic entity electing to be classified as an association taxable as a corporation.
- A domestic entity electing to change its current classification (even if it is currently classified under the default rule).
- A foreign entity that has more than one owner, all owners having limited liability, electing to be classified as a partnership.
- A foreign entity that has at least one owner that does not have limited liability, electing to be classified as an association taxable as a corporation.
- A foreign entity with a single owner having limited liability, electing to be an entity disregarded as an entity separate from its owner.
- A foreign entity electing to change its current classification (even if it is currently classified under the default rule).

Do not file this form for an eligible entity that is:

- Tax-exempt under section 501(a) or
- A real estate investment trust (REIT), as defined in section 856.

Effect of Election

The Federal tax treatment of elective changes in classification as described in Regulations section 301.7701-3(g)(1) is summarized as follows:

- If an eligible entity classified as a partnership elects to be classified as an association, it is deemed that the partnership contributes all of its assets and liabilities to the association in exchange for stock in the association, and immediately thereafter, the partnership liquidates by distributing the stock of the association to its partners.
- If an eligible entity classified as an association elects to be classified as a partnership, it is deemed that the association distributes all of its assets and liabilities to its shareholders in liquidation of the association, and immediately thereafter, the shareholders contribute all of the distributed assets and liabilities to a newly formed partnership.
- If an eligible entity classified as an association elects to be disregarded as an entity separate from its owner, it is deemed that the association distributes all of its assets and liabilities to its single owner in liquidation of the association.
- If an eligible entity that is disregarded as an entity separate from its owner elects to be classified as an association, the owner of the eligible entity is deemed to have contributed all of the assets and liabilities of the entity to the association in exchange for the stock of the association.

Note: *For information on the Federal tax treatment of elective changes in classification, see Regulations section 301.7701-3(g).*

When To File

See the instructions for line 4.

A newly formed entity may be eligible for late election relief under Rev. Proc. 2002-59, 2002-39 I.R.B. 615 if:

- The entity failed to obtain its desired classified election solely because Form 8832 was not timely filed,
- The due date for the entity's desired classification tax return (excluding extension) for the tax year beginning with the entity's formation date has not passed, and
- The entity has reasonable cause for its failure to make a timely election.

To obtain relief, a newly formed entity must file Form 8832 on or before the due date of the first Federal tax return (excluding extensions) of the entity's desired classification. The entity must also write "FILED PURSUANT TO REV. PROC. 2002-59" at the top of the form. The entity must attach a statement to the form explaining why it failed to file a timely election. If Rev. Proc. 2002-59 does not apply, an entity may seek relief for a late entity election by requesting a private letter ruling and paying a user fee in accordance with Rev. Proc. 2002-1, 2002-1 I.R.B. 1 (or its successor).

Where To File

File Form 8832 with the Internal Revenue Service Center, Philadelphia, PA 19255. Also attach a copy of Form 8832 to the entity's Federal income tax or information return for the tax year of the election. If the entity is not required to file a return for that year, a copy of its Form 8832 **must** be attached to the Federal income tax or information returns of **all** direct or indirect owners of the entity for the tax year of the owner that includes the date on which the election took effect. Although failure to attach a copy will not invalidate an otherwise valid election, each member of the entity is required to file returns that are consistent with the entity's election. In addition, penalties may be assessed against persons who are required to, but who do not, attach Form 8832 to their returns. Other penalties may apply for filing Federal income tax or information returns inconsistent with the entity's election.

Specific Instructions

Name. Enter the name of the eligible entity electing to be classified using Form 8832.

Employer identification number (EIN). Show the correct EIN of the eligible entity electing to be classified. Any entity that has an EIN will retain that EIN even if its Federal tax classification changes under Regulations section 301.7701-3.

If a disregarded entity's classification changes so that it is recognized as a partnership or association for Federal tax purposes, and that entity had an EIN, then the entity must use that EIN and not the identifying number of the single owner. If the entity did not already have its own EIN, then the entity must apply for an EIN and not use the identifying number of the single owner.

A foreign person that makes an election under Regulations section 301.7701-3(c) must also use its own taxpayer identifying number. See sections 6721 through 6724 for penalties that may apply for failure to supply taxpayer identifying numbers.

If the entity electing to be classified using Form 8832 does not have an EIN, it must apply for one on **Form SS-4,** Application for Employer Identification Number. If the filing of Form 8832 is the only reason the entity is applying for an EIN, check the "Other" box on line 9 of Form SS-4 and write "Form 8832" to the right of that box. If the entity has not received an EIN by the time Form 8832 is due, write "Applied for" in the space for the EIN. **Do not** apply for a new EIN for an existing entity that is changing its classification if the entity already has an EIN.

Address. Enter the address of the entity electing a classification. Include the suite, room, or other unit number after the street address. If the Post Office does not deliver mail to the street address and the entity has a P.O. box, show the box number instead of the street address.

Line 1. Check box 1a if the entity is choosing a classification for the first time **and** the entity does not want to be classified under the applicable default classification. **Do not** file this form if the entity wants to be classified under the default rules.

Check box 1b if the entity is changing its current classification.

Line 2. Check the appropriate box if you are changing a current classification (no matter how achieved), or are electing out of a default classification. **Do not** file this form if you fall within a default classification that is the desired classification for the new entity.

Line 3. If an eligible entity has checked box 2c or box 2f and is electing to be disregarded as an entity separate from its owner, it must enter the name of its owner on line 3a and the owner's identifying number (social security number, or individual taxpayer identification number, or EIN) on line 3b. If the owner is a foreign person or entity and does not have a U.S. identifying number, enter "none" on line 3b. If the entity making the election is foreign, enter the name of the country in which it was formed on line 3c.

Line 4. Generally, the election will take effect on the date you enter on line 4 of this form or on the date filed if no date is entered on line 4. However, an election specifying an entity's classification for Federal tax purposes can take effect no more than 75 days prior to the date the election is filed, nor can it take effect later than 12 months after the date on which the election is filed. If line 4 shows a date more than 75 days prior to the date on which the election is filed, the election will take effect 75 days before the date it is filed. If line 4 shows an effective date more than 12 months from the filing date, the election will take effect 12 months after the date the election was filed.

Consent statement and signatures. Form 8832 must be signed by:

1. Each member of the electing entity who is an owner at the time the election is filed; or

2. Any officer, manager, or member of the electing entity who is authorized (under local law or the organizational documents) to make the election and who represents to having such authorization under penalties of perjury.

If an election is to be effective for any period prior to the time it is filed, each person who was an owner between the date the election is to be effective and the date the election is filed, and who is not an owner at the time the election is filed, must also sign.

If you need a continuation sheet or use a separate consent statement, attach it to Form 8832. The separate consent statement must contain the same information as shown on Form 8832.

Paperwork Reduction Act Notice

We ask for the information on this form to carry out the Internal Revenue laws of the United States. You are required to give us the information. We need it to ensure that you are complying with these laws and to allow us to figure and collect the right amount of tax.

You are not required to provide the information requested on a form that is subject to the Paperwork Reduction Act unless the form displays a valid OMB control number. Books or records relating to a form or its instructions must be retained as long as their contents may become material in the administration of any Internal Revenue law. Generally, tax returns and return information are confidential, as required by section 6103.

The time needed to complete and file this form will vary depending on individual circumstances. The estimated average time is:

Recordkeeping . . 1 hr., 49 min.
Learning about the law or the form . . 2 hr., 7 min.
Preparing and sending the form to the IRS . . . 23 min.

If you have comments concerning the accuracy of these time estimates or suggestions for making this form simpler, we would be happy to hear from you. You can write to the Tax Forms Committee, Western Area Distribution Center, Rancho Cordova, CA 95743-0001. **Do not** send the form to this address. Instead, see **Where To File** on page 3.

Foreign Entities Classified as Corporations for Federal Tax Purposes:

American Samoa—Corporation
Argentina—Sociedad Anonima
Australia—Public Limited Company
Austria—Aktiengesellschaft
Barbados—Limited Company
Belgium—Societe Anonyme
Belize—Public Limited Company
Bolivia—Sociedad Anonima
Brazil—Sociedade Anonima
Canada—Corporation and Company
Chile—Sociedad Anonima
People's Republic of China—Gufen Youxian Gongsi
Republic of China (Taiwan)—Ku-fen Yu-hsien Kung-szu
Colombia—Sociedad Anonima
Costa Rica—Sociedad Anonima
Cyprus—Public Limited Company
Czech Republic—Akciova Spolecnost
Denmark—Aktieselskab
Ecuador—Sociedad Anonima or Compania Anonima
Egypt—Sharikat Al-Mossahamah
El Salvador—Sociedad Anonima
Finland—Julkinen Osakeyhtio/ Publikt Aktiebolag
France—Societe Anonyme
Germany—Aktiengesellschaft
Greece—Anonymos Etairia
Guam—Corporation
Guatemala—Sociedad Anonima
Guyana—Public Limited Company
Honduras—Sociedad Anonima
Hong Kong—Public Limited Company
Hungary—Reszvenytarsasag
Iceland—Hlutafelag
India—Public Limited Company
Indonesia—Perseroan Terbuka
Ireland—Public Limited Company
Israel—Public Limited Company
Italy—Societa per Azioni
Jamaica—Public Limited Company
Japan—Kabushiki Kaisha
Kazakstan—Ashyk Aktsionerlik Kogham
Republic of Korea—Chusik Hoesa
Liberia—Corporation
Luxembourg—Societe Anonyme
Malaysia—Berhad
Malta—Public Limited Company
Mexico—Sociedad Anonima
Morocco—Societe Anonyme
Netherlands—Naamloze Vennootschap
New Zealand—Limited Company
Nicaragua—Compania Anonima
Nigeria—Public Limited Company
Northern Mariana Islands—Corporation
Norway—Allment Aksjeselskap
Pakistan—Public Limited Company
Panama—Sociedad Anonima
Paraguay—Sociedad Anonima
Peru—Sociedad Anonima
Philippines—Stock Corporation
Poland—Spolka Akcyjna
Portugal—Sociedade Anonima
Puerto Rico—Corporation
Romania—Societe pe Actiuni
Russia—Otkrytoye Aktsionernoy Obshchestvo
Saudi Arabia—Sharikat Al-Mossahamah
Singapore—Public Limited Company
Slovak Republic—Akciova Spolocnost
South Africa—Public Limited Company
Spain—Sociedad Anonima
Surinam—Naamloze Vennootschap
Sweden—Publika Aktiebolag
Switzerland—Aktiengesellschaft
Thailand—Borisat Chamkad (Mahachon)
Trinidad and Tobago—Limited Company
Tunisia—Societe Anonyme
Turkey—Anonim Sirket
Ukraine—Aktsionerne Tovaristvo Vidkritogo Tipu
United Kingdom—Public Limited Company
United States Virgin Islands—Corporation
Uruguay—Sociedad Anonima
Venezuela—Sociedad Anonima or Compania Anonima

See Regulations section 301.7701-2(b)(8) for any exceptions and inclusions to items on this list and for any revisions made to this list since these instructions were printed.

Case Table

Cases found in this book's text and footnotes are listed below.

References are to paragraph (¶) numbers.

References are to paragraph (¶) numbers.

References are to paragraph (¶) numbers.

P

Q

R

S

T

V

W

Y

Finding Lists

Citations found in this book's text are listed below under the following categories: Internal Revenue Code Sections, Regulations, Proposed Regulations, Announcements, General Counsel Memoranda, Letter Rulings, Notices, Revenue Procedures, Revenue Rulings, and Technical Advice Memoranda.

References are to paragraph (¶) numbers.

Internal Revenue Code Sections

References are to paragraph (¶) numbers.

Regulations

References are to paragraph (¶) numbers.

Proposed Regulations

Announcements

General Counsel Memoranda

Letter Rulings

Notices

Revenue Procedures

Revenue Rulings

Technical Advice Memoranda

Index

References are to paragraph (¶) numbers.

D

N

O

P